Politics and Society
in Contemporary China

Politics and Society in Contemporary China

Elizabeth Freund Larus

LYNNE
RIENNER
PUBLISHERS

BOULDER
LONDON

Published in the United States of America in 2012 by
Lynne Rienner Publishers, Inc.
1800 30th Street, Boulder, Colorado 80301
www.rienner.com

and in the United Kingdom by
Lynne Rienner Publishers, Inc.
3 Henrietta Street, Covent Garden, London WC2E 8LU

Library of Congress Cataloging-in-Publication Data
Larus, Elizabeth Freund.
 Politics and society in contemporary China / Elizabeth Freund Larus.
   p. cm.
 Includes bibliographical references and index.
 ISBN 978-1-58826-800-6 (hc : alk. paper)
 ISBN 978-1-58826-825-9 (pb : alk. paper)
 1. China—Politics and government—1949– 2. China—Social
conditions—1949– 3. China—Economic conditions—1949– 4. China—
Military policy. 5. China—Foreign relations—1949– I. Title.
 JQ1510.L37 2012
 320.951—dc23

                                                    2011043123

British Cataloguing in Publication Data
A Cataloguing in Publication record for this book
is available from the British Library.

Printed and bound in the United States of America

     The paper used in this publication meets the requirements
 ∞   of the American National Standard for Permanence of
     Paper for Printed Library Materials Z39.48-1992.

  5   4   3   2   1

Contents

Tables and Figures

Tables

Figures

Acknowledgments

I have witnessed remarkable changes since I first visited China in the summer of 1986. I spent that summer studying Chinese and traveling the country. In Beijing, I bought a bicycle and rode from the university district to Tiananmen Square. It was a wonderful time to be a foreigner in China: the beginning of the reform era with all of its promise, right before the campaign against spiritual pollution. Madonna and Michael Jackson were all the rage. It was three years before the shocking massacre in Tiananmen Square. Since then, I have watched China develop, and I can scarcely believe the changes I have seen there. Now, you cannot ride a bicycle on Beijing's main roads without taking your life in your hands. The number of luxury hotels still astounds me. In Shanghai, bad service from surly salesgirls in state-owned department stores has been replaced with refined politeness in gleaming boutiques.

All of these changes are reflected in this book, the story of China. It is the book I have always wanted to write. I have taught courses and seminars on China for two decades, and I needed a text that would show my students the developments, hopes, and disappointments of China. I was ecstatic when Lynne Rienner Publishers approached me with the project, and I readily agreed to undertake it. I would like to acknowledge the late Marilyn Grobschmidt for navigating me through the proposal stage of the manuscript.

The book would not have been possible without the assistance of many people. I would particularly like to thank Susan Fernsebner, Stephen Phillips, Dawn Bowen, Matthew Cook, George Klosko, and Che-po Chan for reading and commenting on chapters. I would also like to thank Bruce Dickson, Carla Freeman, Lindsay Wei Wang, Bryce Wakefield, Jack Kramer, Shurupa Gupta, Jiang Shiyan, and Ji Lude for answering my questions and offering observations on various topics. Many thanks go to Bobby Durrette, my research assistant. I am grateful to Patrick Brooks-Kenney for his exhaustive research, particularly for Chapters 7 and 9, and for generating excellent graphics. Special thanks go to Jeremy Tan, Alexandre Smith, and Taylor Miller-Freutel, who generated the tables and figures. I thank Stephen P. Hanna for creating a beautiful map to my specifications. Deepest thanks go to Paul Marquard for general editing of the manuscript and to Sean Samuelson for assistance in generating the index. At Lynne Rienner Publishers, I thank Jessica Gribble for her editorial assistance and Shena Redmond for handling the production details. I would also like to thank my copyeditor, Karen Brown, and two anonymous reviewers.

Heartfelt appreciation goes to my parents, Chris and Dutch Freund, for their support throughout the process. Finally, I thank my husband, Tom Larus, to whom this book is dedicated, for his love, patience, and understanding.

—*Elizabeth Freund Larus*

1 Studying Chinese Politics

5:00 P.M., June 12, 1986, Beijing, China
I'm riding my black Flying Pigeon bicycle from northwest Beijing to Tiananmen Square. The air is hot and gritty, but not unpleasant. A man riding on a bike ahead of me sings robustly; he has a nice voice. I begin to pass a slower-moving cyclist. "No! Never pass on the right!" a Chinese friend admonishes me. I'm a bit startled by his vehemence. I'm one of a large flow of cyclists on bike lanes flanking wide boulevards. The cyclists far outnumber buses, taxis, and government sedans. It takes about an hour to pedal from the Central Institute of Nationalities to Tiananmen Square. There, a crowd slowly gathers around me and a classmate taking night exposures of the Monument to the People's Heroes. They ask a lot of questions about my life in the United States, such as do I have a TV? A refrigerator?

5:00 P.M., June 12, 2004, Beijing, China
I'm riding in a taxi going out for a Saturday night in Beijing. The taxi is stuck in traffic. It's not totally unpleasant. The driver is playing a music CD from Taiwan. I strike up a conversation with the driver. I observe that Beijing is a modern city now. I ask where he's from. I'm surprised when he tells me that he's "an old Beijinger." I'm mildly surprised by this news. He's the first Beijing taxi driver I've met this summer; all the others have come from elsewhere in China. I joke that all of the "r"s left New York and ended up in Beijing.[1] I don't think he gets the joke. We arrive at my destination, a five-star hotel. Inside, I'm awestruck by the massive chandeliers lining the lobby. There's a black lacquer baby grand piano, and a Chinese singer crooning Western songs. I order a gin and tonic, amazed at the changes I've witnessed since my first visit to China in the 1980s.

5:00 P.M., June 12, 2010, Fredericksburg, Virginia
I'm giving a tour of my parents' new home to friends visiting from China. They are both members of the Chinese Communist Party (CCP). Who would have

1

thought, during the summer twenty-four years ago, that I'd one day host CCP members in my parents' home in the United States! We take a look at the beautiful furnishings in the master bedroom. The Chinese couple remark that they have similar furniture in China. No wonder they do, because the furniture was made in China! I marvel at how China got to this point so fast. I wonder about how I can explain to my students the dramatic political, social, and economic changes that China has undergone in the last thirty years. In 1986, most Chinese rode bicycles as daily transport; cars were the privilege of Communist Party members and government officials. In 2011, General Motors sold more cars in China than in the United States. In 1986, most Chinese lived in humble apartments. "Living rooms" were pressed into service as dining rooms at mealtimes and bedrooms at night. Furniture was shoddy. Today, about 50 percent of the furniture sold in the United States is made in China. Municipal governments throughout China have razed centuries-old neighborhoods and replaced them with forests of high-rises. Investment in second homes has skyrocketed to the point that the Chinese government is fearful of a housing bubble. Today, China is the world's fastest-growing economy. China has more Internet users than the United States has people. The Chinese Communist Party has jettisoned socialist economics for the market. Fewer and fewer Chinese employees work for state businesses while more and more work in private and foreign firms. An increasing number of private entrepreneurs are joining China's Communist Party, creating perhaps the ultimate oxymoron: the capitalist communist, or the communist capitalist!

What accounts for these dramatic changes? What policies led to these changes, when were they implemented, and who made the key decisions? This book examines the dynamics of China's remarkable political, economic, and social changes. Never have so many people come so far, so fast. Between 1949 and the late 1970s, more than 100 million Chinese people rose out of poverty. Between 1980 and the early twenty-first century, more than 500 million people have risen out of poverty. Once occupied by foreign powers, China has joined those nations on the world stage of international affairs, trade, and finance. China holds the world's largest reserves of foreign currency and contributes mightily to the global economy. China is poised to overtake the United States as the world's largest economy around the year 2020.

Despite these advances, China is still a developing country, and struggles with the problems typical of developing countries. Although China has more millionaires (and billionaires!) than at any time in its history, it is still a poor country. The average per capita income is only $4,382, and the average rural per capita income is even less.[2] Income distribution has become less equal in recent decades as China has moved from a socialist economy to a market-oriented one. There is tremendous income disparity between rural and urban areas and between interior and coastal areas, and life is still hard in rural areas. Rural health care, once rudimentary but widely available, has become scarce. The overwhelming majority of rural residents have no health insurance, and fees are beyond the reach of most rural residents. Poor living conditions and the lack of services in rural areas and in China's interior have resulted in a huge wave of rural-to-urban and interior-to-coastal migration. While these migrants provide cheap labor to construction projects and assembly factories in the cities and coastal areas, their relocation often results in fractured families, the spread of disease, and increased crime. Education is a brighter spot. China has largely eliminated the gender gap in both urban and rural education, although facilities at rural schools often cannot match those in urban areas. Shanghai produces some of the best students in math and science in the world.

China's contemporary history makes a fascinating story. Ruled by emperors for thousands of years, China has an imperial history rich with warring kingdoms, court intrigue, overseas exploration, and foreign trade. In the nineteenth century, both domestic forces and foreign encroachment took their toll on China's imperial order. China's imperial system collapsed in the early 1900s and was replaced by a republican form of government. The new nationalist government lacked cohesion, however, and soon China descended into years of chaos in which the strong ruled and the weak submitted. Out of that chaos rose one man ultimately stronger than the others, General Chiang Kai-shek, who reunited China and restored some semblance of order. This order was short-lived, as imperial Japan entered China in the early 1930s and occupied it during World War II. Forced by Japan to retreat into China's interior, Chiang's Nationalist government could only nominally govern the country during World War II. In China's vast rural countryside, another force—the communists—was gathering strength. Under the leadership of Mao Zedong, the Chinese communists organized the peasantry in revolution. In 1949, they succeeded in overthrowing the Nationalist government and established a new government in which a small, elite group of Chinese communists wielded tremendous power over the vast population. The Chinese communists promised the destruction of the capitalist economy and class-based social system, a new order in which the workers were the masters of society, with lifelong job tenure and state-provided benefits, education and literacy for rich and poor alike, improved hygiene and public health, equality between the sexes, and peaceful foreign relations. The promise of the revolution was betrayed, however, by earth-shattering political campaigns that destroyed lives and tore China's social fabric. By the time of Mao's death in 1976, the Chinese people were exhausted. Under a new leader, Deng Xiaoping, China jettisoned socialist economics and political campaigns and engaged in bold economic reform. By the end of Deng's life, in 1997, China was the world's fastest-growing economy and was becoming a major player on the world stage.

Since 1949, all of China's economic reforms and political campaigns were instigated by the core leadership of the Chinese Communist Party. China is still run by a handful of powerful men. The CCP's 78 million members answer to a handful of men who sit near the apex of party power. The tightly organized and highly disciplined CCP continues to exercise significant control over China's politics, economics, and society. The interlocking membership of party and government personnel means that governments at every level—national and local—carry out party wishes. There is still little transparency in government decisionmaking at any level. In recent years, China has implemented electoral reform by allowing villages to elect committees to make decisions on their behalf. Electoral reform has not advanced beyond the township level, and most elections in China remain indirect. The lack of pluralism and opportunity for people to participate in government and decisionmaking means that people have limited means of voicing their opinion other than in the form of protest. Since the beginning of the reform era in the late 1970s, there has been a sharp increase in both the number and scale of public protest. The protesters air a variety of grievances. In the 1980s many people protested inflation, government and party corruption, and party control of civic organizations. The transition from socialism to a market-oriented economy has created winners and losers. The privatization of state-owned enterprises (SOEs) in particular has resulted in unpaid back wages, loss of pensions and benefits, and layoffs. Frustrated by their treatment and their inability to reverse the trend toward privatization, former state workers have taken their grievances to the street in demonstrations. The Chinese government regularly violates the human rights of the Chinese people. Although the state constitution explicitly states the rights and liberties granted the Chinese people, it also limits those rights when the state feels threatened. The most egregious violations occur against ethnic minority groups and religious organizations.

The goal of this text is to introduce students to the contemporary politics and society of the People's Republic of China.[3] (See Figure 1.1.) The main theme of the book is China's dramatic political, economic, and social transformations under the Chinese Communist Party (CCP). In the ninety years since its creation, the CCP has become the world's largest communist party. Once hunted down and then exiled to the Chinese countryside, the CCP in 1949 succeeded in overthrowing the existing regime and establishing the world's largest communist country. Under Mao Zedong, the CCP reformed and then revolutionized Chinese politics and society. Mao's political campaigns were often brutal, isolating or crushing opposition to the party and causing massive suffering for the Chinese people. By the time of Mao's death in 1976, the CCP's legitimacy was in question. Despite challenges to its legitimacy, membership in the party continues to grow. New recruits to the CCP are pragmatic. Unlike previous generations who joined the CCP for ideological reasons, young recruits now join the party to advance their careers. It is virtually impossible to join the ruling and upper managerial class without being a party member. The CCP is changing, too. The party is becoming increasingly capitalist in view and membership. Deng Xiaoping inaugurated the reform era in 1978, gradually jettisoning socialism for some odd variation of state-led capitalism. Out went most of

Figure 1.1 Map of the People's Republic of China

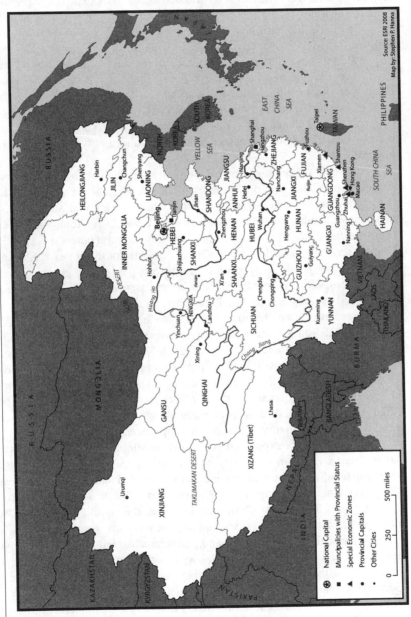

Source: ESRI 2008
Map by: Stephen P. Hanna

the lumbering and slumbering state business and in came foreign investment in private or joint ventures. Foreign-funded businesses exploded in southern China, which provided a seemingly inexhaustible supply of cheap labor from the countryside. Increasingly, many Chinese left state employment for private firms or started their own businesses. Party members even jumped into the sea of private business. The party's embrace of capitalism made it necessary to extend membership to private entrepreneurs. In the past decade, China's capitalists have found it pragmatic to have the seat at the economic and political table by joining the party or running for elective office. Once seated at the table, China's capitalists have had a hand in shaping policy to support their interests, thereby changing both the nature of the CCP and the dynamics of Chinese government.

This book wakens students to the importance of China in world affairs and in their lives. China is important at many levels. First, at the most basic level, the world's most populous country simply cannot be ignored. China's 1.3 billion people are both producers and consumers. Under Deng Xiaoping, China became the world's factory. Its assembly factories and rural businesses stimulated China's economy, resulting in double-digit growth for thirty years. As China's economy grew, so did its appetite for resources, particularly energy and natural resources. China is now the world's largest user of energy, importing much of it to feed its economic growth. In recent years, China has increasingly sought natural resources from abroad. Innumerable Chinese corporations have set up shop in Africa to take advantage of that continent's rich and vast resources. China's desire for resources has driven up the prices of commodities in recent years, affecting prices worldwide. China's consumer demand seems nearly as insatiable. While Americans remain the world's greatest individual consumers, the sheer number of Chinese means that there is simply more demand for goods. China's growing middle class is creating a huge demand for foodstuffs, commodities, and even luxury goods, pushing up prices worldwide.

Second, China's export-led economic development strategy affects the United States. China, in 1978, adopted an economic development strategy based on cheap labor-intensive industry and its undervalued national currency (called the yuan). Unable to compete on their own turf, US businesses moved manufacturing jobs abroad—to China—arguing that they could not compete with other Western and Japanese firms that had moved their operations to China as well. In particular, US businesses and politicians blamed an undervalued yuan for the inability to compete. An artificially low currency makes exports cheaper, and many businesses complained that they could not compete with Chinese exports. However, a stronger yuan and higher wages are unlikely to bring jobs back to the United States. It is more likely that the jobs will merely move on to the next low-wage country. It is increasingly likely that Americans will be working for foreign firms in China or elsewhere as a result of China's three-decades-long strategy of export-driven development. It is also increasingly likely that

Americans will work for Chinese firms in the United States. China's overseas investments have blossomed in recent years, and Chinese firms have opened dozens of plants in the United States since 1995. With trillions of dollars in foreign reserves (composed mostly of US dollars), China is increasingly investing in the United States. Its investment clout is also likely to translate into political clout. China is the largest foreign holder of US debt and uses that position periodically to admonish US politicians for fiscal foolishness. It is no longer impossible to imagine a United States accommodating its largest creditor on some domestic or foreign policy issue.

Third, its geographic location in Asia makes China a key player in the region. China's leaders seek to reestablish the country's preeminence as the Middle Kingdom. Beijing's increasingly aggressive investment in its military is raising eyebrows in the West. There has been much talk in the West about China's military rise. For now, China is sticking to its territorial claims (over Taiwan, the South China Sea, and various islands) and is not seeking to conquer new lands. In recent years, however, Western analysts have noticed a much more aggressive stance on these claims. Chinese ships have harassed ships of its Asian neighbors in disputed territories, compelling some of them to respond with live-fire war exercises, further heightening tensions in the region. China's neighbors are particularly concerned with China's naval expansion in the Asia Pacific and are strengthening military relations with the United States to counter China's rise.

Fourth, China is more engaged in the world than ever. In foreign affairs, China projects itself as a responsible member of the global community. Its membership in international organizations (IOs) has blossomed in recent decades. China's economic rise is helping Beijing wield increasing influence in global issues. Its economic and military weight makes it impossible for Western powers to ignore China. China is increasingly using its voice in foreign affairs, from nuclear proliferation on the Korean Peninsula to international intervention in Sudan and Libya to debt forgiveness for heavily indebted poor countries. The West finds China's engagement with nondemocratic governments, particularly in the developing world, to be particularly irksome. In recent years, China has cut deals with several nondemocratic governments, offering foreign aid in exchange for access to raw materials for its economic expansion. China offers this aid without conditions for political and economic reform, thereby propping up nondemocratic governments in the developing world. Western governments blame China for undoing or undermining much of its work to advance democratic government in the developing world.

China's engagement with the world also is likely to challenge the US position in the world. China's increasing stature in international organizations such as the World Bank, International Monetary Fund (IMF), and World Trade Organization (WTO) is likely to change US dynamics in those organizations. China's naval expansion is calculated to test US military dominance in the Asia

Pacific. Although it is unlikely that China's military would directly confront the United States in Asia, its military modernization and naval expansion may make the United States more hesitant to intervene in the region or could make any confrontation in the region more costly for the United States.

This textbook does not assume that the reader has previous knowledge or experience of China. I have packed this book with detailed information on topics ranging from the rise of the Chinese Communist Party (CCP) and contemporary political institutions to the political economy of the Mao and post-Mao years and the rural-urban gap, and from human rights issues and civil liberties to national defense and foreign affairs. This amount of detail is intended to clarify and elucidate the material, rather than confuse the reader. Individual readers will likely find some details more engaging than others, but I believed it was my academic responsibility to offer as much information as possible to allow all readers a firm understanding of contemporary China's politics and society. The progression of the book is as follows. Chapter 2 sets the stage for the rest of the book. It provides context for understanding contemporary Chinese politics and society. It offers the reader a background on China's geography, demographics, and historical milestones, and traces the progression from imperial order to republican and then communist government. It introduces the reader to the major Chinese schools of thought and examines their impact on China's government and politics. It also traces the rise of the Communist Party and explains Mao Zedong Thought.

China's socialist era is commonly known as the Mao years. From the creation of the People's Republic of China (PRC) in 1949 until the death of Mao Zedong in 1976, China was embroiled in dramatic political, economic, and social revolution. Chapter 3 chronicles and explains this dramatic era. The chapter begins with a discussion of the organization of the early communist government and explains China's socialist transition. It then focuses on several life-changing political campaigns and their impact on China's government and society. The chapter concludes with the end of the Mao era and the beginning of a new chapter in China's history—the reform era—which receives further attention in Chapters 5 and 7. Chapter 4 provides an in-depth look at the organization of the CCP and the state governing apparatus at the national and local levels. It also examines local elections, rural politics, and prospects for China's democratization.

Local elections and prospects for democracy would have been impossible without the reforms of the Deng Xiaoping era. Chapter 5 outlines the dynamics of the post-Mao reform era. The chapter presents and analyzes changes to China's political system in the post-Mao years, with special emphasis on resistance to reforms on the part of China's communist hardliners. It explains the rise of key reformer Deng Xiaoping, and offers the reader an introduction to Deng's early economic reforms, which are examined in greater depth in Chapter 7. The chapter also introduces the reader to China's post-Deng leadership.

Much of the chapter is dedicated to political, constitutional, and legal reforms, with special emphasis on human rights concerns.

While living conditions for most Chinese improved during the reform era, China still confronts significant social issues. Chapter 6 begins with issues that directly affect individuals and the Chinese family. It examines the impact of health-care system reform with special emphasis on the dire consequences for China's rural population, the intended and unintended consequences of population control policies, and the complexities of education reform. Following these sections is one dedicated to civil society and social change. This section chronicles and analyzes the rise of China's middle class and their behavior. It also examines the current state of the arts, media, and Internet in China, with special attention to government attempts to control each of these. The chapter also discusses ethnic minorities in China, emphasizing attempts by the central government to develop minority areas. This section is followed by one dedicated to human rights issues in China, with special reference to violation of the human rights of minorities in China.

Chapter 7 chronicles the amazing economic reforms since 1978. It begins with dramatic reform to agriculture and industry, and analyzes the impact of these reforms on China's rural and urban populations. China's quest for energy for its continued economic development is examined, as well as the negative impact of development on China's environment and China's growing environmental movement. Much of the chapter is dedicated to China's growing presence in the global economy. China not only attracts significant foreign investment but is increasingly investing in other countries. The story of China's remarkable transformation from xenophobic regime during the later Mao years to its propulsion onto the world stage is examined through a discussion of the initiation of a Chinese stock market, the creation of special zones dedicated to foreign trade and investment, and China's quest to attract foreign science and technology. The chapter makes special reference to growing problems in foreign trade and investment, such as violation of intellectual property rights and disputes over the value of Chinese currency and its foreign trade practices.

One of the major problems that evolved out of the reform era is the yawning rural-urban gap. In the early reform years, the Chinese government encouraged foreign investment in eastern China, but failed to channel adequate state investment to rural China. As a result, millions of Chinese fled the countryside for jobs in eastern cities. Those left behind are increasingly discontented as corrupt local officials confiscate land for development. Chapter 8 analyzes the origins and problems associated with this rural-urban disparity and discusses the problems of the hollowing out of rural China. The chapter looks at the rural-urban education and health-care gap and discusses the government response to a looming health-care crisis in rural China. It also examines expression of rural discontent and government responses to address rural poverty as part of a strategy of domestic security.

Chapter 9 addresses issues of national security and introduces the reader to China's military and national defense. It chronicles the creation and modernization of China's military and offers the reader an explanation of the structure of the military and of national defense policy. It discusses recent developments in force projection, cyber warfare, China's space program, and expansion of China's naval power. The author hopes that students interested in this topic pursue their interest by referring to the notes that appear at the end of the chapter and the many resources cited in the bibliography.

Chapter 10 looks at China's foreign policy and its foreign policy making process in historical context and introduces the reader to the philosophy and theory behind China's approach to the broader international community. The chapter then examines China's relations with various regions of the world and with the world's major powers. There is literally nowhere in the world that China has not increased its presence in the last thirty years, and the goal of the chapter is to illuminate the rise of China as a major world player.

That China's leaders aspire to create a rich and powerful nation is undisputed. China's trajectory to reach that goal is less certain. The concluding chapter raises questions about China's future. Chapter 11 assesses major outstanding challenges to China's politics and society, such as government corruption and rising social discontent that challenge domestic security. The chapter offers scenarios for the future direction of domestic politics and discusses prospects for democracy. Finally, the chapter offers perspective on China's future in world affairs.

This book is an introductory text, and I strongly encourage students to explore the wealth of excellent scholarship that is available beyond this book. I have included an exhaustive bibliography not only as a reference for the material in this book, but as a guide to further readings on China's politics and society.

Readers of this book should not be surprised to have some encounter with China in the future. That encounter may be traveling to China, doing business with or working for a Chinese firm in the United States, investing in Chinese firms, or conducting research on China for US businesses or the US government. More and more Americans are living in China and working for US or Chinese firms. My intent in writing this book is to prepare readers for those experiences by helping them to understand China, or at least helping them to understand a world in which China is becoming an increasingly important player.

Notes

1. New Yorkers are notorious for leaving the "r" off the ends of their words; the Beijing accent is heavy in the "r" sound.

2. Income is according to the International Monetary Fund, World Economic Outlook Database, September 2011, http://www.imf.org/external/pubs/ft/weo/2011/02/weodataindex/aspx.

3. The term "China" used in this book refers to the nation-state of the People's Republic of China, which consists of twenty-two provinces, including Tibet, the northwest territory called Xinjiang, and Hainan Island. It does not include the island of Taiwan and its associated territories. Throughout this book, the term "Taiwan" is used interchangeably with the "Republic of China" (ROC), which consists of the islands of Taiwan, Penghu, Jinmen, Mazu, and several islets.

2 The Historical Context

China's geography has had a strong impact on its history and politics.
Its rich loess plateau gave birth to China's civilization, and its rivers allowed a
large population to grow along its banks and in its valleys. China's active ports
were a link with foreigners such as religious missionaries and tradesmen from
other countries. Its fertile central region continues to serve as China's bread-
basket. Much of China is uninhabitable, with vast areas in the west and north
covered by mountains and desert. The difficulty in inhabiting much of its territory has put tremendous pressure on the eastern one-third of the country, which
supports more than 95 percent of the Chinese population. With these attributes
in mind, this chapter begins with an overview of the geography, people, and
key historical events that have shaped contemporary Chinese government and
politics.

Basic Geography

Continental China has a total area of 3.7 million square miles, roughly the size
of the United States, and with a population of 1.33 billion people.[1] China borders on fourteen countries, including Afghanistan, Bhutan, Burma, India, Kazakhstan, North Korea, Kyrgyzstan, Laos, Mongolia, Nepal, Pakistan, Russia,
Tajikistan, and Vietnam.[2] It has 9,010 miles of coastline and maritime claims to
the East China Sea, Yellow Sea, and South China Sea. These shared boundaries
and a claim to vast areas of ocean have resulted in numerous territorial disputes.
For instance, China disputes borders with India, Korea, and Russia, and disputes claims of the Spratly Islands with Malaysia, the Philippines, Taiwan, Vietnam, and Brunei. China occupies the Paracel Islands, which Vietnam and
Taiwan also claim, and the Diaoyu Islands (also known as the Senkaku Islands),
which Taiwan and Japan also claim.

Despite China's size, less than 15 percent of its land is arable. China has
one-fifth of the world's population, but only 7 percent of its arable land. China's

terrain is mostly mountains, high plateaus, and deserts in the west, and mostly plains, deltas, and hills in the east. China's population has historically been concentrated in river valleys and most of its 1.3 billion people live in the eastern one-third of the land. China's climate is extremely diverse and varies from tropical in the south to subarctic in the north. There are frequent typhoons, damaging floods, tidal waves, earthquakes,[3] deforestation, soil erosion, industrial pollution, water pollution, air pollution, and desertification.

The shortage of land suitable for agricultural production has created regional differences (such as in dialects), and prejudices among ethnic groups have made unification difficult. Nearly 92 percent of Chinese are Han Chinese (*huaren*). The remaining 107 million people are considered national minorities (*minzu*). The largest of China's fifty-five ethnic minority groups are the Zhuang, Uygur, Hui, Yi, Tibetans, Miao, Manchus, Mongols, Bouyei, Koreans, and Dai (see Table 2.1).

The Origins of Civilization and Culture

Archeological excavations conducted in the 1920s indicated that China's civilization emerged some six thousand years ago in the Yellow River (Huang He) region with the beginning of settled agriculture in the Loess Plateau (current northern Shaanxi Province). It gradually moved across the North China Plain. About 4000 B.C., the residents of Banpo Village (today's city of Xi'an) lived on

Table 2.1 Population and Geographic Distribution of Major Ethnic Groups

Ethnicity	Geographic Distribution	Population (millions)
Zhuang	Guangxi, Yunnan, and Guangdong	16.2
Manchu	Liaoning, Hebei, Heilongjiang, Jilin, Inner Mongolia, and Beijing	10.7
Hui	Ningxia, Gansu, Henan, Xinjiang, Qinghai, Yunnan, Hebei, Shandong, Anhui, Liaoning, Beijing, Inner Mongolia, Tianjin, Heilongjiang, Shaanxi, Guizhou, Jilin, Jiangsu, and Sichuan	9.8
Miao	Guizhou, Hunan, Yunnan, Guangxi,Chongqing, Hubei, and Sichuan	8.9
Uygur[a]	Xinjiang	8.4
Tujia	Hunan, Hubei, Chongqing, and Guizhou	8.0
Yi	Yunnan, Sichuan, and Guizhou	7.8
Mongolian	Inner Mongolia, Liaoning, Jilin, Hebei, Heilongjiang, and Xinjiang	5.8
Tibetan	Tibet, Sichuan, Qinghai, Gansu, and Yunnan	5.4
Bouyei	Guizhou	3.0
Korean	Jilin, Heilongjiang, and Liaoning	2.0
Dai	Yunnan	1.2

Source: 2000 Census in NBS of China, *China Statistical Yearbook 2010*, 28.
Note: a. Also spelled Uighur and Uyghur.

millet (a cereal grain), fish, and game. Villagers domesticated pigs and dogs, and stored grain in painted pottery (*yangshao*). This Painted Pottery culture spread throughout North China, the Yangtze Valley, and the southeast coast. Neolithic China also began silk production. China had a monopoly on silk production until some silkworms were smuggled to the West in the sixth century B.C. Neolithic farming villages were patriarchal, and relations with other villages were established by marriage or migration. One lineage was headed by a patriarch, with subordinate relations among family and extended family members. Society became more stratified in later centuries.

China's legendary Three Dynasties are the Xia, Shang, and Zhou. The Xia Dynasty (ca. 2000 to ca. 1600 B.C.) is largely considered a mythical dynasty. The Shang Dynasty (ca. 1600 to ca. 1000 B.C.) is China's first documented dynasty. Concentrated in the Yellow River Valley, the Shang Dynasty was characterized by a feudal system of nobles with one ruler or emperor. In addition to highly sophisticated architectural structures, archeologists in the 1920s found Shang "oracle bones," usually the clavicle bone of oxen or a turtle

China's Major Dynasties

Xia (ca. 2000 to ca. 1600 B.C.)
Shang (ca. 1600 to ca. 1000 B.C.)
Zhou (ca. 1027 to 256 B.C.)
Qin (221 to 207 B.C.)
Han (206 B.C. to A.D. 220)
Sui (A.D. 590 to 618)
Tang (A.D. 618 to 907)
Song (A.D. 960 to 1279)
Yuan (A.D. 1279 to 1368)
Ming (A.D. 1368 to 1643)
Qing (A.D. 1644 to 1911)

shell, used for divination. Inscriptions on the bones indicate a highly stratified society, with elites living in post-and beam constructed houses and farmers living in stamped-earth subterranean dwellings. China was decentralized throughout its prehistory. China's independent kingdoms left much control to localities, which were governed by clans and group leaders. For example, irrigation systems were conducted by local initiatives. The Shang also produced magnificent bronzes.

Around 1027 B.C., the Zhou conquered the Shang and built their capital near present-day Xi'an. The Zhou Dynasty (ca. 1027–256 B.C.) is the first dynasty from which there are written records. Zhou kings expanded their power northward and southward to the Han and Yangtze River areas and southeast along the Huai River and established a feudal system, in which sons of the Zhou kings controlled fifty or more vassal states. Despite the power of the Zhou kings, they could not control vassal lords, whose domains became semiautonomous kingdoms and city-states. The Zhou Dynasty is important for the study of China's government and politics because of its limitations on the power of the ruler and for the flowering of Chinese political thought.

China's Imperial Tradition

China's political system has long been characterized by political power concentrated in the hands of a few individuals. China's current rulers, the Chinese
Communist Party (CCP), are only the latest in a long line of leaders who sought
strong and centralized rule. What distinguishes China's current rulers from previous rulers is the extent of control the party has over civil society in China. For
instance, the current Chinese government dictates birth control policy in even
the smallest of Chinese villages. While China's current political system can be
described as authoritarian, for much of China's history, China was governed by
an imperial bureaucracy. In ancient China, rule consisted of the autocracy of
the emperor. Although political power was vested in the imperial authority and
was above the law, it was not without limits. The Zhou devised a concept called
the Mandate of Heaven (*tianming*) to impose limits on the ruler's authority.
Under this mandate, heaven (*tian*) conferred a mandate on any family that was
morally worthy of the responsibility, and kings could rule so long as their conduct was consistent with the will of heaven. The concept of the Mandate of
Heaven also legitimized rebellion. Once a ruler did not act as ruler, the people
had the right to dethrone him. The mandate also required the government to protect people from foreign invasion. Hence, the fall of a dynasty could be explained
in terms of the Mandate of Heaven: heaven could revoke the mandate if it was
dissatisfied with the quality of rule or the character of the ruler, and another ruler
could take his place. The periodic rise and fall of rulers in China was called the
dynastic cycle. The Zhou justified conquering the Shang with the Mandate of
Heaven. Thus endowed, the Zhou kings called themselves Sons of Heaven.

The Mandate of Heaven was reciprocal and conditional. Upon acceptance
of the mandate, the ruler agreed to provide for the people. If the emperor failed
in his responsibility to the people, his mandate would be in danger. Typically,
dynasties fell for one or more of the following reasons: oppressive land taxes,
especially those imposed on peasants; an increase in corruption in government;
inadequate protection of the people; and the inability of the regime to provide
for the people in times of distress. These factors were often coupled with natural disasters, which signaled that the Mandate of Heaven was in danger. Dynasties fell when they were challenged by men of humble origin who led revolts
against oppressive regimes, as in the case of the Han and Ming founders, military strongmen, or when the challengers were aliens or foreigners, such as the
nomadic Mongols and the Manchurians. The mandate would be revoked, and
revolt would result in the establishment of a new dynasty, which would right the
transgressions of the old.

Although China's rulers were autocratic, the emperor's power was not absolute. There were several limits to his rule. First, the Mandate of Heaven served
as a check on the emperor's power. Under the conditional, reciprocal mandate,
Chinese emperors were required to perform certain duties, such as conducting

the proper rituals for a good harvest. If the emperor failed in his duty, the people had a right to revolt. Second, traditions also limited the power of the emperor. Traditions passed down through the generations prescribing particular rules of decorum, or rites (*li*), limited the discretion of individual emperors. Third, China's large and difficult-to-traverse geography meant that emperors often left rule to local authorities, allowing them discretion to deal with parochial issues. China's geography also meant that local authorities often ignored directives from the imperial bureaucracy. The Chinese saying "Heaven is high and the emperor is far away" reflects this sentiment. Fourth, the emperor often relied on recommendations from advisers in his decisionmaking process. Fifth, censors, who were the eyes and ears of the emperor in criticizing the bureaucracy, were allowed to criticize the emperor.

It was during the Zhou Dynasty that Confucius, China's most influential philosopher, was born. No other individual influenced Chinese thought and society more than did Confucius. Although Confucianism's influence may have waned at times when other philosophies came into vogue, it has been an integral part of Chinese society for more than two thousand years and continues to be so today. Confucianism as a philosophy spans centuries and spawned several different philosophical schools. Rather than articulate the evolution of Confucianism over the centuries, the following sections discuss Confucian views of society and government, and introduce Confucianism as a political ideology.

Principles of Confucianism

During the Zhou Dynasty (1027–256 B.C.), China experienced a flowering of intellectual thought, particularly during the Spring and Autumn Period (Chunqiu Shidai, 722–481 B.C.).[4] One of the major philosophies that developed during this time, commonly known as the Hundred Schools era, was Confucianism, which offered views about how society could escape its difficulties. Confucius (Kongfuzi, or Master Kong, 551–479 B.C.) hailed from the Zhou state of Lu, during a time of power struggle and war among feudal lords. With little basis in law and order, rulers used brute force. Some feudal lords and other aristocrats lived in gratuitous luxury, but with a nearly complete lack of ethics. As the number of aristocrats increased, it became impossible to maintain their lavish lifestyles, and some former aristocrats became impoverished. Members of this impoverished group became warriors, government clerks, or philosophers. One of these was Confucius. What is known of Confucius comes from his *Analects* (*Lun-yu*, Conversations) and the *Mencius*, the work of his successor of that name.

A gradual breakdown of government authority and lack of ethics among rulers and the people had led to general chaos in Chinese society. Confucius believed that society was in disarray because standards had deteriorated and people were not living up to their highest ideals. If each individual were perfect in his behavior, society as a whole would likewise be perfect. According to Confucius, proper conduct (*li*) based on moral principles should govern behavior.[5] Hence, society would be harmonious if everyone behaved according to *li*. Confucius also stressed that merit would be rewarded and that hard work and striving for achievement provide the proper approach to life.

Confucius's prescription for the ills and evils of his day was a return to virtue.[6] Specifically, Confucius claimed that only by embracing the ideal of *ren*—humanity, benevolence, or perfect virtue—could society be spared the evil, violence, and cruelty that were destroying it.[7] Confucius believed that social harmony derived only from a hierarchical society in which everyone knew his or her position in society and acted according to the roles prescribed for that position. Relations in Confucius's society were hierarchical and reciprocal. Confucius's hierarchy consisted of superior-subordinate relationships in which the superior commands authority over the subordinate in return for respect and obedience. People would know how to behave in these hierarchical and reciprocal relationships because each role prescribed its own correct, or proper, behavior. The five Confucian relationships are between ruler and subject, father and son, husband and wife, elder brother and younger brother, and friend and friend. For example, a father would raise, nourish, and educate his son; the son would be filial (*xiao*) to his father, obeying him and giving him a commendable funeral. Note that of the five relationships, three were kinship oriented. In traditional Chinese society, the individual's primary duty was to the family rather than to the state. Of course *ren* is not limited to these relationships, but applies to a person's relationship with everyone else as well.

Mencius (372–289 B.C.) is the second great figure who developed Confucian thought. He believed that all men were born with the same kind of human nature and that human nature is good. He also believed that people had an innate sense of right and wrong. His idea that a ruler could not rule without the consent of the people led to the notion of the right to rebel against a ruler who did not take proper care of his subjects, effectively making him lose the Mandate of Heaven.

A second major school of thought, Daoism, questioned the Confucian ideals of social hierarchy and the associated social norms. *Dao,* meaning the path, or way, stemmed from Laozi (Old Master), believed to be an older contemporary of Confucius. In contrast to Confucianism, Daoism was more relativistic, egalitarian, and mystical. The antiauthoritarian Daoists claimed that people should seek to come to terms with the natural forces of the universe. These natural forces are yin and yang. Yin (represented by the female) has elements of passivity and darkness. Yang (represented by the male) has properties of activity and light. Yin and yang are considered complementary, rather than opposite. Harmony is achieved only when yin and yang are in balance, and when there is unity between man and nature.

A major intellectual rival to Confucianism was Moism, based on the ideas of Mozi, who believed in a life of simplicity and undifferentiated love.[8] The notion of undifferentiated love contradicted the Confucian virtue of filial piety in which one's primary duty was to one's family. Mozi shunned war as wasteful. He also believed that people should obey their leaders and that leaders should follow the will of heaven.

Divisions among competing kingdoms in the third century B.C. led to the disintegration of the Zhou Dynasty and the emergence of a new and powerful state, the Qin. Following the collapse of the Zhou, Qin Shi Huangdi, in 221 B.C., unified China into one state.[9] His capital was near modern-day Xi'an (Shaanxi Province), where the Terra Cotta Warriors were found in 1974. Known as the Great Unifier, Qin Shi Huangdi standardized weights and measures as well as currency. He contributed to the building of the Great Wall. To facilitate movement of his armies, Qin Shi Huangdi standardized the length of axles on carts and unified the width of ruts in China's roads made by cartwheels. The Qin created a government bureaucracy in which administrators were chosen not by virtue of birth, but by their performance on competitive examinations. The creation of bureaucratic rule allowed China to localize authority in a centralized state.

Qin Shi Huangdi's key adviser was Li Si, who belonged to the Legalist school of thought. According to the Legalists, the ruler must establish clear and unambiguous laws and strictly enforce them. People would see that violation of the laws would be dealt with severely, so they would quickly change their behavior. It is even better to have arbitrary laws, so that the people would be constantly reminded that power ultimately resided with the state and not with their personal notions of what was just and reasonable. The Legalists' view of human nature was largely negative. The Legalists believed that people were bad by nature and therefore sought punishment and rewards as a regulator of behavior. The Legalists viewed the written law as superior to *li* as regulator of behavior. Qin Shi Huangdi and the Legalists also rejected the concept of the Mandate of Heaven. Qin Shi Huangdi acted as an autocrat, believing that he had the power to do as he wished.

The goal of Legalism, as a political ideology, was to strengthen the state, and in particular to facilitate building a wealthy and strong army. In such a state, an individual's welfare was secondary. The Legalists stressed a strict, written legal code, rather than the *li* of Confucianism. The Legalists established tough punishment for breaking the law. Qin Shi Huangdi burned books of other disciplines and allegedly buried Confucian scholars alive.

Under the Legalists, the term *law* mainly indicated public law. Private law was still governed by custom. Public law is that which is codified to protect society and is not for the protection of individual rights. Chinese law was primarily penal in nature; namely, it was identified by punishment. Three characteristics of Qin Shi Huangdi's legal system were no presumption of innocence, group punishment, and harsh punishment. Contemporary China's legal and penal system continues to bear the heavy handprint of Legalism. Elements of Legalism, such as the lack of presumption of innocence and harsh punishment, are characteristic of China's legal system today.

Legalism, which had contributed to the unification of China, ultimately led to the demise of the Qin Dynasty. Its strict rule led the Chinese people eventually to abandon support for the Qin, and the dynasty collapsed less than four years after the death of its first emperor. The succeeding Han Dynasty (206 B.C. to A.D. 222) began with a strict Legalist code, but eventually adopted Confucianism as its guiding philosophy. Over time, Confucian philosophy evolved into political ideology.

Confucianism as Imperial Ideology

Confucianism became an ideology in the second century B.C. as the Han incorporated Confucianism into the Legalist state. The five key aspects of Confucianism as an ideology are the moral code, virtuous ruler, social harmony, hierarchical society, and group orientation. Confucianism as an imperial ideology stressed the concept of the virtuous and wise ruler whose first duty was to set a proper example of sound ethical conduct. This concept required the emperor to be benevolent and to carry out the requisite rituals. As noted earlier, Confucianism stressed social harmony, which was contingent on strict adherence to reciprocal relationships. Subjects were required to obey the emperor, sons their fathers, and so on. The strict observance of proper behavior reinforced the position of emperor as absolute ruler, so long as he acted properly. Confucianism as an imperial ideology stressed hierarchical society, in which the few learned men comprised the ruling class. One entered this ruling elite through the imperial civil service examination system, begun by the Han in the second century B.C. The examinations tested knowledge of the moral principles embodied in the Confucian classics. Although the exams were open to all males, mastery of the classics required many years of study, and only a small percentage of those who began the process succeeded. The examination system kept the ruling class small and elite, as the sons of the wealthy and powerful with access to a good education had an enormous advantage. The system also ensured that Confucianism would increasingly permeate the government, ensuring a very conservative polity. Although the examination system may be criticized for perpetuating Confucianism to the point of stifling individual intellectual thought, it can be credited with creating an elite stratum of government bureaucrats (mandarins) able to deal with any situation. Given the intellectual depth of Confucianism, the examination system produced extremely competent bureaucrats, who, despite their diverse backgrounds and dialects, shared a common experience and language (Mandarin, the scholar's language) and were capable of holding the empire together. The examination system lasted for two thousand years and fed the imperial bureaucracy with a constant flow of scholar-administrators who carried out the duties of the imperial government throughout China. Confucianism as an ideology put emphasis on the group over individual rights. Individuals who sought their own way threatened to upset the social order and were discouraged from challenging the system.

Confucianism heavily influenced the Chinese political system in three ways. First, it emphasized roles with obligations, duties, and rights. As an ideology, Confucianism posited that good government was fundamentally a matter of ethics and stressed that a ruler's first duty was to set a proper example of sound ethical conduct. For example, if a ruler acts as a virtuous ruler, the subject should then act as a virtuous subject and obey. Second, it was a philosophy that justified autocratic rule, a patriarchal culture, and a strictly hierarchical society. However, the hierarchies that Confucianism suggested involve reciprocity. In other words, in the frames offered by this philosophy, rulers also have a responsibility toward their subjects. One indication of this is the practice of valorizing ministers who corrected wayward rulers. Third, as a group-related teaching, Confucianism emphasized the salvation of society more than the fate of the individual. Throughout Chinese history, there has been no clear concept of protection of individual rights, and certainly not the concept of individual rights over those of society. That theme has been carried on into modern-day Chinese government and politics. For instance, under China's state constitution, the Chinese people enjoy many rights, but the government may suspend those rights if they threaten the state or social harmony.

The incorporation of Confucianism into the Legalist state may seem paradoxical, but the combination of the two made imperial China one of the world's richest and most powerful empires. The people preferred the Confucians' milder form of government to the Legalists' harsh and autocratic rule, and the Legalists found that they needed to call on the Confucians to govern. Through the imperial civil service examination, the Legalists brought Confucian scholars into the state.

The Early Imperial Era

The Han Dynasty expanded China westward through a series of wars. These wars were costly in terms of burdensome taxes and forced conscription into the army. The Han empire broke up into multiple independent kingdoms from A.D. 220 to 581. It was not until 350 years later that China would be reunited under one ruler, with the establishment of the Sui Dynasty in A.D. 590. Like the Qin, the Sui were continuously engaged in war and putting down rebellions, and their reign was brief. The Sui were followed by the Tang (A.D. 618–907), regarded by historians as one of the most cosmopolitan eras in Chinese civilization. Its capital city, Chang'an (present-day Xi'an), was the most populous city in the world at the time. The court was alternately Daoist or Buddhist, but Confucianism eventually revived under the later Tang. The Chinese people enjoyed peace and prosperity for most of the Tang Dynasty, and scholars consider the era the golden age of Chinese poetry and painting.[10] The Tang empire eventually extended into Central Asia and the Korean Peninsula, becoming the greatest power in Asia.

The Song Dynasty (A.D. 960–1279) expanded the civil service test to ensure a continual infusion of young talent into the government.[11] Education flourished and the economy also continued to expand. The Song also reformed the government. Wang Anshi, a counselor to the emperor, early in the eleventh century proposed a sweeping program of reforms designed to invigorate agriculture, revitalize the economy, enrich the country, and strengthen military forces. His major reforms included paying cash for labor to replace *corvee* (forced) labor for public works, providing loans to peasant farmers to be repaid at harvest, and expanding China's irrigation works to boost food production. To increase government revenue, he imposed a progressive tax on wealth. To ensure social order and strengthen local defenses, Wang created the *baojia* system of organizing households. The *baojia* system grouped together households into militias responsible for maintaining law and order. To build up the military, he assigned cavalry horses to each peasant family, who was then obligated to provide the horse and service to the cavalry in time of need. He also increased the number of government schools to compete with the private academies and tried to shift the focus of the examination system away from rote memorization of the classics to more practical problems of administration. To this end, he added tests in law, medicine, and military science to the examination system.[12]

Farm output increased greatly as the Song imported strains of rice from Annam (Vietnam) and improved the cultivation and irrigation of rice. The Song engaged in robust maritime trade and experienced a technological boom. Technical innovations included improved steel production through the use of coal-fired blast furnaces, glass-making, and the use of gunpowder for explosive uses. Papermaking, book printing, and the production of ceramics became established as important commercial industries.[13] The abacus came into use and became the chief calculating device for Asian merchants. Along with commercial expansion and technological advances came urbanization. China's population grew rapidly at this time and more and more Chinese lived in cities. Urbanization had several negative impacts on Chinese society, however. Absentee landlords increasingly exploited tenant farmers, and the status of urban women deteriorated. Although women had always been subordinate to men, urbanization made their work less essential, and it is at this time that we see the growth of the institution of concubinage and the introduction of foot binding. Despite these negative impacts, the Song Dynasty was one of the most prosperous in China's history.

Ironically, it was at this height of Chinese civilization that China was conquered by outsiders, the Mongols, in 1279. The Mongols ruled the Yuan Dynasty from 1279 to 1368. Many Chinese found Mongol culture completely alien and resisted participation in the government. The Mongols established separate systems of law for Chinese and for Mongols, and let the civil service examination system languish so that Confucian scholars no longer had a large presence in the bureaucracy. Although the Yuan eventually moved their capital from

Outer Mongolia to Beijing (Dadu), a large divide between the Chinese people and their foreign rulers persisted. During the Mongol century, many European merchants traveled to China, either through south Russia and the steppe, from Central Asia across the ancient Silk Route (or Silk Road), or by sea through the Indian Ocean and South Asia. The clerics followed, and the Catholic Church established a presence in China in the early fourteenth century.

Court rivalry, floods, famine, and rebellious uprisings weakened the later Yuan Dynasty, and the Mongols were overthrown by a peasant rebellion that established the Ming Dynasty in 1368. Under the Ming, eunuchs acquired considerable power in the imperial court because they, unlike other men, were allowed access to all of the quarters in the court. Numbering in the thousands, court eunuchs were closer to the emperor than were the scholar-officials and became trusted agents of the emperor. The Ming revived and revised the imperial civil service examination system suspended by the Mongols, creating three layers of examinations and three corresponding levels of scholar-officials. Quotas kept the pool of civil servants small, so only the best talent entered the imperial bureaucracy. The Ming also reestablished the tribute system with neighboring states and received tribute missions from Korea, Japan, Annam (Vietnam), Tibet, and others in exchange for military protection from adversaries. They also limited imports from foreign countries, and countries desiring to trade with the Middle Kingdom had first to acknowledge the superiority of the Son of Heaven. The Ming also dispatched maritime expeditions, the most notable being the voyages of court eunuch Zheng He, whose vessels sailed as far as Aden, Mecca, and Africa.

Although the court largely discouraged trade with foreign powers, Chinese merchants found profits in selling Chinese goods abroad and bringing foreign goods back to China with them. As both domestic and maritime trade grew during the later Ming, a thriving handicraft industry developed to support this trade. Despite its achievements, the Ming began its descent in the early seventeenth century as the competence of the emperors declined. The mediocrity of emperors would not have been such a problem if the Ming, like the Yuan before them, had not abolished the position of prime minister and concentrated power in the hands of the emperor. Absolute power in the hands of a virtuous and wise emperor is not a problem; absolute power in the hands of a disinterested emperor is a disaster. The Ming Dynasty was undone as much by inefficiency as by corruption and oppressive land taxes. As rebellion raged around him, the last Ming emperor hanged himself on Prospect Hill, overlooking the Forbidden City.[14]

The Manchurians succeeded in overthrowing the Ming, establishing the Qing Dynasty from 1644 to 1911. The Qing incorporated Taiwan and Tibet into the empire. They continued the imperial examination system, bringing into the government excellent scholar-officials to help administer the empire. Like the Yuan and Ming, the Qing vested all important powers in the hands of the emperor. All executive, legislative, and judicial decisions had to come from the emperor himself.[15] The Qing were blessed to have two good emperors who had especially long reigns. The Kangxi emperor reigned for sixty years (1662–1722) and the Qianlong emperor reigned for fifty-nine years (1736–1795). The Chinese people enjoyed relative peace and prosperity throughout the earlier Qing years. By 1800, however, military ineffectiveness, corruption in the court, and population pressures were beginning to stress the empire.

The Modern Period

The modern era began with earth-shattering events for China. Between the late Ming and Qing Dynasties, China went from being the world's largest and most sophisticated empire to a shattered state occupied by foreign powers. Internal instability coupled with foreign occupation weakened China's centuries-old imperial order. When reform came, it was too little, too late. A world war followed by a civil war further upset China's political system, economy, and society. It would take a small group of loosely organized but disciplined revolutionaries to build a new China out of the wreckage of the old.

The Age of Rebellion

When the West first encroached on China in the beginning of the nineteenth century, the Qing (1644–1911) was already a declining dynasty and was imposing oppressive land taxes. Due to prolonged peace and importation of some agricultural products, China's population had doubled and surpassed 400 million by the mid-1800s. Mounting population put pressure on the land as families divided land among sons, and local authorities and landlords increased land taxes. The people saw no benefit from these burdensome land taxes as the money or goods-in-kind (such as agricultural produce) merely went to corrupt bureaucrats and landlords. During this time of unrest, the Western powers came seeking trade and imperial expansion. China initially snubbed the Westerners, treating them as other barbarians. China's resistance to Western encroachment would lead to military conflict, with the Qing losing territory, legitimacy, and authority.

China under the Qing Dynasty was rocked by a number of rebellions.[16] Although each of these rebellions further weakened the Qing Dynasty, the Taiping Rebellion (1850–1864) had the greatest impact in undermining the authority of the Qing precisely at the time that the Western powers were encroaching on China. Like previous rebellions, the Taiping Rebellion was a peasant revolt. What distinguished it from other peasant rebellions were its religious manifestation and its grievances. The Taiping Rebellion was led by Hong Xiuquan, who proclaimed himself to be the brother of Jesus Christ, and who was inspired to create on earth a Heavenly Kingdom of Great Peace (*taiping tianguo*). Rather than revolt against increasingly oppressive land taxes, the Taiping rebelled against a land shortage as population pressure increased on the land. The rebellion advocated the redistribution of land; sexual equality, namely abolishing the foot binding of females; and prohibitions against slavery, adultery, witchcraft, gambling, alcohol, opium, and tobacco. At their height, the Taiping controlled much of central and eastern China below the Yangtze, capturing the city of Nanjing in 1853. The support of the people was not solid, however. The Taiping lacked a unified, stable leadership, and could not administer what they conquered. As Taiping reforms were contrary to intellectual interests, China's intellectuals sided with the Manchu Dynasty. Eventually put down by Chinese armies in 1864, the Taiping Rebellion was very costly in terms of human lives (an estimated 30 million people died) and in terms of further weakening the Qing Dynasty.

Stimulated by the Taiping Rebellion, separate rebellions emerged throughout China. In 1855, secret-society bandit gangs rebelled in the area between the Huai and Yellow Rivers, and in 1856 Chinese Muslims in Yunnan Province created a new Islamic kingdom in Dali in southwest China. In 1862, Muslims in the northwest also rebelled. It is in this environment of government corruption, mounting population and land pressures, and indigenous rebellion that the Western powers began their advance on China.

The Western Impact

Foreigners came to China several centuries ago. The Jesuit priest Mateo Ricci (Li Madou) (1552–1610) made Western developments in mathematics available to the Chinese in the late sixteenth century. The Dutch established an embassy in China in the seventeenth century and the Dutch East India Company conducted trade with China throughout the seventeenth through nineteenth centuries. The Portuguese actively traded in China in the fifteenth through eighteenth centuries until they were pushed aside by other foreign powers. It was the British, however, who had the greatest impact on the history of China.

Despite early trade with outsiders, over time the Chinese court had forbidden Western traders direct access to the court in Beijing and China's markets. Because of this restriction, foreigners had to conduct trade through their holdings in China. For instance, the Portuguese traded with China through their territory in Macau or via Taiwan. Others had to go through Chinese intermediaries. In the early nineteenth century, Great Britain wanted to deal directly with Beijing and bypass the Chinese intermediaries (called *hongs*) in Canton (present-day Guangzhou). One of Great Britain's key imports into China was *opium*. Opium came to China from Arab tradesmen in the eighth century and was used as a healing drug. Centuries later, the Chinese began to mix opium with tobacco, a practice adopted by Dutch traders in East Asia who mixed opium and tobacco to fight disease. The bamboo pipe facilitated the smoking of opium alone, and by the end of the seventeenth century, people were largely substituting opium for tobacco. By the 1830s, Chinese opium traders organized in brokerage houses were making huge profits. Although the Chinese government banned the selling and smoking of opium in several edicts as early as 1729, the trade offered a new source of corruption for government officials. By the 1830s, both the British and Chinese governments benefited from the China opium trade. Britain's commercial expansion became dependent on opium, while an organized smuggling system fueled Chinese government greed and corruption.

In 1839, the Chinese tried to crack down on the opium trade, resulting in the first Opium War of 1839–1842. The victorious British forced China to cede the island of Hong Kong to Great Britain in perpetuity. They also forced China to open several ports to British residence and trade. Foreign residential areas in these ports were called concessions, which enjoyed extraterritoriality. Under extraterritoriality, foreigners exercised legal jurisdiction over their own nationals. Over time, these concessions created taxation, police forces, and other features of municipal government, all subject to foreign, not Chinese, law. Supplemental treaties with the British, French, and Americans contained a "most-favored-nation" clause, meaning that whatever was promised to each power would be extended to the others. China also had to pay an indemnity to compensate for the confiscated opium and to reimburse the British government for the cost of the war. Finally, the foreign powers gained the right to set tariffs on imports. Without the ability to set tariffs, the Chinese treasury was deprived of important revenue as the foreign powers set low import duties on their manufactured goods. These features of the treaty settlements undermined China's sovereignty and undermined the authority of the imperial Chinese government. Supplemental treaties expanded the Western toehold in China. In 1860, Britain acquired Kowloon Peninsula (the southernmost tip of China across from Hong Kong Island), and in 1899 it leased the New Territories (an undeveloped area south of Guangzhou) from China for ninety-nine years.

When Western powers came to China, groups in China were divided over how to deal with them. The ultraconservatives wanted to maintain and strengthen traditional Chinese ways of life. The self-strengtheners were composed mostly of enlightened officials and scholars who were interested in appropriating Western technology in order to protect the neo-Confucian imperial-bureaucratic system to which they were loyal. They wanted to keep Chinese culture as the structure for Chinese society, but saw Western technology as useful. Most prominent of the self-strengtheners was Li Hongzhang, the Chinese statesman responsible for a number of infrastructure development projects, dealing with foreign powers, and for sending Chinese students to study in the United States. A third group, the institutional reformers, wanted to make China's political institutions more representative. In particular, they proposed introducing a constitution and the creation of a national assembly. The institutional reformers looked to Japan as a model, which had adopted Western political institutions while militarizing.

The Rise of the Radical Reformers: The One Hundred Days of Reform

At the close of the nineteenth century, reformer Kang Youwei offered a series of recommendations to the young Qing emperor. In 1898, Kang Youwei with Emperor Guangxu issued forty reform edicts dealing with almost every conceivable subject, including setting up modern schools, reforming the examination system, and sending students abroad; promoting the development of agriculture, medicine, commerce, and inventions; modernizing China's army and navy; and modernizing the police and postal systems. Chinese conservatives waited to see what the Empress Dowager Cixi, who had been in retirement since 1889, would do.

The One Hundred Days of Reform exacerbated existing tensions between those who advocated radical reform and those who advocated the continuation of a moderate "self-strengthening" course of modernization. Kang Youwei's reforms also threatened the empress dowager by attacking the twin pillars of her

The Empress Dowager Cixi

The Empress Dowager Cixi, popularly known as the "Venerable Buddha," was the widow of the previous emperor, Xian Feng. She had been a minor concubine of the Xian Feng emperor (1851–1861) until the birth of her son, Tongzhi, the emperor's only heir. After the emperor's death, Cixi became regent to Tongzhi, the new emperor, until 1873 when he came of age. Two years later, Tongzhi was dead, and it was rumored that Cixi had a role in his death. Violating the normal succession, Cixi had her three-year-old nephew named the new heir. Cixi acted as regent for her nephew, whose reign title was Guangxu, from his accession to the throne until his marriage and coming of age in 1889, when she went into retirement. Cixi remained a strong force at the imperial court in the Forbidden City and came out of retirement during the One Hundred Days of Reform. After orchestrating his overthrow in 1898, Cixi had the Guangxu emperor imprisoned in one of two prisons. One was on an island known as Ying Tai, whose name signifies Isles of the Blest, or Fairyland, in a lake west of the Forbidden City. The other prison was a windowless pavilion at the imperial Summer Palace. For nearly ten years, Cixi had the emperor shuttled between the two prisons as she traveled from one sumptuous palace to another. When the young emperor's wife, Chen Fei, pleaded with the Empress Dowager Cixi for her husband's release, Cixi had the young empress thrown down a well in the Forbidden City. Cixi ruled China until her death in 1908. It was well known that Cixi would take her place in the dynastic annals as the higher-ranked "grand empress dowager" only if she outlived Emperor Guangxu. In fact, the empress became the "grand" empress dowager for the few hours of her life after the death of the Guangxu emperor in 1908. (Johnston, *Twilight in the Forbidden City,* 28, 48) regime: classical learning and organized corruption in government. On September 21, 1898, she seized the Guangxu emperor, with the help of the warlord General Yuan Shikai, in a coup and began her third reign. With Yuan, she purged leaders of the reform movement. China's opportunity for reform ended prematurely. Cixi died in 1908. The young emperor, ill from neglect and mistreatment due to his imprisonment in a small, windowless pavilion at the Summer Palace, predeceased her by one day.[17]

By the turn of the century, China was a second-rate power. In contrast, Japan responded to Western encroachment by carrying out an aggressive reform agenda. Reformers in Japan believed that the best response to the West was to use Western technology to build "a rich country and strong military" (*fukoku kyohei*). By embracing both Westernization and modernization, Japan embarked on industrialization and political and military modernization. It created a constitutional government with deliberative assemblies, underwent an industrial revolution, and built a strong army. While China lost thirty valuable years to misuse of government authority and thousands of Chinese died in rebellions and famines, Japan largely succeeded in meeting its goals. After all, China had been forced to cede Taiwan and south Manchuria, as well as suzerainty over Korea, to Japan after a brief war with Japan in 1894–1895. China's defeat had come to symbolize the deterioration of the Qing Dynasty.

The Boxer Rebellion

Unlike the 1898 reform movement, which was a daring effort by Chinese scholars to respond to a foreign menace by modernizing the Qing government, the Boxer Movement was a popular initiative led by a secret society. The society, Yi He Quan (known in English as "The Society of Righteous and Harmonious Fists"), studied their own form of Chinese boxing (*quan*) to prepare themselves for battle. Using a combination of Daoist mysticism, proper diet, and martial arts, the Boxers believed themselves invulnerable to foreign bullets.

The sudden rise of the Boxer Movement was fostered by anti-Christian sentiment as well as by economic and political conditions. Yellow River floods had led to widespread famine in Shandong Province in eastern China in 1898, and North China suffered from a drought. Importation of foreign goods depressed domestic cotton and oil industries, and the new railroad threatened the livelihood of carters and canal bargemen. The late 1890s saw disorder, riots, banditry, or local uprisings in every province.

Qing officials used the Boxers, whose slogan was "Support the Qing, Destroy the Foreigner," to challenge the West. In June 1900, Boxers besieged foreign concessions in Tianjin and Beijing, killing foreigners and Chinese converts to Christianity, and looted the cities. The foreign powers called on their militaries to mount a relief effort. In return, the Qing government declared war against the foreign powers. International forces relieved the sieges in Tianjin and

Beijing, and the empress dowager fled Beijing in disguise, staying in Xi'an for a year. In the end, some two hundred fifty foreigners, mainly missionaries, were killed, and approximately one thousand Chinese died at the hands of the combined forces of eleven Western powers. In 1901, the Qing signed the 1901 Boxer Protocol, a formal peace treaty with the foreign powers. Among other things, the treaty forced the Qing to execute many high-ranking officials, destroy several imperial fortifications, suspend imperial examinations in many cities, and pay hefty war reparations to the foreigners. It also allowed the foreigners to expand their residences and to station troops in China. The Boxer Rebellion resulted in the near-dismemberment of the Qing Dynasty.

After her return to court in 1902, the Empress Dowager Cixi saw the need for reform. In particular, she proposed reforms of China's education system, military, and financial system, and encouraged local self-government. Her reforms came too little, too late. By that time, the prestige of the Qing Dynasty was gone.

The Revolutionary Movement

Throughout this turmoil, several groups began to organize against the Qing, seeking its overthrow. The leader of one of these revolutionary groups was Sun Yat-sen (1866–1925). Sun was a revolutionary, founder of the Nationalist Party, and father of the Republic of China. Sun was born into a peasant family in Guangdong Province (formerly Canton). Educated in Hawaii and Hong Kong, Sun began a medical career, but was dismayed by the foreigners' treatment of China. He turned to politics and sought to overthrow the Manchus. Sun advocated the Three Principles of the People, namely, nationalism, democracy, and the people's livelihood. The Three Principles of the People formed the theoretical basis for Sun's revolution. Nationalism (*minzu*) referred to recovering China for the Chinese by driving out the Qing (Manchu) Dynasty and the foreign imperialists and uniting China's Han, Manchu, Mongol, Tibetan, and Muslim minority ethnic groups within one sovereign, independent nation. Democracy (*minquan*) referred to government by the people under a republican form of government. The proposed government would have five powers: executive, legislative, judicial, plus examination and censorial, or control, drawn from Chinese tradition.[18] Under the people's livelihood (*minsheng*), the central government would impose a single tax on unearned appreciation of land values to limit the greed of absentee landlords, and all major productive enterprises would be under state control.

Living in exile in Japan, Sun in 1905 founded the Revolutionary Alliance (Tongmenghui) to bring together various anti-Qing groups seeking revolution. The forerunner of the Nationalist Party (Kuomintang, or KMT), the Revolutionary Alliance used the Three Principles as its manifesto. Young students, and

Chinese living overseas, in particular, supported Sun's Three Principles of the People. For instance, many Chinese students studying in Japan became members of the alliance. Although the Revolutionary Alliance instigated several uprisings from 1906 to 1908, it failed to overthrow the Qing. Despite these failures, by 1911 the Revolutionary Alliance had some ten thousand members, mostly young Chinese who had been recruited and trained in Japan and had returned to their home provinces to agitate secretly for revolution.

Sun's revolution finally succeeded in autumn 1911. On October 9, 1911, a large bomb being made by a revolutionary group in Wuhan exploded by accident. When police invaded, they immediately executed three revolutionaries and found a membership list of other revolutionaries. The list included names of thousands of Qing military troops. Knowing that those on the list faced certain death if caught, the revolutionaries decided to begin the revolution. Three thousand Qing troops rebelled on October 10 (Double Ten Day), forcing the Qing governor general and military commander to flee. In the following months, a succession of Chinese provinces rebelled against the Qing. Sun Yat-sen returned to China from the United States (where he had been seeking funds for his revolution) on Christmas Day 1911, becoming provisional president of the new government. The new government forced the Qing emperor, the five-year-old Pu Yi, to abdicate on February 12, 1912.[19] It was clear, however, that Sun did not have the backing of the military powers of the day. The powerful Beiyang Army refused to recognize Sun's presidency and instead gave the retired Qing general Yuan Shikai full powers to form a new government. In 1912, Yuan Shikai, not Sun Yat-sen, became the president of the new Republic of China (ROC).

The Republic of China

China's young democracy had a bad start. Yuan Shikai used bribery, military force, intimidation, and assassinations to consolidate his power. When the newly formed Nationalist Party (Kuomintang or KMT) elected a prime minister to thwart his power, Yuan had him assassinated.[20] When parliament refused to allow him to revise the constitution at will, Yuan suspended the parliament and local assemblies and declared himself emperor.

The republic lacked a firm foundation. Yuan was a selfish leader, and the Chinese people lacked a sense of nationalism. There was little to keep the republic together. Once the Chinese people had overthrown the Manchus, they drifted along without a common purpose. They also did not grasp the concept of democracy. China's political fortune went from bad to worse. Even though Yuan died in 1916, the impact of his actions lasted for years. His military men were placed in strategic positions in China, becoming warlords whose private armies controlled vast areas of China. The Nationalist government in Beijing nominally governed China, but in reality, the warlords controlled China. Divisions among the warlords fragmented the country and China remained in political chaos from 1916 until 1928.

The Warlord Era, 1916–1928

After Yuan's death, many of his military officers seized control of vast areas of China. Most warlords had no ties to the local population, but imposed arbitrary taxes on inhabitants to train, feed, and supply their forces. They also gained control of provincial revenues to feed their military machines. Lacking political legitimacy, the warlords used the civilian bureaucracy to seal (sign) official documents and issue demands. China in the warlord era had become a failed state.[21] The government of the Republic of China (ROC) only nominally governed China; the warlords were the true powers throughout the country. Even Sun Yat-sen for a time had to seek the protection of the warlord of southern China. Loyalties among warlord troops wavered as one warlord conquered the territory of another, leaving the peasants with yet one more tyrant to exact taxes.

Despite the term *warlord,* China suffered more from neglect than from war during the era. The results of warlordism were inflation, disruption of trade, deterioration in railways and in public works for flood control and irrigation, and the widespread use of opium.[22] The Qing Dynasty in 1906 had begun a concerted attack on opium production and smoking, and with widespread patriotic support, reduced the import and use of British Indian opium. However, the warlords revived Chinese production, which had been on its way to extinction. Warlords levied such high taxes on land suitable for poppy growing that nothing but opium could meet the payments. In sum, the ROC government had little control of China during the warlord era. Awash in arms, warlords ran roughshod

---

Warlords of China

Three of the era's most powerful warlords were Zhang Zuolin, Wu Peifu, and Feng Yuxiang. Zhang, dubbed the "Warlord of Manchuria," became Japan's ally against Russia and had been military governor at Mukden (current-day Shenyang) since 1911. Japan's army in Manchuria assassinated Zhang in 1928. Wu, Zhang's primary rival, represented the British and China's best hopes for peace and order in central China. Feng was called the "Christian General" because he urged his well-disciplined troops to pursue austerity, practical education, social reform, and Protestantism (Fairbank et al., *East Asia,* 760). He was said to baptize his troops with a fire hose. In 1924, Feng double-crossed Wu and allied with Zhang to seize Beijing in 1924. Feng then evicted Emperor Puyi and his family, who had been allowed to remain in the Forbidden City after Puyi's formal abdication.

over the peasants, who found little relief in civilian government and in the ROC government. Sun's ideals of a constitutional republic were ground into the dust of warlord armies.

The 1919 May Fourth Movement

The warlord era was a period of civil war, social and economic upheaval, and political chaos. Despite the chaos, China enjoyed a remarkable era of intellectual ferment. The 1911 revolution had been largely conducted by young revolutionaries, and young Chinese were inspired to take the lead in creating a new China. In 1905, the Qing Dynasty had abolished the examination system, with its emphasis on the Confucian classics. In its place, various Chinese governments as well as Western missionaries had established public and private schools throughout China, particularly in its urban areas. In the first two decades of the twentieth century, China had more young people enrolled in public and private schools than ever. In addition, many students who had studied abroad in Japan or the West had returned and were ready to assume leadership roles in Chinese society and politics. Peking University (also called Beijing University, or Beida), China's premier intellectual institution, became the country's center of intellectual ferment.[23] Peking University's dean of letters was Chen Duxiu. Chen, who had studied in Japan and France and had participated in the 1911 revolution, advocated French Revolution–style individual freedom, and called for students to challenge China's existing social order. Chen's magazine, *New Youth,* became an open forum of discussion among students at Peking University.[24] Chen, along with Peking University chief librarian Li Dazhao, became founders of the Chinese Communist Party (CCP).

These intellectual stirrings included a literary movement. Previously, Chinese writers had used the literary language (*wenyan*) for their works. Literary language was incomprehensible to the non-elite, much like Latin in the West. In 1917, a young philosophy professor, Hu Shih, who had just completed his thesis under John Dewey at Columbia University, proposed that all Chinese who made their living by writing henceforth use the spoken language (*baihua*) instead of the literary language. In recommending the switch, Hu Shih made works of literature accessible to all. He also urged that literature be tied more directly to the life of the people.

Chinese youth, reflecting Chinese society, had grown impatient with the extraterritoriality enjoyed by foreigners in Chinese cities, civil war among warlords, and foreign control of international trade. Western occupation during World War I had revived domestic Chinese industry in the near-absence of competition from foreign goods and had given rise to a thriving merchant class. Students and merchants in particular were becoming increasingly patriotic. This patriotism had been mounting since 1914, when Japan, declaring war on Germany, seized Germany's foreign concessions in Shandong Province. In 1915,

Japan had issued to the Chinese government 21 Demands, a document granting Japan extensive economic and commercial rights in China. The Chinese government's acceptance of the demands sparked nationwide anti-Japanese rallies and boycotts of Japanese goods. This patriotism transformed into nationalism in May 1919 after decisions made at the Treaty of Versailles became public.

The Chinese delegation to the Paris Peace Conference in January 1919 found that the warlord government in Peking in 1918 had signed secret agreements confirming Japan's Shandong position.[25] The Treaty of Versailles affirmed the secret agreements. News of the Versailles affirmation sparked huge protests in China. Some three thousand students protested at Peking University on May 4, 1919. The May Fourth Movement, as this event is commonly known, actually refers to the intellectual movement that followed the protests. The May Fourth Movement had a profound and lasting effect beyond the immediate issue of the Versailles treaty. First, the May Fourth Movement marked the birth of nationalism in China. Although China was still geographically and politically divided by the warlords, urban Chinese in particular began to see themselves more as part of a larger collective identity. While a man from Suzhou might identify more strongly with his hometown than with the Chinese nation, the May Fourth Movement created a sense of identity with China as an independent sovereign nation-state, albeit one that was fragmented and largely under the influence of the Western powers and Japan. One manifestation of this nationalism was China's refusal to ratify the Treaty of Versailles. Second, the May Fourth Movement sparked interest in foreign ideas as young Chinese increasingly turned away from Confucianism and Chinese tradition in their quest to create a strong and modern China. Chinese intellectuals turned to Western thought—such as democracy, socialism, and Marxism—for answers to China's social, economic, and political problems. It was during this time of intellectual stimulation that a handful of Chinese, convinced that communism held the key to China's independence from foreign interference and to national development, created the Chinese Communist Party in 1921. For these three reasons—the birth of nationalism, the increase in intellectual stimulation, and the creation of the CCP—it would not be an exaggeration to state that the May Fourth Movement was one of the most significant events in China's twentieth-century political history.

The KMT-CCP First United Front

Sun Yat-sen was frustrated with the Chinese revolution after 1911. Between 1912 and 1920, first Yuan Shikai and then a series of warlords controlled most of China. Their military rule promoted personal interests and ambitions rather than the good of the country. In 1921, disaffected parliamentarians named Sun president of the Chinese People's Government, located in Guangzhou under the protection of a southern warlord. When the warlord turned against Sun in 1921,

Sun was forced to find a new area of support. The Russian Bolsheviks, who wanted to have diplomatic relations with China, offered to help Sun eliminate the warlords and imperialism. In summer 1922, Sun Yat-sen fled to Shanghai and met with Mikhail Borodin (originally Mikhail Gruzenberg), an agent of the Communist Third International (Comintern) who advised Sun to reorganize the KMT along Leninist lines. In January 1922, Sun signed a joint communiqué with Soviet diplomat Adolf Joffe, the Sun-Joffe Agreement, creating the First United Front between the Nationalists and communists. Reluctant to accept a full KMT-CCP alliance, Sun accepted only individual communists into the KMT, believing that a few communists would have little effect on the KMT. The arrangement was key in tipping the balance of power in favor of Sun. Following the Sun-Joffe Agreement, Sun regained Guangzhou.

The new KMT held its first party congress in January 1924. It made Sun party leader for life and approved his Three Principles of the People as the party's guiding ideology. Borodin had a strong hand in drawing up the first party manifesto. Three key points of the manifesto are worth mentioning. The first point was to attack the role of foreign powers in China. This agenda made anti-imperialism a very important part of Chinese nationalism. The second key point was to appeal directly to Chinese peasants and workers. The communists taught Sun how to broaden his base by appealing to peasants, reorganizing from bottom to top. The third key point called for the organization of a military school called the Whampoa Military Academy. As part of the KMT-Comintern alliance, the KMT sent officers for military training in the Soviet Union. For instance, Sun sent his military assistant, Chiang Kai-shek, to the Soviet Union for three months to study Soviet conditions and to negotiate for Russia's aid, as well as to study the Russian communists' military and political organizations. Upon his return, Sun appointed Chiang head of the new Whampoa Military Academy in Guangzhou. The academy's political commissar was the communist Zhou Enlai (who later became foreign minister under the Chinese communist government). Thus, with the assistance of the Russian communists, Sun reorganized the KMT and created a revolutionary army with political commissars to control the army. The Whampoa Academy built the powerful military army that eventually brought most of China under KMT control.

Sun died unexpectedly of cancer in Beijing in 1925. After much jockeying with rivals for political power, Chiang Kai-shek by 1926 had established himself as Sun's successor. The existence of a common enemy—the warlords in the north and imperialism—kept the KMT and CCP together. But once the enemies were eradicated, the KMT and CCP split apart. Virulently anti-communist, Chiang would soon unleash military terror against China's communists.

The Nationalist Government

In summer 1926, Chiang set out from Guangzhou in a Northern Expedition to defeat the warlords or force their subordination. With the help of the Manchurian

---

The Soong Dynasty

During Chiang's Northern Expedition, KMT left-winger Wang Ching-wei tried to form a government in the tri-city of Wuhan (composed of Wuchang, Hankow, and Hanyang) and wrest control from Chiang. To shift the balance of power in the Hankow government, Chiang sought the aid of the finance minister of Hankow, T.V. Soong. Chiang went through Soong's married sister, Soong Ai-ling, wife of skillful banker H. H. Kung. Madame Kung informed Chiang that she would get the money he needed from her brother on the condition that Chiang agreed to marry her sister, Soong Mei-ling, and also agreed to name her husband prime minister and her brother finance minister in a new government (Seagrave, *Soong Dynasty*, 258). Chiang agreed to all of the conditions, sending his present wife to the United States, and then disclaiming her when she arrived there. (Chiang had married the young Chen Jeizhu [Ch'en Chieh-ju] in 1921, after having divorced his much older first wife. See Ch'en and Eastman, *Chiang Kai-shek's Secret Past.*) After final victory over the warlords in 1928, Chiang Kai-shek named H. H. Kung prime minister and T.V. Soong minister of finance of the new Nationalist government.

---

warlord Zhang Xueliang, Chiang's armies in one year defeated the northern warlord armies.[26]

Bankrolled by the finance minister of Hankow, T.V. Soong, and assisted by Manchurian warlord Zhang Xueliang, Chiang quickly defeated the northern warlord armies and in 1928 established a capital in Nanjing. The KMT split, with the left wing going with the communists to Wuhan. There was considerable attraction for the young and educated Chinese to joining the Nanjing government to strengthen and modernize China. For a time, the Nanjing government offered some peace, stability, and nominal unity to China. Support for the new government came from Shanghai and Nanjing industrialists. The strength of the government, however, was confined largely to China's important industrial areas.

During the Nanjing Decade (1927–1938), the Nationalists tried to implement Sun's Three Principles of the People: nationalism, democracy, and people's livelihood. First, the Nationalists unified the country by defeating or co-opting most warlords, meeting Sun's aim of nationalism. Second, the Nationalists created a republican form of government. Sun had envisioned democracy evolving in China in three stages. In the first stage, military autocracy would establish order and dismantle the old imperial government. It would be followed by a second stage of political tutelage in which the military would still rule, but democracy would gradually be introduced to Chinese society. The third stage envisioned a transition from military rule to democracy. The Nanjing government represented a point between the military and political tutelage stages because it began political tutelage of the people under one-party control. The government proclaimed a draft constitution in May 1936, and called for a national assembly later that year to draw up a constitution based on the draft.[27] The draft established a five-power constitution, based on Sun Yat-sen's idea. Added to the three-power Western constitution (executive, legislative, and judicial branches) were the control and examination branches. The control branch prevented the legislature from controlling the actions of the executive branch; the examination branch made sure that people entered government through exams and not through a spoils system. The executive branch soon dominated the legislature, however, and the judiciary was not very independent-minded. Despite this shortcoming, the Nationalists recruited into the government many qualified individuals and established a relatively modern, efficient government, albeit with the help of the Blue Shirts, a paramilitary police force.

The Nationalist government also tried to fulfill Sun's principle of the people's livelihood by passing a land reduction law that imposed heavy taxes on land owned by absentee landlords. This measure was not fully implemented, however, as many areas were outside Nationalist control. In addition to fulfilling the Three Principles, the Nationalists improved and expanded highways, railroads, communications, and industrial facilities. They expanded elementary education and provided political indoctrination for Chinese youth. Although the Nationalists continued the policy of extraterritoriality, they issued new law codes and secured new treaties, placing many minor foreign nationalities under Chinese jurisdiction. They reduced foreign concession areas from thirty-three to thirteen.

The Nationalists recovered tariff autonomy in 1933, and regained control over maritime customs, the Salt Revenue Administration, and the post office. The government also engaged in monetary reform. The Nationalists substituted managed paper money for silver (the U.S. silver-buying program siphoned off China's silver) and backed the currency partly with reserves of foreign exchange. The Nationalists reorganized administrative divisions of China to reestablish effective administrative control over the countryside: county (*xian*), ward, townships, villages (*cun*) or urban neighborhoods (*li*), and a household registration system, similar to the Qing *baojia* groupings of houses and villages. Groups were supposed to elect headmen and councils, but in practice, officials were appointed from above by the county magistrates.

With these changes, life in the cities improved tremendously, especially for those who had money. Major improvements included more sophisticated medical care, the construction of new hospitals, and the addition of sports grounds and laboratories to schools and college campuses. In the countryside, however, things were as tough as before. Local administrators were often tyrannical or corrupt, and were more sympathetic of local landlords than of the peasants. The worldwide depression of the late 1920s brought disaster to many peasants who had overconcentrated on certain cash crops, and hundreds of thousands, perhaps millions, died when the markets in crops such as silk, cotton, soybeans, and tobacco suddenly plummeted. The need was therefore all the greater for strong political initiative. The central government lacked funds and initiative. The Nationalists were able to govern China from their capital in Nanjing for only a decade. In 1937, they were forced to move the government to Chongqing in the country's interior as Japan seized and occupied China. This wartime displacement rendered the Nationalist government useless.

The Rise of the Chinese Communist Party

Not long after the creation of the KMT, the Chinese Communist Party was established in Shanghai in 1921. It was cofounded by Li Dazhao, a professor of history and chief librarian at Peking University, and by Chen Duxiu, dean of the university's College of Letters. Chen served as the CCP's first secretary-general. Under the control of the Comintern, the CCP participated in an alliance, or First United Front, with the Kuomintang. Two major events, the May 30 Movement and Chiang Kai-shek's White Terror against the communists, contributed to the rise of the CCP, and caused the First United Front to unravel.

In May 1925, Chinese workers were locked out of a Japanese-owned textile mill in Shanghai during a labor strike. Angry at the lockout, the workers broke into the mill and smashed some of the machinery. Japanese guards opened fire, killing one of the workers. This violence was followed by a number of arrests. On May 30, thousands of workers and students assembled outside the

Mao Zedong

One of the early members of the CCP was Mao Zedong. Mao was born in 1893 to a middle-class farming family in Shaoshan, Hunan Province. (Mao's father was a prosperous rice and grain trader, and Mao's sprawling boyhood home is now a museum.) While working at the library at Peking University, Mao met the organizers of the CCP and became a committed Marxist. He returned to Hunan to establish communist organizations there and became an accomplished strike organizer and labor agitator. Mao, like other communists, joined the Kuomintang in 1923 under the First United Front, but relocated to the Jiangxi Soviet during Chiang Kai-shek's Northern Expedition and White Terror. In the 1930s, Mao fought the Japanese occupation of China while rising to leadership of the CCP. He led the Chinese communists to victory over the Nationalists, and presided over the establishment of China's socialist transformation. He used violence and mass campaigns to destroy adversaries and traditional Chinese culture. By the time of his death in 1976, Mao had assumed godlike status among the Chinese people. Along the way, Mao had four wives and ten legitimate children.

police station in the Shanghai International Settlement, demanding the release of six students who had been arrested by the British, and to protest against militarism and foreign imperialism. The British inspector in charge sent a detachment of Chinese and Sikh constables to disperse the crowd. He ordered his men to fire, and eleven of the demonstrators were killed and twenty were wounded. The tragedy of May 30 was followed by huge rallies in Canton and Hong Kong. Those killed were called the May 30 Martyrs. As rage spread all over China, thousands of Chinese joined the CCP.

After its inception, the CCP had infiltrated Shanghai labor unions. Meanwhile, during the Northern Expedition of 1927, Chiang Kai-shek's forces began to root out communists. After taking control of Shanghai in April 1927, Chiang, with the help of the underworld Green Gang (Qing Bang), moved to destroy the CCP-led labor movement by killing thousands of labor organizers, communists, suspected communists, and communist supporters. This attack, known as the Shanghai Massacre, was part of Chiang's larger White Terror campaign against the communists. While some communists were able to survive by hiding in the French concession, others fled to the countryside. Chiang expelled the Soviet advisers from China, ending the First United Front.

In fall 1927, the CCP authorized a series of insurrections, called Autumn Harvest Uprisings, in central and southern China. Mao led attacks on several small towns near Changsha in his home province of Hunan. The communists suffered a series of defeats, resulting in the execution of hundreds, if not thousands, of communists. Survivors were driven underground in the cities or forced into the countryside. The CCP's Central Committee was forced to work in secret in China's foreign enclaves in Wuhan and Shanghai, which provided refuge for the Chinese communists. Mao fled to the Jinggang Mountains (Jiangxi Province),

China's Secret Societies

Shanghai's Green Gang was a secret-society organization that did a brisk business in opium smuggling, heroin trafficking, prostitution, gambling, and protection rackets. It engaged in extortion and pressed businesses for "protection." Gang leaders could be called on to arrange hired guns to break up labor meetings and even kill labor organizers. Many of its leaders were prominent Shanghai businessmen with strong ties to the Kuomintang. One of the gang's most notorious leaders, Big-eared Du (Du Yuesheng), was a close associate of Chiang Kai-shek. A rival secret society was the Red Gang (Hong Bang). The Red Gang was one of the most influential organizations in Shanghai's power circles around the turn of the century. Once involved in the opium trade, by 1910 it had become a club of aging Nationalists, and thereafter left the criminal work to the Green Gang.

The Wives of Mao Zedong

Following the failure of the uprising in Changsha, the Comintern removed Mao from all his Communist Party posts. He retreated to a remote area between Jiangxi and Fujian Provinces. Based in the Jinggang Mountains, Mao carried out bandit raids and married his third wife, He Zichen. Mao was married four times. He married his cousin Luo in an arranged marriage; they apparently never lived together. Mao's second wife was Yang Kaihui, the daughter of one of his teachers. The KMT executed Yang in 1930. Mao's third wife, He Zichen, accompanied Mao on the long march; the marriage ended in divorce. Mao's fourth wife was Jiang Qing, a former actress.

where he began a series of public executions of landlords and aggressive land redistribution to the peasants. He was later joined there by communist military leader Zhu De and a few thousand men. Strengthened by his association with Zhu, the CCP put Mao in charge of the five-thousand-man-strong Red Army.

The Jiangxi Soviet

By the end of 1928, Kuomintang troops had forced Mao and Zhu out of the Jinggang Mountains. They moved southwestward to the Jiangxi-Fujian border, settling in the mountain town of Ruijian. Mao declared the establishment of the Chinese Soviet Republic, known as the Jiangxi Soviet, in November 1931, and declared himself president of the Chinese Soviet Republic. In Ruijian, Mao's land redistribution was so brutal that the communists lost much of the peasants' support.

After Chiang Kai-shek's slaughter of communists in the 1927 White Terror, most communists fled to the countryside and found ample fodder in the peasants for their revolution. The urban communists, however, still represented the Moscow-led Comintern and needed to live furtively and pass directives to the rural areas. Finally, even Moscow realized that a shift from urban insurrection to rural peasantry needed to be made. The early 1930s marked a shift from using the urban proletariat to using peasants as instruments of revolution. In Moscow, however, this was merely a tactical shift. The Comintern fully intended to return to the idea of a proletarian (namely urban-worker) revolution once conditions were ripe in Chinese cities. By 1932, the CCP Central Committee left its secret headquarters in Shanghai and moved to the central base in Jiangxi, where Mao Zedong was president.

Mao's strategy was to implement land reform and to use peasants to liberate China. Chinese peasants were not familiar with the concepts of socioeconomic classes and class warfare. After years spent observing peasant life in rural China, first in the Jinggang Mountain region and then in Jiangxi, Mao believed that peasants first needed class consciousness before they could be inspired to revolt and to overthrow the oppressive class. Mao divided the peasants into four categories: poor peasants, middle peasants, rich peasants, and landlords. According to Mao's strategy, a successful revolution needed the poor peasants and farmhands to unite with the middle peasants against rich peasants, and to liquidate the landlords.

Mao sought the support of the overwhelming majority—the poor peasants—and indoctrinated both peasants and rural bandits in class warfare, inspiring them with promises of land reform. Indoctrinated peasants and bandits were converted into Red Army soldiers. Mao mobilized the peasants and bandits in fighting, production, and propaganda efforts. Because the peasants and bandits knew the land better than did outsiders, Mao was able to mobilize them in guerrilla mobile war. Mao mobilized disciplined forces rooted in the land where they lived and were supported by the masses. More than his position as president of the Jiangxi Soviet, it was Mao's ability to put theory into practice that gave him credibility and legitimacy.

The 1934–1935 Long March

The virulently anticommunist Chiang Kai-shek wanted to oust the CCP from the Jiangxi Soviet. From 1930 to 1934, Chiang organized five "extermination campaigns" against the communist base areas. The first four campaigns were unsuccessful. The fifth campaign was launched differently. In the fifth campaign, Chiang used the *blockhouse method,* which encircled the area with a wall of small fortifications. Those enclosed areas were denied vital supplies and limited the communists' mobility. Chiang's forces gradually tightened the blockade, finally forcing the communists to escape toward southwestern Jiangxi in October 1934. The communists fled across twelve provinces from Jiangxi in eastern China southward through Canton and southern and southwestern China, and then northward through central China to remote northern China. They crossed rivers, mountain ranges, and marshes, and fought cold, fatigue, hunger, thirst, and sickness. They were pursued by not only KMT forces but also local warlords and non-Chinese tribal chiefs. The communists made this arduous trek of some six thousand miles in 368 days, averaging sixteen miles a day, settling in remote Yan'an in Shanxi Province in October 1935. Of the hundred thousand men (and several hundred women) who started out on the Long March, only seven thousand to ten thousand survived.

The significance of the Long March is fourfold. First, survivors of the march became China's political elites for the next sixty years. Many of them gained legitimacy by survival: those who survived were deemed to have the "right stuff." Nearly all of China's political elites through the 1990s could cite their experience on the Long March. The Long March also served as a common experience, binding survivors to each other. As political elites, the Long March survivors enjoyed a large network of supporters and comrades. Survivors of the Long March who assumed key party and government posts include Mao Zedong, Zhou Enlai, Deng Xiaoping, Chen Yun, Peng Dehuai, Lin Biao, and Liu Shaoqi, among others. These individuals are discussed in successive chapters.

Second, the Long March marked the decisive break with the Comintern. In January 1935, the retreating communists stopped in the town of Zunyi in Guizhou Province to hold an enlarged conference of the Politburo, the CCP's executive and policymaking body. Comintern military adviser Otto Braun, who made the Long March with the Chinese communists, and the CCP's Russian-trained element continued to advocate conventional, positional warfare with the Nationalist forces. On the run from the KMT, the CCP membership finally became fed up with the Comintern advisers and opted to follow Mao's guerrilla warfare tactics instead. After the departure of Comintern adviser Otto Braun, the CCP had no contact with Moscow.[28] The CCP's election of Mao without the Comintern's consideration was a decisive break with Moscow. Hereafter, the Chinese communist revolution would be a *Chinese* affair, not merely a part of the larger Comintern program of exporting communist revolution abroad.

Third, it was during the Long March that Mao became leader of the Chinese communists. Mao began to take over the CCP leadership in the course of the Long March, but his position was solidified at Zunyi. Chou En-lai shifted support to Mao and gave Mao leadership of the party's key military post, the Military Affairs Commission (MAC). Of the other communist military leaders at the time, Lin Biao, Peng Dehuai, and Zhang Guotao, only Zhang challenged Mao. Zhang wanted to move to Xinjiang Province to be closer to the Soviet Union. Mao prevailed and was elevated to the position of chairman of the CCP, and Zhang defected to the KMT. Fourth, the march transformed military defeat to triumph and became a key part of CCP mythology and propaganda for decades. In 1935, the CCP settled in Yan'an in remote Shaanxi Province. Safe from Chiang's forces, Mao was able to use the twelve years in Yan'an to develop his political philosophy.

The Yan'an Era

Safe from Chiang's forces, the communists in Yan'an had time to recruit peasants to their forces, carry out agricultural reforms, and purify their ranks. Their effective use of guerrilla warfare against the Japanese in northern China led to fresh recruits among the peasants. Party membership grew to more than 800,000 in 1939 and to about 1.2 million at the end of World War II in 1945. With expanded membership, the party was better able to dispatch activists throughout China's rural north, carrying out experiments in land reform and spreading revolutionary zeal. The communists' penchant for fighting the Japanese and for land reform endeared peasants to the party. The CCP investigated peasants' needs and devised ways to help them meet those needs. The party accomplished this task by providing local peace and order, creating an army of friendly troops who helped peasants in their livelihood, harvesting crops, and by fraternizing with villagers. It also recruited local activists to their causes and began a program of economic betterment for rural peasants by helping to improve crop yields, facilitating agricultural cooperation among farmers, and organizing transportation of produce to markets. It was during this time that many of the practices and experiences of the communists would later fondly be referred to as the "Yan'an Spirit." The United States sent a delegation called the US Army Observation Group, commonly known as the Dixie Mission, to Yan'an to meet with the communists to better understand their agenda and to assess their chances of success in eventually governing China. The mission reported back to Washington that it found morale high and a people infused with a sense of purpose. It also reported that the communists would likely rule China after the end of World War II.[29]

The CCP relied on land reform to maintain a large army. In the vast rural areas under its control, the CCP confiscated landlords' and other opponents' land and tools and redistributed the land by priority to those who joined the army, to the people's militia and their families, and to poor landowners and tenant-peasants. In this manner, the CCP was able to recruit able-bodied peasants, as well as local administrations, into a reserve for the party-controlled army. It also organized old and weak men as well as women into vigilance, production, and military supplies services. The party reorganized the administration at all levels in every locale, placing the army, policy, and people's militia, and all social organizations, under the control of the CCP.[30]

With the peasantry gradually coming under party control, Mao began to purify the CCP of remnants of the Soviet-oriented communists. In practice, the campaign isolated and removed Mao's real or potential opponents. Mao, from 1942 to 1944, undertook a party rectification (*zhengfeng*) campaign against "bureaucratic tendencies." In spring 1942, Mao encouraged members to offer constructive criticism on party operations. After they had come forward, Mao condemned them for their individualism and subjected them to intensive indoctrination in study groups. Some party members were required to make self-criticisms. One scapegoat was Wang Shiwei. Wang was an urban intellectual who migrated to Yan'an after the outbreak of the war with Japan in 1937. In his 1942 work "Wild Lily," Wang denounced party cadres who sought special privileges and lived in relative luxury while young party members like himself were badly nourished and living in dreary conditions.[31] The CCP put Wang on trial and beheaded him. In the wake of these attacks on intellectuals, which Wang's case represented, party cadres lined up to write self-criticisms, eager to avoid harsh punishment. Between 1943 and 1944, all prominent party leaders wrote self-criticisms, openly acknowledging regret and expressing absolute loyalty to the party and to Mao.[32] Mao's security chief, Kang Sheng, then took on a deadly assault against Mao's real or potential opponents. Kang arrested, imprisoned, and tortured more than a thousand party members. Another forty thousand were dismissed from the party. Sixty top party officials committed suicide.[33] Satisfied with the results, Mao in 1944 called off the rectification campaign.

With his opponents silenced, Mao became the undisputed leader of the CCP. In 1943, Mao became chairman of the Politburo and its Secretariat. In 1945, the Seventh CCP Congress claimed that, in order to assure revolutionary success, the party must take Mao as its teacher, and his thought as infallible text. Mao's personality cult had begun. Henceforth, party members, and then Chinese citizens, would refer to Mao by honorifics such as Great Leader, Supreme Teacher, Inspirer of the Masses, Great Savior, and Great Helmsman. By 1945, Mao's authority was supreme.

The experiences at Yan'an, from carrying out land reform to generating peasant enthusiasm for the party to rectifying the party, gave the CCP opportunity to work out any problems associated with these approaches, and helped prepare them to carry out socialist revolution after 1949.

The Collapse of the Nationalist Government and Civil War

The communists were only one threat to the survival of the Nationalist government. The other was Japan. While the Qing Dynasty was teetering on the brink of collapse at the end of the nineteenth century, Japan had gone through a rapid industrial revolution and was building a constitutional democracy. As militarists gained prominence in Japan, the Japanese government channeled much of the fruits of the industrial revolution into military development. At the beginning of the twentieth century, Japan was on the brink of military greatness. At the end of the 1904–1905 Russo-Japanese War, Japan had gained control of Russia's far eastern railways, which extended into China's Manchuria. Japan then stationed troops along this Kwantung Railway. In 1928, Japanese forces had assassinated Zhang Zuolin, the Warlord of Manchuria, believing that his son, Zhang Xueliang, would be more compliant regarding Japan's gradual territorial expansion into Manchuria. In the late 1920s and early 1930s, Zhang Xueliang, dubbed the Young Marshall, was pressed into service with Chiang Kai-shek fighting the communists. In 1931, Japanese army officers in Manchuria set off explosives on a stretch of railway line outside Mukden (today's Shenyang), claiming them to be acts of sabotage by the Chinese. Skirmishes broke out between the Japanese and Chinese, and Japan ordered a full-scale attack against the Chinese barracks. Not wanting a large-scale conflict with a militarized Japan,

Chiang Kai-shek instead ordered Zhang Xueliang to withdraw his forces south of the Great Wall. By year's end, Manchuria was under complete Japanese control. In 1931, Japan established the nation-state of Manchukuo and installed deposed Qing emperor Puyi as emperor of Manchukuo. From 1935 to 1936, Japan was fighting in China, but Chiang used Zhang's forces to fight the communists and warlords.

To get Chiang's forces off their backs, the communists turned the people's attention toward fighting Japan. The Chinese communists offered the KMT a second united front, but Chiang wouldn't agree. Chiang equated the Japanese with a cancer of the skin, but the communists with a cancer of the body. Chiang argued that the cancer of the body was the greater threat. While it is possible to excise a cancer of the skin, a cancer of the body will destroy the body if not totally eradicated. Hence, Chiang saw the Japanese occupation as a temporary threat, but the Chinese communist challenge as a greater, long-term threat. Chiang was less reluctant to pursue the communists than to fight the Japanese. By pursuing the communists, Chiang was able to extend his authority to southwest China, an area not previously under his control.

By 1936, the Young Marshall was fed up with Chiang's unwillingness to fight the Japanese occupation of Manchuria. In December 1936, Chiang Kai-shek flew to the Young Marshall's headquarters in Xi'an to talk with Zhang. Chiang Kai-shek had heard that the Young Marshall was talking with the communists, who wanted the Manchurians to join forces with them. On December 12, the Young Marshall kidnapped Chiang and tried to force him to accept a united front with the communists. Afraid that the Young Marshall would join up with the Chinese communists against him, Chiang agreed, producing the KMT-CCP Second United Front.

Under the terms of the Second United Front, the CCP agreed to abandon the Soviet form of government, reorganize the Red Army as the Eighth Route Army under the jurisdiction of the KMT, and adhere to Sun Yat-sen's Three Principles of the People. In return, the Nationalist government agreed to allow communist semiautonomous regions under the jurisdiction of the KMT. Problems

---

The Arrest of the Young Marshall

The Young Marshall Zhang Xueliang, flew back to Nanjing with Chiang Kai-shek after Chiang's release. In Nanjing, Chiang put the Young Marshall under house arrest as a traitor. Both Chiang Kai-shek and the Young Marshall retreated with the Nationalist government to the island of Taiwan in the late 1940s. Although Chiang Kai-shek passed away in 1975, the Young Marshall stayed under house arrest until his ninety-second birthday in 1989.

in the alliance surfaced after only one year. Infighting began between communist and Nationalist forces. Communist forces, numbering about 40,000 in 1937, grew to 180,000 after only one year of war with Japan. This growth was possibly due to three factors. First, Mao's guerrilla strategy operating behind enemy lines strengthened the communists, while Nationalist troops, who were forced to fight positional warfare in cities, were weakened in the face of Japanese opposition. Urban warfare was disadvantageous to the Nationalists because the Japanese were superior in numbers, weaponry, and air power. Second, the communists, largely based in rural areas, pursued land reform and land reduction, endearing them to the peasants. Third, the communists earned the backing of the rural population by appealing to Chinese nationalism. The communists even got the support of some landlords. At the same time, the party weeded out rightist deviants, indoctrinated their followers, and instilled iron discipline.

In 1937, Japanese troops crossed the Marco Polo Bridge just outside Beijing, beginning an all-out assault against China. For the next eight years, until Japan's defeat in the World War II, Japan would wreak havoc on China. During the Japanese occupation of China, the Nationalists moved not only the capital inland to Chonging, but moved industry and universities inland as well. They dismantled and moved entire factories by brute force, crossing rivers and mountains enroute. The Nationalists moved libraries, their collections of books moved inland by cart. For much of the war with Japan, however, Chiang was more involved fighting communists than the Japanese. Although Chiang appealed to the United States for money and arms to fight the Japanese, he used them to fight the communists. Madame Chiang (Soong Mei-ling) made a particularly impassioned address to both chambers of Congress in 1942. The Chiangs' appeals for more US aid angered General George Stilwell, the US commander in China, who knew that much of the funding for the war material was being siphoned by T.V. Soong, chief of China Defense Supplies.[34] Stilwell complained of lack of cooperation of the Chinese general staff, and of an army shockingly led and brutally mistreated.[35]

Although the Nationalist government had some major achievements and was able to attract the support of people desiring nationalism, it was fraught with factionalism and contradictions in ideology. Sun's ideology was left to different interpretations. Also, the Nationalist government failed to implement economic changes, though this was not entirely its fault. China's existing problems became inflated during the war with Japan. For instance, Japan occupied China's coastal urban cities and ports, denying the KMT an important source of revenue. The KMT was forced to move the government to Chongqing in central Sichuan Province. The Nationalists were at a disadvantage trying to fight the war from China's interior and were forced into positional warfare against superior Japanese forces.

With wartime inflation rising to 235 percent in 1942, rising prices became a nightmare for the middle class, and especially hit hard those people on fixed incomes. Much of the money donated to China by the United China Relief Fund, an American charitable organization, became almost worthless when exchanged at the official rate.[36] China's economic woes had a demoralizing effect on government workers and soldiers, who resorted to graft and corruption. They also affected intellectuals, who were conveyors of Chinese public opinion. In the end, the Nationalists' inability to effectively fight the war with Japan was the main factor in the downfall of the Nationalist government.

In the closing years of the war, US ambassador to China Patrick Hurley was tasked with making peace between the Nationalists and the communists. Hurley flew to Yan'an in late 1944 to meet CCP leaders, delivering a proposal from Chiang Kai-shek offering the communists legal status and a seat on the national defense council in exchange for a surrender of arms to KMT troops. Mao rejected the offer, but agreed to a second offer, proposed by Hurley, that called for communist participation in a coalition government and integration of the CCP armies under central government control.[37] Chiang flatly refused the agreement. Negotiations collapsed in 1945. The communists would not accept a government dictated by Chiang Kai-shek; Chiang would not accept any solution that challenged his authority.[38] By spring 1945, China had become a secondary concern to the United States as its attention was focused on ending the war in Europe.

With the sudden end of World War II in the Pacific, the Nationalists scrambled to maintain a holding in China, and the communists scrambled to expand theirs. Radio Yan'an broadcast a call for the communists to seize and disarm Japanese garrisons. Communist armies raced to Manchuria to collect Japanese arms. The communists were in a good position to expand their reach. They had surrounded railways and towns in North China for five years; they dominated the countryside and established the Anti-Japanese Border Region Government. Chiang claimed that those territories should be controlled by the Nationalist government after Japan's departure.[39] Having fought the Japanese in those areas, the communists were not about to abandon the former Japanese strongholds.[40] Chiang's forces were in a difficult position to negotiate with the communists. Its best troops were located in southwestern China, hundreds of miles from the disputed north and northeast territories and the vital coastal areas. US forces helped move Chiang's forces to the coast, but the communists countered by taking Manchuria. The United States sent Secretary of State George Marshall to mediate between the KMT and CCP, arranging a truce in January 1946. The truce expired in June 1946, with all-out civil war occurring from then until 1949. The decisive battles took place in 1948, and from 1947 through 1949, the KMT moved their Nationalist government to the island of Taiwan, 100 miles off the coast of Fujian Province. In January 1949, the communists took Tianjin and Beijing, and in April took the former Nationalist capital of Nanjing. By mid-October 1949, the communists had taken Guangzhou in southern China. Mao declared the founding of the People's Republic of China on October 1, 1949.

Mao Zedong Thought

Mao Zedong was the leading figure in Chinese politics for more than forty years. Throughout those years, Mao shaped Chinese government and politics through first developing, and then implementing, his own ideology. Mao's greatest contribution to Chinese politics was his ability to link politics and ideology. Mao was both an innovator of ideology as well as an innovator in the relationship of ideology to politics. In short, Mao is the central linkage between theory and practice.

Mao Zedong was born in 1893 to a middle-class peasant family in Hunan Province. A prolific reader, Mao was familiar with the Chinese classics, but did not like them.[41] In 1918, Mao gained a position at Peking University as a library assistant to CCP founder Li Dazho.[42] A member of the May Fourth generation, Mao was a contributor to Chen Duxiu's *New Youth*.[43] Impressed by the Russian communist revolution, Mao became a Marxist in 1920, and joined the CCP soon after its founding in 1921. Mao worked as a KMT political organizer during the First KMT-CCP United Front, but fled to Jiangxi after Chiang Kaishek's White Terror purge of Shanghai in April 1927. In Jiangxi, Mao rose through the ranks of the CCP, first as party secretary of Hunan Province, later as member of the party's Central Committee and of the Politburo, and finally as president of the Jiangxi Soviet. He became party chairman in 1935.

No disinterested scholar of political theory, Mao was committed to putting theory into practice. Mao Zedong Thought can more accurately be referred to as Mao Zedong ideology. *Ideology* is a political term, in which the future is presented as materialistic improvement over the present. In contrast to political theory, which is the study of political behavior, political ideology is action oriented; it is a prescription for change. In particular, ideologies are directed toward the masses, mobilizing huge numbers of people.[44] In short, an ideology shapes belief that inspires people to political action.[45] There are three broad types of political ideologies: status quo, reformist, and radical or revolutionary. A *status quo* ideology seeks to preserve the existing economic, social, and political order. A *reformist* ideology seeks to change the way things are done in the existing economic, social, and political order, but not reshape society. A *revolutionary* ideology seeks to reshape the entire political-socioeconomic order.[46] Mao's political ideology, with its focus on mass mobilization and sweeping change, can be considered a revolutionary ideology.

Mao's years in Yan'an offered him the opportunity to develop his political thought, a process he had begun while situated in the Jiangxi Soviet between 1927 and 1934. Exiled to the countryside by the Nationalist army, Mao saw firsthand that discontent and impoverishment of rural society had created an inexhaustible supply of potential revolutionaries. Contrary to Marx, who predicted the spontaneous uprising of the urban proletariat when conditions were ripe, Mao saw that conditions were ripe for the CCP to give this rural force purpose and direction. The Comintern's program in China was to inspire urban workers to revolution. Marxism, however, was alien to Chinese culture and had proved impractical. In Yan'an, Mao perfected his alteration of Marxism to suit China's needs.

His claim that circumstances drive action was Mao's most significant contribution to Marxism-Leninism. Mao insisted that Chinese communist leaders rely less on theory and "isms" and more on doing the right thing given the circumstances. In his 1937 treatise "On Practice," Mao wrote that there can be no knowledge apart from practice.[47] For Mao, practice is the sole criterion of truth, and knowledge begins with experience.[48] In contrast to Marxism, which emphasizes the importance of theory because it can guide action, Mao argued that "knowledge begins with practice, and theoretical knowledge is acquired through practice and *must then return to practice.*"[49] That is, experience helps flesh out theoretical constructs, but theory must then reflect reality. Mao's contribution to the Marxist-Leninist dichotomy between theory and practice is the implication that anyone can make mistakes in the practical application of theory, but one can learn from mistakes. Mistakes lead to change.

For Mao, it was not merely a question of adapting Marxism to China, but sinicizing it—giving it Chinese characteristics by enriching it with elements drawn from China's experience.[50] Mao reshaped Marxism-Leninism to accommodate Chinese conditions. Marx maintained that urban workers—the proletariat—would spontaneously rise up against their capitalist oppressors when conditions were ripe. They would smash the existing state and replace it with a dictatorship of the proletariat. China, however, was a predominantly peasant society that lacked large numbers of oppressed urban workers. Instead of envisioning an urban-based revolution, Mao advocated a peasant-based revolution with its base in the countryside. For Mao, the proletariat meant the CCP, standing in for the working class. The sinification of Marxism—whereby rural peasants, not the urban proletariat, would be China's true revolutionaries—was Mao's greatest contribution to the Chinese communist revolution.

Over time, Mao developed a popularized version of Marxism, a utopian belief in the powers of the human will (voluntarism), and a form of puritanism expressed in slogans. Mao's voluntarism was a departure from Marx's materialism. For instance, after the split with the Soviet Union in the early 1950s, Mao pushed China to go it alone, and boasted that, by leaping forward, China's industrial development would exceed the USSR's in a number of years. Industry was not confined to the factories; neighborhoods were encouraged to build their factories right in their own backyards, hence the "backyard furnaces," which melted down pots and pans to produce worthless steel.

Mao extolled the virtues of simplicity (frugality). To prevent economic stratification, he lowered everyone's living standards to the lowest level. Communists were to live simple, unadorned lives because then they would not be alienated from the masses. In factories, managers were indistinguishable from workers.

The Private Luxury of Mao Zedong

Despite Mao's call for simplicity, he lived in extreme comfort, bordering on splendor. When he traveled, Mao arranged for his bed to be shipped to wherever he was staying, claiming that no other bed was as good as his. His wife, Jiang Qing, reportedly ordered fur-lined toilet seats. (Li and Thurston, *Private Life of Chairman Mao*, ix)

The Mass Line

One of Mao's most significant contributions to Marxism-Leninism is his concept of "from the masses to the masses," commonly known as the *mass line*. Both Lenin and Mao saw the need for leadership by a revolutionary elite. In *What's To Be Done?* Lenin called for the creation of a communist party to serve as a vanguard of the masses. The party would practice centralized decisionmaking, in which all party members were free to offer comment at the policy formulation level. Once the party leadership made a decision however, all must abide with it without dissent. Whereas Lenin saw organization as key to a revolution system, Mao emphasized the need to involve the whole of the Chinese people. Mao feared that Lenin's "democratic centralism" would create polarity between the leadership's decisionmaking at the top and the people's participation and compliance (which may or may not be enthusiastic) from below. The mass line was a two-way street: it would enable the Chinese communists to be close enough to the people to understand their needs and desires, and the people would embrace party policy because they viewed it as their own. The concept of the mass line is carried out in a multistep process. The party leadership sends party cadres out among the people to gather and summarize their views. The cadres report up the party hierarchy to give the leadership a sense of what the people would welcome and what they would not. Higher party authorities make comments or give instructions based on these ideas and return them to the people. Party cadres then carry out political education and propaganda to test the ideas. Only those policies that had the wholehearted support of the people were to be implemented. The goal of the mass line was to keep the party in touch with the masses, and keep the people politically active.

In all the practical work of our Party, all correct leadership is necessarily "from the masses, to the masses." This means: take the ideas of the masses (scattered and unsystematic ideas) and concentrate them (through study turn them into concentrated and systematic ideas), then go to the masses and propagate and explain these ideas until the masses embrace them as their own, hold fast to them and translate them into action, and test the correctness of these ideas in such action.[51]

As these words indicate, Mao believed that the people, on their own, were incapable of elaborating ideas in any systematic form and needed centralized guidance to help them. Because the ideas originated with the people and because they had confidence in the party as revolutionary elites, the people would, through education and indoctrination, embrace both the ideas and the actions put forth by the party. Mao argued that the mass line, which emphasizes close links between the people and the party, would help the party maintain a close leader-led relationship.

Mao's concept of the mass line was rooted in the CCP's experience in the Jiangxi Soviet. In 1934, in the waning days of the Jiangxi Soviet, Mao called for Chinese communists to mobilize the masses and to deal with the peasants' practical problems.[52] He urged Chinese communists to pay close attention to the well-being of the masses, ranging from the problems of land and labor, to those of fuel, rice, cooking oil, and salt. He urged them to help the peasants send their children to school, repair rural infrastructure, and develop rudimentary health care, all in an effort to win the hearts and minds of the peasants. He argued that it was not enough to ask the peasants to fight alongside the communists at the front, but to raise their enthusiasm for the revolution by helping them first. In short, Mao extolled the communists to organize the revolutionary war and to improve the life of the masses.[53] In this case, he drew a contrast with the marauding Nationalist forces. Nationalist conscripts were so poorly treated that more of them died before reaching the front than died in battle. Nationalist forces commonly looted homes, farms, and livestock, leaving peasant farmers to starve. Mao admonished the communist forces not to confiscate food or livestock, and if they stayed in a peasant's home, to hang up the door (which was used as a bed) when they departed.[54]

At times, the communists went too far in employing the mass line, resulting in bloody mob violence against a specified target. Although Mao and his supporters in the Jiangxi Soviet eventually moderated their use of the mass line, they learned that the mass line was an effective tool for securing the support of the masses. The political system that developed after 1949 further corrupted the mass line. Local officials failed to report bad news, and the leadership would not get the bad news and design policy to rectify the situation. This failure to communicate up the chain of command resulted in tremendous suffering in the 1950s during the Great Leap Forward and again in the 1960s during the Cultural Revolution.

The People's Democratic Dictatorship

In Marxism, the transition phase between the abolishment of capitalism and the establishment of communism is the dictatorship of the proletariat.[55] During the transition, the proletariat would assume state power and suppress all dissent by the bourgeoisie, destroy the social relations of production underlying the class system, and create a new, classless society. In 1949, Mao introduced the concept of the people's democratic dictatorship. The premise of the people's democratic dictatorship is that the party and state work in the best interests of the people, but it may use dictatorial methods when faced with threats to their power. In those cases, evoking dictatorial powers is a necessary evil, without which the regime might collapse and the alternative would be worse than the dictatorship.

Mao deemed the Jiangxi Soviet a "democratic dictatorship of the proletariat and peasantry." Under the people's democratic dictatorship, the army, police, and courts would be strengthened to protect the people's interests by suppressing all those who resist the communist revolution. Under the people's democratic dictatorship, all people who support China in revolution would have their rights preserved and protected. However, anyone who resisted the revolution, such as capitalists, landlords, and Nationalists, would lose for a period of time their right to freedom of speech and their right to vote. Similarly, the dictatorship would protect China from subversion by external enemies. The aim of the dictatorship was to protect the people and the revolution so that China, under the leadership of the CCP, would transform into a modern, industrialized socialist state.[56]

Struggle, Class Struggle, and Criticisms

Mao believed that communist revolution and a communist society could only be born out of violent struggle between the true revolutionaries and the anti-revolutionaries. According to Mao, all individuals could be pegged as members of a particular class and, intentionally or not, behave according to class mores.[57] The first task in instigating class warfare was to help the Chinese people identify with a particular class. In the Jinggang Mountains, Ruijian, and from the Yan'an base, Mao sent party activists among the rural population explaining the concept of class, identifying one's class identity, and then instigating class warfare. Mao's advocacy of violent class struggle in the name of revolution is quite clear in his 1926 defense of violent communist insurrections in Hunan Province. "A revolution is not a dinner party, or writing an essay, or painting a picture, or doing embroidery; it cannot be so refined, so leisurely and gentle, so temperate, kind, courteous, restrained and magnanimous. A revolution is an insurrection, an act of violence by which one class overthrows another."[58]

Mao began using struggle sessions, particularly in instigating class warfare, in the early days of the Jiangxi Soviet and while in Ruijian. As part of his indoctrination of the masses into class warfare, Mao would encourage rural peasants to bring their landlords before mass struggle sessions where the landlord would be hit, spit upon and tortured, and often killed. These struggle sessions served two purposes. First, punishment was group dealt, and the peasants felt that they were the ones meting out the punishment. Second, the masses literally had blood on their hands as a consequence of the struggle sessions, and, as participants in violent revolutionary acts, felt compelled to continue the revolution. The struggle sessions in a sense bound the people to the party. The struggle session proved so effective in dealing with class enemies in Jiangxi and the Jinggang Mountains that Mao continued the practice from his Yan'an base area. After the communist regime was established, Mao used struggle sessions to reconstruct Chinese society. He warned that some people would resist the communist revolution. In the following excerpt from a 1950 speech, Mao argues that each individual must decide which side of the revolution to be on: "Whoever sides with the revolutionary people is a revolutionary. Whoever sides with imperialism, feudalism, and bureaucrat-capitalism is a counter-revolutionary. Whoever sides with the revolutionary people in words only but acts otherwise is a revolutionary in speech. Whoever sides with the revolutionary people in deed as well as in word is a revolutionary in the full sense."[59]

Mao warned the Chinese communists that they needed to maintain vigilance against class enemies even after a victorious revolution because there would be elements in Chinese society that would try to overturn the revolution: "After the enemies with guns have been wiped out, there will still be enemies without guns; they are bound to struggle desperately against us, and we must never regard these enemies lightly. If we do not now raise and understand the problem in this way, we shall commit the gravest mistakes."[60]

Those counterrevolutionaries would have to be dealt with in a likewise violent fashion. One of these "enemies without guns" was the Catholic Church in China. Mao and the CCP made the Catholic Church a major enemy target because of its foreign influence and linkages with the outside world. It also constituted a formidable challenge to the primacy of the CCP in that it possessed its own internal organization and communications systems.[61] As early as 1947, the Chinese communists were torturing and killing priests and closing their monasteries and churches.

Central to Mao's theory of permanent revolution was the thesis that even after the establishment of a new socialist order, individuals and institutions can acquire bourgeois tendencies and change the color of the revolution. Only through constant struggle would these elements be rooted out and socialism prevail. Mao's concept of permanent revolution would take the Chinese people through extreme upheavals over twenty-seven years. By the time of his death in 1976, the Chinese people were absolutely exhausted by constant struggle and were seeking a more settled order.

Campaigns

Mao made liberal use of campaigns (*yundong*), mass mobilization of the people to promote a particular cause or to attack a specified target. These campaigns shared major characteristics. First, they involved massive numbers of people mobilized under the leadership of the CCP. After the communist regime was established, Mao took a new approach to revolution. He—and the party—displayed an unquestioning faith in the possibilities of converting all people to communism and, regardless of class background, everyone was treated as a potential convert. The result was a vigorous application of persuasion and the development of the techniques of self-criticism and public confession. Individuals had to reveal their erroneous views, denounce their past feelings, and dedicate themselves to revolutionary ideas.

> Conscientious practice of self-criticism is still another hallmark distinguishing our Party from all other political parties. As we say, dust will accumulate if a room is not cleaned regularly, or faces get dirty if they are not washed regularly. Our comrades' minds and our Party's work may also collect dust, and also need sweeping and washing. . . . To check up regularly on our work and in the process develop a democratic style of work, to fear neither criticism nor self criticism, and to apply such good popular Chinese maxims as "Say all you know and say it without reserve," "Blame not the speaker but be warned by his words," and "Correct mistakes if you have committed them and guard against them if you have not"—this is the only effective way to prevent all kinds of political dust and germs from contaminating the minds of our comrades and the body of our Party.[62]

Second, the campaigns were aimed at specific targets. Landlords were the targets of the 1950 Land Reform Campaign, and the Catholic Church was one of the main foci of the 1951 Campaign to Suppress Counterrevolutionaries. Estimates of the number of people executed attributable to Mao's early mass campaigns from 1949 to 1952 vary from hundreds of thousands to two million to as many as fourteen million deaths.[63]

Third, the campaigns served to settle perceived contradictions. Mao viewed the world in terms of the law of opposites, such as light and dark, yin and yang, strong and weak. In 1937, Mao wrote the article, "On the Correct Handling of Contradictions," in which he discussed the law of opposites.[64] In mathematics, there is plus and minus; in mechanics, there is action and reaction; in physics, there is positive and negative electricity; in social science, there is class struggle. In war, offense and defense, advance and retreat, victory and defeat are all contradictory. Opposition and struggle of ideas constantly occur within the party as well.[65] In "On the Correct Handling of Contradictions" Mao cited as examples the contradiction between the oppressed class in Chinese society and imperialism, between the proletariat and the bourgeoisie, between the peasantry and the urban petty bourgeoisie.[66] Mao claimed that the contradictions needed to be examined in their various stages and cited the First United Front as an example. During the First United Front, the KMT, on one hand, stood in contradiction to the Chinese masses, but on the other hand stood in opposition to foreign imperialism. The CCP could overlook the contradiction of a KMT-CCP union because the major antagonism at the time was foreign imperialism. The minor contradictions could be put aside until the major one was resolved. The KMT in 1927 became a "reactionary bloc of the landlords and big bourgeoisie" and turned against the CCP, becoming a major antagonist. Still in its infancy, the CCP was not effective in dealing with the KMT forces. After the CCP developed out of the infancy stage, however, it was in a better position to deal with the KMT. It joined with them in a Second United Front against Japanese forces in China because the KMT was also (at least nominally) resisting Japan. The two United Fronts illustrate the complicated state of simultaneous alliance and struggle.[67]

Not all contradictions involved struggle, however. Mao said that there were two types of contradictions: antagonistic and nonantagonistic. Contradictions that exist between the Chinese and their enemies, namely the social forces and groups that resist the socialist revolution, are antagonistic.[68] Antagonistic contradictions can only be resolved by socialist revolution. Other contradictions are nonantagonistic. These contradictions exist among different groups in Chinese society. They may include merely differences of opinion. The contradictions among the people, namely the contradictions within the working class, peasantry, intelligentsia, are not necessarily antagonistic, and could be solved by other means. Contradictions between the classes may be both nonantagonistic and antagonistic.[69]

Under certain circumstances, contradictions among the people could become antagonistic. For example, contradictions between the wage workers and the bourgeoisie are antagonistic. Mao developed his theory of contradictions over many years, and by 1952, clarified that if left unchecked, nonantagonistic contradictions could develop into antagonistic contradictions. Contradictions, antagonistic or not, would have to be resolved in favor of the CCP. Therefore, when necessary, the CCP pursued a united-front strategy, overlooking minor antagonisms in order to accomplish a necessary goal, but then dealing with the minor antagonism so it would not develop into a major antagonism.

In 1945, Mao Zedong Thought was enshrined in the CCP's new constitution where it became the party's guiding ideology. Mao Thought became the basis of all party policies, political campaigns, government guidelines and procedures, and administrative decisions for the next thirty years. As we will see in succeeding chapters, Mao Zedong Thought determined China's politics until Mao's death in 1976.

Conclusion

The Republic of China and the People's Republic that came after it constituted a dramatic break with five thousand years of Chinese history. For most of those five thousand years, China's government and society was strongly influenced by the teachings of Confucius and his followers, the government was staffed by scholar-officials who gained their positions through competitive imperial examinations, the emperor ruled with the Mandate of Heaven and was conscious of rites and rituals as well as the need to meet the needs of his people, and China considered itself the center of civilization. The Chinese imperial system began its long decline in the later Qing Dynasty and Western encroachment in the nineteenth century proved the dynasty incapable of facing powerful and modern foes. The republican revolution of 1911 that finally toppled imperial China brought with it the promise of nationalism, democracy, and better economic conditions. These dreams were as short lived as China's experiment with representative government descended into dictatorship and then anarchy. Out of the confusion of the warlord era, one man—Chiang Kai-shek—was able to muster forces to reunite China under one central government. Chiang took on two opponents: the communists and the Japanese. More inclined to fight the communists than the Japanese occupiers, Chiang forced the communists into China's vast countryside where they found fertile ground for their agenda. Among the communists, one man—Mao Zedong— rose to leadership and used communist exiles in the countryside to develop his political ideology. The Chinese people, exhausted by years of Japanese bombardment and the destruction of China, were catapulted into a civil war. By the middle of the twentieth century, the world's most populous country had jettisoned its past and had begun to follow the communist road, espousing Mao Zedong Thought as its guide.

Notes

1. Population figure is a July 2010 estimate, Central Intelligence Agency, *World Factbook, China, 2011*.

2. China also borders on Macau and Hong Kong, special administrative regions of China, since 1997 and 1999, respectively.

3. The May 12, 2008, earthquake in central Sichuan Province took some seventy thousand lives and made five million people homeless.

4. The Zhou Dynasty is commonly divided into the Western Zhou (1027–771 B.C.) and the Eastern Zhou (770–256 B.C.). In some accounts, the Western Zhou begins around 1050 B.C.

5. In its broadest sense, *li* refers to proper conduct. At the same time, *li* has the more specific meaning of designating ritual and definite rules that constitute propriety and proper behavior. While it is not synonymous with virtue (*de*), *li* is the rules and rituals that can be memorized and practiced in order to cultivate virtue.

6. The five Confucian virtues are humanity or benevolence (*ren*), righteousness (*yi*), propriety (*li*), wisdom (*shi*), and trustworthiness (*xin*).

7. De Barry, *Sources of Chinese Tradition*, 1:16.

8. Undifferentiated love, or universal love, all individuals are loved and respected equally.

9. The term *huangdi* means emperor, and *shi* means first; thus Qin Shi Huangdi means "First Qin Emperor."

10. Two of China's most famous historical poets, Du Fu and Li Bai, belonged to this age.

11. The Song Dynasty is more accurately divided into the earlier Northern Song (A.D. 960–1127) and the later Southern Song (A.D. 1127–1279). The author joins the two for brevity.

12. Opponents of his reforms eventually forced Wang Anshi from office. He spent his remaining days engaged in scholarship and died in poverty in 1086.

13. Song porcelain with a celadon glaze became one of the most desired items in foreign trade.

14. The tree still exists in Jingshan Park, just north of the former Forbidden City.

15. Fairbank, Reischauer, and Craig, *East Asia,* 227.

16. These rebellions included the White Lotus Rebellion (1774–1804), the Taiping Rebellion (1850–1864), the Nian Rebellion (1858–1868), the Southwest Muslim Rebellion (1855–1873), and the Northwest Muslim Rebellion (1862–1878).

17. Visitors to the Summer Palace in Beijing can spot the building, called the Yu-lan Tang, the "Hall of Waters of Rippling Jade."

18. According to Sun's plan, full constitutional government would be realized in three stages and according to a set timetable: three years of military unification, in which the Manchus would be driven from the throne and local self-government would be implemented county by county; six years under a provisional constitution, in a period of political tutelage; and finally, eventual constitutional government with a five-power constitutional government described above.

19. The Emperor Puyi was briefly restored to the throne in summer 1916 following the death of Yuan Shikai.

20. The Revolutionary Alliance and five smaller prorevolution parties merged to form the Kuomintang in August 1912.

21. A failed state is a nation-state in which the central government exercises control over only a small area of the country.

22. Fairbank, *Great Chinese Revolution,* 180.

23. The university was established as Peking University. Using the pinyin system of romanization it is called Beijing University (Beijing Daxue, or Beida as it is commonly known.)

24. Fairbank, Reischauer, and Craig, *East Asia,* 767.

25. China had declared war on Germany in 1917.

26. Zhang Xueliang, also known as the Young Marshall, succeeded his father, Zhang Zuolin, following the latter's assassination by the Japanese in 1928.

27. In 1937, however, Japan invaded China, and the ensuing war delayed China's efforts to implement a constitutional government. The ROC Constitution was finally adopted by China's legislature in December of 1946, after Japan's defeat in WWII. Legislative elections were held in 1947, and elections for the control branch were held in 1948. The president and vice president were elected in 1948. This is the government that ended up in Taiwan in 1949.

28. Bianco, *Origins of the Chinese Revolution.*

29. Many members of the mission were later accused of being communists and either lost their positions in government or were placed in positions of little consequence.

30. Shih, *Urban Commune Experiences,* 8.

31. Wang Shiwei, "Wild Lily," 70.

32. Lynch, *Mao,* 120.

33. Lynch, *Mao,* 121.

34. Tuchman, *Stilwell and the American Experience in China,* 282.

35. White and Jacoby, *Thunder Out of China,* 215.

36. Seagrave, *Soong Dynasty,* 387.

37. White and Jacoby, *Thunder Out of China,* 254.

38. White and Jacoby, *Thunder Out of China,* 255.

39. US general Douglas MacArthur, Supreme Commander for Allied Powers, designated Chiang Kai-shek as the sole authority empowered to accept Japan's surrender in China. Bianco, *Origins of the Chinese Revolution,* 169.

40. White and Jacoby, *Thunder Out of China*, 280.

41. Snow, *Red Star Over China*, 117.

42. Snow, *Red Star Over China*, 139.

43. Schram, *Thought of Mao Tse-Tung*, 13.

44. Baradat, *Political Ideologies*, 8.

45. Macridis and Hulliung, *Contemporary Political Ideologies*, 3.

46. Macridis and Hulliung, *Contemporary Political Ideologies*, 15.

47. Mao, "On Practice," 301.

48. Mao, "On Practice," 305.

49. Emphasis is the author's. Mao Zedong, "On Practice," 304.

50. Schram, *Thought of Mao Tse-Tung*, 71.

51. Mao, "Some Questions Concerning Methods of Leadership," 120.

52. Mao, "Be Concerned with the Well-Being of the Masses," 147–152.

53. Mao, "Be Concerned with the Well-Being of the Masses."

54. Not having guest beds, rural Chinese might take a door off its hinges and use the door as a makeshift bed. Mao instructed the communists to rehang the door when they left the house.

55. Karl Marx, "Critique of the Gotha Program," 525–541.

56. Mao, "On the Correct Handling of Contradictions Among the People," 350–352.

57. Mao, "On Practice," 296.

58. Mao, "Report on an Investigation of the Peasant Movement in Hunan," 28.

59. Mao, closing speech at the second session of the First National Committee of the People's Consultative Conference, June 23, 1950, in *Quotations from Chairman Mao*, 24.

60. Mao, "Report to the Second Plenary Session of the Seventh Central Committee," 316–317.

61. Walker, introduction to Myers, *Enemies Without Guns*, xxi.

62. Mao, "On Coalition Government," 36.

63. Myers, *Enemies Without Guns*, 116n3.

64. Mao revised "On the Correct Handling of Contradictions" in 1957, before he totally socialized the economy and collectivized agriculture.

65. Mao, "On the Correct Handling of Contradictions," 317.

66. Mao, "On the Correct Handling of Contradictions," 322.

67. Mao, "On the Correct Handling of Contradictions," 328.

68. Mao, *Quotations from Chairman Mao*, 41.

69. Schram, *Thought of Mao Tse-tung*, 116.

3 The Mao Years

China's economic and political landscape changed dramatically between the establishment of the People's Republic of China (PRC) in 1949 and Mao's death in 1976. In those twenty-seven years, China was transformed from a fragmented country and a failed state to a unified country with a strong central government. Its economy was transformed from one based largely on agriculture and private enterprise to one controlled by the state, whose goal was rapid industrialization and modernization. Even China's geographical landscape was affected, suffering enormous environmental degradation and waste. While communist policies lifted millions out of poverty, millions of others suffered tremendously at the hands of the communists. Mao's communists mobilized untold numbers of Chinese citizens in innumerable political campaigns in which millions of others would suffer. By the time of Mao's death in October 1976, the Chinese people were exhausted and ready for less radical politics.

Stabilization and Reform

On October 1, 1949, Mao Zedong, with Zhou Enlai and the Chinese Communist Party (CCP) leadership, stood high above the crowds at the Gate of Heavenly Peace and proclaimed the establishment of the People's Republic of China (PRC). The CCP's immediate goals were to create a new government to replace the Kuomintang (KMT), reconstruct China's economy, and reform its armies and foreign relations.[1] To reconstruct and modernize China, the Chinese leadership in 1949 adopted the Soviet model of socialism. The Soviets helped create the CCP and assisted it in its struggle against the Nationalists. The Soviets helped the Chinese communists both monetarily and militarily, so there was a natural tendency for the Chinese communists to lean toward the Soviets. Ideologically, both the Soviet and Chinese communists had in common an antagonism toward imperialism and capitalism, so they shared the same values of collectivization. Also, the Chinese communists were inexperienced in governing a large country, and looked to the more experienced Soviets to guide them in socialist nation building. Although the CCP would largely break with the Soviet communists after 1956, the Chinese communists adopted, often with some modification, Soviet models of economic and political management in the early years of the PRC.

Creating a Government

The communists' first task was to consolidate their power among the Chinese people. To do this, the CCP needed to create a coalition government that would have broad appeal. The CCP applied united-front principles to creating the PRC's first government by building political alliances with elements that would be useful to the CCP. Anticipating victory in the civil war and the need for a new postwar government, the CCP in the last months of the war created a forum for building the new government: the Chinese People's Political Consultative Conference (CPPCC). In September 1949, some six hundred delegates consisting of both party and nonparty members met in Beijing. Technically the highest authority in China, the CPPCC established a government council and wrote a Common Program, which served as a constitution for China. The program declared China a people's dictatorship with four classes: workers, peasants, petty bourgeoisie, and national bourgeoisie. After the CCP sent troops to Tibet in 1950 to assert Chinese control over the territory, the CPPCC claimed to have united Han Chinese, Tibetans, Mongols, Manchus, and Muslims under one flag.

The coalition government was consistent with Mao's views on the dictatorship of the proletariat and defined imperialism, feudalism, and bureaucratic capitalism as enemies of the people. In a people's dictatorship, democracy would be preserved under a coalition government that served as a big tent, but the people's enemies would lose their economic and political rights. The Common Program proposed gradually squeezing out Western companies (imperialists), eliminating the landlords (feudal forces), and confiscating large enterprises connected with the KMT (bureaucratic capitalists). Thus, in a united-front fashion, democracy would be preserved while flushing out the enemy. The people's democratic dictatorship would be led by the working class based on an alliance of workers and peasants. As the vanguard of the proletariat, the CCP would clearly lead the new government.

The Chinese adopted the Soviet model of political organization by setting up parallel party and government offices at each level of the political system in China. The political and administrative levels, from top to bottom, with the center located in Beijing, include province (*sheng*), city (*shi*), county (*xian*), town (*xiang*), and village (*cun*). Each level has government and party offices, and a legislature or assembly. The national legislature is the National People's Congress (NPC), which enacts laws and ratifies treaties. One of the NPC's earliest laws was the 1950 Marriage Reform, which voided arranged marriages if women wanted out of them. It also gave unmarried, divorced, or widowed women the right to hold land in their own names. The State Council (cabinet), headed by a premier (prime minister), housed central government ministries and agencies. In 1950, the CPPCC named Zhou Enlai premier, a position he held until his death in 1976. The central government initially had some thirty ministries, most headed by non-CCP personnel. Of the fifteen economic ministries and agencies, however, more than 55 percent were headed by CCP members. Once there were suitable party members available, they replaced the nonparty members. In this manner, China was unified under a strong central government. In local governments, the CCP left KMT officials in their posts simply because there were not enough communists to fill those ranks.

The second major task was to stabilize and reconstruct the economy. After a decade of war with Japan and several more years of civil war, the Chinese economy was in a shambles; most of its urban infrastructure had been destroyed. First, the new government needed to deal with the problem of inflation. Its first move was to balance the government budget by collecting agricultural taxes in kind and by collecting sales and businesses taxes in the cities. Second, the government took over the banking system, thereby gaining control of all credit. Third, it paid personnel in market-basket terms. Salaries were calculated not in money terms, but in terms of basic commodities, such as oil, grain, and cloth. By summer 1950, the government had largely stabilized prices.

The next task was to restore production facilities and transportation. The CCP promoted the formation of labor unions, and workers and citizens were organized into small study groups wherein group members were encouraged to explore their innermost thoughts as a preliminary step to transforming themselves from "experts" (individuals with technical expertise) into "reds" (individuals with political commitment). By 1952, production was restored to prewar levels.

The CPPCC followed a policy of *gradualism* in socializing China's economy. Initially, landowning peasants kept their land, and the bourgeoisie kept their private businesses. Gradualism in nationalization meant there was no outright confiscation of private industry. Large foreign businesses willing to work with the Chinese communists, such as Shell International Petroleum Company, were encouraged to stay and work for the new society. National ministries saw to it that privately owned industries obtained needed raw materials. These industries were eventually transformed into joint state and private enterprises and finally into completely state-owned operations through the "buying off" policy, under which former owners of private enterprises were paid interest on their shares at a rate fixed by the state.

Early Political Campaigns

To consolidate its hold on power, the CCP made full use of mass campaigns to achieve social and economic goals and to involve the populace. The campaigns employed group mobilization and self-criticism, and in areas like Yan'an, these tactics were characterized by the selective targeting of victims, mass struggle sessions, and mass participation in punishment. The early mass campaigns were the Campaign to Suppress Counterrevolutionaries, the Three Antis, the Five Antis, and the 1950 land reform campaign.

To have broad appeal, the coalition government initially included KMT members, but it was not long before the CCP had trained enough members to take over the positions occupied by former Nationalists. With more than 2 million KMT members still in China, the CCP wanted to crush any potential resistance to its reforms. In October 1950, the CCP launched the Campaign to Suppress Counterrevolutionaries, a series of mass rallies against millions of Chinese who had been in KMT party or youth organizations or had served in Nationalist armies. Millions of people were put under the category of class enemies, bandits, and spies. Nearly a million people died in this yearlong national campaign.

In 1951, the CCP launched the Three Antis Campaign against embezzlement, waste, and bureaucrats, with government officials as the target. The main goal of the campaign was to root out government officials who might put their hands in the cookie jar of public money. Nearly 4 million officials were put under enormous psychological and physical pressure to confess pilfering public funds. In the end, very few officials had actually been found guilty, but Mao's purpose was served. Public officials were terrified of Mao's power and dropped any resistance to his policies. The 1952 Five Antis Campaign targeted the capitalist class. The vices were bribery, tax evasion, theft of state property, cheating on government contracts, and stealing state economic information. Workers were encouraged to snitch on employers. Industrialists, bankers, and business leaders were forced to undergo group criticism sessions and confess their past economic crimes. Many employers were brought to trial. Some were killed and others lost their businesses to the government and were left to work as government employees in their own firms.

In 1950, the CCP departed from gradualism and implemented radical agrarian reform. Agrarian reform was not new to the party. Mao carried out land reform in the Jiangxi Soviet and Ruijian, and the CCP carried out land reform in the areas that came under communist control during the civil war. The goal of the 1950 Agrarian Reform Law was to confiscate and redistribute land previously held by the landlords. To accomplish this goal, the CCP organized rural work teams that would identify all individuals in villages according to class. The teams then confiscated and redistributed land according to class. Rich peasants retained their land and property and landlords retained some land for their own use, but the communists confiscated and redistributed the rest to poorer peasants. The work teams encouraged violent confrontations between peasants and landlords to wreck the power base of the landlords. Consistent with his policy of mass mobilization, Mao ordered that the executions take place in public. The CCP encouraged peasants to publicly criticize and struggle against the landlord, who would be taken to a field and shot. Some 1 million people were executed during this campaign.[2] By the end of the land reform campaign in 1952, almost half of the country's agricultural land had been redistributed to about 60 million peasant households, comprising more than half of China's population. Peasants gained title to land, and had the party to thank for it.

The purpose of these early campaigns was to break the backbone of the resistance of anyone who was in a position to challenge the new regime, namely, anyone who had influence in pre-1949 China. Bringing in the masses to participate in campaigns and punishment against KMT officials, capitalists, and landlords legitimized the people's dictatorship. Survivors of these early campaigns learned to keep critical comments to themselves and not to test the regime's authority.

The campaigns were effective in four ways. First, the CCP revealed that it would no longer protect private businesses or tolerate semilegal practices that had continued in China after 1949. Chinese capitalists were threatened. Second, it meant upward social mobility and involvement for some, but for others it meant fear and uncertainty because movements often involved excesses and terror. Third, they helped the CCP assert government control and influence over workers' organizations and strengthened CCP power. Fourth, the campaigns broke the back of resistance by putting an end to independent modes of operation of capitalists and bureaucrats.

In 1954, China's communist leadership increased centralization and consolidation of political control. China moved to a tightly centralized system in which provincial party secretaries supervised the dissemination of CCP orders through local party offices. The CCP reorganized China into twenty-one provinces, five autonomous regions (Xinjiang, Tibet, Inner Mongolia, Ningxia, and Guangxi), and two municipalities with the status of province (Beijing and Shanghai).[3] Below these levels were some two thousand county governments that supervised about one million branch offices or cells of the CCP in towns, villages, army units, factories, mines, and schools.[4] Parallel to these CCP offices were government administrative offices, which, although distinct from the party, were responsible for implementing party policy. A new state constitution reaffirmed the dual structure of party and government.

Urban Reform

The CCP was also active in reforming and reviving China's cities after years of war. It established street committee branches in neighborhoods to work on such tasks as street cleaning, water supply, health and vaccination programs, running children's bookstores, and establishing night schools. These street committee branches also had some responsibility for public security and could be used to track criminals, enforce curfews, and mount local patrols. The CCP launched campaigns against prostitution and opium addiction. It cut back on prostitution through a system that registered all housing and monitored male visitors and their departure time; it reduced opium addiction with enforced "cold turkey" methods and by making the former addicts' families responsible for their staying clean.

To maintain order in urban neighborhoods, the communists in the early 1950s began to organize city dwellers into *residents' committees,* whose function was to resolve problems and disputes affecting residents, organize literacy and sanitation work, prevent fires (many residences were constructed of wood), and look into the welfare problems of residents. Most important, each residents' committee had a public-security section that was responsible to the local police station. One of the tasks of the residents' committees was to keep an eye on the population under their jurisdiction and to report regularly to the local police station.[5] The residents' committees therefore served two purposes. First, they served as the eyes and ears of the police and kept order through the resolution of disputes or through fear of spilling the beans to the police. Second, because they existed only in residential areas, the committees served to organize people not already organized in schools, factories, or other work units. For instance, housewives, retired individuals, and the elderly, who did not belong to any formal organization, were organized under the residents' committee system. The residents' committees were thus a low-level unit in the communists' overall organization scheme. By late 1954, the communists extended the residents' committee system to all Chinese cities. They were largely unpopular because they interfered with private life and were often regarded as instruments of the police.[6]

The CCP in 1958 also created the household registration system (*hukou*), in which all families in a neighborhood were registered in books that were kept on file at the local police station. The goal of this system was to check on people attempting to evade the rural land reform campaign. But it also served to limit rural-to-urban migration, so urban centers could be developed without overtaxing facilities. In 1950, 90 percent of China's population were farmers. China's urban population increased nearly 30 percent from 1953 to 1956. China's cities would be overwhelmed if large numbers of farmers continued to migrate to urban areas. In reality, city governments often did not enforce the *hukou* system if they needed labor for industrial or infrastructural programs. For example, municipal governments relaxed *hukou* restrictions during the 1958–1962 Great Leap Forward as some 20 million peasants flocked to China's cities to participate in industrial production. Governments strictly enforced the *hukou* after the Great Leap to force the peasants back to the countryside. The *hukou* system still exists in China today, although the need for labor in the booming coastal areas has made rural-urban migration easier than in Mao's day.

Household registration also became important to qualify for government benefits such as education and health care, and for ration coupons for staples such as grains and cotton cloth. It became nearly impossible to enjoy such benefits without the proper registration. Parents passed their registration to their children, solidifying the rural-urban distinction.[7] The household registration system served a political purpose as well. Local police bureaus kept personal dossiers (*dang' an*) on every resident of a neighborhood.[8] The dossier contained personal information and information on one's background, such as family class level. Classes were assigned in the early 1950s and were hereditary. The labels were particularly important during the political campaigns. Individuals could be targeted as class enemies simply by having inherited a politically incorrect class label. A black mark in one's dossier, such as having a relative from one of the enemy classes, could adversely affect one's educational and employment opportunities, and even affect one's marriage prospects. The fear of having a black mark in one's dossier, which could negatively affect future generations, was an effective political tool in ensuring the cooperation of the people with party and government policy.

Socializing Agriculture and Industry

After the 1950–1951 land reform, the CCP gradually began to collectivize agriculture. Although agriculture would not be thoroughly collectivized until 1958, the CCP began the transition to socialist agriculture by first creating farmers' cooperatives. The CCP organized peasants into mutual-aid teams to pool draft animals, implements, and shared labor. In 1954, these teams gave way to larger co-ops, the agricultural producers' cooperatives (APCs). The APCs were a unified management system of farm production wherein individual peasants pooled their land, draft animals, tools, and houses in return for shares in the enterprise. After making deductions for expenses and collecting taxes, the communists distributed income to APC members based on their contributions, stated in shares. In the mid-1950s, the CCP accelerated agricultural reform. In the third stage of agricultural reform, all peasants worked for wages with no return from their input of property, tools, or land. By 1956, the entire country was involved in this stage of collectivization, just one step short of communization.

The CCP applied a policy of gradualism to industry as well. In 1949, three-fifths of China's labor force in manufacturing was self-employed craftsmen.[9] Inadequate numbers of trained and experienced CCP members prevented the party from immediately socializing industry. Industry owners and managers, many of them KMT members, kept their positions while the CCP trained cadres to replace the capitalists. Some of the work in socializing industry was already done for the Chinese communists. Under the Nationalists, the National Resources Commission (NRC) had gained control of two-thirds of China's industrial investment. After the communist revolution, the NRC's top officers and some two hundred thousand employees stayed in China.[10] The CCP used the NRC to build a state-controlled economy. By 1952, state-owned industry contributed 42 percent of gross industrial output value, as opposed to individually owned industry, which contributed only 21 percent.[11] The NRC engineers drove the engine of China's economic growth and development until their fall from grace in the 1958 Great Leap Forward.

The Transition to Socialism

Less than four years after the founding of the PRC, the Chinese communists had built a new government, confiscated and redistributed land, taken over much of China's private industry, eliminated or intimidated landlords and capitalists, crushed any remaining KMT resistance, and trained enough cadres to deepen socialization of the Chinese economy. Nationwide economic planning began in 1953 with the adoption of China's First Five-Year Plan (1953–1957). China's leaders adopted the Soviet model of economic growth and development in this plan by putting emphasis on heavy industry at the expense of agriculture and light industry, and by creating a centralized and planned economy. For instance, in the first year of the plan, China's leaders increased investment 84 percent over the previous year's levels, with most of the investment going to industry; half of the industrial investment went to 156 large-scale and capital-intensive projects aided by the Soviet Union.[12]

Under the First Five-Year Plan, the Chinese government transferred all industries and commerce to state control. The socialization of industry allowed Mao to devise a cellular economy around the work unit (*danwei*), a company or organization that functions as an employer, but also offers housing and social services. With the contraction of the private economy, the state began to disburse services through state enterprises. Social services such as education and health care became work-unit based. Large state-owned enterprises (SOEs), which might employ tens of thousands of people, had on their industrial campuses housing blocks, schools, entertainment venues, restaurants, shops, medical clinics, or even hospitals. The state also began to act as an employment agent, assigning workers to jobs in state work units, rather than having them look for jobs themselves. Universities, colleges, and schools became responsible for placing graduating students in jobs according to state direction. The state might assign young graduates to jobs hundreds of miles away in remote provinces if that is what China needed.

China experienced impressive economic growth during the First Five-Year Plan. National income grew about 9 percent, and agricultural output grew at nearly 4 percent, outpacing the population growth (2.4 percent). To provide plentiful cheap food for the cities, however, China's leaders implemented a *planned purchase and supply system,* requiring peasants to sell their produce at below-market prices. This system created a disincentive for farmers to increase production, and farmers had difficulty buying goods because of the high prices of finished products. To correct this imbalance, Mao urged the CCP to press ahead with total collectivization, which it accomplished, with disastrous consequences for the Chinese people, during the 1958 Great Leap Forward.

The 1956 Hundred Flowers Campaign

It was during the First Five-Year Plan that Chinese-Soviet relations began to fray as CCP resentment grew over Soviet unwillingness to forgive millions of yuan in loans. In February 1956, Soviet Communist Party leader Nikita Khrushchev made a secret speech to the Soviet Communist Party attacking Stalin's memory. This was a shattering event for the Chinese, who still saw much merit in maintaining the memory of a great Stalin. Mao, showing his first sign of serious dissatisfaction with Khrushchev, began to champion liberalization within the communist bloc while still upholding the virtues of Stalin at home. In the early stages of the First Five-Year Plan, Mao began to see that intellectuals—writers as well as scientists—of all political persuasions would be needed if there were to be a surge in China's productive capacities. Some advocates of compromise also entertained the hope that the authorities in Taiwan, still led by Chiang Kai-shek, might be encouraged to look to some eventual peaceful reunification with the PRC if China's former bourgeoisie were treated well.

Alluding to ancient China's Hundred Schools era (about 500 B.C. to 300 B.C.), which had produced China's great philosophies, Mao in 1956 proclaimed: "Let one hundred schools of thought contend; let one hundred flowers bloom." This Hundred Flowers Campaign, as it became known, represented both political and intellectual liberalization. China's intellectuals had been reticent in their comments since the political campaigns of the 1950s. Mao wanted to win back to the party the loyalty of China's intellectuals, and he encouraged scientists, writers, technicians, and professionals to come forward to offer criticism of economic, administrative, and political policies. In 1956, an economy that made significant growth in the early years was beginning to slow down, and Mao urged China's intellectuals to offer help in reviving a slowing economy. In Poland and Hungary, discontent with communist bureaucracy exploded into violent conflict. Mao wanted to avoid such a political meltdown in China by encouraging intellectuals to speak out before they reached the boiling point. Intellectuals, who for the past five years had been forced to undergo self-criticism sessions and confess their antiproletariat sentiments, doubted Mao's sincerity and were extremely cautious in responding to his invitation. Seeing their reticence, Mao in February 1957 offered a series of speeches to encourage intellectuals. On February 27, Mao made his famous speech "On the Correct Handling of Contradictions Among the People," in which he blamed bureaucrats for popular discontent and urged nonparty intellectuals to criticize the CCP.[13] Mao claimed that the intellectuals' constructive criticism would represent a nonantagonistic contradiction among the people, and was therefore permissible.[14]

In May 1957, intellectuals began to express critical views. The CCP organized a series of "speaking out" sessions. In Beijing, more than 160 professors and professionals from scientific and technical circles held a symposium in which they criticized the party for forcing them to spend so much time in political activities that they did not have adequate time for their research.[15] It soon became apparent that there was widespread and deeply felt resentment against the regime. Intellectuals, and the Chinese people in general, resented party domination of all aspects of society. They complained of special privileges for party members, criticized the party for giving direct orders to the people without going through the proper channels, commented that China lacked an effective legal system, and claimed that the CCP discriminated against people outside of the party. Others claimed that some party cadres, once promoted, were no longer accountable to the people.[16] Young people were some of the loudest critics. At Peking University, students covered a "democracy wall" with posters critical of the CCP.

Mao was shocked at the intensity of the criticism. Instead of mentioning failings for the system that could be quickly put aright, the intellectuals began to raise fundamental questions about communism. As in his 1957 essay "On the Correct Handling of Contradictions Among the People," Mao stated that some forms of conflict were healthy and could be expected even in a completely socialist and classless society, while others reflected class differences and had to be sharply repressed. He drew a line on criticism, however, and on June 7 an editorial for the *People's Daily,* the party's mouthpiece, stated that challenging the party was forbidden. The Hundred Flowers Campaign was over, and the Anti-Rightist Campaign began, bringing all critical intellectuals under severe attack for being counterrevolutionaries.

Among the intellectuals branded rightist was Ding Ling (1904–1986), one of China's best-known female writers. A former revolutionary, Ding Ling had become a member of China's literary establishment. During the 1942 party rectification campaign, Mao condemned her famous essay "Thoughts on March 8 (Women's Day)" as narrowly feminist for its criticism of the inequality between the sexes during the Yan'an era. During the Anti-Rightist Campaign, the CCP criticized and purged Ding Ling as an "inveterate antiparty element" and banished her to a border farm in Heilongjiang.[17] The CCP similarly penalized a whole generation of bright young party activists, among them some of China's finest social scientists, scientists, and economists, such as the astrophysicist Fang Lizhi and journalist Liu Binyan.

By the end of 1957, the CCP had branded half a million intellectuals as rightists. It sent many intellectuals to labor camps or to jail, others to the countryside. Some committed suicide. It did not rehabilitate many until 1979, many of them posthumously. The Anti-Rightist Campaign had a detrimental effect on China's political and economic development for at least a couple of reasons. First, because the intellectuals were sidelined in jail, in penal labor camps, or exiled to the countryside, there was no real voice of opposition to Mao and his

Liu Binyan, Journalist and Political Campaigner (1925–2005)

Liu Binyan joined the CCP in 1944, and by the mid-1950s was a star reporter for *China Youth News*. His ability to travel throughout China to cover news stories allowed him the opportunity to witness conditions in China in the early Mao years. Traveling throughout China in 1956, Liu saw rising discontent as the once-robust economy slowed and prices soared. Workers complained that the communists pushed them to the point of exhaustion to meet state production quotas and complained about constant party interference in their daily lives. In Shanghai, labor strikes were becoming the norm. During a lull in the "speaking out" sessions in late May 1957, Liu wrote a letter to Mao expressing his concerns that party conservatives were trying to halt the party rectification process, and that they were contributing to the deterioration of relationships between the CCP and the people. In March 1958, the CCP officially branded Liu an "extreme rightist." Of the six charges against him, the last referred to his letter to Mao. It claimed that Liu had tried to "influence Chairman Mao with his own vicious thinking." The CCP expelled Liu from the Party and sent him down to the countryside (*xiafang*) in Shanxi Province for reform through manual labor.

Liu bore the rightist label for twenty-one years. For thirteen of those years, Liu labored in the countryside, separated from his family. In his memoir, Liu claims that the stigma of being labeled a rightist, making one lower than a criminal, was worse than the exile. The stigma could even be extended to one's family members. The CCP labeled Liu's sister an extreme rightist for defending Liu. The party rehabilitated Liu in 1979, and he became the leading investigative reporter for the *People's Daily* (*Renmin Ribao*), the CCP's mouthpiece. The CCP expelled him from the Party in 1987 for criticizing abuses within the party. He moved to the United States in 1988, where he lived until his death from cancer in 2005. (Liu, *A Higher Kind of Loyalty*)

policies. After the teasing out of criticism in the Hundred Flowers Campaign and the ensuing party rectification and Anti-Rightist campaigns, no one dared to question Mao. The lack of discussion allowed Mao to become absolute dictator of China, retarding the country's political development. Second, it retarded China's economic development as Mao had effectively silenced those who were in the best position to guide China's economy with sound economic principles. Free from real opposition and sober restraint, Mao was free to pursue radical political and economic policies. The lack of political and economic development would have deadly consequences for the Chinese people.

Deepening China's Socialist Reforms

By the end of the First Five-Year Plan it became apparent to China's leaders that the Stalinist model of heavy industrialization did not fit China's needs. As increases in industrial productivity began to decline, China's leaders saw an urgent need to rapidly boost agricultural production to both feed the cities and maintain rapid development of heavy industry. Furthermore, the rising power and prestige of managers and technicians conflicted with the egalitarian ideals of the revolution. Mao's disdain for intellectuals and bureaucrats and his infatuation with the resolve of the masses, once properly stimulated by the CCP, led him to break with the Stalinist model of development. Mao appealed to self-reliance, decentralized planning, cooperation, and mass participation to accelerate the pace of socialist development and technological advance.

Discontent with the Soviet model of economic development had begun as early as 1955, when PRC vice chairman Liu Shaoqi proposed a systematic review of the rigidly centralized economic system. Mao wanted more scope for localities and state enterprises under the state plan. In April 1956, Mao called for the state to give more discretion to production units and localities. The Second Five-Year Plan (1958–1962) legitimized the decentralization of administrative authority to localities and individual production units.

Mao had taken up the issue of decentralization in a surprise move at the third plenum (meeting) of the CCP's Eighth Congress in fall 1957. At the end of the plenum, Mao argued for greater speed in economic development and took up the political issue of the nature of contradiction. To the consternation of the congress participants, Mao forced adoption of the class contradiction between the proletariat and the bourgeoisie as the main contradiction.[18] Mao's discussion of class contradiction had no bearing on economic policy, but contributed to tensions that would become critical to his new program for national construction. Congress proceedings reveal that party leaders had serious reservations about Mao's plans for China's economic development. Several of China's leaders had disagreed with Mao's 1955 collectivization of agriculture and sought to shift the party away from emphasis on Mao's individual leadership and more toward collective leadership. Concern among China's leaders over Mao's growing personality cult led the congress to drop Mao Zedong Thought from the party constitution. Mao relinquished his position as head of state and retreated to the "second line of leadership," professing to need time to ponder policy considerations. Liu Shaoqui was elected president of the PRC and chairman of the National Defense Commission and became Mao's heir apparent. The party left its day-to-day matters in the hands of President Liu, CCP general secretary Deng Xiaoping, and CCP vice chairman Zhou Enlai.

Mao's professional retreat did not diminish his political power. Dissatisfied with the Second Five-Year Plan, which called for only a modest increase in farm production, Mao reiterated an earlier call for a "great leap" in agricultural and industrial production. Mao began his call for a great leap in the mid-1950s as he became disillusioned with the Soviet model of economic modernization that was housed in huge bureaucracies. Mao was ardently antibureaucratic, particularly because he believed that bureaucrats, like intellectuals, were too removed from the people, were more involved in protecting their turf than in working to solve real problems, and were not directly engaged in production. Thinking that agriculture and industry had gotten bogged down in bureaucratic organization and procedures, Mao in 1957 decentralized administration of the economy by handing decisionmaking powers over to provincial and local officials. Consistent with his belief that if properly mobilized the masses could achieve any goal, Mao ordered mass mobilizations. The earlier mobilizations were to boost agriculture through improved irrigation. In September 1957, the CCP and the State Council announced a new movement to build and improve waterworks.

Mass mobilizations such as that for the Red Flag Canal Project spurred more mobilizations. In winter 1957–1958, the CCP mobilized a number of APCs to work on gigantic new water control and irrigation projects. By the end of the year, more than 600 million people throughout China were involved in waterworks projects.[19]

The Great Leap Forward

In November 1957, Mao and other communist leaders gathered in Moscow to commemorate the fortieth anniversary of the Bolshevik Revolution. After Mao arrived in Moscow, Khrushchev announced that, on the basis of its newly announced Seven-Year Plan, the Soviet Union would overtake the United States in per capita as well as total output of major industrial and agricultural products by 1970. Even before Mao heard the speech, Mao had convinced China's leaders to launch a new, radical program of economic development based on the slogan "more, faster, better, and cheaper." At the CCP's third plenum a month earlier, Mao had stated that there were two methods of doing things, "one producing slower and poorer results and the other faster and better ones."[20] While

---

Red Flag Canal Project

One of China's highly ambitious irrigation schemes was the Red Flag Canal Project. In 1956, millions of peasants worked day and night in an effort to complete a 940-mile canal in three months. The building of this massive waterway became a model for the rest of China in its exemplification of the values of self-reliance, self-sacrifice, and perseverance. The CCP used the canal as an example of the people, guided by Mao, harnessing nature. Together with the terraced show fields of Dazhai and the model Daqing oil field, the party held up the Red Flag Canal for study and emulation. The time frame was too ambitious, and in fact the canal took ten years to complete.

still in Moscow, Mao committed China to overtake Great Britain in industrial production in fifteen years.

From January until May 1958, Mao attended a series of meetings throughout China, gaining the support of provincial leaders for his policy initiatives. Critics who urged restraint were forced to write self-criticisms. China launched the Great Leap Forward in May 1958. The Great Leap Forward broke sharply with certain development principles of the First Five-Year Plan and embarked China on a new path. China had made impressive advances under the First Five-Year Plan. China's gross national product had increased 9 percent on average per year during the plan and industrial production had increased nearly 19 percent, owing partially to the many large-scale projects provided by the Soviet Union. The emphasis on heavy industry contributed to growing sectoral and regional imbalances, however. Despite collectivization, China's agricultural production grew less than 4 percent and in 1957 grew by only 2 percent. Meanwhile, China's population continued to grow. From 1952 to 1957, China's population had grown 12 percent, with urban population growing 40 percent, particularly as people migrated from rural to urban areas to work in industry.[21] The CCP claimed that urban food consumption would have to be cut because agriculture could not support existing levels.[22] Mao and his supporters argued that China's industrial growth could not be sustained if agriculture continued to lag. In his closing speech to the fall 1957 third plenum of the Eighth Central Committee, Mao called for "more, faster, better, and cheaper" results in economic construction, marking the beginning of the Great Leap Forward.

Formation of People's Communes

The aforementioned waterworks brigades were forerunners of the rural commune system. In an attempt to increase work production under the slogan "more, faster, better, cheaper," party officials in Henan Province abolished private plots in April 1958 and merged cooperatives into a *people's commune* of nearly ten thousand households. The galvanization of peasants through the organization of a commune impressed Mao, and he saw communes as a way to achieve greater economies of scale. The communes served four purposes: to completely collectivize agriculture, to amalgamate state and society, to gradually eliminate the difference between town and country, and to eliminate the difference between industry and agriculture.

Collectivize agriculture. With the establishment of the communes, the party abolished ownership of private land, tools, and draft animals. Consistent with the militarization of life and labor, each commune consisted of large production brigades, which in turn consisted of a number of smaller work teams. Work teams corresponded to former neighborhoods and averaged twenty-six households. The brigades, which averaged seven or eight work teams, often corresponded to old villages. Communes were composed of thirteen to fourteen brigades. Work teams cultivated land held in common according to targets set by the brigades, the communes, and other higher-level units. When establishing production targets, Mao believed that larger meant more. Traditional Chinese plots were small because a father's land was divided among sons upon his death. Over time, these small plots were insufficient for even subsistence farming. Mao believed that larger agricultural units would produce more food. Thus, the early communes were huge; the average commune was made up of five thousand households, twenty-five times larger than higher-level APCs. Some of the early communes had more than one hundred thousand members. By the end of 1958, more than 1 million households, or 99 percent of rural households, belonged to twenty-five thousand communes.

The communes changed the most basic work organization of China's peasants. Under the APCs, farmers had continued to work on their own land, following the traditional cycle of plowing, planting, irrigating, and harvesting. Under the commune system, however, farmers lost their private land to the communes and were placed on production teams that were assigned specific tasks. Although they stayed in their home villages, they worked with people with whom they had not previously worked and with whom they did not maintain informal ties. Their teams went from field to field to cover all of the arable land in the commune, working on land unfamiliar to them. Instead of working with the idiosyncrasies of their own land, farmers found themselves merely carrying out tasks assigned to them on completely anonymous land.[23] The loss of the ability of China's farmers to work out the idiosyncrasies of the land would have a devastating effect on China's agriculture and the Chinese people.

The alienation from the land also contributed to a lack of motivation. Farmers lacked zeal for producing for the collective and for the cities. China relied on government procurements to secure sufficient supplies of grain to fuel industrialization. According to the state plan, communes had to fulfill a given state quota of production. One part of this quota stayed at the commune to meet expenses and to feed work teams. The remainder was called the surplus. Surpluses were not enjoyed by members of a commune, but were sent off to state warehouses to be distributed in the cities. While the concept of surplus implies excess grain, in reality the surplus was a convenient method of extracting large amounts of grain from the communes. The state strictly limited commune expenses to maximize surpluses. Neither the communes nor the peasants were satisfied with their share of the harvest.[24]

Members of work teams drew incomes from the commune based on a "half supply, half wages" formula in which 50 percent of peasant wages were paid in goods and services and 50 percent in cash. The first half corresponded to the "to each according to his needs" axiom in which households received the "seven guarantees" of food, clothing, medical care, childbirth, education, housing, and marriage and funeral rites, according to the number of family members.[25] The latter part of the formula may be translated as "to each according to his labor," in which remuneration was based on how many hours one worked at tasks graded according to difficulty. If the commune exceeded its quota, the state simply took more produce from the commune, removing any incentive to beat the quota. Commune farmers found there was little incentive to work hard, and a general malaise set in among commune workers as they lost enthusiasm for toiling for the collective good. Although people who worked enthusiastically were rewarded with bonuses, the differential was not great enough to inspire people to work hard. Households generally depended on the collective income distributed by the commune for 70–80 percent of their livelihoods, with the remainder coming from their small plots or household sideline activities.[26] The lack of incentive structure resulted in disappointing levels of agricultural production. Agricultural production actually fell during the 1958–1961 Great Leap Forward.

Amalgamate state and society. To create a truly communist society, the CCP needed to narrow the gap between state and society. The communes merged with the local township (*xiang*) government. Members of the township people's council served concurrently as members of the commune's management committee, and members of the township party committee served concurrently as members of the commune party committee.[27] Thus, commune and township party committees became one and the same, although real power rested with the party committee, which made all of the decisions regarding agricultural, educational, commercial, and welfare functions of the communes.[28]

The organization of the communes significantly altered family life and Chinese society. The early communes had residential dormitories for the two sexes and nurseries for the children, which broke up families. To free women from family matters so as to allow them to work in the fields, elderly relatives lived in hostels and children spent their days in nurseries. Children attended commune schools, and the ill sought care in commune health clinics. The communes served meals in huge canteens. A common slogan in rural communes was "Eat as much as you can, work as much as you must."[29] Mao thought that by ridding peasants of any housework or need for a private plot they would have time and energy to increase production.[30] Commune conditions varied widely. Many families continued to live in their homes, paying rent to the commune. Some nurseries preferred mothers to come and pick up their children in the evening because there were inadequate facilities or staff for their care.

The communes also destroyed another vital part of Chinese society: the market town. In traditional China, the marketing community played an important role in Chinese society. A market town served a marketing community of six to forty villages whose individual populations were too small to support a market. The market town would commonly open on selected days of the week. The market town would attract farmers selling produce and townspeople selling other services, such as doctors, dentists, barbers, and fortune-tellers. The market town was where residents of several villages would meet to gossip, arrange marriages, and carry on other social activities. The communes eliminated the market towns, disrupting the Chinese social system.

Profile of a Commune: The Weixing (Sputnik) People's Commune

The first commune in China, known as the Sputnik, was the Chayashan People's Commune of Suiping County, Henan Province, established in April 1958. Citizens over sixteen years old were admitted as full members of the Weixing (Sputnik) Commune. Consistent with the people's dictatorship, former landlords, rich peasants, counterrevolutionaries and other people deprived of political rights were accepted as unofficial members and became official members only after having their political rights reinstated. When the APCs merged into the commune, all members had to turn over their collectively owned property to the commune, as well as privately owned plots of farmland, house sites, livestock, and trees. In addition to expanding agricultural output, the Weixing Commune required members to build irrigation works, improve the soil, use good strains of seed over large areas, breed draft animals, prevent and control insect pests and plant diseases, apply careful cultivation, and adopt mechanization of agriculture as the countryside acquired electrification.

The commune instituted a system of universal, compulsory education combined closely with labor and established primary schools and continuing education schools so that all school-age children could attend school and all young people reach senior primary school. A system of citizen soldiery also operated throughout the commune. The commune organized militia units whose members undertook regular military training, fulfilled tasks assigned by the state, and received wages for their service.

An elected committee of representatives carried out the management of the commune, and production contingents (which supervised a number of production brigades) carried out the day-to-day affairs of the commune. Production contingents had discretion to organize production, undertake capital construction, handle production expenses, and distribute rewards.

Commune members received wages, taking into account the intensity and complexity of the task, as well as members' physical condition, skill level, and attitude toward work. The commune paid wages monthly, but could vary depending on the commune's income in a given month. Commune members who worked harder than others received awards, and the commune penalized lazy or slovenly workers through a reduction in their wages. It offered female members one month's maternity leave at half wages.

(continues)

Profile of a Commune:
The Weixing (Sputnik) People's Commune (cont.)

The commune set up community canteens, nurseries, and sewing teams to free women from household labor. Members did not need to use the canteen if they did not want to and could prepare their own meals. The commune also set up a hospital with inpatient wards for serious cases. Every production contingent had an outpatient clinic, and brigades had health officers and a midwife. Commune members paid a yearly fee in accordance with the number of family members, but no other fees were charged for medical care. Authorities destroyed the existing houses of commune members, and used the building materials to build new homes for the commune. The occupants paid rent equivalent to the cost of maintenance and repair. The commune also provided social, recreational, cultural, and athletic activities. The commune encouraged each production contingent to have a club room, amateur theatrical troupe, choir, and sports team, as well as a small reading room and radio sets. ("Tentative Regulations of the Weixing People's Commune," 61–77)

Eliminate the difference between town and country. Mao was disturbed that large disparities in standard of living existed despite the egalitarian promises of the 1949 revolution. One of the goals of the Great Leap Forward, albeit not as major as the others, was to diminish urban-rural disparity. Under a program called *shangshan xiaxiang* (literally, "up to the mountains and down to the villages"), the CCP sent more than 1 million urban youth to the countryside between 1956 and 1966. It sent 12 million more between 1968 and 1975, during the Cultural Revolution.

   Shangshan xiaxiang was a revolutionary program in which urban youth were to be integrated with the peasants, who were the true revolutionaries. What was truly revolutionary about the program, however, was the idea that educated urbanites would not merely live alongside peasants, but would *become* peasants. In spring 1957, Liu Shaoqi argued that more educated young people should be sent to the countryside because the urban and educational sectors could not absorb their growing numbers. The demand for educated people was well satisfied in urban settings, but rural areas still needed large numbers of educated youth.[31] Of course the policy of sending urban youth to the mountains or countryside would help alleviate urban youth unemployment, but the greater objective was rural and frontier development. Mao wanted young people to have some connection with the socialist transformation of agriculture: "All people who have had some education ought to be very happy to work in the countryside if they get the chance. In our vast rural areas there is plenty of room for them to develop their talents to the full."[32]

In 1958, CCP general secretary Deng Xiaoping ordered communes to be set up in the cities. Liu Shaoqi, vice chairman of the party's Central Committee, stated that "the development of people's communes would eliminate the differences between the cities and the countryside and between industry and agriculture; it would also make the countryside more like the cities and the cities more like the countryside."[33] In May 1958, the communists created experimental urban communes. Typically, inhabitants of several streets and employees of area businesses were reorganized as a commune. Urban communes consisted of two thousand to three thousand households and ten thousand to twenty thousand people. Each commune had canteens, nurseries, and kindergartens, freeing the women for work outside the home. There were services such as barbers, swimming pools, stores, and clubhouses. The communes mobilized residents to eradicate pests, repair buildings, improve water delivery systems, and participate in movements such as the Eradicate Pests program and the Sweep Away Illiteracy movement. Production in an urban commune was coordinated with the production plans of the local state-owned industrial enterprises, and their production plans were fitted into the state's production plan. After the floods, drought, and other calamities in the second half of 1960 robbed state enterprises of raw materials, the communes turned to production of small commodities. Throughout the second half of the Great Leap Forward, the CCP directed the urban communes away from supporting state industry to light industry.

A major issue in implementing the urban communes was the distribution of incomes and the effective control of consumption. Before the appearance of communes, wages in state-owned factories were largely based on seniority and amount of output produced. State firms sometimes offered bonuses based on productivity. The urban communes replaced this system with a system in which workers were paid according to hours worked. Communes controlled consumption by limiting wages and rationing necessities; low incomes prevented any resurgence of capitalism.[34] The urban communes stressed collectivization in all aspects of life: commune members worked, lived, and socialized together. After a day of working together, work team members would retire with their families to work team dormitories. They used the same canteens, nurseries, and laundry facilities. The communes required women, unchained from household duties, to engage in production in neighborhood industries, such as making cement, selecting coal, or working a backyard furnace.

Forcing people to work, live, and socialize together was supposed to create a stronger socialist atmosphere. In fact, it nearly destroyed the Chinese family because the communes organized and absorbed family members into the commune according to age and sex. The communes estranged and destroyed the relationship among family members as their daily activities (sewing, cooking, childrearing, and tending to the old and infirm) were all transferred to the commune's welfare organizations and were handled collectively. Families had little privacy as they lived in close proximity to other families from the same work unit in commune-provided housing. As a result, the collective became more important than the family.

Eliminate the difference between industry and agriculture. Mao and the CCP intended that industry would be the engine of China's economic growth. To accelerate industrial production, Mao and the CCP put forward the general policy of developing agriculture.[35] Under the commune system, the party mobilized the population to develop agriculture and local industrial enterprises. In addition to farming, the party required communes to build massive infrastructure projects, such as land reclamation and dams. In Guangdong, the communes built 21 large reservoirs and 155 medium-sized ones for electrical generation, flood prevention, and irrigation between 1957 and 1964.[36] These projects often took the farmers away from their farming, thereby decreasing agricultural production. However, Mao believed that by developing agriculture and industry side by side, within fifteen years China would overtake Great Britain in industrial development. The communes eliminated the need for residents to do anything but farm for China and produce metal.

One of these industrial projects was steelmaking. Under the First Five-Year Plan, steelmaking was the responsibility of large state-owned enterprises located in urban areas. Consistent with Mao's decentralization of administration, steelmaking became the responsibility of all rural and urban residents. Communes, and most urban work units, built their own mini-mills called backyard furnaces. These furnaces were made of whatever material was available, usually mud and straw, and were sometimes reinforced with human hair offered up by commune members to strengthen the structure of the mills. More than a million backyard furnaces ran day and night. Wood fuel for the mills came from China's woodlands, denuding entire forests. People contributed anything of metal—pots and pans, bed frames and window frames, even doorknobs and jewelry—to the making of pig iron. The irony is that perfectly good materials were fed into the backyard furnaces to make goods that were shoddy and useless.

Mao had ambitious goals for steel production during the Great Leap Forward. China's planners had set a steel production goal of 30 million tons for 1959, a 600 percent increase over 1957. Although Mao asked that the goal be dropped to 20 million tons (a 400 percent increase over 1957), even this goal was unrealistic. Production reached only 8 million tons in 1958; 3 million tons were useless, produced in the backyard furnaces. Industrial production increased 66 percent from 1957 to 1959, but the momentum was unsustainable. In 1960, industrial production fell below 10 percent, in 1961 it fell by 38 percent, and in 1962 fell a further 16.6 percent. Twenty million workers lost their jobs and were sent back to their rural villages.

The party affirmed the "correctness" of the people's communes in late 1958. Because of good weather, China's communes produced a bumper crop that year. Believing that it was the collectivization of agriculture that had resulted in the good harvest, the party set ambitious targets for output for the following year and encouraged communes to compete in busting their agricultural production quotas. Communes pledged to increase their production beyond the state-mandated quotas. The pledges became ridiculous as the communes tried to outbid one another, but no commune wanted to be seen as a laggard. Wheat yields were typically five hundred pounds an acre, but some communes pledged fifty thousand pounds an acre. The absurd pledges led to falsifying records to meet the quotas. No one could possibly believe these figures, but few dared speak up.

Growing concern over the Great Leap Forward's radical policies came to a head at the Central Committee's eighth plenum in Lushan in August 1959. Mao critic Peng Dehuai was particularly critical of the enormous financial cost of the backyard furnaces and their unquantifiable benefits, and he also targeted the habit of exaggeration. Peng's greatest insult, however, was to put the blame on Mao for all of the disasters of the Great Leap Forward. At Lushan, Mao argued that the gains outweighed the losses, and gave People's Liberation Army (PLA) brass an ultimatum to side with him or Peng. Nervous PLA officers defected from Peng, and he was isolated. At Lushan, Peng lost the Defense Ministry to Lin Biao, but remained a member of the Politburo and vice premier. The party moved him from the government residential compound at Zhongnanhai to a dilapidated house on the outskirts of Beijing, where he lived for six years. He apparently tried his hand at gardening and farming, and became an exhaustive reader. Once they knew who he was, neighbors frequently visited. Life seemed rather pleasant until his persecution a few years later during the Cultural Revolution. Peng's was the only voice critical of Mao's Great Leap Forward policies, and the party dismissed him from office. In his showdown with Peng, Mao had proven that his word was absolute. Unconstrained by criticism, Mao plunged China ahead in his Great Leap, with disastrous consequences.

A combination of bad weather, lack of an incentive system, pressure to meet targets, and poor procurement and pricing policies was compounded by a lack of specialists and managers in the communes to teach the peasants methods of large-scale agricultural production. As a result, peasants produced less grain in 1959 than prior to 1958. Many of the peasants were not farming at all. Instead, they were smelting metal, most of which was useless. Grain production fell sharply from a high of 200 million tons in 1958 to 170 million tons in 1959 and possibly as low as 143.5 million tons in 1960. China's grain exports, however, continued to grow, topping 4 million in 1959 and exacerbating the growing agricultural crisis. Unaware of the looming crisis in the countryside, China's leaders in 1959 ordered that one-third of China's arable land lie fallow, otherwise the supposed surplus would rot in government storehouses. Out of fear, commune leaders fudged production numbers, which only meant that the state took more grain away from the communes and sent it to the cities. Reserve stocks of grain cushioned the 1959 drop in agricultural production, but the worst impact on food supplies occurred in 1960–1961. Rural commune members were not aware that their dire situation had become a national phenomenon. Some tried to escape their communes for the cities. The CCP prevented residents from leaving the communes by commandeering any mode of transportation, from overland vehicles to boats. Commune militias shot those who tried to escape. Many people committed suicide.

The crisis became nationwide in 1959, with all eighteen of China's predominantly rural provinces recording above-normal mortality rates. In 1960, national food production fell 25 percent. The Chinese diet was largely dependent on food grains, but the average yearly grain consumption per capita of China's rural population fell 25 percent after the launch of the Great Leap Forward. It took the government three years to respond to the famine, however. The result of these policies was the greatest man-made famine in history. Some 30 million Chinese died of starvation and starvation-related illness during this time. It would take a decade for per capita production of grain to surpass the 1957 level on a sustained basis (see Figure 3.1).

The increase in China's mortality rate (the number of deaths per thousand people) indicates the depth of the famine. China's mortality rate had declined during the 1950s due to a cessation of warfare, a reduction in extreme poverty, and better access to health care. Increased fertility also contributed to the decline. This downward trend was reversed after the launch of the Great Leap Forward. China's mortality rate in 1957 was eleven deaths per thousand people; by 1960 it had risen to more than twenty-five deaths per thousand people. In

Figure 3.1 China's Grain Production

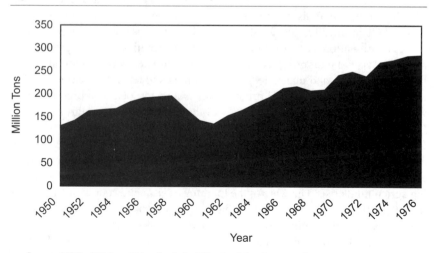

Year

Source: NBS of China, *China Statistical Yearbook* (various years).

1960 Sichuan and Guizhou, mortality reached more than fifty per thousand.[37] The Great Leap Forward also created a fertility crisis, which is defined as a drop in fertility of more than 15 percent from the average of the previous years. By 1961, China's fertility rate had dropped more than 45 percent below pre-Leap figures.[38] Some 30 million children were not born as women could not conceive because of severe malnutrition.[39] For China as a whole, the net fertility loss amounted to about 90 percent of a normal year's births; in only three provinces was it less than 40 percent.[40]

Although urban residents did not experience such severe famine, they did find a shortage of food. The chief source of food for urban populations was government supply. Urban residents received a fixed ration of grain at a fixed price. With the growing grain deficit, the government had to dip into grain reserves to feed the cities. People had to queue in long lines for bread and fish. The need to feed the cities meant that the central government took more grain from rural areas. In Heilongjiang, one of China's major grain-exporting provinces, the rate at which the government procured grains climbed from 44 percent in 1957 to 63 percent in 1960. In Sichuan Province, the procurement rate climbed from 30 percent to 49 percent in 1959. In Fujian, the procurement rate was 40 percent in 1959.[41] Anti-Rightists languishing in prison camps had an especially hard time.

Post-Leap Retrenchment

The disastrous policies of the Great Leap Forward led to a period of economic entrenchment from 1961 to 1965. During that time, Mao fell out of favor and once again moved from the first line of leadership to the second line. Concern over the radical plans of the Great Leap Forward led party leaders in December

---

Tragedy of the Camps

"Early in 1961, my mother gave birth to my older sister. It was a particularly bad time. Famine had begun. Even though she was working in a labor camp—actually a labor farm—there was not enough to eat. Food was sent to the cities instead. Communist Party members got plenty. Not so for my parents; rightists were given less food than others in the camp. As a result, my sister Ying died a few days after she was born. My mother told me so many times that my sister was so beautiful even though she, my mother, had not eaten well during the pregnancy. She said Ying was born healthy, but had died from malnutrition because my mother was unable to breastfeed. Officials in the camp refused to provide milk." *Lindsay L. Wang, as told to John Franklin Copper* (Wang, *Dog's Daughter*, 27)

1958 to convince Mao to relinquish the post of president of the PRC to Liu Shaoqi. During the period of retrenchment, President Liu and CCP general secretary Deng Xiaoping, as well as Premier Zhou Enlai, played a large role in China's economic recovery. The CCP brought ousted economic planner Chen Yun back to power.

In 1959, the party leadership eased off the extreme measures of the Great Leap Forward. Deng Xiaoping reduced the sizes of the communes by breaking them down into smaller units. He also allowed the communes to move away from extreme egalitarianism. The state reduced the amount of surplus grain extracted from the communes and focused on raising peasant enthusiasm for production. It kept to a minimum the amount taken from the collective and increased the portion that could be distributed to peasants, thereby linking reward more closely with labor output.[42] It allowed peasants plots for their own use and to keep agricultural surpluses. Deng encouraged peasants to engage in sideline occupations and to trade in the reopened free markets. Local cadres moved quickly to decollectivize arable land. In 1958 there was no quantifiable acreage available for individual production. By 1964, more than 8 percent of China's arable land was available for individual production.[43] These plots produced on average more than twice as much as community-owned land and helped Chinese agriculture to recover rapidly from the 1959–1961 disaster. They also increased family income. One study of ten Chinese communes indicates that in 1964, 20 percent of family income came from plots for individual use, and yet, despite these achievements, less than 8 percent of land was available for individual production.[44]

The retreat from collective production facilitated growth of petty capitalism in the countryside. As prices were higher in the free markets than state procurement prices, farm families tended to put more effort into their noncommune holdings than into collective work. By the mid-1960s, noncommune production accounted for about one-third of peasant income.[45]

To stimulate collective effort, the communes introduced more effective incentive structures. The commune paid peasants according to a complex system of work points based on their individual productivity rather than according to hours worked. This change benefited the physically stronger, more experienced, and more driven commune members, and led to significant income differentials. Some peasants and work team leaders colluded in the allocation of work points, to the advantage of both.

Liu Shaoqi implemented similar reforms in industry. He shifted emphasis from heavy industry to light industry and revived material incentives to inspire labor. He closed thousands of small and economically inefficient factories and shops in China's cities. He dismissed most of the workers in larger enterprises hired during the Leap and froze new employment. Out of economic necessity, the state sent some 20 million laid-off workers to the countryside in what was called the "return to the village" movement. By taking these measures, Liu cut China's total industrial workforce in half.

To clear the cities of rural migrants and send them back to the countryside, the CCP strictly enforced the *hukou* (household registration) system. Municipal governments distributed ration coupons for much-needed staples to residents with the requisite *hukou*. Urban dwellers without the correct *hukou* found it impossible to receive the ration coupons and had no choice but to return to the countryside. The household registration system effectively built a fence around the cities and protected the higher standard of living of urban dwellers at the expense of those who lived in rural areas.

With Mao's political retreat, Liu and Deng recentralized authority in the party and state bureaucracies. The failures of the Great Leap—food shortages and famine, disruption of social life, and chaotic economics—all called for recentralization of economic and political controls. Putting the CCP at the forefront of this effort, Liu and Deng put aside Maoist-style mass campaigns for bureaucratic rule in favor of economic stability and sociopolitical order. Liu in particular was intent on reestablishing the Leninist authority and legitimacy of the party. He restored firm lines of command within the CCP and restored the party's command over society in general. To exonerate the party for the Leap's failures, the CCP made lower-level party cadres, particularly the Maoist-inspired rural cadres, scapegoats of the disasters of the Great Leap. Party officials dismissed many local cadres and ordered the remainder to strictly follow higher-level party directives. Middle- and higher-level party cadres regained administrative authority at the provincial, regional, and urban levels, and the party reinstated many officials purged in the Anti-Rightist Campaign. It recruited people with technical and administrative expertise. Much to Mao's chagrin, Liu was transforming the CCP from a revolutionary organization into a professional bureaucratic apparatus. Mao believed that the party was becoming more concerned with self-preservation and perpetuation than with pursuing permanent revolution. He believed that, by downplaying ideology, the CCP was attracting opportunists rather than revolutionaries, which only reinforced careerist tendencies already present in the party.[46]

The failure of the Great Leap Forward highlighted a growing division within the CCP leadership. Mao was clearly aware that many party leaders shared Peng Dehuai's criticisms of the Leap, even if they did not voice them. After Mao stepped aside in 1959, the party put its policies into the hands of cautious leaders who stressed deliberation and gradual progress rather than Mao's swift and sweeping changes. The most prominent of these were Liu Shaoqi and Deng Xiaoping. The rise of Liu and Deng restored the authority of party bureaucrats whose power had been eclipsed during the Great Leap Forward. Along with leading party officials such as Peng Zhen and economic planners Chen Yun and Bo Yibo, Liu and Deng began to dismantle Mao's Great Leap policies and return China to a more stable economic order. Aware of Mao's tremendous following among the people, the party bureaucracy invoked Mao's name as a symbol of national unity even as they undid much of his order. Invoking Mao's thoughts would come back to haunt them in just a few years, however, when Mao regained power and unleashed a mass campaign against the party bureaucracy in the Cultural Revolution.

Origins of the Cultural Revolution

The origins of the Cultural Revolution can be understood in the context of the failure of the Great Leap Forward, China's split with the Soviet Union, and Maoist theory of contradiction in practice. After the demise of the 1957 Hundred Flowers Campaign, China's leaders had jettisoned the highly centralized, bureaucratic Soviet model of economic growth for a more decentralized approach. This approach resulted in the communes of 1958 and the mass mobilizations of peasants to carry out large infrastructure projects and industry, culminating in projects such as the Red Flag Canal and the backyard furnaces. Just as the peasant-based Red Army had been victorious by depending on men rather than weapons, Mao believed that the CCP could mobilize peasants in a *mass line* to stimulate agricultural production and to facilitate the rapid development of industry. This belief in voluntarism—the triumph of the will over material limitations—departed from the Soviet model, which relied on material resources and technology to develop industry and the economy. During the Great Leap Forward, Mao saw the communes as a national phenomenon, each commune being a self-sustaining economy, cultural center, and military unit held together and led forward by the CCP. The communes would also engender a sense of comrades-in-arms against reactionary (counterrevolutionary) foes. The hopes of the Great Leap Forward were never realized, resulting in the severe economic crisis of 1959–1962 and the 1960 retreat. In the "three bad years" immediately after the Great Leap Forward, President Liu Shaoqi took over the running of the party from Mao. The most devoted Leninist of China's leaders, Liu set about creating a bureaucratized, elitist party machinery. He stressed technocratic expertise over revolutionary zeal, and elevated party careerists over pure revolutionary cadres. Under Liu, the party apparatus by 1962 had become tightly structured, hierarchically centralized, and managerially efficient.[47] The unleashing of the Cultural Revolution in the mid-1960s was Mao's attempt to wrest party control back from Liu and his supporters.

The Cultural Revolution was also an attempt to undo Liu and Deng's post-Leap economic policies. In the "three bad years" after the failure of the Great Leap Forward, Liu reintroduced capitalism to industry by reinstating material bonuses to reward hard work, introducing a more comprehensive wage-grading system with bigger differentials based on skill and performance, and offering material rewards for inventions and technical improvements.[48] Deng Xiaoping allowed peasants to farm their own plots and reopened free rural agricultural markets. These material incentives contradicted Mao's mass line economic theory, and he branded these reforms "revisionism." Liu's revisionism, which marked the return to market-oriented economics, stressed expertise and the scientific method rather than mass mobilizations and strict observance of ideological orthodoxy. Mao claimed that without clear ideological goals and correctly politicized people to administer those goals, science and technology would serve the wrong purposes and would not achieve rapid results.[49] Mao's Cultural Revolution was an attempt to turn back the clock on Liu-Deng revisionism.

The China-Soviet split, which became public in 1960, also contributed to the launch of the Cultural Revolution. After Stalin's death in 1953, Mao saw the Soviet Union as departing from Marxist-Leninist principles. Mao took exception to Khrushchev's 1956 speech before the Soviet Communist Party's Twentieth Congress (commonly known as the "de-Stalinization speech"), in which the Soviet leader criticized Stalin's excesses. Mao believed the speech was a veiled criticism of him. Also, Soviet criticism of the Great Leap—the Soviets branded the Leap as economically unsound and dangerously fanatical—and the failure of the Soviets to follow through on a promise to offer China nuclear weapons assistance angered Mao. Mao also denounced Khrushchev's policy of peaceful coexistence with the West. Mao criticized these moves as Soviet revisionism. He believed that the Soviet Union was moving away from the concept of continuous revolution and egalitarian principles and toward a new ruling class of specially privileged, urban-centered technocrats. He saw the same pattern in Liu's reforms and unleashed the Cultural Revolution to check those tendencies.

The Cultural Revolution was an integral part of Mao's uninterrupted revolution. Mao and his supporters believed that revisionism, namely capitalist tendencies, had reemerged in China after the Great Leap Forward. As revisionism endangered the creation of a classless socialist society, Mao needed a "cultural revolution" to revitalize the revolutionary process and move China toward the ultimate socialist goal.[50] In the broadest sense, revisionism meant everything deviating from Marxism-Leninism-Maoism. It also described techno-bureaucrats who substituted science and technology for ideological orthodoxy in the quest for economic development. Revisionism also described the decline of the relevance of revolutionary norms and values to the solution of modern-day problems. Sidelined, but not without power, the Maoists still believed that proper ideology and mass mobilization would bring about desired results. The Liuists were more apt to use the party organization and state apparatus to achieve results. The difference between the two became known as the "red versus expert" dichotomy. Mao equated bureaucrats with the bourgeoisie, and equated bureaucratic dominance with revisionism, or capitalist tendencies. Leaders of the bureaucratic class were the leaders of the CCP. To regain his political power, Mao would unleash a radical political campaign against revisionism, and against the party, in the Cultural Revolution.

The Rise of Lin Biao

Mao increasingly turned to the military for support. Strongly against professionalization of the PLA, Mao in 1958 denounced the PLA's attempt to establish "bourgeois military thinking," and in 1959 purged Defense Minister Peng De-haui, in part for his support of the professionalization of the army and for advocating obtaining modern military supplies and equipment from the Soviet Union. Mao replaced Peng with Lin Biao, who pushed for politicization of the PLA. Lin compiled Mao's quotes into a "little red book" as part of his indoctrination program. He revived the political commissar program (a party or government appointee who oversees a unit of the military), downplaying the professionalization of the military. In 1963, Lin Biao intensified indoctrination in the army by starting a mass campaign within the PLA to emphasize the basic values of service to the party. The focus of the campaign was a young PLA soldier, Lei Feng, who had left behind after his untimely death a diary detailing a life of service and obedience to the PLA and party.[51] Although the diary was fictitious, it served to launch an attack against those people who lacked revolutionary spirit, such as the intellectuals and writers. The Lei Feng campaign sparked a larger Learn from the PLA political campaign. Lei Feng's diary was introduced into China's schools and Mao gave it his imprimatur by signing the diary with his own calligraphy. The Learn from the PLA Campaign broke with the precedent in the CCP that militarism must be kept subordinate. As early as 1938, Mao had argued that because political power comes out of the power of the gun, the party commands the gun and the gun must never be allowed to command the party.[52] Further indication of Lin Biao's politicization of the PLA was the placement of PLA-staffed political bureaus in schools and factories. The presence of the PLA in schools, where minds are shaped, was instrumental in building Liu's power base.

The Mao Cult

Lin's politicization of China's military greatly contributed to the creation of the Mao personality cult. The cult of Mao had actually begun as early as the Yan'an days and grew larger during the rectification campaigns of the early 1940s, which simultaneously attacked opposition to Mao while popularizing his writings. The communists' victory over the Nationalists in 1949 secured Mao's place in China as a "savior" and "star of salvation." Although the disasters of the Great Leap Forward temporarily retarded the growth of the Mao cult, it roared back to life in the 1960s. After his efforts in 1960 to turn the PLA into a "great school of Mao Zedong Thought," Lin Biao moved to use the PLA to educate the entire nation, while deifying Mao in the process. In 1964, the PLA's political department published *Quotations from Chairman Mao Zedong* (commonly known as Mao's "Little Red Book"), a collection of short extracts drawn from Mao's writings and speeches. The book distilled Mao Thought and presented it as a fountain of wisdom. In the following three years, the PLA printed nearly a billion copies of the book, along with 150 million copies of Mao's *Selected Works*. Lin ordered the book as required reading in schools and universities, and classes began and ended with readings from it. During the Cultural Revolution, it was common practice for everyone to carry a copy, and bands of Red Guards beat hapless souls who neglected to have it on their person.

The cult of Mao reached new heights during the Cultural Revolution. Mao's writings were set to music, and performers and common citizens performed loyalty songs and loyalty dances. Mao's cult portrayed him as larger than life. Posters and portraits superimposed Mao's visage on the sun, its rays emanating from Mao, the "shining sun" of the people. Mao became the Great Leader, the Great Helmsman, the Great Teacher, and the Supreme Commander of the Chinese people. Even Edgar Snow, the American who had extolled the virtues of Mao and the communists in his 1938 book *Red Star over China,* was puzzled by the inordinate amount of glorification of Mao. In a visit to China in 1964–1965, Snow found giant posters of Mao hung in the streets, busts in every chamber, and his books and photos displayed everywhere, to the exclusion of others.[53]

The Great Proletarian Cultural Revolution

The Great Proletarian Cultural Revolution lasted from 1966 until 1976. The most intense years, from late 1965 to April 1969, can be broken down into four phases: (1) the 1965–1966 leadership struggle, (2) the 1966 revisionism campaign, (3) the 1967–1968 Red Guard phase, and (4) the 1968–1969 attempt to rebuild the government.

In late 1962, with the economy stabilized, Mao began his political comeback. In September, he launched his Socialist Education Movement, which made Maoist ideology a criterion for all political and government institutions. Disguised as a movement to reform the thought of lower-level cadres, the education movement was actually a major purge of Mao's potential adversaries. By the end of the three-year campaign, the CCP had dismissed some 1 million cadres.

Mao's reemergence on the political scene caused a rift in the party, called the "two-line struggle." Party politics forced cadres to align either with Liu Shaoqi and Deng Xiaoping, who disdained Mao's mass mobilization approach, or with the PLA under Lin Biao, who embraced Mao. Liu and Deng believed that the Great Leap Forward was a disaster on such a scale that it never could be repeated. They argued that people were most motivated by material incentives, such as bonuses and higher wages, as reward for hard work. The Liu-Deng line also valued the application of science and technology to manufacturing and economic development. Mao argued that the sneaking of capitalism into socialist values smacked of revisionism, a bastardization of Marxism. Deng valued pragmatism; Mao valued ideological purity. Mao became convinced that party cadres were reluctant to accept new socialist values and that the CCP was no longer an instrument for revolution. Putting his faith in the Chinese people,

Mao began to disdain the party leadership and claimed that true socialist change needed to come from the people. To truly effect change, Mao believed he needed to cleanse the party of revisionists and wipe out traditional culture so that a revived party could truly rule.

Mao made his move in 1965. The precipitating cause of the Cultural Revolution was a disagreement over the play *The Dismissal of Hai Rui from Office*. Written by the playwright and deputy mayor of Beijing Wu Han, *Dismissal* was a sympathetic portrayal of a sixteenth-century official who was dismissed from office because he showed compassion and understanding for the lot of the peasants. When Wu Han had Hai Rui recommend returning land to the peasants, he was really suggesting the worth of private plots of land, allegedly condemning Mao's communes and policies of total collectivization. Chinese audiences saw Hai Rui as symbolizing Peng Dehaui, whom Mao had dismissed for criticizing his commune policies. Mao organized a Five-Man Group, led by Beijing mayor and Politburo member Peng Zhen, the member of the Politburo most directly responsible for cultural and ideological education, to evaluate the play. Much to Mao's ire, the group concluded that the play should be taken at face value and not as an allegory. Mao asked Yao Wenyuan, editor of *Wen Hui Bao,* Shanghai's influential daily newspaper, to write a criticism of the play. Published in early November 1965, Yao's letter is largely seen as the opening shot of the Cultural Revolution.

Wu Han was only one of several writers whose allegorical and critical works angered political leaders. Mao and his supporters found it difficult to censor these works because they were carried in newspapers and magazines controlled by Mao's opponents. Fed up with the criticism of his policies by communist and noncommunist writers and intellectuals, Mao ached to completely reform Chinese society and intellectual life. In late May 1966, Mao created the Central Cultural Revolution Small Group (CCRSG) as an organ of the Politburo Standing Committee to direct the Cultural Revolution. The CCRSG was composed of Mao's personal supporters, headed by Mao's personal secretary Chen Boda, and included Mao's wife Jiang Qing and her Shanghai allies— Yao Wenyuan and Zhang Chunqiao—and Kang Sheng of the public security apparatus and secret police operations. Creation of the CCRSG gave the radical Maoists greater voice in Beijing, in addition to their media base in Shanghai. The CCRSG skirted the party Secretariat and became the top decisionmaking office of the party, directly answerable to Mao. The CCRSG became the preeminent organ for promoting the Cultural Revolution.

Leadership Struggle

From autumn 1965 until July 1966, the CCP was embroiled in a hidden leadership struggle. In November 1965, Mao left Beijing for Shanghai and Hangzhou. Mao felt that Beijing was too tightly controlled by Mayor Peng Zhen and believed that he could command the support of the Shanghai branch of the CCP. Also, Mao had trouble persuading the editor of Beijing's *People's Daily* to publish his statements. Throughout spring 1966, members of the Cultural Revolution Group were successful in stirring up unrest on university campuses in Beijing, particularly at Peking University and Tsinghua University. At Peking University, President Lu Ping was more interested in high academic standards than in political indoctrination and had disbanded student groups that had formed to study the political works of Mao. He also resisted a 1958 government policy requiring students to work in fields and factories as part of the regular curriculum. When the central government required discussion of Wu Han's *Dismissal,* Lu Ping confined the discussion to an academic debate. In May 1966, philosophy professor Nie Yuanzi and six colleagues hung a big-character poster attacking the university administration and party committee for supporting the original Five-Man Group.[54] Mao had the poster broadcast and published all over China, and students responded by organizing protest teams to challenge the authority of school administrators and party committees through mass struggle sessions. Student groups at Peking University and Tsinghua University were particularly vicious in their attacks. Liu Shaoqi tried to restore order to campuses. He sent work teams of party cadres to schools to prevent the outbreak of mob rule and keep the movement under party control. The work teams tried to contain the violence by allowing the posting of big-character posters and the organization of rallies, parades, and demonstrations inside schools but not on the street, banning beating and insulting, and preventing any attacks on private residences.[55] These measures clashed with the CCRSG because they blocked the kind of mass movement Mao envisioned.

Revisionism Campaign

In May 1966, Mao returned to Beijing, and in the name of the Central Committee declared the official opening of the Great Proletarian Cultural Revolution. Mao ousted Politburo member and Beijing mayor Peng Zhen, and Mao's supporters took over the *People's Daily.* In July, Mao ordered the withdrawal of all work teams from college campuses, removing any restraint against the students. Mao criticized the work team policy as being repressive, and targeted Liu for future denunciation. In August 1966, Mao convened a plenum (the eleventh) of the Central Committee packed with his supporters. The plenum attacked revisionism in the party, government, and army, and orchestrated an all-out attack on Liu and Deng, branding them as "Khrushchevite revisionists." It demoted Liu from the number-two post of party vice chairman to number eight, and promoted Lin Biao to number two, thereby tagging Lin as Mao's successor. It promoted members of the CCRSG and PLA marshals to the Politburo. The CCRSG took over the Secretariat, assuming Deng's power base. Mao removed Liu's work teams from the campuses, and ordered leadership of the Cultural

Revolution on campuses to be the work of revolutionary teachers and students. The CCP instructed college and middle-school students to set up Cultural Revolution committees for their campuses and Cultural Revolution small groups for each class. The CCP suspended classes and instructed students to devote themselves full-time to the revolution.

Red Guard Phase

Militant students organized themselves as Red Guards (*hongweibing*), inspired by the slogans "It is justified to rebel" and "Learn revolution by making revolution." During the extended summer vacation, streams of out-of-town students traveled to Beijing to demonstrate their loyalty to Chairman Mao. From August through November, some 13 million Red Guards gathered in eight massive rallies in Beijing, shouting portions of *Quotations from Chairman Mao Zedong,* the Red Guards' bible. The announced purpose of the Red Guards was to destroy the Old World and to establish a New World of the proletariat. Standing high on the Gate of Heavenly Peace above Tiananmen Square, Chairman Mao offered the Red Guards his blessings and urged them to destroy the Four Olds: old ideas, habits, customs, and culture.

With the blessing of Mao—their Great Leader, Great Helmsman, Red Sun, and Supreme Commander—mobs of Red Guards wreaked havoc on Chinese society from late 1966 through early 1968. Distrustful of his own party cadres, Mao instructed the Red Guards to help oust Liu and CCP general secretary Deng Xiaoping. In early 1967, Liu and Deng suffered humiliation and beatings in several struggle sessions. Mobs denounced Liu at mass meetings as the "biggest capitalist-roader within the party," and denounced Deng as China's number-two capitalist-roader. In summer 1967, party leaders put them under house arrest. Branding him a "traitor, spy, and renegade," the CCP leadership stripped Liu of his official positions and expelled him from the party in October 1968. Chinese officials escorted Liu from Beijing and moved him to solitary confinement. Liu died of pneumonia, alone and naked on the floor of a dirty cell in 1969. The party did not reveal his death to the public until after the Cultural Revolution lest he be made into a martyr and sentiment turn against Mao. Liu's wife and first lady of China, Wang Guangmei, an important political figure in her own right, was lured from her home on the pretext that her child had been injured in an accident. Red Guards dressed her as a whore and dragged her before tens of thousands of people at Tsinghua University where she was taunted and humiliated. Under the orders of Chairman Mao, Wang was thrown into prison, where she lived in solitary confinement for a decade. She was released from prison and rehabilitated in 1979.

The most violent phase of the Cultural Revolution began in the summer of 1966 when Red Guards mobilized off their campuses and began searching homes and confiscating property belonging to targeted families. Targeted families commonly belonged to the so-called Five Black Categories of land-lords, rich peasants, counterrevolutionaries, "bad elements," and rightists. Waves of Red Guard units would raid entire neighborhoods, ransacking one house after another. They would smash everything related to the Four Olds: books, paint-ings, anything that struck them as bourgeois would be taken out and burned in bonfires. The Red Guards usually confiscated anything of value, such as gold bars, jewelry, antiques, and rare books. Then they would seal up the houses. The Guards subjected victims to humiliation and beatings. The Red Guards often forced their victims to appear before large public gatherings and to wear dunce caps. The Guards and the crowd denounced and spit upon their defense-less victims; relatives and former friends often joined in the denunciations. Usu-ally, the Guards forced the victim to wear a large signboard around his or her neck with a criminal label written on it and with the victim's name crossed out in red ink. The most common form of physical abuse and humiliation the Red Guards used at struggle sessions was the jet-plane style (*penqishi*). Guards forced the person being denounced to stand or kneel down, in front of the crowd, usually on a platform. Two guards standing behind the person would press his or her head down while holding his or her arms and raising them up high, like two wings of a jet.[56] The Guards might hold their victim in this position for hours while others read speeches of accusation and shouted slogans. They forced others to kneel for long periods of time on broken glass.

Thousands of Chinese were driven to suicide by the Red Guard intimida-tion and terror. Wu Han's daughter suffered a mental breakdown and commit-ted suicide in 1976. Some suicides were actually murders. The well-known and much-loved Chinese author Lao She either drowned himself or was drowned by Red Guards in a lake. It was not uncommon for Red Guards to throw people from the roof of a building, or from upper-floor windows, and call it a suicide. Deng Xiaoping's elder son, Deng Pufang, was paralyzed from the waist down by a fall from the roof of a building at Peking University, where he was a physics student.[57] In some cases, people murdered family members in suicide pacts to avoid torture.

Red Guards also destroyed public property and cultural relics. By the end of the Cultural Revolution, gangs had destroyed 73 percent of Beijing's 6,843 officially designated places of cultural or historical interest. Zhou Enlai was successful in protecting the Forbidden City (now called the Palace Museum, or *gugong*) after receiving advance warning of an attack and ordering Beijing Gar-rison troops to defend it.[58] In Shandong Province, local teachers and students joined forces with teachers and students from Beijing in destroying the Confu-cius Temple in Qufu county. They destroyed more than six thousand cultural ar-tifacts, including paintings, books, stone steles, and graves. They organized rallies to denounce Confucius, particularly for his educational philosophy, which "only produced cowardly bastards." Red Guards from three middle schools in Shandong exhumed the corpse of Wu Xun, a founder of several

Human Tragedy of the Cultural Revolution

In August 1966, a female doctor made a suicide pact with her parents: "We were sitting on the foyer floor, racking our brains for a way to kill ourselves. . . . My parents both insisted that I go ahead with it. I had never thought myself capable of killing anyone, let alone my parents. But under these circumstances I was capable of it, and I had no other choice. . . . I felt for my father's strong artery and pierced it. Immediately the hot blood spurted out. He even asked me to see if his pulse had stopped. He said he wished it could be faster."

The doctor, who survived a jump out of a third-story window in a suicide attempt, was sentenced to life in prison for resisting the Cultural Revolution through collective suicide, including murder, as a means of escaping punishment. She was released in 1979, wearing the same hospital pajamas that she had worn for ten years. (The doctor's story is recounted anonymously in the piece entitled "Was I Really Guilty?" in Feng Jicai, *Voices from the Whirlwind*, 42.)

schools in China, broke it into pieces, and burned it. On Hainan Island, Red Guards destroyed the grave of Hai Rui, the virtuous Ming official who had been dismissed from office.[59] Red Guards also attacked religious sites. Virtually all churches were looted and ransacked, and most were converted into warehouses, offices, and workshops. Catholic, Protestant, Muslim, and Buddhist places of worship were attacked and stripped of their religious symbols. Gangs chiseled or blasted stone crosses, statuary, and other architectural features from the exteriors of churches and toppled entire steeples from Christian churches. Many Buddhist temples and monasteries, because of their large size, were converted into factories.[60] Some Chinese tried to resist the Red Guards. For example, in 1966 several thousand people prevented the Red Guards from ransacking the Revolutionary Museum and destroying the relics and curios. Fights broke out between factory workers and intruding Red Guards at several factories in Beijing in late 1966.[61]

The violence extended beyond Red Guard atrocities and China's cities. Scattered reports of mass killings indicate that local zealots attacked and killed people in towns and villages throughout rural China. One of the most egregious displays of violence was the 1967 Dao County Massacre in Hunan Province. Spurred by rumors that Chiang Kai-shek's Nationalist troops were going to attack China with the support of people belonging to the Five Black Categories, rebel organizations and militias slaughtered more than four thousand people belonging to the categories. The oldest victims were in their seventies; the youngest was a ten-day-old infant. More than one hundred households were wiped out, and more than three hundred people committed suicide. The massacre, which had spread to neighboring counties, ended only after the personal intervention of Premier Zhou Enlai.[62]

Rebuilding the Government

The Cultural Revolution escalated in January 1967. That month, the Workers Command Post, controlled by Zhang Chunqiao and Yao Wenyuan, tried to take over power from the Shanghai party committee and the city government. The attempted takeover, in what was dubbed the January Revolution, or January Storm, made Shanghai a revolutionary model in a nationwide power-seizure campaign. Chinese communists compared the power-seizure phase of the Cultural Revolution with the Russian October Revolution of 1917 and the French Paris Commune of 1871. As a consequence of the January Revolution, Mao urged the Red Guards to openly challenge the state structure at all levels and, with other mass organizations, to take over local and provincial governments and the leadership of all schools, state institutions and organizations, factories, and communes in 1967 and 1968. Mao eventually favored the creation of *revolutionary committees,* which consisted of a triple alliance of the Revolutionary Rebels (older students who focused on destroying the older, less revolutionary cadres) and Red Guards, the Revolutionary Cadres (former party members who had remolded themselves and were certified as loyal Maoists), and army officers.

China began to descend into anarchy in summer 1967. Red Guard units and other rebel groups had broken down into factions, carrying out extreme acts of violence among themselves and against more conservative groups in attempts to prove themselves more "red" than the other. Mao ordered the PLA not to intervene in factional fighting. In Wuhan, a radical faction seized trains loaded with arms for North Vietnam, and the PLA armed a more conservative faction (the Million Heroes) for their defense against the radicals. The commander of the Wuhan military region staged a counterrevolutionary coup, taking over the city government and kidnapping Mao's two emissaries, provoking a radical group to attack the army, seeking its overthrow. Although the attempt failed, the Wuhan Incident was a watershed event in the Cultural Revolution for it shifted the conflict from between the radical groups and the CCP to between the radical groups and the military. The Wuhan Incident set off a violent frenzy of activity by the left, and radical groups used it as an excuse for all-out attack on the PLA. Mao's wife, Jiang Qing, supported the leftists, extending and deepening the most violent phase of the Cultural Revolution. Lin Biao excused the chaotic situation by declaring that chaos was necessary to expose the reactionaries and was a normal part of revolution. He instructed the PLA to respond only to people who were against Mao and to those who attacked the military. He also ordered some PLA soldiers who had made "mistakes" to receive training with the Revolutionary Rebels as their teachers and to use their own mistakes as teaching materials.[63]

Things got so chaotic by late summer 1967 that China was on the brink of anarchy. Red Guard factions were fighting armed battles in virtually every city in China. Gangs attacked foreign dignitaries remaining in China. Mobs seized and burned the British diplomatic compound in Beijing. In September 1967, Mao finally instructed Lin Biao to use the PLA to restore order by disarming the Red Guards and warring factions. Mao no longer favored Red Guards and honored more conservative workers and peasants. In the Seizure of Power of spring and summer 1968, a fresh round of violence erupted between remnant Red Guard units and the PLA. Jiang Qing reportedly encouraged this phase. In Guangzhou, old factional disputes became so violent that the PLA imposed a dawn-to-dusk curfew.[64] Bloody fighting continued in China's more remote provinces, often at the hands of the PLA, which was trying to repress Red Guards and remaining radicals. The bloodiest violence occurred in Guangxi, where massacres and mass executions were sometimes followed by cannibalization of the dead.[65] At Tsinghua University in Beijing, battles between Red Guard units escalated from launching stones, bricks, and concrete chunks to rockets and projectile missiles carrying firebomb warheads against rivals' dormitories. Several students were burned alive.[66]

The CCP recognized that it needed to remove many of the students from China's cities. In 1968, schools began to assign graduating students to jobs in rural areas. Educated youth were sent to the countryside to settle permanently among the peasants. Faced with resistance from educated youth, in May 1968, *Wen Hui Bao,* the mouthpiece of Jiang Qing's Shanghai clique, ran a series of editorials to convince Chinese youth of the importance of settling down in rural areas. It extolled workers, peasants, and soldiers as the best teachers of revolutionary youth, and urged youths to integrate with the workers and peasants and temper themselves for the rest of their lives.[67] The editorials branded students who resisted rustication "counterrevolutionaries."

The most violent phase of the Cultural Revolution ended with the meeting of the Ninth Party Congress in April 1969. Although the congress declared the Cultural Revolution ended, in reality it continued under the military until 1971 and under Mao's wife and cronies until Mao's death in 1976. Mao ordered the PLA to disarm the Red Guards and break up their units. The CCP sent more than 10 million Red Guards to the countryside to be reeducated by the peasants, China's true revolutionaries. China's leaders also required each urban family to send one adolescent youth down to the countryside. Believing their rustication to be permanent, many of these "sent-down youth" descended into depression and suicide. Also sent to the countryside were hundreds of thousands of party cadres who had resisted the Cultural Revolution. All intellectuals were sent "down under" (*xiafang,* literally "downward transfer") to the countryside to "cadre schools" under military control. A cadre school was not a school in the real sense of the term, but a center for reeducation through labor. Residents of the "schools" underwent thought reform through criticism and struggle. From 1966 to 1971, the party sent 20 million intellectuals to the countryside as their research institutes closed down and universities suspended teaching. It branded intellectuals "the stinking ninth category," derived from the classification of people into eight classes during the Yuan Dynasty. Living conditions at the schools were quite bad, and many intellectuals, who were not used to such harsh conditions, died in the process of reeducation.

An estimated four hundred thousand to five hundred thousand Chinese were killed from 1966 to 1969, the most violent phase of the Cultural Revolution. The Cultural Revolution claimed, among others, the lives of head of state Liu Shaoqi, authors Lao She and Wu Han, Wu Han's wife, Yuan Zhen, and Peng Dehaui. Other casualties of the Cultural Revolution include thousands of people who committed suicide and millions of people who had been tortured but survived with long-term disabilities and trauma.

Literature and the Arts During the Cultural Revolution

The Cultural Revolution was a national phenomenon devoted to radically remaking Chinese society. As its name implies, culture was the focus of change. In addition to wreaking havoc on Chinese society, the Cultural Revolution succeeded in attacking literature and the arts, education, and health care.

Mao's wife, Jiang Qing, was instrumental in destroying traditional Chinese culture. In July 1966, Mao instructed Jiang to purify Chinese culture. As head of the CCRSG, Jiang censored all art forms by requiring that all written works be vetted by a bureau over which she presided. To be approved, the works had to be proletarian in nature and further the socialist cause. She banned old books and nearly all foreign works. Under Jiang, literature and the arts were an important contribution to the creation of Mao's personality cult. New books featured Mao's quotations on every other page. Songs and printed art all exalted Mao. Posters were a popular form of revolutionary propaganda. Posters encouraged the Chinese people to "make revolution all one's life, read Chairman Mao's books all one's life," and claimed that "the People's Liberation Army is the great school of Mao Zedong Thought."

Throughout the Cultural Revolution, music consisted largely of songs extolling the greatness of Chairman Mao and of rebel songs to inspire Red Guards to engage in revolution. Mao's poems were set to music and performed by choruses nationwide. Other songs, such as "Wishing Chairman Mao a Long Life" and "Chairman Mao Is the Red Sun in the Hearts of the People of the Whole World," inspired loyalty. The latter was particularly popular among schoolchildren. One song, "A Song of Triumph for Chairman Mao's Proletarian Line on Public Health," asserts that devotedly reading Mao's works can result in faith healing.

From 1966 until 1976, virtually the only performing arts allowed were eight "model performances." Even the beloved and ancient Peking opera was transformed into a revolutionary venue. Five of the eight model performances were modernized Peking opera, in which Red Guards and the PLA replaced princes and princesses as main protagonists. Two of the eight model performances, *The White-Haired Girl* (*Baimaonü*) and *The Red Detachment of Women*, were ballets. The former tells the story of a slave girl who flees an oppressive landlord and is aided by a communist army officer. Under the soldier's guidance, the girl becomes a disciplined fighter who turns her grievance against the landlord into broader class warfare. The latter ballet has a similar theme, in which a slave girl is rescued from her tyrant master by a communist soldier, who instructs her to join a female detachment of the Red Army, where she becomes a heroic fighter. Film versions of the operas and ballets were distributed to reach a broader audience. Production of non-revolutionary-themed films was put on hold, and foreign films that were dubbed into Chinese were labeled "poisonous weeds" and banned. At film studios across China, personnel were labeled counterrevolutionary and were beaten, struggled against, imprisoned, or sent to labor camps.[68] The rich and varied centuries-old Chinese arts had become not only dull and banal but dangerous.

Even fashion was subject to reform. Jiang imposed a dress code on urban residents. Men and women living in urban areas adopted the unisex outfit of blue cotton-padded jacket with baggy pants, a cap with a red star on the crown, and black cotton shoes (*buxie*). Women cut their hair in pageboy-style haircuts. Red Guards confiscated women's dresses and lipstick as "bourgeois."

Education During the Cultural Revolution

China's Confucian society traditionally has placed great emphasis on the importance of education. In communist China, families still sought their children's admission to the best schools. In the 1960s, admission to schools at all levels of education was based on a student's performance in the entrance examination. Competition was keen. Children of intellectuals did well in the examination, and made up a majority in the good schools. Cadre children, some of whom were good students, were often admitted based on family ties. In colleges and universities, the bulk of the student body was increasingly from urban, middle-class families. Intellectuals and their children commonly had more education than the average party member. Mao's post-1949 goal had been to educate the masses, eliminate bookish and abstract knowledge, combine practical and theoretical work, and put politics in command of education.[69] With none of these goals realized, Mao, in the early 1960s, began a massive attempt to overhaul China's education system.

Yao Wenyuan, the editor of Shanghai's *Wen Hui Bao* daily newspaper and author of the attack on the play *The Dismissal of Hai Rui from Office*, began to attack the educational, cultural, and propaganda officials of the Beijing Municipal Party organization in 1965. On college campuses, militant students at Peking University were the first to respond to Yao's call. Frustrated by high academic standards at Peking University, students from peasant and worker-class backgrounds organized campaigns against university president Lu Ping and his administration in summer 1966. Their attacks against the university establishment inspired college and university students throughout the country to do the same. Students in Shanghai, Nanjing, Wuhan, and other cities followed their fellow radicals in Beijing and began to dismiss school administrators and sometimes criticized, interrogated, imprisoned, or physically punished them. In some places they set up cultural revolutionary committees to replace the school administration. The members of the committees were usually student leaders or popular teachers, but they lacked administrative ability. They tended to give in to student demands, which eroded any authority the committees might have had. After the organization of the Red Guards, classrooms emptied out. Schools commonly had several Red Guard units. Only those students of the correct bloodline could join the Red Guards. Only children of families from the Five Red Categories—revolutionary martyrs, revolutionary cadres, soldiers, workers, and peasants—could join. To prove their revolutionary fervor, students from the "not-so-good family backgrounds" created their own Red Guard units.[70] In 1966, both Peking University and the Beijing Foreign Languages Institute had more than seventy units each. Some groups had just two or three members; larger ones had hundreds and adopted army organization with platoons, squads, and battalions. These units organized larger umbrella organizations that developed contacts with other local groups and with those across the nation. For example, Beijing had 120 liaison stations representing Red Guard groups from the provinces. Tsinghua University's major unit had forty-seven stations outside Beijing.[71] The member units deployed to assist each other when necessary. For example, the arrival of Red Guards from Beijing incited students to violence at the Shanghai Experimental Primary School. They broke windows and lightbulbs; destroyed laboratory specimens, tables, and chairs; and even made a hole through the three floors to the roof so that the sky could be seen from the ground, just to show their revolutionary fervor.[72]

With the Red Guards taking over the administration of their schools, most schools cancelled classes in late spring 1966. Out-of-town students took the extended summer holiday to travel to Beijing to gather in Tiananmen Square to receive Mao's blessing. Red Guards crisscrossing the country commandeered train cars, straining the transportation system. In February 1967, the central government issued a directive to "resume classes and make revolution." The success of this directive was limited to primary schools, where the Cultural Revolution was the weakest, primarily due to the students' age. By September 1966, most primary schools had reopened, but the atmosphere was never the same as before the Cultural Revolution. Young children were not as respectful to their teachers. Teachers had been criticized and struggled against, so the teachers' status had dropped in the children's eyes.[73]

The Cultural Revolution was stronger in the high schools and universities. Many high schools held no classes and the students continued their fighting, even among the few schools that reopened in early 1967. School schedules commonly consisted of an hour of studying Mao's thoughts and directives, an hour of criticism meetings and the study of wall posters, a couple of hours of study of industrial and agricultural skills or military training, followed by evening meetings focused on the Cultural Revolution. Regular classes could not be held because many students did not have the patience to sit through them, nor the teachers the authority to enforce discipline. Teachers were afraid to use textbooks that had been criticized earlier in the movement, and the only safe readings were Mao's works. Since students regarded Mao as their sacred leader, they could not refuse to study Mao.[74] Most universities held no classes because of the continuous fighting and the low attendance. Most universities cancelled classes until 1969 and did not admit new students until 1970 or 1971.

After all peaceful means proved ineffective in dealing with the radical students, as a last resort the central government dispatched propaganda teams of workers to the schools, who finally overwhelmed the radical students. With the workers' success, schools reopened. Students returned in a trickle. Some students returned after finding it boring at home, and others returned after being told the schools would assign them a job. A major problem in resuming classes was getting the teachers' cooperation. Faculty members had been divided between party members, who valued political enthusiasm, and intellectuals, who valued academic achievement. The party supervised teaching, and teachers were required to infuse the regular curriculum with a heavy dose of ideology. The party members and intellectuals distrusted one another, and the Cultural Revolution became an occasion to settle scores. Party cadres singled out intellectuals for criticism. Now they were being asked to return to work with the same people who had criticized and taunted them. Many teachers complied with the workers' requests to resume their teaching, but without much enthusiasm.

The resumption of classes began very slowly. Many revolutionaries were reluctant to surrender their freedom, and saw no purpose in resuming classes until schools reformed their curricula. They also did not want to submit to PLA political and military training, including daylong indoctrination in Mao Thought.[75] With the encouragement of the central government, the reopened schools revised their curricula. As early as 1964, Mao had wanted to shorten the period of formal schooling. In 1967, a new educational program shortened primary schooling from six to five years, and secondary education to four or three years. Teachers and cadres visited factories and the countryside to ask workers and peasants what kind of graduates they needed. Based on this information, education reform committees throughout China eliminated courses deemed irrelevant to meeting the needs of society. They eliminated history, geography, and literature because of their lack of direct practical value. Students learned industrial skills rather than chemistry and physics, and agricultural techniques instead of biology. The party required students to work on farms or in factories.[76] Curricula downplayed academic excellence and threw out anything theoretical.

Schools admitted students based on their behavior, not merit, increasing the enrollment of students from worker and peasant stock.

One of the beneficiaries of Mao's education reforms was residents of rural China. The central government reduced state aid to relatively well-off urban districts and redirected funds to the poorer areas. It introduced at least five years of primary schooling in rural areas. From 1966 to 1976, there was a dramatic increase in primary and secondary enrollments in the countryside. Primary enrollment increased from about 116 million to 150 million and secondary enrollment from 15 million to 58 million.[77] The government revised admission to universities, making it possible for more peasants and workers to enter. It downgraded entrance examinations in favor of a system of recommendation from local production units and selection on the basis of political criteria as well as academic ability. The new system gave priority to poor farmers, workers, soldiers, and lower-level cadres.

Health Care During the Cultural Revolution

During the Cultural Revolution, the central government put increased emphasis on rural health care. During the retrenchment period after the Great Leap Forward, most of China's rural health clinics had closed, while the number of urban clinics nearly doubled.[78] After his political comeback, Mao called for doctors to move their practices to the countryside, where most people lived. In 1965, Mao proposed expanding China's pool of health-care workers by extending medical education beyond higher middle-school graduates to graduates from higher primary schools. These students would receive both classroom instruction and on-the-job training, and would be sent down to the countryside. Mao argued that even these medical students would be better than "quacks and witch doctors," even if they were not talented in medicine.[79] He proposed leaving in the cities a few of the less capable doctors and moving the rest to the countryside. Mao also suggested a greater emphasis on preventive medicine and the treatment of common illnesses rather than the study of rare and more complicated diseases.

Many of the rural clinics were staffed by "barefoot doctors" (*chijiao yisheng*), who were part farmer and part doctor, with minimal training in both Chinese and Western medicine.[80] Although they lacked professional skills, they often possessed a wealth of practical knowledge and experience. The barefoot doctors helped alleviate the shortage of professionally trained doctors in rural areas and contributed to the limited improvement of health and hygiene in the countryside. Some barefoot doctors were even assigned work in urban hospitals, often with disastrous results. Barefoot doctors assisted in surgeries, delivery of babies, and other serious medical procedures. As the barefoot doctors frequently provided services well beyond their capacity, patients often died in their care.

After medical schools reopened following the disruptions of the Cultural Revolution, the state reduced the program of study from six years to three years in order to graduate enough doctors to meet immediate needs. The curriculum focused on common illnesses. Classes admitted for study in 1971 included a greater number of students from rural areas. Many of these students were the younger barefoot doctors. Urban hospitals established clinics and teaching institutes in rural communes and provided doctors to staff them. Urban medical personnel served on mobile medical teams dispatched to rural areas, or at a commune medical center on a rotating basis. In 1969, the central government increased funding of the training of barefoot doctors. By 1973, more than a million such paramedics were engaged in preventive medicine. They offered health education and birth control information and devices, and treated common illnesses while referring more seriously ill patients to commune or city hospitals.[81]

Post–Cultural Revolution Reorganization and Recovery

September 1968 through April 1969 was a period characterized by an attempt to rebuild party and government. The party's Ninth Congress in April 1969 marked Lin Biao's rise to power. The CCP wrote a new party constitution, in which it was written that Lin Biao would succeed Mao. Inserting the transfer of power into the party constitution formalized Lin Biao's position as China's undisputed leader second to Mao. Indicative of its growing clout, the military had a strong showing at the Ninth Party Congress. Forty percent of the representatives at the congress were army officers; 50 percent of the twenty-five-member Politburo was military.

Lin Biao's fortunes were short-lived. Lin Biao had become so powerful that Mao began to feel uncomfortable. That was the beginning of the end of Lin Biao. Mao began to complain of the military's primacy soon after the 1969 Ninth Party Congress, which put the PLA in leadership positions in Beijing and in the provinces. For instance, by 1970, more than half of all provincial party secretaries were serving military officers.[82] Mao also lost patience with Lin's apparent lack of enthusiasm for rebuilding the party and government and his ambition to succeed Liu Shaoqi as head of state. Mao also resented Lin's push to intervene in foreign affairs at a time when Mao and Zhou Enlai were planning an opening to the United States.

Mao was certainly aware of Lin's role in creating the Maoist cult, and Mao knew that Lin had been key executor of Mao's wishes during the Cultural Revolution. He wanted to cut Lin's power before Lin could use his position as head of the military to challenge Mao.[83] By 1970, Lin realized that his power was eroding. He allegedly planned an assassination of Mao. There is scant academic evidence of an actual assassination plot. Speculation is based on a memo kept by a group of Lin's supporters, led by his son Lin Liguo. The memo claimed that

B–52 (a code name for Mao) enticed followers with sweet words, but later put them to death for fabricated crimes. The memo, once leaked, was considered reflective of Lin's thoughts. Mao began to cut Lin down. A morphine addict, Lin would try to attend major public functions, where Mao would intentionally ignore Lin, and he began to undercut Lin's influence in the military. Rumors circulated that Lin, under the pretext of civil defense, had built secret getaway tunnels from his house, in case a planned coup against Mao failed. On September 12, 1971, Lin Biao, his wife, and his son tried to flee Mao's retribution to find sanctuary in the USSR. The plane crashed in Outer Mongolia, killing all on board. There is speculation that Mao had the plane shot down, as Lin's daughter had informed Zhou Enlai of the flight. It simply may have run out of fuel.

With Lin Biao gone, Foreign Minister Zhou Enlai became premier. Zhou was occasionally able to put a brake on Mao's directives, but became ill with cancer. Mao brought Deng Xiaoping, the former CCP general secretary, back from the purge. Deng spent much of the Cultural Revolution in Jiangxi Province, working part-time in a tractor-repair plant. He was somewhat protected from persecution through his close relations with the military, as he had been political commissar of the Second Field Army since 1949 and had been associated with two of China's five field armies. Because of Deng's connections with the PLA, as well as his reputation as a proven administrator, Mao agreed to bring Deng back to Beijing in 1973 as vice premier, the same rank he had enjoyed when he first came to Beijing twenty-one years earlier.

One of Deng's key tasks was to help Mao reshuffle military regional commanders. In the provinces, party committees were taking back most of the powers lost to the revolutionary committees. The military men who had dominated those committees refused to give up power, however, and were entrenched as members of reconstituted party committees or as party secretaries. Mao wanted to replace the military officers with civilians. In December 1973, Mao promoted Deng to the Politburo and the party's Central Military Commission (the party organ that controls the military). These positions in the government and military put Deng at least on level terms with party radicals Wang Hongwen and Zhang Chunqiao. The radicals and Jiang Qing were beginning to lose the support of Mao, who was eager to rebuild the party and government. Feeble with Parkinson's disease and nearly incapacitated due to a stroke or heart attack in 1972, Mao had increasingly put power in the hands of his wife, Jiang Qing, and her three collaborators, commonly known as the Gang of Four. By 1974, however, Mao told Jiang he no longer wanted to see her and claimed that she had wild ambitions and that she was not allowed to speak his name.[84] The radicals' fall from grace gave Zhou Enlai room to recover control of the media, which the Gang of Four had used for their propaganda.

Ill with stomach cancer, in early 1974 Zhou Enlai gave Deng day-to-day responsibility for foreign affairs. With the country coming out of the isolationist shell of the xenophobic Cultural Revolution, Deng in 1975 led the first Chinese delegation to the UN. In 1975, China's legislature appointed Deng first vice premier. Deng immediately began to tackle China's pressing social and economic problems, convening ten conferences in nine months. Deng devised a strategy to revive and modernize China's economy. Based on Zhou's 1965 "four modernizations," Deng called on the National People's Congress (the highest state legislative body) to modernize agriculture, industry, science and technology, and national defense by the end of the century. In late 1975, however, Deng made a couple of missteps, raising Mao's ire. First, Deng stated that the key links to China's economic development were stability and unity; for Mao, the only key link was class struggle. Second, Deng endorsed an attempt by Tsinghua University to dismiss two of the Gang of Four's most active supporters there. The two appealed to Mao, who supported them.[85] When the Gang attacked Deng in a March 1975 meeting, Deng simply turned off his hearing aids and declared that he had not heard a word of what was said.[86]

In January 1976, Zhou Enlai died of stomach cancer. Mao appointed Politburo member Hua Guofeng, not Deng, acting premier. Mao, who refused to have any member of the Gang succeed him, chose Hua as a compromise candidate because Deng was opposed to the Gang of Four. Jiang Qing wanted her crony Zhang to succeed Zhou Enlai, but he was unacceptable to senior members of the Politburo. In a reckless move, the Gang tried to defame Zhou, whom they hated, and Deng. In April 1976, at the spring homage to the deceased (the Qingming Festival), Zhou's faithful left wreaths and banners eulogizing Zhou but critical of Jiang Qing. The Politburo claimed that Deng must have been responsible, and Mao ordered the army to remove any wreaths commemorating Zhou. The next day, crowds staged a demonstration in Tiananmen Square, and Deng was again purged, but was protected by anti-Mao elements in the military because of his influence and connections. Deng moved from place to place throughout summer 1976. He returned to Beijing only after Mao's death in fall 1976.

Conclusion

Several significant events occurred in 1976, signaling that Mao's reign was over. First, Premier Zhou Enlai died in January 1976. In July, PLA founder Zhu De died, and the massive Tangshan earthquake killed some two hundred thousand people. These ill-fated events signaled that Mao, like emperors before him, was losing the Mandate of Heaven.

Mao, who had achieved emperorlike status through his personality cult, had begun to lose the mandate a couple of years earlier. Mao began to lose his revolutionary and ideological zeal, and became more like an emperor than ever. He groomed his wife to be his successor but became disillusioned, and even disgusted, with her. Despite his rejection, Jiang and her Gang continued to push Mao's revolutionary policies of egalitarianism and class struggle against bourgeois tendencies. During Mao's final years, Jiang Qing tried to negotiate with the military, but it refused to work for her. She wanted to be chief of the party, but Mao rejected her and put Hua Guofeng in charge. Mao died on September 8, 1976. One month later, the Politburo ordered the arrest of the Gang of Four. The Politburo elected Hua Guofeng chairman of the party's Central Committee and Central Military Commission, and confirmed his appointment as premier. Thus, the Cultural Revolution finally came to an end with the death of Mao and the arrest of the Gang of Four in the fall of 1976. Deng returned to Beijing, and the CCP rehabilitated him in 1977.

Notes

1. The CCP determined the goals at the March 1949 second plenum (meeting) of the Seventh Central Committee of the CCP.
2. Barnett and Vogel, *Cadres, Bureaucracy, and Political Power in Communist China*, 228.
3. Taiwan and Hainan Islands were later added as provinces; Tianjin and Chongqing were added as municipalities with the status of provinces.
4. Spence, *Search for Modern China*, 542.
5. Schurmann, *Ideology and Organization*, 376.
6. Schurmann, *Ideology and Organization*, 377.
7. Since 1998, children can choose either their mother's or their father's *hukou* location and type (agricultural or nonagricultural status).
8. The KMT also established police stations in various sections of cities to supervise their populations, which residents found intrusive. Schurmann, *Ideology and Organization*, 369.
9. Fairbank and Goldman, *China*, 357.
10. Fairbank and Goldman, *China*, 357.
11. State Statistical Bureau, *China Statistical Yearbook 1998*, 433.
12. Most of the investment from the Soviet Union came in the form of loans, all of it to be repaid. Fairbank and Goldman, *China*, 359.
13. Mao made the February 27, 1957, speech at the Eleventh Session of the Supreme State Conference. He went over the verbatim record and made certain additions before its publication in the *People's Daily* (*Renmin Ribao*) on June 19, 1957.
14. Mao, "On the Correct Handling of Contradictions," 351.
15. Benton and Hunter, eds., *Wild Lily*, 88.
16. Benton and Hunter, eds., *Wild Lily*, 85–87.
17. Ding Ling was rehabilitated in 1979, when she became a senior member of the Writers' Association.
18. Teiwes, *China's Road to Disaster*, 67.
19. Schurmann, *Ideology and Organization*, 466.
20. Mao, *Selected Works*, Vol. 5, 490.
21. State Statistical Bureau, *China Statistical Yearbook, 1998*, 105.
22. Bachman, *Bureaucracy, Economy, and Leadership in China*, 87.
23. Schurmann, *Ideology and Organization*, 471.
24. Oi, *State and Peasant in Contemporary China*, 15.
25. Hughes, *Chinese Communes*, 22.

26. Putterman, "Ration Subsidies and Incentives," 236.

27. "How to Run a People's Commune," *Renmin Ribao* [*People's Daily*] editorial, September 4, 1958, in *People's Communes in China* (Peking: Foreign Languages Press, 1958), 86.

28. For an authoritative discussion of rural commune organization, see Schurmann, *Ideology and Organization*, chapter 7.

29. Smil, "China's Great Famine," 1620.

30. "How to Run a People's Commune," *Renmin Ribao* [*People's Daily*] editorial, September 4, 1958, in *People's Communes in China* (Peking: Foreign Languages Press, 1958), 84.

31. Bachman, *Bureaucracy, Economy, and Leadership in China*, 182.

32. Mao Zedong, *Socialist Upsurge in China's Countryside*, 378, 383, in Bernstein, *Up to the Mountains*, 61.

33. "Comrade Liu Shao-chi in Hsu-sui," *Renmin Ribao* [*People's Daily*], September 13, 1958, in Shih, *Urban Commune Experiments*, 33.

34. Shih, *Urban Commune Experiments*, 40.

35. Tao, *People's Communes Forge Ahead*, 5.

36. Tao, *People's Communes Forge Ahead*, 11.

37. Peng, "Demographic Consequences," 647.

38. Peng, "Demographic Consequences," 641.

39. Becker, *Hungry Ghosts*.

40. Peng, "Demographic Consequences," 643.

41. Peng, "Demographic Consequences," 657.

42. Oi, *State and Peasant in Contemporary China*, 71.

43. Burki, *Study of Chinese Communes*, 35.

44. Burki, *Study of Chinese Communes*, 38, 40.

45. Meisner, *Mao's China and After*, 263.

46. Meisner, *Mao's China and After*, 250–251.

47. Chiou, *Maoism in Action*, 47.

48. Richman, *Industrial Society in Communist China*, 316.

49. Chiou, *Maoism in Action*, 49.

50. Chiou, *Maoism in Action*, 46.

51. Lei Feng allegedly died after being backed over by a truck as he was trying to help a comrade in trouble. Another account claims that he died when he ran his bicycle into a telephone pole.

52. Mao, "Problems of War and Strategy," 224.

53. Meisner, *Mao's China and After*, 281.

54. Big-character posters (*dazibao*) are wall posters written in the Chinese language.

55. Ahn, *Chinese Politics and the Cultural Revolution*, 216.

56. Guo, Yongyi, and Yuan, *Historical Dictionary of the Chinese Cultural Revolution*, 124.

57. Deng Pufang eventually resumed movement of his arms and neck as a result of at least two operations in Canada. In the 1980s, he became the president of the Chinese National Welfare Fund for the Handicapped, which he established to assist China's handicapped people.

58. MacFarquhar and Schoenhals, *Mao's Last Revolution*, 117.

59. MacFarquhar and Schoenhals, *Mao's Last Revolution*, 120.

60. Myers, *Enemies Without Guns*, 229.

61. Pan and de Jaegher, *Peking's Red Guards*, 223–224.

62. Guo, Yongyi, and Yuan, *Historical Dictionary of the Cultural Revolution*, 66.

63. Singer, "Educated Youth and the Cultural Revolution in China," 46.

64. Meisner, *Mao's China and After,* 344.

65. Zheng, *Hongse jinian bei* [Scarlet memorial]; Sutton, "Consuming Counter-revolution."

66. Schoppa, *Revolution and Its Past,* 348.

67. Singer, "Educated Youth and the Cultural Revolution in China," 66.

68. Clark, *Chinese Cultural Revolution,* chapter 3.

69. Pye, *China,* 277.

70. Kwong, *Cultural Revolution in China's Schools,* 33.

71. Kwong, *Cultural Revolution in China's Schools,* 34.

72. Kwong, *Cultural Revolution in China's Schools,* 69.

73. Kwong, *Cultural Revolution in China's Schools,* 114.

74. Kwong, *Cultural Revolution in China's Schools,* 115.

75. Singer, "Educated Youth and the Cultural Revolution in China," 37.

76. Kwong, *Cultural Revolution in China's Schools,* 142.

77. Meisner, *Mao's China and After,* 362.

78. Meisner, *Mao's China and After,* 359.

79. Meisner, *Mao's China and After,* 360.

80. The idea of a farmer as a doctor originated in rural parts of Shanghai, and peasants were usually barefoot while working in the wet rice fields; hence, the term *barefoot doctor.* Guo, Yongyi, and Yuan, *Historical Dictionary of the Cultural Revolution,* 10.

81. Meisner, *Mao's China and After,* 361.

82. Teiwes and Sun, *Tragedy of Lin Biao,* 128.

83. Lynch, *Mao,* 194.

84. Evans, *Deng Xiaoping,* 202.

85. Evans, *Deng Xiaoping,* 207.

86. Evans, *Deng Xiaoping,* 209.

4 The Structures of Politics

The sweeping changes described in the previous chapter completely transformed China's politics, economics, and society. Soon after the establishment of the People's Republic of China (PRC) in 1949, China's communist leaders carried out a series of political and economic campaigns to marginalize or eliminate political competition, socialize the economy, and break down traditional values. They took the Chinese people on a dizzying roller-coaster ride of highs and lows: radical land reform, rapid industrialization, terrorizing persecution of intellectuals and adversaries, a Great Leap into misery and starvation, and a violent Cultural Revolution. How were Mao Zedong and the other Chinese communists able to so completely transform China's economy and mobilize millions in the name of revolution? Mao and the Chinese communists were able to carry out the sweeping changes and political campaigns because they exercised complete control over China's political institutions. They had created a political party that enforced strict discipline and had tentacles that reached into the state governing apparatus and the military. The Chinese communists who founded the Chinese Communist Party (CCP) in 1921 created the party in the likeness of the Russian Communist Party: they vested power in the hands of a few top leaders and put all executive power in the hands of a supreme leader. To exercise monopoly power over the state and military, the founders of the CCP established party organs responsible for the recruitment, training, and discipline of party members and placed party elites in key administrative positions in government, industry, agriculture, education, and the military. It is virtually impossible to join China's ruling and managing elite without being a member of the Communist Party. Although the policies of the party have changed over time, the structure remains largely intact.

This chapter introduces the structure and process of China's political system and illuminates the power that the CCP exercises over the state and military. It also explains the resiliency of the CCP. Its ability to survive while other communist parties around the world have crumbled is a testament to its ability to adapt and respond to changing situations in China.

107

China's political institutions are the party, state, and military. Although China's state government apparatus is organizationally and functionally separate from the party, the party directly or indirectly controls government organizations and personnel. State government and the party have overlapping memberships, and high-ranking government personnel are important CCP leaders. Of the three institutions, the party is the strongest politically, and the other two serve the interests of the party. The triumvirate of party, state, and military has kept the CCP in power for more than sixty years. The paramount leadership of the CCP and the subordinate relationship of the state and military to the party largely explain why the PRC has never experienced a military coup. Despite the democratization of southern European and Latin American countries and the fall of authoritarian governments in Eastern Europe in the late twentieth century, the Chinese communist government continued to maintain political power.

The Chinese Communist Party

Although China has eight so-called democratic political parties, the Chinese Communist Party is China's ruling party.[1] The CCP allows no public discussion of multiparty elections and, aside from a few experiments at the grassroots level, there are no popular elections at all for party posts. With 78 million members, the CCP is the largest communist party in the world. Founded in 1921 with help from the Russian communists, the CCP is a Leninist party by nature. A Leninist party maintains its unity by emphasizing hierarchy and concentration of power in the hands of its top leaders (see Figure 4.1). The CCP is organized according to the Leninist principle of democratic centralism (democracy under centralized guidance), which demands that subordinate levels of organization follow the dictates of superior levels. Its highly structured organization forms a pyramid that reflects the concentration of power at the top of the party.

The party is organized along territorial-administrative lines. The most basic level of party organization is the 3.5 million grassroots branches, or cells, based in neighborhoods, work units, and villages with three or more full-time party members. Above these branches are party committees at the county, provincial, and national levels. The central organs of the CCP, in ascending order of importance, are the National Party Congress, the Central Committee, the Political Bureau and its Standing Committee, and the General Secretary. (The Central Commission for Discipline Inspection ensures that all party work conforms to party doctrine. The Central Military Commission controls China's military.)

The National Party Congress

The National Party Congress (Daibiao Dahui) is in theory the highest body of the CCP. It should be distinguished from the National People's Congress, the

Figure 4.1 Structure of the Chinese Communist Party

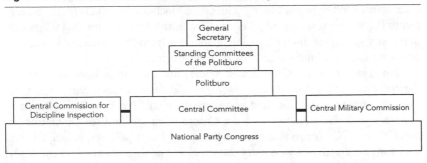

highest state legislative body, first mentioned in Chapter 3 and discussed below. The CCP has convened seventeen congresses since the first in 1921. After coming to power in 1949, the CCP held no congress until 1956. Between 1956 and 1969, disruptions caused by the Great Leap Forward and Cultural Revolution meant that the party convened only three congresses. Since 1977, the CCP has consistently held congresses every five years, as its constitution stipulates. Each National Party Congress is identified by a number. The First National Party Congress convened in 1921, the Sixteenth in 2002, and the Seventeenth in 2007.

The National Party Congress is the largest meeting of party members and usually convenes for several days. In recent years, the numbers of delegates have exceeded two thousand. Party members choose delegates in nationwide regional elections held over several months. In an attempt to democratize the selection process, the Central Committee instructed that delegates to the 1982 congress be elected by secret ballot and that the number of candidates exceed the number of seats to be filled. It also recommended the election of experts in economics, science, and technology, and of women and minorities. In recent years, the party has encouraged the election of delegates from among workers. In 2007, more than 28 percent of the 2,217 party congress delegates to the Seventeenth National Party Congress were grassroots people such as workers, policemen, doctors, or teachers.[2]

The National Party Congress convenes in the Great Hall of the People in Tiananmen Square. Its primary function is to elect representatives to the CCP's Central Committee and its Standing Committee. The term *election* is a bit misleading in this case. In reality, key party leaders draw up a list of those to become members of the Central Committee and present it to the party congress for formal ratification. (Since 1982, however, delegates have the right to nominate write-in candidates.) In 2007, the party congress elected 183 people to the Seventeenth Central Committee after the party sent investigation teams around the country to review the credentials of some 43,300 party officials!

A major task of the congress is to select a new Central Committee, Politburo, and Standing Committee. The Standing Committee elected in 2002 consisted mostly of engineers, or technocrats, reflecting the Sixteenth Party Congress's commitment to the promotion of science and technology. In 2007, the Seventeenth Party Congress elected a Central Committee that is more than 92 percent university graduates, including nine academics from the Chinese Academy of Sciences and the Chinese Academy of Engineering.

The National Party Congress also hears and examines the work report of the previous Central Committee, discusses and decides major party issues, revises the party constitution, and approves the next Five-Year Plan. The party congress also elects members to the Central Commission for Discipline Inspection, the CCP organ that ensures that party lines, policies, principles, and decisions are consistent with party doctrine, and hears and examines the report of the previous commission.

The sheer size and short duration of the National Party Congress make it impossible for the congress to devise and initiate party policies. Rather, the congresses legitimate decisions made by party elites and approve leadership changes. For example, in 1957 the Eighth Congress approved Great Leap Forward policies; in 1966 the same congress branded Liu Shaoqi and Deng Xiaoping revisionists and demoted Liu from the post of party vice chairman; in 1982 the Twelfth Congress adopted a new party constitution; and in 1987 the Thirteenth Party Congress affirmed Deng's economic reforms and Open Door policy to the outside world. Basically, the National Party Congress rubberstamps decisions that top party leaders make in private meetings held before the convening of the congresses. Many of these decisions used to be made at the annual party retreat at Beidaihe, a seaside resort some two hundred miles east of Beijing. CCP chief Hu Jintao ended the practice in 2004, but party decisions are still made privately before their formal acceptance by the National Party Congress.

The Central Committee

The party constitution vests in the much smaller Central Committee supreme power for party decisions and policies when the National Party Congress is not in session. When the National Party Congress is not in session, the Central Committee carries out its decisions, directs the work of the party, and represents the CCP in its foreign relations. The Central Committee convenes the National Party Congress and approves or endorses policies, programs, and major changes in membership of leading party organs. Under the principle of democratic centralism, all party members are eligible to express their opinions, but once a decision is made by the party leadership, all members are obliged to support the decisions of the Central Committee.

Each National Party Congress elects a Central Committee, and each Central Committee is identified by the congress from which it sprung. For example, the First National Party Congress elected the First Central Committee of the

CCP, the Sixteenth National Party Congress elected the Sixteenth Central Committee, and so on. Each Central Committee stands for five years.[3] During that time, the Central Committee holds annual meetings, called plenums, to discuss and ratify party and state policies. The Seventeenth Central Committee of the CCP held its fifth plenum in October 2010. The Seventeenth Central Committee had 204 members, with 167 alternates, in 2011.

The major organizations under the Central Committee are the Organization Department, International Department, United Front Work Department, Propaganda Department, and Party Central Academy. The Organization Department is the party's personnel office and is vital for maintaining party control over the country. It places party cadres in thousands of high-ranking positions—collectively known as the *nomenklatura*—in the party, government, military, and judicial system, as well as in large businesses, hospitals, flagship universities, research centers, museums, libraries, and the media.[4] The Organization Department also keeps extensive files, or dossiers, on all future party leaders. The International Department operates worldwide. In the past, its activities ranged from subverting foreign governments and smuggling weapons to insurgents to supporting despotic regimes such as the Khmer Rouge in Cambodia. As China has moved from a revolutionary state to a status quo state, the mission of the International Department has changed. More recently, it has served as a secret envoy in sensitive negotiations with North Korea (and possibly Iran), a means to introduce foreign officials and experts to China, and as an outreach organization to build ties with foreign societies and political parties. The United Front Work Department conducts relations with noncommunist political parties in China and abroad. The Propaganda Department is in charge of ideology work, controls the Chinese media, and monitors media personnel. The Party Central Academy indoctrinates and grooms principal party cadres.

The Politburo, Standing Committee, and General Secretary

The Leninist principle of *democratic centralism* vests political power in the hands of a few party elites who occupy positions in the Politburo and in the smaller Standing Committee. The Central Committee elects the Politburo, its Standing Committee, and the general secretary. In reality, the Central Committee approves candidates selected by party elites. The Politburo and the exclusive Standing Committee are the real decisionmakers. The Politburo carries out the day-to-day functions of the party when the Central Committee is not in session, and the Standing Committee runs the daily party affairs when the Politburo is not meeting. The full Politburo tends to include party secretaries from big municipalities like Beijing and Shanghai, and from important provinces like Guangdong. Members of the Politburo and Standing Committee live in the walled compound called Zhongnanhai, next to the former Forbidden City (the former emperor's palace in Beijing). The Politburo typically has fourteen to twenty-four members, and its members form the CCP's power elite. In 2010, the Politburo had sixteen members; the Standing Committee had nine members. Also noteworthy are the ages of the Politburo members. The average age of the new members of the Politburo is more than three years younger than at the Sixteenth Party Congress. The party can claim that it is working toward making its leadership younger in age. The Politburo controls three other important bodies and ensures that the party line is upheld. These are the Central Military Commission, which controls the armed forces; the National People's Congress, or parliament; and the State Council (cabinet), the government's administrative arm.

The Politburo's Standing Committee works as a kind of inner cabinet and groups together the country's most influential leaders. The Standing Committee usually has fewer than ten members and meets weekly. Members of the Standing Committee hold the posts of party general secretary, premier, chairman of the National People's Congress, and head of the Central Discipline Inspection Commission. Until 1982, the chairman of the CCP headed the party with the assistance of several vice chairmen. Since the position of chairman was retired in 1982, the general secretary has been the party's top bureaucrat. The general secretary of the Central Committee calls sessions of the Politburo and its Standing Committee and is in charge of the work of the Secretariat of the Central Committee—the administrative arm of the Politburo—and of the Standing Committee. Deng Xiaoping was general secretary of the CCP from 1954 to 1966, a position that made him long and lasting contacts that would serve him well after his rehabilitation and rise to power in the late 1970s. There is only one general secretary.

The office of the party Secretariat carries out the day-to-day work of the CCP. It is the party's inner cabinet and serves under the direction of the Politburo and its Standing Committee. The party's Central Committee approves nominees provided by the Standing Committee. Several members of the Secretariat held concurrent positions on the Politburo. This overlap in membership allows party leaders to exercise control over policy implementation and gives Secretariat members sitting on the Politburo a role in party policymaking. Most important, the Secretariat is a proving ground for successors to senior party leaders. After accruing many years of experience on the Secretariat, members aspire to become general secretary of the party.

Other Party Organs

The Central Commission for Discipline Inspection is responsible for maintaining party morale and discipline. It controls the performance of party organizations and investigates breaches of discipline. The commission is answerable to the Central Committee. Party discipline is maintained through the concept of democratic centralism in which all members are free to express diverse opinions, but lower levels of party members are subordinate to superior levels, and individual members are subordinate to the organization.

Below the central level, there are party committees and congresses in each of China's provinces, autonomous regions, and municipalities directly under the central government. The party is also represented in various county subdivisions. At the bottom of the party hierarchy are committees and branches set up in state-run factories, shops, schools, offices, and neighborhoods.[5]

Party Recruitment and Discipline

Chapter 1 of the 2007 CCP Constitution states that party membership is open to any Chinese worker, farmer, member of the armed forces, intellectual, or "any advanced element of other social strata" who is at least eighteen years old and who accepts the party's program. The most significant departure from the 1992 party constitution is substitution of the term *farmer* for *peasant,* and the elimination of revolutionaries from the list.

Membership is prestigious and exclusive. Only about 6 percent of China's population belongs to the CCP. The first step to joining the CCP is to join the Young Pioneers in primary school and then the Communist Youth League (CYL) in high school and college. The CCP selects only the most promising members of the CYL to join the party. Another way to join the party is to be recruited by a party member. The CCP maintains more than 3.3 million cells at the grassroots level, and party activists in these cells seek out appropriate new members and recruit them. For instance, party members try to recruit coworkers or college classmates. Interested individuals submit a written application, and applicants who are accepted study ideology and theory under a period of tutelage. Candidates for party membership must go through a one-year probationary period. In the post-Mao era, the party places emphasis on applicants' technical and educational qualifications rather than on ideological criteria. The process from application to full party membership typically takes a couple of years.

Recruitment is exclusive because the CCP is an elite Leninist party. The CCP's authority rests on the claim that China must be led by a crack force   a vanguard—of only the most enlightened members of society who know what is best for the masses. Almost all of the founders of the party were young radical revolutionary intellectuals, as were most of the party's top leaders in the early years. Since its founding in 1921 (with the exception of the Cultural Revolution years), the CCP has emphasized the recruitment of intellectuals, including college students. Early party constitutions stipulated that one needed to be a worker, poor peasant, lower-middle peasant, revolutionary soldier, or any other revolutionary who had reached the age of eighteen. After abolishing the college entrance examination in 1966, the party accepted "worker-peasant-soldier" college students based on recommendation by local work units or party organizations.[6]

Since the reform era began in the late 1970s, the party has recruited talented people from all classes and occupations, putting more emphasis on one's skill set than on one's class orientation. Although the party continues to recruit new members among China's college students, the proportion of party members among college students declined from 26 percent in 1975 to 5 percent in the 1980s as a reflection of students' disillusionment with communist ideology as well as their disgust with party corruption.[7] Since the late 1980s, however, more and more college students have expressed interest in joining the party, though their motivations vary. The post–Tiananmen Square Massacre college student body is more pragmatic than those who joined earlier. Many college students join primarily for the perks or for career advancement. Surveys taken among China's college students in the past decade indicate that the overwhelming majority of applicants want to join the party to promote their own advancement. Few applicants indicate that they want to join out of a belief in communism.[8]

Although college students join the party for personal reasons, they bring with them the technical skills necessary for the party's scientific and technocratic development strategy. Particularly valuable are management science majors (which includes economic planning, finance, and accounting) and engineering majors (which includes textile engineering, civil engineering, mechanical engineering, chemical engineering, and transportation). In the reform era, the party recruits candidates with both technical education and political loyalty for leadership positions.[9]

Elite recruitment has transformed the party leadership from revolutionaries to technocrats so that the party can better deal with the more technical problems facing China in the twenty-first century. Since the Fifteenth Party Congress, all members of the Standing Committee are technocrats, with a majority trained in engineering. Most new recruits of the CCP's Central Committee are also more educated. The percentage of college-educated members in the Central Committee has increased from 44 percent in 1956 to 92 percent in 1997. In addition, in the early twenty-first century, the CCP voted to open party membership to private entrepreneurs. The party actively recruits private entrepreneurs as a strategy for co-opting capitalists.[10] In 2007 alone, 1,554 private entrepreneurs joined the party, including the chairman of the Wanfeng Auto Holding Group, Asia's largest aluminum wheel producer; the chairman of the Lifan Group, a motorcycle producer; and chairman of the Chuanhua Group, a detergent manufacturer.

The 2007 Seventeenth Party Congress

The Seventeenth Party Congress of the CCP met from October 15 through 21, 2007. In his report to the congress, CCP general secretary Hu Jintao admitted that the party fell short in living up to the expectations of the people. He pinpointed China's unresolved problems of environmental degradation, urban-rural disparity, regional disparity, poor agricultural growth, and rising social problems. In surprisingly candid comments, Hu admitted that the governance capability of the party failed to deal with these problems.[11] Claiming that it is necessary for the CCP to lead the country through its current problems, Hu promised to reform the party's internal organization. Hu's comments are important because they set the tone for China's direction for the next five years. The congress formalized proposals to approve intraparty democracy, inserted the term *scientific development* into the party constitution, encouraged consumption rather than investment, promoted protection of the environment, and put forward peace talks with Taiwan. This chapter discusses each of these initiatives by turn.

Arguably the most important action taken by the Seventeenth Party Congress was the approval of intraparty democracy. Income disparity due to uneven economic growth, and corruption due to a concentration of power in the hands of a few people, have created an unstable economic and political situation that challenges the legitimacy and authority of the CCP. To maintain legitimacy, the Seventeenth Party Congress formally approved Hu's concept of intraparty democracy (*dangnei minzhu*). *Democracy* in this case does not mean rule of the majority, but rather improving law-based governance to ensure that the party leads the people in effectively governing the country. Under Hu's vision of intraparty democracy, the CCP's survival is dependent on its ability to clean up corruption and carry out law-based governance.

Rather than introducing rule of the majority to the CCP, intraparty democracy involves expanding democracy within the concept of democratic centralism. In reality, in the 1970s Mao was the absolute and undisputed leader of the CCP and gave little, if any, consideration to lower-level party cadres. He did not attend Politburo meetings, preferring to send instructions to the party's leaders through intermediaries, usually pretty young women who were often in his company. After Mao's death, the party amended its constitution to forbid all forms of personality cult, a clear reference to Mao's godlike image and power. Although Deng Xiaoping never became the autocratic ruler that Mao was, he nevertheless exercised enormous power. In both the Deng and post-Deng eras, secretaries of party committees at all levels of government have had final say in any decision. They have taken their cues from the CCP, which follows the Politburo's directives. Top party leaders and party secretaries at all levels have enjoyed enormous power, and there has been little respect for lower-level party cadres. Despite talk of democracy, the general secretary has had most of the decision-making power, and his decision has been binding on all subordinates. In other words, democratic centralism has been more central than democratic.

The Seventeenth Party Congress approved the gradual implementation of intraparty democracy.[12] Although it refers to the term only once (in its general program), the 2007 party constitution spells out procedures for achieving intraparty democracy. At the national level, beginning in 2007 the Politburo is to report regularly to the Central Committee and accept its supervision.

A second change is the gradual increase in the number of candidates approved by the Central Personnel Office to fill delegate seats. Chapter 2, article 11

Democratic Centralism

"Individual Party members are subordinate to the Party organization, the minority is subordinate to the majority, the lower Party organizations are subordinate to the higher Party organizations, and all the constituent organizations and members of the Party are subordinate to the National Congress and the Central Committee of the Party." (2007 CCP Constitution, chapter 2, article 10)

of the constitution stipulates that the number of candidates nominated be greater than the number of persons to be elected. Although the constitution does not stipulate the number of candidates to be nominated, party leaders have approved the gradual expansion of the number of candidates, increasing competition among candidates. In 2007, the ratio of multiple candidates for members of the Central Committee increased from 5 percent at the Sixteenth Party Congress to 10 percent, and the ratio of multiple candidates for alternate members of the Central Committee expanded from 5.7 percent at the Sixteenth Party Congress to 13 percent. Third, the same article also indicates that the party will create a tenure system for delegates to all levels of party congresses.

A fourth change is the retention of some delegates in local party offices after the conclusion of a party congress. In years past, delegates to party congresses would break from their career responsibilities for several days to participate in national, provincial, or local party congresses. The delegates would return to their careers, such as mayor, professor, or doctor, at the conclusion of the congress. The Seventeenth Party Congress allows some delegates to remain with the relevant party committee at the conclusion of congresses and not return to their careers. In this fashion, the delegates can ensure that the local party committees are carrying out the policies of the congress. For example, if a county conference has five hundred delegates, perhaps ten of the delegates will remain with the county party committee to ensure that the committee considers the decisions of the five hundred delegates. Another procedure to implement intraparty democracy is the *majority vote rule*. Rather than vest complete decisionmaking power in the hands of the party committee secretary, under the majority vote rule, party committee members vote on decisions, which are binding and cannot be ignored by the party secretary. The secretary honors the majority vote.

Carrying out intraparty democracy is important for the party's survival for two reasons. First, the later generations of CCP leaders lack the stature of Mao and Deng. Mao and Deng came from the first and second generations of party leaders, respectively. Like their contemporaries, Mao's and Deng's legitimacy stemmed from their pre-1949 participation in the early years of the party, the Long March, and war against the Nationalists. Their successors do not have the authority commanded by Mao and Deng. After Mao's death, the CCP and the Chinese people recognized that Mao made serious mistakes, and the party wants to ensure that no leaders can rule China with the godlike status that Mao enjoyed and abused. Second, in the reform era when capital is king, the CCP recognizes that the power of the party secretaries has led to a serious corruption problem in China. Party secretaries commonly engaged in nepotism to fill positions in party and state offices and in nonstate enterprises. In elevating the status of regular party cadres, the CCP is diluting the power of the party secretary.

Another major development of the Seventeenth Party Congress was the approval of the inclusion of Hu's "scientific outlook on development" in the party constitution. *Scientific development* refers to the need for economic, political, and social development that benefits all. Party leaders recognize that China's reform-era development has been remarkable but uneven. In the past, China's leaders emphasized economic growth, even to the point of degrading the environment and compounding economic inequality. The Seventeenth Party Congress recognized that the growing gap in income distribution, urban-rural disparity, and regional income disparity has led to social discontent, and in some cases, violence. Hu Jintao's report stated that the foundation of China's agriculture remains weak, and that rural areas still lag behind in development. Hu admitted that China's society had become more stratified, and that the Chinese people have higher expectations for economic development. The party's task regarding income disparity is to "narrow the urban-rural and interregional gaps in development and promote a balanced economic and social development."[13] The congress approved Hu's call to make economic development the party's top priority, concentrating on construction and development, improving science and education, better training of personnel, and embracing sustainable development.

The Seventeenth Party Congress encouraged increased domestic consumption. Much of China's economic growth has been based on exports of goods. Chinese household savings rates average around 25 percent of household income, and compared with Western countries, domestic consumption is quite low. To lessen China's reliance on exports, China's leaders are calling for greater domestic consumption. Also, the congress called for greater protection of the environment. China's environment is discussed in detail in Chapter 7.

The Seventeenth Party Congress approved Hu Jintao's call for China and Taiwan to discuss a formal end to hostilities and to reach a peace agreement. However, the party maintained its long standing demand that Taiwan accept the One-China principle, which states that there is one China, and Taiwan is a territory of China. In his report, Hu indicated that Beijing was willing to talk to any party that recognizes that both sides of the strait belong to one and the same China.[14]

One omission, that of Hu's Harmonious Society—a road map to smooth social and economic inequalities while growing the economy—was notable. Hu's proposal of a Harmonious Society is an indication that society is not in harmony. Specifically, there is animosity among segments of society. Urban-rural and coastal-interior disparity has led to discontent among those who feel left behind by China's economic boom. This discontent has spilled over into riots, demonstrations, and other displays throughout China. The Seventeenth Party Congress did not endorse Hu's program, indicating continued division in the party ranks.

The PLA's Relations with the Party and the State

The military comprises the third leg of China's governing apparatus and is discussed in greater detail in Chapter 9. The party-military relationship is best described as symbiotic. Consistent with Mao's edict that "political power comes out of the barrel of a gun," the military is subordinate to and works for the party. The idea that the CCP would have its own military comes from Lenin's theory of revolution. Marx believed that a communist revolution would come about when the conditions were ripe for the oppressed proletariat to rise up spontaneously against their capitalist oppressors. Lenin discounted Marx's belief in a spontaneous uprising and argued that socialist revolution needed leadership to educate the masses and guide them in revolution. As the capitalists and the bourgeoisie class would control the state military force, a revolutionary group would need its own military.

Because the Russian-dominated Comintern helped create the CCP, the CCP adopted the organization and propaganda structure of the Russian Communist Party. Initially, the Comintern worked closely with Sun Yat-sen's Kuomintang and helped establish the Whampoa Military Academy in Guangzhou to train KMT and CCP military officers for a revolutionary army. After the collapse of the First United Front in 1927, the CCP realized that it needed an army loyal to the party. In August 1927, the party established a revolutionary army and gave its Central Military Commission (CMC) responsibility to command the military and manage military affairs. The CMC created branches in the provinces to direct army activities there. After the 1927 KMT-CCP split, the party used the Red Army to fight against the Nationalist army and to spread the message of communist revolution throughout China. The party's propaganda machine was partly redirected toward military work, and communist soldiers carried out radical land redistribution and recruitment of peasant youth into the Red Army. Army officers conducted both military and political operations. The mobilization of the army to rural areas required that army officers engage in political propaganda, mass mobilization, and local administration. Party cadres received military training, and army officers received political training. Hence, interlocking military-party relations date from the founding of the PLA, and top Red Army officers who were members of the CMC include such military men as Zhu De, Peng Dehuai, and Lin Biao.

Elected by the Central Committee, the CMC exercises authoritative policymaking and operational control over the military. The CMC directs unified command for all of China's armed forces (army, navy, and air force). Tradition-ally, China's top party and state leaders have led the CMC. For example, former CCP general secretary and PRC president Jiang Zemin served as CMC chief at the same time, as do current general secretary and PRC president Hu Jintao, demonstrating the interlocking relationship among party, state, and military. Since 1982, the CMC has had a counterpart organization in the *state* Central Military Commission. The leadership of both bodies is identical, further illus-trating the tightly connected membership of party, state, and military organs.

The integration with the party at the top decisionmaking level ensured the military's support for the CCP throughout the 1945–1949 civil war, the post-1949 nation-building phase, the Mao years, and the post-Mao years. Under Lin Biao, the military played an unusually prominent role in state and party affairs during the Cultural Revolution. From 1968 to 1975, military officers chaired 68 percent of provincial, autonomous regions and centrally administered municipal revolutionary committees (see Chapter 3) throughout China. Only 32 percent of chairmen were party cadres. In 1971, military officers served as secretaries for more than 60 percent of China's provincial party committees. After the fall of Lin Biao, the CCP moved to reduce the role of the military in China's politics. By 1975, only 47 percent of provinces had a military officer as party secretary. Military representation on the Politburo and Central Committee likewise declined. In 1969, thirteen PLA senior officers (52 percent) served on the Politburo, but this fell to only seven military officers (33 percent) in 1973. Since 1969, military representation on the Central Committee has declined from a high of 43 percent of members to an average of about 21 percent since 1987, indicating that the in-terlocking party-military relationship is still an established pattern.

Although the percentage of military represented on the Central Committee has declined since its height during the early years of the Cultural Revolution, the PLA and the party still enjoy close relations. It was the military that built Mao's personality cult. In the 1960s, Mao's supporters in the military promoted Mao Zedong Thought as undisputed orthodoxy and built a personality cult around the man. China's leadership has called on the PLA to intervene in poli-tics at various times in PRC history. For instance, when Red Guards got out of hand during the Cultural Revolution, Mao called out the PLA to disarm and disband the Guards, and Deng called on the PLA in spring 1989 to crack down on nationwide protests. Until recently, military commanders served as party leaders at provincial, regional, and national levels. Although the party and mili-tary relationship is not as symbiotic as in the past, there is no concept of a military independent of the CCP. The CCP general secretary still acts as chairman of the CMC, and the party political branch is established at all levels of the military and implements the decisions of the party's Central Committee. Close party-military relations have ensured that the PRC has never experienced a military coup, nor has the military ever taken society's side in political disputes. After the collapse of the Berlin Wall and the collapse of authoritarian governments in

Eastern Europe, many Western eyes turned to China in anticipation of the same. China's authoritarian government received its greatest challenge in spring 1989 as demands for political liberalization spread throughout China. Despite this mass movement, the CCP maintained power largely because it commanded the loyalty of the army. Long after Mao's death, political power still comes out of the barrel of a gun.

The Organization and Role of State Political Institutions

China's key state political institutions are the executive, prime minister and cabinet, legislature, and the bureaucracy (see Figure 4.2). China's chief executive is the president of the PRC. China's state political institutions have interlocking memberships with the CCP and military. The president, vice president, premier, and chairman of the national legislature all serve on the CCP's Standing Committee of the Politburo. China's four vice premiers also serve on the Politburo.

The Executive

The president of the PRC is the head of state. He is the supreme representative of China in both domestic and foreign affairs. China has had six presidents between 1949 and 2011: Mao Zedong, Liu Shaoqi, Li Xiannian, Yang Shangkun, Jiang Zemin, and Hu Jintao. According to China's state constitution, the president has the power to promulgate laws; appoint and remove the prime minister (premier), vice premiers, state councilors, ministers of ministries, and state commissions; confer state medals and honorary titles; issue orders of special amnesty; proclaim martial law and a state of war; as well as issue orders of mobilization (according to decisions of the NPC and its Standing Committee). Although the president represents China in foreign affairs, his position is largely symbolic and ceremonial. In reality, the president acts according to decisions of the national legislature.

The National People's Congress (NPC), China's highest legislative body, elects the president and vice president to five-year terms. There is a two-term limit for the presidency. According to the constitution, candidates for the president and vice president must be PRC citizens who have the right to vote and to stand for election and must have reached the age of forty-five.[15] Candidates for the president and vice president are proposed by the NPC presidium for deliberation by all NPC deputies. Then the presidium officially decides on the candidates, one for the presidency and one for the vice presidency (making them noncompetitive positions), for election through voting by the NPC. China's leaders have vowed to gradually replace the current single-candidate practice, but no date has been set for the change. Because the NPC theoretically elects the president and vice president, it is the only body that can remove the president and vice president from office.

Figure 4.2 Organization of the PRC Government at Respective Administrative Levels

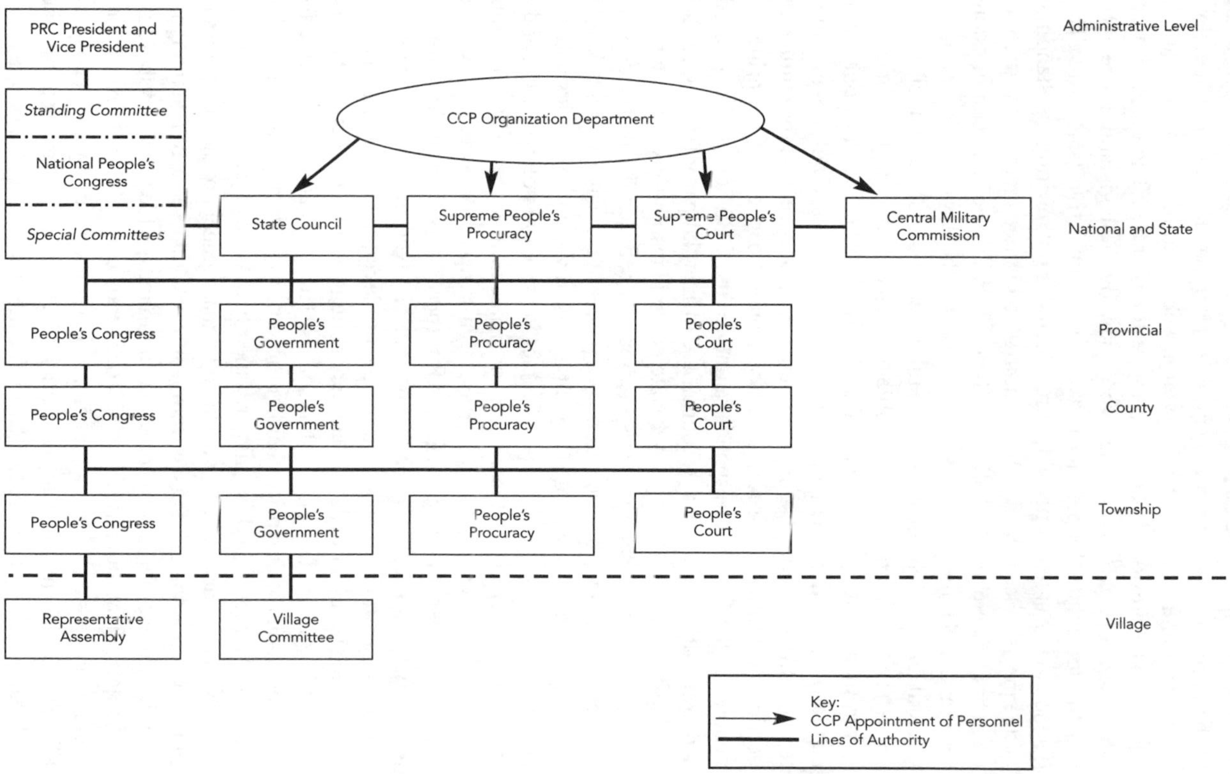

PRC President and Vice President	

National People's Congress
- Standing Committee
- Special Committees

Administrative Level: National and State
- State Council
- Supreme People's Procuracy
- Supreme People's Court
- Central Military Commission

CCP Organization Department

Provincial
- People's Congress
- People's Government
- People's Procuracy
- People's Court

County
- People's Congress
- People's Government
- People's Procuracy
- People's Court

Township
- People's Congress
- People's Government
- People's Procuracy
- People's Court

Village
- Representative Assembly
- Village Committee

Key:
→ CCP Appointment of Personnel
— Lines of Authority

The State Council

The top executive apparatus is the State Council (cabinet), led by the prime minister (premier). The membership of the State Council includes, in addition to the premier, four vice premiers, a secretary, and five state councilors. The president nominates the premier, who is subject to review by the national legislature. The president also can remove the premier. The premier nominates other members, who are subject to review by the legislature. The PRC state constitution limits the premier to two consecutive five-year terms. The State Council meets at least once a month. When it is not meeting, its Standing Committee meets twice a week. The Standing Committee includes the premier, vice premiers, a secretary, and all of the heads of ministries and commissions. The secretary, under the premier, is responsible for the day-to-day work of the State Council and is in charge of the general office of the State Council.

The State Council is responsible to the national legislature in carrying out government functions. For instance, the State Council carries out regulations and laws adopted by the legislature and deals with such affairs as China's internal politics, diplomacy, national defense, finance, economy, culture, and education. In reality, however, the State Council carries out the principles and policies of the CCP and responds mainly to the CCP Secretariat. Accordingly, senior members of the State Council are influential party leaders, further consolidating the party's control over state political institutions. The interconnected state-party membership obscures distinctions between the party and state government, resulting in a concentration of power in the hands of a few key leaders.

Subordinate to the State Council are twenty-eight ministries and commissions, which constitute the State Council's principal policymaking and supervisory offices. Heads of the central government ministries and other important offices in the central government are high-level party leaders as well and are usually members of either the CCP's Politburo or its Central Committee. There are *ministries* and *commissions* at the central government level, *departments* at the provincial level, *divisions* at the county level, and *sections* at the township level. The size of China's bureaucracy is huge, with bureaucrats at every level of Chinese government. China has some 40 million cadres—the name for people in positions of authority in either the state or party apparatus. Not all cadres are party members, and not all party members are cadres.

To better manage their workload, China's leaders organize into four broad functional areas: party affairs, government work, state security, and foreign affairs. The first three groupings oversee and command a wide array of subordinate bureaucracies. Traditionally, the top leader heads party affairs. Government work focuses on economic development and is typically led by the second or third highest-ranking member of the leadership hierarchy. State security includes both public security and state security (counterintelligence). Foreign affairs naturally focuses on relations with other countries. Under each of these functional arrangements are subgroups called leadership small groups (LSGs) in charge of policy areas. Leadership small groups coordinate implementation of policy across the bureaucratic network. Each LSG consists of a Politburo Standing Committee member and other members of the Politburo and Central Committee.[16] By straddling party and government, LSGs serve as links between China's leaders and the bureaucracies that implement policy. Leadership small groups for the Seventeenth Party Congress ranged from finance and economic affairs and political and legal affairs to foreign affairs and tourism. Some LSGs are ad hoc. For example, China's leaders in April 2003 created an LSG to oversee the work of control and management of severe acute respiratory syndrome (SARS) and to coordinate their efforts with the World Health Organization.

Under the leadership small groups is a group of functional bureaucracies, called *xitong* (system). *Xitong* link related bureaucracies (government ministries and departments and party offices and their subordinate organs) under functional areas (such as energy, finance, economics, and so on). The *xitong* serve as bridges between party and government organs to enable them to work together on important issue areas. Different *xitong* cover different policy areas. There are six key *xitong:* party affairs, organization and personnel, propaganda and education, political and legal affairs, finance and economics, and the military.[17]

Although the *xitong* link the bureaucracies with China's leadership, they are not particularly effective because bureaucratic coordination is too complicated in China. The main problem stymieing bureaucratic coordination is the tension between vertical and horizontal rule. Because China's political system is highly authoritarian, one would think that China's leaders could govern by fiat, that is, they could simply issue orders down the bureaucratic chain of command and the bureaucrats would deal with the task the leaders want performed. The process gets muddied because there are both vertical and horizontal lines of rule in China. Vertical rule (*tiao,* or line) flows from central government ministries to subordinate agencies at lower levels of government. Leaders at each level in the hierarchy take direction from above and also pass decisions down to lower levels. Horizontal coordination (*kuai,* or chunk) works out policy differences at each territorial level (such as at the provincial or county level of government). The relation between the two lines is called *tiao-kuai guanxi.*

For example, the Shandong Provincial Water Resources Department is a component of the provincial government responsible for the administration of water affairs in the whole province. It has vertical authority to issue directives to county water departments. County water departments are part of county government. Under the *tiao-kuai* system, county water departments must follow the directives of both the Shandong Provincial Water Resources Department (*tiao*) and the county government (*kuai*). In addition, the county water departments must take directives from the county party committee and other offices in the provincial government (see Figure 4.3).[18] China scholar Kenneth Lieberthal accurately claims that the *tiao-kuai* system resulted in fragmented authority, that is, the problem of having too many bosses.[19] To rectify the problem, China's leaders in the late 1990s began to eliminate oversight by local (*kuai*) authorities and to centralize authority in administrative superiors (*tiao*) at the provincial level. This transformation remains incomplete.

Center-Local Relations

Below China's central government are thirty-one provincial-level bodies (see Table 4.1). They are divided into twenty-two provinces (the PRC considers Taiwan to be its twenty-third province) and five autonomous regions (Inner Mongolia, Guangxi, Tibet, Ningxia, and Xinjiang).[20] In addition, there are four municipalities directly under the central government (Beijing, Shanghai, Tianjin, and Chongqing) and two special administrative regions (SARs), consisting of Hong Kong and Macau.[21] Provinces and municipalities under the central government have the status of central government ministries. Because they are equal in political rank, they cannot issue binding orders on any other. The four levels of government below the provincial level are cities, counties, townships, and villages (see Figure 4.4).[22]

China is a unitary state, with final authority resting in the central government's State Council located in Beijing. Unlike states in the US political system, China's provinces do not have their own constitutions and must accept the leadership of the State Council (cabinet). The State Council has the power to decide the division of responsibilities between the central and provincial governments and also has the power to annul inappropriate decisions and orders of provincial governments.

Center-local relations in China swing back and forth between centralization and decentralization. When the communists established the PRC in 1949, they established provincial and local governments in six regional districts governed by both military and administrative committees. These six regions were grouped as the Northeast, Northwest, North, East, South Central, and Southwest bureaus. The leadership of each bureau consisted of a government chair, party secretary, military commander, and army political commissar—reflecting the close relationship among state, party, and military. Sometimes one man would have all four posts, as in the case of Gao Gang in the Northeast bureau. Deng Xiaoping, who later became China's paramount leader after Mao's death, held two of the four posts in the Southwest bureau. By embedding the party into the state's administrative apparatus, the bureau system allowed the CCP to extend its influence throughout China. Although the bureaus no longer exist and the military is far less powerful in the administration of these regions than in the early days of the PRC, the regional categorizations still exist (see Table 4.1).

Figure 4.3 Lines of Authority

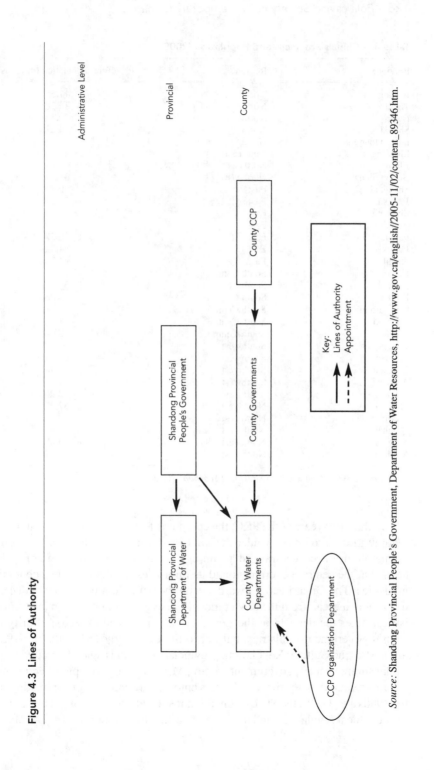

Administrative Level

Provincial

County

Shandong Provincial People's Government

County CCP

Shancong Provincial Department of Water

County Governments

County Water Departments

CCP Organization Department

Key:
Lines of Authority
Appointment

Source: Shandong Provincial People's Government, Department of Water Resources, http://www.gov.cn/english/2005-11/02/content_89346.htm.

Table 4.1 China's Provinces and Population (2009)

Province	Region	Total Population (millions)
Beijing	North	17.55
Tianjin	North	12.28
Hebei	North	70.34
Shanxi	North	34.27
Inner Mongolia	North	24.22
Liaoning	Northeast	43.19
Jilin	Northeast	27.4
Heilongjiang	Northeast	38.26
Shanghai	East	19.21
Jiangsu	East	77.25
Zhejiang	East	51.8
Anhui	East	61.31
Fujian	East	36.27
Jiangxi	East	44.32
Shandong	East	94.7
Henan	South Central	94.87
Hubei	South Central	57.2
Hunan	South Central	64.06
Guangdong	South Central	96.38
Guangxi	South Central	48.56
Hainan	South Central	8.64
Chongqing	Southwest	28.59
Sichuan	Southwest	81.85
Guizhou	Southwest	37.98
Yunnan	Southwest	45.71
Tibet	Southwest	2.9
Shaanxi	Northwest	37.72
Gansu	Northwest	26.35
Qinghai	Northwest	5.57
Ningxia	Northwest	6.25
Xinjiang	Northwest	21.59

Source: NBS of China, *China Statistical Yearbook 2010,* 97.

In the early years of the PRC, the communists permitted a good deal of autonomy in the provinces. Under the First Five-Year Plan, however, the communists introduced centralized planning, which required that authority be housed in the central government and its ministries, particularly the economic ministries. The Great Leap Forward swung the pendulum back toward decentralization, a break from the Soviet model of development based on large ministries. After the debacle of the Leap, Liu Shaoqi recentralized authority in central government ministries, but not to the extent enjoyed in the pre-1957 days. After the Cultural Revolution, provincial authorities again benefited from a relaxation of central government control. Many of Deng Xiaoping's economic reforms required that provincial leaders enjoy discretion in decisionmaking. In the 1980s and 1990s, the State Council granted local people's congresses power to adopt local regulations and mandated that standing committees at and above

Figure 4.4 Levels of Government

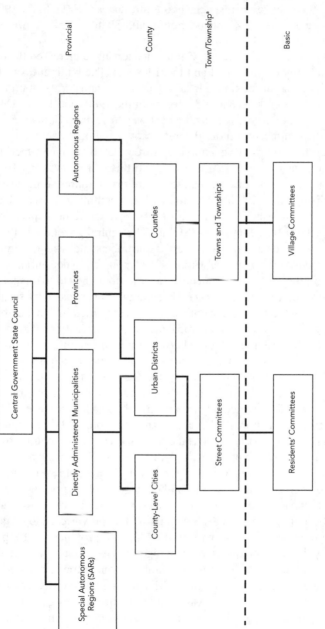

Note: a. Smaller rural areas have townships; larger rural areas have towns.

the county level carry out the work of the congresses. For example, in 1981, the Standing Committee of the National People's Congress granted legislative power to Guangdong and Fujian Provinces to make exceptional economic laws and regulations for their special economic zones (SEZs). In the 1990s, the NPC gave the Shenzhen, Xiamen, Zhuhai, and Shantou SEZs power to pass local legislation.

In the past two decades, China's leaders have increased the decisionmaking authority of provincial and local leaders. The willingness of the center to grant increased discretion to local governments and party committees is a direct consequence of the economic reforms of the 1980s and 1990s. Deng Xiaoping and his supporters argued that the best way to develop China's economy was to give local authorities more discretion over regional economic development. Rather than control the economy by direct fiat, the center directs the economy through macroeconomic policy. Key to this change was the 1994 reform of China's fiscal system. The road to this reform requires some discussion. After establishing the PRC in 1949, the Chinese communists created a highly centralized fiscal system in which most state revenue came from collecting profits from state-owned enterprises (SOEs). The central government then distributed this revenue to central government departments and local governments. In the early Deng years, however, China's leaders opted to decentralize fiscal policy. In 1980, Beijing gave provincial authorities more power to retain profits and allocate resources, thereby increasing the provinces' capacity for planning and developing their local economies. Revenue retained by local authorities, however, meant fewer revenues for central government coffers. With fewer resources to distribute, the central government lost significant fiscal control over localities and had to look elsewhere for revenue, which was difficult because China's sole national tax authority, the State Administration for Taxation, collected taxes only from SOEs.[23] As a result, the central government relied on local authorities, particularly the provinces, to collect revenue. China's revenue collection was bottom up. Local governments collected tax revenues and passed them up to the next level, until the money reached the central government.

There were two problems with this system. First, some money disappeared at each level of local government, cheating Beijing of revenue to fund the central government budget. Second, although some of the revenue was redistributed back to the provinces, the central government kept most of the money.[24] In the 1980s, Beijing struck tax deals with individual provinces, allowing them to keep more revenue. The objective of allowing the provinces to keep more of the money they collected was to encourage provincial authorities to develop their own economies without draining central government coffers. To this end, Beijing implemented a national program in which a negotiated percentage or amount of locally collected revenues was remitted to the central government. This program also had some difficulties. First, the central government could unilaterally renege or change the terms of the negotiation. Second, loopholes allowed local authorities to direct investment to localities in their jurisdiction that had lower tax rates. Because of these negotiated deals, the central government's share of total government revenue fell from around two-thirds in 1978 to only one-third in 1993.[25]

In the early 1990s, China's leaders sought to end subnational bargaining with the center for tax revenue. In 1994, Beijing introduced a three-tiered tax system. The 1994 tax reform allocates all revenue from the consumption tax to central government coffers and allocates all revenue from the individual income tax and sales taxes to local budgets. In addition, Beijing imposed a value-added tax (VAT) of 17 percent on goods and services. The VAT is the single largest source of Chinese government revenue and is divided between the central government (75 percent) and local governments (25 percent).

As a result of these reforms, the central government's share in total revenue more than doubled to about 50 percent of all revenue and has made it possible for the central government to redistribute resources to local governments to achieve national objectives. The redistribution takes two forms: general transfers and special (earmarked) payments. General transfers are based on a tax rebate system, so the more a locality pays the more it gets back. General transfer distribution is uneven among China's provinces, however, because the richest ones receive the bulk of resources, leaving the poorer ones to fund expenditures without the necessary funds. As a result of decentralization and tax reform, county and township governments in poorer regions face increasingly serious financial constraints. In many cases, expenditures for local governments are much higher than their revenues, leaving them unable to pay teachers' salaries or even run tax-collecting offices. In 2007, total local government debt was between 800 billion and 1 trillion yuan ($123 billion and $154 billion).[26] Local governments also levy illegal fees and charges to fund projects, many of which never come to fruition.

A major weakness in the transfer system is the siphoning of funds at each level of subnational government. Lower levels of government depend on transfers from higher levels to help fund their budgets, which are usually running deficits. Provincial governments often hold on to funds that should be transferred down to local governments. The provinces' sticky fingers only make it more difficult for county and township governments to fund programs. Increasingly, local governments have had to rely on extrabudgetary revenue, including proceeds from land sales and real estate development. For instance, in 2005, Beijing ordered directives to cool rapidly rising house prices. Local governments, which control land supply, resisted the directive because land-use transactions have become a critical source of their revenue.

In addition to the general transfers, there are more than two hundred kinds of special earmarked transfers for which provincial governments may apply.

Provincial officials travel to Beijing to directly lobby central government ministries for the earmarked transfers, avoiding the national legislature. The process of allocation lacks transparency because more than a dozen ministries are involved in transferring funds, with no centralized review and coordination among them. The availability of special payments makes it easier for provincial governments to disregard their budgets. The Chinese saying "Heaven is high and the emperor is far away" illustrates current center-subprovincial relations. It means that the further one goes from the center of government, the more likely it is that local leaders will follow local rules rather than edicts from the capital.

Representation

The source of political power for each level of government is the people's congresses.

Before 1982, only the National People's Congress had the power to make laws. In the spirit of self-government, China's 1982 state constitution also allows people's congresses at the provincial level (and of autonomous regions) to issue administrative regulations and local rules. Later, the revised Organic Law of the Local People's Congresses and Local People's Governments (commonly called the Organic Law) extended legislative power to the people's congresses of cities where provincial and autonomous regional governments are based and to other large cities that the State Council approves.

The National People's Congress

The NPC is the highest organ of state power. The Presidium sits at the top of the NPC's structure and decides whether to permit draft laws to be considered by the NPC sessions.

Representatives to the NPC are called *deputies*. In recent years, the number of deputies has exceeded or numbered about three thousand. NPC deputies are elected for a term of five years by people's congresses at the provincial level as well as the PLA. Candidates are nominated on the basis of electoral districts or electoral units and are nominated by the political parties and various people's organizations. The number of deputies to the NPC is determined by the population in each province, autonomous region, and municipality directly under the central government. Each of these units has no fewer than fifteen deputies. Any voter, with the support of at least ten people, may also nominate a candidate. The number of candidates for deputies must be greater than the number of deputies to be elected. Elections are conducted by secret ballot. The Communist Party has undue representation in the NPC. Although the CCP accounts for less than 6 percent of China's population, its members accounted for more than 70 percent of the 2,987 delegates elected to the NPC in 2008.

The Major Functions of the National People's Congress

The major functions of the NPC are to:

- Amend the state constitution and enact laws
- Supervise the enforcement of the state constitution and the law
- Elect the president and the vice president of the republic
- Decide on the choice of premier of the State Council upon nomination by the president
- Elect the major officials of government
- Elect the chairman and other members of the state Central Military Commission
- Elect the president of the Supreme People's Court and the procurator-general of the Supreme People's Procuratorate
- Examine and approve the national economic plan, the state budget, and the final state accounts
- Decide on questions of war and peace
- Approve the establishment of special administrative regions and their governing bodies

Because of the infrequent meetings, the NPC functions through a permanent body, the Standing Committee, elected by NPC deputies. The Standing Committee's powers were enhanced in 1987 when it was given the ability to "enact and amend laws with the exception of those which should be enacted by the NPC," thus giving the committee legislative powers. The Standing Committee presides over sessions of the NPC and determines the agenda, the routing of legislation, and nominations for offices. The NPC also has nine permanent committees (one for education, science, culture, and health, and one each for finance and economics, foreign affairs, law, internal and judicial affairs, ethnic minorities, overseas Chinese, the environment, and agriculture). Leaders of the Standing Committee are invariably influential members of the CCP. The Standing Committee normally meets every two months, but can convene extraordinary meetings if necessary.

The Standing Committee undertakes a large amount of work when the NPC is not in session. The Standing Committee enacts and amends statutes (with the exception of those that should be enacted by the NPC); interprets China's state constitution and laws; supervises the work of other state organs, such as that of the State Council, Central Military Commission, Supreme People's Court, and Supreme People's Procuratorate (prosecutor); annuls administrative rules and regulations, decisions, or orders of the State Council as well as those of local governments that violate the constitution; appoints and removes ministers in charge of ministries or commissions; selects the vice chairs of the Central Military Commission and members of the commission according to the nomination of the chair of the Central Military Commission; and appoints and removes vice presidents and judges in China's judicial system. It also makes key decisions concerning foreign affairs, such as deciding on the ratification and abrogation of treaties and important agreements concluded with foreign countries.

The Legislative Process

According to Chinese law, the NPC Presidium, Standing Committee, and various special committees, as well as the State Council, the Central Military Commission, the Supreme People's Court, and the Supreme People's Procuratorate (prosecutor), may submit bills to the NPC. A group of at least thirty deputies can also submit bills. Bills are discussed at group meetings as well as in related special committees (see Figure 4.5). A bill is passed if more than half of the delegates attending the NPC session agree. Voting is electronic, and laws adopted by the NPC go into effect once they are promulgated in the form of the decree of China's president.

Western observers of China's NPC often dismiss it as a rubber-stamping body, meaning that it merely approves policy initiatives handed down from China's leaders. While the NPC is too large and too tied to the CCP to be a truly deliberative body, there have been occasions when the NPC has registered displeasure or has even voted against (albeit not in the majority) proposals presented before it. One such example concerns the Three Gorges Dam. The Three Gorges Dam is a six-hundred-foot dual-use dam, generating power and irrigating farmland, on the Upper Yangtze River. Critics charged that the dam's four-hundred-mile reservoir

Figure 4.5 National People's Congress

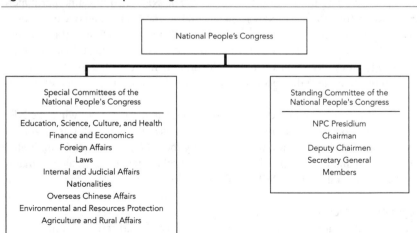

would flood towns and farmlands, displace more than 1 million people, submerge thousands of towns and villages, destroy hundreds of archeological sites, and cause unacceptable river silting. When the project was presented to the NPC for a final vote in April 1992, one-third of NPC delegates abstained or voted against the $10 billion project. The dam was finally completed in 2008, but NPC disagreement over the dam was one factor that led to a decision to delay consideration of the project for at least six years.

Subnational Political Institutions

Legislative bodies below the national level (provincial, county, and township) are called local people's congresses. Congresses at the provincial or county levels meet once a year and township congresses generally meet two or three times a year.[27] When congresses are not in session, their functions and powers are exercised by their standing committees at and above the county level. The administrative arm of these people's congresses is the local people's government. People's governments exist at three levels: (1) provinces, autonomous regions, and special municipalities; (2) counties, autonomous counties, cities, and municipal districts; and (3) administrative towns.[28] Municipalities directly under the central government and large cities are subdivided into districts, and counties are subdivided into townships and towns. The administrative towns replaced people's communes as the basic level of administration (see Figure 4.6). Village government consists of two bodies, the village committee and the representative assembly. The village committee acts as the executive branch of local government; the assembly acts as the deliberative, consultative, and policymaking branch.

Provincial governments have the power to implement local laws, regulations, and decisions of the provincial people's congresses and their standing committees. Provincial people's congresses and their standing committees have the power to supervise the work of provincial governments and to change and annul inappropriate decisions of the provincial governments.

People's congresses at the subnational level elect the leaders of their local governments. They include provincial governors and deputy governors, municipal mayors and deputy mayors, and heads and deputy heads of counties, districts, and towns. The congresses can also recall these officials and demand explanations for their actions. Local congresses examine and approve budgets as well as plans for the economic and social development of the areas under their jurisdiction. They also maintain public order, protect public property, and safeguard the rights of the people guaranteed by China's constitution. Just as at the national level, the CCP is well represented in the local congresses. Party members occupy between 60 and 70 percent of China's lower-level congresses.

Figure 4.6 Structure of Provincial and Local Government

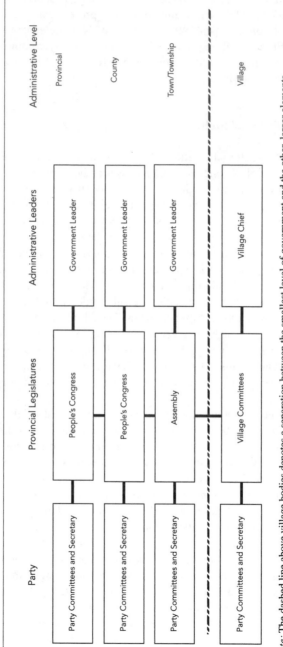

Note: The dashed line above village bodies denotes a separation between the smallest level of government and the other, larger elements.

Elections

China's constitution stipulates that all citizens of the PRC who have reached the age of eighteen have the right to vote and stand for election, regardless of ethnic status, race, sex, occupation, family background, religious belief, education, property status, or length of residence.

China has both direct and indirect elections. Direct election means voters directly elect deputies to the people's congresses by casting their votes. Counties, districts, townships, and towns all carry out direct election of deputies to people's congresses. Election committees preside over elections. The 1982 election stipulated that voters residing in counties and townships directly elect deputies to their own people's congresses. Each county is divided into electoral districts, each of which elects delegates to the county people's congress. (See Figure 4.6.) Deputies to the provincial congresses are elected for five-year terms; deputies elected to the township and county congresses are elected for three-year terms.

Deputies to provincial people's congresses, like those to the National People's Congress, are indirectly elected, meaning that they are elected by the people's congresses at the next lower level. For example, deputies to each of China's twenty-two provincial congresses elect deputies to the National People's Congress, and deputies to county legislatures elect deputies to their provincial legislature. Deputies to the people's congresses of the autonomous regions, municipalities directly under the central government, and cities divided into districts are also elected by the people's congresses at the next lower level.

Candidates for deputies to the people's congresses are nominated on the basis of electoral districts. They may be nominated jointly or independently by political parties, mass organizations, or a group of at least ten voters. Each electoral district has a quota of deputies to be elected, and since 1979, there may be twice as many candidates as seats in direct elections. Above the local level, there may be 50 percent more candidates than seats.

The relevant election committee establishes voting stations and mobile voting boxes. Voters obtain ballots by presenting their ID cards or voter's cards. Elections are conducted by secret ballot. Before voting begins, election committee staff tally and declare the number of voters, examine the ballot box in front of voters, and organize voters to choose those to supervise ballot casting and help tally the votes. The election is valid when more than half of the voters in a constituency have cast their votes. The election has to be held another time if less than this figure has cast votes. When the casting of ballots is over, election committee staff check the number of people who have cast their votes and the total votes received, and make a record, which is signed by the voting supervisors. A candidate wins the election when he or she receives more than half of the votes cast. If more than one candidate receives the same amount of votes, they must stand for a runoff election and the candidate with more votes wins the election. When the counting of votes is completed, the election committee of each constituency confirms the validity of the election and announces the results.

Rural Politics

Legislative bodies in rural China are called *village representative assemblies.* They usually consist of several dozen people. In many cases, assembly members are also party members, and it is not uncommon for a majority of assembly members to come from the CCP. The method of selecting representatives to the village representative assemblies varies from selection by higher authorities to election by small villagers' groups, which have replaced the communes' production brigades as the smallest unit of local political organization. Election is usually done by a show of hands rather than secret ballot.

The assembly meets several times a year to discuss major decisions concerning the village and to issue policy guidelines to the village committee and to the executive branch of the local government (discussed below). Discussions often concern economic issues, such as expansion of a school or securing funding to build a bridge or road.[29]

Since the 1980s, China has expanded rural self-governance through popular elections. The need for rural self-governance came about as a direct result of economic reforms launched in 1978. The breakup of the people's communes at the end of the Cultural Revolution had left rural villages void of local government. The communes' production brigades had served as both an economic organizing body and the local government. Their dissolution meant that villages

---

Election Committees

China has election committees at all levels of government. The committees preside over the election of deputies to people's congresses at the corresponding levels; decide on the date of election; conduct registration of voters, examine the qualifications of voters, and publicize lists of voters; look into appeals of disagreement lodged by voters concerning the lists of voters and make due decisions; decide on the division of constituencies and allocate the number of deputies to the constituencies; tally and publicize the names of candidates for deputies; and, according to the opinion of the majority of voters, decide and publicize the official lists of candidates for deputies, dispatch staff to preside over ballot-casting stations or the election of electoral meetings, decide on whether the election is valid, and publicize the lists of names of deputies elected; and process reports and charges against violations during the election.

had no administrative offices to lead the villages; manage schools, health clinics, and welfare benefits; mediate disputes; and manage public utilities. Decollectivization of agriculture shifted power from party cadres to peasants and gave them more discretion over economic decisions. Some party cadres abandoned their posts for the private sector. Other cadres took advantage of their positions for their own benefit, exploiting the local population by imposing arbitrary fees and taxes and by confiscating agricultural land for private enterprise. The decline of the relative power of rural party cadres and the rising corruption created the necessity for a new form of local governance. In response to this need, farmers in Guangxi Province organized a village committee (VC), essentially the executive branch of the village government, to govern their affairs. Meanwhile, Deng Xiaoping was trying to get the support of farmers for his economic reforms. To gain momentum for his reforms, Deng and his supporters wanted to strengthen grassroots work and so encouraged the spread of village committees in China's rural communities. In 1982, the NPC amended China's constitution to formalize the establishment of village committees throughout rural China. In 1987, the NPC passed the Organic Law of Village Elections (experimental), which stipulated, but did not require, village elections for members of the village committee and for its chairperson. As an experimental law, it did not specify how elections should be carried out, but gave provincial governments latitude in designing the election process.[30] In addition, the Organic Law advanced market-oriented economic reforms, consistent with Deng Xiaoping's desire to gain the support of China's rural population for his reforms. Article 5 states that village committees shall assist villagers in their efforts to establish cooperatives and other economic enterprises and promote the development of rural production under a market economy. Again, the central government gave local governments wide discretion in implementing this part of the law.

Early implementation of the law was spotty. Some villages held elections, while others did not. Some local leaders argued that empowering residents would make their jobs harder. They tried to frustrate local elections by blocking or rigging elections or refusing to convene elections. Some leaders monopolized nominations, held last-minute elections, required that party members vote for favored candidates, or banned unapproved candidates from making campaign speeches. Others insisted on votes by a show of hands, annulled results when the "wrong" candidates won, forced committee members from office, or rejected villagers' demands for recalls.[31] To better facilitate grassroots representation, the NPC in 1998 passed a revised and updated Organic Law, mandating that all villages hold competitive elections and adding specific requirements such as secret ballot, open counting of votes, and the immediate announcement of the winner. According to the Organic Law, VCs have three to seven elected members, who serve for three years. All registered adults are eligible to vote and to stand for election. Voting is conducted by secret ballot, and the number of candidates must exceed the seats to be filled by the election.

Villagers are encouraged to fight election fraud by lodging reports with local governments. Because the VCs are elected by the people, no organization can remove a village committee member.

Village committee elections are increasingly competitive and open, with candidates campaigning door-to-door. Speeches are limited to election-day statements to voters, however. The sick, elderly, and migrants away from home can vote by proxy, and roving or mobile ballot boxes are used in extremely rural areas. The use of these unsecured boxes has raised questions of ballot tampering, however. Township governments, which certify the election results, have been known to annul elections if the leaders disapprove of the results.[32]

Voter interest in local elections is on the rise. Initially, voters appeared reluctant to participate in village committee elections, but this may have changed since the passage of the revised 1998 Organic Law. Voter interest increased after villagers saw that they could replace corrupt and inept cadres with people more to their liking. Village committee elections have resulted in the turnover of members, ousting older and less economically savvy members with younger and more entrepreneurial ones. Because the village committee manages the village's finances and seeks to improve the village's economy, many committee members are successful entrepreneurs or were involved in managing businesses or factories. Doctors are often a popular choice for VC chief as they have had personal interactions with the villagers. Farmers who have skill in expanding their output have been elected in Fujian. Because the village chief manages the village finances and can increase village wealth by developing rural businesses, many village chiefs have a background in business or management.[33] Village committees elected by the people are also more responsive to villagers' concerns. One of the functions of the committee is to manage village finances. Villagers have found that the popularly elected VCs give a better accounting of village spending.[34] Elected officials tend to tax people less and are more accountable to the people, providing them with more public services and checks and balances against village leaders than do appointed cadres. The result is more economic growth.[35]

The village committee has its limitations, however. The Organic Law states that the CCP constitutes the core of the village leadership. Hence, the village party branch is superior to the village committee. Township and village party secretaries play a role (albeit an ambiguous one) in the nomination of candidates for the committee. The VC chair is often also the village party secretary, and village committee and local party committee membership often overlap. The overlap between the VC chair and the party secretary protects, rather than undermines, the CCP's rule in rural China as party cadres can claim some legitimacy through VC elections. On the one hand, the party-VC overlap may render local self-governance merely a formality. On the other hand, the elections are paving the way for a democratic transition, particularly given the rising interest in VC elections.

There also appears to be friction between the popularly elected VCs and the township government directly above them. Before the Organic Law, township leaders appointed village chiefs, giving the township governments greater control to force villages to conform to township policies. Some township governments annulled VC election results after the committees rejected township directives.[36]

Elections are extending beyond the village committee level. Currently, township residents directly elect delegates to their congresses, but higher authorities appoint township chiefs. From 1999 to 2001, Sichuan, Shanxi, Shenzhen, and Henan Provinces carried out experimental direct elections for township chiefs, although the CCP formally stopped the process. However, other townships have carried out such illegal elections.

Democratization and the Future of the CCP

As most Chinese still live in rural villages, competitive elections at this level involve nearly 57 percent of the country's population. Depending on the legitimacy of these elections, rural elections may create the paving stones for grassroots democracy in China. Village elections have positively altered the village power structure. Before the implementation of village elections, the VC chief, who was usually a party member, often merely carried out the party secretary's wishes, and the village assembly merely approved his decisions. But village elections have given the VC chief more legitimacy, and the chief's legitimacy is further enhanced by the villagers' increased interest in local elections.[37]

Grassroots democracy in the form of competitive village elections does not necessarily indicate that China is moving down the path of democracy, however. Democratization is a process, not an endpoint. The CCP's efforts to implement intraparty democracy and the passage of the Organic Law only go so far if there is still interlocking membership of state and party organs. China's democratization needs to involve self-governance at each level of government (village, township, county, province, and national), but the people's congresses at each level are subordinate to the CCP at each level. Prospects for self-governance in China depend on the willingness of the CCP to introduce political reform. For the CCP, stability is number one. Introducing reform risks instability.

Conclusion

The CCP is one of the world's strongest and best organized political parties. It commands and receives extraordinary discipline from its members. Its Leninist structure ensures that only a few members maintain tight control of the party, and its interlocking membership with the state apparatus and its bureaucracy ensure that its programs are carried out. Democratic centralism further strengthens the party by offering its members the opportunity to voice opinions, but requiring that they obey party orders.

The character of the party has changed over the decades and reflects the flavor of Chinese politics. In its early days, the party focused on revolution and its leadership was largely made up of revolutionaries. In the 1960s, Mao leaned on the military for support, so the military had a significant presence in the party leadership. After Mao's death, the party oriented China toward reform and modernization, and the leadership favored reformers and technocrats. To advance the current party agenda of deepening reforms and enhancing China's presence worldwide, the CCP leadership currently favors individuals with scientific education and training. Party membership has likewise changed, and now counts capitalists as its members.

As far as state politics goes, Chinese citizens participate in elections and directly elect their village chief, members to their village committee, and deputies to township and county congresses. The impact of these elections is muted by the fact that China is in reality a one-party state, and in fact, the party trumps local government officials in decisionmaking. However, scholars are seeing more competitive elections, complete with vigorous campaigning. As long as China's leaders are committed to a one-party state, these local elections are the closest China will come to democracy.

Notes

1. China has eight officially recognized political parties in addition to the CCP. They do not contest the CCP's power, and they act in consultation with the CCP.

2. "More Grassroots Delegates to Attend Communist Party's Seventeenth Congress," *Xinhua,* August 3, 2007.

3. Each Central Committee now sits for five years, but the Seventh Central Committee lasted from 1945 to 1956, and the Eighth from 1956 to 1969.

4. The Chinese borrowed the *nomenklatura* system from the Russian communists. The *nomenklatura* are a small elite group within China who hold various key administrative positions in all spheres of the country's activity, such as in government, industry, agriculture, education, and so on, whose positions are granted only with the CCP's approval.

5. Party committees at the provincial level are elected by provincial-level congresses that convene every five years. County-level party congresses convene every three years and elect a committee, standing committee, and secretary. Below the county, the general branch committee meets twice a year and is elected for a two-year term. The party branch, or lowest level of party organization, meets four times a year and elects a branch committee for a two-year term.

6. Gang Guo, "Party Recruitment of College Students in China," *Journal of Contemporary China* 14, no. 43 (2005): 374.

7. Gang, "Party Recruitment," 376.

8. Gang, "Party Recruitment," 385.

9. Jiang Xiaowei, "An Assessment of Major Theoretical Perspectives of Elite Recruitment."

10. For more information on the CCP's strategy for recruiting capitalists, see Dickson, *Wealth into Power.*

11. Hu Jintao, "Hold High the Great Banner of Socialism."

12. Gradual implementation will take time. The September 2009 Third Plenum of the Seventeenth Party Congress omitted reference to intraparty democracy.

13. Hu Jintao, "Hold High the Great Banner of Socialism."

14. Hu Jintao, "Hold High the Great Banner of Socialism."

15. The 1982 constitution raised the age from thirty-five to forty-five.

16. Lieberthal, *Governing China,* 216.

17. Lieberthal, *Governing China,* 219–232.

18. Adopted from "Brief Introduction to Shandong Provincial People's Government," http://www.gov.cn/english/2005-11/02/content_89098.htm.

19. Lieberthal, *Governing China.*

20. An autonomous region is a provincial-level administrative division largely populated by one or more minority ethnic groups. Like a province, an autonomous region has its own local government, but has more legislative rights. China's five autonomous regions are Guangxi, Inner Mongolia, Ningxia, Tibet, and Xinjiang.

21. A special administrative region (SAR) is a local administrative area directly under the central government. China's constitution specifically empowers the state to establish special administrative regions when necessary. China currently has two SARs: Hong Kong and Macau.

22. Some provinces also have prefectures between the province and county levels. Prefectures are administrative rather than political entities, so they do not have people's congresses or people's governments, and their leaders are appointed by higher levels.

23. The State Bureau of Customs collected customs duties.

24. Zhang Le-Yin, "Chinese Central-Provincial Fiscal Relationships."

25. Wang Shaoguang, "China's 1994 Fiscal Reform," 801.

26. "Fiscal Reform: Disentangling the Public Purse Strings," *China Development Brief,* January 25, 2007. Monetary equivalents for yuan are given in US dollars unless otherwise noted.

27. The duration for meetings is different at each level of government. Generally, it takes one to two days for meetings at a township level, three to five days at a county level, and seven to ten days at a province level.

28. Autonomous counties are minority-populated areas within nonautonomous provinces. For example, Sichuan Province has autonomous counties populated by Tibetans.

29. International Republican Institute, *People's Republic of China: Election Observation Report,* 14.

30. The National People's Congress gave the central government's Ministry of Civil Affairs responsibility for overall guidance on implementing the Organic Law.

31. O'Brien and Lianjiang, *Rightful Resistance in Rural China,* 55.

32. O'Brien, "Villagers, Elections, and Citizenship in Contemporary China," 422.

33. International Republican Institute, *People's Republic of China: Election Observation Report,* 14.

34. For an examination of voter interest, see O'Brien, "Villagers, Elections, and Citizenship in Contemporary China," 407–435.

35. International Food Policy Research Institute, *China: Impact of Public Investments at the Village Level.*

36. Congressional-Executive Commission on China, *Village Elections in China.*

37. For more information on the political impact of rural elections, see O'Brien, "Villagers, Elections, and Citizenship in Contemporary China."

5 Political Reform

The Chinese people reacted to the announcement of Mao's death in September 1976 with anxiety and bewilderment. Although some people were genuinely grieved by his passing, in many cases displays of grief were staged for the benefit of others who might question one's reverence for Chairman Mao. Beyond their grief at the loss of the Great Helmsman, the Chinese people lost a sense of national direction. Mao had purged or demoted each of his heirs apparent—Liu Shaoqi, Deng Xiaoping, and Lin Biao. The issue of Mao's succession and the direction of post-Mao China raised questions concerning China's political future. Would Mao's successor follow Mao's political and economic philosophies, or would a successor make radical changes to China's political economy? Would China's leaders continue mass political campaigns, or follow a more moderate path?

In October 1976, the party leadership ordered the arrest of the Gang of Four. Unlike the announcement of Mao's death, the Gang's arrest was met with raucous celebration. The Cultural Revolution had torn the fabric of Chinese culture and society. It had destroyed Chinese values, banned Western ideas of democracy, and corrupted socialism, leaving an ideological vacuum. It had hurt the legitimacy of the Chinese Communist Party (CCP), and millions of Chinese were left with physical and psychological scars. China had a stagnant economy and largely isolationist foreign policy. Mao's death and the incarceration of the Gang of Four gave China's leaders the opportunity to change the direction of the country's politics and economy. The initial years after Mao's death were a time of seeking direction. Mao's successor, Hua Guofeng, tried to continue Mao's policies, earning him the label "whateverist" for his penchant to argue that China should continue whatever policies Mao had ordained. In an attempt to depart from the whateverist line, Hua initiated a program of grand infrastructure projects. His tenure as China's leader was limited, however, as he lacked Mao's history, credentials, and charisma. The most dramatic changes to China's political and economic order came after Deng Xiaoping consolidated his position as China's paramount leader in the early 1980s. Deng's initial goals

143

were to restore the legitimacy of the CCP, reform the Chinese economy, and open China to the world. Noticeably absent was any agenda to liberalize—to open or democratize—China's government and politics. Deng and his supporters, the so-called reformers, would run into opposition by party hardliners (leftists) at nearly every turn. Deng's death in 1997 ushered in a new generation of party leaders with their own agendas. China's second, third, and fourth generations of leaders each initiated new programs and policies. This chapter examines the progression of political reform in China under Deng Xiaoping and his successors.

The Rise and Fall of Hua Guofeng and the Whateverists

Soon after the deaths of Mao and of Premier Zhou Enlai, Hua Guofeng became acting premier, passing over Deng Xiaoping, who had been recently rehabilitated. In spring 1976, the CCP leadership had blamed Deng and his supporters for riots that had taken place over Zhou Enlai's memorials in Tiananmen Square. After denouncing Deng and removing him from his party posts for a second time in his career, party leaders appointed Hua premier and first vice chair of the CCP. In the last days before his death, Mao allegedly wrote to Hua, "With you in charge, I am at ease." In October 1976, within a month of Mao's death, Hua ordered the arrest of Mao's widow, Jiang Qing, and the rest of the Gang of Four, effectively ending the Cultural Revolution.[1] Jiang Qing and her associates became scapegoats for the Cultural Revolution, shifting political heat away from the party leadership. In October, the CCP made Hua chair of the party and chair of the Central Military Commission (CMC). Wearing these three hats, Hua assumed the ultimate power of the party, state, and military.

Hua's political career, which had blossomed during the Cultural Revolution, was rooted in his loyalty to Mao and Mao Zedong Thought. Once in power, Hua had little room to maneuver away from Mao Zedong Thought. In 1977, Hua publicly espoused his "two whatevers" formula: "Whatever decisions made by Chairman Mao, we must resolutely uphold; whatever directives were issued by Chairman Mao, we must follow without fail." Hua built a large public mausoleum in Tiananmen Square to house Mao's sarcophagus, and he led a committee to edit the remainder of Mao's *Selected Works.*[2]

Despite his annunciation of the whateverist line, Hua was critical of the excesses of the Cultural Revolution. He gradually repealed many Cultural Revolution edicts and practices. He allowed the performance of once-banned movies, plays, and operas, and the publication of literary journals. This latter move evoked the outpouring of bridled-up emotion concerning the pain of the Cultural Revolution. Several young writers published accounts of their experience as Red Guards or as "sent down" youth. One of the earliest of these accounts available in the West was Liang Heng's *Son of the Revolution.* Hua also undid many of the Cultural Revolution's egalitarian educational policies, returning

China to the elitist educational system of the 1950s. Hua intended that his cultural and educational reforms would gain the support of China's intellectuals for the Four Modernizations, a plan to update China's agriculture, industry, science and technology, and national defense.[3] Most intellectuals remained skeptical of Hua because of his close relationship to Mao during the Cultural Revolution. His policies, however, would soon allow them to express their anti-Mao sentiments.

Hua was convinced that greater incentives and higher investment would achieve rapid rates of growth. In 1978, Hua announced an ambitious ten-year development program as part of his "Great Leap Outward" to transform China into a great, modern, and socialist country by the end of the century. Hua encouraged mechanization of agriculture and instituted material incentives for farmers to stimulate agricultural output. To modernize industry and increase industrial production, Hua proposed 120 large-scale projects, all of which required imports of foreign technology and large infusions of cash. China's leaders poured state funds into the projects. China's rate of investment rose to 36.5 percent of national output in 1978, higher than at any time since the founding of the People's Republic of China (PRC) other than the Great Leap Forward.[4] The investment was to be funded by China's oil exports, but China's leaders expanded imports faster than they raised foreign currency to pay for them. China's leaders turned to foreign governments, particularly to Japan, for loans. With the loans, China's leaders signed contracts worth hundreds of millions of US dollars.

Hua's Ten-Year Plan was too ambitious, and it was abandoned after one year. China's central leadership forced Hua to resign his position as premier in September 1980 and as chairman of the CCP and the CMC in June 1981.

The Rise of Deng Xiaoping and the Reformers

After Mao's death, Deng Xiaoping had secretly returned to Beijing. Although Deng was able to come out of hiding after the Gang's arrest, Hua was reluctant to rehabilitate Deng because he posed a challenge to Hua's authority. In July 1977, however, Deng's supporters in the party and military were instrumental in reinstating him. Deng enjoyed the support of the military and party and state bureaucrats because he had forged strong and lasting relationships with many of them as a leader in the Jiangxi Soviet and participant in the Long March, as a political commissar of the army during Japanese occupation and the Chinese civil war, and as general secretary of the CCP from 1956 to 1966.

Deng also enjoyed widespread support because he challenged Mao ideologically. Whereas Mao stressed strict adherence to ideological orthodoxy, Deng was more pragmatic. Deng argued that the correct approach was to "seek truth from facts," and to adapt Marxism to China's political and economic realities.

Deng's "white cat–black cat" adage—"No matter whether a cat is black or white, if it catches mice, it's a good cat"—encapsulates his philosophy that it does not matter what method one uses so long as it gets the job done. This meant that it did not matter if China's leaders used socialism or capitalism to achieve its goals. Unlike Mao, Deng put economics, and not politics, in command. Rehabilitated again in 1977, Deng was directly responsible for education, science and technology, military affairs, and foreign affairs. He immediately began to prepare a reform agenda.

Deng was convinced that China's existing economic system retarded economic growth and development and that reform would achieve rapid improvement. Deng's chief opponent in reforming the economy was Chen Yun. Chen Yun in the 1950s was the architect of the relatively successful First Five-Year Plan and claimed that socialism was the best way for China to develop its economy. He argued that the failures of the 1960s and 1970s came not from the system per se but from mistakes, inadequate controls, and poor implementation. He argued that China was too poor and its population too large to produce enough goods to meet demand, and that price controls were necessary to avoid inflation.[5] Chen Yun espoused the birdcage theory of economic development. He argued that the economy was like a bird. If the government allowed the economy complete freedom, it would get out of hand. If the government controlled the economy with a tight fist, the economy would die. But if the government managed the economy with set limits and parameters, the economy, like a bird in a cage, would be free to grow and develop, but not fly out of control.

To move ahead with his agenda, Deng needed the support of reformers like himself as well as of those who had the power to block his reforms. After his return to Beijing, Deng Xiaoping had been working to reinstate his supporters, and he consolidated his authority by bringing his protégés into power. In 1978, Deng began to move his supporters from the provinces, where they held powerful party and state positions, to the central government in Beijing. His two key protégés were Hu Yaobang and Zhao Ziyang. Other supporters were Hu Qiaomu, Peng Zhen, and Wang Zhen. The Third Plenum of the Eleventh Party Central Committee in December 1978 endorsed Deng's philosophy. Despite Hua's official government and party positions, Deng Xiaoping was the de facto leader of the plenum. The plenum moved the party's focus from class struggle to economic modernization and announced that the era of mass movements was over. In the ensuing months, Deng and his supporters outlined an ambitious program of agriculture, industry, intellectual, and political reform. Between December 1978 and February 1980, several of Deng's supporters and fellow reformers joined the Politburo or Standing Committee. They included Zhao Ziyang, Hu Yaobang, Peng Zhen, and Wang Zhen. Zhao Ziyang was also appointed vice premier.

In February 1980, the CCP reinstated the position of party general secretary, which had been suspended during the Cultural Revolution. Deng appointed reformer Hu Yaobang to the position and gave him responsibility for national policymaking. Previously, national policymaking had been vested in the Politburo under Hua's leadership. Hu's appointment undercut Hua's authority as party chairman, and in August 1980, Hua Guofeng resigned the premiership. Zhao Ziyang succeeded Hua as premier.

Early Economic Reforms

Deng and his fellow reformers claimed that economic development necessitated moving away from a planned economy, which the Chinese had adopted from the Soviets soon after establishing the PRC. Under the First Five-Year Plan (1953–1957), China created a socialist economy, with economic planning housed in huge central government bureaucracies, and placed emphasis on heavy industry with a high rate of investment. Throughout the 1950s, 1960s, and 1970s, various political campaigns disrupted production and transportation of agricultural and industrial goods. By the time of Mao's death in 1976, agricultural productivity and income were flat. Communes had locked the rural population into agriculture. State control over food supplies kept farmers poor because the state set prices for agricultural produce artificially low, depriving farmers of much-needed revenue for investment in their farms and causing government agencies to ration food to urban consumers and rural households, limiting the population's caloric intake. Industrial production was growing, but it was not contributing to China's economic development in a meaningful way. Productivity and income stagnated because China was engaged in extensive rather than intensive economic growth. While extensive growth of a country's gross domestic product (GDP) increases production and demand, intensive growth (per capita GDP growth) increases resource productivity as well as production and consumption rates. Industrial economies tend to gradually replace extensive growth with intensive growth, allowing for both population growth and a substantial rise in GDP per capita.

China's reformers began economic reform immediately after consolidating their positions in the 1978 Third Plenum of the Eleventh National Party Congress. At the December 1978 plenum meeting, Deng had announced the Four Modernizations: the drive to improve agriculture, industry, science and technology, and national defense. The goal of the modernization program was to achieve a comparatively comfortable standard of living by the end of the twentieth century.[6]

Achievement of the Four Modernizations required a radical restructuring of China's economy, in essence a second revolution. The restructuring began in experimental fashion and moved in cycles of advancement and retrenchment throughout the 1980s and 1990s. By the end of the twentieth century, China's economy had been radically transformed into a market-oriented economy.

Deng Xiaoping and the reformers began their market-oriented reforms in the agricultural sector because it was increasingly apparent that Chinese agriculture was inadequate to support the modernization drive and because further urban development would require a strong agricultural base. In 1978, communes in several of China's provinces introduced an experimental "responsibility system," which assigned production teams production quotas. After the requisite produce was turned over to the collective, production teams or households could dispose of any production surplus as they wished. They could consume it, sell it to the state at state-mandated prices, or sell it on revived local agricultural markets at market prices. In 1980, the party's Central Committee recommended adoption of a household responsibility system (HRS), which returned agriculture to family-based farming. The HRS allowed the dismantling of the communes as individual families were able to lease land from their local government for a period of fifty-five years. Households were allowed control of agricultural goods produced above the state quota and could keep profits after remitting taxes to the state. The HRS was the first major capitalist reform promoted by the state. By 1984, 98 percent of China's farm households were participating in the HRS. In 1979–1980, the central government increased procurement prices for agricultural products. It also froze quotas for mandatory deliveries to the state and allowed farmers to sell quota surpluses at the higher prices on open markets. Price reform and implementation of the HRS changed the landscape of China. The ability to make and keep a profit provided farmers the necessary material incentive to boost production. Agricultural production shot up 9 percent and farmers branched out into sideline trades, such as cash crops and husbandry. This trend continued until the state shifted the focus of reform from the countryside to the cities in 1984.

The spectacular success of the early agricultural reform made a strong case for extending market-oriented reforms to state industry, and disarmed critics like Chen Yun who were skeptical of changes in the state factories. From 1978 to 1985, Deng moved full speed ahead in implementing radical reform in agriculture and industry. Not until grain production leveled off in the second half of the 1980s did Chen Yun and his followers start to make serious trouble for the reforms and the leaders identified with them, namely Hu Yaobang and Zhao Ziyang.

China's reformers followed agricultural reform with reform of industry. Under the Soviet model of development, China had invested heavily in heavy industry to the neglect of light industry, particularly consumer goods. During the Mao years, the few industries that produced consumer goods made such shoddy goods that no one wanted to buy them. The Chinese people made do with their old furniture and household goods rather than buy shoddy new ones. Millions of Chinese people literally stuffed their meager household savings under the mattress. By the early reform era, the Chinese people had accrued substantial savings. Tapping into these funds, China's reformist leadership actively encouraged collective and private enterprises after 1978. The main rationale for this policy was the need to provide jobs for millions of unemployed urban youth.

In rural areas, town and village enterprises (see Chapter 7), which were collectively owned by local governments and private investors, sprang up and employed farmers displaced by the abandonment of the communes. Once legalized, collective and private enterprises flourished because they operated outside the plan and met market demand. In 1979, Deng announced his Open Door policy to encourage foreign investment in China. To attract foreign investment, Deng opened four special economic zones (SEZs) in the coastal cities of Shenzhen, Zhuhai, Xiamen, and Shantou (see Chapter 7).

In the early years of reform, the central government nurtured private, nonstate firms with preferential treatment that gave them competitive advantages over state enterprises. First, the government offered them low tax rates. For instance, in 1983, the government granted nonstate enterprises a 35 percent tax rate versus a 55 percent rate for state firms. Second, it allowed collectives and nonstate firms to retain all their own profits, while it still required state firms to submit some profits to the state. Third, the state placed no restriction on employees' salaries, thereby allowing collective and nonstate firms to attract the employees who were not reliant on state benefits from state firms. These new employees included the young, better-educated, and better-skilled sector of the workforce who was willing to forgo state benefits for much higher pay.

In the early reform era, resistance by China's leftists would have made it impossible for the reformers to replace the command economy with a market one. Instead, China's reformers found it easier to legalize the nonstate economy than to deregulate the state economy. Hence, they began to allow the private, nonstate sector to develop as a supplement to the state economy. Allowing the nonstate sector to merely supplement the state sector had the added advantage of not appearing to threaten anyone's vested interests in the state sector. In 1979, China's reformist leaders began to allow urban authorities to issue business licenses to private entrepreneurs, thereby allowing the nonstate sector, which would operate totally in the market, to operate alongside the state sector. As discussed in Chapter 7, when the nonstate sector took off, managers of state enterprises were forced for the first time to compete with nonstate (collective and private) factories. Soon, many managers of state enterprises began to advocate expanding market freedoms for their firms.

While reformers were pushing for economic liberalization, party hardliners wanted to maintain the socialist road. Ironically, the early economic reforms gave the conservatives adequate ammunition to challenge the reforms. As mentioned in Chapter 4, tax reform allowed state firms and local (subnational) governments to retain a larger share of their profits and revenue, causing a shortfall at the national level and a sizable national budget deficit. Imports, especially of capital goods needed to support large infrastructure projects, well exceeded exports, resulting in an unparalleled trade deficit of $3.9 billion. At the end of 1980, opponents of reform mustered enough political support to force economic retrenchment. The central government halted thousands of investment projects in response to overextended capital investment and a high inflation rate. The Sixth Five-Year Plan (1981–1985), however, gave a green light to some 288 projects, and in 1982, overall large-scale investment began again. In 1983, China's leaders ordered national implementation of the household responsibility system, and in 1985 replaced the mandatory state procurement of grain with a more voluntary contract system.

In 1984, Deng announced the beginnings of the *socialist commodity economy,* which meant that the production of goods and services would be determined by the market rather than by central government planning. Although the central government would still set goals for the economy, the government would increasingly use taxes as well as price, wage, and interest rates to regulate the economy. In addition to this marketization of the economy, the socialist commodity economy redefined property-use rights. Land and other means of production would continue to be owned collectively or by the state, but individuals could use and even inherit the land. The party adopted these reforms at the Central Committee's plenary session in 1984. At this meeting, the Central Committee stressed the need to "build socialism with Chinese characteristics," meaning reforming the economy using capitalist techniques while retaining the centralized Leninist party-state.

China's GDP grew an average of 10 percent throughout the Sixth Five-Year Plan (1981–1985), making China one of the world's fastest-growing developing nations. Agriculture and industry overfulfilled their targets set for annual growth, however, and China's economy once again began to overheat. China's economy grew 12 percent in 1984 and 1985, and state investment grew 25 percent in 1984 and 43 percent in 1985. Industrial production increased by 20 percent in 1984. The wage bill, bloated by bonuses paid to workers as part of their wages, rose by more than 17 percent from 1983 to 1985.[7] Despite this economic growth, many Chinese people felt that capitalist development was actually hurting them. Lifting price controls on agricultural products, and later consumer goods, had resulted in inflation. Inflation in Beijing reached 30 percent in early 1985, hurting factory workers and lower-paid government employees. At the same time, the fast flow of money and the expansion of government programs fed official corruption, which exploded into several financial scandals. In agriculture, many farmers had moved out of grain production into more lucrative cash crops, causing a decline in the supply of grain and an increase in food prices.

By 1985, China suffered from overextended capital investment, raging inflation, and a visible decline of the living standard of the people. The Chinese people were beginning to criticize Deng Xiaoping openly. By early 1986, the overheating of the economy and tensions forced the party to suspend further experimental economic reforms. China's leaders tightened import controls and imposed austerity measures, including slashing credit to state and nonstate firms, forcing factories to close and lay off employees. This tightening of credit had the desired effect of slowing the money supply and cooling the economy. By the end of the year, however, Deng and Premier Zhao Ziyang had garnered enough support among the reform-minded leadership to resume market-oriented reforms. Zhao encouraged further foreign trade and investment along China's coast and an expansion of the SEZs. He also suggested that state enterprises operate as independent economic units and that they eliminate job security and a host of employee benefits.

After coming to power in the late 1970s, Deng Xiaoping focused his efforts on revitalizing the Chinese economy because Mao's policies had retarded China's economic growth and development. However, Deng also recognized that Mao's penchant for continual revolution and his political campaigns had caused the Chinese people much suffering and that China's politics needed reform if the CCP were to continue to have the support of the people. If Deng had run into resistance in reforming the economy, he had to tread even lighter in reforming China's politics.

Early Political Reforms

The Cultural Revolution cost the CCP much legitimacy. In the months following Mao's death, in September 1976, Hua Guofeng did what was necessary to restore the party's legitimacy. He arrested the Gang of Four, rehabilitated purged urban intellectuals and party members, and substituted intraparty collective decisionmaking for Mao's absolute dictatorship. Hua left China's political institutions largely unchanged, however. Deng Xiaoping and his fellow supporters took reform a step further and sought to reform China's political institutions, within limits. In 1978, the Eleventh Party Congress adopted a new state constitution. Its immediate predecessor, the 1975 constitution, had a strong Maoist influence with its stress on mass politics and party supremacy. The 1975 constitution removed most provisions on individual rights and freedoms, eliminated the chairman of the PRC from the state structure, institutionalized the party's direct control of the state, and proclaimed China as a "socialist state of the dictatorship of the proletariat," as opposed to "a people's democratic state." It made the national legislature subordinate to the party and put the military under the control of the chairman of the party's Central Committee. The 1978 state constitution restored many provisions on legality and individual rights that had been removed in the 1975 constitution. For instance, it provided for freedom of speech, correspondence, publication, assembly, association, procession, demonstration, and freedom to strike. Deng Xiaoping was also responsible for the removal of denigrating class labels from certain groups of people in China, such as those released in June 1978, and the labels of other rightists.

Under Deng, China's leaders in 1979 restored political and civil rights to property owners and rich peasants, whom the party had labeled "enemies of the people" for thirty years. They ended discrimination against members of former class enemies and their descendants with respect to school enrollment, job assignment, and political activity (but only as long as they supported socialism). Deng and his supporters also reversed the verdict of the 1976 Tiananmen Square incident, and rioters were relabeled "revolutionary heroes" instead of "counter-revolutionaries." Deng Xiaoping ordered the release of some political prisoners, and in 1980 rehabilitated former president Liu Shaoqi posthumously. From 1977 to mid-1980, party leaders reversed the verdicts of and rehabilitated more than 2.8 million people, some posthumously.[8]

In 1977 and 1978, China experienced a brief period of political liberalization under Deng Xiaoping. During this so-called Beijing Spring, the CCP granted the Chinese people greater freedom to criticize the government, particularly the excesses of the Cultural Revolution and the Gang of Four. The Beijing Spring culminated in the Democracy Wall Movement, an outpouring of pent-up sentiment among a broad spectrum of Chinese society. Although the spring would be followed by a chill in January 1979, the Beijing Spring set the stage for the 1986 and 1989 protests at Tiananmen Square.

Beijing Spring: The Democracy Wall Movement

In 1978, Deng Xiaoping, in an acknowledgment of the disastrous effects of the Cultural Revolution on the Chinese people, advocated revising the state constitution to grant more political freedoms and was able to insert into the new constitution the Four Big Rights (*sida*) of "speaking out freely, airing views fully, holding great debates, and writing big-character wall posters" (*dazibao*). These freedoms, coupled with the need to express angst over the excesses of the Cultural Revolution, spurred the Democracy Wall Movement in the fall of 1978.

The first poster appeared in mid-November on a large wall near the Beijing bus station. The poster attacked Mao by name and criticized him for his "wrong judgment" in calling for class struggle throughout the Cultural Revolution. Within a short time, activist organizations not formally associated with the CCP formed the Democracy Wall Movement, composed mostly of young factory and office workers and former Red Guards. The wall, dubbed the Democracy Wall, was soon covered with large-character posters, poems, drawings, and photographs criticizing Mao, the Gang of Four, and the instigators of the 1976 Tiananmen incident, and praising Zhou Enlai and Deng Xiaoping. The wall led to discussions of human rights, democracy, political reform, and other previously dangerous topics. Deng claimed that it was necessary to let the Chinese express their angst over the Cultural Revolution in a positive way so as to avoid emotion spilling over into criticism of the party. Deng also encouraged public pressure on China's leadership to rehabilitate victims of the Cultural Revolution. New posts went up on a nearly daily basis.

Within a few short months, however, the Democracy Wall Movement had gone from a random assemblage of posters and gatherings to a vociferous attack on Deng Xiaoping, the lack of personal freedoms, and human rights abuses. On December 5, 1978, Wei Jingsheng, an electrician at the Beijing Zoo and former Red Guard, posted his *dazibao,* "The Fifth Modernization." His poster argued that without democracy the Four Modernizations could not succeed. Wei's argument was a direct challenge to Deng Xiaoping, whose Four Modernizations embraced economic but not political liberalization as a sufficient basis for transforming China. Instead of using a pseudonym on his poster, as others had done, Wei brazenly included both his real name and address in Beijing.

Wei expanded on this theme in two articles in his journal, *Exploration (Tansuo)*. Wei claimed that Deng would turn into a dictator if the current political system persisted, and that there could be no modernization without democracy.[9] He argued that Marxism was the main source of socialist totalitarianism, and that Confucianism provided a better path for China's political liberalization. He also claimed that genuine reform was impossible under the existing system and under Deng's leadership.

Although Deng Xiaoping had been quietly supportive of the movement, he reversed course when the movement escalated to demonstrations throughout China. Deng Xiaoping, in March 1979, stated that realization of the Four Modernizations could not happen without upholding the Four Cardinal Principles: (1) adhering to upholding the socialist road, (2) dictatorship of the proletariat, (3) primacy of the CCP, and (4) Marxist Leninist–Mao Zedong Thought. Authorities

Democracy or a New Dictatorship?

"Everyone in China knows that the Chinese social system is not democratic and that this lack of democracy has severely stunted every aspect of the country's social development over the past thirty years. In the face of this hard fact there are two choices before the Chinese people. Either to reform the social system if they want to develop their society and seek a swift increase in prosperity and economic resources; or, if they are content with a continuation of the Mao Zedong brand of proletarian dictatorship, then they cannot even talk of democracy, nor will they be able to realize the modernization of their lives and resources. . . .

"Furthering reforms within the social system and moving Chinese politics toward democracy are prerequisites for solving the social and economic problems that confront China today. Only through elections can the leadership gain the people's voluntary cooperation and bring their initiative into play. Only when the people enjoy complete freedom and expression can they help their leaders to analyze and solve problems. Cooperation, together with policies formulated and carried out by the people, is necessary for the highest degree of working efficiency and the achievement of ideal results." (Wei Jingsheng, "Democracy or a New Dictatorship?" *Explorations,* March 1979) arrested activists throughout the spring. They arrested Wei Jingsheng on March 29, 1979, when his poster went too far, challenging the fundamental principles of the CCP. The government charged that his writing was "counterrevolutionary" because his posters slandered Marxism-Leninism and advocated abandonment of the socialist system, counter to the Four Cardinal Principles. Chinese authorities sentenced Wei to fifteen years in prison after a show trial in which he defended himself because there was no opportunity to hire a lawyer. One year later, the government deleted the Four Big Rights from China's constitution.

In April 1981, Deng ordered a nationwide crackdown on democratic activists and their unofficial journals and banned all wall posters. The Democracy Wall Movement fizzled out after the activists' arrests largely because it failed to garner the support of China's political elites. Deng's political supporters, such as Hu Yaobang and Zhao Ziyang, were not willing to jeopardize the reforms by backing an unorganized movement led by idealistic youth. Despite the apparent attractiveness of its demands to many of the Chinese people, the movement did not gain widespread popular support. Still recovering from the struggle of the Cultural Revolution, the Chinese people were leery of another mass movement. China's youth would renew their calls for democracy ten years later.

The Second Stage of Reform

Although Deng halted political liberalization when he crushed the Democracy Wall Movement in 1981, he returned to the issue with a new state constitution

Incarceration of Wei Jingsheng

In prison, Wei Jingsheng became China's best-known symbol of China's human rights abuses. His health deteriorated and his heart weakened. He lost most of his teeth and suffered from high blood pressure, arthritis, headaches, and depression. After Wei served fourteen years in prison, the Chinese government released him in 1993 on the eve of the International Olympic Committee's decision on whether to award the 2000 Olympic Games to Beijing. After speaking with dissidents and meeting with US assistant secretary of state John Shattuck, Wei was rearrested and sentenced to another fifteen years. His health deteriorated to such an extent that the government feared he would die in prison, making him a martyr. In 1997, the Chinese government released Wei on medical parole, putting him on a Northwest Airlines flight to Detroit. He was told that he would have to complete his sentence if he ever returned to China. Since 1997, Wei has traveled throughout the United States speaking out on China's human rights abuses and educating members of Congress on human rights in China.

in 1982. It gave the Chinese People's Political Consultative Conference (CPPCC) a larger role in policymaking. The new constitution aimed to distinguish between the functions of the party and state, thereby curbing the party's interference in state affairs. The 1982 constitution also restored the post of chairman of state, currently called the president. It established a *state* Central Military Commission to lead the military (although the membership is virtually the same as the party's CMC). The 1982 state constitution also puts the law above the party by declaring that the party is to carry out activities *within* the extent of the constitution and the law. Deng was responsible for the 1982 constitution, which, at least formally, institutionalized the rule of law. For instance, the 1982 state constitution specified for the first time that all Chinese citizens are equal before the law. It specified that all organs of state, political parties, the military, public organizations, enterprises, and institutions must abide by the law. It also put more emphasis on individual rights than did the 1978 constitution and restored or expanded most provisions on individual rights and freedoms that appeared in the 1954 constitution. The 1982 constitution dropped the right to propagate atheism (as contained in the 1978 version) and allowed "normal religious activities," but prohibited foreign domination of religious affairs. While the 1982 constitution restored many individual rights contained in the 1954 constitution, the state reserved the right to suspend individual rights if they appeared to contravene state security or social harmony, and there was no provision to interpret and supervise enforcement of the constitution. The 1982 constitution, however, was a victory for the reformers over the old Maoists. Despite its many shortcomings, the constitution's strength lay in its attempt to separate the functions of the party from those of the state.

After halting the Democracy Wall Movement, China's leaders tried to reassert control through a series of rectification campaigns. The campaigns included the Civilization and Courtesy Educational Movement, which emphasized good manners, discipline, and morality; the campaign against "bourgeois liberalism," directed against Western democratic influences; the 1986 campaign against "spiritual pollution," directed against pornography, greed, and decadent fashions; and a campaign against "unhealthy tendencies," such as vulgarity in the arts, corruption, extravagance, and waste. None of these campaigns got much traction, as the Chinese people had no interest in returning to the Maoist practice of mass campaigns against selected targets.

In 1986, Deng renewed his quest for economic and political reform and called for socialist democracy. In 1985, several of Deng's younger supporters had joined the Politburo, preparing the ground for realization of socialist democracy. One of these supporters was reformer and Politburo member Hu Qili. In a May Day 1986 speech, Hu Qili called for democratization of China's political system. He gained the support of Deng Xiaoping, who claimed that corruption and abuse of power were the result of the unchecked power of some party officials. In fall 1986, the party Secretariat, headed by Zhao Ziyang, created a task force to recommend political reforms. Prominent Chinese intellectuals and journalists supported Deng's call for political reform, and in the second half of 1986, began publicly to question Marxism. Most important, they called for an academic environment free of government censorship and political reprisals. In June 1986, Yan Jiaqi, director of the Institute of Political Science at the prestigious Chinese Academy of Social Sciences (CASS), wrote a broad critique of China's political system. Other intellectuals echoed Yan's critique and called for greater freedom of inquiry and further development of socialist democracy. Although Deng Xiaoping never defined socialist democracy, he nevertheless favored restructuring China's political system to make it more democratic. One method of democratizing China's political system was to make elections to people's congresses more competitive.

In November 1986, the National People's Congress passed an election law for selecting delegates to local people's congresses. Reformers and intellectuals were disappointed that the law left the nomination process in the hands of party-controlled election committees. Disappointment over the law and Deng's limited reforms was first expressed at the University of Science and Technology (known as Keda) in Hefei, the capital of Anhui Province. In December, students at Keda demonstrated against the election law and the lack of choice of candidates in forthcoming local elections. They demanded that China reform its one-party system into a multiparty system with competitive elections and abandon official ideology. Their protests won the support of Keda's vice president, astrophysicist Fang Lizhi, who earlier had equated the Four Cardinal Principles with superstition, dictatorship, conservatism, and dependency, and who had said that change could only come from below and from individuals, not from above. Throughout December, student protests spread to eleven provinces, leading to several arrests. At Keda, Fang Lizhi encouraged students to return to their classrooms, which they did in January 1987 in anticipation of their final exams.

China's leaders acted swiftly to punish demonstration participants and their supporters. Although they ordered the release of student demonstrators who had been arrested in December, workers who had been detained during the demonstrations remained in jail as counterrevolutionaries. The CCP expelled Fang Lizhi and removed him from his post as vice president of Keda. It removed journalist Liu Binyan from the staff of the *People's Daily* and expelled him from the party for the second time.[10] The party removed CCP general secretary Hu Yaobang in 1987, partly because of his efforts to curb corruption among the "princelings," the children of senior party leaders who enjoyed unusual privilege and wealth and many of whom were engaged in gross acts of corruption. Also, Hu's close ties to democratic intellectuals had angered party elders. Skirting formal party procedures, Deng and party elders at an informal meeting forced Hu to accept responsibility for the student demonstrations. The party appointed Zhao Ziyang CCP general secretary, and appointed Li Peng, a Soviet-trained technocrat, to replace Zhao as premier. Although Hu kept his seat on the Politburo and its Standing Committee, he was stripped of any political power. By the middle of January 1987, the government tried to suppress dissent by initiating a campaign against "bourgeois liberalization." Although the students terminated their protests, their demands had not been met. Their unmet grievances would lead students to return to nationwide protests in 1989, resulting in devastating consequences for the students, some of China's leaders, and prospects for democracy in China.

After the 1986 demonstrations, Deng put political reforms on hold as the party redoubled its efforts to reform the economy. Zhao Ziyang worked with Deng to accelerate the pace of economic development in the late 1980s. To prevent the economy from overheating, Beijing set a modest target growth rate of 7.5 percent in the Seventh Five-Year Plan (1986–1990) and scaled back government investment in the economy. Despite these measures, industrial production expanded by 18 percent in 1988, more than double the government's goal, indicating that the economy was overheating and spinning out of control. The overheating economy also played havoc with people's pocketbooks. In 1988, China's leaders imposed an austerity program designed to control inflation by imposing limits on borrowing and investment. The inflation rate reached 25 percent in early 1989, in spite of the austerity measures, exacerbating social discontent.

The 1989 Tiananmen Square Massacre

Social discontent came to a head in Tiananmen Square in spring 1989. Tiananmen Square is the geographical center of Beijing and is the world's largest public square. It is bound to the north by the Gate of Heavenly Peace (Tiananmen) and the Forbidden City, the former residence of the emperors. Ringing the three other sides of the square are the Great Hall of the People, the National Museum of China, and Mao's mausoleum. The square also houses the obelisk known as the Monument to the People's Heroes. The square has been the site of many historical events, such as Mao's proclamation of the establishment of the PRC, the gathering of millions of Red Guards during the Cultural Revolution, and the site of mourning for former premier Zhou Enlai, to name a few. More recently, the square has become a site for attempted protests, but more frequently for tourists and kite flying. In spring 1989, it became the site of massive protests and an infamous massacre.

By spring 1989, there was significant unrest in China's cities due to raging inflation, corruption, intraparty corruption, and the unfair privilege of the princelings. Retail price reform, initiated by Zhao Ziyang, resulted in inflation of more than 30 percent. Social discontent boiled over into student and then societywide demonstrations in spring 1989. Student discontent had been brewing for a long time. Although no large-scale student unrest had occurred since the

1986 protests, pent-up dissatisfaction had already boiled over into street demonstrations several times during 1988. The immediate cause of the protests varied. For example, at a dance at Hohai University in Nanjing, in December 1988, a brawl between some African students and Chinese students and staff had prompted angry protest marches denouncing the Africans for allegedly assaulting Chinese women and beating up other students. In other cases, the trigger had been an attack on students by hooligans. Thus, in spring 1988, after three unemployed youths killed a Peking University (Beijing University, or Beida) student in a confrontation in a restaurant near the campus, over a thousand Beida students marched to Tiananmen, demanding retribution and measures to improve school security and public order. But in each instance, the underlying cause for the demonstrations was the students' feeling that education and intellectuals were undervalued by the party and government. For instance, some Hohai University students had expressed resentment that the African students (who constituted the majority of third world students in China on Chinese government scholarships) received far larger living stipends and lived in less crowded and superior dorms. The Beida students saw evidence of the government's failure adequately to safeguard intellectuals from rougher elements of Chinese society.

Amidst this campus turmoil and social discontent, Beida students planned a demonstration for the seventieth anniversary of the 1919 May Fourth Movement. But an unanticipated event forced them to move up the date of the demonstration. Deposed party leader and reformer Hu Yaobang died on April 15, a week after suffering a heart attack at a Politburo meeting. Of peasant stock, Hu participated in the 1934 Long March and rose through the party ranks to become Deng Xiaoping's right-hand man. In the early and mid-1980s, Hu was in charge of day-to-day matters during China's economic and political liberalization. Standing only about five feet tall, Hu joked that Deng selected him because he was the only man in China shorter than the diminutive Deng Xiaoping. A Marxist to the end, Hu nevertheless pushed for rapid economic and political reform, particularly a freer political system. His forced resignation in 1987 after the student demonstrations angered those people clamoring for democracy and freedom. Many students had hoped Hu would be brought back one day to lead China in reform.

Upon hearing of his death, students at many of Beijing's universities made posters memorializing Hu and placed memorial wreaths in Tiananmen Square. Someone placed a large portrait of Hu Yaobang at the top step of the Monument to the People's Heroes. However, student response to Hu Yaobang's death quickly moved beyond mourning to heated protests for democracy, an end to corruption in the CCP, and freedom of the press. On the night before Hu Yaobang's state funeral, student activists gathered classmates from more than twenty universities in an overnight march to Tiananmen Square. During Hu's funeral on April 22, student leaders tried to deliver a petition to the Standing

Committee of the National People's Congress. The petition demanded that the government restore Hu Yaobang's reputation, repudiate the campaigns against bourgeois liberalization and spiritual pollution, allow citizens free speech and free press, lift restrictions on street protests, end official corruption by revealing the salaries and other wealth of party and government leaders and their families, increase funding for higher education, and raise salaries for teachers and other intellectuals. To the students' frustration and anger, no representative of the Standing Committee came out to meet them. In response, leaders of the newly established Beijing Students' Autonomous Union Preparatory Committee—with Wang Dan, Wu'er Kaixi, Ma Shaofang, Zhang Kai, and Zhou Yongjun as officers—voted to start a citywide class boycott. The student movement had begun.

After Hu's funeral, China's leaders turned their attention to the student protestors. On April 26, the *People's Daily*—the CCP's mouthpiece—published an editorial condemning the protests as "turmoil." The state China Central Television Service (CCTV) broadcast the editorial nationwide. The editorial was designed to send a clear message to the students that the government would not tolerate further demonstrations, but had the opposite effect of inflaming student passion.[11] In defiance of the editorial, 150,000 students from more than forty universities marched on Tiananmen the next day. In the following weeks, the student protests escalated in size and membership, with the public joining the marching students. Reporters from the official New China News Agency (Xinhua) joined hundreds of journalists from different Beijing publications, including the China News Service, the *Workers Daily,* and even the *People's Daily.* Protests also took place in China's other major cities and provinces and included not just students, but workers, government officials, and other residents.

In May, some students dropped out of the movement and returned to their classes while others, organized by the more charismatic student leaders—Wang Dan, Wu'er Kaixi, and Chai Ling in particular—favored stronger action and called for a hunger strike. Word of the hunger strike spread to students in other parts of China. Thousands of students flocked to Beijing to support their classmates.[12] In addition to their initial demands, students began calling for autonomous student unions to replace the official student organizations controlled by university party committees. China's leaders were losing patience with the occupiers of the square and tried to persuade the students to vacate before the arrival of Soviet leader Mikhail Gorbachev in mid-May. Talks with students collapsed, and the hunger strike continued when Gorbachev arrived in China. It was the first state visit between the former Soviet Union and China in thirty years and marked the ending of hostile relations between the two countries. It had been touted as a major diplomatic breakthrough, and China's leaders had planned a state welcoming ceremony in Tiananmen Square. Because the hunger strikers were occupying the square, China's leaders welcomed Gorbachev at the Beijing Airport, delaying for two hours the first meeting between China's president, Yang Shangkun, and Gorbachev at the Great Hall of the People. Tensions between the reformers, who believed they had tried a moderate approach with the students, and the old-guard party elders, who wanted to use a firmer hand, were coming to a boil. Deng Xiaoping began to wait impatiently for Gorbachev to leave so he could restore order in Beijing and elsewhere.

Sympathy for the hunger strikers and strong support for the student movement grew as ambulances sped to and from Tiananmen Square day and night. Even the official news media gave positive coverage of the movement. By May 16, the number of people fasting rose to 3,100, and many of those who had been fasting for days were beginning to collapse. Ambulances could be seen leaving the square as students began to pass out from lack of nutrition. The students' plight garnered the sympathy of the Chinese citizenry, and people demonstrated to urge the government to negotiate with the students to resolve the standoff. It was the participation of people of all occupations—journalists, office workers, manual laborers, government bureaucrats, police, and even PLA officers—that made China's leaders concerned that society in general might turn against the government. For instance, railway maintenance worker Han Dongfang and other workers established the Beijing Workers' Autonomous Union to advocate for nonofficial labor unions.

Although talks between the students and the government continued, they failed to result in any satisfactory agreements. During Gorbachev's visit, the size of demonstrations in Beijing swelled to more than a million people, with millions more protesting in at least a hundred other cities throughout China.[13] The foreign media, which had descended on Beijing to cover the Soviet leader's historic visit, set up operations in Tiananmen Square to offer worldwide coverage of the protests. Losing patience, Deng Xiaoping ordered the mobilization of troops from nearby provinces to Beijing. The troops began arriving in mid-May, but stayed in the rail yards outside of Beijing. Camped for weeks, the troops became weary waiting in their train cars. Local citizens trekked to the rail yards to greet the soldiers and offer them food. The CCP was in a hard place, exacerbating divisions between Li Peng and the hardliners and Zhao Ziyang and the reformers. Li Peng steadfastly refused Zhao's demand that the April 26 editorial be remanded.

At this point, Deng could not wait for Gorbachev to leave. Over Zhao's objections, the Politburo Standing Committee, led by Li Peng, Chen Yun, and their supporters, voted to impose martial law in Tiananmen Square. The martial law conditions banned processions, demonstrations, boycotts, and strikes and authorized the army and security apparatus to use all "means to handle matters forcefully," if necessary.[14] Hearing the decision, Zhao visited the students at Tiananmen Square, telling them that he had come "too late" and asking their forgiveness.[15] He disappeared from the square and was stripped of his party post soon thereafter.[16] On May 29, the Goddess of Democracy statue arrived in Tiananmen Square. Designed and constructed by students at a fashion institute, it was moved from the institute to the square in pieces to avoid detection and confiscation.

When troops moved into Beijing on the night of June 3–4, residents and workers stalled the tanks. Swarming the PLA vehicles, they argued that "the PLA are the friends of the people!" Residents built barricades to stop the troops, and some people even tried to block PLA trucks with their bodies. Despite these efforts, the PLA troops and vehicles moved on, the army tanks crushing the barricades and crushing people beneath their tracks. As defiant citizens attacked army vehicles, burning trucks and tanks and killing soldiers, the troops advanced on Beijing. They opened fire as they marched toward the square, killing civilians on their way to work. Most of the people who died outside of Tiananmen Square were not students. Many were innocent bystanders and commuters. Some of the victims were women and children. Most were killed on Chang'an Avenue, Beijing's main thoroughfare between Muxidi, a western suburb, and Tiananmen Square. When the troops moved to outside Tiananmen Square on June 3, student leaders Wu'er Kaixi, Wang Dan, Shen Tong, and Chai Ling wanted to clear the square. But other student leaders wanted the students to take a "democratic vote" on whether to leave the square. Students, many of them out-of-towners who had nowhere to go and no arrangements to return to their schools, voted to stay in the square. After midnight, troops, which had been ordered to clear the square, shot up the public address system and shut off the lights. The student leaders negotiated with the military a peaceful withdrawal of occupants of the square through the square's southwest corner. As they processed out of the square early on June 4, an infantry unit in the square fired into a large crowd of civilians, which had gathered in front of it, killing and wounding many people. Shooting continued throughout June 4. Several hundred, and possibly thousands, of civilians were killed on June 3–4.[17] Student leaders Wu'er Kaixi, Shen Tong, and Chai Ling were able to escape to Hong Kong and the West.[18] Wang Dan was number one on the list of "most wanted" students and was arrested on July 2 and sentenced to four years in prison. Union organizer Han Dongfang went into hiding, but unable to stay underground, turned himself in to authorities. He contracted tuberculosis in detention and was later released.

China's leadership imposed a news blackout for several days after June 4, followed by broadcasts of photos and identifications of movement activists, calling for Chinese citizens to turn them in. Broadcasts also memorialized members of the PLA and security apparatus killed on June 3–4 and aired scenes of the PLA helping ordinary citizens across China.

What had set off the spring 1989 movement, and why did it end so tragically? There are three explanations for the origins of the spring 1989 demonstrations: leadership struggle, social disaffection, and the failure of institutional reform. The first explanation posits that the Tiananmen Square protests were the catalyst of a power struggle being waged between CCP hardliners and reformers.

In the early 1980s, China's key reformers were paramount leader Deng Xiaoping, then CCP general secretary Hu Yaobang, and then Premier Zhao Ziyang. With Hu Yaobang sidelined after 1987, party hardliners who had fiercely resisted economic and political reform stepped up their criticism of newly appointed CCP general secretary Zhao Ziyang. Zhao thought that the protests were patriotic, but the hardliners, who viewed protests as a threat to stability, called for tough action to end the demonstrations.[19] Li Peng informed Deng that the demonstrators were making personal attacks by dropping little bottles (Xiaoping sounds like "little bottle" in Chinese) and shouting critical slogans to express their displeasure with Deng Xiaoping. Walking a political tightrope between the hardliners and reformers, Deng opted for martial law. The decision to impose martial law brought to a conclusion the power struggle that had been waged throughout the decade of reform. Temporarily, at least, the hardliners had won, and the result was tragic for China.

The second explanation is that popular dissatisfaction with the consequences of economic reform resulted in a societywide movement.[20] Economic reforms from 1978 through the mid-1980s were characterized by an equitable distribution of opportunities. Employees of China's state-owned enterprises worried that they would lose job tenure and benefits, the 1988–1989 austerity program forced rural businesses to close, and former farmers flocked to urban and coastal areas looking for work. By 1989, resentment against the new-moneyed elite reached explosive proportions, and all that was needed was a catalyst. Hu Yaobang's death in April 1989 was that catalyst. The students' demands focused on anticorruption and institutionalizing pluralist decisionmaking, not the development of opposition political parties or elections based on universal suffrage. Democracy to the students meant institutionalized rights of speech, demonstration, free press, independent student and labor unions, and an independent judicial system. Because Chinese history is replete with students (as intellectuals) at the forefront of movements, it was not the student movement per se that disturbed China's leaders but the added participation of labor that made them nervous. According to Leninist theory, the Communist Party is the leader of the proletariat. In May 1989, it appeared to China's leaders that the urban masses were turning against the party, and the party acted to maintain its control of society.

A third explanation for the demonstrations and their tragic end is the failure of Deng Xiaoping to change institutional structures of politics in China, namely, to resolve conflict through negotiations, bargaining, compromises, and accommodation. China scholar Tang Tsou claims that Tiananmen signified the latest in a series of failures in the twentieth century to rebuild the Chinese state, to restructure its society, and to establish a viable state-society relationship.[21] The students were at the forefront of an emerging civil society (defined as organizations, associations, and institutions organized by the citizenry, rather than forced by the government). Students wanted the right to form independent student unions. Deng, however, was a strong disciplinarian who valued the maintenance of ideological orthodoxy. Recognition of the legal status of the students' autonomous association would have required a fresh look at the Chinese communist system in which only one officially recognized association, under the strict guidance of the party, can carry out activities. The students were well aware of this impediment to their demands. The more radical of the student leaders—Chai Ling and her husband, Feng Congde, Wu'er Kaixi, and Wang Dan—were obstinate when they refused to leave the square. The CCP hardliners were likewise obstinate and refused to consider the students' demands. The result was defeat for the party moderates, and the hardliners won in a zero-sum game. The result was tragic for the students.

Post–Tiananmen Square

The protests of 1989 were the culmination of dilemmas experienced during the decade of reform from 1978 to 1988. The crackdown silenced society but did not solve the dilemmas themselves, primarily because Deng failed to reform China's political institutions. The Four Cardinal Principles continued to stifle debate on party and state policy. Infiltration of the party into every aspect of

---

Twenty Years After the Massacre

June 4, 2009, marked the twentieth anniversary of the massacre at Tiananmen Square. The Chinese Communist Party still maintains that military force was necessary to prevent "chaos." On the twentieth anniversary, China's leaders ordered the square closed, and hundreds of police patrolled the area surrounding the square. Government authorities prevented distribution of some foreign newspapers and blocked access to websites that contained sensitive material, including Twitter, the microblogging service. Ding Zilin, a former professor and party member, whose son Jiang Jielin was killed on June 3, 1989, planned a memorial at the square to mark the twentieth anniversary of her son's death. Although Chinese authorities allowed her organization, Tiananmen Mothers, to meet near the square, they prevented Professor Ding from leaving her apartment and joining them. Former student leader Wu'er Kaixi, who has been living in Taiwan for the past several years, said he intended to surrender to Chinese authorities to stand trial for his involvement in the demonstrations and to visit his parents on the mainland. Immigration authorities denied him entry to China.

Chinese textbooks refer to the 1989 protests as "political turmoil," and to the "barbaric masses" of Beijing citizens, rioting and burning army vehicles, killing soldiers, and attacking government ministries. The Chinese government refuses to release an official count of the dead and injured.

one's life by means of the secret police, a comprehensive network of neighborhood and village organizations, and a dossier system of files to keep watch on all citizens continued to stifle individual freedoms. The state continued to function as owner of the major means of production and communication, stifling entrepreneurial talent. The major obstacle to political development in China, however, was the inability of China's leadership to tolerate and harness society's discordant voices. After the tragedy at Tiananmen, students lost much of their enthusiasm for structural political reform.

In the early 1990s, Deng began a gradual retirement. At the same time, however, he made some of his strongest moves to open China's economy to the world. In November 1989, Deng Xiaoping resigned as chair of the party's CMC, and in March 1990 he resigned as chair of the state CMC. Deng Xiaoping now held no government or party posts. Retirement, however, did not mean that Deng completely removed himself from China's political scene. In the aftermath of Tiananmen, Chen Yun had successfully challenged Deng's authority in the party. Chen and his supporters were effective at blaming Deng for the crackdown and ensuing international ostracism, and they used Deng's vulnerability to undermine his reform agenda. Chen Yun's camp advocated central planning and slow growth. As a consequence, the 1991–1995 Eighth Five-Year Plan set a slower growth rate of about 6 percent a year. Despite challenges from the Chen camp, Deng, from 1990 until 1992, worked to revive party support for rapid growth. In January 1992, the eighty-seven-year-old Deng embarked on a Southern Tour to personally bless market-oriented reforms. He visited booming Guangzhou and delivered speeches aimed at setting off a new wave of economic growth. He urged Guangdong Province to try to join the ranks of the Asian Tigers by the year 2010. He visited the SEZs of Shenzhen, Shekou, and Zhuhai, where he supported the continuation of special policies to attract foreign investment. He reiterated the white cat–black cat theory about the acceptability of market forces and proposed the creation of stock markets in Shenzhen and Shanghai.[22] Deng's message was simple: China needed to move briskly ahead with economic growth and not slow the pace as Chen Yun, Yao Yilin, and Li Peng had recommended. Deng's Southern Tour reignited China's economy and reinstated his power as China's paramount leader. Deng reemerged as China's dominant leader at the October 1992 Fourteenth Party Congress.

Deng passed away in February 1997, ending the second generation of Chinese leaders.[23] The mantle passed to Jiang Zemin and the third generation of Chinese leaders. Jiang solidified his leadership position by elevating many of his supporters from Shanghai (commonly called the Shanghai Clique) to high government positions. In 1998, the Fifteenth Party Congress elevated Deng's economic czar, Zhu Rongji, to premier. It moved Li Peng, who had to step down after serving the maximum of two terms allowed by the constitution, to the National People's Congress to replace the retiring Qiao Shi. Li's change of position was the first by a top leader in response to constitutional requirements.[24]

After moving to the National People's Congress, Li lost a substantial portion of his political base and never again exercised the political power that he had commanded in the late 1980s.

The Third Generation of Chinese Leadership

At his ascension to full leadership of the CCP and PRC in 1997, Jiang Zemin was considered by many to be a consensus candidate, one who would be a temporary officeholder until a stronger leader rose through the party ranks to lead China. This belief was based on Jiang's apparent lack of the kind of relations

---

Jiang Zemin

The third of five children, Jiang was born in 1926 in Yangzhou in Jiangsu Province. He earned a degree in electrical engineering at Shanghai Jiao Tong University and joined the CCP in 1946 while still a student. After training in Moscow, Jiang served as an executive for several state industrial enterprises. He eventually transferred to government service and held various positions in the Chinese bureaucracy. In 1982 he was elected to the Central Committee and in 1983 became minister of electronics industries. Elected mayor of Shanghai in 1985, he subsequently became party chief of Shanghai in 1985. He was elected to the Politburo in 1987.

Jiang Zemin ascended to power during the spring 1989 purges and was part of the decisionmaking apparatus even before the imposition of martial law on May 20. He closed Shanghai's *World Economic Herald,* earning him the praise of the hardliners. After Zhao's purge, Jiang was elected a member of the Politburo's Standing Committee. He became CCP general secretary in 1989, becoming Deng's heir apparent. In late 1989, he was elected chair of the party CMC, and in 1990 was elected chair of the state CMC. After the crackdown at Tiananmen, however, Jiang sided with those who wanted to put the brakes on capitalist-oriented reform. Deng's Southern Tour seems to have converted Jiang. Although Jiang held China's key party and state leadership positions, he lacked the authority that Deng possessed. Many observers both in and outside of China believed that Jiang was merely a transitional figure until a more powerful leader could be found. Needing Deng's support to maintain his legitimacy, Jiang, in 1992, began to push for the more rapid economic growth that Deng was calling for. In particular, Jiang favored more foreign investment in China. In 1993, Jiang coined the new term *socialist market economy* to describe the transformation of China's centrally planned socialist economy into a government-regulated, capitalist market economy. He became PRC president in 1993 and assumed full leadership of the state, party, and military after Deng's death in 1997.

with the PLA that Mao and Deng had enjoyed. Much of Mao's and Deng's legitimacy was rooted in their participation in the Long March and because they were part of the generation that fought both the Japanese and the Nationalists, leading the Chinese communists to victory in 1949. Mao is considered one of the founding fathers of the PLA and, as CMC chairman, was China's supreme military authority. Deng served as the political commissar of the PLA Second Field Army and worked closely with military leaders in the southwest administrative region in the early years of the People's Republic. The Long March and the Sino-Japanese War solidified both Mao's and Deng's relations with the PLA, and during their tenures as China's leader, the PLA lent first Mao and then Deng their support. Jiang did not have that history. He lacked military experience, knowledge of military affairs, and connections in the PLA.[25] Jiang appears to have been elevated to CMC chief only because Deng Xiaoping put pressure on the military chiefs to back him. The military's tepid response to Jiang as leader of the armed forces weakened him politically. During his tenure as party chief and state president, Jiang could not count on the military's unconditional support and was continuously aware that he would need to compromise to gain their support at the time of any potential crisis.

Despite his relatively weak position and some early doubts about his legitimacy, Jiang exercised considerable political power for a decade. His leadership positions in the party and state hierarchy (CCP general secretary, PRC president, and party and state CMC chief) gave him the authority necessary to lead China. He also moved his trusted supporters (the Shanghai Clique) into positions of power in the central government and party hierarchy. He enhanced his standing with the military by supporting the modernization of the PLA. Under Jiang, China doubled its military expenditures not once, but twice. At the same time, Jiang undermined the ability of the PLA to intervene in politics by interviewing every senior officer prior to his promotion and promoted each one based on his qualifications rather than on personal connections. Jiang's position also benefited from the fact that none of his potential rivals had close relations with the military that could undermine his authority in a future struggle.[26] He also ordered the PLA to divest from its commercial enterprises. During the 1980s reform era, China's leaders had given economic development priority over the military. Faced with decreasing funding, the PLA turned to producing its own weapons and matériel as well as opening businesses to generate extra funds. By 1997, the PLA had built a commercial empire that included as many as twenty thousand businesses involved in everything from manufacturing to hospitality. The PLA's businesses earned an estimated $25 billion a year. Due to concerns that these commercial pursuits were breeding corruption in the PLA and interfering with military effectiveness, in July 1998 Jiang ordered the PLA to divest from its commercial interests no later than the end of the year. This order also applied to officials in the judiciary and other security agencies. The PLA largely complied with Jiang's order, though not within the set deadline. PLA officers were reluctant to give up the wealth provided by their business interests.[27]

During his tenure, Jiang is also credited with sustaining China's economic boom, making inroads to cracking down on corruption, overseeing the 1997 handover of Hong Kong from Great Britain to China, China's 2002 accession to the World Trade Organization, and Beijing's successful bid to host the 2008 Summer Olympics. Under Jiang and Zhu Rongji, China sustained an average of 8 percent GDP growth annually, achieving the highest rate of per capita economic growth in major world economies. This feat was mostly achieved by continuing the process of transition to a capitalist economy. China carried out reform of state-owned enterprises during the Jiang years, either closing or merging weaker firms with stronger ones, converting state firms into shareholding corporations, privatizing smaller state enterprises, and letting the weakest go bankrupt. By the end of Jiang's presidency in 2003, the private sector accounted for nearly 50 percent of GDP. China became the most attractive foreign direct investment (FDI) destination in the world. In 2003, FDI in China reached $53.5 billion, up from $41.7 billion at the beginning of Jiang's tenure in 1997. Total foreign trade exceeded $800 billion, more than double the 1997 figure. In 2003, China held more than $404 billion in foreign reserves, up from $143 billion in 1997.

Throughout his tenure as party and state leader, Jiang struggled to get a handle on official corruption in China. In the 1980s and 1990s, many Chinese took to heart Deng's statement that "to get rich is glorious." The booming economy offered them boundless opportunities and many entrepreneurial Chinese had entered the class of the nouveau riche. Much of these riches were ill-gotten gains, however. Party members and their offspring, the princelings, were in a unique position to use their party positions and personal connections (*guanxi*) for self-gain. Public anger at official corruption had been one of the key issues in the demonstrations of the winter of 1987 and spring of 1989. Fearing that official corruption would undermine the legitimacy of the CCP, Jiang made an effort to combat and punish corruption. At his keynote speech at the Fifteenth Party Congress in 1997, Jiang called official corruption "a grave political struggle" challenging the very existence of the party. The biggest fish Jiang caught in his anticorruption campaign was Politburo member and Beijing mayor (and former Beijing party chief) Chen Xitong.[28] Chen was mayor of Beijing during the spring 1989 demonstrations and claimed that only a few hundred people had been killed in the June 4 massacre. He ruled the city with such control that Beijing residents called it the "Chen System," a play on his given name––Xitong (a homonym for *system* in the Chinese language). Chen took advantage of China's market-oriented reforms for huge personal gain, accruing several mistresses and private secretaries, and luxury villas. Despite launching anticorruption campaigns in 1989 and in 1993, in which Jiang promised to catch both "tigers" (high-level party and state officials and their offspring) and "flies" (ordinary citizens), Chen remained untouched.

The unraveling of the Chen System began in late 1994 when the McDonald's fast-food restaurant on the corner of Wangfujing Avenue was sold to make way for a huge new $2 billion Hong Kong–financed real estate development.[29] In the mid-1990s, Chen embarked on a modernization of Beijing in a bid to host the 2000 Olympic Games and sought to build the massive Oriental Tower on the McDonald's site. He and his staff demanded major bribes in return for construction contracts. In 1995, Jiang ordered that Chen be removed from the Politburo and be expelled from the party. Chen's expulsion lifted his immunity from criminal prosecution and sent a signal that Jiang would not tolerate corruption by high party officials and their offspring.[30] Investigators had shown that Chen had taken $67,000 from state funds and drained $2.5 billion from public coffers to "support a decadent and corrupt life." Chen was sentenced to sixteen years' imprisonment for corruption and dereliction of duty. Chen's conviction was part of a five-year-long crackdown on corruption. Another forty officials were arrested, and a Beijing court sentenced his son to twelve years' imprisonment for accepting bribes and embezzling funds. Soon after, Zhou Beifang, a close associate of Deng Xiaoping's son Deng Zhifang, was sentenced to a two-year suspended death sentence for offering and taking bribes while serving in the Hong Kong–based International Trade and Engineering Company and Concord Grand, both subsidiaries of Beijing's Capital Iron and Steel Company (Shoudu). The day after his arrest, his father, Zhou Guanwu, a close associate of the late Deng Xiaoping, stepped down as Shoudu company chair. The Zhou case indicated that Jiang had accumulated enough power to face down Deng's former associates and firmly take the reins as leader of the third generation. Chen Xitong was the highest-ranking communist official to be indicted since Mao's wife, Jiang Qing, was tried after Mao's death in 1976.

Jiang followed his anticorruption campaign with the development of his own political thought. In 2000, Jiang announced his Theory of Three Represents (*sange daibiao*), which proclaimed that the CCP represented advanced productivity, advanced culture, and the fundamental interests of the majority.[31] The first represent signified that the party would lead China toward a market economy and that private entrepreneurs, who played a significant role in China's market economy, also were important political actors. The second represent signified integrating the finer aspects of foreign culture with Chinese culture to contest the decadence associated with capitalism. The third represent signified the party's role in safeguarding the common interests of the people.

The Three Represents provides a guideline for the party to act in the twenty-first century, but also gives the party and Jiang credit for China's booming economy. In November 2002, the Sixteenth Party Congress enshrined the Three Represents into the party constitution alongside Marxism-Leninism, Mao Zedong Thought, and Deng Xiaoping Theory (building socialism with Chinese characteristics).[32] The addition of the Three Represents to the party constitution was an attempt to cement Jiang Zemin's historical legacy as a Marxist theorist on the level of Marx, Mao, and Deng. At the same time, the first represent, which implies that the party is the faithful representative of China's development, legitimizes the inclusion of "red capitalists"—businessmen, small-business owners, and private entrepreneurs—within the party. In the 1990s, China's non-state sector had grown beyond the state sector. Private businesses were the engine of China's economic growth and development, and their owners sought membership in the CCP to protect their business interests. They were shut out of the party, however, by an official ban on entrepreneurs.[33] At the same time, however, many party members left administrative positions in state enterprises for managerial positions in private firms, in a process commonly called "jumping into the sea" (*xiahai*). Despite transferring to the private sector, they remained party members and kept their party posts. Recognizing the fact that private entrepreneurs wanted to join the CCP and that party members were increasingly participating in private business, Jiang in 2001 indicated that it was time for the CCP to allow entrepreneurs party membership. In a speech celebrating the eightieth anniversary of the founding of the CCP, on July 1, 2001, General Secretary Jiang Zemin stated that "worthy people from all sectors who are loyal to the motherland and socialism"—private entrepreneurs who met key conditions—should be admitted to the party.[34] Jiang's statement alluding to CCP inclusion of entrepreneurs was remarkable in that it broke with the Marxist-Leninist principle that the CCP is the vanguard of the working class, and as such advocated class struggle. Jiang's inclusion of entrepreneurs was tantamount to instructing the CCP to abandon class struggle, which represented a huge break from Mao Zedong Thought. The CCP dropped its ban on private entrepreneurs after Jiang's speech. Although thousands of private entrepreneurs had quietly joined party organizations throughout China, Jiang's speech officially sanctioned their membership. As early as the mid-1980s, the CCP co-opted entrepreneurs into the party. By the late 1980s, up to 15 percent of private business owners were party members.[35] There were at least seven private entrepreneurs among the 2,100 delegates at the November 2002 Sixteenth Party Congress. One week after the congress amended the party constitution to allow private businesspersons to join, the party admitted about 1,700 private entrepreneurs.[36] The number of private entrepreneurs holding government posts or belonging to the party has likewise increased. By the late 1990s, more than 5,400 private businesspersons participated in people's congresses at the county level or higher, and more than 8,500 participated in political consultative conferences at the county level or higher.[37] In 2003, there were at least fifty-five private entrepreneurs in the National People's Congress. In 2006 alone, 1,554 private entrepreneurs joined the CCP.

There are several explanations for the party's reversal of its ban on private entrepreneurs. First, as mentioned above, as early as the late 1980s the party had been co-opting entrepreneurs into its subnational offices. In the early 1990s, the party leadership identified entrepreneurs as targets of its united-front policy. The party's Central Document No. 15, issued in 1991, stipulated that entrepreneurs be "united, helped, guided, and educated" by the party. The rationale was that it was better to integrate entrepreneurs into China's political process and turn them into "red capitalists" than to exclude a large and growing group that had considerable economic resources to challenge the party.[38] Soon thereafter, the party began to incorporate entrepreneurs into its political order by arranging for them to participate in people's congresses and political consultative conferences.[39] The 2001 lifting of the ban merely made official what had been going on for some time. Second, although Jiang faced resistance to their membership, the resistance was not as strong as in earlier years. Party elders were retiring or dying off. Surviving elders such as Deng Liqun could still mount fierce opposition to reforms, but the character of the party was changing. As the party became younger and more educated in science and technology, it became less resistant to reform. Third, private entrepreneurs were influential in having the ban lifted. As drivers of China's economic growth, entrepreneurs had influence that grew as China's economy boomed. In 2003, the private sector accounted for more than 59 percent of China's GDP.[40] In sum, the state had benefited from the growth of the private sector and recognized that it needed to respond to the private sector's interests.[41] Private entrepreneurs sought positions in government (as delegates to people's congresses and consultative bodies) and admission to the party to protect and advance their interests. Having positions in the congresses or political consultative bodies and joining the party would also help raise their political status.[42]

The Rise of the Fourth Generation of Leaders

The transition from the third to the fourth generation of China's leaders was the first planned succession in the history of any major communist state. At the Sixteenth Party Congress in November 2002, Jiang Zemin handed over his post as party general secretary to Hu Jintao, thus ordaining the fourth generation of Chinese leadership. This was the first time in PRC history that the transition of government authority was not accompanied by violent party infighting. Despite Hu's elevation, the transition process from third to fourth generation would actually take several years. Although Hu Jintao was elevated to CCP general secretary, six out of the nine new members of the Standing Committee were part of Jiang's Shanghai Clique, a group of Jiang supporters that, to Hu's chagrin, ultimately served as a check on his power and kept Jiang's influence strong in the upper echelons of the CCP. Jiang also retained his post as chair of the party's CMC in an attempt to exercise dual leadership with Hu. In March 2003, the National People's Congress elected Hu Jintao president of the PRC. Jiang still clung to the chairmanship of the CMC, despite this having been a good time to relinquish the post to Hu.

Jiang retired from the CMC in September 2004, giving Hu a clean sweep of the three key leadership hats in China: president of state, general secretary of the CCP, and chairman of the military (CMC).

Contemporary Political, Constitutional, and Legal Reforms

China's leaders suspended their efforts to pursue political, constitutional, and legal reforms for a decade after the tragedy at Tiananmen. By the late 1990s, however, China's leaders once again turned their attention to those reforms.

Political Reforms

There has been growing recognition among the third and fourth generations of Chinese leaders of the need for political reform in China. At the September 1997 Fifteenth Party Congress, Jiang Zemin called for efforts to press ahead with reform of China's political structure. In his address, Jiang claimed that the main tasks of political restructuring were to develop democracy, strengthen the legal system, separate government functions from those of state-owned enterprise (SOE) management, streamline government organs, improve the democratic supervision system, and maintain stability and unity. To improve the systems of democracy, Jiang proposed improving the system of people's congresses by ensuring that they function according to law, and that they establish closer ties between deputies and the people they represent. He also proposed increased participation of the noncommunist Chinese People's Political Consultative Conference in the deliberation of state affairs. At the grassroots level, Jiang called for more competitive local elections and more open reporting to constituents of administrative affairs. Jiang also criticized China's existing political structure, arguing that unmanageable organization and overstaffing had led to waste and redundancy. His remedy was to reduce the number and scale

---

PRC President Hu Jintao

Hu Jintao was born in Anhui Province in 1942 and joined the CCP in 1964. Hu holds an engineering degree from Tsinghua University, where he specialized in the study of hub hydropower stations. He worked for the Ministry of Water Conservancy and worked his way up the party hierarchy. In 1985, he was named party secretary of Guizhou Province. From 1988 to 1992, Hu served as party secretary of Tibet (he did not spend much time in the region, however, because he suffered from severe altitude sickness). In spring 1989, Hu called Chinese troops to the region and imposed martial law to restore order as part of the "strike hard" (*yanda*) policy against Tibetan separatists. In 1992, the party leadership rewarded Hu with a seat on the Politburo Standing Committee for his role in the campaign against Tibetan separatists. In the 1990s, he served on the Standing Committee as well as on the Secretariat of the party Central Committee, and in 1998–1999 served President Jiang as vice president of the PRC. He was named party general secretary in 2002, president in 2003, and chief of the party CMC in 2004.

of government economic departments and to professionalize the civil service by making admission and promotion more competitive. Perhaps more important were his comments on the need to fight official corruption. He demanded that the party operate under the scope of the law and that it do a better job in supervising cadres and punishing those who abuse their powers. He also demanded the punishment of law enforcement officers who break the law or who accept bribes.[43]

Jiang's comments reignited interest in political reform. Progress on Deng's political reforms had been largely suspended after the spring 1989 demonstrations and government crackdown. In his 1997 address, Jiang put political reform back on the agenda. For Jiang and Chinese leaders, political reform does not encompass Western political institutions and traditions such as multiparty competitive political systems, checks and balances, or parliamentary systems. China's leaders consider those institutions and traditions as leading to chaos and destruction, much along the lines of the collapse of the Soviet Union under Gorbachev's glasnost and perestroika.[44] Rather, China's leaders limit political reform by adhering to the Four Cardinal Principles (upholding the socialist road, dictatorship of the proletariat, leadership of the CPP, and Marxism–Leninism–Mao Thought). Consistent with the third principle, the leadership of the CCP, Beijing views politics as the job of the party and restricts the role of noncommunists in China's government and politics. The priority for China's post-Deng leaders has been to develop China's economy, namely, building socialism with Chinese characteristics. Political reform is only considered for its value in promoting economic development. China's leaders recognize that China needs to strengthen the rule of law to provide a stable environment for economic development. For China's leaders, political reform is about managing state affairs according to the law under the leadership of the CCP, and not about limiting the powers of government or expanding civil rights and liberties.

One indication of political reform is the increased role of the National People's Congress in deliberating policy. Long considered to be a rubber stamp of the party, NPC deputies have increasingly revised or proposed bills in the legislature, voiced objection of bills, voted against bills, or refused to vote for party-proposed bills. Deputies have increasingly displayed their displeasure by refusing to support government reports wholeheartedly. The NPC has also become more active in selecting and confirming candidates for senior government positions.[45]

Another major development in political reform has been the emergence of grassroots democracy (described in Chapter 4). The most significant development there has been the promulgation of the 1987 Organic Law of Village Elections and the revised 1998 Organic Law. The initiative for improving local governance, hence the Organic Law, originated with local leaders. Efforts to expand direct elections to the township level were likewise pushed by local leaders. Initially, China's top leadership neither condoned nor banned these reforms. Over time, however, China's leadership has accepted some of these reforms, and in 1997 made the 1988 experimental Organic Law permanent. By the late 1990s, the concept of local governance spread to urban areas. In 1998 and 1999, residents of several Chinese cities voted in direct elections for representative to their residents' committees. Residents' committees have existed since 1954 but were limited to menial neighborhood tasks and neighbor snooping. They were usually led by an elderly woman appointed by the municipal party office. In the reform era, increasing unemployment due to the dismissal or layoffs of urban SOE employees, coupled with the influx of rural immigrants, created massive social and economic change in China's cities. Urban residents needed an organization able to respond to these changes. As in rural areas, the initiative for direct elections came from local officials, not Beijing. Although China's leaders neither condoned nor condemned the direct elections, the central government allowed elections for urban residents' committees on an experimental basis. As an indication of his support for grassroots political engagement, Jiang in his 1997 address advocated improvement of both rural and urban grassroots associations and self-governing mass organizations. One decade later, China is practicing elections in both urban and rural areas. It appears that China's leaders are willing to allow grassroots organization and reform so long as reform does not jeopardize party leadership or economic stability.

After he relinquished the offices of president and party secretary to Hu, Jiang still retained considerable influence as the head of the party and of the state Central Military Commission as well as through allies on the Standing Committee of the Politburo. The outbreak of severe acute respiratory syndrome, which was identified around January 2003, became an opportunity for Hu to assert his authority as the head of the party and government. Jiang and his allies initially underreported the number of infections and imposed severe restrictions on media coverage (see Chapter 6). Despite these measures, some newspapers and medical professionals argued that the outbreak was much more severe and widespread than official reports claimed. Demands for the government to be honest in confronting the deadly outbreak began to appear in newspapers. On April 20, Hu broke from the cover-up policy, and dismissed the public health minister, Zhang Wenkang, who had claimed that the outbreak was under control. Hu also instituted a policy of honest disclosure of the outbreak by the government and the media, and he made well-publicized visits to places dealing with the disease. Even as Hu was acknowledging the crisis, however, Jiang continued to downplay its severity, costing him support and popularity to Hu's benefit. Hu's policy was not a push for greater media freedom, but it did display a willingness of China's leadership to respond to crises with honesty and openness instead of secrecy and denial.

In early 2008, scholars at the CCP's top think tank, the Central Party School in Beijing, issued a report calling for democratic reforms to limit the power of the party, encourage competitive voting, and rein in government censors. They argued that failure to reform China's political system would lead to economic disarray, an increase in corruption, and worsening public discontent.[46]

Constitutional Reforms

The PRC constitution is China's highest law and sets parameters for political power and legal development in China. It differs, however, from the US Constitution in two key ways. First, they differ in their approach to the concept of rights. The US Constitution limits the powers of the federal government because it is based on the philosophy that a government cannot take away rights that God has given to the people. The authors of the PRC constitution do not share this philosophy and claim that because the state grants rights to the people, it has the authority to take those rights away. Second, the two state constitutions differ in their approaches to the powers and authority of subnational government. The US Constitution limits the power of the national government to make decisions on behalf of state governments. The United States has a federal form of government, with constitutions at both the central and state levels of government. The US Constitution does not profess to be a complete scheme of government, and so presupposes the state governments. The administrative, legislative, and judicial functions of the national government are those relating to matters that must be deemed common to the whole nation.[47] Any powers not specifically given to the central government are retained by the states. This is not the case in China. China is a unitary government, in which ultimate political power and authority rest in the central government. China's provinces do not have their own constitutions and therefore do not retain any powers separate from that of the central government. As with individual rights, provinces have powers only because the central government awards them, and these rights can be retracted at any time.

China's constitutions have at times expanded or contracted the powers of the state and legal protections of the rights of Chinese citizens. The 1954 constitution, China's first, established the country's organs and institutions of power (executive, legislative, and judicial). It proclaimed China as a "people's democratic state" and as such granted the Chinese people several rights, including the right to freedom of speech, correspondence, demonstration, and religious belief. Citizens could vote and could run for election. They also acquired the right to an education, work, rest, material assistance in old age, and the ability to lodge complaints with state agencies. It protected individuals from arbitrary arrest and detention, and granted each citizen the right to a public trial and to offer a defense aided by a "people's lawyer." It granted citizens equality before the law and granted women equal legal rights.

In contrast, the 1975 constitution, set forth during the Cultural Revolution, proclaimed China as a "socialist state of the dictatorship of the proletariat," eliminated the chair of the PRC from the state structure, and institutionalized the party's direct control of the state. Even the National People's Congress was put under the leadership of the CCP. It drastically reduced the number of provisions regarding citizens' basic rights, from nineteen articles to four. Specifically, it omitted provisions on the freedom of residence, to change residence, and of scientific research and literary and artistic creation. Although it retained the freedom to believe in religion, it added the freedom not to believe in religion and to propagate atheism. It included new "people's rights," including the freedom to strike and to "speak out freely, air views fully, hold debates, and write big-character posters."[48] These rights, however, applied to only those people loyal to the party and who obeyed PRC laws. The constitution also eliminated provisions containing such "bourgeois" concepts of due process as equality before the law, public trials, right to defense, and protection against arbitrary arrest. It also dropped provisions for judicial independence. It politicized China's legal order by subjecting the people's courts to revolutionary committees at all levels of government, introduced the mass line as the operational principle for trial work, reintroduced mass trials in "major counterrevolutionary criminal cases," and legitimized the dominant position of the police in law enforcement by stipulating that the functions and powers of the procuracy (prosecutors) be exercised by the public security bureaus (police).[49]

In 1982, the National People's Congress adopted a new constitution to replace the 1975 Maoist one.[50] The new constitution restored many of the 1954 provisions on legality and individual rights omitted by the 1975 constitution. It described China as a socialist state under the people's democratic dictatorship instead of as a "dictatorship of the proletariat." It took as China's guiding ideology the aforementioned Four Cardinal Principles. To curb the party's interference with the state, it restored the post of chairman of state, established a *state* Central Military Commission, and removed the direct command of the PLA by the Central Committee of the party. Perhaps more important, the party was expected to carry out activities within the extent of the constitution and law, as required by every individual and organization. It strengthened the system of people's congresses and enlarged the powers of the Standing Committee of the National People's Congress.[51] The new constitution also tried to institutionalize the rule of law, as opposed to the rule by man typical of the Mao years. It also restored equality before the law for all PRC citizens and restored the authority of the people's courts and procuracies to exercise authority independently according to the law. The 1978 constitution reinstated judicial independence. Judicial independence does not mean the protection of judges from interference in the exercise of judicial authority. Rather, it means that the courts carry out judging power exclusively and do not share that function with other organizations, as was the practice during the Cultural Revolution.[52] The constitution states that the people's courts "exercise judicial power independently" and are not subject to interference by administrative organs, public organizations, or individuals. Because the National People's Congress and CCP are not listed, it is not clear that they cannot be involved. In fact, local party commit-tees have the power to resolve disagreements among local courts, police, and procurators, and local party authorities often issue directives to local courts on how to decide specific cases. In addition, the courts are constitutionally subor-dinate to the legislative branch. Although a people's congress cannot lawfully interfere in an individual case, it can report on a case and organize an investi-gation of the case.[53] The prospect of being challenged can have a chilling effect on judges and affect their performance.

Although the 1982 constitution restored certain of the individual rights omitted in its predecessor, many of those rights have limits. Take, for instance, the exercise of religion.[54] The 1982 constitution specifies that the state protects "normal religious activities," but leaves undefined the term *normal,* so state of-ficials can limit what activities are allowed. It further stipulates that no reli-gious affairs may be "subject to any foreign domination," which means that the Roman Catholic Church in China cannot recognize the authority of the pope in Rome. The provision also greatly limits the activities of other Christian denom-inations in China. The 1982 constitution guarantees the freedom and privacy of correspondence, but permits public security bureaus to censor correspondence to "meet the needs of state security or investigation into criminal offenses."

In 2004, the Tenth National People's Congress revised the constitution for the fourth time since its adoption in 1982.[55] Although the authority to revise China's state constitution is vested in the National People's Congress, the CCP plays a large role in the revision process. Since 1975, each party congress has proposed revisions to the state constitution.[56] After the party congress adopts a new direction, it is then incorporated into the state constitution. The National People's Congress then meets to engage in a new round of constitutional revi-sion.[57] In 2004, outgoing party chief and state president Jiang Zemin wanted to leave his mark on China's government and politics. Under his direction, the party recommended that the NPC revise the constitution to reflect Jiang's val-ues. The four most important revisions encourage private entrepreneurs to act as a force driving China's economy, further protect private property, recognize human rights, and revisit the use of military force in response to civil unrest and other emergencies.

Foremost, the 2004 revisions incorporate Jiang's Three Represents, mak-ing it a national guiding ideology. The amended preamble references the first represent (that the party represents the development trend of China's "advanced productive forces"—meaning the emerging professional, technical, and entre-preneurial middle class) to indicate that capitalism is not inherently contradic-tory to communism and that the CCP should recruit private entrepreneurs as a new force in its united-front work of constructing Chinese socialism.

A second revision offers greater protection for private property. Amend-ments to article 11 of the constitution protect the individual and private sectors of the economy, including foreign investment in China, declaring that the state protects their rights and interests. The 2004 changes also protect the right of citizens to own and inherit private property and deem "inviolable" the lawful private property of citizens. The revision to article 13 requires compensation for private property confiscated by the state in the name of the public interest.

A third change to China's state constitution is the declaration of recognition and protection of human rights. Article 33 of the constitution simply declares that "the state respects and guarantees human rights." China's leaders use a socioeconomic definition of human rights that includes food, shelter, safety, education, and medical care, rather than the Western definition, which protects individual freedoms and civil liberties, such as freedom of speech, assembly, and religion. Previous constitutions used the term *citizen's rights,* which rejected the universality of human rights and implied that rights were class-based. That is, one's rights depended on one's class status. The unqualified declaration of human rights may signal that China accepts a universal definition of human rights.

A fourth major change in the 2004 constitution is the reconsideration of the use of military force to respond to civil unrest and other emergencies. Article 67 of the 1982 constitution provided the Standing Committee of the National People's Congress with the authority to impose martial law. The 2004 version removes that language and instead states that the Standing Committee has only the authority to declare a state of emergency, leaving vague the conditions under which this authority would be invoked. More important, the revision leaves open the option for the civil police, rather than the PLA, to respond to the emergency. The change in wording requires that the 1996 Martial Law of the PRC be changed to allow the use of police in an emergency situation and to more clearly establish the details of the procedures and criteria for declaring a state of emergency.

Despite these changes, China's leaders do not subscribe to the philosophy of constitutionalism. *Constitutionalism* is the idea that government can and should be legally limited in its powers, and that its authority depends on its observing these limitations. However, the 2004 revisions are significant for the limits they impose on the power of the national government. Since 1975, continual and gradual changes to China's constitutions have for the most part moved in the direction of constitutionalism, namely, in further limiting the powers of the central government, protecting economic rights, expanding individual rights, and recognizing human rights. Before he departed as party chief in 2002, Jiang checked the power of the CCP by amending the preamble of the party constitution to state that the CCP rules the country according to law.

Legal Reforms

China's legal development has been spotty. With the exception of a phase from 1954 to 1956, when they tried to adopt a legal system based on the Soviet model, China's leaders actually played down the rule of law. For most of the Mao years—particularly in the later years of his reign—and into the Deng years, China practiced more rule by man than rule of law. China's various constitutions and legal system reflect this mentality. In 1978, however, China began to reform its legal system. The Chinese public, angry over the injustices of the Cultural Revolution, called for legal reform. China's leaders, well aware of the abuses that occurred during Mao's time in power and during the Cultural Revolution, recognized the need for reform. Reform of the legal system was an important step in helping the CCP regain the legitimacy it lost during the last ten years of Mao's rule.

Traditional Chinese society had two forms of law: *fa* (positive or jural law) and *li* (societal or moral law based on a moral code or rites). Positive law stands for formal and codified rules enforced by a judiciary. Societal or moral law is informal and is a set of socially approved norms and values, enforced by administrative agencies and social organizations. In Confucian China, positive law played only a supplementary role to societal law as a regulator of human behavior and social order. The Chinese people traditionally stayed away from the courts of law and considered litigation as a last resort. Offenses and disputes were more often handled by clan elders, the village council, or some other social group.[58] Just as positive law and the Confucian moral code coexisted in traditional China, jural (formal) and societal (informal) law coexisted in Maoist China. Formal rules played a secondary role in both traditional and Maoist China. Mao's influence on China's legal development is reflected in the emphasis on the societal model of law over the jural model. Mao assimilated traditional attitudes toward law, such as subordinating law to a dominant political philosophy, into the Soviet system that China adopted after 1949. Marxist-Leninist ideology and the Soviet system subordinated law to political dictates. Central to the Soviet legal system was the concept of class struggle. Using the class line approach, Mao provided a theoretical framework for differentiating and resolving social conflicts. In his 1957 speech "On the Correct Handling of Contradictions Among the People," Mao drew distinctions between the people and the enemy. Conflicts among the people would be dealt with by methods of democracy, but conflicts between the people and the enemy would be dealt with by the method of dictatorship, which called for severe sanctions.

After 1957, the jural model declined as the CCP put greater emphasis on the extrajudicial methods of law enforcement and dispute resolution.[59] During the Great Leap Forward, there was a definite shift from the jural model to the societal model. China's formal legal system was often ignored as the words of party and government officials took on new weight. Circulars and party regulations began to take the place of a code of criminal law or judicial procedure. Party committees completely controlled the legal system, and public security organs meted out justice. This trend continued during the Cultural Revolution as the party totally dismantled the "bourgeois" legal system and replaced it with mass line devices and the imposition of military control.[60] The 1975 constitution, written during the Cultural Revolution, further reduced restraints on the Maoists. It eliminated the procuratorate (prosecutors) and transferred its functions and powers to the police. Public security forces gained the power to arrest without having to go through other judicial organs. It also subjected people to instant, arbitrary arrest. Police officers, revolutionary committees, or mobs conducted impromptu trials and meted out spur-of-the-moment justice.

After Mao's death and the arrest of the Gang of Four, China's leaders recognized that it needed to reinstitute the rule of law. In 1977, Premier Hua Guofeng began to reconstruct China's formal legal institutions based on the spirit of the 1954 constitution. For example, he directed the military to turn over responsibility for public security to the civilian sector. Central government leaders began to reorganize judicial procedures and establish codes of criminal law and judicial procedure, reopened law schools, and hired professors to staff them. Bookstores and libraries stocked legal books and journals. By the end of the year, China's legal system and the courts reportedly were stronger than at any time since the 1954–1956 period.

China's Judicial System

Hua's most immediate task in reconstructing China's formal legal institutions was the restructuring of a judicial system severely damaged by the Cultural Revolution. In 1979, China reestablished the Ministry of Justice, which had been abolished in 1959. Led by a justice minister (attorney general), the ministry's main tasks are to handle all judicial administrative work of the courts at all levels, direct and supervise the work of reeducation through labor, direct and supervise the practice of lawyers and legal advisors and the work of legal aid, publicize law and educate the population on the Chinese legal system, cooperate with the NPC and State Council in the drafting of relevant legal laws, and participate in the formulation of laws for the Hong Kong and Macau special administrative regions.[61] The Chinese legal system has its roots in the Continental legal tradition with its dependence on statutory law. Unlike Anglo-US case law, court decisions in China are not the source of Chinese law and do not have legally binding effect in judicial practices.

In 1980, China adopted the Organic Law of the People's Courts. The law guarantees equality before the law, open trials, the right to defense, and the right to appeal. It maintains the court system composed of the Supreme People's Court, local people's courts, and special people's courts.[62] China's highest court is the Supreme People's Court in Beijing, China's ultimate court of appeal. Under the Supreme Court is a three-tiered system of local courts (courts of first instance): the higher and intermediate courts of provinces, autonomous regions, and municipalities directly under the central government, and the basic people's courts of counties, townships, and municipal districts. People's courts at all levels are composed of a president, a number of vice presidents, chief judges, associate chief judges, and judges. By law, court president and judges of the Supreme Court, higher, and intermediate courts are elected by the corresponding people's congress for a maximum of two consecutive five-year terms. Corresponding personnel for the basic courts can be elected to a maximum of two consecutive three-year terms. Chief judges and other judges are appointed by the Standing Committee of the corresponding people's congresses. The courts at all levels have a criminal division and a civil division, each headed by a chief judge and associate chief judges. In addition, the Supreme Court and the lower courts have established economic divisions to deal with economic crimes such as graft, fraud, bribery, and counterfeiting.

Prosecutors and Defense Attorneys

Parallel to the courts is a hierarchical system of prosecuting offices called people's procuratorates, the highest being the Supreme People's Procuratorate. The procuracy carries out investigation of criminal cases, oversees the activities of the police in the criminal process, institutes prosecution, scrutinizes the trial activities of the courts, and supervises the execution of judgments and the activities of correctional facilities.[63] One task of the post-Mao leadership has been to reinstate the Chinese bar, which had disappeared from China's legal scene during the 1957–1958 Anti-Rightist Campaign. In 1980, China adopted a statute that classified lawyers as "workers of the state." Their primary duty was to safeguard the interests of the state rather than the rights of Chinese citizens, and they received their salary from the state. The 1996 Lawyers Law changed the nature of the profession from that of public service to private practice, redefining a lawyer as one who provides legal service to society.[64] Today, lawyers safeguard the legitimate rights and interests of their clients and are paid by their clients. Lawyers in China are defense lawyers and most are engaged in criminal defense (prosecutors work for the People's Procuratorate). China has some 165,000 lawyers, far too few for a population of more than 1.3 billion, but up from 3,000 thirty years ago. Beijing alone has 16,000 lawyers. Lawyers in China are very well paid, and many are among China's new wealthy elite.

Criminal Process

As a unitary state, the public security apparatus, including the police, is part of the central government. Because of China's vastness, however, the central government is often unable to monitor local public security units. The process of justice in China is uneven, and there is considerable room for abuse. China's criminal process is highly politicized because of interference by the party and government. The CCP institutionalized party intervention in the judicial process by creating an interlocking system of vertical control by public security organs, with horizontal control by local government and party organs. The public security apparatus performs all the police tasks in China, is responsible for maintaining law and order, and investigates all criminal cases. The apparatus is headed by a Ministry of Public Security, and there are public security *departments* at the provincial and special municipality levels, public security *bureaus* at the county and municipal levels, *subbureaus* at the rural or urban district level, and public security *stations* at the city district level. The public security apparatus cooperates with local party and government organs. Thus, the police are subject to the leadership of both high-level public security organs and the party committees and governments at the same level.[65]

The stages of a criminal process are arrest and detention, investigation, trial proceedings (investigation, debate, appraisal, and judgment), and sentencing. Police must produce a warrant to carry out an apprehension or to make an arrest. Authorities are supposed to notify the family of the detainee of the reason for action and the place of confinement within twenty-four hours. This is often not the case, however. Particularly in the case of the detention or arrest of political dissidents, the family is not notified of the place of detention. Under "shelter and investigation," police may detain people without charge for up to three months, and under "administrative detention," police may send detainees to labor camps for up to four years without being charged. In reality, police have nearly unchecked powers. Police commonly use torture, beatings, inadequate food, and poor hygiene to elicit confessions and ensure compliance. They regularly tamper with evidence, and have nearly unlimited powers to suppress or cover up information necessary for a defense lawyer to adequately defend a client.[66]

The Criminal Procedure Law codifies the criminal process. According to the law, the public security bureau detains the individual and must begin interrogation within twenty-four hours. It must release immediately detainees for whom it finds no legitimate grounds. When the public security bureau deems it necessary to declare a detainee arrested, it should seek approval from the procuratorate within three days (or within seven days for special circumstances). If the procuratorate approves arrest, it then initiates investigation. Investigation tasks include interrogation of the detainee and witnesses, search and seizure, examination of evidence, and preparation of indictment. Despite these protections, many public security and procuratorate personnel violate the law. They illegally detain people, arbitrarily interrogate them, and unlawfully search people's homes. Illegal detention or excessive detention takes place with such regularity that many lawyers take on nearly as many detention cases as criminal cases. Although the Criminal Procedure Law forbids the use of torture in extracting confessions, the practice of torture remains widespread in China.[67]

When the procuratorate finds sufficient evidence for prosecution of the accused, it files an indictment with a court and the case goes to trial. The people's court tries the defendant. Trials are conducted by either a panel of judges or a judge and a people's jury. Judges receive no special education and more often than not have no background in legal studies. Juries are made up of assessors who are laypeople elected by local residents or people's congresses, or who are appointed by the court for their expertise. In contrast to the US system—in which the judge does not intervene on the side of either the defense or prosecution and is thus said to be impartial—in China, both judges and assessors actively question witnesses. In practice, the assessors commonly defer to the judges and do not act as an independent jury. According to China's constitution and the Criminal Procedure Law, the accused has the right to defense. The accused may defend himself or herself (as did Wei Jingsheng), hire a lawyer, or have a relative or guardian defend him or her. If a defendant does not have a defender or the financial means to hire a lawyer, the people's court will designate a lawyer who is obligated to provide legal aid to serve as defender. Chinese law firms must agree to be willing to take on pro bono work. The defense lawyer has the right to question witnesses, experts, and the defendant; summon and question new witnesses; introduce new evidence; and participate in courtroom debates.

Despite changes in the legal system that allow lawyers to serve as independent defenders of their clients, lawyers still face several difficulties. First, the Criminal Procedure Law is often used to intimidate or harass defense lawyers. Article 306 of the law holds criminal defense lawyers personally liable if they destroy or forge evidence, help any parties involved destroy or forge evidence, or coerce or entice their client or a witness into giving false testimony or changing testimony in defiance of the facts. Lawyers counseling their clients to repudiate a forced confession, persuade a witness to retract false testimony extracted under torture, or turn up evidence disadvantageous to the prosecution can be charged with evidence fabrication and be sentenced to prison. From 1997 to 2002, some five hundred lawyers were jailed under this law. More than 90 percent of these lawyers were cleared, indicating that the law is often abused or invoked to intimidate defense lawyers.[68] In 2003, prominent defense lawyer Zhang Jianzhong was tried on charges of assisting in the fabrication of evidence in a major corruption case. His case raised concerns that some prosecutors are using criminal provisions on evidence fabrication to intimidate defense lawyers.[69]

Second, although forensics is increasingly used in reaching verdicts, it is still common for verdicts to be handed down based on incomplete evidence. Third, despite a lawyer's best efforts, chances are great that his client will be found guilty. The Criminal Procedure Law states that no one is to be considered guilty until found so by a court. Despite the law, more than 99 percent of the individuals prosecuted by the people's procuratorates at all levels are found guilty. Fourth, lawyers engaged in defense of political dissidents have been harassed, intimidated, and sometimes lost their licenses.[70] Fifth, the Ministry of Justice keeps lawyers under control by policing the profession and issuing licenses.

Lawyers belong to government-controlled bar associations, compromising their independence. Sixth, party and government officials often interfere in adjudication. Although the Organic Law of the People's Procuratorates states that the procuratorates exercise the authority independently of administrative organs, organization, or individuals (including the party and party cadres), this is often not the case. Party and government officials at all levels of government commonly interfere with procuratorial work. If the case involves a party member, the CCP Discipline Inspection Department will most certainly interfere in the case.

According to the Criminal Procedure Law, all cases are to be heard in public, except those involving minors or state secrets. In the past, this provision was likely to be ignored, but trials now are increasingly open to the public. Interested parties can receive tickets to a trial by showing personal identification. After the judge and assessors rule on a case, they pass sentence. An aggrieved party can appeal to the next higher court. Criminal cases in which the guilty face immediate execution undergo first trials in intermediate courts, second trials in provincial high courts, and final review by the Supreme Court. If defendants are found guilty of minor offenses, the court will sentence them to probation or detention. Under probation, offenders continue to work at their place of employment and receive their normal wages, while undergoing the supervision of the public security organs. Under criminal detention, offenders are confined in a detention house by the local public security bureau rather than incarcerated in prison. The penalty for more serious offenses is fixed-term imprisonment, life imprisonment, or death. Most people found guilty but not sentenced to death are sent to labor camps (*laogai ying*) maintained by the public security apparatus, where the state tries to reform convicts through political indoctrination (*xi nao*, or brainwashing), self-criticism, and hard labor. China's prisons are penal as well as economic entities and are supposed to make money for the state. Prisoners are regularly engaged in factory production, often for export, with most profits going to the state. Prisoners' sentences can be extended if they do not show repentance. Release from prison does not guarantee that they can return to their hometown. It is unlikely that a former employer or any employer would willingly hire a former convict, and released prisoners may be ordered to stay at the prison under a forced labor assignment. Juveniles who commit minor offenses are turned over to neighborhood organizations, parents, and teachers for intervention. Juveniles who commit more serious offenses are sent to reform schools for youth, run jointly by the Ministry of Education and the Ministry of Public Security, where offenders spend half a day on study and half a day on work.

Death Penalty

China carries out more executions than any country in the world, and nearly three-quarters of the world's executions occur in China. Exact figures are hard to come by because China classifies these statistics as state secrets. Based on media reports and publicly available official documents, Amnesty International estimated that China carried out 1,718 executions in 2008, more than the rest of the world combined.[71] This high number reflects the fact that the death penalty can be applied to more than sixty-eight crimes, including nonviolent crimes such as drug trafficking, pornography distribution, and disclosing state secrets, and economic crimes such as tax evasion, counterfeiting, smuggling, and money laundering.

China's leaders began reform of the death penalty in 2006. Before the 2006 reforms, China had no official position on the frequency of imposing the death penalty. After reforms began, the Chinese government officially stated that it intends to "kill fewer, (and) kill more humanely."[72] China's Supreme Court has authority of final review over all death sentences handed down for immediate execution.[73] Each death sentence must be reviewed by three judges, who are required to check facts, laws, and criminal procedures and precedent. In March 2007, the Ministry of Public Security and the Ministry of Justice introduced reforms to reduce the incidence of wrongful death sentences. The ministries revised procedures for witnesses at trial and reaffirmed that confessions extracted under torture cannot be used as the basis for conviction.[74] The Supreme Court in the first half of 2008 overturned about 15 percent of the death sentences sent by provincial courts for final review.[75] Many China legal experts and foreign human rights organizations argue that China should end, and not just curb, its use of execution.[76] China's criminal law calls for the use of capital punishment for "criminal elements who commit the most heinous crimes."[77] This provision is very broad and includes nonviolent crimes such as drug trafficking, official corruption, and disclosing state secrets abroad. Many government leaders and most of the Chinese population want to retain the death penalty. Government officials support the use of capital punishment because they see it as a deterrent to future crimes. Many people in China support the death penalty because they see it as vindication for the victim. An estimated 90 percent of the population oppose the abolition of capital punishment and have pressured government and judiciary officials to continue the practice.[78]

Conclusion

The major thrust of Deng's reformism was to satisfy the material aspiration of the people, without sacrificing the leadership of the CCP. Hence, Deng and his fellow reformers undertook courageous economic reforms, while maintaining extreme caution with regard to other reforms, such as reforming China's political institutions and legal system. Political reform in post-Mao China has been characterized by periods of liberalization and of retrenchment. A predictable pattern soon became apparent: limited political reform followed by retrenchment as China's older, more leftist leaders tried to restrict reform to the economy only.

The first stage of political reform occurred from 1978 to 1983, followed by a more dramatic second stage beginning in 1986. The first stage of political reform included steps taken to construct a new legal order, such as the adoption of new state and party constitutions; resumption of elections of local legislatures, with some competition among candidates nominated by the party; increased participation by the national legislature in discussions on national policy; and streamlining and restaffing the state bureaucracy. Political relaxation had its costs, however. These costs included increases in crime and corruption, the expression of opinions by intellectuals and students that challenged the state, and experiments with new styles of expression by writers and artists. Frustration with these problems resulted in social upheaval in 1987 and appalling violence in 1989.

In the decades since the 1989 Tiananmen Square Massacre, China's leaders largely avoided political liberalization, but focused on restoring the party's legitimacy. Among other things, they welcomed private entrepreneurs into the party, amended the constitution to protect property rights, and reformed the legal system. While these reforms constitute a major improvement over the tyranny of the Maoist state, it is clear that the reforms are designed still to maintain the position of the party and state at the top of China's power structure.

Notes

1. The Gang of Four, Chen Boda, and Lin Biao's supporters were tried from November 1980 to late January 1981. Jiang Qing and Zhang Chunqiao were given suspended death sentences. The other defendants were sentence to long terms in prison. Chen Boda and Lin Biao's supporters were released in the 1980s.

2. The mausoleum is open to the public and draws long lines of people even on the most sweltering of summer days. Foreigners must display a passport for entry.

3. Zhou Enlai first used the term *Four Modernizations* in 1964 and again in 1975, but never implemented them due to the politics of the Cultural Revolution. In 1978, the CCP and central government leaders promulgated the term in the party and state constitutions. Deng Xiaoping brought the plan to fruition in the 1980s and 1990s.

4. State Statistical Bureau, PRC, *China Statistical Yearbook, 1998,* 38; Harding, *China's Second Revolution,* 55.

5. Vogel, *One Step Ahead in China,* 77.

6. In comments to former Japanese prime minister Masayoshi Ohira in December 1979, Deng specified that a comparatively comfortable standard of living meant a per capita GNP of US$800.

7. Harding, *China's Second Revolution,* 72.

8. Leng and Hungdah, *Criminal Justice in Post-Mao China,* 40.

9. Wei, "Democracy or a New Dictatorship?"

10. See Chapter 3 for more information on Liu Binyan.

11. Zhao Dingxin, *Power of Tiananmen,* 155.

12. For detailed accounts of the various demonstrations, see Shen Tong, *Almost a Revolution,* and Zhao Dingxin, *Power of Tiananmen.*

13. For reports on protests in the provinces, see Unger, ed., *Pro-Democracy Protests in China*.

14. Evans, *Deng Xiaoping and the Making of Modern China*, 295.

15. Zhao Ziyang, *Guojia de qiutu* [Prisoner of the state].

16. Zhao Ziyang died in January 2005, after spending more than fifteen years under house arrest in Beijing for his support of the 1989 student demonstrations in Tiananmen.

17. The Chinese Red Cross estimated 2,600 military and civilian deaths based on counts from local hospitals, but retracted the figure under government pressure.

18. Shen Tong is president of VFinity, a company he founded in New York that offers a web-based content management and collaboration platform for video, audio, and text.

19. Zhao Ziyang, *Guojia de qiutu* [Prisoner of the state].

20. Anita Chan, "The Social Origins and Consequences of the Tiananmen Crisis."

21. Tang Tsou, "The Tiananmen Tragedy."

22. Gilley, *Tiger on the Brink*.

23. Mao was the leader of the first generation, Deng the leader of the second generation, Jiang of the third, and Hu Jintao of the fourth.

24. Lieberthal, *Governing China*, 211.

25. Joffe, "The People's Liberation Army and Politics," 103.

26. Swaine, "Modernization of the People's Liberation Army," 127.

27. "The Song of Jiang Zemin," *Economist*, August 8, 1998, 35; "No Longer the Army's Business," *Economist*, May 8, 1999; "Asia's Boardroom Brass," *Economist*, July 10, 1999.

28. Chen Fang wrote a novel, *The Wrath of Heaven: Scandal at the Top in China*, based on the events that led up to the jailing of Chen Xitong.

29. Gilley, *Tiger on the Brink*, 241.

30. In the past, the CCP ordered "party discipline" for wayward members.

31. The Three Represents is actually the brainchild of Wang Huning, professor of international politics at Fudan University in Shanghai. He is a member of the Central Committee of the Seventeenth Party Congress and is director of the policy research office of the Central Committee.

32. Deng Xiaoping, "Build Socialism with Chinese Characteristics," *People's Daily*, June 30, 1984.

33. The party imposed a ban on the admission of private entrepreneurs in 1992. However, many party members quietly participated in the nonstate sector.

34. Jiang Zemin, full text of the speech at the meeting celebrating the eightieth anniversary of the founding of the Communist Party of China, July 1, 2001, http://www .china.org.cn.

35. Dickson, *Red Capitalists in China*, 98.

36. Kim, "From the Fringe to the Center," 121.

37. Dickson, *Red Capitalists in China*, 100.

38. Dickson, *Red Capitalists in China*, 166.

39. Kim, "From the Fringe to the Center," 118.

40. According to data from the National Bureau of Statistics, in *China by Numbers 2007*, 80.

41. Kim, "From the Fringe to the Center," 126.

42. Kim, "From the Fringe to the Center," 129.

43. Jiang Zemin, from a report given to the Fifteenth Party Congress, 1997, http:// www.fas.org/news/china/ 1997/970912-prc.htm.

44. *Glasnost* refers to political liberalization; *perestroika* refers to economic restructuring of the Soviet economy.

45. Lee, "Political Reforms in Post-Deng China."

46. Chris Buckley, "Elite China Think-Tank Issues Political Reform Blueprint," *Reuters*, February 18, 2008, http://www.reuters.com.

47. Bryce, *American Commonwealth*, 33.

48. Leng and Hungdah, *Criminal Justice in Post-Mao China*, 19.

49. China abolished the procuratorate system in 1969, and the 1975 constitution formally confirmed this reality. The procuracy is now part of the Public Security Bureau (which also maintains the police functions in China). Leng and Hungdah, *Criminal Justice in Post-Mao China*, 20.

50. The National People's Congress revised the constitution in 1978, striking a compromise between the more liberal document of 1954 and the Maoist document of 1975.

51. Leng and Hungdah, *Criminal Justice in Post-Mao China*, 42.

52. Nathan, "China's Constitutionalist Option," 184.

53. Nathan, "China's Constitutionalist Option," 185.

54. The 1982 constitution removed the right to propagate atheism as contained in the 1978 constitution.

55. The state constitution of the PRC should not be confused with the CCP's party constitution. The National People's Congress revised the 1982 constitution in 1988, 1993, 1999, and 2004.

56. Each revision coincides with the end of the term of the five-year party congress and the beginning of a new National People's Congress. For example, the Fifteenth National Party Congress (1997–2002) and the Sixteenth National People's Congress (2002–2007) revised the constitution in 2002. Thus, revisions in the 2004 constitution contained changes proposed by the Sixteenth Party Congress (2002–2007). Party congresses, such as the Sixteenth Party Congress, report on the previous five years and devise a policy direction for the new leadership.

57. Chen Jianfu, "The Revision of the Constitution in the PRC."

58. Leng and Hungdah, *Criminal Justice in Post-Mao China*, 7. See the Chinese movie *Chiu Ju* for a contemporary portrayal of one woman's quest for justice.

59. Leng, "Role of Law in the People's Republic of China as Reflecting Mao Tsetung's Influence."

60. Leng and Hungdah, *Criminal Justice in Post-Mao China*, 14.

61. Ministry of Justice, People's Republic of China, http://legalinfo.gov.cn.

62. The special courts include military, railway transport, water transport, and forestry courts.

63. Article 5, Organic Law of the People's Procuratorates.

64. For more information on the legal profession in China, see Lo and Snape, "Lawyers in the People's Republic of China."

65. Tanner and Green, "Principals and Secret Agents," 646.

66. Tanner and Green, "Principals and Secret Agents," 647.

67. Nowak, "Civil and Political Rights, Including the Question of Torture and Detention."

68. Ip, Liu, and Ling, *China's Death Penalty Reforms*, 32.

69. Congressional-Executive Commission on China, "Defense Lawyers Turned Defendants: Zhang Jianzhong and the Criminal Prosecution of Defense Lawyers in China," May 28, 2003, http://www.cecc.gov/pages/news/zhang_052703.php.

70. US Department of State, "Country Reports on Human Rights Practices—2007."

71. Amnesty International, *Amnesty International Report 2009: The State of the World's Human Rights*.

72. Ip, Liu, and Ling, *China's Death Penalty Reforms*, 29.

73. Some death sentences are suspended for two years as the convicted person undergoes reform, and they are commuted to life imprisonment if the convicted person does not commit any additional crimes during the two years.

74. Ip, Liu, and Ling, *China's Death Penalty Reforms*, 28.

75. "Top Court Overturns 10 Percent of Death Sentences," *China Daily*, June 27, 2008.

76. Ng Tze-wei, "Quashing of Death Penalties Hailed, 'But More Action Needed,'" *South China Morning Post*, June 28, 2008, 4; "Welcome Reduction in Use of Capital Punishment in China," *Dui Hua Human Rights Journal*, June 27, 2008.

77. Criminal Law of the People's Republic of China, section 5, article 48 (adopted July 1, 1979, and amended March 14, 1997), http://www.com-law.net/findlaw/crime/criminallaw1.html.

78. Ng Tze-wei, "Quashing of Death Penalties Hailed, 'But More Action Needed,'" *South China Morning Post*, June 28, 2008, 4.

6 Social Dynamics

Mao's socialist economy provided Chinese workers with employment, housing, and social benefits, all through the work unit (*danwei*). Under the "iron rice bowl" and "one big pot" systems, state enterprise employees enjoyed life-long job tenure and egalitarian wages (detailed in Chapter 7). Although the iron rice bowl and one big pot systems had many drawbacks, they nevertheless provided Chinese workers with security in a country that had no social safety net. In the countryside, communes provided similar security. The collective provided wages, housing, meals, health care, and education. All of this changed after 1978. Reform of state-owned enterprises (SOEs) broke the iron rice bowl and eliminated the one big pot. Under reform, SOEs began to require employees to contribute to their health care insurance and pensions and to pay more for housing. Most employees, many of them older and less skilled, resented the fact that they now had to pay for something that the firm had once provided them. Many SOE employees saw their situations deteriorate as they now had to pay out of pocket for health care and other social security benefits, reducing their disposable income. At the same time, China's leaders introduced sweeping controls on family planning, reducing China's population growth rate, but resulting in sobering unintended consequences.

Since 2006, China's leaders have dedicated more attention to improving key issues that impact the country's development, particularly addressing health care concerns, boosting education standards, and raising the standard of living for ethnic minorities. This chapter examines party and government efforts to address these key social issues.

Health Care

During the Mao years, all Chinese citizens had access to basic health care under a socialist health-care system. Urban workers received health benefits from their work units, and many larger SOEs had their own health clinics or hospitals.

Rural residents had access to local or community health clinics, which offered basic, if rudimentary, health care. The government owned and ran all care centers, from large urban hospitals to rural clinics, and physicians were employees of the state. Nearly all Chinese citizens had health insurance. The Government Insurance Scheme covered government employees. The Labor Insurance Scheme covered state-owned enterprise workers, and the commune-based Cooperative Medical System covered rural workers. The Cooperative Medical System operated village and township health centers commonly staffed by "barefoot doctors," practitioners who had only the most basic medical training. China's near-universal coverage was a major factor in improving public health from the 1950s through the 1970s. Improvements in public sanitation and health care in the early days of the PRC helped increase life expectancy in China from about thirty-five years to sixty-eight years, far above that of other low-income countries (even taking into account the 1961–1963 famine and the 1966–1976 Cultural Revolution). The increase in life expectancy was largely due to government investment in urban health insurance and rural primary health care.

In the reform era, however, per capita income increased but access to health care deteriorated, especially in rural regions. In the 1980s and 1990s, state work units such as SOEs shed their responsibility to provide basic health care, and paying for health care became the responsibility of the individual worker. In rural areas, health clinics shut down due to lack of funding, and most health-care professionals vacated their rural clinics for urban ones. The percentage of population covered by health insurance decreased dramatically from more than 90 percent in the late 1970s to only about 20 percent in 1993.[1] This decrease was borne mostly by rural residents. In 1993, while approximately 49 percent of China's urban population remained insured, only 13 percent of rural residents had such insurance. In some areas, less than 5 percent of rural residents were insured.[2] Out-of-pocket medical spending for Chinese rural households has increased tremendously since the collapse of the rural health system. Approximately 95 percent of rural residents have to pay out-of-pocket fees for their health service. The percentage of household expenditures dedicated to health care and medical services also increased. In 2009, 7.2 percent of rural household expenditures were for health care and medical services, up from 3.3 percent in 1990.[3]

From 1997 to 1998, the average share of public spending on health in low-income countries was 1.26 percent, but in China it was only 0.62 percent. Of the health systems in 191 countries in the world, China ranked 144 in terms of overall performance and 188 in the equity of health-care financing.[4] From 1978 to 1999, the central government's share of national health-care spending fell from 32 percent to 15 percent. The government shifted much of the responsibility to provincial and local authorities, who funded their portion through local taxes. Wealthier coastal provinces could better afford to invest in health care than the less wealthy rural provinces.

Impact of Health Care Reform

The lack of adequate health care slowed advances in public health, and if it were not for the increase in income, life expectancy in China would have likely declined in the 1990s.[5] The decline in government expenditures for rural health care and the increasing reliance on out-of-pocket expenses resulted in a marked deceleration in the increase in life expectancy in rural areas. This deceleration forced the Chinese government to reexamine its policies and reassert government's leading role in health care. In 1997, the State Council released the "decision on health reform and development," setting forth a goal of providing every Chinese citizen with basic health care. In 1998, the central government created a new "basic medical insurance" system for urban employees, combining social pooling with personal accounts. National guidelines stipulated that it be financed by 6 percent of the wages paid by the employer and 2 percent of the wages earned by the employee. By 2008, however, only 17 percent of medical costs were covered by the insurance system.[6]

Access to health care in China is determined by who can pay. In 2004, 71 percent of Chinese had no health insurance; 90 percent of the rural population had no health insurance.[7] Between 1991 and 2000, individual out-of-pocket spending as a share of total health spending increased from 38 percent to 60 percent. Although the government continued to cap charges for surgeries, standard diagnostic tests, and routine pharmaceuticals, it permitted health-care centers to earn profits from new drugs, new tests, and technology, with profit margins of 15 percent or more.[8] Also, the government allowed hospitals to award bonuses to physicians determined by the revenue a physician brought into the hospital. These changes resulted in an increase in sales of expensive pharmaceuticals and high-tech services, such as imaging. A common complaint is overprescription. Many patients complain that doctors at public clinics prescribe more drugs because their bonus is related to the volume of the drugs they prescribe.[9] The result is a bifurcated health-care delivery system: most rural Chinese could not afford care, but a growing class of rich Chinese has access to Western-style, high-tech care.[10]

In January 2009, China's State Council announced that it would spend $124 billion on medical reforms over the following three years in an effort to increase participation for both urban and rural populations and to reform public hospitals. The goal is to reduce public hospitals' reliance on profits from drug sales and medical service fees to cover expenses.

SARS Outbreak and Crisis of 2003

The 2003 SARS (severe acute respiratory syndrome) crisis highlighted the problems with China's health-care system. SARS is a viral respiratory illness caused by a coronavirus. It was first reported in Asia in February 2003. Over the next few months, the illness spread to more than two dozen countries in North America, South America, Europe, and Asia before being contained. According to the World Health Organization (WHO), a total of 8,098 people worldwide became sick with SARS during the 2003 outbreak. Of these, 774 died. SARS begins with a high fever, headache, and body aches. After two to seven days, SARS patients may develop a dry cough. SARS spreads by close person-to-person contact. The virus that causes SARS is thought to be transmitted most readily by respiratory droplets produced when an infected person coughs or sneezes. It also can spread when a person touches a surface or object contaminated with infectious droplets and then touches his or her mouth, nose, or eyes. SARS causes a buildup of mucus in the lungs, causing victims to struggle for breath. As they struggle for breath, SARS victims often spit up mucus and phlegm, infecting health-care workers who try to treat them. Initially, Chinese doctors misdiagnosed SARS as pneumonia because its symptoms are similar to those of pneumonia and because most SARS patients develop pneumonia.

The first cases of SARS in China occurred in Guangzhou in November 2002, but Chinese physicians did not diagnose the disease as SARS. Although the disease had begun to spread to hospital personnel as well, the authorities were not alarmed as the disease did not spread to the larger community and seemed to die out on its own. By late January, however, an alarming number of doctors, nurses, and assistants were falling ill. As political authorities claimed that the disease was under control, a team of experts from Beijing and Guangzhou began to investigate the outbreak and devise a strategy to thwart its spread. A member of the investigative team, Dr. Zhong Nanshan, disputed the claim from Beijing that the disease was chlamydia and could be treated with antibiotics. He submitted a report to Guangzhou authorities that set out a range of medical techniques to prevent infection. The Guangzhou authorities failed to share the report's recommendations with other countries, which would soon be hit by the disease.

Word of the disease began to trickle out of the hospitals, but there was no news of the disease in the official media. Residents of Guangzhou, who were text-messaging each other about the virus, began to administer home remedies, such as boiling vinegar, to ward off infection. The central government told the public not to panic, and imposed a news blackout on the virus.

China's denial of the severity of the crisis allowed the disease to spread overseas. In early February, a WHO organization based in Hong Kong, which monitors disease outbreaks, alerted WHO headquarters in Geneva of the Guangdong epidemic. The WHO immediately sent a team to investigate the outbreak, but Chinese authorities did not give the team permission to travel to Guangdong until two months later. Meanwhile, in late February, a physician who had treated patients in Guangzhou fell ill on a visit to Hong Kong, infecting numerous guests at the Metropole Hotel. These guests took the disease with them when they returned to their homes in Singapore, Toronto, and Vietnam. Those infections set off epidemics, prompting the WHO to issue a global health alert recommending against travel to infected countries. By early March, the virus had spread to Canada, Vietnam, Australia, the Philippines, Singapore, Ireland, and the United States. The WHO opened an investigation into the pandemic and on March 15 issued a global warning about the threat of SARS, but Li Liming, chief of China's Center for Disease Control, denied that a coronavirus was causing the epidemic. By mid-April, Hong Kong would be reporting one thousand cases and at least thirty deaths.

The virus quickly spread to Beijing, where more people would die of SARS than anywhere else in the world. Of all the SARS cases reported worldwide, more than 31 percent occurred in Beijing. The first SARS case in Beijing occurred in March 2003, and on April 2, Premier Wen Jiabao held a ministerial meeting to discuss the severity of the infection. Chinese news agency Xinhua's report of the meeting stated that the disease had been brought under control. Apparently Premier Wen did not have full information on the epidemic. Many of the SARS cases were in military hospitals, which did not report information to civilian authorities. Beijing city authorities withheld information on the number of cases in city hospitals from the central government because they were afraid the government would blame them for the spread of the disease.[11] On April 2, the WHO recommended that travelers postpone travel to China and Hong Kong. In response, China's minister of health, Zhang Wenkang, held a press conference on April 3 claiming that it was safe to work, live, and travel in China. He declared that Beijing had twelve SARS cases, three of whom had died. In fact, city hospitals were admitting more than 100 cases a day.

Meanwhile, China's leaders began to gather in Beijing for the National People's Congress to elect Hu Jintao as president. Not wanting bad news to overshadow the congress, Chinese president and party leader Jiang Zemin refused to lift the news blackout. Angry with the party's refusal to deal with the growing epidemic, retired military surgeon Jiang Yanyong wrote to the government and media criticizing China's leaders for playing down the deadly disease and for failing to cooperate with a WHO investigation. In particular, Dr. Jiang took exception to the health minister's claim that Beijing had only a dozen cases of SARS and three deaths, and countered that he knew of at least 120 cases at the city's military hospitals. Dr. Jiang e-mailed copies of his letter to CCTV and Hong Kong–based Phoenix TV, and to friends who might contact the foreign media. Although the Chinese media did not report on Dr. Jiang's letter, *Time* magazine picked it up and ran a story on its website where people living in China could read it. China's central government was forced to acknowledge the severity of the epidemic. On April 20, the central government reversed itself and President Hu and Premier Wen publicly stated that the situation was "extremely grave." Central government authorities ordered an investigation of the virus, and fired health minister Zhang and Beijing mayor Meng Xuenong for not taking appropriate health measures.

After their April 20 acknowledgment, central government authorities acted swiftly to prevent and minimize new infections. They initiated programs for early identification of the disease and for the quarantine of known cases. The party set up infection-control checkpoints and established fever wards. Beijing city officials tried to minimize public crowding by canceling most public gatherings and closing schools. Wu Yi, acting minister of health and a vice premier, established a national SARS headquarters in Beijing and ordered the Ministry of Health to classify SARS as an infectious disease, making it subject to reporting requirements. Officials at all government levels began daily reporting of infections as well as their control measures, and Chinese authorities reported all new and suspected SARS cases to the WHO. The central government built a SARS hospital outside Beijing to quarantine suspected and confirmed SARS patients, and health officials quarantined people who had come into contact with SARS victims as well. China's leaders even took the unusual step of cancelling the traditional weeklong May Day holiday to minimize travel, also setting up fever checks for travelers at airports and bus and train stations. The usually teeming Beijing subway system was nearly empty of commuters, and the few people who dared to ride wore surgical-type face masks. Most foreign students left Beijing as academic exchange programs ended the spring semester early. The travel bans succeeded in stopping the spread of SARS, and China's efforts to treat infected people stopped the epidemic. In summer 2003, the WHO declared China SARS-free.

The SARS epidemic had been able to rage in China for several reasons. First, political attention and energy were diverted to the timing of transfer of China's leadership. The transfer of leadership to Hu Jintao and Wen Jiabao began at the Tenth Party Congress in November 2002 and was settled at the Tenth National People's Congress in March 2003. Once the political transfer was complete, China's leaders turned their attention to the SARS epidemic. Second, China's health institutions were not adequately prepared to deal with a catastrophic illness. The main problem with the health care system was not with its delivery, but with its institutions. The strength of the system was China's health care providers. Doctors, nurses, and assistants took grave risks in caring for SARS patients, and many lost their lives to the disease for their efforts. Their efforts were stymied, however, by institutional roadblocks that prevented various units in the health care system from sharing information vital to stopping the epidemic. For instance, the Ministry of Health is subordinate to party offices at the local level of government, but local party bosses are unsure about what information to pass on because, under Chinese law, epidemics are state secrets. As such, local authorities do not have the jurisdiction to announce epidemics until the Ministry of Health first makes the disclosure. Any local official who publicly disclosed the disease without ministry disclosure would be liable to prosecution. The regulations on disclosure created a disincentive for transparency. The lack of transparency and the failure of China's leaders to act until mid-April allowed the disease to spread worldwide, at the cost of hundreds of lives. The lack of transparency, at all levels of government, meant that China's political and health-care institutions were not prepared to deal with a catastrophic disease. For instance, Guangdong party secretary Zhang Dejiang, a close supporter of former president and CCP general secretary Jiang Zemin, knew of the disease in early January. On January 4, the *Heyuan News* published a fax from the provincial center for disease control designed to calm the local population. Instead, the *Heyuan News* story created a frenzy of reporting, alarming Guangdong authorities, who responded by prohibiting all negative reporting of the disease. The limited press coverage they did allow, however, claimed that reports of an epidemic were merely a rumor. Provincial authorities were concerned that the reports would create a general panic that would disrupt the upcoming Chinese New Year holiday and hurt the local economy. Although they informed doctors and nurses that the disease was highly infectious and that they needed to isolate patients and protect themselves with masks, provincial authorities kept the public in the dark. Guangdong provincial authorities did not inform Beijing of the disease until early February. The Ministry of Health sent the vice minister of health to Guangdong to investigate. Thus, the State Council certainly knew of the disease in early February. Moreover, as a member of the party's powerful Politburo, Guangdong party chief Zhang Dejiang would have had the opportunity to bring the matter to the attention of China's leaders. However, it was not until April 8, when it was clear that the disease was not particular to Guangdong, that the Ministry of Health listed SARS as an epidemic. Also, the People's Liberation Army (PLA), which ran the military hospitals where many of the Beijing SARS cases were discovered, covered up the SARS situation. By early April, China's leaders knew that the PLA was withholding information, but the military did not divulge information until required to do so on April 20.

The Chinese government was also slow to respond because it lacked knowledge about the disease. The investigation team from the Guangdong Institute for Respiratory Diseases had to start from scratch in establishing a cause of the disease, method of transmission, incubation period, symptoms, and treatment. Once public knowledge of the Guangdong infections reached the outside world, the WHO had to go through the same process. With far less knowledge of the disease, WHO officials devised a broader definition of the disease. Arriving in Guangzhou in April, they found that much of their work had already been done. The lack of information sharing between Chinese authorities and the WHO cost the WHO valuable time in devising a plan to prevent a global pandemic.

The government's lack of rapid response had severe political consequences as well. The lack of preparedness and transparency led to a crisis in confidence in China's government. The government and party failed to take command and control of the situation until embarrassed by international public disclosures of the epidemic. In late April, President Hu and Premier Wen were the picture of concerned leaders, convening meetings, visiting hospitals, meeting medical workers, and expressing condolences to the families who had lost loved ones to the disease. Despite their efforts, the SARS crisis profoundly affected public trust in China's health authorities and in the government. The dismissal of health minister Zhang and Beijing mayor Meng raised questions about government accountability to the public. The central government fired the two men from their posts the same day *Caijing Magazine* published an eighteen-page report on SARS, announcing the epidemic to the international community. The fact that the government came forward only after being exposed, coupled with the ability of the party to suppress information, illustrates both the lack of transparency and lack of accountability on the part of the CCP and the government. The international community found the SARS case to be another situation in which the Chinese government was less than forthcoming and fueled cynicism about the government's sincerity. After the SARS case, both the CCP and central government have tried to regain legitimacy and have been more willing to share information on diseases. For instance, the Chinese government began more reliable reporting on HIV/AIDS in China. In 2009 when the swine flu (H1N1) emerged, China took no chances. In late April, a Mexican tourist who had flown to Shanghai and then Hong Kong was diagnosed as infected with the virus. The Chinese government tracked down one hundred of his fellow passengers in China and quarantined them for seven days.

Population Control and Family Planning

Perhaps there is no greater intrusion of the state into society (and particularly into family life) than the government's attempts at population control. Since the 1950s, China's leaders have viewed population growth as a problem requiring state intervention, with little or no thought given to individual rights in the matter. The PRC conducted its first census in 1953, revealing a population of 583 million. The period of peace and prosperity that followed the civil war, coupled with advances in health care, contributed to a rise in births and a drop in mortality. Concerned that unchecked population growth would create a drag on China's economic progress, China's leaders began population control measures in the 1950s. Influenced by Beijing University economist and National People's Congress (NPC) member Ma Yinchu, who argued that China needed to slow population growth, the party in 1956 launched a campaign promoting the use and production of contraceptive devices. China's leaders suspended the birth control campaign during the Great Leap Forward, however, and persecuted Ma along with other intellectuals. In 1964, the central government created a Birth Planning Commission and Birth Planning Office to begin work on designing a national population control plan. Shortly thereafter, China's leaders suspended the plan, as they did other national programs, during most of the Cultural Revolution. In 1971, China's leaders began a third family-planning campaign. In response to two baby booms in the 1950s and 1960s, Zhou Enlai introduced a national population control policy emphasizing late marriage, smaller family size, and longer spacing between births. For the first time, China legally obligated all newly married couples to use artificial contraception. One of the criticisms of the programs to limit family size, however, is that until 2001 they were policy but not law, and yet were rigorously enforced as if they were law. But because it was not against the law to violate the policy, the enforcement of the policy has taken arbitrary and barbarous forms.

Urban health-care practitioners and rural barefoot doctors worked to educate couples on the virtues of family planning. Policies carried out during the Mao era reduced births in cities, but had little effect in the countryside. It was not until the early 1980s, however, that China's leaders established central government–level offices to impose birth control on China's population. By the 1990s, more than 80 percent of Chinese married couples were using contraception. Today, the most common methods of contraception, in order of frequency, are tubal ligation, use of the intrauterine device (IUD), and vasectomy. Overwhelmingly, women bear the burden of sterilization. Of the 151 million people sterilized between 1971 and 2001, nearly 75 percent were women, many of them "volunteered" by their husbands, who refused to be sterilized.[12] Thirty-seven percent of Chinese women of reproductive age have been sterilized.[13] Abortion is commonly used as a family-planning tool by local cadres when couples exceed the state quota for the number of children allowed. Between 1971 and 2001, birth planning officials performed 264 million abortions, many of them late-term abortions.[14]

The state implements its population control program through China's administrative and education systems. The State Family Planning Commission, under the State Council's Office of Family Planning, carries out China's population program. The commission conveys its policy decisions to local authorities, who transmit the policies to cadres in rural communities and urban districts for enforcement. Family-planning offices in government offices and SOEs chart women's menstrual cycles, provide contraceptives to married women, and offer sterilization and abortion services. In rural areas, each township (previously commune) has a family-planning committee to coordinate and supervise family-planning work. Subcommittees disseminate family-planning information and contraceptives, organize and lead study groups, persuade (and in some cases, force) reluctant individuals to practice family planning, and monitor the results of these programs.[15] The State Family Planning Commission uses newspapers, radio, television, publications, theater, music, local performances, and schools to propagate family planning. Each city, county, and township has a family-planning publicity and education center, which produces television programs, videotapes, and other publicity materials.[16] The state also publicizes family planning through the education system. A number of Chinese villages and neighborhoods have set up population or marriage education schools where people of child-bearing age receive information about population, childbirth, contraception and birth control, maternity, and childcare through the lectures or advice given by doctors, teachers, and cadres. The primary purpose of these schools is to en-courage participants to practice family planning more conscientiously. Consid-ering the high participation rate of couples of childbearing age, it appears that the programs are compulsory.

The most zealous family-planning officials are found at the local level. Local family-planning offices record the number of local women of childbear-ing age, their monthly cycles, their form of birth control, and their number of pregnancies and live births. Local cadres put enormous pressure on women who exceed the quota for live births to submit to an abortion. Local cadres are eager to carry out China's population control policies because promotion to higher office is not determined by their record of economic development but by their record in keeping births below the prescribed limit. One party boss in rural Anhui Province boasted that he would rather see seven grave mounds than one extra birth, referring to women who died from botched abortions.[17]

China's One-Child Policy

It was Mao's successors who introduced the most sweeping and draconian of China's family-planning campaigns, the one-child policy. Mao's successors were increasingly concerned that the baby booms of the 1950s and 1960s would create echo effects. As the baby boomers entered their reproductive years, China would almost certainly experience baby boomlets. Deng Xiaoping's attempt to drastically reduce China's population growth rate was a reaction to baby boom-lets projected for the 1980s and the 1990s. Even if fertility were reduced by mandatory birth limits, China's population would increase again when people born in those boomlet years reached childbearing age, peaking in the early twenty-first century. Deng argued that, unless the state enacted drastic popula-tion control measures, these large population increases would seriously hinder China's economic progress. Obsessed with "scientific decisionmaking" in ad-dressing the country's problems, China's leaders tasked mathematicians from China's space program with creating plans for developing the national econ-omy. The mathematicians projected a population of 1.5 billion by 2020.[18] China's leaders instructed Marxist statisticians and economists at Beijing's Peo-ple's University to develop a "scientific policy" plan on population. They argued that China's huge and rapidly growing population was worsening problems of unemployment, accumulation, livelihood, and education.[19] In particular, they determined that such an increase would delay achievement of the Four Mod-ernizations, the party's key program for China's development. The statisticians

viewed rapid population growth as a problem and claimed that overly reproductive individuals were a burden to the state.[20] Influenced by Malthusian theory, in which population would outstrip food supply, and by Western alarmists
who warned of a population explosion in the third world, China's Marxist statisticians claimed that the only way to avoid such a crisis was to mandate that
couples have only one child.

In January 1979, China put into effect a one-child policy for most of the
country's population. Under the policy, couples sign a pledge to have only one
child. Since 1983, the national guideline has been "after first child, IUD; after
second child, sterilization." There are exceptions to the one-child limit. People
living in rural areas and ethnic minority groups are generally allowed to have
two children. Rural farmers and herdsmen in Tibet have no limitations on the
number of children they can have.[21] However, local cadres commonly enforce
the one-child policy among China's minority families as well.

Initially, rural residents resisted the one-child policy. To counter resistance
in the countryside, central authorities in 1983 launched a mass campaign of
forced sterilization and abortion. That year, family-planning officials carried
out nearly 21 million tubal ligations and vasectomies and more than 14 million
abortions.[22] Since implementation of the one-child policy, many pregnant
women have fled their villages and have given birth in the mountains, leaving
their children with relatives. Other women have abandoned their children, many
of whom are placed in orphanages. Two-thirds of Chinese children put up for
adoption are female.

In the 1990s, coercion had become the norm as targets had to be achieved,
no matter how. To ensure enforcement, the party initiated the "five procedures"
against resisters and violators. The five procedures are seizing grain, livestock,
and furniture; demolishing houses; and incarceration. Coercion, which continues in the twenty-first century, includes locking people in township offices until
they comply, confiscating the property of noncompliers to substitute for unpaid
fines, and physically damaging the property of people who have fled.[23]

In the early 1990s, Peng Peiyun, minister of the State Family Planning
Commission, linked birth control to rural economic development. Based on an
experimental program in Jiangsu Province, Peng adopted the slogan "fewer
children, faster prosperity" (*shaosheng, kuaifu*). China's leaders later integrated
the program into the Develop the West Campaign, designed to develop the backward western region of China (see Chapter 8). In particular, the program sought
to create incentives for couples to practice birth control.[24] In 2004, Hu Jintao
shifted China's birth control program from reliance on negative penalties toward positive rewards. In particular, Hu had in mind the rural poor of China's
western regions who could not pay the fines imposed for exceeding the birth
quota. Integrating birth control into the western development plans, couples
who did not have a second child, even though they were legally able to do so,
would be rewarded with payments. Also, under a new system of "rewards and

supports," elderly Chinese whose compliance with the birth limit prevented them from having a son would receive an award of modest support payments for the rest of their lives. Couples whose only child had died or become disabled would also receive support.[25] The long-range goal of this system is to encourage young couples to observe the birth limit, as well as to have daughters, knowing that they will be covered by social retirement funds in their old age.

Consequences of the One-Child Policy

The drop in the birth rate is not without its costs, however. The one-child policy has had several tragic consequences. First, it has led to *selective abortions.* Women often wait until the second trimester to determine the sex of their child, and end the pregnancy if it is a girl. Many abort several female fetuses until they become pregnant with a boy. Late-term abortions carry more health risks for the mother. More recently, improvements in technology have made sex selection easier. Although Chinese law forbids the use of ultrasound for sex selection, it is commonly used for such purposes. Chinese culture prefers sons, who will carry on the family line, maintain the ancestors' graves, and provide labor for the family farm. China's ancient system of land distribution also favors sons. A farmer who does not produce a son can be stripped of his inheritance of land by the family's clan. Girls, on the other hand, are a bad investment because they need to be fed, clothed, and sheltered until marriage, but after marriage will leave the family and bring their labor to their husband's family.

A second consequence is *female infanticide.* If sex-selective abortions are not available or possible, a couple might kill a female baby soon after birth so they can try for a son. Rural couples may have a second child if the first one is disabled. In cases where a couple's first child is a girl, the family might neglect the child to the point of impairing her mental and physical health, allowing them to have a second child so they can have the male they desire. The law allowing rural residents to have a second child if the first is a girl does not apply in urban areas. District birth planning officers fine couples who violate the one-child policy. However, richer citizens can afford to pay the fine and have more than one child, creating resentment amongst the less wealthy.

Third, the one-child policy has resulted in a *gender imbalance* in China. The Chinese preference for boys and sex-selective abortions has created an excess of males and a shortage of females. In 2005, births of Chinese boys exceeded births of girls by more than 1.1 million. Nationwide, there is a ratio of 120 males to 100 females, but rising as high as 146 males to 100 females in the one-to-four age range in some rural provinces. The world average ratio is 101 males to 100 females. Provinces that allow rural residents to have a second child if the first is a girl had the highest gender ratios.[26] China has 32 million more males than females aged under twenty, and for the next twenty years, China will have increasingly more men than women of reproductive age.[27] By the early twenty-first century, the generation of only children born in the 1980s and early 1990s has entered marriageable age. It is difficult in rural areas in particular to find a bride.

The gender imbalance has thus resulted in a fourth consequence, the *trafficking of women*. The scarcity of young women, coupled with the migration of women to the coast in search of jobs, has resulted in a shortage of marriage partners for rural males. The shortage has created opportunities for human traffickers. Traffickers lure or kidnap women in provinces with more females or from neighboring countries such as Burma, Thailand, and Vietnam. Traffickers lure unsuspecting females with promises of jobs in southern coastal China to help sustain their impoverished families in their home countries. They then sell the women to unmarried Chinese men, who force the women to stay in China and raise new families. In some cases, police have tried to rescue such a woman only to be beaten off by her husband's family and neighbors who argue that they paid a good price for her and she belongs to her husband. The price for a wife brought to China can vary. A wife from Burma, for example, can range from $2,400 to $6,000, depending on the youth and beauty of the girl. After having children, most of the women are reluctant to leave their children to escape to freedom.

The one-child policy has also led to a wave of child abductions. According to some estimates, as many as seventy thousand babies and toddlers are being stolen every year and sold by organized crime. Primary abductors are human traffickers and gangs of beggars. Most abducted children are boys because of the premium that Chinese society puts on boys. Families want to secure a male heir, something they may not be able to do given the limitations of the one-child policy. Traffickers can sell boys for as much as $6,000, but girls may fetch as little as $500. Abducted girls are raised as future wives for boys and to look after the adopted families. Gangs of beggars use abducted children as pawns for their begging schemes. Migrants are particularly vulnerable, as they often live illegally in cities and are afraid to go to the police to report abduction. Parents who report abduction complain that the police are not doing enough to find the child or abductor. Although Beijing has recently acknowledged the problem of child abduction, many local authorities remain indifferent to the problem.[28] Frustrated by the lack of police action, parents have turned to private investigators and family advocacy groups for help in finding their missing children.

A fifth consequence of the one-child policy is the *emotional and mental toll* that abortion has taken on women. There are about five hundred female suicides in China per day, a rate three times higher than for males. In rural areas, the suicide rate for women is three to four times higher than for men. Suicide is the leading cause of death for Chinese women, and China is the only country in which the suicide rate for females is higher than that for males. Although suicides may not be directly linked to the one-child policy and the abortions that occurred as a consequence, the number of suicides in rural China has risen since the enforcement of the one-child policy.

As a sixth consequence, the one-child policy has created an *underclass of children* who are the products of unplanned pregnancies. Because they are illegal, these children cannot be registered as ordinary citizens for health, education, and other benefits. There are no official statistics on the number of illegal births, but the State Statistics Bureau has discovered undercounts of up to 40 percent in some rural villages.[29] A survey done in 1995 of three provinces showed that the actual number of girls alone was 22 percent more than was registered.[30] Unregistered children from unapproved pregnancies are collectively known as the "black population." There may be as many as 5 million such children in China. Because of the underreporting of births, no one really knows the population of China. While the lower births in the cities may offset the higher births in the countryside, not knowing the country's population makes it harder for the government to engage in economic and social planning.

Another consequence of the one-child policy is a *graying population.* In 2009, nearly 10 percent of China's population was aged sixty-five or over, up from less than 5 percent in 1982.[31] The graying of China creates two problems. First, China will begin to experience a labor shortage. Since 1979, China's leaders have relied on an export-driven economy based on labor-intensive industry. In 1999, there were ten workers per retiree. By 2020, the expected ratio is six retirees per worker, and in 2050 it is expected to reach only three workers per retiree. As much as a quarter of China's economic growth between 1978 and 1999 was due to the huge population caused by the baby booms of the 1950s and 1960s. By 2012, however, the dividend will have turned into a deficit. By 2035, nearly one in five Chinese will be sixty-five years of age or older, constituting a staggering 280 million senior citizens.[32] There will be fewer employees to work in Chinese factories, thereby pushing up wages and causing China to lose its cheap labor force as a competitive edge. Second, there will be fewer young people to support the elderly in their retirement years. Third, the dependency ratio, which is the ratio between the economically dependent population and the economically active population, is rising in China. This ratio is described as the *one-two-four problem,* in which one child takes care of two parents and four grandparents. In response, China's leaders have allowed only children married to other only children to have two children. The relaxation of the one-child policy makes it possible for one child to take care of the mother and one to take care of the father in their old age.

It is possible that a decline in the number of births would have happened without the one-child policy. Malthus, in his 1798 tract *Essay on the Principle of Population,* argued that population tends to grow more rapidly as incomes or living standards of the population rise; that the natural tendency of population is to grow more rapidly than the food supply; and that per capita food production would thus decline over time, putting a check on population. Writing on the eve of the Industrial Revolution in the West, Malthus did not foresee the future contribution of invention and technology. In fact, after 1870, population growth in most Western nations began to decline just as living standards and real wages grew most rapidly. Peacetime fertility rates in England and Western Europe began to fall in the 1930s, before the advent of the pill or IUD.[33] While modern-day neo-Malthusians argue that contraception is the primary method of slowing population growth, these declines in population growth and fertility rates challenge that belief. Critics of the neo-Malthusians argue that development is the best contraception, and development—not government-run family-planning programs—is the best way to slow population growth.

In China, the fertility rate was already falling in the ten years before Deng introduced the one-child policy. The most dramatic decrease occurred before the draconian policy was imposed, between 1970 and 1979, when the largely voluntary "late, long, few" policy (later childbearing, greater spacing between children, and fewer children) had already resulted in a halving of the total fertility rate, from 5.9 to 2.9 children per family.[34] After the one-child policy was introduced, there was a more gradual fall in the rate until 1995. In 1998, fertility in China dropped below replacement rate (2.1), and it has more or less stabilized at approximately 1.5.[35] Consider the fertility rates of China's neighbors in East Asia. Many of them have had substantial declines in fertility during the past thirty years and have some of the lowest total fertility rates in the world: 1.2 in Japan, 1.1 in Singapore, 1.07 in Hong Kong, and 1.05 in Taiwan.[36] Although each of these countries had policies encouraging lower birthrates, none of the policies came close in scope, expense, and strict enforcement to China's one-child policy.

There also appears to be a positive correlation between increasing female education and decreasing fertility, and between the incidence of women working and decreasing fertility. Namely, better-educated and working women have fewer children. In other developing countries, fertility rates are declining as those countries are becoming more urbanized, and as women are better educated and are working more outside the home. Fertility rates have decreased, particularly in those developing countries where national income has increased and where voluntary family planning is available.[37] It is entirely possible that Chinese women would have had fewer children anyway had China's leaders continued the voluntary policy of the 1970s and put more resources into female education.

In the twenty-first century, population control has become even more important. Until the early 2000s, population control was a plan—in 2001 it became law. The 2001 Law on Population and Birth Planning codifies state justification for population control. The law provides a legal basis for state determination of both the quantity and quality of China's population. Chapter 1 of the law declares that population control is a "basic national policy of the state." The attempt to limit the number of Chinese births is only one part of China's family-planning programs. The law legitimates eugenics. With the question of quantity largely under control, China's leaders are currently obsessed with raising the quality of births in China. In particular, they are determined to create a superior race (*yousheng*), which will help China achieve world-leader status in the twenty-first century. Article 2 specifically refers to the state's mission in improving the quality of China's population. Each year, approximately 6 to 8 percent of births in China (between 80,000 and 120,000) involve some sort of state-defined "defect." The Chinese government tries to head off the problem as far in advance as possible by conducting premarital examinations and screening pregnancies for defective fetuses.[38] Chinese couples are encouraged, and often coerced, into aborting fetuses that exhibit any defects.

Domestic and Foreign Adoption of Chinese Infants

Adoption in China increased after the implementation of the one-child policy in 1979. Most of the children adopted are girls because there are relatively few boys available for adoption. Couples adopt for a variety of reasons: infertility, death of a child, desire to circumvent family-planning policies, and desire to create families of one child of each gender. Chinese law makes it difficult to legally adopt abandoned children. China's adoption laws serve more as a deterrent to couples who might exceed the one-child rule and less to help find homes for abandoned children. Because the Chinese government considers adopted or abandoned children unplanned and therefore illegitimate, it is difficult for adoptive parents to acquire household registration papers for the children. China's adoption law restricts adoption to couples who are childless and over thirty years of age. Since few couples meet those restrictions, some 80 percent of adoptions are done informally. These couples often turn to an informal adoption system in which birth parents seek suitable families for their child, leaving the infant on a doorstep, for example, and in which villagers take abandoned children to their homes and take care of them as birth children. In Beijing, one poor couple who had been scrounging in dumpsters collected five disfigured infant girls and took them home to raise.[39]

International adoption has helped some Chinese children find homes and has alleviated the crowding at some Chinese orphanages. By the end of 2007, some 120,000 Chinese orphans had been adopted worldwide. American families adopted many of these children. Families in the United States have adopted some 40,000 Chinese children since China began international adoption in 1989, and they adopted 7,906 Chinese children in 2005, up from 115 children in 1992. In 2007, however, the Chinese government imposed more stringent adoption requirements, which had the effect of reducing international adoptions. US adoptions fell by half, to only 3,909 in 2008 and 3,400 in 2010. The Chinese government currently limits adoption to heterosexual married couples where the husband and wife are both at least thirty but not older than fifty years of age; are physically and mentally healthy, which excludes individuals taking antidepressants and those who are overweight (those with a body mass index of forty or more); either husband or wife holds a stable occupation, in which annual income is at least $10,000 per family member, and family net assets should be at least $80,000; both husband and wife have at least a high school diploma or vocational degree, and do not have any criminal history; and the family does not exceed five children, four of whom can be under the age of eighteen.

While it can take up to five years to adopt a Chinese child, the wait for a special-needs child is much shorter. Many American couples adopt special-needs children from China. Although figures on adoption of Chinese special-needs children by US families are hard to find, Children's Hope International, an adoption service that helps special-needs children find homes, claims that it has placed more than 3,500 Chinese babies with adoptive families.[40]

Education

China's contemporary education system and the academic inclination of the Chinese people are rooted in the Confucian tradition. Confucian values found in China's education system include motivation, achievement attribution, and learning strategies. Confucianism emphasizes knowledge and self-cultivation. This value system has instilled in the Chinese people a firm belief that educational achievement is vital to individual betterment and social well-being. Confucius and other philosophers of the Zhou Dynasty held that people had a capacity for constructing a harmonious social order that would be realized only when they were both free from physical want and properly instructed. Throughout Chinese history, people have placed a high value on formal education because of its intrinsic worth in personal growth and its external reward for higher socioeconomic status in society. In Chinese literature, numerous folk songs, folk stories, and fairy tales convey the same message stressed by the Confucian philosophy, that is, that education is the most important thing in life. The cultural emphasis on academic achievement serves as a source of inspiration for student motivation, but also as a source of societal pressure for the parents. Chinese parents hold high educational expectations and press their children to achieve academically at nearly any cost.

History of China's Education System

China's formal education system began in 124 B.C. when the Han emperor Wu Di founded the Grand Academy (*daxue,* or great learning), an institution of higher learning designed to educate and train men for the administrative service of the imperial state. Until the end of the imperial era, successive dynasties maintained a central education system. Recruitment into the imperial bureaucracy was by means of officially conducted written examinations. This system was based on the philosophy that appointment to office should be made not on the basis of one's family privileges or social status, but on the grounds of one's intellectual talents. The early philosophers believed that most men, as it was men who filled these positions, were by nature endowed with similar faculties, but that they should be selected on the basis of the skills and qualities that education and moral training had given them.

The main examinations were the *jinshi* and the *ming-qing*. Competition was intense; the success rate for *jinshi* candidates was only 2 to 3 percent. In the *jinshi*, candidates were tested in two forms of literary composition, in knowledge of certain Confucian classics, and in ability to analyze contemporary administrative problems. In the *ming-qing*, the main test was for rote knowledge of a limited number of the Confucian classics and their interpretation by earlier scholars. Both the *jinshi* and *ming-qing* required memorization of the classics. Because mastery of the classics required one to absorb and regurgitate large amounts of material, the traditional Chinese learning strategy was largely based on book study and memorization. Over the centuries, the content of the examinations became increasingly rigid. From the mid-fifteenth century onward, the *jinshi* was dominated by a stereotyped form of composition, called the "eight-legged essay," which was never more than seven hundred characters.[41]

During the Qing Dynasty (A.D. 1644–1911), Christian missionaries had established a network of schools, colleges, and universities throughout China. At the same time, Chinese reformers were debating the *ti-yong* dichotomy. *Ti* (substance) represented traditional Chinese values; *yong* represented Western technical skills. Qing Dynasty reformers tried to modernize the education system. They jettisoned the classical learning system for programs in foreign language (English, French, German, Russian, or Japanese), Western science, mathematics and astronomy, international law, engineering, and geography. Christian missionaries, eager to educate recent converts, provided basic primary-level education and established colleges and universities as a means of gaining access to the upper class. St. John's College became one of the most celebrated academic institutions in China. The Jesuit order of Catholic priests established Aurora University in Shanghai, which taught mainly in French and provided faculties of arts, law, science, civil engineering, and medicine. In 1898, the old "eight-legged essay" was abolished. In 1905, Qing reformers abolished the old *jinshi* examinations and established a Ministry of Education. In 1912, Peking University admitted its first students.[42] Both official and mission colleges and universities flourished. The Chinese government also sent students abroad to learn Western methods. Many of these students brought Western ideas of philosophy and politics back to China when they returned. After spending several years abroad, many of the returning students were discouraged by the backwardness they perceived in their homeland and agitated for political change.

After defeating the warlords in 1928, the Nationalist government began to establish schools and enroll students nationwide. The Japanese invasion and occupation of China disrupted educational plans. After Japan's defeat in 1945, the Nationalists again tried educational reform, but were soon embroiled in civil war with the Chinese communists. The Chinese communists engaged in education reform soon after establishing the PRC in 1949. To raise literacy rates, the Chinese communists revised the writing system by simplifying many Chinese characters. Character simplification involved reducing the number of strokes needed to write a given character. The State Council approved and issued lists of more than three thousand simplified characters (*jiantizi*) each decade between 1956 and 1977. In 1979, the State Council adopted the Chinese phonetic alphabet, *pinyin,* to romanize Chinese proper nouns.

The Education System Under Mao

The communist government infused China's education system with heavy doses of political indoctrination. Teachers were the first targets. The party labeled most teachers as bourgeois in class background and thinking, and required them to undergo thought reform, or political indoctrination. The CCP appointed party members to key posts throughout the educational system and subjected teachers to political campaigns designed to break their resistance to passing on Marxist principles to their students. The party labeled teachers who resisted the indoctrination as "counterrevolutionaries" or "rightists." However, the party invited compliant teachers to join the CCP, which enhanced their career opportunities.

As part of the CCP's political indoctrination, primary-level students memorized moral slogans while upper-level students memorized political slogans and Marxist texts. The communists integrated Marxism into academic subjects as well. For instance, the study of Chinese literature stressed social realism, and students interpreted the stories of heroes and villains in terms of the socioeconomic classes they represented. Foreign literature portrayed the worst features of capitalism. History courses used Marxist theory to explain the progression of history, and special courses on the CCP portrayed the party as ending China's backwardness and promoting China's advances.

From the founding of the PRC until his death, the education system in China reflected Mao's philosophy on education. For Mao, the purpose of education was to develop students' morality, knowledge, and physical condition, and to create laborers with both knowledge and socialist beliefs. Specifically, China's education system had to pursue three revolutionary goals. First, education was the key to achieving wealth and power. To end China's backwardness, China needed to train engineers, scientists, technicians, and others with "modern skills." Second, education was to serve the social revolution by eradicating the "three major differences" between town and country, worker and peasant, and mental and manual labor. Third, education was to create a New Man, one who would be motivated by his love of the collective interest rather than of the individual.

Education During the Cultural Revolution

At no time was Mao's philosophy of education more evident than during the Cultural Revolution. During the Cultural Revolution, China's schools and education institutions became centers for indoctrination rather than for sophisticated learning. Beginning in the 1950s, political content became central. After the Hundred Flowers movement (see Chapter 3), Mao saw the need to bring China's colleges and universities under control and to bring them into line with Marxism–Leninism–Mao Zedong Thought. During the Cultural Revolution, revolutionary committees replaced administrators in running the colleges and universities. The committees based the selection and promotion of teaching faculty on correct political views rather than on skill, expertise, or seniority. In rural areas, and then in urban areas, people-managed (*minban*) schools replaced state-managed (*gongban*) schools. Neighborhood revolutionary committees or street committees ran primary schools, and neighborhood revolutionary committees and local factories ran the secondary schools. In rural areas, brigades ran the primary schools and communes ran the secondary schools under the direction of revolutionary committees. *Minban* teachers were paid in rations and cash subsidies; state teachers received government salaries. Putting revolutionary committees in charge of urban and rural schools met two goals. First, it prevented the growth of the "revisionist educational line," and second, it relieved the state from having to finance all primary and secondary education.

Class background became the deciding factor in admissions to colleges and universities. Universities rejected applicants from "bourgeois" backgrounds or those who had black marks in their families' dossiers. Admission of students with peasant or worker backgrounds, however, increased to 50 percent in 1960, from 20 percent a decade earlier. Consistent with Mao's philosophy on education, colleges and universities sought to bridge the gap between knowledge and labor. They substituted vocational training for general knowledge, and turned out large numbers of technicians. Universities sent faculty members to factories to learn from the masses and hired politically correct technicians as teaching faculty. Mao's policies were largely successful in promoting educational access and equality. In the 1970s, the share of teachers and students in rural areas above the elementary level increased, as did the share of urban students of lower socioeconomic status. There also appeared to be a narrowing of gender gaps in primary and secondary education. Inequality increased again after the Cultural Revolution.

During the most violent phase of the Cultural Revolution, Red Guard factions disrupted instruction in primary, secondary, and tertiary educational institutions.

Red Guards and student rebels dismissed school administrators and often criticized, interrogated, tortured, and occasionally killed them. Student rebels viewed the revolutionary committees that replaced school administrators as democratic, with members elected from the schools at large. Teachers still reported to work, but spent their time engaged in political indoctrination rather than in instruction. From 1966 to 1968, most high schools and all universities held no classes due to the disruption of the Red Guards and student rebels. Schools and university campuses became gathering centers for Red Guards and student rebels to criticize and punish teachers and administrators, to write big-character posters, to study Mao Thought, and to promote the revolution.

The central government ordered all schools reopened in 1968 and shortened the combined primary and secondary instruction from twelve to nine years. The state required students who completed secondary school, usually at the age of fifteen or sixteen, to work on farms or in factories for three years to gain practical experience before applying to university. The requirement to work before considering application to higher education was consistent with Mao's philosophy that the purpose of education was to develop students' knowledge and physical condition, and to create laborers with both knowledge and socialist beliefs. Some universities reopened in 1970, but many did not open until a year or two later. The central government abolished the annual entrance examination on the grounds that it represented a "revisionist line of education," and based admissions on a system of nominations and recommendations. The new system called for self-nomination of the applicant, nomination by the masses, and recommendation by the party leadership. The new system favored students from a so-called revolutionary social background, such as workers, peasants, members of the army, and some "sent-down youth." At the same time, the system discriminated against students with "bourgeois" backgrounds. With an influx of students who were largely unprepared for academic rigor, universities had to lower standards and offer remedial classes.

The Cultural Revolution set China back twenty years in education. Without any formal education, students of the 1966–1976 decade were completely lost. When the high schools and universities reopened, students were ill-prepared to engage in intellectual debate, having studied Mao Thought and little else. Primary and secondary school curricula had been compressed, from six to five years each. After working on farms or in factories for three years, most high school graduates were unable to handle the sophisticated material required at the university level. Mao and his supporters had closed more than 100 research institutes associated with the Chinese Academy of Science and had persecuted the faculty. The universities also offered an abbreviated curriculum of only three years. Students and faculty spent most of their time putting theory into practice by working in university-associated factories. When they did study, students used only those materials the state deemed politically correct. By the end of the Cultural Revolution, many high school students were barely literate and many university students were studying at a lower, high school level. Mao's successors were left to clean up the mess that China's education system had become.

Education in the Reform Era

Despite the urgency for education reform, Mao's successors disagreed on the direction of reform. Mao's immediate successor, Hua Guofeng, wanted to continue Mao's model of mass education and the inclusion of manual labor in the curriculum. Deng Xiaoping and other reformers wanted to return to an emphasis on merit and expertise. The debate raged for two years, until Deng was able to consolidate his political position and push his reforms. Deng Xiaoping recognized that education had to be the center of China's modernization. In a speech to the 1978 National Educational Work Conference, Deng Xiaoping proposed educational policy that would meet the needs of China's modernization. In particular, Deng claimed that primary and secondary education needed to be strengthened. He also called for renewed respect for teachers, and for better working conditions and higher compensation.

The Chinese people were quick to try to catch up. Even during the Cultural Revolution, many Chinese families tried to homeschool their children. Although the Red Guards destroyed many "bourgeois" books, they exempted science and math books from destruction. Many of China's educated families believed that the Cultural Revolution would not last forever and always believed that their children would one day go to college. To prepare their children for that day, many Chinese families dusted off their old math, science, and, in some cases, literature books and taught themselves or their children. Despite Mao's efforts to completely reform Chinese culture, he could not kill the passion for education that was rooted in millennia of Confucian culture and the legacy of the imperial examination system. Even adults, including senior citizens, tried to catch up on what they had lost. For instance, Shanghai residents learned English from listening to BBC broadcasts; workers enrolled in extended learning courses or weekend education.

In rural areas, the breakup of the communes meant that they were no longer responsible for education, and localities lacked the resources and manpower to take on the schools. Rural school enrollment declined in the early 1980s after the closure of the commune schools. Families that had returned to farming under the Household Responsibility System kept the children home to help on the farm rather than send them to school. In 1985, the party's Central Committee published a major review of education policy. The review emphasized the need to restructure China's education system to meet the Four Modernizations in agriculture, industry, science and technology, and national defense. To meet this need, in 1986 the central government enacted the Nine-Year Compulsory Education Law, requiring the most developed areas of the country to offer nine years of compulsory schooling by 1990. Areas of "medium-level development" had until 1995 to meet this goal. The state set no goal for the less developed areas. The government claimed to have reached near-universal education at the primary and secondary levels by 1995. These figures are unreliable, however, as the central government relied on local governments to collect the statistics.

Deng and the reformers also made important changes to the curriculum. They phased out most political education, such as political theory and socialist ethics classes, which had crept in during the 1986 "spiritual pollution" campaign and after the 1986 and 1989 student demonstrations. After the Tiananmen Square crackdown, the state required university students to undergo one year of military training and political study.

Education Today

Today, elementary and middle school education is compulsory in China. In some areas of China, the common pattern of five years of primary school, three years of junior high, and two years of senior high school (five-three-two) are giving way to a six-three-three sequence. A system of *key schools,* which are similar to college preparatory schools, operates at national, provincial, county, and city levels. They are highly selective, and entrance to these schools is through competitive examination. They receive additional state funding and have resources superior to other, non-key, schools. They receive from two to three times as much money and have one-third more staff than non-key schools. Nearly 100 percent of students who attend key schools are accepted into higher education, 85 percent of them being accepted to China's top universities. Key schools constitute about 2 percent of primary schools, 8 percent of junior high schools, 4 percent of senior high schools, and 9 percent of universities. It is debatable if the key schools can take all of the credit for graduating excellent students. Because key schools attract above-average students in the first place, their success in graduating excellent students might hinge more on the caliber of student who enrolls in the key schools than on the school's superior resources.

The Ministry of Education develops a standard curriculum for all junior and senior high schools. The People's Education Press is responsible for compiling textbooks according to central guidelines. The Ministry of Education has prepared two tracks of instruction. Key schools use the more advanced track, and non-key schools use the lower-level track that consists of a core of basic knowledge. Consistent with China's modernization goals, both tracks are putting increasing emphasis on science. China's leaders are increasingly putting emphasis on vocational, technical, and agricultural high schools. Secondary schools teach physics, chemistry, biology, and health sciences as separate courses.

Despite China's economic boom, China spends less of its national income on education than do most developing countries. In 2008, the central government spent only 3 percent on education, well below the average of 5.5 percent in developed countries and 4.2 percent in developing countries. In 2006, the central government pledged to increase education funding to 4 percent of GDP, a goal not yet achieved. Until recently, students had to pay tuition and fees to attend public schools.

Having to pay tuition and fees put an undue burden on rural families and severely hindered education prospects for rural children. In 2004, the average primary school fees in rural China were 260 yuan ($32), while junior high school fees were 440 yuan ($54). According to the World Bank, a rural family living on a dollar a day at the poverty line would have about 888 yuan ($108) total resources per child for a year. Sending a child to middle school would take half of that.[43] In the poorest rural areas, elementary school fees might be only 160 yuan ($20), and junior high fees 240 yuan ($30) for the academic year, but with the average farm income only about 640 yuan ($78), education was considered a luxury. Also, parents who had never attended school often did not see the value in educating their children.[44]

It was evident to China's leaders that putting the burden of education on local governments had created regional gaps in education opportunity and quality. In 2006, China recentralized education funding by transferring payments from the central government to local governments.[45] In 2008, the central government began waiving tuition and fees for nine-year compulsory education, first in rural areas and then in all urban areas nationwide.

Despite the waiver, disparities in the availability and quality of education remain. It makes sense that local governments in wealthier counties are able to spend more on education than those in poorer counties. In fact, many schools, particularly those in rural areas, continue to suffer from lack of adequate funding. Many rural schools are physically run-down and lack basic teaching materials; schools are forced to pay various fees and taxes; teachers are absent, lethargic, or inadequately prepared.[46] In response to these problems, poor rural communities have started their own schools, and enterprising young people have started their own home-based schools. Throughout rural Chinese villages, young people too poor to afford a university education but with higher education ambitions have opened private schools in homes to educate peasant children. Gansu Province, one of China's poorest, has at least 586 such schools. One of these schools charged 18 yuan ($2.64) a term and had fifty-two students, thirty-eight girls and fourteen boys. The gender imbalance stemmed from the fact that the area's state-run school charged four times as much. Local families sent their sons to the state school, and sent their daughters to the less expensive private school.[47]

Rural poverty and lack of adequate funding have thus resulted in gender inequality in education. There is a positive correlation between rural poverty and gender inequality in enrollments. Boys have a higher probability of enrollment at all levels, and children whose mother has a higher education level than the father tend to be in school, especially boys. Children in more wealthy families tend to do better in school and are less likely to repeat a grade. Children in poorer families are less likely to go to school. Girls who are doing poorly in school are more likely to drop out of school, but boys usually stay in school through junior high.[48] In recent years, however, there has been a decrease in the educational gap between boys and girls. Although gaps still exist between boys and girls in illiteracy rate, years of school attainment, enrollment rate, and drop-out rate, the gender gaps have been narrowing.[49] Between 1990 and 2000, the enrollment rate for China's school-age children rose from 76 percent to 96 percent, with simultaneous improvement rates for both boys and girls. The World Bank finds no gender gap in terms of enrollment rates in urban areas, and only small gaps in rural areas.[50] For instance, although enrollment rates for school-age children in China's poorer provinces were lower than the national average, the gap between boys and girls was not significant.[51]

Recent trends in higher-level education. Despite the relatively low level of national income committed to education, Chinese urban primary and secondary schools offer students rigorous instruction, particularly in math and science. Consistent with the Chinese philosophy that learning is hard work, Chinese parents push their children to excel academically. Aware that they need to compete with large numbers of students for a limited number of seats in China's premier universities, Chinese students study long hours to try to rise above the crowd. Both parents and students view teachers as role models, or as "engineers of the soul."

In contemporary China, as in imperial China, academic success remains a primary path for individual advancement. In the collectivist Chinese culture, academic success not only holds the promise of future prosperity, but also brings honor to the family. The ultimate goal is to gain acceptance into one of China's top ten universities. The competition for slots in China's elite universities begins in primary school. Parents hire tutors, enroll their children in weekend language programs, and set high expectations for academic excellence so that their children will be accepted into key junior and senior high schools. Entrance to university is through a national standardized exam, called the National College Entrance Examination (NCEE). Administered annually, the NCEE is extremely competitive because it is a vital step toward a university education that promises higher socioeconomic status in society. Under this standardized system of selection, every student, regardless of family status or background, can achieve upward mobility through a university education. After the NCEE was suspended during the Cultural Revolution, in 1977 the Chinese government officially resumed the NCEE to admit university students on the basis of academics. Since then, successful performance in the NCEE has become a ticket to a quality university education and to a prosperous life. Given the disparity between China's population and limited space in higher education, the rate of university admission is much lower than the availability of higher education in the West.

China's leaders continue to be committed to upgrading China's education system, particularly at the tertiary level. The Tenth, Eleventh, and Twelfth Five-Year Plans all contain commitments to continue high economic growth through quality upgrading and the production of ideas. A key priority for the Twelfth Five-Year Plan (2011–2015) is to transition from "Made in China" to "Designed in China" by investing heavily in science and technology, and research and development, and by supporting next-generation information technology. To meet its needs, China is graduating an increasing number of college and graduate students. The number of undergraduate and graduate students in China has been growing at approximately 30 percent per year since 1999, and the number of graduates at all levels of higher education in China has approximately quadrupled in the last six years. In 2007, nearly 5.3 million students graduated from China's colleges and universities, a threefold increase from 1999.[52] The number of enrollments quintupled between 1998 and 2005. The state has increased spending on tertiary education, with most of the new spending focused on elite universities.[53] Elite universities are the top ten universities in China, which receive the largest education funds from central and local governments. They have priority in selecting students through national entrance exams and have the best faculty and research resources in China. Under tertiary education reform, China's leaders seek to elevate a small number of universities to world-class status, while enlarging them. In recent years, the central government has instructed all universities in China to substantially increase enrollments. Many universities have responded by increasing undergraduate enrollments 30 percent.

Market-oriented reforms are transforming tertiary education in China as well. Before the reform era, the state assigned jobs to high school and university graduates, and graduates had little choice in their job assignment. The Chinese government phased out job assignment in the 1980s and 1990s, allowing graduates to apply directly for jobs in which they were interested. One's skill set became increasingly important as graduates were forced to compete with each other for employment. High school and university students began to take courses that reflected their interests and that would make them more competitive in the job market. High schools and universities have responded to this interest by offering more vocational-oriented curricula. In poorer regions of China where there is little chance for someone to earn a university degree, many junior high school students are opting out of regular academic senior high schools and are enrolling in secondary technical schools. Technical schools are particularly attractive to rural students and students of little means because they are less expensive to attend and often offer a stipend. While it takes four years to earn a university degree, it takes fewer years to graduate from a technical school. Because university and technical school graduates earn similar wages, many students opt to attend a technical school and begin work earlier rather than later, enabling them to begin the move up the seniority ladder earlier than their university counterparts. In urban areas, some students are opting first for technical school and later for a university education. In the past, enrollment in a technical school precluded university entrance. That is no longer the case, and many students who enroll in technical schools later attend university.

With salaries in the technical fields becoming increasingly attractive, more students are opting for vocational programs in upstart entrepreneurial colleges. Despite their low ranking in the hierarchy of education, colleges of economics and trade schools enjoy high enrollment. The tuition for vocational schools is quite reasonable, and many students receive some funding from their employer to attend. Some students gain university admission by having their employers designate them as commissioned training students.[54] China's elite universities, such as Peking University and Fudan University, have responded to the student interest in foreign business, economics, and law by establishing schools of business management or finance.

The emergence of private schools. China's economic expansion and lack of adequate government funding have created opportunities for the establishment of private schools at all levels of education. The reemergence of a wealthy class presents entrepreneurs with opportunities to make money in for-profit education. In the early years of the real estate boom (1992–1996), real estate developers established elite private schools to attract buyers to their residential development projects.[55] One of the first private schools was the Guangya Primary School, founded in 1992 in Chengdu in Sichuan Province. The school offered Western-style teaching methods in superior facilities complete with air-conditioning, computers, TVs, and pianos, all for expensive tuition and fees. Guangya led the way for other private schools, and by 2005, some 15 million students were enrolled in 77,000 nonstate schools. One such school, the Oriental Pearl College, has 2,600 students from kindergarten through high school. Allowing students to move out of the state-funded system lessens the burden on the government. These institutions charge higher fees than state schools and claim to offer better facilities and equipment, smaller classes, and better teachers. The elite private schools charge more than 10,000 yuan ($1,587) in tuition and fees per year, putting them beyond the reach of most Chinese.[56] In coastal China, parents pay up to $3,000 a year to education their child in a reputable private boarding school. Families are increasingly able to afford the cost of a private education because of the rise in salaries and because most couples have only one child, due to the one-child policy. But not all of China's private schools are elite. China has many ordinary private schools that cater to the new middle class. They charge more moderate fees than the elite schools and usually have more modest facilities. The demand for education also created opportunities for the creation of private universities. The first private universities appeared in 1982, usually as weekend or night programs providing remedial education. By 1997, however, China had more than 1,200 private universities. Private universities are more independent of government bureaucratic control, which gives them more autonomy in administration and decisionmaking as well as flexibility in meeting student demands. Private universities must obtain the approval of the Ministry of Education to confer degrees. In 2005, only twenty-four private universities had won approval from the Ministry of Education to offer undergraduate degrees.[57]

Despite their economic situation, even the poorest people in China value education, and private schools increasingly serve the at-risk population. In urban China, most migrant children attend unregistered schools. Migrant-sponsored schools emerged as self-organized educational institutions, outside of the public system, in the 1990s. The migrant-sponsored schools were cheaper than the conventional schools and required monthly payment, which was a more manageable arrangement than the semester or annual fees required by conventional schools.[58] Although migrant children should be able to receive free compulsory education, many cities are unwilling or unable to provide such services. A rare case is the city of Shanghai, which made a major effort to enroll migrant children in free public schools and to help support private schools for children. Today, many migrant parents still prefer to send their children to the migrant-sponsored schools because of the savings and because they believe that their children will not be looked down upon or be teased by the children of local residents.

Civil Society and Social Change

In 1978, China's leaders adopted an Open Door policy (*kaifang zhengce*) toward foreign trade, investment, and borrowing. In addition to helping finance China's economic development, this foray into international economics introduced McDonald's, Michael Jackson, Madonna, and even concepts of democracy to the Chinese public. This open policy, coupled with political and legal reforms, transformed the social landscape of China. In the past thirty years, the Chinese people have become more consumption-oriented, more receptive to foreign culture and ideas, and more interested in the concept of human rights.

The Rise of the Middle Class

Three decades of economic growth have created a sizable middle class in China, identified by its relatively high level of education and income and by consumption patterns. China's middle class largely consists of private entrepreneurs, business professionals and managers, government officials, university professors and schoolteachers, technicians, and specialists. Members of the middle class enjoy more job security and higher income than rural residents, the urban working class, and laid-off laborers. Their annual income ranges from 60,000 ($9,524) to 500,000 yuan ($79,365).[59] Their lifestyles also distinguish them from others. They can afford cars and housing, take vacations abroad, and consume a variety of luxury goods. They also have more social influence than members of the lower socioeconomic classes.

Members of China's middle class are aware of social and political affairs, but are not particularly politically active. Because the party continues to be the nexus of power in China, most members of the middle class are outside of the political process and have little ability to change conditions in China. Because of government censorship of the media, the middle class is increasingly turning to the Internet for information and discussions of social and economic issues.

Chinese youth are increasingly turning away from politics and toward consumerism. In the 1980s, educated youths in China challenged the official ideology as well as the regime. At the same time, they challenged traditional Chinese culture. Chinese youth saw the market economy and Western democracy as a panacea for Chinese social and political ills. Since the 1989 Tiananmen Square crackdown, however, China's educated youth are less interested in directly challenging the regime and are more focused on activities that bring them foresecable results and personal satisfaction. In the 1980s, many educated young people viewed themselves as intellectuals and chose intellectual pursuits over commercial activities. Today, pervasive commercialism has transformed them. They are more likely to identify themselves as professionals in the modern society and believe that earning money is legitimate and preferred. In the 1980s, private businesses, which were often small owner-operated operations, were often run by the least educated people. Today, many large enterprises are managed by those who once considered themselves to be intellectuals.[60] They may not be completely satisfied with the current economic, social, and political orders, but are appreciative of China's economic prosperity and political stability. Thus, they would rather accept the existing establishment than try to change it.

While it is difficult to generalize attitudes and behaviors of Chinese youth, it can be said that young Chinese in wealthy coastal areas are cosmopolitan and strongly affected by global trends. Most young Chinese are apolitical, which means that they abstain from political participation, stemming from their lack of concern for politics. For instance, a Communist Youth League survey indicated that although 75 percent of young people interviewed expressed a willingness to participate in politics, 73 percent had not actually participated at all.[61] Political scientist Stanley Rosen found that most young Chinese viewed party membership as valuable for one's future success, such as in finding a well-paying job and good housing in a major city, and that most applicants have little knowledge or interest in most party activities and goals.[62]

Despite their apparent political inactivity, young Chinese express a high level of interest in social and political affairs. Rather than join political organizations to express their social and political views, they communicate in relative anonymity on the Internet. Internet chat rooms and blogs allow Chinese youth to communicate directly with one another, without the inconvenience, or the risk, of joining a political-oriented organization. Many journalists also use blogs to publish stories that the party finds too sensitive to print in the press. After being posted on blogs, these stories might make it into the press. For instance, a judge who was in custody died under suspicious circumstances. A blogger put pictures of his corpse on a blog, illustrating that the judge could not have died of natural causes. The story ended up in the press. In another case, a reporter covered an investigation of the death of schoolchildren who had drowned in a flood. Prohibited from saying much in his newspaper article, the reporter passed information on the investigation to several blogs. The story eventually made it into Chinese newspapers.[63]

Propaganda and the Arts

The Chinese government uses the print, broadcast, and electronic media to propagate views and party ideology. Soon after its creation in 1921, the CCP began to use propaganda to spread its message. Mao used propaganda to consolidate and maintain the party's power. Because approximately 80 percent of the population was illiterate, the party initially relied on China's centuries-old culture of storytelling to spread its message and cause. The stories often featured liberated peasants and better lives under the direction of the CCP. The CCP created its own newsreels and documentaries. The CCP also used poster art as a form of propaganda. Posters portrayed workers, peasants, and the party all working together to bring prosperity to China. The party also formed mobile cinema teams and took over the press. To influence China's youth, the CCP printed its own cartoons and comic books, which typically displayed class heroes and communist war victories. Posters typically featured healthy children engaged in some activity to further the gains of the motherland. Chinese communist propaganda also spread to theater plays. The first play the communists created was *The White-Haired Girl (Bai mao nü)*, a modern Chinese ballet about an abused woman who escapes to the mountains and survives on pilfered temple offerings. She descends from her mountain hideout as the communists arrive in her village and lives on to tell of the glories of the party.

Chinese communist propaganda reached its zenith during the Cultural Revolution. In remaking Chinese society, Mao attacked traditional values and "bourgeois things." Mao used propaganda in an effort to purge old ideas, customs, and thoughts from Chinese culture. As noted in Chapter 3, the party's criticism of the play *The Dismissal of Hai Rui* (1960) sparked the Cultural Revolution, with Jiang Qing and her associates as the primary instigators who purged all literature, films, art, and music of traditional Chinese culture. All music and visual arts had to meet Jiang's propagandist standards as well. Poster art typically depicted Mao as a deity. In every poster, he is part of the sun, above everyone or larger than life. Artists who resisted state control of their artistic expression were persecuted and imprisoned. Instead of engaging in self-expression, detained artists were forced to write self-criticisms. Under these conditions, many artists worked in secret or stopped creating art as self-expression.

Jiang Qing, who had been a B-grade actress and movie critic, radically reformed the Beijing Opera, eventually banning all but five. These five operas, called "model operas" (*Taking the Bandit's Stronghold, On the Docks, Raid on the White Tiger Regiment, Sparks Amid the Reeds,* and *The Red Lantern*), offered heroic representations of the proletariat and the CCP. To these operas, Jiang Qing added one symphony and two revolutionary modern ballets (one of them being *The White-Haired Girl*) to comprise a group of "model" performance pieces.

Many theater actors returned to the stage after Mao's death and the arrest of Jiang Qing and the Gang of Four. Beijing Opera enjoyed a revival in the late 1970s, but competition from television and the movie industry in recent years has reduced public interest in opera. Chinese art has enjoyed a revival. Much of the early post-Mao art expressed emotions over the injustices and abuses of the Cultural Revolution. Increased artistic freedom and the economic boom of the 1980s and 1990s yielded an explosion of Chinese art. Cynical realism has become one of the most important movements in contemporary Chinese art. Today, China has a thriving arts scene, and commercial and private art is largely uncensored. Private galleries and artists' colonies openly show nudity and sexually explicit pictures, but Chinese authorities balk at most depictions of China's leadership. Rather than confiscate such pictures, Chinese authorities usually request that the gallery remove the works. For instance, authorities asked a Beijing gallery to remove a painting of China's leaders all wearing the same dark suit and sporting identical hairstyles.

Cinematic Control

Chinese cinema began in 1896, only one year after it was invented in France. The thriving theater and movie industries that existed in Shanghai and other Chinese cities throughout the Nationalist years lost ground under the communists. Chinese communists used theater and the cinema for propaganda purposes during their rise to power and throughout the Mao years. Mao and China's communist leaders stifled the performing arts. From 1966 to 1972, not a single film was made in China. Throughout the Cultural Revolution, Jiang allowed the showing of only eight sample movies, one of them being the 1950 cinematic adaptation of the book and play *The White-Haired Girl*.

China's movie industry enjoyed a revival during the Deng years. In 2005, China produced 260 films, third behind India and the United States. Box office receipts in 2005 totaled 2 billion yuan (about $244 million). This revival, however, was tempered by government censorship. The State Administration of Radio, Film, and Television (SARFT) vets all films made in China and bans those that delve too deeply into topics of sex, violence, horror, religion, or politics. It requires that films with explicit sex and fear-provoking elements be cut or revised before release. SARFT claims that these moves are necessary to purify screen entertainment and create a more harmonious and "green" film environment for the public, especially children. SARFT bans films with content involving murder, violence, horror, evil spirits and devils, and excessively terrifying scenes, conversations, background music, and sound effects. Other films that are banned include those that distort the Chinese civilization and history; tarnish the image of revolutionary leaders, heroes, important historic characters, members of the armed forces, police, and judicial bodies; reconstruct crimes; or advocate environmental damage and animal abuse. For instance, the government banned Zhang Yimou's *Raise the Red Lantern* for its perceived criticism of the Chinese bureaucracy and Chen Kaige's *Farewell My Concubine* for its perceived negative portrayal of the CCP. Both movies had won international film awards. SARFT also banned international prize-winning movies such as *Cry Woman,* an offbeat tale of a woman who uses her distinctive voice as a professional mourner to pay off her husband's debts, and *Blind Shaft* for its depiction of life in China's illegal coal mines. SARFT also banned *To Live,* for its negative portrayal of various CCP policies and political campaigns. SARFT banned the film's director, Zhang Yimou, from making films for two years. *To Live* won the 1994 Cannes Film Festival's Grand Jury Prize. The justification for SARFT regulations is a belief on the part of party leaders that art should glorify and propagate, not inform or alienate. Chinese film directors often stifle their own creativity in producing films that pass SARFT regulations.

SARFT also bans foreign films that fail to meet its standards, or requires that they be edited before they are shown in China. For instance, SARFT in 2006 banned the animated film *Over the Hedge* because it depicted killing of animals. In 2007, SARFT demanded that *Pirates of the Caribbean: At World's End* cut Chow Yun-fat's portrayal of a Singaporean pirate, which SARFT claimed depicted a negative stereotype of Chinese people. Chinese authorities allow only twenty foreign films a year to be released in China on a revenue-sharing basis. China has too few movie theaters for its population, and many of its theaters are old. In recent years, the number of movie screens in China has doubled, although many of the new theaters are expensive. New movie theaters charge 40 to 120 yuan ($6 to $18) for a ticket, well beyond the means of most Chinese. China's movie industry competes with television and pirated DVDs, which are cheaper ways to watch the latest movies.

Media Control

The media in China consists of television, radio, newspapers, and magazines. Freedom of the press is guaranteed under article 35 of the Chinese constitution. However, other articles subordinate these rights to the national interest. China has one of the worst records of media freedom.[64] Based on measures of legal environment and political and economic controls, Freedom House in 2010 gave 84 points out of 100 (a score of 0 indicating a completely free media, and a score of 100 indicating a complete lack of media freedom) to China; 81 points were given to Russia, 33 to Hong Kong, 24 to Taiwan, 19 to the United Kingdom, and 18 to the United States. Finland and Iceland were given 10, the lowest score (most free).[65] Reporters Without Borders ranked China 171 in its sample of 178 countries. Only Sudan, Syria, Burma, Iran, Turkmenistan, North Korea, and Eritrea were ranked worse than China.[66] The US Department of State's annual *Country Report on Human Rights Practices in China* is rife with accounts of harassment, persecution, and incarceration of journalists and bloggers. For instance, its 2008 report claims that twenty-nine journalists and fifty-one cyber dissidents were imprisoned in China.[67]

The Chinese government owns all of the country's media outlets and controls the media through its Central Propaganda Department, particularly through censorship of any news or discussion that the party considers a threat to the regime legitimacy, political stability, or national image. The department controls the print media in conjunction with the State Press and Publication Administration; controls the broadcast media in cooperation with the State Administration of Radio, Film, and Television; and controls the Internet industry with the help of the Ministry of Information Industry. The party controls the media largely through appointment of media managers. The party's Organization Department and Central Propaganda Department appoint managers of national media outlets, such as the television station CCTV, *People's Daily,* and Xinhua (New China News Agency). At the provincial and local levels, party committees cooperate with the party's Central Propaganda Department to appoint managers to media outlets. The party also controls media content. Local offices of the CCP's Propaganda Department work with local party and government officials and the relevant media authority (such as the local branch of the State Press and Publication Administration) in transmitting guidelines to the local media. Editors and journalists must enroll in a national registration system and participate in ideological training sessions. Topics covered at the training sessions include Marxism, party leadership in the media, libel law, national security law, and regulations concerning news content. Editors and journalists must also attend additional political indoctrination retreats to study CCP ideology.[68] Membership in the party is key to career advancement and promotion to the upper echelons of media administration. Media executives, executive directors of television channels and radio stations, and key newspaper editors are party members.

The party determines news content and censors the media, and the Central Propaganda Department issues propaganda circulars instructing all media outlets on the handling of sensitive topics or specific news stories. For instance, the media must refer to the Falun Gong (see below) as an evil cult and portray the

Taiwan independence movement as separatism. The party requires media outlets to use Xinhua as the only news source, giving it a monopoly on domestic news.[69] In addition to government censorship of the media, Chinese journalists engage in self-censorship. The party expects Chinese journalists to know the party's priorities and expects them to know the limits of what they can say. Penalties for wayward journalism include cancellation or rebroadcasts of television news programs, dismissal of individuals associated with specific articles or series, cancellation of the license of a media organization, and imprisonment of editors or journalists.

Despite government and party controls of the media, China's journalists are able to pass a surprising amount of sensitive material past the censors. In recent years, there has been an increase in independent and investigative journalism. Part of this rise is due to the increase in the number of newspapers and media outlets in China. The increase can be traced to the decentralization of state ownership of the media and commercialization of the media in the 1980s. To better broadcast plans for economic reform, the CCP ordered party committees at all levels of government to establish "party papers." The number of newspapers in China increased fivefold by 1985 and eightfold by 1990. The central government soon allowed the newspapers to carry advertisements, making them profit-seeking ventures. The party also created a system of nationwide programming by ordering the establishment of broadcast stations at all levels of government. Local stations could produce their own news in addition to carrying mandatory broadcasts from CCTV1, the national television station.[70]

Chinese authorities began to loosen media controls after the Tiananmen Square crackdown, when they faced a legitimacy crisis. The CCP relaxed controls on material it deemed nonsensitive while maintaining tight control over the dissemination of sensitive material. At the same time, China's leaders began to commercialize the media by cutting subsidies and encouraging outlets to prove their viability by attracting advertisers and boosting circulation among the public. In 2002, the central government began to limit party and government ownership of media outlets, throwing the newspapers and broadcast stations into the market. The media responded by offering news that was informative and interesting, leading to the rise of investigative journalism that often pushes censorship boundaries.

To survive in the market, China's media organizations must promote the party ideology but do so in ways that are attractive to their audience. Journalists who can do both tasks are handsomely rewarded. Broadcast stations and print media encourage editors and journalists to report interesting news stories by offering them performance bonuses. In determining performance bonuses, media executives take into account reader or viewer responses to a journalist's report. Journalists risk losing performance bonuses if their stories are too sensitive or sensational. Journalists working in the for-profit media receive a base salary, sometimes only 15 to 20 percent of their total salary, with the rest being made up by performance bonuses. A journalist can make as much in a month in base salary as a farmer makes in a year. The addition of the performance bonus makes journalism a lucrative career in China. Good journalists quickly learn to balance their desire to earn performance bonuses with the need for news reports to meet party requirements.

Under Hu Jintao, however, Beijing has tightened control over journalists, forcing them to become increasingly adept at blurring the boundary between what the state deems as acceptable and unacceptable reporting. For instance, political journalists are increasingly adept at playing "edge ball" with Chinese censors. "Edge ball" is a term in ping-pong, referring to a hit on the very edge of the table. An edge ball is a legitimate ball as it is within bounds, but nearly impossible to defend by opponents. By playing "edge ball," Chinese journalists are testing the limits of politically acceptable news reporting without breaking the law. Chinese journalists have actually created a gray zone between what is acceptable to the censors and what is not.

Under Hu Jintao, there has been a rise in contentious journalists who engage in highly visible, clearly intentional, and overt investigative journalism.[71] Beijing-based *Caijing Magazine* is at the forefront of investigative journalism in China and regularly plays "edge ball" with Chinese censors. The *Southern Weekend, Southern Metropolis Daily, China Youth Daily,* and the *Beijing News* also engage in investigative journalism. For instance, Guangzhou's *Southern Metropolis Daily* published reports on the prison murder of Sun Zhigang. Sun was a twenty-seven-year-old college graduate who worked for a graphic design company in Guangzhou. In March 2003, the police stopped Sun on the street and required him to show residency papers. The police took him to the local precinct station for not having identification. He was transferred to one of the city's *shourong* stations—detention centers for vagrants and those without proper residency permits—where he died after being brutally beaten. The official media did not report the event, due to its sensitive nature. A reporter from the *Southern Metropolis Daily* picked up a letter posted on the Internet from Sun's parents and reprinted it on the Internet, where it was copied and disseminated throughout China. Although the reports led Premier Wen Jiabao to abolish the *shourong* system, the editors and journalists responsible for the series were sentenced to prison terms for the revelation.[72] In another case, the influential Guangdong Province weekly, *Southern Weekend,* in 2001 revealed the crimes of a corrupt local party boss. Journalists who report on topics counter to the party's approval suffer harassment or imprisonment. For instance, in 2007 the editor in chief of the monthly *Bai Xing* was removed from his post after investigating harsh living conditions in rural areas. In a similar case, in 2004, Larry Lang, a Chinese TV commentator based in Hong Kong, publicized how SOE managers were profiting greatly from privatization deals, while workers saw little benefits or were even laid off. While his work helped to stem the practice, government officials cancelled his show in 2006.[73] The Central Propaganda

Department and the government-sponsored All-China Journalists' Association called for the dismissal of an investigative reporter for the *China Economic Times* who had reported that substandard materials had been used on concrete employed in the construction of the Wuhan-Guangzhou railway.[74] In December 2009, the CCP's Propaganda Department demoted the chief editor at the *Southern Weekend* after he conducted an interview with US president Barack Obama without the department's prior approval.

Despite the party's attempts to censor sensitive material, however, readers clearly want the information. The rise in popularity of newspapers such as *Caijing, Southern Weekend,* and *Metropolis Daily* has resulted in the decline in circulation of party newspapers such as the *People's Daily.*

Internet Freedom

China has the largest population of Internet users in the world, with 485 million users in 2011. The Chinese government encourages Internet use for education and business, while asserting control of the actual flow of information available. The Chinese government and CCP control the Internet with the help of the Ministry of Information Industry, the Internet Propaganda Administrative Bureau, the Bureau of Information and Public Opinion, and the Internet Bureau. The Internet Propaganda Administrative Bureau issues licenses to commercial websites and allows them to reproduce reports from the official media, but not from independent news organizations. The Bureau of Information and Public Opinion organizes meetings with commercial sites to discuss public opinion and passes the findings on to party officials. The Internet Bureau exercises ideological control by forcing employees of propaganda agencies to take bureau-sanctioned courses on censorship and requiring online company executives to take an annual trip to the birthplace of communism and write an article on the trip. A fourth agency, the Beijing Internet Administrative Bureau, evaluates nineteen of the leading websites based in Beijing and determines what subjects will be covered the coming week, what articles will be written, and which articles will be eliminated. These four organizations report to party members and help keep dissent on the Internet to a minimum.

To avoid detection, many Internet users use proxy servers to access banned content. Some use online gaming as a way to communicate sensitive information. In 2006, political dissidents successfully used Internet instant messaging (IM) to hold large-scale, virtual meetings. The central government is increasingly concerned about the use of the Internet to undermine government and party authority. In 2006, President Hu Jintao called for "purifying" the Internet environment and stated that the party's ability to control the Internet is a matter affecting state stability.[75] The government has tightened restrictions to increase government control of the Internet. These restrictions include stricter website registration requirements, enhanced official control of online content, and an expanded definition of illegal online content. The government completely bans some overseas websites, such as YouTube, Facebook, MySpace, and Twitter. Having blocked these foreign sites, the Chinese government is encouraging domestic versions. In 2009, Chinese authorities approved new China-based microblogging services called *weibo,* which employ thousands of censors. Like Twitter in function, the largest providers have millions of users. For instance, Sina Weibo has 140 million users. Even the CCP's own mouthpiece, the *People's Daily,* opened one. China plans to launch an English version of Sina's *weibo* in the United States in the near future.

Websites are required to be licensed by, or registered with, the Ministry of Information Industry (MII).[76] The government pressures Internet companies in China to sign the "Public Pledge on Self-Discipline for the Chinese Internet Industry." Signatories promise not to disseminate information that "may jeopardize state security and disrupt social stability" or that "contravene laws and regulations and spread superstition and obscenity." The government requires Internet companies to monitor the information appearing on websites and remove the harmful information promptly. Internet regulators require all of China's search engines—including Google, Baidu, Yahoo!, Sina, and Sogou— to delete "all harmful information." To ensure that sensitive items do not see the light of day, the government gives both domestic and foreign Internet businesses in China a confidential list of banned items. The list changes over time to reflect current events, so Internet companies must consistently review the lists. In addition, Chinese authorities filter the Internet with technology that intermittently blocks sites that contain sensitive terms. This Internet-filtering system, known informally as the Great Firewall, blocks access to a range of foreign content, from criticism of China's leaders to information about sensitive historical events and political terms.

Much of the technology used to filter Internet content is designed by foreign companies. Cisco Systems, Microsoft, Nortel Networks, Sun Microsystems, and Websense all have provided sophisticated technologies that help the Chinese government censor the web. The technology filters words such as *human rights, democracy,* and *freedom.* The MII monitors the Internet under guidance from the central government's Central Propaganda Department. The MII employs more than thirty thousand people to police electronic communications. Two cartoon characters, Jingjing and Chacha (*jingcha* is the Chinese word for police) redirect Internet users away from forbidden information. The characters pop up on the computer screen when a user strays into dangerous territory. The government blocks sites discussing Taiwan and Tibetan independence; underground religious and spiritual organizations, such as Falun Gong and other suspect Qigong clubs; democracy activists; and the 1989 Tiananmen Square Massacre. In 2006, the Ministry of Public Security began to monitor all major portals and online forums as part of a campaign against online pornography. From April to September 2007, the Ministry of Public Security shut down

18,400 illegal websites either for carrying pornographic content or because they were unregistered.[77]

Like journalists, operators of web portals and blog-hosting services engage in self-censorship to ensure their servers are free of politically sensitive material. Internet cafes must install software that allows government officials to monitor customers' Internet usage. Internet cafes are subject to surveillance, and many cafes require patrons to provide identification. Authorities detain or arrest Internet users who dare to criticize the government. Bloggers, journalists, and activists who post political or dissenting views on the Internet have been sentenced to four- to six-year prison terms, or have been committed to mental hospitals. China imprisons more bloggers than any other country. In 2007, fifty of the sixty-four cyber-dissidents imprisoned worldwide were in Chinese prisons.[78]

The Cases of Yahoo!, Google, and Microsoft

American Internet companies Yahoo!, Google, and Microsoft are all active in China. Yahoo! entered the Chinese market in 1999, one of the first foreign Internet companies to do so. In 2005, Yahoo! invested $1 billion in the Chinese Internet firm Alibaba and transferred ownership of Yahoo! China to Alibaba. Yahoo! is a 40 percent minority shareholder in Alibaba. As a result, Yahoo! argues that cooperation with Chinese authorities is in the hands of Alibaba, and not Yahoo! In 2002, Yahoo! signed the Public Pledge on Self-Discipline for the Chinese Internet Industry, which requires, among other things, that Yahoo! refrain from producing, posting, or disseminating harmful information that may compromise national security or disturb social stability. Since signing the pledge, which Yahoo! was under no legal obligation to do, Yahoo! has censored search results through the Chinese version of its search engine.[79] In 2005, Yahoo! provided Chinese authorities with information leading to the arrest and imprisonment of two journalists, Li Zhi and Shi Tao. Shi had sent an e-mail summarizing the content of a Central Propaganda Department communiqué on party efforts to control the Chinese media. Shi sent the e-mail using his Yahoo! account to the editor of a Chinese prodemocracy website based in the United States. Chinese authorities accused him of "illegally providing state secrets to foreign entities" and demanded that Yahoo! Holdings (Hong Kong) provide account-holder information.[80] A Chinese court used the Yahoo! evidence in the case against Shi Tao, which resulted in a ten-year prison sentence.

Microsoft acquiesces to direction from the Chinese government to restrict content available through MSN Spaces (a program that allows individuals to create and maintain personal websites). MSN blocks blog titles with terms including *democracy, human rights, freedom of expression, Tibet independence,* and *Falun Gong.* Microsoft's China-based search engine, MSN China, filters the results of searches for politically sensitive terms. A search of these terms results in only official and government-approved sites. Google also filters sensitive information. Although Google.com is available in China, searches pass through a firewall, which censors terms, websites, and services that the party deems offensive or subversive. The firewall is intended to control foreign-based websites. It consists of routers that connect to the main fiber-optic cable lines in China, which connect China to the global Internet. Web browsers send out requests to websites, and while the information is traveling over the pipeline, the router will serve as a filter. If the requested site is one that is on China's list of banned sites, then the request will not be completed and there will be no access. If the site is not completely banned, but there are certain pages that contain banned key words, then only those links to the specific pages will be available. Critics claim that self-censorship contradicts Google's pledge to "do no evil." As a concession to critics, Google informed users when information was being censored and decided not to launch Gmail or other services that hold private information until it feels confident that it can protect users' privacy.

Despite these controls, some websites are able to post uncensored news. For instance, during the winter 2006 SARS outbreak, many people stayed at home and kept in touch through the Internet. Word of the disease spread by e-mail, computer, and text message, thwarting government efforts to block news of the outbreak. Information technology has allowed political and environmental activists to organize protests against local party organizations. In 2007, an anonymous text message on their cell phones prompted thousands of citizens

The Case of Google.cn

In 2006, Google launched Google.cn, a self-censoring Chinese search engine as an alternative to Google.com, which is based outside China. In March 2010, Google stopped censoring Google.cn, citing major cyberattacks that appeared to target the e-mail accounts of human rights activists. It automatically redirected mainland Chinese users to an uncensored Chinese-language version of its service hosted in Hong Kong, Google.com.hk. Hong Kong, a special administrative region (SAR), enjoys freedom of speech not protected in China. Chinese authorities called Google's decision to stop censoring "totally wrong" and stated that Google must follow Chinese laws. Although Google was not censoring the Hong Kong site, China's Internet filters, collectively known as the Great Firewall, blocked politically sensitive search results for users in China. In particular, Chinese authorities insisted that users perform more than just a single mouse click to reroute to the Hong Kong site. As a compromise, Google agreed to impose a "double click" rule so as not to automatically reroute searches, thereby saving face for the Chinese government. Soon after, Chinese authorities renewed Google's license in China. Google continues to provide web search and local products to users in China.

in Xiamen (Fujian Province) to protest against plans to build a massive chemical factory in residential areas. They protested that the factory would be hazardous to residents' health. Residents heard of the potential hazard and criticism of the project from blogs and chat forums. In response to the demonstrations, the State Environmental Protection Administration forced a halt in construction pending an environmental impact study.[81] In 2006, reports of slave labor appeared in the Internet discussion forum *Tianya*. The forum reported that boys were being abducted from poor villages in Shanxi and Henan Provinces and were held captive and forced to work in deplorable conditions despite the knowledge of local police. *Tianya* posted a petition by the boys' fathers, and official media reported the story. Within eight days, China's leading politicians intervened, ordering the release of hundreds of the boys and the arrest of their bosses.[82]

Ethnic Minorities in China

China is a multiethnic state.[83] China has fifty-six officially recognized ethnic groups. Some 91.5 percent of the population is Han Chinese. The other fifty-five minorities, called national minorities (*minzu*), number approximately 106 million people. Several of the ethnic minorities exceed 1 million people. The largest of the minority groups are the Zhuang (16.2 million), Manchus (10.7 million), Hui or Chinese Muslims (9.8 million), Miao (Hmong) (8.9 million), Uygur (also spelled Uyghur and Uighur, 8.4 million), Yi (7.8 million), Mongols (5.8 million), Tibetans (5.4 million), Bouyei (3 million), and Koreans (1.9 million) (see Table 2.1).[84] The ethnic minority groups' percentage of the total population increased from 6 percent in 1953 to 8.5 percent in 2000. The increase was due to improvements in traditionally poor health care in minority-concentrated areas and to the minority exemption to the one-child policy. While most Han Chinese are limited to only one child, the policy has not been applied to most ethnic minority groups. The exemption partly explains the increase in the percentage of minority groups between 1953 and 2000.[85]

The ethnic minorities are scattered throughout sixteen of China's provinces. In the autonomous regions of Tibet (Xizang) and Inner Mongolia, the minorities make up the majority. Many of China's ethnic minorities live in autonomous regions. Autonomous regions are named by combining the geographical name, followed by the name of the specified minority population, followed by the name for the administrative level. For instance, the heavily Zhuang-populated area of south(west) China is called the Guangxi Zhuang Autonomous Region and the Muslim northwest is called the Xinjiang Uygur Autonomous Region. Most of the minorities are concentrated in five provincial-level ethnic minority autonomous regions: the Tibet Autonomous Region, the Xinjiang Uygur Autonomous Region, the Inner Mongolia Autonomous Region, the Ningxia Hui

Autonomous Region, and the Guangxi Zhuang Autonomous Region. Most of the autonomous regions and provinces are located in China's borderlands, and more than 90 percent of China's land bordering with foreign countries is occupied by ethnic minorities. Hence, China's policies toward its ethnic minorities are largely influenced by the need to secure its border areas. For instance, in the early 1990s, some Chinese Muslims living in the Xinjiang Autonomous Region along China's northwest border began to agitate for more autonomy, or even independence, from the PRC, just as many regions in Central Asia had been able to do after the collapse of the Soviet Union.

For most of China's history, ethnic minorities lived largely in isolation from the Han. They spoke their own languages, and most did not speak Mandarin. In the 1930s, the Chinese communists entered minority areas as they tried to establish support among the rural population. Largely ignorant of local customs, the communists recruited minority elites to help them win the hearts and minds of the people. After creating the PRC in 1949, the Chinese communists set out gradually to integrate China's ethnic minorities into the unified state. China's leaders recognized that it could not enter minority group areas and dictate policy; it needed leaders from minority groups who would be familiar with the ethnic minority language and culture. When the CCP created new administrative divisions (see Chapter 3), it created five autonomous regions for those areas largely populated by minorities and allowed minorities to maintain their customs and habits in these areas. Because the party lacked cadres with knowledge of minority groups' languages and culture, it selected prominent minority elites as leaders.

In the early 1950s, the CCP began the process of classifying minority groups as separate nationalities. To identify national minority groups, the CCP used four characteristics—common language, territory, economy, and culture—that Joseph Stalin had set out in his 1914 work *Marxism and the National Question*. Work teams applied this definition to China's ethnic minority groups, basing their classifications on particular economic conditions, historical background, and international relations in a defined area. The classification teams labeled some individuals and communities as belonging to a particular minority group even if they disagreed. The teams often classified individuals and groups according to where they lived rather than on the above criteria.[86]

The CCP believed that ethnic minority autonomy would be a temporary arrangement. According to Marx, nationalism was a construct of the ruling class and would fade away after a communist revolution. Hence, the CCP tolerated and even offered national recognition to some groups that had not been considered ethnic minorities, because it did not see the arrangement as permanent. The recognition of ethnic minorities and the creation of the autonomous units would later become problematic for the CCP. Rather than facilitate assimilation, the autonomous designation largely froze ethnic divisions. Administrative divisions, based on ethnicity and led by minorities, conferred on minority groups political legitimacy that previously did not exist.[87]

After 1956, the Chinese government began a more assertive policy of assimilation. It forced minorities to replace their "feudal customs," such as religious practices, with the "scientific" values of socialism. For instance, the central government required schools in minority areas to teach Mandarin and introduced socialist concepts of collectivization of agriculture. The CCP extended the Anti-Rightist Campaign into minority areas, targeting those who advocated local nationalism. These policies led to clashes between Han Chinese and minorities, especially in Tibet and Xinjiang, resulting in a relaxation of policies. The Chinese government resumed radical assimilation during the Cultural Revolution, and Red Guards targeted and persecuted many prominent minority leaders. Efforts to eliminate the Four Olds during the Cultural Revolution (see Chapter 3) led to the destruction of minority temples, artifacts, historical sites, and texts. After the Cultural Revolution, the Chinese government again modified its assimilation policy, allowing for greater diversity. Chinese cadres began to learn minority languages, and the government encouraged the preservation of minority culture, traditions, music, dance, and dress. After the relaxation of China's assimilation policy led to challenges to Beijing's authority, the central government tightened up restrictions in Xinjiang and reimposed martial law in Tibet. Although the government lifted martial law in the 1990s, it has kept security tight in Tibet through a series of "Strike Hard" campaigns. For instance, in spring 2008, China's top leaders cracked down on human rights protests on the eve of the Beijing Olympics, and in 2009, they launched a Strike Hard campaign on the eve of the fiftieth anniversary of the March 1959 suppression of a rebellion in which the PLA drove the Dalai Lama into exile in India and established more direct control over Tibet.

Amendments to the 2004 constitution state that all ethnic groups in the PRC are equal, and the amendments contain a number of special provisions for minorities, as outlined below. However, many of these rights have not been observed. Many Western analysts note that political expression and representation are more tightly controlled in autonomous areas than in nonautonomous areas.[88] On paper, the constitution obligates the state to protect the rights and interests of the minority ethnic groups. For instance, China's ethnic groups have the freedom to use and develop their own spoken and written languages and to preserve or reform their own folkways and customs. With the exception of the 1975 constitution, all of China's state constitutions since 1954 have contained provisions for self-government in autonomous regions. Autonomous areas exist at all subnational levels of government and can be provinces, prefectures, counties, or townships. The principal institutions and organs of self-governance are the people's congresses and people's governments of autonomous regions, prefectures, counties, and ethnic townships. Either the chair or vice chair of the standing committee of the people's congress, as well as the head of any autonomous government, must come from the dominant ethnic minority. The Chinese constitution grants autonomous regions more rights, at least on paper, than it grants to provinces. Autonomous regions have a chairperson, whereas provinces have governors, who are required by law to be from the minority ethnic group as specified by the autonomous region.

As the principal organ of self-governance, the people's congresses can enact regulations in light of the political, economic, and cultural characteristics of the ethnic minorities in their areas. The Standing Committee of the National People's Congress must approve these regulations before they can go into effect. The people's congresses and governments at the subnational levels are responsible for local economic development under the guidance of state plans. Consistent with the concept of self-governance, the governments of the ethnic autonomous areas independently administer educational, scientific, cultural, and public health agencies in their respective areas. The constitution stipulates that the organs of self-government of the ethnic autonomous areas use their own spoken and written languages in performing government duties.[89] The central government organ responsible for ethnic minority policy is the State Ethnic Affairs Commission. The Eleventh Party Congress initially selected a Han Chinese as commission minister, but reversed its decision after China's top leadership determined that it was politically inappropriate for a Han Chinese to hold the position. Instead, the congress selected Yang Jing, a Mongolian and former governor of Inner Mongolia, as commission minister.[90] The Law on Regional National Autonomy (LRNA) is the basic law for the implementation of the system of regional national autonomy.[91] Although the LRNA stipulates local self-governance of autonomous areas, the practice of self-governance is no different from that of the provinces. Unlike the United States, where each state has a constitution with reserved powers, China is a unitary state in which provinces and autonomous regions are subordinate to Beijing. Although China's autonomous regions have people's governments and people's congresses, autonomous regions are still subject to the arbitrary will of the central government. Each of the five provincial-level autonomous regions has CCP chiefs whose political power exceeds that of the region's chairperson.

Chinese history is fraught with considerable hostility between Han Chinese and ethnic minorities. Under Deng Xiaoping, the Chinese government made a concerted effort to increase the number of cadres with ethnic backgrounds serving in minority areas. In Tibet, historically the most nationalistic of the minority areas, the number of ethnic Tibetan cadres as a percentage of all cadres in Tibet increased from 50 percent in 1979 to 62 percent in 1985. In Zhejiang Province, the government formally decided to assign only cadres familiar with nationality policy and sympathetic to minorities to cities, prefectures, and counties with large numbers of minority people. In Xinjiang, the leaders of the region's fourteen prefectural and city governments and seventy-seven of all eighty-six rural and urban leaders were of minority nationality by the late 1980s. Since the 1980s, all Han cadres working in minority areas are required to learn the local spoken and written languages. In recent years, unrest in Tibet and terror plots by Uygur separatists seeking independence have threatened Hu Jin-tao's goals of building a "harmonious society." To defuse ethnic tension, China's leaders have begun to recruit more ethnic elites into the country's political apparatus. For the first time in PRC history, all of the chairs of China's five provincial-level autonomous regions have ethnic minority backgrounds.[92] It should be pointed out that all of these leaders are state leaders and not party leaders. The latter are overwhelmingly Han and are the real holders of power.

Economic Development in Ethnic Minority Areas

The 2004 constitution obligates the state to assist ethnic minority areas in their economic and cultural development.

Although minority groups constitute only 8.5 percent of China's population, they inhabit 64 percent of China's land, mostly vast areas in China's southwest, northwest, and northern periphery. Much of this land is uninhabitable mountain and desert terrain, but other lands have important natural resources such as timber, oil, natural gas, coal, and minerals. Mao Zedong Thought highlights the importance of ethnic minority lands to China's economic development. "The Han nationality has the population, the minority nationalities have the land. . . . It is thus imperative that the Han assist the minorities in raising their standard of living and socialist ideological consciousness, while the minorities provide the natural resources necessary for the industrialization and development of the motherland."[93]

In 1999, President Jiang Zemin expressed the desire to seize a historic opportunity to accelerate the development of western China. A key component of this strategy is the Develop the West Campaign (further explored in Chapter 8). Launched in 2000, the campaign directs state investment, foreign investment, and private capital into modernizing China's poor interior. It is an attempt by China's leaders to narrow the economic gap between the more prosperous coastal regions and the poorer interior. After rising to power, Deng Xiaoping in the early 1980s advocated an economic development strategy in which coastal China would develop first, and the west would follow. The state bestowed favorable economic and investment policies on eastern China, which attracted both domestic and foreign investors to coastal special economic zones (SEZs) and town and village enterprises. Meanwhile, the interior remained undeveloped and poor, resulting in a serious coastal-interior gap. By the late 1990s, Deng's promise that western development would follow eastern development still had not come to fruition. After twenty years of economic development, the western provinces attracted only 5 percent of foreign investment in China. The Develop the West Campaign is an ambitious, long-term development program designed to modernize the interior regions where most ethnic groups live. It covers six provinces (Yunnan, Gansu, Sichuan, Guizhou, Qinghai, and Shaanxi), three autonomous regions (Ningxia, Tibet, and Xinjiang) and one provincial-level municipality (Chongqing). The aims of the Develop the West Campaign are to promote development by exploiting the west's natural resources and to pacify the region with Han migration. The exploitation of the west's resources perturbs many of the ethnic minorities living there. According to the aforementioned Law on Regional National Autonomy (LRNA), the central government owns all of the country's natural resources, but allows localities to protect and manage them. Ethnic minorities living in the west complain that the revenue generated by the exploitation of natural resources in their backyards by state firms flows east and is not invested in the local economy. They also are increasingly disturbed by Han migration westward, which is diluting ethnic concentrations in the west.

An alternate aim of the Develop the West Campaign is to pacify a restive west, where ethnic tensions threaten China's stability and security. Although portrayed as an effort to alleviate poverty in minority-populated areas and to reduce interior-coastal economic disparity, the campaign is as much an attempt to control the restive minority groups as to homogenize Chinese society. This social homogenization is realized by further integrating ethnic minority groups into the Han-dominated Chinese nation.[94] The two areas that concern Beijing the most are Xinjiang and Tibet. The Xinjiang Uygur Autonomous Region is located in far northwest China. Literally the "New Frontier," Xinjiang is the nexus at the crossroads of Russia, Central Asia, Mongolia, the Indian subcontinent, Tibet, and China. It occupies a sixth of China's landmass. Its Tarim Basin contains large oil deposits, and Lop Nor is China's premier nuclear test site. Xinjiang is home to the Uygur nationality, a predominantly Muslim ethnic group with a population of approximately 8 million. Although Xinjiang has experienced rapid economic growth under Deng's economic reforms, the Uygurs remain poor. The growing disparity between Han Chinese living in Xinjiang and the Uygurs has created significant tension between the two groups. Part of the Uygur-Han conflict stems from migration of Han Chinese to Xinjiang in the 1990s. The breakup of the Soviet Union exacerbated tensions that had long existed in Xinjiang. In 1990, Han police and soldiers clashed with Uygurs, whom Beijing labeled "counterrevolutionary plotters" belonging to the Islamic party of East Turkestan. In an effort to "civilize" and pacify the restive region, the state offered subsidies to Han Chinese who were willing to migrate. Over time, Han Chinese bought out or bought up businesses in Xinjiang's cities. By the late 1990s, Han ownership of businesses in Urumqi, Xinjiang's key city, exceeded that of Uygurs.

In the 1990s, Beijing put down periodic outbursts of ethnic violence with military force. In 1996, the central government carried out a Strike Hard (anticrime) campaign against the Uygurs. The Public Security Bureau claimed to have captured more than 2,700 terrorists, murderers, and other criminals in two months. Instead of stemming the tide of separatism, the Strike Hard campaign further alienated Xinjiang's population. In February 1997, hundreds of Uygurs took to the streets demanding independence for Xinjiang, only to be met with military force. Uygur separatists carried out several bus bombings in Urumqi to coincide with Deng Xiaoping's funeral and exploded a pipe bomb on a bus in Beijing. After the September 11, 2001, attacks, Beijing increased surveillance and control of Uygurs in Xinjiang. Violence flared in February 2009 as Uygurs chafed under limitations to religious practices. Nearly two hundred people were killed in the ensuing riots. In recent years, China's leaders have moved some forty thousand troops to Xinjiang to quell separatist activities and maintain security.

Tibet is a second area of concern for central authorities. In 1950, the CCP declared PRC jurisdiction over Tibet and stationed troops there to control it. Chafing under PRC rule, Tibetans rose up in 1959, but were put down by Chinese troops. During the crackdown, the Dalai Lama, spiritual leader of the Tibetans, fled to Daramsala, India. From his exile in India, the Dalai Lama has sought autonomy for the Tibetans and maintains that Tibetans need more control over their own affairs to maintain their culture and ethnicity. As in the case of Xinjiang, the central government has encouraged Han Chinese to migrate to Tibet and has offered willing Han Chinese subsidies and tax breaks to open businesses there. Today, Han entrepreneurs own most of the businesses in Lhasa and other areas of Tibet, creating resentment among the Tibetans. The Tibetans argue that the Han entrepreneurs discriminate against the Tibetans; Han businessmen argue that the Tibetans are insufficiently proficient in Mandarin Chinese and do not share the Han work ethic. Throughout the decades, armed Tibetans have periodically clashed with Chinese authorities. Beijing responds with Strike Hard campaigns and martial law. For instance, in spring 1989, China's leaders sent troops to the region and imposed martial law to restore order as part of the Strike Hard policy against Tibetan separatists. Anti-Chinese riots erupted in March 2008, after a peaceful demonstration by monks. The riots were triggered by a desire on the part of monks and other Tibetans to commemorate the forty-ninth anniversary of Chinese occupation of Tibet.

Education and Health Care of Ethnic Minorities

Ethnic minority educational levels are below those of Han Chinese. Approximately 8.5 percent of minority youths have had no formal schooling, compared with 2 percent of Han.[95] While the national illiteracy rate (and that for urban Han) is 7 percent, the illiteracy rate for national minorities as a whole averages 25 percent. At 40 percent, Tibetans have the highest illiteracy rate among China's urban population, followed by the Dai (28.2 percent), Yi (13.65), Hani (13.48), Miao (also known as Hmong) (12.6), and Bouyei (12.58).

High illiteracy rates for most minority groups, and for rural minorities in particular, are likely to continue because primary-school attendance for most minorities is low. For instance, less than 20 percent of Tibetans have a primary education. Enrollment in junior high school is less than 25 percent. Although urban enrollment is high, many remote areas of Tibet have universalized only three-year primary education.[96] In 1986, the central government enacted the Compulsory Education Law, mandating nine years of school (six years of primary school and three years of junior high school). The law would be carried out nationwide in three phases: developed areas, moderately developed areas, and underdeveloped areas. Although all areas were required to have met the goal of universal primary education by 1990, the moderately developed areas and underdeveloped areas were not expected to realize compulsory junior high school by then. At the secondary level, fewer ethnic minority children attend school than the Han. Considering the low numbers of children attending primary and secondary school, it is no surprise that minority college attendance is low.

The state has implemented a number of measures to increase school attendance and decrease the dropout rate for minority students. It provides subsidies for education in minority areas and has built boarding schools where transportation between home and school makes attendance difficult. Some minorities can teach in their native language and use books in minority languages. A type of affirmative action program adds points to scores of minority students for college and university entrance examinations; some students may take the entrance exams in their native language. Some universities offer remedial classes for minority students. The state also subsidizes nationality schools and colleges, including ethnic minority teacher-training colleges.[97]

Although minority education attainment continues to lag behind that of the Han, there have been increases. The numbers of ethnic minority students attending school have continually increased, as has the number of minority teachers. The 2000 census indicates that illiteracy rates in minority areas decreased between 1990 and 2000.

Human Rights Issues

China is a signatory to twenty-one UN conventions on human rights. In 1988, China's National People's Congress ratified the Convention Against Torture, and in 1998 signed the International Covenant on Civil and Political Rights (ICCPR).[98] In 2004, the National People's Congress amended China's state constitution to include the protection of human rights.[99] These protections, however, are greatly diminished by the existence of articles 51 through 54, which explicitly state that individuals exercising their rights may not infringe on the interests of the state; must not commit acts to compromise the security, honor, and interests of China; must keep state secrets; must protect public property; and must observe labor discipline and public order.[100] The limitations noted in these articles affect all rights protections in China.

Human rights abuses are common in China today. These include controls on expression and association (including restrictions on freedom of speech and the media, assembly and association, and religion), torture and ill-treatment of prisoners, lack of due process, and repression of minority groups.

Restrictions on Freedom of Speech, the Media, Assembly, Association, Procession, and Demonstration

Article 35 of China's constitution guarantees citizens freedom of speech, the press, assembly, association, procession, and demonstration. In reality, China tightly controls the flow of information. A censorship bureaucracy licenses and monitors all media outlets and publishers and must approve all books before publication. Beyond official censorship, journalists engage in self-censorship. All journalists, editors, and publishers are aware of party propaganda department guidelines, such as the requirement that news coverage be 80 percent positive and 20 percent negative. They purposely avoid sensitive topics such as environmental degradation, the one-child policy, and social discontent. Authorities block websites and filter Internet content based on specified words and topics. Some thirty journalists and fifty individuals were in prison in 2007 for reporting on sensitive topics or posting their views on the Internet.[101] The government also imposes severe restrictions on contact between foreign news media and dissidents and routinely imprisons dissidents who meet with foreign news media.

Chinese authorities also tightly control citizen associations. All civic organizations in China fall under the umbrella of the CCP. There are no autonomous unions or organizations. There are no true nongovernmental organizations or independent think tanks in China because they all must accept party oversight. Although article 35 guarantees citizens freedom of assembly, association, procession, and demonstration, under state law demonstrators must receive a permit to gather. These permits are commonly denied. Citizens who process and demonstrate without a permit are subject to arrest and detention. The government also prohibits protests against the political system or national leaders and quickly suppresses demonstrations involving expression of dissenting political views. Chinese law stipulates that such activities may not challenge party leadership or infringe upon the interests of the state.

Freedom of Religion

China's five government-recognized religions are Buddhism, Catholicism, Islam, Protestantism, and Daoism. Article 36 of the constitution guarantees Chinese citizens the right to freedom of religion. This right is limited, however, with prohibitions against proselytizing and other activities deemed to "disturb public order." According to the constitution, "The state protects normal religious activities." The term *normal* is subjective, and the state has the sole power to determine what activity is normal and what is not. Perhaps more important, the constitution states that "no one may make use of religion to engage in activities that disrupt public order, impair the health of citizens, or interfere with the educational system of the state." All religious venues are required to register with the State Administration for Religious Affairs or its local Religious Affairs Bureaus. Together, they are responsible for monitoring and judging whether religious activity is "normal" and therefore lawful. Both the State Administration for Religious Affairs and the party's United Front Work Department provide policy guidance and supervision over implementation of government regulations on religious activity.[102]

Government authorities used these limitations on religious freedom in 1999 to ban the Falun Gong ("Skills of the Wheel of Law") movement. The Falun Dafa (popularly called Falun Gong) is a spiritual movement based on a form of Qigong (deep breathing exercises) and emphasizes the unity of physical and spiritual healing. Adherents combine physical and spiritual exercises with moral cultivation. Founded by Li Hongzhi, a former government official, Falun Gong took root in China in 1992. Chinese found its slow, meditative exercises combined with teachings from Buddhism and Daoism a balm for their hectic lives. Aware of a 1994 law requiring religious activity to be supervised by an official, "patriotic" religious organization, Li called his organization a "cultivation system" or a "spiritual belief system" to avoid confrontation with the government.

Membership in Falun Gong grew exponentially in the 1990s and included common citizens, civil servants, journalists, academics, and party members. By 1999, Falun Gong had more than 70 million practitioners inside China, outnumbering the party membership and making it one of the largest nongovernmental organizations in Chinese history. Its phenomenal growth and ability to organize protests against state-organized criticism of the movement threatened party and government officials.[103] In April 1999, more than ten thousand Falun Gong practitioners from all over China held a peaceful demonstration outside the Zhongnanhai party and state compound in central Beijing, seeking official recognition of the organization. The event that triggered the protest was the detention of up to fifty Falun Gong practitioners in Tianjin who had been protesting a media report critical of the organization. Over the next three months, the official Chinese media ran articles and editorials critical of Falun Gong, which spurred more protests. In July, the Ministry of Civil Affairs banned the Falun Gong "cult" on the pretext that it was a political force opposed to the CCP and the central government and that it "preaches idealism, theism, and feudal superstition." The central government accused Falun Gong of organizing large-scale illegal gatherings and trying to persuade people to give up their ideals and pursuits and eschew social practice, in contradiction to the building of socialism with Chinese characteristics.[104] China's leaders followed the ban with massive state repression, confiscating and destroying materials and prosecuting organizers. Since 1999, thousands of Falun Gong adherents have been imprisoned in China, some dying in captivity. Thousands of practitioners have been sent to labor camps or to mental hospitals, and more than two thousand have been tortured to death. Others have lost their jobs and their homes.[105]

China's authorities also limit relations between Chinese religious institutions and foreign churches. China's constitution states that "religious bodies and religious affairs are not subject to any foreign domination." Before 1949, churches in China operated freely, usually under the direction of foreign missionaries and with foreign sources of funding. In the 1950s, China's communist leaders began to remove foreign "imperialist" influence from China's Christian churches and bring them under state control. They forced Protestants and Anglicans to dissolve their denominations and unite under the Three-Self Patriotic Movement (*sanyi yundong*). The three selves of self-governance, self-support, and self-propagation rejected foreign church leadership, foreign financing, and foreign administration. Autonomy meant that the Chinese communist government cut off the churches' foreign sources of funding and expelled the Western missionaries. China's leaders also forced the Catholic Church in China to disassociate itself from all "imperialist contact" (namely the Vatican and the pope) and to submit to the direction of the CCP. China's leaders created the Chinese Catholic Patriotic Association, which broke ties with the Vatican in 1957. The Chinese government imprisoned, confined to labor camps, or killed clergy who remained faithful to the Vatican.[106]

During the Cultural Revolution, China's leaders banned all religious activity and closed all Three-Self and Catholic churches. Bands of Red Guards destroyed churches, sometimes even pulling the spires off the buildings. Other churches became government offices or warehouses. Red Guards and other mobs beat, tortured, and imprisoned priests and nuns. Many Christians and Catholics joined underground house churches. In 1979, the government reinstated the Three-Self Patriotic Movement under Nanjing bishop Ding Guangxun, a liberal theologian and former Anglican. The Three-Self Patriotic Movement is the only Protestant denomination that the communist leadership tolerates. The Three-Self Patriotic Movement forbids teaching of the Second Coming of Christ, the resurrection of the dead, the gifts of the Holy Spirit, and the establishment of the Kingdom of God.[107] The Three-Self Patriotic Movement bans the biblical books of Daniel and Revelation because they prophesy the end of time. Bishop Ding also started a theological reconstruction campaign among the official seminaries to change the focus of teaching from justification by faith in Jesus Christ to justification by love in doing good deeds. It was thought the move would make Christianity more compatible with socialism.[108] Priests and ministers are discouraged from preaching about salvation for believers because it divides believers from nonbelievers, creating confusion and "sorrow."[109] The Three-Self Patriotic Movement continues to limit the freedom of religion in China. The state is the head of the church. Religious groups must register with a government-affiliated patriotic religious association. These official religious organizations administer local religious schools, seminaries, and institutes to train priests, ministers, imams, Islamic scholars, and Buddhist monks. Students who attend these institutes must demonstrate "political reliability" and all graduates must pass an examination on their political, as well as theological, knowledge to qualify for the clergy.[110] The state also reserves the right to review sermons to guarantee that they comply with government restrictions; oversees clergy education; requires that all Christians register with their local Three-Self church; mandates that preaching should be on the social rules and the social benefits of Christianity; prohibits preaching outside the Three-Self church buildings; forbids evangelizing or distributing tracts; and prohibits government officials, schoolteachers, soldiers, and police officers to be Christian. Although there are no laws prohibiting the religious instruction of children, in practice, local authorities in many regions prohibit children from attending services at churches, temples, and mosques, and prevent religious instruction outside the home.

In 2008, the state relaxed its control of the distribution of Bibles. In recent years, Bibles were available only to those who registered at a Three-Self church.[111] China continues to prohibit the importation of Bibles and the printing of Bibles by unapproved sources. Amity Printing Company is the one state-approved printer of Bibles in China, and has been printing as many as 3 million copies each year. In 2007, the Three-Self Patriotic Movement asked the Public Security Bureau to shut down all house church meetings and arrest house church leaders and traveling evangelists. Despite the ban, in some regions unregistered house churches meet openly. Authorities continue to harass unregistered Catholic bishops, priests, and laypersons, including by means of government surveillance and detentions. Many of those detained remain unaccounted for or have died in detention.

Official figures indicate there are 16 to 17 million Protestants, but researchers estimate the figure is likely to be 50 to 70 million. Official figures indicate there are 4 million Catholics in China, but the Vatican estimates there are between 8 and 18 million Catholics in China.[112] The huge discrepancies exist because more Christians belong to unregistered house churches than to official Three-Self churches or the Chinese Catholic Patriotic Association. Although it is impossible to estimate the number of underground Protestant and Catholic churches, signs indicate that the underground church is growing.

Torture and Ill-Treatment of Prisoners

The use of torture in China is illegal. China has ratified the United Nations Convention Against Torture, and articles 247 and 248 of China's Criminal Law prohibit the use of torture. Chinese law forbids prison guards from extracting confessions by torture, insulting prisoners' dignity, and beating or encouraging others to beat prisoners. Nonetheless, the government has been ineffective in enforcing the prohibition. Although it appears that the use of torture in urban areas has decreased, it is still widespread in rural areas. In November 2006, the

Supreme People's Procuratorate deputy secretary Wang Zhenchuan acknowledged that illegal interrogation by "atrocious torture" occurred throughout China and that almost all mishandled criminal cases in the previous year involved some sort of illegal interrogation. Wang estimated that at least thirty wrongful convictions were issued each year because of torture.[113]

The police commonly use torture to coerce confessions of crimes. The use of torture to extort confessions is the major cause of false convictions in China. Suspects do not have the right to remain silent or the right to a lawyer during interrogation, so there is no one to prove that the suspect was tortured. They may come to trial long after the interrogation, so any wounds incurred by torture are likely to be healed by the time of trial. Illegally obtained evidence, including confessions by torture, is permissible at trial, encouraging police to use torture to extract confessions. More than 80 percent of China's prisoners serve their sentences in labor camps, most of them in cold, remote, and tornado-prone Qinghai Province. Prison conditions are harsh and degrading. Prisoners are subject to beatings by guards using electric batons, long periods in handcuffs or leg irons, long periods in solitary confinement, and denial of food or medical treatment. Prisoners and detainees often are kept in overcrowded conditions with poor sanitation. Food often is inadequate and of poor quality, and many detainees rely on supplemental food and medicines provided by relatives.[114] Political prisoners often receive the worst treatment. Authorities typically restrict prominent dissidents to solitary confinement and deny them food and medicine provided by relatives. Dissidents are sometimes imprisoned in small cells with other prisoners with highly communicable diseases. For instance, the authorities put labor activist Han Dongfang in a cell with tuberculin prisoners. He quickly contracted the disease and became so ill that the Chinese government opted to release him rather than see him die a martyr in prison.

Repression of Minority Groups: Tibetans and Uygurs

The Chinese communists took control of Tibet in 1950, creating the Tibet Autonomous Region.[115] The Dalai Lama, spiritual leader of Tibetan Buddhists, fled in 1959 after an uprising against oppressive Chinese rule. Over the past fifty years, thousands of Tibetans have been incarcerated for peacefully expressing their political and religious beliefs. China's leaders strongly criticize the Dalai Lama as a "false religious leader" and associate Tibetan Buddhist religious activities with separatism. Authorities severely restrict religious practice in Tibet. Monks are prohibited from venerating the Dalai Lama, an activity the central government describes as "splittist." Authorities force monks to denounce the Dalai Lama and subject them to intense patriotic education at their monasteries. Although government officials maintain that possessing or displaying photos of the Dalai Lama is legal, authorities view possession of such photos as evidence of separatism when detaining individuals on those charges.[116] The central government also interferes in the process of finding and educating reincarnated lamas. The Panchen Lama is the second most sacred Tibetan Buddhist figure after the Dalai Lama. The government insists that Gyaltsen Norbu is the Panchen Lama's eleventh incarnation, despite the Dalai Lama's recognition of Gendun Choekyi Nyima. Although most Tibetan Buddhists recognize the latter as the Panchen Lama, Tibetan monks are forced to sign statements pledging allegiance to the government's choice. Government authorities deny access to Gendun Choekyi Nyima, and his whereabouts are unknown. Human rights organizations have named Gendun Choekyi Nyima China's youngest political prisoner. In an attempt to ensure that its pick becomes the next Dalai Lama of Tibet, China's state religious bureau requires that Tibetan Buddhists planning to be reborn fill out an application and submit it to several government agencies. The government deems reincarnations of individuals who fail to follow procedures illegal or invalid.[117]

China's central government encourages the migration of ethnic Han Chinese to Tibet. Critics of this migration claim that Han migration threatens to destroy Tibet's national, religious, and cultural identity. Han Chinese own most businesses in Tibet's capital of Lhasa and often discriminate against the local Tibetans. The Chinese government responds to periodic violent and nonviolent demonstrations against Chinese rule with crackdowns against Tibetans or with military force. In 1987, Chinese state media broadcast footage of the Dalai Lama's visit to Washington, where he gave a speech at the invitation of the Human Rights Congress. China broadcast the Dalai Lama's visit, accompanied by condemnation by Chinese officials. The image of the United States receiving the Dalai Lama incensed China. Three days after the Dalai Lama's speech on Capitol Hill, Chinese authorities executed a pair of Tibetan prisoners in Lhasa. The Tibetans viewed the executions as a political statement and responded with demonstrations and riots until Beijing declared martial law in March 1989. Chinese police brutally suppressed the demonstrations over eighteen months, killing and injuring hundreds of Tibetans.

Anti-Chinese riots erupted again in March 2008 after monks and other Tibetans held a peaceful demonstration to commemorate the forty-ninth anniversary of the Chinese occupation of Tibet. Protests soon erupted in Tibet and other Tibetan-inhabited regions, turning violent. In the ensuing riots, largely Tibetan mobs torched hundreds of Han Chinese–owned businesses and homes, and killed at least eighteen civilians. The violence spread to nearby provinces with significant Tibetan populations, with Han Chinese retaliating. The government put down the riots with military force, killing scores of Tibetans and jailing or detaining thousands.

Another area of ethnic abuse and discrimination is the Xinjiang Uygur Autonomous Region (XUAR), home to 19 million people, most of them Muslim. In the 1990s, the area was engulfed in both separatist and antigovernment violence. In 1990, Beijing began tightening controls on the Uygurs during the collapse of the Soviet Union as some Turkish-speaking Uygurs, the dominant ethnic grouping in Xinjiang, sought to reestablish an independent East Turkestan Republic.[118] Although most Chinese Muslims (Hui) and Ugyurs sought to maintain regional autonomy, others began to call for independence. In 1990, and again in 1992–1993, separatists carried out a series of explosions and attempted bombings. Beijing responded to this violence with arrests and a crackdown on religious establishments. Meanwhile, Beijing tried to tie the historically autonomous territory to China by accelerating Han migration to Xinjiang. It also tried to step up economic development of Xinjiang, mostly by exploiting oil and gas resources there. Large numbers of Han Chinese laborers flocked to Xinjiang to participate in infrastructure development schemes and to start up businesses. Most of the economic gains benefitted the Han, and Uygurs began to feel marginalized in their homeland. Antistate and anti-Chinese sentiment turned violent, and in response, Beijing began a Strike Hard campaign in spring 1996 to round up suspected separatists.[119] The campaign lasted one year and was accompanied by protests, explosions, and assassinations of Uygur officials.[120]

In February 1997, Uygurs staged a demonstration to protest the Strike Hard campaign and other Chinese policies in Xinjiang, including restrictions on religious and cultural activities, as well as the migration of Han Chinese settlers to the region. The protestors appealed for Beijing to respect their local autonomy. China's security forces violently put down the protest and shot a number of demonstrators, leading to three days of rioting and further harsh reactions by the authorities. The authorities responded with arrests of thousands of Uygurs, and Beijing instituted sweeping new policies that focused on religion as a source of opposition. It closed mosques and schools. In March 1997, separatists exploded bombs nearly simultaneously on three buses in Urumqi, killing nine people and injuring sixty-eight.

By 1998, the number and severity of acts of violence had decreased in Xinjiang. Throughout the violence, the Chinese government had maintained that the violence was the work of a few separatists. After the September 11, 2001, attacks on the United States, however, Beijing changed its tune and claimed that the violence in Xinjiang was connected with international terrorism. In 2001, Beijing began to crack down on the "three forces" of religious fundamentalism, separatism, and terrorism. Officials in the XUAR used the crackdown to raid, detain, and punish individuals suspected of promoting the three forces.[121] Cases do still arise, however, such as the planned separatist attack during the Beijing Olympics. In April 2008, the Public Security Bureau announced that it had arrested thirty-five people in Urumqi who were planning attacks on hotels in Beijing and Shanghai during the 2008 Summer Olympics. In recent years, Chinese authorities have used the war on terrorism to justify harsh repression of ethnic Uygurs, resulting in serious human rights violations.[122] In China, most political prisoners undergo thought reform through hard labor. Uygur individuals are the only known group in China executed for political crimes, such as "separatist activities."

China's leaders accelerated Han Chinese migration to Xinjiang in the 1990s to colonize the region in an attempt to dilute the region's ethnic and cultural identity. Due to migration the traditional Han-Uygur ratio in Urumqi shifted from 20 percent Han and 80 percent Uygur to 80 Han, 20 percent Uygur. Like the Tibetans, Uygurs strongly resent the Han migration. Han Chinese own most businesses in Urumqi and discriminate against Uygurs in hiring, sometimes on language concerns. The XUAR has reduced ethnic minority language instruction and currently requires schools to teach both Mandarin Chinese and local minority languages, or to teach Chinese only. The XUAR tightly controls Koranic education and prohibits the use of Arabic in public schools.

Conclusion

To claim that the post-Mao reforms have deeply impacted social and life issues in China would be an understatement. Many employees of state firms have lost health care benefits, while nonstate firms often do not offer health insurance. Although most urban Chinese have access to health care, many cannot afford it because they must pay up front and with cash for services. The same practice is true in rural areas, where residents have even less cash to spend on health care. Moreover, the dismantling of China's rural health system has made adequate health care rare. As a result, many Chinese who need treatment go untreated. Moreover, the SARS epidemic is an illustration of politics over public health. More sobering are policies that affect one's family and one's quality of life, namely the one-child policy. While millions of children, mostly girls, have been aborted, millions of others have been born outside of the official system, and their parents have abandoned them, hidden them from authorities, or have been forced to pay hefty fines. A few lucky ones are adopted.

Education has fared better. After Mao's death, school curricula put less emphasis on ideological indoctrination and more on instruction in subjects that would enhance China's development, such as math and science. China's reformers made admissions to colleges and universities based on merit rather than class background. Although it continues to underfund education, the Chinese government now requires all students to have nine years of education. Gender disparities in education have decreased, and advances have been made in rural education.

Chinese consumers have experienced a sea change in habits from that during the Mao years. Consumerism has replaced frugality as gleaming shopping malls have replaced drab state-run department stores. Designer labels have replaced the unisex clothing of the Cultural Revolution. Automobile traffic has replaced bicycle traffic in many cities, causing traffic jams. Urban families with only one child have replaced those with siblings. While the community telephone is all but obsolete, cell phones and the Internet make it easier to communicate with people with common interests in distant places. Since 1978, there has been an exciting revival of the arts in China. Although the state tries to control the arts scene through censorship, Chinese artists are adept at exhibiting their art in urban galleries and artists' colonies. The state has had more success in censoring Chinese and foreign cinema in China, allowing only a few movies a year beyond the censors. The Chinese government encourages use of the Internet for business and education, and China has more Internet users than the United States has population.

Despite these advances, the state and party maintain tight control on social order. Chinese authorities control and censor the media (although savvy Chinese say they can easily surmount the Great Firewall of China), arbitrarily detain and incarcerate people without effective defense, tightly control organized religion and civic organizations, and persecute Tibetans and Muslims in the northwest. There is no evidence that China is willing to relax these controls anytime soon.

Notes

1. Ho, "Market Reforms and China's Health Care System"; Liu Yuanli, Hsiao, and Eggleston, "Equity in Health and Health Care."

2. Bogg, Dong, Wang, Cai, and Diwan, "The Cost of Coverage: Rural Health Insurance in China"; Henderson et al., "Distribution of Medical Insurance in China"; Ministry of Health of the PRC, *Research on National Health Services.*

3. National Bureau of Statistics (NBS) of China, *China Statistical Yearbook 2010,* 367.

4. World Health Organization, *World Health Report 2000,* Annex Table 1, 152.

5. World Health Organization, *World Health Report 2000.*

6. "China to Spend $124B on Health Care," *China Economic Review,* January 22, 2009.

7. Meng-Kin, Hui, Tuohong, Wen, and Zijun, "Public Perceptions of Private Health Care," 222.

8. Blumenthal and Hsiao, "Privatization and Its Discontents," 1167.

9. Meng-Kin et al., "Public Perceptions of Private Health Care," 227.

10. Blumenthal and Hsiao, "Privatization and Its Discontents," 1167.

11. Abraham, *Twenty-first Century Plague,* 46.

12. Philip Pan, *Out of Mao's Shadow,* 305.

13. Liz Gooch, "Skewed Gender Ratio Leaves Mainland Men out in the Cold," *South China Morning Post,* June 16, 2008, 16.

14. Philip Pan, *Out of Mao's Shadow,* 305.

15. Veeck, Pannell, Smith, and Huang, *China's Geography,* 115.

16. Information Office of the State Council of the People's Republic of China, *White Paper on Family Planning in China,* Beijing, August 1995, http://www.cntravel .biz/c/d/White-Papers-From-China-Family-Planning-in-China-913.shtml.

17. Chen and Wu, *Will the Boat Sink the Water?* 101.

18. Greenhalgh and Winckler, *Governing China's Population,* 105.

19. See Greenhalgh, *Just One Child,* for a detailed account of the birth of the one-child policy.

20. See Greenhalgh, *Just One Child,* 113.

21. Cheng Li, "Ethnic Minority Elites in China's Party-State Leadership," 3.

22. Philip Pan, *Out of Mao's Shadow,* 303.

23. Greenhalgh and Winckler, *Governing China's Population,* 140.

24. Greenhalgh and Winckler, *Governing China's Population,* 142.

25. Greenhalgh and Winckler, *Governing China's Population,* 175.

26. Gooch, "Skewed Gender Ratio," *South China Morning Post,* June 16, 2008.

27. Zhu, Li, and Hesketh, "China's Excess Males, Sex Selective Abortion, and One-Child Policy."

28. Clare Dwyer Hogg, "Has Anyone Seen Our Child?" *Observer,* September 23, 2007; "China's Stolen Children," *101 East,* Al Jazeera English broadcast, January 30, 2010, http://english.aljazeera.net/programmes/101east/2010/01/201012665955553360 .html.

29. Elisabeth Rosenthal, "Rural Flouting of One-Child Policy Undercuts China Census," *New York Times,* April 14, 2000.

30. Hesketh, Li, and Zhu, "Effect of China's One-Child Policy," 1173.

31. NBS of China, *China Statistical Yearbook 2010,* 96.

32. Nicholas Eberstadt, "The Demographic Implication of China's One-Child Policy," *Far Eastern Economic Review,* December 4, 2009.

33. Fertility rates represent the number of children an average woman is likely to have during her childbearing years, usually ages fifteen through forty-nine.

34. Hesketh et al., "Effect of China's One-Child Policy," 1172.

35. Central Intelligence Agency, *World Factbook: China,* 2011.

36. Central Intelligence Agency, *World Factbook: China,* 2011, and the Government Information Office, Republic of China, *Republic of China Yearbook, 2008.*

37. "Go Forth and Multiply a Lot Less," *Economist,* October 31, 2009, 29–30.

38. Greenhalgh and Winckler, *Governing China's Population,* 171.

39. Greenhalgh and Winckler, *Governing China's Population,* 270.

40. Emily Chang, "Finding a Home: Fewer Children Up for Adoption in China," CNN.com/asia, April 12, 2009, http://www.cnn.com/2009/WORLD/asiapcf/04/10/china .adoptions/.

41. The "eight-legged essay" was the primary test for people to attain ranks as scholars in the Ming and Qing Dynasties. It tested students on their knowledge of the Confucian classics and their ability to write commentaries on them in a formal, prescribed manner. It gained its name from the fact that it had eight sections.

42. The university was first formally established as the Imperial Capital University during the Hundred Days of Reform in 1898. It was renamed Peking University in 1912.

43. Dollar, "Poverty, Inequality and Social Disparities," 12.

44. See Wright, *Promise of the Revolution,* on rural education, particularly 81–87 and 131–137.

45. For more information on financing for rural education, see Guo, "Persistent Inequalities in Funding."

46. Guo, "Persistent Inequalities in Funding," 62–63, 135–136.

47. Tooley, *Beautiful Tree;* Ministry of Health of the PRC, *Research on National Health Services.*

48. Connelly and Zhenzhen, "Educational Access for China's Post–Cultural Revolution Generation," 69.

49. World Bank, *Gender Gaps in China,* 1.

50. World Bank, *Gender Gaps in China.*

51. Specifically, enrollment rates for school-age children in China's poorer provinces were 92 percent for boys and 91 percent for girls. The national average was 97 percent for boys and 96 percent for girls. World Bank, *Gender Gaps in China.*

52. NBS of China, *China Statistical Yearbook 2010,* 753.

53. China spends more per student at the higher education level than at the basic level. In 1993, the Chinese government spent twenty-five times more on college students than on elementary school students. In 1998, China dedicated 1.6 billion yuan (US$193 million) *each* for its two top universities, Peking University and Tsinghua University, while total nonsalary budgetary spending for all rural elementary schools in China *combined* was only 2.3 billion yuan (US$278 million). Guo, "Persistent Inequalities," 216.

54. Rosen, "Education and Economic Reform."

55. Jing Lin, "Emergence of Private Schools in China," 50.

56. Jing Lin, "Emergence of Private Schools in China," 50.

57. Jing Lin, "Emergence of Private Schools in China," 58.

58. Yiu Por Chen and Zai Liang, "Educational Attainment of Migrant Children," 125.

59. "China's Middle Class Defined by Income," *People's Daily,* January 20, 2005. China's definition of middle class is based on the World Bank's criteria of the medium level of international GDP per capita, ranging from $3,470 to $8,000, adjusted for currency exchanges and purchasing power parity.

60. Zhao Dingxin, *Power of Tiananmen,* 438.

61. Rosen, "Contemporary Chinese Youth and the State," 364.

62. Rosen, "Contemporary Chinese Youth and the State," 365.

63. Rebecca MacKinnon, "Bloggers and Censors."

64. Tang Wenfang, *Public Opinion and Political Change,* 82.

65. Freedom House, *Freedom of the Press 2010.*

66. Reporters Without Borders, *Worldwide Press Freedom Index 2010.*

67. See the US Department of State, *Country Reports on Human Rights Practices,* for the years 2007 and 2010.

68. Esarey, *Speak No Evil,* 4.

69. Tang Wenfang, *Public Opinion and Political Change,* 81.

70. Esarey, "Cornering the Market," 41.

71. For particular cases of contentious journalism, see Hassid, "China's Contentious Journalists."

72. Philip Pan, *Out of Mao's Shadow,* 266.

73. "The Second Long March," *Economist,* December 13, 2008, 30–32.

74. Freedom House, *Freedom of the Press 2010.*

75. US Department of State, *Country Reports on Human Rights Practices—2007.*

76. US Department of State, *Country Reports on Human Rights Practices—2007.*

77. US Department of State, *Country Reports on Human Rights Practices—2007.*

78. Reporters Without Borders, *Worldwide Press Freedom Index 2007.*

79. Amnesty International, *Undermining Freedom of Expression in China: The Role of Yahoo!, Microsoft, and Google.*

80. A major criticism of Yahoo! in the Western press is that it actually did not have to provide the information to the government, particularly with no warrant and in Hong Kong.

81. "Mobilised by Mobile," *Economist,* June 23, 2007, 48–49.

82. "Mobilised by Mobile," *Economist,* June 23, 2007, 48–49.

83. Constitution of the PRC, preamble, amended 2004.

84. NBS of China, *China Statistical Yearbook 2010,* 28.

85. Cheng Li, "Ethnic Minority Elites in China's Party-State Leadership," 3.

86. Kaup, *Ethnic Politics in China,* 88.

87. Katherine Palmer, "China's Nationalities and Nationality Areas," 278.

88. See the Special Focus on National Minorities section in the Congressional-Executive Commission on China's *Annual Report 2005,* http://www.cecc.gov/pages/annualRpt/annualRpt05/2005_3a_minorities.php.

89. Article 121, Constitution of the People's Republic of China, amended 2004.

90. Cheng Li, "Ethnic Minority Elites in China's Party-State Leadership," 2.

91. National People's Congress, PRC, Law on Regional National Autonomy, promulgated May 1984, http://www.novexcn.com/regional_nation_autonomy.html.

92. Cheng Li, "Ethnic Minority Elites in China's Party-State Leadership," 2.

93. Mao quoted in Chien-Peng Chung, "'Regional Autonomy' for Minority Nationalities in the People's Republic of China: Rhetoric or Reality?"

94. Goodman, "Campaign to 'Open Up the West'," 326–327.

95. Hannum, Park, and Kai-Ming, "Introduction: Market Reforms and Educational Opportunity in China," 9.

96. Postiglione, "School Access in Rural Tibet," 93–116.

97. Postiglione, "School Access in Rural Tibet," 95.

98. ICCPR protects the right to life, to liberty, and to freedom of movement, to equality before the law, to presumption of innocence until proven guilty, to appeal a conviction, to be recognized as a legal person, and to privacy and protection of that privacy. It protects individuals' freedom of thought, conscience, religion, opinion and expression, and assembly and association. It also forbids torture, inhumane or degrading treatment, and arbitrary arrest and detention; restricts the death penalty to the most serious crimes; and forbids the death penalty for minors.

99. A third paragraph added to article 33 states that the state respects and preserves human rights. Constitution of the People's Republic of China, http://english.people daily.com.cn/constitution/constitution.html.

100. Constitution of the People's Republic of China.

101. Amnesty International, *Amnesty International Report 2008,* 94.

102. US Department of State, *Country Reports on Human Rights Practices—2007.*

103. Millions of party members belong to Falun Gong.

104. "Xinhua Commentary on Political Nature of Falun Gong," *People's Daily Online,* http://english.peopledauly.com.cn/english/199908/02/enc_199908020.

105. US Department of State, *Country Reports on Human Rights Practices—2007.*

106. See Myers, *Enemies Without Guns,* for more information on the government's treatment of the Catholic Church.

107. "China's Protestant Churches to Adhere to 'Three-Self' Principles," *People's Daily Online,* http://english.peopledaily.com.cn/english/200009/21/print20000921_51066.html.

108. "The Underground Church," China Aid Association, http://chinaaid.org/persecution/the-underground-church/.

109. "China's Protestant Churches to Adhere to 'Three-Self' Principles," *People's Daily Online.*

110. US Department of State, *Country Reports on Human Rights Practices—2007.*

111. In 2004, the author was able to buy Bibles from the gift shop of a Catholic cathedral in Beijing, without registering.

112. Vatican City State, "Interview for the Newspaper *Yomiuri* of Japan," Kyoto, Japan, May 14, 2007, http://www.vaticanstate.va/IT/Stato_e_Governo/Strutturadel Governatorato/Presidenza/Presidente/2007/14_maggio_2007-p-2.htm.

113. US Department of State, *Country Reports on Human Rights Practices—2007*.

114. US Department of State, *Country Reports on Human Rights Practices—2007*.

115. The autonomous region called Tibet is smaller than the historical Tibetan territory. After 1949, the Chinese communists moved the province's boundaries, and Tibet lost territory to the neighboring provinces of Qinghai, Gansu, and Sichuan.

116. US Department of State, *Country Reports on Human Rights Practices—2007*.

117. *Zangchuan Fojiao huofo zhuanshi guanli banfa* (Law on the Management of Reincarnation of Living Buddhas in Tibetan Buddhism), State Administration for Religious Affairs of the PRC, Beijing, July 13, 2007, http://www.sara.gov.cn/GB//zcfg /89522ff7-409d-11dc-bafe-93180af1bb1a.html.

118. In the middle of the twentieth century, the western part of the region enjoyed independence as the Soviet-aligned East Turkestan Republic. China did not achieve effective control of the area until soon after the establishment of the PRC in 1949. As a result, certain sections of the community have retained memories of a distinct political and administrative identity.

119. "Strike Hard" campaigns are periodic drives against serious crime, but are commonly directed against agitation by ethnic minorities.

120. Millward, *Violent Separatism in Xinjiang: An Assessment*, ix.

121. US Department of State, *Country Reports on Human Rights Practices—2007*.

122. Amnesty International, *Amnesty International Report 2008*.

7 Political Economy

China is experiencing an economic rise unparalled in history. China is the world's second largest economy after the United States, with a GDP of $5.36 billion in 2010.[1] China has the fastest-growing economy in the world. In 2009, China's economy was ten times larger than it was in 1978. Between 1978 and 2007, China's per capita GDP quadrupled, something it took Britain fifty-eight years, the United States forty-seven years, and Japan thirty-four years to do. China also has a major presence in the world economy. By 2008, China's share of global GDP had risen to 6 percent from 1.8 percent in 1978 when Deng initiated his political and economic reforms.[2] China is also the world's largest trading nation, the world's largest exporter of goods, and the world's second largest importer of goods. In 2010, China's world trade was worth $3 trillion. Most Chinese are living better than ever as a result of this economic rise. Life expectancy, infant mortality, and per capita income have all dramatically improved. Some 500 million people have been lifted out of poverty in a generation.

China's meteoric economic rise is the direct result of Deng Xiaoping's decision in the late 1970s to jettison socialism for market-oriented economics and to open China to the world economy. The watershed event for the shift from socialist to market economics was Deng's 1978 adoption of the Four Modernizations. The seeds of reform had actually been sown earlier, in 1975, by an ailing Zhou Enlai, the genesis of the Four Modernizations, but Deng recognized that China's economy had stagnated during the Cultural Revolution, and at the Third Plenum of the Eleventh Central Committee in December 1978, Deng announced plans to implement Zhou's vision to modernize agriculture, industry, science and technology, and national defense. At the same meeting, the Central Committee endorsed Deng's Open Door policy to promote the expansion of economic relations with the rest of the world. Over the succeeding thirty years, China's reformers liberalized the Chinese economy and made China a key player in the world economy. At the same time, however, economic liberalization created social dislocations for many Chinese. Price reform led to spiraling inflation, eating into the wages and savings of most Chinese; state enterprise reform resulted in massive layoffs, especially of older and less skilled workers; lack of government oversight of China's nascent stock exchanges resulted in myriad opportunities for corruption for the well connected and loss of financial security for many others. By 2010, however, most of these issues had been resolved, and China was on its way to becoming one of the world's economic powerhouses. The evolution of a market-oriented economy in China, with all of the accompanying political and social dislocations, has been a thrilling, if dizzying, ride for most Chinese.

Agricultural Reforms

By the late 1970s, Deng was committed to the restructuring of the Chinese economy. The Third Plenum of the Eleventh Party Central Committee in November and December 1978 gave him his chance. In endorsing the Four Modernizations, the party signaled that its focus would no longer be on class warfare but on economic modernization.

The first of Deng's economic reforms was to revitalize agriculture. Following collectivization of agriculture in the 1950s, the central government determined production quotas, procured agricultural produce from farmers at state-determined prices, and sold agricultural produce at state-controlled markets. The state determined what agricultural products the communes had to grow, regardless of local conditions. To maintain low food prices in the cities, the state procured commune produce at below market prices. The low prices benefited urban residents, but kept farmers poor.

Food availability also was a problem in the Mao era. Although China's grain production grew 2.5 percent a year, exceeding population growth of 1.9 percent, most Chinese had barely enough to eat. Sharp reductions in agricultural production and availability contributed to the massive famine of 1959–1961. In the late 1960s and 1970s, China began to import grain, mostly wheat. In the 1970s, the average level of consumption in urban areas was still only 2,328 calories per capita. Rural residents consumed even less, barely meeting the United Nations' average daily minimum requirement of 2,100 calories.[3] Not only was the quantity of caloric intake limited, but so too was the quality. The average Chinese diet consisted of strictly rationed coarse grains (corn, sweet potato, millet, and sorghum). Most people did not have daily access to cooking oil, sugar, meat, and vegetables on a regular basis.[4]

Despite the promises of the revolution, rural peasants were no better off in the 1970s than they were before collectivization in the 1950s. Deng Xiaoping in 1979 initiated a series of reforms. To spur production, the central government boosted credit by offering loans at market or below-market interest rates. Looser credit allowed farmers to borrow to invest in the purchase of fertilizer, seeds, pesticides, fuel, and farm machinery. To encourage production and raise farm income, the state in 1979 raised procurement prices of goods sold to the government by about 20 percent. It also raised state procurement prices for above-quota surpluses to 50 percent (from 30 percent) of the state fixed price. It also gradually reduced the number of crops under state pricing, letting the market determine prices for an increasing number of agricultural goods. Finally, in the early 1980s the state began to dismantle the communes. This process had actually begun as an illegal experiment in the late 1970s. Following Mao's death in 1976, some communes quietly adopted an experimental system that allowed production teams (usually thirty to fifty households) to keep or sell any agricultural goods they produced above the state-mandated production quota. The local experiments became more widespread in the late 1970s and caught the attention of Deng Xiaoping. As a result of these experiments, the central government in 1983 announced a national policy called the Household Responsibility System (HRS). The most dramatic change under the HRS system was the reestablishment of the household as the primary unit of farm production. Under the HRS, the collective (later, village and township authorities) assigned plots of land to farm, but not to own. Initially, families leased the land for fifteen years; the contracts were later extended to up to fifty years. In return for the use of land, the families agreed to meet state production quotas. After meeting the quotas, families could do anything they wanted with the surplus, such as keep or consume it, sell it to the state, or sell it on newly revived farmers' markets. By 1984, most communes had been abolished, and agriculture had returned to household farming.

The result of these reforms, coupled with good weather in 1981–1982, was a dramatic increase in agricultural production. Agricultural production more than tripled to 8.2 percent in the early reform years, much higher than the 2.7 percent it grew in the 1970s. Yields increased across the board. For instance, grain production increased an average of 5 percent per year from 1978 to 1984. Rice production increased more than 4 percent, wheat 8 percent, corn 4 percent, and cotton 19 percent between 1978 and 1984. The planting structure also began to change. During the Mao years, agricultural policy, detailed in China's Five-Year Plans, focused largely on grain (rice, wheat, corn) production. Between 1952 and 1978, grain had accounted for more than 80 percent of sown area. In the early reform era, however, Chinese farmers began to produce a greater variety of agricultural goods and began producing higher-value cash crops, horticultural goods, livestock, and aquaculture products. By 1983, some 85 percent of peasants had allocated land to the production of cash crops and had undertaken some kind of sideline operation. As a result, by 1985 the percentage of total area sown in China dedicated to grain production had dropped 4 percent as farmers shifted to more profitable crops. Chinese farmers also became more productive. For instance, per capita output of grain increased from 702 pounds in 1978 to 794 pounds in 1985.[5] Newly reinstituted farmers' markets served not only the rural population, but urban Chinese as well. In 1980, farmers' markets accounted for a quarter of all fish, eggs, and poultry bought in Chinese cities.

The early reforms resulted in a surplus of grain in 1984, causing grain prices to fall dramatically and causing farmers to turn to more lucrative cash crops. To avoid further surpluses, the government in 1985 lowered the purchase price for grain and initiated a second round of agricultural reforms. The government abolished mandatory production quotas and instead set targets for a limited number of agricultural products (grain, cotton, corn). Farmers had the option of contracting with the state, where they would receive a set price for produce and have access to a guaranteed buyer. Or they could sell their produce on the open market at market prices. The result of the new procurement policy was a 6 percent drop in grain output as farmers shifted production to cash crops.

Rural Industrialization

After the dissolution of the communes, China had a surplus of rural labor. Deng Xiaoping encouraged the creation of rural industry to both employ former commune members and produce consumer goods, which had been neglected under Mao's model of economic growth. Under Mao, China adopted the Soviet model of economic growth, which emphasized investment in heavy industry at the cost of light industry. Any consumer goods that were produced during this period were shoddy. In the 1980s, there was tremendous pent-up demand for better-quality consumer goods because of their shortage during the Mao years. In the 1980s, Deng and other reformers began to encourage collectives, individuals, and families to pool their money and start small businesses, making consumer goods such as lamps, small electrical appliances, and even baby formula. These rural businesses, called town and village enterprises (TVEs), soon sprang up all over the countryside. The number of TVEs exploded between 1985 and 1992 and succeeded in employing rural residents. Employment in TVEs increased from 28 million in 1978, surged to 93 million in 1990, and exploded to 135 million in 1996. By 2008, TVE employment reached 156 million people, constituting 31 percent of rural employment (see Figure 7.1).[6] The creation of TVEs spurred rural economic growth and development. Throughout the 1990s, TVEs were the engine of China's economic growth, and the best TVEs were producing for export.

TVE development contributed to increases in both the rural economy and rural incomes. Rural net per capita incomes increased from 133 yuan in 1978 to more than 5,153 yuan in 2009 (Figure 7.2). Rural incomes in coastal provinces, where most TVEs were located, grew more rapidly than rural incomes in central and western China. Also, income derived from rural industry (TVEs) exceeded incomes derived from farming. Some farmers opted to leave farming to work in TVEs. TVEs also limited out-migration because better-educated

Figure 7.1 Employment in Town and Village Enterprises

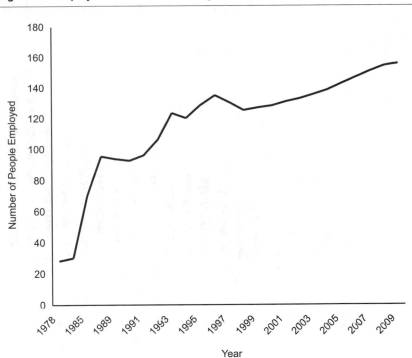

Source: NBS of China, *China Statistical Yearbook 2010,* 119.

farmers found they could work in their hometowns for a decent wage. The share of nonagriculture income in net household income increased from 22 percent in 1990 to 52 percent in 2004. Most of the nonagricultural income came from wages.[7] With the development of the TVEs, the growth of industry and services in rural China has been two to three times faster than the growth of agriculture.

Having reformed agriculture, the state redirected investment after 1985 from rural to urban areas. Government investment in rural China dropped precipitously, and since the early 1980s, the countryside has once again lagged behind urban China. While rural incomes steadily increased during the reform era, prices for farm inputs such as fertilizer rose faster than market prices for farmers' produce. Increasingly, it did not pay to farm. The small scale of household plots (about .34 to .68 hectare, depending on the size of the family) often could not support economies of scale or offered limited effective mechanization. Some families eventually gave up their plots, or allowed other households to lease their plots. In fact, the movement of farmers to nonfarm employment accounts for the increase in rural incomes.

Figure 7.2 Net Income in Rural Areas

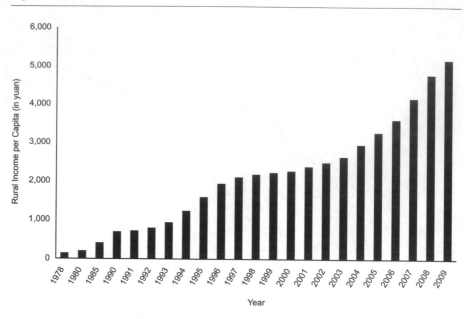

Source: NBS of China, *China Statistical Yearbook 2010,* 342.

Throughout the 1980s and 1990s, TVEs bought up much agricultural land, arguing that rural industry, not agriculture, was the engine of rural economic growth. Many farmers were coerced into giving land that they leased, but not owned, to local governments for the development of TVEs. The result was a net loss of agricultural land and environmental degradation as TVEs skirted environmental regulations and dumped toxic waste directly into streams, rivers, and agricultural land. The loss of agricultural land, drop in farm prices, and diversion of state investment from rural to urban areas pushed more than 100 million residents out of rural China and into towns and cities. Most of this migrant population was young men, depriving villages of their most productive farmers.

In the late 1980s, local officials in rural areas were commonly diverting state procurement funds for agriculture to the more lucrative TVEs. In 1988, the state was forced to issue IOUs to farmers. At the same time, local officials began imposing various fees on rural residents to pay for local development initiatives, many of which never came to fruition. Fed up with the IOUs and official corruption, farmers rioted in 1992 and 1993. Beijing reacted by redeeming farmers' IOUs and enacting the Law on Agriculture, giving farmers the right to refuse to pay improper fees.

The record on China's agricultural reforms is mixed. The increase in rural incomes masks their geographic disparity. Income in coastal rural areas, where most TVEs are located, is higher than in the interior. The dissolution of the communes (and later the shuttering of many state enterprises) contributed to the unemployment of some 200 million rural Chinese and the out-migration of some 100 million more. The drop in grain production after 1985 forced China to import grain, a staple of the Chinese diet. Although China in 2004 reversed this trend, increasing grain production about 3 percent a year, the production of higher-value products, such as fruit, vegetables, melon, livestock, and aquacultural products, has grown at about 9 percent per year or more. The structure of agriculture has changed, as China has moved beyond grain as its production priority. By 2009, grain constituted 68 percent of area sown, down from 80 percent in 1978.[8] The output of aquatic products increased nearly 52 percent between 1978 and 1985, and increased a whopping 166 percent between 1978 and 1990.[9] China even became a net exporter of agricultural products. Many Chinese agricultural and aquaculture products can be found in American grocery stores. For instance, China is now the third largest source of US agricultural and seafood imports. China is now a price setter for honey, apple-juice concentrate, frozen shrimp, crayfish, mint and other essential oils, condiments such as garlic and hot pepper sauces, frozen vegetables, and flowers.[10]

Despite these advances, many Chinese farmers are desperately poor and cannot afford health care or education for their children. Rising discontent over rural-urban disparity, unemployment, and local corruption threatens stability in many rural areas. In the past decade, the central government eliminated the agricultural tax, expanded an experimental health-care insurance scheme to most rural counties, and eliminated tuition and fees for rural students pursuing compulsory education. The central government has also pledged to spend more on rural infrastructure.

Despite these initiatives, central government spending in the countryside has not increased appreciatively and continues to average around 9 percent each year. And although the central government increased spending for rural infrastructure 14.7 percent since 2008, it is only slightly higher than the 14 percent average increase for all government spending, and it is less than the 15 percent average rise in military spending.

The inability of farmers to own their own land keeps many of them poor. Thirty years after the introduction of the HRS, farmers in China still do not have title to their own land. Land in rural China is owned by the collective (village or town). Farmers cannot mortgage the land they farm to invest in it, nor can they sell it and use the proceeds to start a new life in the cities. The lack of private property rights also leaves farmers vulnerable to exploitation by local authorities. Farmers are increasingly distressed as local officials confiscate rural land—without compensation—to develop into industry or housing. Local officials are eager to develop agricultural land because it helps build their careers and because they are promoted on the basis of their ability to develop the local economy. In contrast, forced appropriations by local governments have deprived some 40 million farmers of some or all of their land since the early 1990s, with little or no compensation.[11] From 1999 to 2002, three hundred thousand acres of farmland were illegally seized from 1.5 million farmers. Chinese law allows land confiscation in the name of the public interest. In March 2003, the National People's Congress passed the Rural Land Contract Law, which stipulates that villages cannot illegally alter or annul contracts with farmers. It also stipulates that local authorities cannot reclaim contracted land during the farmer's contract period. Despite this law, local authorities continue to claim land illegally. Nearly ten thousand square miles of farmland were transformed by development in 2003 alone, becoming, among other things, factories, apartment blocks, and golf courses.[12] Farmers have used courts, petitions, and appeals to officials at all levels to seek compensation for lost land. One village near Fuzhou, in eastern China, fought for over a decade in seeking compensation for two hundred acres of rich farmland confiscated by local officials and sold for development.[13]

Industrial Reform

At the beginning of the reform era in the late 1970s, Chinese industry was mainly state-owned and urban. In 1978, state-owned enterprises (SOEs) accounted for 78 percent of industrial output and employed 76 percent of all industrial workers. SOEs were the backbone of China's socialist economy and enjoyed monopoly status. SOEs operated under the mandatory state plan and under the direction of the appropriate ministry. They procured raw materials at state-fixed prices, produced a quota of goods under the state plan, and sold their goods to other state firms at state-determined prices. SOE profits were the most important source of government revenue.

Despite occupying the commanding heights of Chinese industry, SOEs had several weaknesses. Many SOEs used outdated Soviet-era technology, and enterprise directors could not reinvest profits in updated equipment and technology. Instead, SOE profits flowed to state coffers. SOE directors deferred to enterprise party committees on important decisions concerning the firm. The state plan required most SOEs to employ surplus numbers of employees. Managers lacked the authority to offer material incentive to productive workers and to dismiss unproductive ones. As a result, SOEs suffered from low productivity, and the quality of their goods was often shabby.

In December 1978, the Third Plenum of the Eleventh Central Committee began a program of industrial reform. The plenary session recognized that the overcentralization of authority was a serious shortcoming in China's economic management and that it was necessary to shift authority from the central government to local authorities. This decentralization of authority would allow SOEs greater decisionmaking power. Thus, the first phase of reform focused on relaxing state control of industry and allowing market forces to play a greater role in the allocation of resources. The second stage focused on the reform and restructuring of state industrial enterprises.

Price Reform and National Planning

One of the earliest reforms to affect industry was price reform. Under China's planned economy, the state rather than the market had determined prices for procurement and distribution of agricultural and industrial goods. During the Mao years, China planners set prices low and rarely adjusted them. Prices had become distorted and had no relation to supply and demand. As China's reformers moved toward a market economy after 1978, they needed to move the economy away from state-fixed pricing. In 1980, Premier Zhao Ziyang established three categories of prices: fixed prices, negotiated prices, and market prices. State industry used the first two prices under a two-tier pricing system, called the dual-track pricing system (*shuang guizhi*). Under this system, a single commodity would have both a low state-fixed price and a higher negotiated price. State-run factories procured a particular amount of a commodity through the planning system at state-fixed prices and additional amounts of the same material at higher negotiated prices. Nonstate firms used market prices for all of their transactions. In agriculture, Beijing initially raised state procurement prices for agricultural products and gradually replaced state-determined prices with market prices.

Another aspect of price reform was allowing state enterprises to sell some of their production at market prices. Under China's planned economy, state firms had been required to sell any output produced under the state plan at state-determined prices. These prices were usually below market prices. Under reform, this practice continued, but anything the firm produced beyond the quota could be sold at market prices, or at prices that floated within a state-established range near market level. The exact price was determined either by the market or in negotiation between buyer and seller. Being able to sell the above-quota product at a higher price led to greater incentive to produce more. China scholar Barry Naughton calls this strategy "growing out of the plan."[14] As the state reduced the number of goods produced under the state plan, it decreased the number of fixed prices. By 1985, the number of industrial products sold at fixed prices fell from 256 to 29, and the number of consumer goods sold at state-fixed prices fell from 85 to 37. The number of agricultural commodities also dropped, from 113 to 25.[15] By the early twenty-first century, the state had largely ended fixed pricing for raw materials.

As one can imagine, the various pricing schemes created opportunity for hoarding. Individuals with access to certain commodities would buy a good at the lower state-fixed price and keep it off the market until they could negotiate a higher price for it. This hoarding led to shortages of a number of key commodities. Relaxation of pricing also resulted in inflation. Negotiated prices pushed prices up, and the relaxation of agricultural prices pushed up both food and retail prices. Inflation increased to 9 percent in 1985 and 19 percent in 1988. The price of food rose by double digits. For example, the price of meat and eggs rose 22 percent in 1985 and rose 10 percent in 1986, and the price of fish rose 34 percent in 1985 and 12 percent in 1986. The price of vegetables rose by one-third in 1985.[16] China's leaders fought to control inflation throughout the 1980s. Inflation was one of the complaints culminating in the protests of spring 1989.

Deng Xiaoping and his fellow reformers accompanied price reform with a loosening of control of SOEs. They realized that it was necessary to reduce the excessive interference of the state in enterprise affairs and to link enterprise decisionmaking to economic consequences. This task called for decentralization of authority in two steps. First, they had to reduce the number and responsibilities of the central and provincial government administrative agencies and to streamline the bureaucracy. Second, they needed to make enterprise directors responsible for the operation of their firms. China's leaders began to streamline the central bureaucracy in 1982 with the reorganization of the central government. They reduced the number of central government organs from ninety-eight to sixty-one. The following year, China's reformers cut the number of provincial-level party and state officials and reshuffled leadership in party committees at the county, district, and municipal levels. By reshuffling cadres, Deng Xiaoping was able to place many of his key followers in key leadership and decisionmaking positions across China.

In addition to reducing the number of government agencies, Deng Xiaoping and his reformers tried to restructure the central planning system. Under the central planning system, the central government had directed production planning through administrative decrees. In the 1980s, China's reformers shifted decisionmaking authority from centralized authorities (ministries) to local authorities. Throughout the 1980s, increasing numbers of commodities were produced outside the planning system. By the late 1990s, nearly all production, save for large infrastructure programs, was outside of the state plan.

Coinciding with price reform and the decentralization of authority were plans to allow the nonstate sector to grow as a supplement to the state sector. To this end, China's reformers began to encourage the development of nonstate industrial firms. The number of industrial enterprises jumped from fewer than a million in 1980 to 7.34 million in 1995. Many of these firms were town and village enterprises (TVEs). These nonstate firms were mostly owned by local governments and employed, among others, former farmers from the dissolved communes. Outside of the state plan, the TVEs benefited from the dual-track pricing system. In the 1980s, the number of TVEs exploded, especially in the countryside. By the late 1980s, TVEs employed some 90 million workers. At the same time, Deng and his reformers invited foreign investors to China to join up with Chinese businesses in joint-venture firms. Concentrated in special economic zones (SEZs), these joint ventures benefited from preferential tax treatment and lower tariff barriers. Both the TVEs and joint ventures began to compete with China's industrial SOEs, forcing China's leaders to reform state industrial enterprises.

Reform of State-Owned Enterprises

The shift away from centralized planning resulted in major changes in the management of SOEs. As state firms that could be affiliated with central, provincial, or county governments, SOEs were often merely appendages of government agencies. Enterprise directors had little decisionmaking power regarding the operation and management of their firms. They also had no discretion in hiring employees, but merely had to accept the employees assigned to the firm. To keep unemployment low, Chinese authorities filled SOEs with surplus numbers of employees, hampering the overall productivity of the firm. Once employed, however, workers enjoyed lifelong job tenure and cradle-to-grave benefits. Under Mao's cellular economy, SOEs had been miniature societies responsible for providing their employees with housing, health care, childcare and education, retirement pensions, and unemployment insurance, as well as producing goods and services (see Chapter 3). Lacking a comprehensive national social safety net, the state channeled social welfare benefits through these work units to individual workers or their families. The "iron rice bowl" of guaranteed employment with associated benefits could not be taken away or broken.

The "one big pot" system of egalitarian wages also stifled worker initiative, however. Under the system of everyone eating from "one big pot," employees with the same job title, skill level, and seniority received equivalent wages regardless of initiative. Managers could not reward industrious employees with material rewards, and workers had no incentive to work harder because the "iron rice bowl" prevented managers from threatening to lay off lazy or incompetent employees. In 1978, China's leaders began a series of reforms to expand enterprise autonomy. In 1979, Chinese leaders granted some, and later all, SOEs the rights to retain a share of their profits, to enjoy accelerated depreciation, and to sell commodities produced above the state-mandated quota.

In the 1980s, China's leaders also began a series of reforms designed to replicate market forces in state firms (marketization). In 1984, the Twelfth Central Committee launched the economic reform process by coining the phrase "to build socialism with Chinese characteristics," meaning reforming the economy using capitalist techniques while retaining the centralized Leninist-CCP state. The Central Committee's Decision on Reform and Economic Structure linked problems of bureaucracy and overcentralization of authority with poor economic development. It stated that the primary obstacle retarding China's economic development was abysmally low productivity among urban SOEs. The underlying assumptions were that overcentralization of authority in SOEs had stifled worker initiative and resulted in those enterprises acting merely as administrative appendages of the party and state, rather than as productive, economic entities. Low productivity was seen as a response to the inability on the part of SOE directors to persuade or coerce workers to work harder because the managers were subordinate to directives from the party and the state. At the same time, there was no incentive system with which a director could reward an energetic employee who did more than his share of work. Even if a bonus was awarded, it tended to be distributed in an egalitarian fashion rather than used as an award for exemplary work. To alleviate the problem of overcentralization of authority and the low level of productivity, the 1984 Decision on Reform proposed stepping up efforts to draw a greater distinction between ownership and operation of enterprises and called for a "director responsibility system," in which the enterprise director is responsible for the production function of the firm. The 1988 Enterprise Law further increased managerial authority of directors over their enterprises by granting them responsibility and power to make important economic decisions facing the firm. It also made enterprise directors accountable for both the profits and losses of their firms. Taking on responsibility for the profits and losses of their firms meant that SOE directors needed to be able to break the "iron rice bowl" and "one big pot" systems of cradle-to-grave job tenure and associated benefits and egalitarian wages. SOE directors gained the ability to recruit and dismiss employees, offer fixed-term labor contracts to new employees, offer bonuses to energetic workers, and provide unemployment insurance to employees. The law also removed party committees from the day-to-day operations of the firm. The party would still be responsible for guaranteeing and supervising the implementation of the principles and policies of the party and state, and it would continue ideological and political work among employees by continuing its leadership over the enterprise trade union and Communist Youth League.

In 1988, China's SOEs employed an estimated 15 to 20 million surplus workers. One solution to the problem of having too many employees was the implementation of an in-house employment system. Enterprises that used this system in the 1990s redeployed redundant workers by establishing new businesses, retraining them, and allowing infirm, disabled, or elderly workers to take early retirement. Many firms opened service companies, such as restaurants, hostels, and tourist offices that utilized existing fleets of company buses, to absorb excess numbers of employees. Redeployed employees received lower wages than they received in their previous posts, but could earn generous bonuses if they proved particularly enterprising.

Despite these reforms, increasing numbers of industrial SOEs lost money. In 1985, about 10 percent of industrial SOEs were losing money; by 1995 this figure had increased to 44 percent. One of the reasons for the increase was reluctance on the part of China's leaders to allow state firms to lay off redundant workers for fear of social unrest. To keep unproductive firms afloat, and therefore protect jobs, the state heavily subsidized SOEs throughout the late 1980s

Wage Reform

At the start of SOE reform, an employee's basic wages were distributed according to his or her grade on the eight-grade system. After 1988, wage distribution became much more complex, and was based on a variety of criteria designed to reflect the individuality of workers. Most SOEs adopted a structural wage system in which an individual's total wages were composed of a basic wage consisting of technical, position, and seniority wages, and a supplementary wage consisting of a bonus. Before reform, the state determined employee wages. After wage reform, SOE managers gained authority to determine wages according to the aforementioned structural wage system. Wage reform benefited younger and more skilled workers because they could earn higher bonuses than under the previous wage system. However, many older and less skilled workers saw their total wages decrease as bonuses became a more important component of their total wages. Depending on circumstances, workers might receive no bonus at all. For instance, workers employed in loss-making factories and those that suffered from chronic power shortages would receive a basic wage, but in all likelihood no bonus. Under these conditions, total wages for these employees would be lower under the new wage system than they would have been under the old eight-grade system. Although employees of profitable SOEs saw their total wages increase, employees of loss-making SOEs complained that their total wages were being cut, through no fault of their own.

and 1990s. These subsidies were necessary to offset costs incurred by the "iron rice bowl" that had proven to be nearly impossible to break. Subsidies to unprofitable enterprises soaked up more than 44 billion yuan (about $7.48 billion) in 1992 alone. In addition to subsidies, the state supported inefficient enterprises by forcing state banks to lend them money. Because of debt problems, many enterprises never repaid the loans.

In 1986, the central government had tried to get tough with unprofitable SOEs by threatening to cover losses only up to a certain fixed level and to gradually reduce the money it handed out to make good on the losses. Despite these efforts, the number of money-losing SOEs continued to escalate. By 1998, more than half of China's large and medium-sized industrial SOEs were losing money, and debts exceeded assets at one-third of these firms. SOE losses were largely due to three factors. One factor was the central government's *tightening of credit*. The central government tightened credit in the late 1980s to try to bring down inflation that had heated up soon after the introduction of price reform. At the same time, China's government began running increasingly large budget deficits and it cut lines of credit in an effort to reduce enterprise financial dependency on the state. As a result, SOEs lost the easy money they had previously enjoyed. A second factor contributing to the increase in loss-making firms was *outdated production technology and low utilization of existing equipment*. Since the founding of the PRC, China had been successful in building an extensive industrial base. China's rapid rate of industrial growth, however, was not accompanied by development of technical, managerial, and worker skills. Hence, China's industrial development had been extensive, rather than intensive, which would have involved better use of existing capital equipment, development of managerial methods, and worker skills. Finally, productivity remained low, largely due to the *employment of surplus workers* in SOEs. For instance, in 1997 there were 10 million surplus workers employed in China's industrial SOEs.

One option for reforming SOEs was to privatize them. Although China in the 1990s privatized some of its smaller state firms, most notably in the industrial city of Wuhan, China's leaders in general hesitated to privatize firms for theoretical and politically strategic reasons. Privatization was anathema to China's socialist economic system, and privatization threatened existing coalitions of bureaucrats, managers, and labor. Rather than privatize its state firms, China in the 1990s adopted the policy of closing, stopping, transforming, or merging operations of SOEs. China's leaders adopted this policy not because it might be less painful than privatization, but because it was more politically palatable. China's leaders were concerned that privatization would upset social order as workers perceived a threat to their security. As an alternative, China in the later 1990s allowed some SOEs to become stock corporations, thereby allowing them to generate their own revenue.

Corporatization of State Firms

The marketization of SOEs in the 1980s was followed by their corporatization in the 1990s. Corporatization involves converting state firms into shareholding corporations. After the development of a stock market system, China began to offer shares of stock in SOEs to domestic and foreign investors.

Under the modern enterprise system (MES) reforms, primary ownership would remain with the state (as the enterprises' largest shareholder) but the enterprises would be reorganized and run as corporations. The state would refrain from directly interfering in the production and management of SOEs, and enterprises would organize production according to market demand. The 1994 Company Law made shareholding SOEs answerable to shareholders. Perhaps most important, corporatization relieved the state of its unlimited responsibility for SOEs. Under the previous system, SOEs were obliged to care for their employees from cradle to grave, providing housing, medical care, education, and other social welfare benefits. When an enterprise becomes a shareholding corporation, however, the state is no longer liable for the entire plant and its employees. It is liable only for its investment in the originally appraised assets. Thus, MES reforms redrew the boundaries of the state and firm.[17]

Despite the change in ownership composition, however, state enterprise managers had difficulty adapting to the need for transparency and disclosure necessary for operating in a market-oriented economy and for maintaining foreign investor confidence in their firms.[18] The Tsingtao Brewery flotation in Hong Kong is a good illustration of the difficulty SOE managers encountered in transitioning to capitalism. In July 1993, China's premier beer maker, the Tsingtao Brewery, offered for sale shares in the brewery on the Hong Kong Stock Exchange. Instead of using the funds to expand the brewery production facilities as the prospectus for the initial public offering (IPO) proposed, Tsingtao management took the proceeds from the Hong Kong listing to lend to other state firms at high interest rates. Investors and market analysts complained that Tsingtao's management saw nothing wrong with what they had done, and brewery management assured investors and financial analysts that the money had been returned. Part of the problem was that Tsingtao had begun to act as a bank. By loaning money from the brewery's flotation at high interest rates to other state firms, Tsingtao's management took the risk of not getting the money back. Loaning the money to other state firms was very risky, considering that state firms are in debt to their suppliers because they are not being paid by their customers for goods delivered. If one enterprise were to default, Tsingtao would lose its investment.[19]

Tsingtao's lack of disclosure was not uncommon. Corporatized state firms often failed to divulge information on how investments were actually used, and managers often engaged in other questionable financial practices. For instance, the Ma'anshan Iron and Steel Company in 1994 tried to artificially inflate dividend payments to Hong Kong investors by withholding dividend payments to its own holding company. In 1995, Zhou Beifang, the chairman of Shougang Holding (Hong Kong) and son of Capital Iron and Steel Works chief Zhou Guanwu, was arrested on corruption charges. In 1996, the wife of the chairman of Siu-fung Ceramics Holdings dumped 80 million shares of company stock ahead of an announcement of a poor interim result, fueling an investigation of the company's chairman and wife on charges of insider trading. In 1999, there were several high-profile cases of dubious financial practices. That year, the chairman and two board directors of the Dongfang Boiler Group were arrested for stealing more than 1 million shares of stock meant for staff; the former chairman of Guangdong International Trust and Investment Corporation (GITIC) was placed under investigation for the multibillion-dollar failure of GITIC; five Hong Kong–listed companies linked to Guangdong Enterprises (Holdings) were charged with using funds raised from the market for purposes not stipulated in fundraisings; and the chairman and executive director of China Everbright, a firm associated with China's State Council, was investigated for economic irregularities.

Based on these and the Tsingtao cases, it is clear that the legacy of the state plan was still strong into the 1990s. Although managerial autonomy increased under the MES, state enterprise managers often still acted as agents of the state, rather than responding to the demands of investors. The lack of interest in investors' concerns was largely due to the fact that the corporations' boards of directors were made up of former bureaucrats and party cadres. Several Chinese universities, such as Fudan University in Shanghai, began management training programs in the 1990s designed to educate managers in the way of the market. Courses ranged from management methods to portfolio management.

Despite the problem of lack of transparency, the issuing of stock allowed China to raise the revenues necessary for industrial expansion at a time when the economy was slowing down and the state was unwilling to inject massive amounts of investment into SOEs. By the early 2000s, most of China's SOEs had converted into shareholding corporations.

SOE Reform and Labor Discontent

SOE reform created winners and losers. Winners included younger and better-skilled workers who stood to earn higher wages, and managers of productive SOEs who enjoyed more perks and greater power. Losers included older and less skilled workers who were concerned about job security and welfare, and managers of less profitable enterprises. Many workers had seen their total wages decrease under the structural wage system. SOE employees also found that they had to pay for what they once received as benefits through their workplace. Many of the older employees were dissatisfied with the reforms because they now had to contribute to retirement pension plans and had to pay out of pocket for expenses such as health care and housing. Formerly, the SOE had provided these benefits to employees for free or for a minimal fee.

In the late 1980s and early 1990s, SOE reform and high inflation caused many discontented workers to protest the reforms. They engaged in work slowdowns, work stoppages, strikes, acts of sabotage against their firms, and legal street demonstrations. Between June 1989 and summer 1991, more than fifty thousand Chinese workers engaged in strikes or other protests.[20] Some workers took more extreme measures. In early 1992, workers in Tianjin rampaged through the Seagull Watch Factory smashing equipment to protest efforts by management to trim staff by sacking almost half of the firm's four thousand employees. In a separate incident, angry Chongqing Knitting Mill workers went on strike and besieged the plant. When the head of the city's textile department came to negotiate, workers took him hostage. Workers were afraid that the mill's closure would mean they would lose their housing, education, and medical retirement benefits. Retired workers eventually saw their pensions cut 25 percent. Other workers took their anger out on enterprise managers. Disgruntled employees attacked managers, causing their hospitalization, and even death, claiming ill-treatment by the managers. Liaoning provincial authorities claimed that incidents of factory managers being beaten up or attacked had increased in the early 1990s. In one case, the general manager of the Shenyang City People's Hotel was killed by a meat chopper–wielding employee whose salary had been cut after his position had been made redundant. In Sichuan, a factory worker nicknamed "the monk" went on a rampage with a hunting rifle, killing three colleagues inside the factory and killing five others before being killed himself when a taxi he stole plunged over a cliff. "The monk" began the shooting spree after an argument with a supervisor over timekeeping.[21]

Despite these incidents of labor violence, reformers in China's leadership and many workers wanted to continue enterprise reform. Labor tensions were undoubtedly high in the 1980s and 1990s. However, many SOE employees welcomed the changes. For some workers, the reforms were not as threatening to their security and interests as they initially seemed. They also realized that the reforms offered unprecedented economic opportunities and labor mobility. At the beginning of the reform era, the state appointed employees to SOEs and workers could rarely transfer to another firm. The worker seeking transfer had to acquire prior approval from his work unit. After reform, all employees signed fixed-term contracts with their enterprises. At the expiration of their contracts, employees could continue with the firm under a new contract, or leave for another job. Also, they found their total wages increased under the structural wage system. Many workers welcomed the ability to increase their incomes through higher bonuses.

The labor contract system contributed to this increased labor mobility, but more important, the explosive growth of the nonstate sector increased economic opportunities. For some it meant that they could moonlight easier. Many SOE employees retained their state jobs so they could continue to receive benefits associated with those jobs, but took on second jobs, usually in the private sector, to supplement their incomes. The development of nonstate enterprises allowed skilled employees to seek jobs outside the state sector. In the early reform era, much nonstate employment was characterized by self-employed individuals (*getihu*). Beginning in the 1980s and 1990s, however, many of these budding entrepreneurs expanded their operations. Some SOE employees, including party cadres, took leave or quit to "jump into the sea" (*xiahai*) of private entrepreneurship. As a result, the number of mid-sized and larger private firms (*siying qiye*) grew throughout the 1980s and 1990s. In 1992, there were 910 million employed in urban private firms, up from 320,000 in 1979. By 2000, there were nearly 13 million, and by 2009 this figure had risen to more than 55 million.[22]

When Deng Xiaoping coined the phrase "socialist commodity economy" (also known as socialist market economy) in 1984, his intent was to maintain state industry as the backbone of China's socialist economy, but to allow the nonstate sector to supplement the state sector. Today, the nonstate sector of China's economy far exceeds the state sector. Fewer Chinese are employed in SOEs. By 2008, only 20 percent of urban employed persons worked in an SOE. More people were employed by nonstate urban firms.[23] Large-scale enterprises, which play a key role in China's economy, continue to be state-controlled, but other industries have been restructured as shareholding corporations or mixed forms of ownership, such as joint ventures. Industries that the state continues to control include those related to China's state security, those that are natural monopolies, those that supply public-use products or services, and large enterprises in new and high-technology industries.

Since 1997, China's strategy for SOE reform has been *zhuada fangxiao* ("grasping the big while letting go of the small") to get rid of many nonstrategic small and medium-sized SOEs.

The remaining SOEs are making significant profits for the state and are required to pay a portion of after-tax profits to the central government. SOEs are estimated to have given Beijing $6.16 billion in payouts in 2010.[24]

In the twenty-first century, both state and nonstate industries are contributing to China's dramatic economic rise. In particular, these industries are contributing to fulfilling China's energy needs, which are discussed in the next section.

Energy Needs

China's continued economic rise is contingent on a plentiful and stable supply of energy. China overtook the United States in 2009 to become the world's largest energy user. China's demand for energy is projected to increase by 75 percent between 2008 and 2035.[25] Fossil fuels, such as coal and oil, will be the dominant source of energy over this period, although renewable energy sources and nuclear power will rise. China meets about 70 percent of its total energy needs through coal, and coal has fueled China's rapid, double-digit economic growth for the past thirty years. To maintain that pace of growth, China must tap all of its energy resources, including coal. China is the world's largest producer and consumer of coal. It produces 35 percent of the world's coal, and China consumes 1.3 billion tons of coal a year. China draws some 80 percent of its coal from small, privately owned mines that are often illegal and poorly run. In 2009, 2,631 coal miners lost their lives in the mines. As coal reserves have become increasingly difficult and treacherous to access, China's leaders have stepped up efforts to secure other sources of energy, such as oil, hydroelectric power, and "green" sources of energy such as wind turbines and solar panels.

Oil is another precious energy resource for China. In 2008, China imported 56 percent of its oil and will likely import four-fifths of its oil by 2030.[26] The PRC was an oil-importing country at its inception, and suffered a shortage of oil in the early 1960s when the Soviet Union ended assistance and oil to China. This shortage led to exploration of the Daqing oil field, which began production in 1963. From 1965 through the 1980s, China was self-sufficient in oil. As its domestic economy and energy consumption increased, however, China in the early 1990s became a net importer of oil.

While industry is responsible for 72 percent of China's total energy consumption, this pattern is changing as more affluent Chinese purchase cars and build larger residences.[27] These changes will increase energy consumption and shift China's demand toward petroleum and gasoline. Although China has increased domestic production of oil and natural gas, it cannot meet the increasing demand. China consumes approximately 7.85 million barrels of oil per day. By 2015, China's oil consumption could rise to 10 to 12 million barrels per day. Since 1996, China has been a net importer of crude oil, and in 2008, China became the world's second largest importer of crude oil, surpassing Japan. About half of its oil imports come from the Middle East, and almost a quarter from Africa. Five percent of China's oil imports come from East Asia. China's largest suppliers of oil are Saudi Arabia (20 percent), Angola (17 percent), Iran (12 percent), Oman (8 percent), and Russia (7 percent).[28] In 2004, China began building a strategic petroleum reserve that will ultimately have a capacity of 500 million barrels. Considering China's appetite for oil, it is unlikely that even this large amount is enough to adequately cushion severe disruptions.

The great Daqing field in Heilongjiang Province is China's largest producer of crude oil, followed by the Shengli fields in Shandong Province and the Dagang field in Hebei Province. New fields are needed to meet domestic demand for oil. Many multinational firms, such as Royal Dutch Shell, Exxon, Marathon, and British Petroleum, and joint ventures have played a significant role in exploration, especially in the far northwest and in the South China Sea fields. Although fields in Xinjiang Province once held great promise as potential sources of oil, the government is concerned that the fields may not be as extensive as once thought.

To increase energy security, China and Kazakhstan developed a massive pipeline to transmit oil from the Caspian Sea to refineries in China. Another pipeline connects Russian oil fields to Xinjiang refineries (Chapter 10).

Disappointed by land-based oil exploration, China has turned to the sea in its quest for oil. Exploration in the South and East China Seas has heightened political tensions with some of China's neighbors, however. Many other nations contest all or part of the Chinese claims in the South China Sea, particularly in the areas around the Spratly Islands. Hence, China's quest for oil in the seas is not only an economic issue, but a foreign policy one as well.

China's oil corporations are currently involved in oil exploration and production abroad. In 1992, China's leaders put forth a "going out" strategy, which advocates channeling China's vast foreign currency reserves toward Chinese companies for overseas expansion and acquisitions, especially in energy and natural resources. This policy was actually initiated by China's biggest oil companies: CNPC (China National Petroleum Corporation), Sinopec (Chinese

National Petrochemical Corporation), and CNOOC (China National Offshore Oil Company). Since the 1990s, the "going out" strategy has largely been directed at Africa, and is discussed in Chapter 10.

China is trying to reduce its dependency on coal and oil by looking toward alternative energy sources. The Eleventh Five-Year Plan (2006–2010) calls for a doubling of renewable energy generation (wind, solar, biogas, and hydroelectric power) to 15 percent of the country's needs by 2020.[29] For instance, China is poised to become the world's largest market for wind energy and the world's largest center for the manufacture of wind energy–generating equipment. At this time, however, the industry's key technologies are dependent on imports. China has begun to use biomass energy and biofuels, although their use is still quite limited. In Chongqing, a biomass waste plant generates power from city household waste, which is distributed through a power grid. In Henan Province, an agricultural-waste energy power plant uses wheat, corn, and other agricultural waste stalks to generate power. The State Power Grid Corporation, a state-owned enterprise that builds and operates power grids, uses cotton, forestry waste, and other "gray" biomass to produce energy. China is just beginning to explore geothermal power and power derived from methane. Sinopec and Glitnir Bank of Iceland are developing geothermal resources near Xi'an in northern Shaanxi Province. Methane gas fuels more than 40 million households in China. Chongqing city alone has 860,000 households using methane gas.[30] China needs to step up use of solar energy. China is the world's biggest producer of photoelectric cells, but exports 99 percent of them.

China's Twelfth Five-Year Plan (2011–2015) sets new targets to reduce China's reliance on energy imports and to improve energy efficiency. China has great hydropower potential. The Three Gorges Dam on the Upper Yangtze is the world's largest-capacity hydropower station and produces 22,500 megawatts of electricity, well ahead of Brazil's 12,600 megawatts from the Itaipu Dam. The promise of energy generated by water is compromised, however, by a drop in water flows along China's major rivers. In recent years, the Yangtze River has been running so low that hydropower production along the river has been slowing.

The Environment

China is a vast country with a great many resources. China historically has had an abundance of coal, iron ore, petroleum, natural gas, mercury, tin, titanium, tungsten, salt, manganese, aluminum, lead, zinc, and uranium. It also has the world's largest hydropower potential. Industrialization under Mao and post-1978 economic development schemes have depleted many of China's natural resources and seriously degraded the environment. After seizing power, the Chinese communists sought to rebuild China through rapid industrialization.

With their emphasis on heavy industry, the early Five-Year Plans required that the government exploit China's natural resources. Industrial ministries, which set production targets for relevant state firms, were more interested in meeting those targets than in protecting the environment. The plans also failed to adequately assess the value of natural resources. The central government deflated the value of natural resources to make raw materials for state industry as cheap as possible. The practice of setting artificially low resource values encouraged the excessive exploitation of resources.

Political campaigns such as the Great Leap Forward and Cultural Revolution also wreaked havoc on China's environment. Like the Chinese folklore story, "Yugong yishan," which tells of a foolish old man who wanted to move a mountain, Mao believed that mass mobilization would overcome any material limitations. His belief in voluntarism (Chapter 3) led him to invest in many environmentally damaging projects. Massive deforestation of China's forests during the Great Leap Forward and terracing of fragile lands during the Cultural Revolution permanently scarred China's landscape. Great bonfires and cooking stoves in commune kitchens also consumed great amounts of firewood. Many Chinese were unhappy about the destruction of forests and the cutting of trees that they had known since childhood, which had provided them with shade, hunting grounds, firewood, and chestnuts.[31]

Rapid economic development since 1978 has depleted many of China's natural resources, and China continues to suffer from soil, air, and water pollution.[32] The major causes of China's environmental degradation are point and nonpoint source pollution, and ecological problems. Point source pollution derives from industrial effluents, airborne releases from factories, and particulates from power plants. Nonpoint source pollution derives from agricultural activities such as fertilizer and pesticide runoff from farmland and infiltration of livestock waste. These trends increase nutrient flows into lakes, creating algae blooms that choke off oxygen supplies to fish and plant life. Ecological problems stem from deforestation, desertification, salinization, pollution from fertilizers and farm chemicals, and erosion brought about by poor land-use practices. The World Bank estimates that 750,000 people die prematurely in China annually from air and water pollution alone. The following sections examine the scope and negative effects of each of these types of pollution in China.

Soil Pollution

China can be divided into three physiographic regions: the rugged terrain of the western regions, the southwest high plateaus, and the lush eastern alluvial and coastal plains. Westerly winds from Central Asia render west China cold and very dry throughout the winter, and precipitation is limited year-round. The southwest plateaus are also water-deficient. The east-west trend of the Qingling Mountains, which extend eastward to the East China Sea along the Huai River, divides China into regions of water surplus and water deficit, having serious implications for agriculture. Rainfall generally refreshes annual groundwater supplies in southern China and the southern part of the northeastern plains. The remainder of China north of the Qingling Mountains is water-deficient where groundwater exists, but is inconsistently replenished by precipitation. Some of China's worst environmental problems are in the dry, ecologically unstable regions of the north and west.[33]

Due to these conditions, less than 15 percent of China's land is arable. Although China has enough food to feed its population, regional disparities perpetuate malnutrition. Since the 1980s, China has lost much agricultural land to nonagricultural purposes, particularly in China's coastal provinces where population density is high and economic reform the most rapid. Excessive use of chemical fertilizers and pesticides has damaged China's soil. Fertilizer use in China increased from less than 5 million tons in 1950 to 40 million tons in 2003.[34] Industrial waste and mining also contribute to the pollution of China's soil.

One of the leading causes of land degradation and soil pollution in China is *deforestation*. Between 1958 and 1982, China carried out a series of deforestations known as the "three great cuttings." The first great cutting occurred at the beginning of the Great Leap Forward. Government policies encouraged the cutting down of massive forests to make way for industry or to use as fuel. For instance, massive forests were cut down to fuel the "backyard furnaces." Not only was the steel made in these furnaces useless, but many of China's hills were entirely denuded of trees. Roughly 10 percent of China's forest cover was felled in the course of a few months to fuel these rudimentary furnaces. The second great cutting occurred during the Cultural Revolution when the Chinese state sent 20 million youths to the countryside for land reclamation. They cleared more than 1.3 million hectares. The third great cutting occurred from 1980 to 1982, after Mao's death. In addition to cropland, the states contracted out to families forests that had been state-owned. People feared the government would renege and take back the land, so they rapidly cleared it to get as much use from it as possible.[35] This deforestation has contributed to the blowing away of topsoil and a loss of agricultural land. Since 1949, China has lost one-fifth of its agricultural land to soil erosion and economic development. Deforestation along the Yellow River and in the Upper Yangtze has increased the incidence and intensity of flooding.

Desertification also afflicts China. *Desertification* is the degradation of land from human activities as well as climatic variations. It is the consequence of livestock overgrazing, increased salinization of river basins, wind and water erosion, and poor cultivation practices. China loses approximately nine hundred square miles a year to desertification. Worsening desertification in Inner Mongolia and the Gobi Desert region has caused crippling sandstorms hundreds of miles away in Beijing. The incidence of sandstorms is increasing. Sandstorms afflicted Beijing once every seven or eight years in the 1950s, and every two to three years in the 1970s. By the early 1990s, however, they had become an annual problem. Residents claim that dust from the sandstorms works its way through keyholes and window frames, dirtying homes, clothes, and even bedding. Sandstorms have become a significant health problem, causing respiratory problems not just for the elderly, infirm, and very young, but for the healthy as well. Some sandstorms are so powerful that the remnants reach North America. In March 2010, Hong Kong, 1,240 miles to the south, recorded high pollution levels, partly due to an unusually ferocious sandstorm. Schools were advised to cancel outdoor activities and elderly people sought medical attention for shortness of breath. Across the 100-mile Taiwan Strait, island residents covered their mouths to avoid breathing the grit. Sand covered cars in ten minutes, and some airlines cancelled flights due to poor visibility caused by the sandstorm. The most significant and comprehensive government response to China's land degradation problems is the Three-North Shelterbelt Program, a reforestation program commonly known as the Great Green Wall. The Great Green Wall is a seventy-three-year development plan to reforest 35.6 million hectares (4 million square kilometers) by the year 2050. According to official Chinese statistics, China, by 2009, had reforested more than 6 million hectares of land.[36]

Water Management and Pollution

China is also a country of rivers. China's three major rivers are the Yangtze (Chang Jiang, or the Long River), Yellow River (Huang He), and West River (Xi Jiang). As its name implies, the Yangtze is China's largest and longest river. It flows eastward from Tibet to the East China Sea at Shanghai. In central China, the Yangtze irrigates farms. It serves as China's major west-east transit route and makes central China accessible to maritime transportation. The Yellow River is China's second longest waterway. It flows from the North China Plain, carrying yellow loessal silt, which is deposited along its riverbeds. Farmers since antiquity have used the rich loess for agricultural cultivation. And since antiquity, farmers have built levies to protect their land and homes. When the levees break, the river pours into the plains, causing massive property damage and loss of life, earning the river the name "China's Sorrow." For the past thirty years, however, excessive withdrawal of river water has caused the river to dry up before reaching the sea. In 2011, water levels along the mighty Yangtze River reached record lows, slowing hydropower generation, reducing agricultural output, and curtailing shipping traffic. Ships have been running aground in the drought-stricken river at Hankow in Wuhan, snarling shipping traffic there.

Despite the existence of these great rivers, availability of water has long been a major issue in China. China's earliest attempt to irrigate central China was the Dujiangyan Irrigation System. It is the oldest surviving nondam irrigation system in the world. Built on the Minjiang River more than 2,200 years ago,

Dujiangyan still irrigates the plains outside of Chengdu in Sichuan Province. A more recent attempt to irrigate China is the Three Gorges Dam Project.

China's water supply is 25 percent below the global average, and pollution from agriculture, industry, and households exacerbates water scarcity. Damming and excessive exploitation of China's river water have diminished river flows, depriving rivers of the ability to self-cleanse and contributing to further degradation. Many of China's natural lakes are also disappearing. The shortage of clean and available water resources has led to the overpumping of groundwater, lowering China's water tables and groundwater reservoirs.

Nearly all water in China has been polluted. More than 70 percent of water in five of China's seven river systems is unsuitable for human contact. The Yellow River, the main water source for North China, has become increasingly polluted, and its wastewater drainage far exceeds capacity. The underground water of a majority of China's cities is polluted, and the situation worsens every year. Two-thirds of China's major cities face a serious shortage of clean water. The main sources of water pollution in China are sewage, industrial, and household contaminants. As many as 700 million people drink water so polluted by human and animal feces that it falls well below the minimum government standard. For instance, pollution of the Tuojiang River in Jianyang City (Sichuan Province) in March 2004 prompted the provincial government to suspend municipal drinking water supplies. The city spent thirteen days without water. A chemical plant had dumped lethal wastewater containing synthetic ammonia and nitrogen directly into the river. In May 2004, the river was polluted a second time when a paper company discharged excessive amounts of wastewater into the river. In July 2004, an eighty-three-mile-long black and brown substance flowed along the Huai River, one of China's seven big rivers, killing wildlife and millions of fish. It occurred because too much water had been taken from the river system for industry and irrigation, reducing its ability to clean itself. Numerous factories dumped untreated waste directly into the river as well. China's largest monosodium glutamate plant ignored environmental regulations and poured untreated industrial waste into the Huai River.[37]

China produces approximately 3.7 billion tons of sewage per day. China would need ten thousand wastewater treatment plants, at a cost of some $48 billion, just to achieve a 50 percent treatment rate. Rural areas are particularly affected by water pollution. In rural areas, about 300 million people rely on unsafe drinking water. Rural water wells commonly have iron, manganese, and nitrate that far exceed state health standards. Water pollution also hurts China's rural economy. Agriculture consumes 70 to 80 percent of China's water, and much of that is polluted by runoff from farms, industry, and mines. Farmers depend on clean water to irrigate crops, but no one wants to buy crops irrigated with toxic water. As a result, rural incomes derived from agriculture remain depressed. Water pollution affects the livelihood of China's fishermen as well,

Three Gorges Dam Project

The Three Gorges Dam (San Xia) is the largest dam project in history. China's leaders have proposed damming the Yangtze ever since Sun Yat-sen proposed a dam in his plan for industrial development eighty-eight years ago. The proposal for the Three Gorges Dam ran into serious opposition when presented in China's parliament and passed with the smallest margin in the legislature's history. The dam's primary purposes are to raise the water level to allow larger-tonnage ships to reach Chongqing, and to control the Yangtze's regular flooding and provide energy, in the form of hydroelectric power, to downstream provinces, particularly Hunan and Hubei. To benefit Hunan and Hubei, however, involves displacement of more than 1 million people, the flooding of farms, and the destruction of historic and prehistoric archeological sites. The environmental impact is great, as the dam will affect local climate, flora and fauna, soils, geology, and agricultural ecology. It is possible that the dam will increase malaria and schistosomiasis, due to slower water velocity in the reservoir in front of the dam.[38] Critics of the project charge that by trapping silt the dam could actually make downstream riverbanks more vulnerable to flooding. Water quality is already deteriorating because of the dam, and soil erosion has led to riverbank collapses and landslides along the shores of the Yangtze's tributaries.

Despite these factors, the final concrete has been poured to complete the 606-foot-high barrier that stretches 7,575 feet across the Yangtze River. The dam required twenty-five thousand workers and cost $180 billion, but Chinese officials say it has the strength to hold back more waters than Lake Superior and power twenty-six generators to churn out 85 billion kilowatt-hours of electricity a year. The scope and consequences of this project show China's determination to be among the world's great economic powers, and the Communist Party's willingness to trade individual rights to get there. The project has displaced 1.4 million people, many of whom have not been compensated. The Chinese government promised displaced people new houses and livelihoods, but in many cases, the compensation was taken by corrupt local officials. Without a new home or job, the displaced people have been unable to survive in their new locations. It was reported as early as 1999 that millions of dollars in compensation funds were being embezzled; many officials were prosecuted but the complaints have not stopped.

There has been political opposition within China's normally pliant government when it comes to the environmental issues, however. The opposition demonstrates that the Chinese government is at least realizing that something needs to be done to address the country's serious ecological concerns. Although the issues created by the Three Gorges Dam are very problematic, it is possible that the worst effects can be dealt with if the government takes the problem seriously enough.

who face a shrinking fish catch. In many areas, farmers compete with industry for water resources. In Shandong Province, several thousand farmers rioted after Chinese officials prevented them from drawing from the local reservoir.

Water pollution also causes skin lesions and cancer. According to official government statistics, every year about 2 million Chinese people suffer diseases such as cancer from drinking water that is rich in arsenic.[39] A World Bank study found that lack of clean water contributed to liver, stomach, and bladder cancer in rural areas.[40] Pollution of rural drinking water has resulted in the emergence of so-called cancer villages. More than ten thousand tons of inklike chemical wastewater is dumped into the Qiantang River daily. In two villages near the river in Zhejiang Province, more than sixty people have died from cancer, representing 3 percent of the population of the two villages. The same picture emerges along the Huai River. Between 1994 and 2004, a total of 1,838 people died in eight villages of Ludian Township near the basin of the Hong River, a tributary of the Huai. The average mortality rate during the period was 9.7 percent, which far exceeds the 5 percent rate considered normal. In 2004 alone, a total of 209 people died, representing more than 12 percent of the population. The main causes of their deaths were lung cancer, liver cancer, and various cancers of the digestive system, which could all be traced back to river pollution.[41] In the coastal village of Xietang in Guangdong Province, men of the village died at a young age, leaving only women and children. Most living villagers were sick from diseases. Tests of a sample of water from a well, the main water source for the village, found that iron, manganese, and nitrite in the water far exceeded state health standards.[42]

In the past twenty years, China has passed legislation to protect water resources. Some of these laws are the Water Law, Water Pollution Prevention and Control Law, Water and Soil Conservation Law, Flood Control Law, and Fishery Law. The central government and local governments have passed numerous regulations on the use and protection of water resources as well. The central government has also made an effort to strengthen law enforcement. For instance, the Ministry of Water Resources and the Ministry of Environmental Protection make announced and unannounced visits to sites to improve the enforcement of laws and regulations.[43]

Despite these measures, China's environmental protection departments find it increasingly difficult to deal with the country's growing water pollution problem. According to China's Environmental Protection Law, environmental departments have no teeth to enforce the rules, but can merely impose fines.[44] Until recently, polluters faced a maximum 100,000 yuan (about $12,500) fine for violating environmental regulations, a mere pittance compared with the money invested in development projects, which often amounted to billions of yuan. The newly amended Water Pollution Prevention and Control Law, effective June 1, 2008, imposes stricter penalties against noncompliance. Under the law, the fine for pollution causing massive damage is calculated as 30 percent of the direct costs, with the fine not exceeding 1 million yuan (about $122,000). For example, the Chuanjiang Corporation, which had polluted the Tuojiang River in 2004, paid 1 million yuan in penalties and 11 million yuan (about $1.34 million) in compensation. Although the amended law strengthens punishment against polluters, the amount is still limited, and for some companies, it is financially worthwhile to break the law. Thus, the amount of fines is too low and too limited to deter companies from breaking the environmental regulations.

Air Pollution

Sixteen out of the twenty most polluted cities in the world are in China. Approximately three hundred thousand people a year die prematurely from respiratory diseases. The main causes of China's air pollution are industrial and automotive. The major source of air pollution is the burning of coal for industry, transportation, and electricity generation. China has been using coal for energy for thousands of years. Coal-fired power stations generate approximately 70 percent of China's electricity, compared with 50 percent in America. The first use of coal on a large scale was the major industrial plans under Mao Zedong, which started the widespread combustion of coal in 1949. During the First Five-Year Plan, from 1953 to 1957, China constructed industrial and mining enterprises, including industries for coal mining. At the time, the Soviet Union played a major part in the construction of many industries fueled by coal. These industries later posed a problem in China because of their inefficient and wasteful use of coal. The Great Leap Forward also boosted the use of coal because many Chinese workers in the countryside used coal as energy for backyard furnaces to make steel. Between the Great Leap Forward and the Cultural Revolution, the small-scale mining industry boomed, particularly in the coal-mining sector.

Since 1979, China has used coal as its primary source of fuel for its industries. While other sources of consumption include oil, natural gas, hydroelectric power, and nuclear power, coal unmistakably outweighs all other sources of energy. The main reason for the heavy consumption is the vast amount of mineral deposits in China's mountainous regions, making China the largest producer of coal in the world. China's coal reserves are nearly depleted in the northern regions, forcing miners to dig deeper, making coal mining increasingly dangerous. Coal mining in China is one of the world's most dangerous professions, and is unquestionably the most deadly job in China. Although China produces 35 percent of the world's coal, 80 percent of deaths in coal mine accidents occur in China. In 2002, 6,995 miners were killed in Chinese mines, an average of twenty deaths per day. In 2009, small private mines accounted for about 30 percent of China's coal supply, but 70 percent of the fatalities. Government efforts to shut illegal mines and toughen enforcement of private mines reduced the number of deaths to 2,631 in 2009. Although China closed 1,054 illegal coal mines in 2008, nearly 80 percent of China's mines are illegal, which makes enforcement and further reductions difficult. Coal mining also contributes to health problems. In 2004, six hundred thousand miners were suffering from pneumoconiosis, a disease of the lungs caused by long-continued inhalation of dust. The figure increases by seventy thousand miners every year.[45]

Although coal is a relatively cheap source of energy, it is highly polluting. China's coal has high sulfur content and goes through a less stringent desulphurization process than that found in the West. The higher the sulfur content in the coal, the more particulate matter the coal produces. Also, much of China's coal industry uses an outdated Soviet-era technology in which the use of energy is wasteful and inefficient, creating unnecessary pollution. However, the demand for coal is unlikely to diminish anytime soon. The growth of a consumer-driven middle class has created more demand for coal-generated electricity. Many of China's cities commonly experience blackouts because of the inability to keep up with demand. As a result, China plans to build 544 new coal-fired power stations to meet this insatiable demand for energy.

Pollution from the combustion of coal creates serious health problems. Highly concentrated air pollution, primarily in cities, accounts for some four hundred thousand premature deaths each year. Various respiratory diseases such as chronic bronchitis and pneumoconiosis typically cause these deaths. Heavy pollution has contributed to serious ecological concerns both within China and internationally. Soot is one of the major effects of the combustion of coal and is measured in total suspended particles in the air, which accounts not only for respiratory diseases but for environmental damage as well. Soot, which contains acid droplets from the burning of coal, mixes with precipitation and falls back onto the country. This type of precipitation, called acid rain, falls on 30 percent of the country, damaging and rusting buildings, eroding soil, and harming the ecosystem. Coal burning in China affects Japan, Taiwan, North and South Korea, and the Philippines as wind currents blow pollution from China across Asia, causing respiratory diseases and causing acid rain to fall on regional countries. Many countries in the region are concerned about a brown haze consisting of a two-mile-thick cloud of soot that sometimes stretches across South Asia from Afghanistan to Sri Lanka. The brown haze causes acid rain, cuts sunlight, and possibly accounts for thousands of lung disease–related deaths each year.

Global warming is another troubling aspect of the combustion of coal. Burning coal releases greenhouse gases such as carbon dioxide into the air. Although the greenhouse effect is a natural process, in which gases reflect and warm the earth, China's rapid industrialization contributes to what many scientists are calling *global warming*. At its current level of growth, China by 2015 will surpass the United States as the highest producer of greenhouse gases. International pressure is mounting on China to reduce the amount of carbon dioxide it releases into the environment. The Kyoto Protocol is one of the main international agreements designed to reduce the emission of greenhouse gases. The agreement, signed in 1999 under the United Nations Framework Convention on Climate Change, states that Annex 1 countries, or developed countries, are committed to reducing overall carbon dioxide emissions by at least 5 percent below 1990 levels between 2008 and 2012. However, under this agreement, China is not an Annex 1 country, or developed country, and therefore is not required to commit to reducing emissions even though it signed and ratified the treaty in 2002. In fact, China's carbon dioxide emissions are likely to have risen by 11 percent per year from 2008 to 2010. If that is the case, by 2010, China's emissions of greenhouse gases will have outstripped reductions achieved by all of the countries that have signed the Kyoto Protocol combined.[46] China's Twelfth Five-Year Plan (2011–2015) sets new targets to improve energy efficiency, thereby cutting down on waste, and to slow the pace of environmental degradation.

Protecting China's Environment

Citizen groups and nongovernmental organizations (NGOs) have organized to demand a stronger government response to pollution. However, the demand for economic growth makes the drive to protect the environment difficult. Local leaders are rewarded more for economic development of their areas than for their protection of the environment. Shutting down polluting factories increases unemployment, and may be politically unpopular. Nevertheless, the Chinese government has taken some steps to protect the environment.

China is responding to the environmental crisis by trying to pass the internationally recognized Leadership in Energy and Environmental Design certification for more of its buildings. As part of the Eleventh Five-Year Plan, the Ministry of Construction in March 2006 issued an edict requiring that all new construction in China be 50 percent more energy-efficient. These buildings use the flow of the sun and the rain to save energy and use 40 percent less water than conventional buildings. Despite these efforts, it is not likely that China will meet the 50 percent mark. The reality of China's nation-building policies, ambitious construction firms, and a massive floating population needing urban housing in coming decades makes the reality of these projects hard to enforce.[47]

In recent years, the Chinese government has also begun to express concern over threats to China's biological diversity.[48] Uncontrolled deforestation, overgrazing of rangelands, overexploitation and use of animal and plant resources, atmospheric pollution, poor utilization of water resources in arid areas, overfishing, and adverse affects of tourism, mining, and wetland reclamation all threaten China's biodiversity. China's leaders have made some efforts to protect the country's biodiversity, however. For instance, in 1992, China signed the Convention on Biological Diversity. Not all aspects of China's biological diversity are being covered, however. Most government efforts focus on charismatic megafauna (large animal species that have widespread popular appeal, such as the giant panda), not insects. In recent years, the central government's focus on megafauna has led to the creation of ecotourism programs. Although those programs generate revenue, they often degrade natural habitats.[49]

Environmental NGOs

Both domestic and international NGOs are active in China. China had no environmental NGOs before 1994. The first Chinese environmental NGO was the Friends of Nature. It has been key to protecting the habitat of the golden monkey, which was being destroyed by illegal logging. Two other pioneering environmental NGOs are the Global Village of Beijing and Green Home. By 2006, there were 2,768 environmental NGOs in China with millions of participants. International nongovernmental organizations (INGOs) that lobby for environmental protection provide information to the government, lobby the government on behalf of environmental interests, educate the public, and engage in conservation, species protection, and policy advocacy. The central government appreciates the presence and work of INGOs given its own limited capacities and because of their common interests. In fact, the Ministry of Environmental Protection (MEP) works closely with environmental INGOs. Local governments are less enthusiastic, however, because INGOs tend to check up on local problems.[50] For example, in 2003 the Yunnan provincial government drew up plans to build a series of reservoirs and dams along the Nujiang River for the generation of electricity. Project backers claimed that the development would also provide water for irrigation and drinking, provide flood control, and enhance local tourism. According to official statistics, the project would increase the annual income of the local administration by 2.7 billion yuan (about $415 million).[51] The MEP (formerly the State Environmental Protection Administration) opposed the project in the absence of a persuasive environmental assessment, as required by the 2003 Environmental Impact Assessment Law. A coalition of Chinese NGOs urged the central government to hold hearings on the project and to report the findings to the public. After the hearings, other NGOs, such as the Green Earth Volunteers, Friends of Nature, and Yunnan-based Green Watershed, joined the coalition in an antidam movement. The NGOs conducted field surveys of the area, published articles, organized seminars, and delivered speeches. Finally, in April 2004, Premier Wen Jiabao suspended the project and called for more detailed evaluation.[52]

Of the international NGOs, the World Wildlife Fund (WWF) has been in China the longest, having maintained offices and funded environment-related projects in China since the mid-1980s. The International Crane Foundation (ICF) began conducting research in China in the late 1980s. Most INGOs are engaged in projects that promote energy efficiency and energy conservation in China. In the two years between 2000 and 2002, thirteen INGOs and four US university–affiliated research centers launched thirty-nine energy-related projects in China.[53] The second largest area of INGO activity concerns conservation and biodiversity protection. The WWF leads all other INGOs in program implementation. Other environmental INGOs active in China include Wetlands International, Greenpeace, Friends of Nature, International Fund for Animal Welfare, and Worldwide Fund for Nature.

Many environmental activists complain that government regulations and emphasis on economic development limit the influence of NGOs. Government regulations affecting NGOs prevent environmental movements from growing into societywide movements. For example, strict regulations prohibit more than one organization of a particular nature from being established at the same administrative level. Another regulation requires social organizations to register with the appropriate civil affairs department, making it impossible for local groups to enroll members from different areas. Many members of Chinese NGOs claim that the government often ignores them and, in some cases, has tried to shut down their operations. For example, after the suspension of the Nujiang Dam project, Chinese NGOs brought local peasants to Beijing to participate in an international conference. The peasants and NGO representatives demanded a greater say in use of public lands. Not long thereafter, party officials ordered an investigation of Chinese NGOs and restricted the ability of NGO leaders to travel abroad. NGOs also had to submit reports on activities to the government.[54]

Since 1979, China has passed more than forty environmental protection laws and many regulations. Although the national level of government has shown interest in protecting the environment, local governments are less enthusiastic. Environmental protection plans contradict or get in the way of economic development programs. Because local government officials often build their careers based on the success of their economic programs, they tend to favor economic development programs over environmental protection. For instance, commercial activities such as logging and fishing run counter to environmental protection projects and often continue despite NGO efforts to stop them. Basically, the Chinese government is experiencing a conflict of values between economic development and sustainable development.[55] Most regions that need protection for biodiversity are located in minority-populated areas that have less clout in Beijing than the more prosperous Han-majority regions.

The Internet and cell phone technology have helped environmentalists organize protests. In 2007, citizens united in Xiamen against the construction of a chemical factory and, in 2008, in Shanghai over plans to extend a magnetic levitation train line. Chinese are increasingly taking their grievances to the courts. Environmental activists travel the country taking on cases and are increasingly winning cases against polluters and even environmental protection officials who have been negligent in their work, resulting in fines or prison sentences. However, justice and restitution for damage can take years.[56] The Chinese government has established pilot environmental courts to hear and try cases against polluters. The first such case occurred in September 2009, when the All-China Environment Federation, a public-interest group affiliated with the Ministry of Environmental Protection, filed a lawsuit alleging that the local land bureau was negligent in protecting local resources. Residents of Qingzhen in southern China filed a complaint against the local land resources bureau for not razing an unfinished factory, as required by law, which was polluting a local lake. It was the first time a Chinese court accepted a lawsuit brought by an environmental group against a government body. The land bureau issued an administrative order to resolve the complaint rather than let the case go to trial. China has only two other such courts, in Yunnan and Jiangsu. As pilot projects, the environmental courts have not been officially sanctioned by the people's court or backed by national legislation.

China in the World Economy

In December 1978, the Third Plenum of the Eleventh Central Committee adopted the Open Policy (*kaifang zhengce*), a set of policies to promote China's participation in the world economy. After a decade of xenophobia, the policy opened China to foreign trade, foreign direct investment (FDI), and foreign borrowing. Under the Open Policy, China in 1979 created four special economic zones (SEZs) in Guangzhou and Fujian Provinces to attract FDI, and in 1984 opened fourteen coastal cities to attract technology-intensive production.

Foreign Trade and Investment

An important part of Deng's economic reforms was bringing China into the world economy so that it could benefit from increased trade, foreign investment, and foreign technology. Several international and domestic factors presented obstacles to foreign trade during the Mao era. In the 1950s and 1960s, China faced a trade embargo from Western capitalist nations. Consequently, China's main trading partners were the Soviet Union and Soviet satellite states. China's trade suffered further as a result of the Sino-Soviet split in the early 1960s. Domestically, government trading agencies strictly controlled China's international trade, and there were tight restrictions on foreign investment and loans. Party leaders were concerned about the increased foreign presence and influences, as well as the possible instability that would come from opening China's economy to the world. Since the end of the Mao era, China's leaders have pursued a number of economic reforms that have transformed China from an economy largely closed off from the rest of the world to an important and integral member of the international economy.

Special Economic Zones

One of the first steps in China's economic reforms was the establishment of special economic zones. Reformers planned the SEZs to open China to the world economy and to experiment with economic decentralization, while at the same time maintaining economic stability and party control. Deng Xiaoping and Zhao Ziyang, Deng's protégé, were key advocates of the zones. In 1979, Beijing designated Shenzhen, Zhuhai, Xiamen, and Shantou as SEZs. These locations were chosen because of their proximity to the overseas Chinese communities in Hong Kong, Taiwan, and Macau. China's leaders hoped to take advantage of connections of language, culture, and family to establish economic cooperation with these communities. Beijing looked to attract trade, investment, modern technology, and successful Western business practices from overseas Chinese firms. The government sought to attract foreign firms to these SEZs by supplying cheap labor, infrastructure, and preferential treatment. By concentrating the influx of foreign business within several SEZs, the Chinese government was trying to shield domestic industry from new competition and limit exposure of Chinese citizens to undesirable foreign ideas, such as an expansion of civil liberties and human rights. During the 1980s, China's leaders designated Hainan as China's fifth SEZ and opened fourteen coastal cities to foreign trade and investment, extending to them favorable conditions similar to those enjoyed by foreign firms in the SEZs. China's leaders aimed many of these policies at Taiwanese trade and investment with political goals in mind. By encouraging greater economic interaction, China's leaders hoped to foster PRC-Taiwan interdependence and ease the process of unification.

While the SEZs attracted foreign investment, created jobs, and fostered trade, they also engendered some resentment and criticism. Party hardliners took exception to the legal exceptions and preferential treatment granted to foreigners within the SEZs and other development areas. They compared the zones to the treaty ports of the previous century, where Western countries exploited China's resources and people and operated outside of Chinese law. They saw the SEZs as a way that modern capitalists could repeat that humiliation. In addition to these nationalistic and ideological criticisms, there were more tangible problems arising from the SEZs. In trying to create a preferential environment for foreign business and investment, the government allowed serious violations of Chinese labor laws to take place in the development zones. There were numerous government investigations and media reports of underage workers, dismal living conditions, and marathon work schedules. This mistreatment of workers led to labor strikes and further denunciations from party hardliners. The type of businesses growing in the SEZs was also an issue. In their early years, the SEZs failed to attract much of the advanced technology that China's leaders saw as critical to making Chinese firms more efficient and competitive as the country transitioned to an open, market-oriented economy. Instead, they attracted labor-intensive and highly polluting industries to China's nearly inexhaustible supply of cheap labor and lax environmental standards. The SEZs and other development areas also exacerbated China's regional economic disparity. In the early reform years, most of these zones were located along China's coast. From 1979 to 1987, 90 percent of foreign investment projects in China were located in that region. Despite these problems, China's SEZs have succeeded in being the engines of economic development that China's reformers had hoped for. For instance, Shenzhen, China's largest SEZ, has grown at a rate of around 28 percent for the last thirty years.

Hoping to repeat the success of the first five major SEZs, China has continued to establish other economic development and technology zones (EDTZs) throughout the country. These sixty-nine zones focus on various aspects of economic development, such as trade, advanced technology, and bilateral economic cooperation with other nations. China's EDTZs are powerful engines of regional economic growth and development and contribute 11 percent to China's economic growth. While China's use of SEZs and other EDTZs has contributed significantly to China's economic development, their future is uncertain. The government subsidies and similar preferential treatment within the zones could be challenged under China's World Trade Organization (WTO) commitments as unfair. However, even without the preferential treatment, those zones that are already developed would still offer firms needed infrastructure and proximity to labor and an established business community.

China and the World Trade Organization

China became a member of the WTO on December 11, 2001, after fifteen years of negotiations. Jiang Zemin and Zhu Rongji had been key proponents of China's accession. They and other reformers faced opposition from party hardliners who believed that the WTO, like the International Monetary Fund and the World Bank, was a tool by which the United States could advance its economic interests in China. As reformers offered changes and concessions to the United States and the West to gain entry to the WTO, party hardliners accused them of selling out China to foreigners just as China's leaders had done almost a century earlier. The continued delays and rejection that China's accession faced over the fifteen years of negotiations also spurred a nationalistic response against international integration among some of China's people and leadership. In addition to such ideological resistance, reformers faced concerns that further opening China's economy, which joining the WTO would require, would harm China's domestic firms in the near term. Even the reformers acknowledged that China might pay this short-term price of membership, but they believed that joining the WTO was necessary if China were to become a major player in the world economy.

One of the effects of WTO membership was trade liberalization—the removal of trade barriers—between China and other WTO member countries.

Barriers, such as quotas and tariffs, placed on Chinese goods by WTO members were restricting China's economic growth. While China's leaders saw membership as necessary to maintaining China's rapid growth, there were also fears that China's economy would suffer in the near term from increased competition from foreign firms as China removed its own barriers. However, these fears were not realized. Instead, in 2002, the year after accession, China's economy grew by 7.8 percent and then grew by 9.3 percent in 2003. Despite complaints that the Chinese government uses mercantilist policies to restrict imports, China has been reducing trade barriers since the early days of Deng's economic reforms, and it has been doing well in abiding by its WTO agreements. By 2005, China did away with any remaining import-licensing requirements (which are permissions from the government to import specific goods). Also in 2005, China removed its import quotas, except for quotas on certain goods allowed under its WTO agreements. Further, when comparing China with other developing economies, China as of 2007 had a lower applied tariff rate than Mexico, Brazil, India, and South Korea.

China's accession to WTO membership was a major achievement for China's reformers, who saw WTO membership as a way to overcome resistance to further economic reforms from party hardliners and those with financial interests in existing policies. The aforementioned liberalization of foreign trade and investment created a more competitive market for China's businesses. The inefficiency of SOEs, and Chinese firms in general, was a severe restriction on China's economic growth, but shutting them down was very unpopular because they supported so many workers and government bureaucrats. Reformers also faced ideological resistance from hardliners who viewed SOEs as an integral part of China's communist nature. China's open trade commitments as a WTO member gave reformers leverage against such resistance.

China's remarkable economic growth can be attributed in part to the increased efficiency and productivity of Chinese firms, which were brought on by opening China's economy to greater foreign competition. This competition comes not just from imports, but also from foreign-owned and joint-venture firms within China. In addition to increased efficiency, pursuing WTO membership helped China attract foreign capital. Pursuing membership in the WTO was a strong signal to the outside world that China was committed to the open market reforms that are crucial to private investment. By September 2001, with China's accession to the WTO drawing near, foreign investment had grown by more than 20 percent over the same period for the preceding year.

Being a member of the WTO has greatly benefited China. China's foreign trade, especially exports, has grown substantially since joining the WTO. However, real and perceived failures by China to uphold its WTO commitments are a source of criticism and possible economic retaliation from other WTO members. Since China's ascension, its trade surpluses with the United States and Europe have grown significantly, and so has criticism of China from within the United States and European Union for its unfair trade policies, discrimination against foreign or joint firms in China, weak protections for intellectual property rights, and limiting the appreciation of the yuan.

China's accession to the WTO has also hurt certain sectors of China's domestic economy. The accession has increased regional disparities and negatively impacted farmers. Most of the assembly factories benefitting from the WTO are located in southern coastal China, and far fewer are located inland, exacerbating the already growing disparity between coastal and interior China. Subsidies, which once helped rural farmers, ended under the WTO, hurting rural farmers. Textile manufacturing was also hurt. As a result of a sharp reduction in the import tariffs and a gradual abolition of quotas, export orders decreased by 5 to 10 percent in 2002 compared to the year before. Export prices also fell by 10 to 15 percent. The United Nations Development Programme (UNDP) anticipates an increased feminization of agriculture, in which men migrate to urban areas to work in assembly factories, but women stay behind as farmers in rural areas. The economic well-being of women is likely to deteriorate as demand for land-intensive crops such as soybeans, cotton, and corn declines due to a drop in import tariffs on those products. Falling demand is likely to be accompanied by rising rural unemployment, causing greater migration from rural to urban areas. The UNDP also claims that women would be further marginalized in industry. While China's accession to the WTO will bring more capital-intensive and high-technology industry to China, women's participation in these areas tends to be low, and the UNDP found little evidence that women would move up the industry food chain.[57]

China's trade situation deteriorated in 2011 when it registered its first quarterly trade deficit in seven years. The deficit reflects the rising prices of imported commodities and spurred concerns that China's export-oriented development model may be reaching its limit. In recent years, China's leaders have encouraged Chinese to spend more. Boosting domestic consumption will make China's economic development less dependent on exports.[58] Despite government urging, household spending in China has actually declined in the last decade. In 2000, household spending contributed about 47 percent to China's gross domestic product (GDP), but in 2009 had fallen to about 36 percent.

China's Stock Market

An important part of a market economy is the free flow of capital from individuals and firms to enterprises that can use that money to increase efficiency and productivity. In capitalist countries, the stock market serves as a medium for this flow of capital. The origins of China's modern stock market can be traced back to 1980 when some Chinese firms began to issue shares of stock. These securities were not standardized or regulated. It also was illegal for individuals to trade these shares on a secondary market (with people or firms other than the firm that issued the shares), so informal (i.e., illegal) markets emerged for trading stocks. In 1984, the Chinese government established regulations for shares and the stock market.

In 1984, Beijing designated the People's Bank of China (PBC) as the government body responsible for regulating both securities and markets. However, the PBC's regulation of securities proved to be problematic. First, there was an inherent conflict of interest. Bank officials knew that the more money Chinese put into securities, the less money they would leave in bank accounts. The PBC used its regulatory power to limit investment in securities by dictating prices and dividends, by placing high taxes on share trades, and by interfering with firms' trying to issue shares. A second problem stemming from the PBC's role as regulator was that the actual oversight of stock issuance and trading was largely delegated to local PBC branches. These branches were controlled by local officials who often put local and personal gains before central government policy.

China established its first over-the-counter (OTC) stock markets in 1986 in Shanghai and in Shenyang. It opened another OTC market in Shenzhen two years later. These were legal, secondary markets where Chinese could buy and sell shares among themselves. Also in 1986, China's nascent stock market began to find high-level party support. Premier Zhao Ziyang endorsed selling shares as the way for SOEs to raise their own capital, as opposed to relying on government loans and subsidies. This objective of ending the SOEs' dependence on government financing was a key reason Chinese leaders came to support the stock market. The same year as Zhao's endorsement, Deng Xiaoping greeted the chairman of the New York Stock Exchange in Beijing and presented him with a share from a Chinese enterprise. In 1987, the Thirteenth National Party Congress proclaimed the socialist nature of owning stocks. However, support for this capitalist institution suffered severely during the political turmoil of 1989. Despite the renewed hardline condemnation of political and economic reforms, market reformers were busy planning the next step in developing China's stock market, establishing stock exchanges.

Stock exchanges are enterprises that facilitate and standardize the trading of shares. In 1990, China established the Shanghai Stock Exchange (ShSE) and the Shenzhen Stock Exchange (SzSE) with ten listed companies. Party officials came to support establishing stock exchanges as a way to overcome weak local oversight of the OTC markets. China's OTC markets were decentralized and poorly monitored, which facilitated corruption, fraud, and black market trading. Within a stock exchange, shares, trading, prices, and payments would be centralized, which allows for better supervision and control of the market. This improved oversight meant that stock exchanges could advance stability and party control, two perennial top priorities of CCP leaders. The two stock exchanges did poorly at first because of the lingering conservative political climate in the years after 1989. After a year, only fourteen firms had listed their shares on the two exchanges and they had raised 500 million yuan ($62 million) in capital.[59] Investors wondered if party hardliners might win out and close down the stock market. In 1992, Deng helped end such fears during his southern tour when he endorsed China's "experiment" with the stock market. By the end of 1992, the fifty-three firms listed on the two stock exchanges had raised 9.4 billion yuan ($1.64 billion).[60]

Initially, only Chinese citizens could buy shares on China's stock market. In the early 1990s, however, China introduced a special type of share for purchase by foreigners. Today, shares on the Chinese stock market for Chinese investors are designated A shares, and shares for foreign investors are designated B shares. There are also legal-person shares and state shares that are not traded on the market but are held by Chinese firms and the government, respectively (see Table 7.1). These nontradable shares make up the majority of listed companies' shares, preventing any foreign (or private Chinese) investor from acquiring a controlling share of listed companies. As of 2007, the B shares available to foreigners accounted for only 1.5 percent of total issued shares on China's stock market. Chinese firms also issue H shares and red chips, listed in Hong Kong, as well as N shares, listed in New York.

The central government maintains tight control of the stock market through the ministry-level China Securities Regulation Commission (CSRC). Most firms listed on the official exchanges are large SOEs. The dominance of SOEs on the exchanges makes sense given that the main objective in creating a stock market was to replace government financing for SOEs with nongovernment financing. However, the restricted listing on the official exchanges leads small or private enterprises in search of capital to take part in informal (illegal) trading. Such trading persists, despite attempts by the CSRC to shut them down. Informal

Table 7.1 Chinese Shares of Stock

Share Type	Description	Percentage of Shares of Listed Firms (as of 2002)
A shares	Listed in mainland China, available to Chinese investors (and a few designated qualified foreign investors)	23
B shares	Listed in mainland China, available to foreign investors (and as of 2001, Chinese investors)	3
Legal-person shares	Not tradable on the official market (but sometimes traded informally), held by Chinese firms	20
State shares	Not traded, held by the state	46
H shares	Listed in Hong Kong	8
Red chips	Listed in Hong Kong	8
N shares	Listed in New York	8

Source: Table generated from Green, *Development of China's Stock Market,* 29; Fung and Zhang, eds., *Financial Markets and Foreign Direct Investment,* 140, 143; Liu Ti and Green, "China's Informal Stock Market," 5; and Chiu and Lewis, *Reforming China's State-Owned Enterprises and Banks,* 211.

trading takes place in a range of settings, from person-to-person trades to sophisticated markets. An estimated one thousand firms and 3 million investors are a part of China's informal stock market.[61]

Today, China's official stock exchanges operate under the sole supervision of the CSRC. Starting with ten listed companies in 1990, the ShSE and SzSE listed 1,718 companies as of 2010.[62] The amount of capital raised annually on the ShSE and SzSE has also seen impressive, though jagged, growth since their inception (see Figure 7.3). In 1990, the ShSE and SzSE raised 500 million yuan ($62.5 million). In 2010, the amount of capital raised in the market was 868 billion yuan ($131.77 million).[63] As of 2009, China's stock market had 171.5 million investors.[64] Although the majority of Chinese investment firms are controlled by the government, the stock market is furthering China's progress toward a market economy and encouraging foreign investment, which contributes to China's overall economic growth.

Science and Technology

The third of China's Four Modernizations is science and technology. China has increased spending on education by double digits almost every year for over a

Figure 7.3 Capital Raised on the ShSE and SzSE Stock Markets Annually

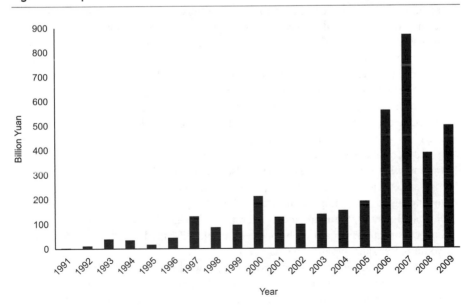

Source: Generated from NBS of China, *China Statistical Yearbook 2010,* 742.

decade. In 2008, China increased education spending by 20 percent over the previous year.[65] Likewise, China's expenditures on research and development more than doubled between 2003 and 2007.[66] Although the quality of China's education system and the level of China's technological advancement are improving, they are doing so from a very low point relative to advanced Western countries. For example, in 2006, the Organization for Economic Cooperation and Development (OECD) estimated that China's gross domestic research and development spending was $86.8 billion, which was far lower than that of Japan ($138.8 billion) or the United States ($242.8 billion).[67] As for China's education system, a 2005 study by the McKinsey think tank found that 90 percent of Chinese earning degrees in engineering or technology fields lacked the skills to compete in the global market.[68] In 2009, Shanghai Jiao Tong University ranked the two hundred best schools in the world and not a single Chinese university was on the list.[69] An increasing number of Chinese are studying overseas. In 1990, fewer than 3,000 Chinese were studying abroad. A decade later, 38,989 Chinese students were studying overseas. By 2007, the number had jumped to 229,300.[70]

One of the goals for China's opening to the world was to stimulate the advancement of science and technology. In the 1980s, most foreign investment in China involved low-tech manufacturing. However, since then, foreign firms have been setting up increasingly advanced operations in China, even some research and development operations. One of the main problems still holding back high-tech foreign investment is China's weak protection of intellectual property rights. Fear of having their technology stolen and counterfeited or reverse-engineered still deters some foreign firms from bringing high-tech industry to China. The Chinese government plays on the allure of its large domestic market to override such concerns. Foreign firms that do bring advanced technology to ventures in China are given preferential treatment.

Another aspect of China's technological advancement is espionage. Chinese espionage is seen as a major problem in Western countries. The type of spying taking place varies widely. Those involved include native Chinese citizens, native Chinese with citizenship in the country in which they are spying, or native citizens of a second country working with Chinese contacts. Determining whether spies are working for Beijing or whether they merely are private entrepreneurs seeking a profit is not always easy. A major focus of Chinese technological espionage is military technology, especially from the United States. However, there are also numerous incidents of civilian industrial espionage, particularly against advanced economies like the United States, Europe, South Korea, and Japan (see Chapter 9).

A good indicator of China's position in the world in terms of technology is its share of trade in high-technology goods (see Figure 7.4). In 2006, China's share of global high-tech exports was 16.3 percent, up from just 4.9 percent in 2000. In the same period the US and Japanese shares fell and the EU share rose slightly.

Figure 7.4 Share of Global High-Tech Exports, 2006 (in percentages)

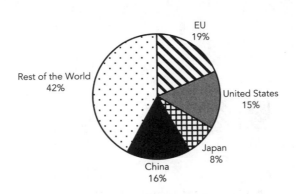

Source: Generated from Loschky, "High-Technology Trade Indicators, 2008," 29–33.

However, when the share of high-tech exports is broken down by sector, it becomes apparent that much of the increase in China's share of the high-tech export market is made up of less advanced technologies. The high-tech sectors in which China has made significant gains are in computers, telecom, and electronics, including many common consumer goods (such as laptops and DVD players). While China is making progress in the more advanced sectors (such as scientific instruments, aerospace, and pharmaceuticals), the United States and the European Union still make up the largest shares of those sectors (see Figure 7.5).

Though China still lags behind the most advanced countries in science and technology, there is no question that it has made considerable progress since opening to the world. China is also involved in biotechnology, including genome sequencing, cloning, and gene therapy. While China lags behind in the pharmaceuticals sector, it has developed drugs approved by the WHO and the US Food and Drug Administration. China has more Internet users than the United States or Europe. In the military field, China is one of a few countries in the world that builds and operates nuclear submarines. China is an exporter of satellites and related technology. In 2003, China became only the third country in history to launch a man into space.

Trade, Foreign Investment, and Today's Economy

China has changed dramatically since reform began in the 1980s. One of the greatest changes is the transition from a state-planned economy to an increasingly market-driven one. During the 1980s, the establishment of SEZs and

Figure 7.5 Global Export Market Share in Selected High-Tech Sectors, 2006

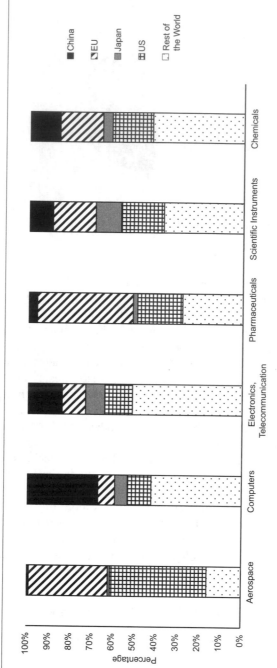

Source: Estimates based on Loschky, "High-Technology Trade Indicators, 2008," 29–33.

China's stock market spurred a tremendous growth in foreign trade and the influx of foreign investment. China further eased its tight restrictions on foreign trade and moved closer to a market economy as it pursued accession to the WTO. Opening China to foreign trade and investment has helped to bring about incredible economic growth. Between 1978 and 1988, China's economy grew by more than 300 percent (see Figure 7.6). Over the next ten years China's economy grew by more than 460 percent. Almost a decade later, in 2009, China's economy had grown by 300 percent.[71]

As of 2007, China was the world's second largest exporter and third largest importer of goods. China's top five trading partners (in descending order) are the United States, Japan, South Korea, Taiwan, and Germany. China's major exports are electrical machinery and equipment, power generation equipment, apparel, textiles, iron and steel, furniture, optical and medical equipment, chemicals, ships and boats, footwear, and vehicles. China's major imports are electrical machinery and equipment, oil and mineral fuels, power generation equipment, optical and medical equipment, metal ores, plastics, organic chemicals, and copper. China has maintained a positive trading balance since 1994 (see Figure 7.7). In 2010, China enjoyed a trade surplus of $183 billion.

China is the world's second largest recipient of foreign direct investment (FDI) after the United States. Investors are attracted to a nearly inexhaustible

Figure 7.6 China's Economic Growth

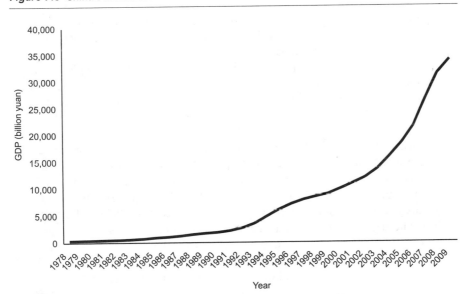

Source: NBS of China, *China Statistical Yearbook 2010*, 38.

Figure 7.7 China's Foreign Trade

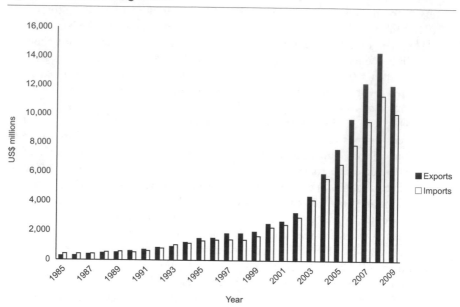

Sources: State Statistical Bureau, PRC, *China Statistical Yearbook 1998,* 55; and NBS of China, *China Statistical Yearbook 2010,* 230.

supply of low-cost labor and a promising market of more than 1.3 billion consumers.[72] China had virtually no FDI at the start of Deng's Open Door policy in 1979 (see Figure 7.8). China's leaders opened the country to FDI in stages. First, China's leaders restricted foreign investment to export-oriented joint ventures with Chinese firms located in the newly created SEZs. In the early 1990s, China's leaders went a step further, permitting foreigners to produce goods for the China market. Finally, by the mid-1990s, foreign investors could establish wholly foreign-owned enterprises in China. By the end of 2008, foreigners had invested a total of $899 billion in China. Thirty-eight percent of this investment came primarily from Hong Kong and Macau.[73] Foreigners invested $108 billion in 2008 alone. Although the manufacturing sector is the largest recipient of FDI in China, accounting for 52 percent of all FDI, inflows have surged since the country joined the World Trade Organization in 2001.[74] Joining the WTO forced the Chinese government to open up the services sector.

Foreign investment in China has historically been concentrated in the coastal areas of the country. More than four-fifths of accumulated FDI inflows are in the eastern region. In recent years, however, more and more FDI is going to central and western China—a direct result of the central government's Develop the West Campaign (discussed in detail in Chapter 8), which encourages development of China's interior. Another factor encouraging the

Figure 7.8 China's Actual Foreign Direct Investment

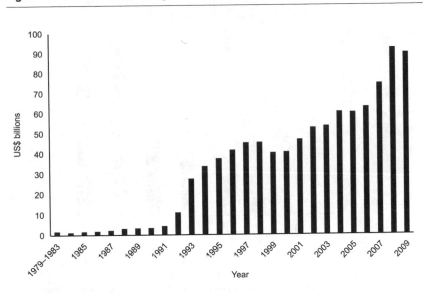

Sources: NBS of China, *China Statistical Yearbook 2008,* 729, and *China Statistical Yearbook 2010,* 251.

westward trajectory of FDI is the rising costs of labor in the east. Improved infrastructure has also made transportation to the interior cheaper and more convenient than in the past.

China's Outward Foreign Direct Investment

China also aggressively invests overseas. In the 1980s, China's outward foreign direct investment (OFDI) averaged $453 million a year and $2.3 billion in the 1990s. While global FDI declined during the global recession of 2008, China's nearly doubled. China's total OFDI was $52.2 billion in 2008, nearly double the $26.5 billion in 2007 (see Figure 7.9).

China's outward FDI accelerated after 2000 as a result of the government's adoption and promotion of a "go global" policy aimed at establishing China as a major player in the world economy. The strategy required that China's leaders relax restrictions on outward capital and simplify administrative requirements. State-owned enterprises dominate China's OFDI, where their average investment size far exceeds that of China's private firms. Most SOEs investing overseas invest in the natural resources sector as Beijing seeks to secure natural resources to fuel the country's economic growth. However, the service sector is also increasingly investing overseas, largely because of the large number of nonstate firms that need goods and services, such as insurance. More than 70

Figure 7.9 China's Outward Foreign Direct Investment

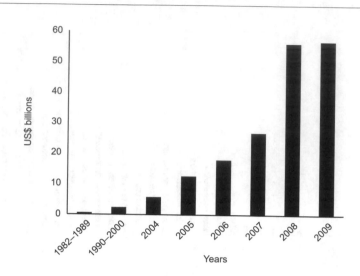

Sources: Generated from UNCTAD, *World Investment Report 2009,* 53; NBS of China, *China Statistical Yearbook 2008,* 736, and *China Statistical Yearbook 2010,* 257.

percent of China's OFDI is in services. The acquisition of local brands, such as Lenovo's purchases of IBM's personal computer business, has also driven up China's OFDI figures, as has the diversification of large SOEs into international markets. Moreover, some Chinese firms have moved their labor-intensive operations overseas to Vietnam and Africa, where wages are lower than those in China.

The bulk of OFDI flows to developing countries and to Africa, in particular. Chinese investments in Africa have increased sevenfold in the period 2003–2006. China is now a leading source of FDI in Africa, and China has invested in forty-eight countries on the continent. Most of the FDI is aimed at accessing natural resources and is invested in the resource-rich countries of Algeria, Nigeria, South Africa, Sudan, and Zambia. Increasingly, however, Chinese are investing in the manufacturing and construction sectors in Africa.

Trade and Investment Issues

Despite the global financial crisis of 2008, foreign investment and trade in China remain robust. Increasingly, however, other countries are finding fault with China's business practices. Two of the major complaints that countries make against China are violation of intellectual property rights (IPRs) and an artificially low-value currency that benefits Chinese exports.

Intellectual Property Rights

Foreign businesses often accuse China of ignoring trademarks, copyrights, and other forms of intellectual property rights (IPRs). The United States is one of the major complainants against China. In 2007, the United States brought a complaint against China to the WTO, arguing that China did not do enough to protect IPRs. The International Intellectual Property Alliance (IIPA) estimated that in 2008 alone, the counterfeiting of music, films, books, and computer software in China cost US firms $3.5 billion.[75] In 2009, the IIPA argued that China's policies on IPRs failed to live up to China's WTO commitments.[76] The European Union charges that China engages in counterfeiting. In 2007, the EU trade commissioner stated that 80 percent of all the counterfeit goods in Europe were produced in China.[77] While the European Union acknowledges that China has made some progress on enforcing IPRs, the EU ranks China as the worst country for IPR violations.[78]

A key problem with enforcing IPRs in China is that local officials have significant influence on how or if China's commitments are enforced. This problem stems from the fact that local officials have authority over the money and manpower of the local offices responsible for enforcing China's IPR laws. These same local officials stand to profit from counterfeiters operating in their area. Beijing's efforts to enforce IPRs are mostly limited to well-publicized raids on specific offenders to show other countries that China is making an effort to uphold IPRs.

The concept of patents and patent protection is new to China, having passed its first patent law only twenty-five years ago. China's IPR enforcement regime remains very weak, with vague laws, soft punishments, and lax enforcement. However, the importance of IPRs within China is growing. In recent years, Chinese firms have been applying for more and more patents, not just in China, but abroad as well. The number of lawsuits concerning IPR violations brought by Chinese firms against other Chinese firms, as well as firms overseas, has also increased in the past few years. As Chinese firms become more vested in strong IPRs, it is likely that China will bring its IPR enforcement in line with other advanced economies because it will be in Chinese interests to do so.

The Yuan, the Dollar, and Global Economic Stability

Within the modern global economy, nations' economies are extremely interdependent. The worldwide ripple effects of the 2008 financial crisis illustrated how trouble in one nation's economy can cause problems around the world. The greater the role a country plays in the global economy, the more it can benefit international trade and finance, and the more it can suffer. As previously covered in this chapter, China has benefited tremendously from opening its economy to the world. However, three major issues concern China in the world economy today. These issues are the value of the yuan (China's currency), the role of the US dollar as the major currency of international exchange, and China's role as the largest financier of US national debt (see Figure 7.10). These issues are sources of tension with China's trade partners, the United States and the European Union in particular, and these issues are interrelated.

Until 2005, China pegged the value of the yuan directly to that of the US dollar. This peg helped to keep Chinese goods cheaper relative to US goods, making them more attractive to the American consumers. US manufacturers, and more recently US politicians, claim that China pegs the yuan 25 to 40 percent below its real worth. They argue that the artificially devalued yuan creates a positive trade environment for China that results in trade surpluses for China, but trade deficits for the United States. In 2011, two-way trade between China and the United States totaled $457 billion, with China enjoying a trade surplus of $273 billion.[79]

US politicians also claim that China's undervalued currency causes US manufacturing to relocate to China, costing the United States jobs. After years of pressure from the United States, China's leaders announced in 2005 that they would shift from a decade-old peg against the dollar to a managed float, based

Figure 7.10 Share of US Trade Deficit, Selected Countries

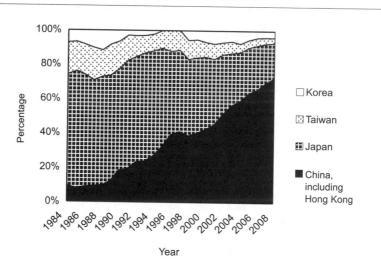

Sources: Bureau of Economic Analysis, "US International Transactions Accounts Data," Tables 2a and 2b.

on a basket of several currencies, to value the yuan. Since 2005, the yuan has strengthened 25 percent against the dollar.[80] Despite the shift to a managed float, Beijing continues to intervene in foreign exchange markets to keep the value down. China keeps the yuan low against the dollar by buying dollar-denominated assets, primarily US government securities. The US government issues foreign debt (Treasury bills or bonds, also called Treasuries) to finance its operations. Although most US debt is held by Americans, chronic government budget deficits have forced the US government to find foreigners to buy US debt. In the past five years, China has spent as much as one-seventh of its entire economic output on the purchase of foreign debt—largely US Treasury bonds and American mortgage-backed securities. China is the top foreign holder of US Treasuries. As of March 2011, China held more than $1.14 billion in US Treasury bonds, more than one-fifth of the total held by foreign nations (see Figure 7.11).

To manage the value of the yuan against the US dollar, China's central bank continually wades into foreign exchange markets. As a result, China has an enormous and growing stock of foreign exchange reserves. As of March 2011, China had foreign exchange reserves of $3 trillion. An estimated two-thirds of

Figure 7.11 China and Other Major Holders of US Public Debt (as of March 2011)

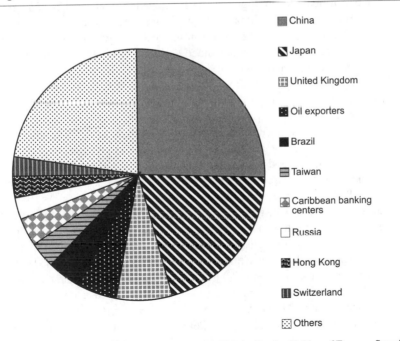

- China
- Japan
- United Kingdom
- Oil exporters
- Brazil
- Taiwan
- Caribbean banking centers
- Russia
- Hong Kong
- Switzerland
- Others

Source: US Department of the Treasury, Table of Major Foreign Holders of Treasury Securities, accessed May 16, 2011, http://www.treasury.gov/resource-center/data-chart-center.

these are held in dollar-denominated assets. The buildup of foreign exchange reserves suggests that the People's Bank of China continues to intervene in the markets to support the yuan at an artificially low level.

Concerns over ballooning US government deficits caused Beijing to slow its purchases of US debt in late 2010 and early 2011. China's leaders are increasingly critical of America's tremendous debt load and have admonished US government officials to get their financial house in order and to protect China's investments. At the same time, US politicians and the public have become increasingly concerned about the political and economic power that creditor status confers on China. They fear that creditor status will allow Beijing to force concessions from the US on issues of both domestic and foreign policy. The penchant for the US government to spend what it does not have and China's willingness to buy US debt have created an uneasy debtor-creditor relationship between Washington and Beijing.

Conclusion

In the thirty years since the start of the reform era in 1979, China carried out major agrarian reform, largely denationalized industry, professionalized the military, made significant technological advances, opened stock markets, and embraced international trade. China's reformers dreamed that opening China's economy to the world would bring in foreign technology, which would help China leap forward to the level of advanced Western countries. Instead, foreign investors merely transferred low-tech, labor-intensive, and highly polluting industries that were no longer welcome at home. In the international economy, one of China's main roles is still as a source of low-skilled labor. Despite China's impressive economic gains of the last three decades, China is still a relatively poor country with a lower GDP per capita than many countries. China's low-skilled, low-paid workers do not actually build the goods that China exports, but merely assemble those goods from parts shipped to China from other countries. China's role as the final assembly point for the goods it exports is illustrated by a shift in trade between the United States and East Asian countries. As foreign firms shift final assembly of goods to China, their share of the US trade deficit has gone down while China's has risen (see Figure 7.10). This relationship is also reflected by the fact that China's biggest trade deficits are with Japan, South Korea, and Taiwan.[81] Most of China's own exported goods are assembled in China from imported components. China's leaders are trying to change this scenario by creating world-class universities with strong emphasis on research in science and technology. The central government is investing heavily in the country's top universities—Fudan, Nanjing, Peking (Beida, or Beijing University), Shanghai Jiao Tong, Tsinghua (Qinghua), Xi'an Jiaotong, Zhejiang, and Tongji—hoping to turn them into world-class research centers. Being a world-class university means being able to attract a top-notch faculty. Chinese universities are increasingly competing for outstanding faculty worldwide. Many of the new faculty members are Chinese nationals who earned doctorates in science and engineering abroad and who see opportunities in their home country.[82]

China's economic reforms have created opportunities for the Chinese that previous generations never had. In less than two generations, China has blossomed from an isolationist dinosaur to a dynamic economy. To maintain China's economic boom, China needs greater and greater amounts of energy. As coal becomes more difficult to extract, China is increasingly relying on oil and gas. Chinese energy companies are sealing deals on oil and gas projects in the Middle East, Africa, and Central Asia as part of China's "going out" strategy. China has also increased efforts to secure alternative sources of energy, such as hydroelectric, wind, and solar power. The future of hydroelectric power is compromised, however, by drought. For instance, drought has reduced water flow along the mighty Yangtze River, compromising energy generation of the Three Gorges Dam hydroelectric project.

China's economic drive has not been without its costs. Perhaps the greatest of these has been the further degradation of China's environment. China's environmental problems adversely affect the health of millions of Chinese. China's environment has suffered from decades of degradation during both the Mao years, with their emphasis on heavy industry and focus on quantity of production, and the reform years, when economic growth trumped environmental protection. Recent efforts to protect the environment should be applauded, as should the central government's tolerance of and even cooperation with environmental NGOs.

Notes

1. Monetary amounts are in US dollars unless otherwise noted.
2. "The Second Long March," *Economist*, December 13, 2008, 30–32.
3. Huang, Otsuka, and Rozelle, "Agriculture in China's Development," 472. The United Nations' average minimum requirement is 2,100 calories, enough to meet minimum physiological needs.
4. Huang, Otsuka, and Rozelle, "Agriculture in China's Development," 467.
5. National Bureau of Statistics (NBS) of China, *China Statistical Yearbook 2010*, 496.
6. NBS of China, *China Statistical Yearbook 2010*, 119.
7. Park, "Rural-Urban Inequality in China," 51.
8. NBS of China, *China Statistical Yearbook 2010*, 481.
9. NBS of China, *China Statistical Yearbook 2010*, 494.
10. Veeck et al., *China's Geography*, 225.
11. "How to Make China Even Richer," *Economist*, March 25, 2006, 11.
12. Edward Cody, "China's Land Grabs Raise Specter of Popular Unrest," *Washington Post*, October 5, 2004, A1.

13. Cody, "China's Land Grabs," A1.

14. Naughton, *Growing Out of the Plan.*

15. Harding, *China's Second Revolution,* 111.

16. Harding, *China's Second Revolution,* 112.

17. Freund, "Falling Flat," 167–182.

18. For a study of the corporatization of China's state industry, see Freund, "Falling Flat"; and Larus, *Economic Reform in China.*

19. Freund, "Fizz, Froth, Flat."

20. Perry, "From Native Place to Workplace," 50.

21. "Eight Die in Sichuan Worker's Gun Rampage," *South China Morning Post,* April 6, 1993, 1.

22. NBS of China, *China Statistical Yearbook 2010,* 119.

23. NBS of China, *China Statistical Yearbook 2010,* 118.

24. "Beijing May Raise Profit Pay-outs for SOEs," *China Economic Review,* April 8, 2010.

25. International Energy Agency, *World Energy Outlook 2010.*

26. US Department of Defense, *Military Power of the People's Republic of China, 2010,* 20.

27. NBS of China, *China Statistical Yearbook 2010,* 270.

28. US Department of Defense, *Military Power of the People's Republic of China, 2010,* 20.

29. Central People's Government of the People's Republic of China, *The Eleventh Five-Year Plan,* http://www.gov.cn/english/special/115y_index.htm.

30. Louis B. Schwartz, *China Renewable Energy and Sustainable Development Report,* 7.

31. Shapiro, *Mao's War Against Nature,* 83.

32. Having depleted the store of accessible coal, Chinese miners now must dig deeper into the earth to access hard-to-reach coal reserves.

33. Veeck et al., *China's Geography,* 17.

34. Brown, "China Replacing the United States as World's Leading Consumer."

35. Shapiro, *Mao's War Against Nature,* 80.

36. NBS of China, *China Statistical Yearbook 2010,* 441.

37. Economy, *The River Runs Black.*

38. Schistosomiasis is a disease caused by parasitic worms carried by freshwater snails. It causes fever, can damage internal organs, and can cause impaired growth and cognitive development in children.

39. Feng Jianhua, "A Polluter's Paradise?" *Beijing Review,* September 14, 2006, 18–19.

40. Jian Xie et al., *Addressing China's Water Scarcity,* 19.

41. Wang Hsin-hsien, "River Pollution," *Taiwan Perspective* (Taipei: Institute for National Policy Research, 2004), http://www.tp.org.tw/document/detail.htm?id=20011976.

42. Feng Jianhua, "A Polluter's Paradise?" 18. It is not clear why men were affected by the pollution more than women and children.

43. Jian Xie et al., *Addressing China's Water Scarcity,* 43.

44. Feng Jianhua, "A Polluter's Paradise?" 18.

45. Zhao Xiaohui and Jiang Xueli, "Coal Mining: Most Deadly Job in China," *China Daily,* November 13, 2004.

46. Auffhammer and Carson, "Forecasting the Path of China's CO_2 Emissions Using Province-level Information."

47. Robert Marquand, "A 'Green' Building Rises amid Beijing's Smog," *Christian Science Monitor,* April 3, 2006.

48. Biological diversity (or biodiversity) refers to the variety of living organisms within an ecosystem, the range of species and genetic variability within each species, and the varied characteristics of ecosystems.

49. For more information on biodiversity in China, see McBeath and Leng, *Governance of Biodiversity Conservation in China and Taiwan.*

50. Lin Teh-chang, "Environmental NGOs and the Anti-Dam Movements in China," 156.

51. Lin Teh-chang, "Environmental NGOs and the Anti-Dam Movements in China," 170.

52. Lin Teh-chang, "Environmental NGOs and the Anti-Dam Movements in China," 171.

53. Zusman and Turner, "Beyond the Bureaucracy," 132.

54. Lin Teh-chang, "Environmental NGOs and the Anti-Dam Movements in China," 172.

55. Sustainable development is the pursuit of economic growth in ways that can be supported for the long term by conserving resources and protecting the environment.

56. For more information on environmental cases, see Economy, "Environmental Enforcement in China."

57. For more information on the negative impact of WTO accession on China's economy, see United Nations Development Programme, *China's Accession to WTO: Challenges for Women in the Agricultural and Industrial Sectors,* and Huang and Rozelle, "Impact of Trade Liberalization on China's Agriculture and Rural Economy."

58. The four factors that fuel GDP growth are investment in physical assets, household spending (consumption), government spending, and net exports of goods and services.

59. NBS of China, *China Statistical Yearbook 2010,* 743.

60. NBS of China, *China Statistical Yearbook 2010,* 743.

61. Liu Ti and Green, "China's Informal Stock Market," 5.

62. NBS of China, *China Statistical Yearbook 2010,* 743.

63. The amount of capital raised declined, however, to 385 billion yuan in 2008 and 496 billion yuan in 2009. NBS of China, *China Statistical Yearbook 2010,* 743.

64. NBS of China, *China Statistical Yearbook 2010,* 742.

65. NBS of China, *China Statistical Yearbook 2010,* 779.

66. NBS of China, *China Statistical Yearbook 2008,* 804.

67. Organization for Economic Cooperation and Development (OECD, *OECD Science, Technology, and Industry Outlook, 2008,* 21.

68. Fred C. Bergsten et al., *China: The Balance Sheet,* 103.

69. "The Future Is Another Country: Higher Education," *Economist,* January 3, 2009.

70. NBS of China, *China Statistical Yearbook 2010,* 757.

71. Derived from figures in NBS of China, *China Statistical Yearbook 2010,* 38.

72. For an entertaining look at foreign investment in Chinese consumers, see Browning, *If Everybody Bought One Shoe.* Also worth reading is McGregor's *One Billion Customers.*

73. Ministry of Commerce of the People's Republic of China, *Invest in China: Statistics of FDI from Selected Countries/Regions for 2008,* April 27, 2010, http://www.fdi.gov.cn; NBS of China, *Actual Foreign Direct Investment (FDI) by Country of Origin, 1990–2004.*

74. NBS of China, *China Statistical Yearbook 2010,* 254.

75. The IIPA is a private-sector coalition of trade associations representing US copyright-based industries designed to improve international protection and enforcement of

copyrighted materials. IIPA, "2009 Special 301 Report on Copyright Protection and Enforcement," 84–109.

76. IIPA, "2009 Special 301 Report on Copyright Protection and Enforcement."

77. Jonathan Eyal, "The End of a Sino-EU Love Affair: Decades-Old Good Relations Soured by Quarrels over Trade and Human Rights," *Straits Times* (Singapore), November 28, 2007.

78. European Commission, *Intellectual Property: IPR Enforcement.*

79. US-China Business Council, *US-China Trade Statistics and China's World Trade Statistics.*

80. The Chinese yuan has strengthened to 6.5 yuan to the dollar from 8.2 yuan in June 2005.

81. NBS of China, *China Statistical Yearbook 2010,* 238–241.

82. Levin, "Top of the Class."

8 The Rural-Urban Divide

Only a couple of years after Mao's death, Deng Xiaoping and his fellow reformers began an ambitious plan to restructure the economy and open China to foreign investment. Reform and opening brought about an unparalleled economic boom. Economic reforms have contributed to a more than tenfold increase in GDP since 1978 (see Figure 7.6). Between 1979 and 2008, China's GDP grew on average 10 percent annually, about three times greater than the world average. Between 1978 and 2008, China's per capita gross domestic product (GDP) increased fiftyfold, lifting about 500 million people out of poverty.[1] Reform and opening improved the quality of life for millions of Chinese. Life expectancy increased from 64 years in 1978 to 73.5 years in 2010. The adult illiteracy rate fell by more than half, from 37 percent in 1978 to 5.8 percent in 2010.[2] The infant mortality rate fell from forty-one per thousand live births in 1978 to nineteen in 2009.[3] These numbers do not tell the whole story, however. Although the pie is getting bigger, it is not being distributed equally. Economic development has been more rapid in coastal areas than in the interior, and rural income lags far behind urban income.[4] In 2006, Chinese rural households' annual per capita income averaged 5,000 yuan ($641) in the east, 3,300 yuan ($423) in the center, and less than 3,000 yuan ($385) in the west. Using the Gini coefficient, a commonly used measure of income inequality, China's wealth gap is growing at an alarming rate. China's Gini coefficient before the reform period was 0.16, soaring to 0.415 in 2007.[5] Zero indicates that income is perfectly distributed and a higher coefficient corresponds to greater inequality, maximizing at 1.0; a Gini coefficient of more than 0.4 is widely considered a sign of serious social inequality. China is experiencing the largest income gap since it began economic reform in 1978. In 2008, the average urban resident earned 3.36 times more than his or her rural counterpart, up from 2.79 in 2000.[6] The ratio is even wider between interior and coastal regions. The ratio between per capita GDP in Shanghai and Guizhou Province, for example, is nearly ten to one.

Although the number of people living on a dollar a day fell by nearly 400 million between 1990 and 2005, there are still more than 200 million people living on that amount. Most of the poor live in remote and resource-poor areas in central and western China. Many of them lack access to clean water, arable land, or adequate health and education services. Availability and quality of services in rural areas fall far short of those in urban areas. Education and health care are substandard for much of China's rural population. More than half of China's population lives in rural areas. While many Chinese are indeed becoming rich or at least comfortable, the rural population remains poor and desperate.

The Rural-Urban Divide in Chinese History

China's remarkable economic growth has been accompanied by massive rural-to-urban migration. In general, when a country's GDP per capita increases from $700 to $1,500, its rate of urbanization increases, so that the urban population accounts for 40 to 60 percent of the total population. In 2003, the proportion of China's people living in cities exceeded 40 percent of the total for the first time. The pace of China's urbanization is unprecedented. For instance, by 2004, the proportion of China's population living in cities reached over 40 percent, double the urbanization rate twenty-five years prior. The same increase in urbanization took fifty years in the United States in the nineteenth century.[7] By 2007, the share of China's population living in cities had reached 45 percent. More than 160 of China's cities have populations of more than 1 million. Chongqing, with a population of more than 31 million, is the world's fastest-growing urban center. Shanghai has a population of more than 19 million, Beijing more than 17 million, and Tianjin more than 10 million. Shenzhen, a city that did not exist a generation ago, now has 9 million inhabitants. Millions of residents in each of these cities are migrant workers.

China's urbanization has not been accompanied by the shantytowns so prevalent in other developing countries. One major explanation for the lack of shantytowns ringing Chinese cities is the *hukou* residency permit system. As described in Chapter 2, the *hukou* system was based on the traditional *baojia* system of rural organization. In 1958, the communist government made the *hukou* system law. Under the regulations governing household registration, local authorities assigned every citizen both an occupation and a location *hukou*. An agricultural *hukou* provides one with access to farmland; a nonagricultural *hukou* allows one access to state-provided jobs, housing, health care, and pension benefits. The residency *hukou* indicates the location where one is entitled to receive these benefits. *Hukou* are nontransferable, and until recently it was nearly impossible to change one's *hukou,* which parents passed down to their children. Without the proper residency *hukou,* one simply could not access state benefits. Until the 1980s, the *hukou* system effectively prevented rural Chinese from moving to cities because once they got there, they would not be eligible for housing, a job, education benefits for their children, health care, or food ration cards. The residency system thus segregated urban populations from rural ones and prevented migration on any significant scale.

The system began to change in the mid-1980s. Until then, no employers (the vast majority being state-owned enterprises) would hire a potential employee without the requisite *hukou*. The Open Door policy changed that. Chinese-foreign joint ventures in coastal special economic zones (SEZs) were eager to hire cheap labor and did not care that applicants did not have the requisite *hukou*. The joint ventures offered higher wages than could be made in China's interior, but did not promise benefits. Young, healthy, single men were willing to forgo state benefits for wages three times the amount they would have earned in a state-owned enterprise (SOE) in China's interior. In 1985, the Ministry of Public Security allowed rural laborers to apply for temporary residency permits. In the 1980s, some city governments began to charge migrants high fees in exchange for *hukou* in towns and cities. In the 1990s, Shanghai and Shenzhen offered blue-stamp *hukou* to highly skilled migrants who were able to make sizable investments. The blue-stamp *hukou* could be converted into an urban *hukou* after a specified period and offered highly skilled migrants the chance to live in those cities permanently, benefited their employers by providing a highly skilled and permanent employee base, and deposited money into municipal coffers.[8]

In the late 1990s, the State Council introduced experimental reform of the *hukou* system. It allowed rural migrants who lived and worked in selected towns and small cities for more than two years to receive an urban *hukou*. Today, migrants who have a permanent and legal address and have stable employment are allowed to obtain urban *hukou* without paying a large fee. It is more difficult for migrants to work in large cities, however. Only a few migrants who meet strict criteria on educational attainment, skills, financial ability, and health are able to obtain urban *hukou* in large cities.[9]

The Urban Bias

Given the opportunity, most Chinese would prefer to live in an urban area rather than a rural area because the cities draw a greater share of the nation's wealth. Like other developing countries, China suffers from limited financial resources, and like the others, it dedicates more resources to industry than agriculture because it sees industry as an engine of economic growth. Hence, there is conflict between rural and urban classes over limited resources. Generally, urban classes dominate because political power is concentrated in the towns and cities. Public and private services are more extensive in towns and cities than in rural areas. State and market mechanisms generally function in favor of towns by extracting surplus from agriculture. The imbalance between rural and urban development is called *urban bias*. Urban bias pulls resources from agriculture and concentrates them in towns and cities. As a result, the rural poor remain poor.

One way to eliminate urban bias would be for government to invest more resources in agriculture—allowing farmers to own agricultural land, for example—because urban industry has been unable to absorb much of the fast-growing labor force. Chinese living in rural areas cannot own the land they farm because it still belongs to village collectives, whereas in urban areas, property can be bought and sold. The lack of rural property rights means that local government and party officials can confiscate land for development projects, which incidentally boosts their career-burnishing credentials. As of 2004, an estimated 70 million rural Chinese have been removed from their farms so that the land could be used for urban and industrial development.[10] It is not unheard of for villagers to take matters into their own hands. For instance, in September 2008, a villager in Xiashuixi village in Shanxi Province stabbed the local party chief to death after villagers alleged that the official ran a gang that used harassment and violence to take over their farmland. The attacker's mother had spent a year in detention after she complained to authorities about property damage she attributed to the party boss.[11] In Wangying village in Anhui Province, villagers conducted a tax revolt against a "shock team"—officials who force villagers to cough up tax money or confiscate property in lieu of taxes—only to lose their jobs. Other peasants have been tortured and beaten to death by police for campaigning against illegal taxes and fees. In another case, peasants were murdered for trying to audit the accounts of corrupt officials.[12]

Poor Agriculture Structure and Infrastructure

A chief factor explaining rural poverty is poor agriculture structure and infrastructure. Under collectivization, the rural communes existed for the sole purpose of providing cheap food for China's urbanites. The state provided the communes with fertilizer and equipment; in return, the communes produced food for the state to distribute in urban areas. Farms were on their own to produce enough to support themselves. The communes lacked any meaningful incentive structure. The land had been confiscated from individual families, removing any incentive for individuals or families to benefit personally from additional production. Furthermore, commune directors were rather like absentee landlords in the sense that they were too far removed from the day-to-day operations of the commune.

The lack of incentives was exacerbated by a weak procurement and marketing structure. To keep food cheap in the cities, the state paid artificially low prices to farmers for their agricultural produce. These low prices kept food cheap for urbanites, but also kept China's farmers poor. After the return to household farming, the central government in 1985 introduced a dual-price system designed to increase production incentives and farm income. Households contracted with the state to sell a fixed amount of produce at state-mandated prices. The households could sell any surplus on the open market, pocketing the income. The new price system succeeded in increasing agricultural production. Output of grains, for example, increased 46 percent between 1978 and 1990.[13] Meanwhile, farm incomes more than doubled between 1990 and 1995.[14]

In the late 1980s and 1990s, farmers increasingly turned toward cash crops to reap higher profits. Cash crops are those grown specifically for profit (often having higher market value), while subsistence crops are those grown to feed the producer's own family or livestock. Cash crops pay better than grains, so many farmers abandoned grain production for more profitable goods. Examples of Chinese cash crops are peanuts, sesame, tea, tobacco, fruit, and peppers. Concerned about the drop in production of grains, in the mid-1990s the state mandated that farmers grow more grain. With more grain produced, grain prices dropped, as did farm incomes. The decrease in farm incomes caused many farmers to migrate to the cities for jobs, earning higher wages. In 2007, Beijing eliminated government control of grain purchasing, leaving the purchasing and sale of grain to the open market.

Rural-Urban Economic Disparity

Since 1978, urban incomes have grown faster than rural incomes, with the exception of two periods. The first was in the 1980s when the household responsibility system (see Chapter 5) returned agricultural decisionmaking from collectives back to individual families. Between 1978 and 1984, China's agricultural production grew 7.4 percent annually, compared to an annual growth rate of 1.8 percent in the previous seven years.[15] The incentives and government investment in rural areas spurred agricultural activity. Relaxation of price controls increased prices for agricultural goods. Increased activity and increased prices increased farm incomes. The second period was in 1994–1995 when the urban economy suffered retrenchment and the rural economy grew due to higher production yields and prices. Despite these two phases, urban incomes have outpaced rural incomes. By 2005, the rural-urban income gap reached a historic high. That year, rural incomes were only 39 percent of urban incomes.[16]

In 2009, the average annual income of rural households was 5,153 yuan (about $758, or about $2 a day) while the average annual income of urban households was 17,175 yuan ($2,526), a gap of more than 12,000 yuan (about $1,765), up from a gap of 9,646 yuan ($1,419) in 2007 (see Figure 8.1).[17] The urban-rural income gap is even more egregious when one compares China's richest cities with the nation's poorest areas. For example, the average per capita income in Shanghai was 18,645 yuan ($2,421) in 2007, but in Qinghai Province was only 8,058 yuan ($1,046).[18] According to official statistics, more than 14.7 million people living in rural areas lived in absolute poverty in 2007, and more than 28 million lived on one dollar a day.[19]

Figure 8.1 Per Capita Income for Rural and Urban Areas

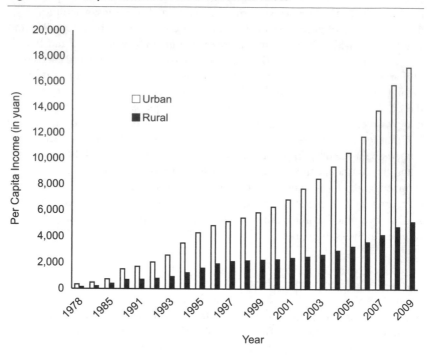

Source: NBS of China, *China Statistical Yearbook 2010, 342.*

Rural Taxation

Further compounding the insult of low rural incomes is the indignity of regressive rural taxation. In 1984, the Twelfth National Party Congress announced the launch of comprehensive urban reform. As the focus of reform shifted from rural to urban China, capital investment was redirected to China's cities. The 1984 tax reform decentralized tax collection, decreasing subsidies from the central government and forcing local governments to raise their own revenue for community welfare, local officials' salaries, health care and education, transportation and public works, and social welfare benefits for veterans. With less money coming from Beijing, local authorities have imposed ad hoc fees on the rural population. To raise revenue for rural areas, the central government gave the administrative townships (former communes) taxing authority. Township bureaucracies took on responsibility for transportation, health services, education, infrastructure repair and development, irrigation, family planning, and more. The growing bureaucracy required more money, which was taken from the peasants in the form of various taxes and fees. These taxes and fees are regressive rather than progressive, meaning that local authorities often impose fees on households regardless of income, creating a greater burden on the poor. Much of the time, rural residents are nickel-and-dimed into paying fees for services they never receive. Between 1990 and 2000, the peasants' tax burden averaged 146 yuan per person, six times the average urban resident's tax burden of 37 yuan.[20]

Governments at all levels impose taxes and fees. In addition to the ninety-three categories of fees and charges devised by the State Council and ministries, local governments have devised another 269 types of taxes. These taxes include devious rural tax schemes, such as including fundraising for building township movie theaters or setting up the township technology website; management fees to repair public buildings and to pay for village cadres' allowances for business trips and entertainment; stipends for the village's nonproduction personnel, such as the party secretary, newspaper delivery man, guard of sliding slopes, and forest guard; and education expenses, including the salary of schoolteachers, office expenses, and purchase of sports equipment. Other rural taxation burdens may include village birth control projects, such as nutrition allowances for postabortion operations and stipends for members of the village committee for birth control; militia training, such as stipends for safeguarding firearms and cartridges and living expenses during training; and social services, such as stipends for residents of the village old people's home and for village health workers, as well as for preferential treatment for surviving members of revolutionary martyrs and retired army personnel, for workers hurt in work-related accidents, for families in hardship, and for the aged who have lost their families. There is also a live pig tax, and a pig-killing tax. Finally, there is an "attitude tax" to ensure that all taxes are promptly paid. Delinquency in paying taxes results in a "bad attitude" tax.[21]

One township levied various taxes associated with getting married, including fees for a letter of authorization from the couple's employers, for the notary, for the marriage license, and for premarital physicals, and deposits for commitment to the one-child policy, for commitment to deferred pregnancy, for "mutual devotion," and for a "golden wedding." There is also a tax for banquet-related environmental hazards, and a donation to the "Happy Children's Center."[22]

The imposition of taxes and fees led to serious rural protests in the 1990s and the early twenty-first century. Although the NPC passed legislation to limit rural fees, local authorities continue to impose taxes and fees. To help ease the burden for China's rural population, President Hu Jintao's administration eliminated the rural education surcharge.

In addition to imposing taxes and fees, many local authorities engage in outright extortion. Local party cadres and township and village authorities commonly hire thugs to arbitrarily seize innocent people on trumped-up charges and illegally detain them until family members pay for their release. These illegal detentions make a lot of money for local authorities. In one case, in Lixin

County in Anhui Province, three cadres had hired thugs to arrest and detain more than two hundred people from twenty-two villages in the township. Although the case came to trial, there was no justice for the victims. The three cadres received only light sentences of one to three years, with probation, while many of the victims' lives were destroyed. After paying exorbitant extortion fees, many people had to take loans and sell their houses or whatever they owned, and were left destitute.[23]

Rural-Urban Social Disparity

Merely looking at the rise in China's GDP does not offer an accurate picture of development in China. To get a better picture of development in China, one should look beyond GDP to a broader definition of well-being. The United Nations' Human Development Index (HDI) provides a composite measure of three dimensions of human development: longevity (life expectancy at birth), knowledge (literacy and average years of schooling), and income, according to purchasing power parity (PPP). Based on this formula, each country of the world is assigned an HDI rating between 0 and 1; the closer a country is to 1, the better is its level of human development. In 2010, the average life expectancy in China was 73.5 years. The adult literacy rate for people aged fifteen years and older was 94.2 percent. The combined primary, secondary, and tertiary gross enrollment ratio was 68.7 percent. GDP per capita (according to PPP) was $7,206.[24] In 2010, then, China's HDI was .66, giving it the rank of 89 out of 177 countries.[25]

The HDI can be used to examine China's rural-urban social disparity. According to official statistics, life expectancy in Beijing, Shanghai, and other developed areas in the coastal region was about eighty years, but in the western province of Guizhou it was less than seventy years. The under-five child mortality rates in Beijing and Qinghai were 5.1 per thousand live births and 35 per thousand live births, respectively. The illiteracy rate of the population over fifteen years of age was only 3.9 percent in Beijing, while it was about 14 percent in Gansu, Qinghai, Ningxia, and other underdeveloped regions of western China.[26]

The rural-urban social disparity can be partly explained by the shortage of social services in rural areas. Social services faced financial difficulties when tax reforms were carried out in the 1980s and 1990s. Under the 1994 tiered tax system, all revenue from the consumption tax goes to central government coffers, and all revenue from the individual income tax and sales taxes go to local budgets. Local governments, particularly counties and townships, were made responsible for providing social services, such as schools and clinics, in their areas. Localities with strong local revenue bases were able to finance social services, but in poorer areas, the tax revenue did not cover the expense of providing social services. The lack of financial resources resulted in the widespread policy of making public service providers, such as clinics and schools, responsible for their own financing through the collection of fees. The lack of public funding for social services also means that poor families cannot afford health care and cannot afford to send their children to school. The lack of education further inhibits one's future earning potential, almost certainly guaranteeing that poor children will later become poor farmers or wage-labor migrant workers.

Police departments are also failing in rural areas. Chinese living in rural counties suffer clan warfare, criminal gangs, and indifferent or corrupt police officers. For instance, in late 1998 and early 1999, two neighboring villages in Lanshan County battled each other using makeshift cannons. The fighting destroyed sixty homes and killed twelve, including five people from a nearby village bombarded by accident. The local police ignored the events because an investigation would reveal a public safety problem in the area, which would hurt the officers' chances for advancement. More than fifty murders in the county have similarly been ignored, often due to bribery or political influence. Beyond such indifference and greed, police officials in some rural areas cooperate with criminal gangs or engage in their own criminal enterprises, such as drug trafficking and money counterfeiting.[27]

The Education Gap

Education and health care are good indicators of the rural-urban divide. In 2008, the central government budgeted 3.6 percent of GDP for education, well below the average of 5.5 percent in developed countries and 4.2 percent in developing countries.[28] Elementary and middle school education is compulsory in China. Many poor rural schools have failed to implement the nine-year mandatory education law, mostly because poor families cannot afford the school fees.

Until the early 1980s, the central government was responsible for compulsory education. However, the 1983 education reform outline and the 1986 Compulsory Education Law made the central government responsible for setting education policies and regulations, but made subnational governments responsible for funding and implementation of policies. After 1986, provincial governments made plans for the development of education and coordinated the education spending of county governments. Between 1994 and 2001, town and township governments paid nearly 80 percent of China's compulsory education costs. Provincial governments paid less than 11 percent, and county governments 9 percent. Less than 2 percent of resources came from the central government.[29] In rural areas, county governments shifted funding responsibilities down to township governments. Because of a weak tax base, most rural township governments could not afford to pay teacher salaries on a regular basis, or to keep the schools running. The financial burden then fell on local people, who had to pay tuition and other fees. Many teachers left the schools or failed to show up for class.[30] The 2006 abolition of the agricultural tax, which helped raise farm income, deprived county governments of revenue. To make up the difference, localities have turned to unauthorized charging of fees. Unauthorized charging of fees was the leading complaint about prices of goods and services in 2006.[31]

The central government is working to narrow the rural-urban social disparity. Elementary school enrollment rates are almost 100 percent in the most developed eastern provinces, but are only 60 to 70 percent in the poorer western and central regions. In 2002, the central government capped educational fees, and in 2004 launched a "two frees and one subsidy" program for rural compulsory education in the western provinces. The program provides free textbooks and tuition, along with living allowances for poor students in rural schools. In 2006, the central government directed 70 percent of new funding to rural education and provided subsidies to primary and middle schools to eliminate collection of education surcharges. In 2007 and 2008, the Chinese government waived all tuition and fees for compulsory education in rural and urban areas to give China's poor more equal education opportunities.

The cost of education has led to gender disparity in education. Given the burden the cost of education places on rural families, many have opted for their sons, but not their daughters, to attend school. Girls have had less access to educational opportunities at both the primary and middle school levels. In the early 1990s, girls represented about 70 percent of all primary school–age children (between seven and eleven years) who were not enrolled. At the same time, the primary school completion rate was significantly lower for girls (89 percent) than for boys (94 percent). Females have constituted a high proportion (often 70 percent) of the illiterate population in the poor areas.[32] Over the past two decades, education levels have increased in rural China, and gaps between boys and girls have been diminishing. By 2000, moreover, more than 96 percent of boys and 95 percent of girls were enrolled in primary school, a rate only slightly lower than that of their urban counterparts.[33] The rural dropout rate also improved for girls. In 2000, only 3 percent of rural school-age girls dropped out of school, down from more than 16 percent in 1990.[34]

The remaining disparities are in the quality of compulsory education. Gaps remain, particularly in financing, school conditions, and teacher qualifications. In 2005, the average per student education expenditures at the primary and junior high school levels were 1,823 and 2,277 yuan ($222 and $277), respectively. In rural areas, however, the average expenditure was only 166 yuan and 233 yuan ($20 and $28), respectively. The difference between the most well funded (Shanghai) and the least well funded (Guangxi and Anhui Provinces) was at least twenty-seven-fold. The expenditure per junior high school student in the western region was only 40 percent of that in the eastern region.[35]

Insufficient funding of schools led to an uneven allocation of education resources. Chinese schools are characterized as "key" and "non-key." The practice of distinguishing between key and non-key schools dates back to the 1950s when the government was in desperate need of professional talent to rebuild the country. The government created key schools to identify and educate the most promising candidates for higher levels of education. Shut down during the Cultural Revolution, the key schools were restored by the Chinese government in the 1980s to revive the country's lapsed education system. Schools with a strong financial base, superior teachers, and modern equipment and resources are designated key schools and become stronger with the backing of more government assistance. Weaker programs become non-key and continue to receive fewer government resources, becoming less competitive and less attractive. Rural and urban areas have both key and non-key schools. Naturally, key schools favor urban students and the children of more affluent Chinese and of government officials. Children of migrants find it difficult to be admitted to a key school. Most rural schools, particularly in western China, are non-key schools, where students are subject to differentiated treatment at a very young age. Despite a Ministry of Education ban on key schools in the mid-1990s, the system still exists, perpetuating inequitable access to quality education. Many rural schools are not safe, and rural children are more likely than their urban counterparts to study in an unsafe environment. Although only 64 percent of primary and middle school students live in rural areas, 86 percent of unsafe school facilities are there.[36] This fact became tragically apparent during the spring 2008 earthquake in Sichuan Province, where most of the buildings that crumbled were schools. Some nineteen thousand students died in collapsed schools while other buildings remained standing.

Rural schools are cramped and lack the equipment and technology found in urban schools. Rural primary schools have nearly 3 percent less floor space than their urban counterparts. Dormitories, canteens, and toilets at rural schools are below national standards. The per student value of primary school instruments (including lab equipment, computers, and Internet access) is also below national standards. The per student value of primary school instruments in the eastern region was nearly twice as high as that in the central and western regions. Only 51 percent of rural primary schools reach national standards for teaching instruments for the subjects of math and nature, as opposed to 73 percent of urban schools. Less than 6 percent of rural primary schools have Internet access, as opposed to 43 percent of urban schools. Only 23 percent of rural junior high schools have Internet access, as opposed to 52 percent of their urban counterparts.[37]

There are still large gaps in the educational background of teachers in rural and urban schools. At the primary school level, 83 percent of teachers in urban schools had a higher education background (junior college or above), but only 54 percent of rural teachers had higher education. More than 68 percent of junior high school teachers in urban schools had higher education, but only 30 percent did in rural schools.[38] The quality of instruction is also inferior in rural schools. Many rural parents question the value of education, especially if the teachers are uninterested and frequently absent. The poor quality and high cost of education have led to high dropout rates in rural regions. Fewer rural children continue their education beyond middle school than do their urban counterparts. In 2002, the average number of years of schooling for urban workers was eleven, but less than seven for rural workers. Many dropouts leave school for economic reasons, the major causes being families needing children to work and the cost of schooling.

Health Care

During the Mao years, rural residents had access to basic, if rudimentary, health care. The communes provided health care through the Cooperative Medical System (CMS). Staffed by practitioners with minimal medical training (village medical practitioners, or "barefoot doctors"), the rural medical system emphasized public health measures, such as inoculations and hygiene. Despite the basic nature of rural health care, the rural health-care system improved the overall health of rural residents. Immunization and other health measures, such as better sanitation and control of mosquitoes for malaria, helped control infectious diseases and increased life expectancy. As mentioned earlier, life expectancy in the better-developed coastal regions is about eighty years, but in the poorer interior areas is less than seventy years. The infant mortality rate in remote Qinghai Province is 2.89 percent, ten times that of Shanghai at 0.3 percent.[39]

The rural health system has nearly collapsed in the reform era, and inequalities in health and access to health care have increased. In the 1980s, China's leaders began to extricate the state from the provision of social services. They shifted the burden for financing social services from the central government to provincial and local governments and mandated that they fund their portion through local taxes. Central government expenditures are now less than 1 percent of GDP. According to the World Health Organization, China ranks 156 out of 196 countries in the ratio of government health spending to GDP.[40] From 1978 to 1999, the central government's share of national health-care spending actually fell from 32 percent to 15 percent.[41] The result has been a growing disparity in urban and rural health care. Wealthier coastal provinces, which have stronger financial bases, can better afford to invest in health care than their poorer counterparts. Rural local governments do not have the financial means to provide health care to residents. The allocation of government funding nationwide is also disproportionate. Only 25 percent of public health resources are devoted to rural residents, although they account for more than 50 percent of China's population.

Without the Cooperative Medical System, rural Chinese could no longer pool funds for their health care, and became uninsured. During the Mao years, 85 percent of rural Chinese were covered by health insurance. Today, less than

10 percent of rural residents have health insurance; a mere 3 percent of rural residents in China's poorest, rural western provinces have health insurance. With no rural health insurance system, rural residents pay for health-care costs out of their own pockets or take out loans. Between 1993 and 1998, the average cost of a visit to a rural health practitioner increased 175 percent and the cost of admission rose 140 percent. At the same time, the percentage of rural residents who had health insurance decreased 22 percent to only 9 percent of residents.[42] By 1998, out-of-pocket spending on health care increased the number of rural households living below the poverty line by more than 44 percent.

The high cost of medical care coupled with the lack of insurance reduced the health-care utilization rate in China. In 1985, the bed occupancy rate of township health centers was 46 percent and that of county hospitals was 83 percent. By 2000, these rates had dropped to 33 percent and 61 percent respectively. Naturally, poorer households use fewer medical services. On average, 45 percent of the discharges from medical care in rural China are patient-initiated against medical advice. Nearly 80 percent of these discharges occur because patients cannot afford to stay longer in the hospital.[43]

With the dissolution of the commune system, qualified medical personnel were no longer forced to serve in China's rural collectives, and in most cases left for the cities. Many rural health clinics closed, and the rural poor were left with no health care. The barefoot doctors became unemployed. They either left the health services field or sought employment as private practitioners. Working in the poorly regulated private sector, the barefoot doctors have stopped providing public health services, for which they are no longer compensated, and have turned to more lucrative technical services, for which they have no training.[44] They have also found that selling prescription drugs is a moneymaker. Drug sales have ballooned throughout rural China, their prices well beyond what rural residents can afford. Many of the drugs are counterfeit, to boot.

Public health and medical agencies have begun to collect fees for medicines and services to cover their costs, and they link the salaries of health and medical workers to the money they collect. As a result, they tend to overprescribe medications and procedures that generate fees. Not only has it become more expensive to get medical care, but access to care has decreased. Private practitioners and many public ones see patients only if they are paid up front, something most rural residents cannot afford. Unable to afford medical care and aware of the inferiority of rural medical care, seriously ill patients bypass local practitioners and facilities and seek outpatient care in the nearest urban hospital. Care in hospital-based services costs even more than in rural facilities, increasing the burden on the rural poor. The search for better medical care contributes to rural-to-urban migration and overtaxes urban health units.

Uninsured and unable to pay high user fees, most rural Chinese are shut out of the health-care system. The lack of basic health care has led to an increase in the spread of disease and premature death. Infant and child mortality is almost 2.7 times higher in the western than in eastern regions, 2.4 times higher in rural than in urban areas, and even 5 times higher in the poorest rural counties than in large cities. Almost 1.6 times as many mothers die during childbirth in rural areas as in urban centers.[45] There has been a resurgence of some infectious diseases, such as schistosomiasis, which was nearly controlled in the past.[46]

The prevention of the spread of communicable disease is the responsibility of epidemic prevention stations, which operate at each level of subnational government. The stations conduct health surveillance, including collecting information on infectious diseases from hospitals. Each lower-level station is to report to the next higher-level station in the chain of vertical command. The system is weak, however. The stations report to the government health bureau at the same administrative level rather than to upper-level stations, which in turn reports to the Ministry of Health. The Ministry of Health's annual statistical report indicates that there are no data from many localities, so the ministry does not have a complete picture of the incidence of infectious diseases in China. SARS and other viruses, such as avian flu, are known to have, or are believed to have, animal hosts. These viruses can be spread to humans from human-animal contact. Given that most of the Chinese who live in rural areas are engaged in agriculture and animal husbandry, human contact with animals is inevitable. Clinics or hospitals that treat infected patients are not required to share information.

During the SARS epidemic of 2003, the lack of information sharing and the failure of epidemic prevention stations to report diseases up the chain of command rendered China's rural health-care system inadequate to respond to the outbreak. Because of the expense of health care, most rural residents did not consult a health-care provider when ill, which posed a great challenge to the detection of SARS. Only after the detection of hundreds of cases and the deaths of several residents were villages required to set up reporting centers. These centers passed the case information on to the county's epidemic prevention station, which sent an ambulance to the villager's home to make a diagnosis. The SARS epidemic in rural China was compounded by the return of infected migrants from southern coastal China, the epicenter of the outbreak. Infected migrants, who were afraid to report the illness to authorities, traveled home to rest and hide. In the end, it was largely the mass mobilization of rural residents that prevented a SARS pandemic in rural China. Local health-care practitioners quarantined villages and took the temperature of all people seeking entrance to the village, including returning migrants. Schools and many work units carried out daily health examination of students. Local authorities disinfected every passing vehicle and required villagers to disinfect their houses daily.

HIV/AIDS

The breakdown in the rural health system, domestic migration, and rural poverty all have contributed to the spread of the human immunodeficiency virus (HIV) and an increase in deaths due to acquired immunodeficiency syndrome (AIDS). HIV/AIDS is the third deadliest communicable disease in China. Although AIDS was first reported in China in 1985, the Chinese government refused to divulge statistics on the disease's rate of infection. Until the early 2000s, the Chinese government denied having an HIV/AIDS problem. Only after the 2003 SARS debacle did the government acknowledge the disease and begin to report HIV and AIDS data. In 2011, there were approximately 780,000 HIV/AIDS cases in China. In 2011 alone, there were 48,000 new infections.[47] An estimated 44 percent of China's HIV carriers are intravenous drug users, and nearly 20 percent are prostitutes and their clients.[48] There are 190 new infections every day, and an estimated 1 percent of all pregnant women are infected with HIV.

The three main causes of HIV/AIDS transmission in China are intravenous drug use (IDU), a thriving sex trade, and blood-selling schemes. First, nearly 90 percent of IDU occurs in Guangxi, Xinjiang, Yunnan, Guangdong, Guizhou, Sichuan, and Hunan Provinces. These seven provinces either border the "Golden Triangle" of Vietnam, Laos, and Myanmar (Burma), which is the source of the world's major illicit drugs, the Central Asian republics, or are along inland trucking routes. According to official statistics, China in 2006 had 1.16 million registered drug abusers.[49] The estimated number is closer to 3.5 million.[50] Most IDUs are under the age of thirty-five, a key factor contributing to the spread of HIV. This age group is more sexually active, having more unprotected sex and sexual partners than the rest of the population. The majority of IDUs are within the migrant population, making the disease even harder to identify.

Economic liberalization and migration contributed to the second major method of transmission, the commercial sex industry. The Chinese communists had been effective in abolishing the sex trade in China in the early 1950s. In the reform era, commercial sex is a thriving industry. The establishment of joint ventures and foreign firms in southern coastal China encouraged migration from the poorer interior. The migrants, mostly men, seek partners in locations where they work. The sex trade responds to this need, with both local and migrant women participating in the trade. Separated from their families, overseas Chinese businessmen from Hong Kong and Taiwan also participate in commercial sex. Estimates of the number of prostitutes in China vary from 4 to 6 million to six to eight times those figures. The majority of commercial sex workers are young female migrant workers, many of whom have no ties to the community and are very mobile. Others are former female workers laid off from state-owned enterprises. They turned to prostitution because they do not have alternate means of supporting their families. Even some student participants of the spring 1989 protests, who were blacklisted and thereby could not find jobs, found employment in the sex trade in southern coastal China. Unprotected sex is common among commercial sex workers. Migrants and businessmen who become infected through unprotected sex spread the disease to their wives when they travel home again. The proportion of commercial sex workers who are

HIV-positive women grew from 10 percent in 1990 to 39 percent in 2004.[51] In the 1990s, AIDS in Taiwan exploded among housewives of businessmen who had traveled to China.

The third method of transmission is the selling of blood, particularly in Henan, Hubei, Anhui, Shanxi, and Hebei Provinces. Because of a cultural taboo against blood donation, China's blood supply is chronically low. The lack of supply opened the door to a lucrative blood-buying and -selling industry in China. In the 1980s and 1990s, many poor Chinese sold their blood to "blood-heads" (*xuetou*) for 40 to 100 yuan (about $5 to $12) each. Poor farmers, accustomed to incomes of $200 to $300 per year, sold their blood, sometimes in the course of months and years, to supplement their incomes. The bloodheads sold the farmers' blood to collection centers. These collection centers were unregulated and performed procedures known as blood pooling. After pooling the blood in a centrifuge and collecting the plasma, the blood was returned intravenously to the donors. The centers reused needles and syringes, and failed to sterilize them between uses. These procedures quickly spread bloodborne diseases such as HIV and hepatitis. By 2000, blood donors began showing signs of AIDS and began dying in large numbers known as "hot spots." Villages close to collection centers and villages where several donors traveled together to distant collection centers became known as "AIDS villages," as the infection rate among adults ranged from 20 to 80 percent.[52] In 1998, the Chinese government made blood selling illegal. By the time the schemes were stopped, however, some thirty-five thousand people had been infected through commercial blood donation and transfusion.[53] Additionally, there are some seventy-five thousand orphans, many of whom are infected.[54]

In 2003, China's leaders made AIDS a national priority and introduced a program to address the spread of AIDS and care for HIV-infected people. They created the China Comprehensive AIDS Response (China CARES), China's first national AIDS treatment plan. Both the central government and the Global Fund to Fight AIDS, Tuberculosis, and Malaria financially support China CARES. The program focuses on providing free antiretroviral therapy to those who cannot afford the drugs. In 2007, approximately thirty-two thousand people were being treated.[55]

Since coming to grips with the gravity of the HIV/AIDS situation in China, the Chinese government has increased spending on combating HIV/AIDS from $12.5 million in 2002 to $185 million in 2006. Local governments provide additional funding. In 2006, both the Chinese government and international groups invested approximately $388 million to combat HIV/AIDS.

In 2003, the central government implemented the policy of "Four Frees and One Care," in which the government provides free antiretroviral drugs for rural AIDS patients and urban AIDS patients facing financial difficulties, free HIV testing and counseling, free drugs for pregnant women and testing of newborns to reduce mother-child transmission of HIV, free education for AIDS orphans, and care and economic assistance to households of people living with HIV/AIDS. Additionally, the Chinese government mandates that all entertainment spots make condoms available. In recent years, free HIV testing expanded to all provinces. From 2004 to 2006, central and local governments tested millions of people, especially in high-prevalence areas such as Henan and Yunnan Provinces. China's Center for Disease Control and Prevention tested some 2 million former blood donors. China's Health Ministry launched a nationwide system to collect AIDS data from county health authorities directly through the Internet instead of by paper reports, which are commonly passed through a hierarchy of officials who are loathe to pass on bad news. The ministry requires that local disease prevention authorities visit HIV patients twice a year and AIDS patients four times a year, writing a record of each visit.[56]

Although the Chinese government provides antiretrovirals free to citizens, only a few actually benefit from the policy. Unfortunately, some HIV/AIDS patients in China have developed resistance to antiretrovirals. The central government has approached international pharmaceutical company Abbott Laboratories about distributing its second-line drug, Kaletra, in China.

The Chinese government is also trying to treat IDUs. China established its first pilot methadone site in Gejiu City in Yunnan Province. The center offers tests for HIV and dispenses methadone to drug addicts. There is also a drop-in center where parents of drug users can gain information on how to prevent the spread of HIV. In another center, a nonprofit group offers counseling and support for HIV- and AIDS-infected people.[57] By the end of June 2007, Yunnan Province had fifty-three methadone maintenance-treatment clinics serving more than five thousand drug users. The success of these centers is questionable, however, as 83 percent of participants in the Gejiu treatment program dropped out of the program in the first month and returned to heroin addiction. Addicts claimed that the program did not remove their exposure to the drug-taking environment, such as heroin availability and drug friends.[58]

The Chinese government estimates that 80 percent of those it believes to be HIV-positive are unaware that they are infected. The government does not know who they are because of incomplete testing and reporting, especially among the IDUs, commercial sex workers, and homosexuals. Medical professionals lack the necessary equipment and technologies to diagnose, counsel, treat, and monitor HIV/AIDS patients. This problem is particularly acute in rural areas where the health-care system is nearly nonexistent. Under such circumstances, it is unlikely that rural local governments can carry out the Four Frees and One Care program. Another explanation for the gap in the data is the social stigma that HIV/AIDS patients carry in China. Because of the stigma, many people will have nothing to do with HIV-positive people or AIDS patients. Doctors commonly refuse to treat AIDS patients, and many Chinese who suspect they are infected are hesitant to be tested, putting their sex partners at risk. Some HIV carriers, real or pretend, have found a way to make the disease lucrative. They resort to petty crime, such as pickpocketing. When they are caught by the police, the petty crooks claim that they are HIV-positive. Police and other law enforcement officers are wary of contact with HIV- and AIDS-positive lawbreakers and rarely detain them.[59] To help reduce the stigma associated with AIDS, the Chinese government recruited NBA basketball star Yao Ming to advocate for people living with HIV. In 2006, Yao was featured in a public-service announcement, with HIV-positive basketball legend Magic Johnson, that included key messages on stigma and discrimination. The announcement was widely broadcast throughout China and was used in the UNAIDS (Joint UN Programme on HIV/AIDS) and International Olympic Committee AIDS leaflet. Yao Ming was also featured in a leaflet that accompanied all condoms distributed at the Beijing Olympics as part of that campaign.[60]

In recent years, the Chinese government has welcomed foreign assistance in its fight against HIV/AIDS. The US government funds HIV/AIDS programs through the President's Emergency Plan for AIDS Relief (PEPFAR). Through PEPFAR, China has received more than $30 million for prevention, care, and treatment programs as well as support for AIDS orphans and vulnerable children.[61] In 2007, the Bill and Melinda Gates Foundation launched a major partnership with the Chinese government to fight the spread of AIDS in China. The foundation committed an initial $50 million toward expanding HIV-prevention efforts in high-risk populations, such as IDUs, sex workers, and men who have sex with men. Of the total, $20 million would go to the Ministry of Health and $30 million to local, national, and international NGOs.[62]

The Government Response to the Rural Health-Care Crisis

In 2002, the central government announced plans to increase state investment in hospitals, maternal and health-care institutions, disease prevention and control centers, health supervision agencies, and village health clinics. It planned to finish building and refurbishing hospitals and medical services in all counties and townships by 2010, and pledged to ensure that there was at least one public hospital per township. It also asked colleges to offer specific training for rural medical workers, and doctors in urban areas were required to work in rural areas for one year if they wanted a promotion.[63]

Despite these measures, many rural residents lack the finances to pay for health care. Between 1992 and 2003, health-care affordability worsened in rural areas. In 1998, 19 percent of rural residents who felt ill did not seek health care because of cost concerns. By 2003, the rate of foregone health care in rural areas had risen to 22 percent. In 2003, 83 percent of rural patients who refused to seek medical care cited inability to pay, as opposed to 20 percent in 1998.[64] In 2003, the average visit to a rural health clinic cost 100 yuan ($12), which was 75 percent higher than in 1998. The average cost of hospitalization was

3,227 yuan ($394), and the average cost of drugs purchased at pharmacies was 50 yuan ($6).[65] Considering that the average per capita income in rural China in 2003 was 2,622 yuan (about $320), these costs are well beyond the means of most rural residents.

In 2002, China's leaders created a New Rural Cooperative Medical Care System (NRCMCS), a basic insurance program to provide for the treatment of serious diseases. Rural residents voluntarily participate in the plan, funded by individuals, organizations, and governments. Since 2003, the central government and local governments have subsidized medical care for rural residents. The Ministry of Civil Affairs provides additional subsidies for rural patients nationwide who need expensive medical treatment and to the poorest 5 to 10 percent of people in China's provinces as well. The new system has its shortcomings, however. The plan covers only inpatient care, with a very high deductible, and still leaves rural residents without adequate primary care services and drugs.[66] There is also a question of the ability of local governments to help fund the annual subsidy. Because the plan focuses exclusively on catastrophic costs, many rural poor delay consulting a doctor until the illness becomes so severe that they must seek catastrophic assistance from the cooperative medical care system. In addition, people might not join the program if they believe that they do not need major medical coverage. If the young and healthy refuse to join, or drop out of the program, the system would begin to lose money, particularly if it needed to cover older and less healthy people. Local governments may need to raise contributions, which would lead to a greater exodus of the young and healthy, and the eventual collapse of the program.[67] Although nearly all of China's villages have health service clinics, there is only one doctor and health worker for every thousand rural residents. Health-care utilization rates also remain low. Only 78 percent of hospital beds are used in county hospitals, and only 48 percent of beds are used in township hospitals. Inability to pay for care and the inconvenient location of hospital facilities are the two major causes of the low utilization rates.[68]

Living Conditions and Social Security

China has made advances in reducing rural poverty. In 2009, farmers' net income per capita was 5,153 yuan ($758), a growth of 8 percent over the previous year. The low-income population in rural areas (those with a per capita net income below 1196 yuan, or $176) numbered 36 million.[69] Despite these advances, nearly 15 million people in rural areas live in absolute poverty, with annual incomes below 785 yuan ($115).[70] Recognizing the large numbers of poor and very poor, China's leaders established several programs to improve living conditions for the rural poor.

Rural Old-Age Insurance

In 1991, China's leaders began an experimental, rural old-age insurance program, with pilot programs in several counties. The program draws on individual contributions supplemented with government subsidies. Both are put in an individual account, and the insured person can receive a pension of the accumulated funds when he or she is sixty years of age. Although the Ministry of Labor and Social Security is responsible for the program, some local governments are experimenting with reform of the system, including providing more public financing. The goal is to establish a pension system that combines individual contributions, collective contributions, and government subsidies, and that can attract more rural participants. Widening the pool of participants puts more money in the program, thereby raising the level of security.[71]

A similar program provides old-age insurance for farmers who lost their land to government requisition. Local governments commonly requisition agricultural land for their development goals. Farmers who have had their land requisitioned have no income, future earnings, or pension. In 2003, some 20 million farmers had lost their land to development, and as a result had been granted urban *hukou*. They received only minimal compensation for their land. With few nonagricultural skills to fall back on, many became unemployed.[72] In 2006, the State Council proposed establishing a social security system specifically for farmers whose land had been requisitioned. Under the plan, farmers whose land has been expropriated for urban development receive a basic minimum living allowance and pension. The actual amount of benefits is determined by a formula that considers the condition of the local economy and the recipient's age group.

The rural old-age insurance program is complemented by a new minimum living allowance. This minimum-living-standard subsidy program covers 48 million rural residents.[73] The program focuses on the sick, disabled, elderly, and those without the ability to work. It helps the rural poor meet basic living expenses. The program is funded by local governments, with subsidies from the central government for those areas with financial difficulties. The average monthly benefit is 71 yuan (about $11).

Migration

China is experiencing the largest human migration in history. China has an estimated 200 million migrants, more than 15 percent of its population. The mobility rate is actually quite low compared with that of industrialized developed countries, but the sheer numbers involved have created economic and social stresses. Large-scale job losses among migrant workers, such as the 20 million lost in early 2009 during the global economic downturn, exacerbate these stresses. Migrant unemployment causes problems not only where the migrants are living, but also in their home villages, which then suffer from a drop in remittances.[74] The Chinese government increasingly needs to orchestrate responses to the problems created by such large numbers of migrants.

Most migrants are not permanent, earning them the moniker "floating population" (*liudong renkou*) because they are more likely to "float" between their rural homes and urban areas, or between interior and coastal regions. Most of China's migrants come from rural areas in China's interior, and most migrate to cities within their home province, while others migrate to coastal regions. Much of the floating population performs construction or other heavy labor in the cities, returning home to help during the planting and harvest seasons. The trek from central to coastal China is arduous. It takes three days to travel from the Shenzhen special economic zone (SEZ) to Sichuan Province by train. The train cars are packed with so many migrants that many are required to stand for the entire thirty-odd hours of the journey.[75]

Both push and pull factors inspire rural Chinese to migrate. The most common push factors (generally negative developments and circumstances that motivate people to leave their homes) are lack of land, unemployment, and poverty. China's migrant population consists of former farmers and laid-off urban factory workers. The dismantling of the rural communes left too many farmers with not enough land. Some farmers returned to their family farms or found employment in newly established town and village enterprises (TVEs). Some farmers migrated to urban areas. Other farmers found that they could not afford to run family farms after the central government began in 1984 to divert investment from rural areas to cities, and so left them for work in the cities. Other rural residents migrated because of the effects of urban bias. As resources flowed from rural to urban areas, so did migrants. China suffers from a serious shortage of arable land. Less than 15 percent of its land is suitable for agriculture. Land has actually become more scarce in the reform era as farmland is converted into industrial land. Due to development, China has less farmland than it did in 1978. Between 1987 and 1992, for example, China lost close to a million hectares of farmland each year to urbanization and the expansion of roads and industries.[76] Local authorities have been known to confiscate farmland for development projects, such as industry or luxury housing, claiming that the development benefits all. Urban sprawl has also encroached on China's farmland. As a result, 30 to 40 percent of China's agricultural labor force is surplus. The loss of farmland and lack of jobs have caused some farmers to migrate to urban areas or to coastal provinces in search of wage labor.

The closing of state-owned enterprises has also forced people to migrate. Many of the cities in China's interior were developed around state industry. When the SOEs collapsed, millions of people lost their jobs. To mask the extent of the unemployment, the Chinese government calls former SOE employees "off-post" (*xiagang*) workers. Off-post workers are not registered as unemployed and are still contractually tied to their work units, even though in most cases they no longer receive any wages or living expenses from the SOE.

Pull factors (generally positive conditions encouraging migration) include demand for unskilled labor in urban construction, demand for labor in private enterprise, and the desire for better education and health care. In the last few years, Shanghai alone built one thousand new skyscrapers, all with the help of cheap migrant labor. Cheap migrant labor made possible the east's rapid expansion of infrastructure and urban sprawl. Plentiful and cheap migrant labor also staffs private businesses. Nonstate market or retail jobs account for 80 percent of all markets in Beijing. Migrants stock inventory, store goods, and provide service for Chinese and foreign customers. Most of these jobs require little training, and migrants easily fill these roles. Migrants also perform the "dirty" jobs shunned by local residents. Migrant workers are often willing to take any jobs that will help them escape the poverty of subsistence farming. Roles as maids and street cleaners fall to migrant laborers. Migrants also make up a majority of employees in joint-venture enterprises (JVEs). JVEs require significant labor to help sell and monitor merchandise in places like Hong Kong and Beijing. Famous shopping districts function on the ability of the JVEs to move, load, unload, and sell vast quantities of goods. Jobs at JVEs require some training, and may help migrants improve their skills and marketability.

Most migrants are young, single, and male. There are two tracks of migrants. One track consists of *temporary migrants* who tend to come from rural areas and migrate to urban areas for a while before returning home for months or years. They tend to have less education than permanent migrants do and generally do not seek an urban *hukou. Permanent migrants* tend to come from urban areas in the interior, are more skilled, and have more years of education. Temporary migrants generally perform labor that urban residents are not willing to do, such as working in construction and other occupations demanding heavy labor. They are usually paid less than urban or local residents for their labor as well. Migrants earn 450 yuan to 800 yuan a month ($71 to $127), and per capita income for rural migrants living in urban areas is 60 to 78 percent that of local residents.[77] (Migrants who lack an urban *hukou* are also ineligible for social benefits.) The poverty rate is 50 percent higher among urban migrants than among permanent residents. The exception is permanent migrants, who often seek an urban *hukou.*

Since the 1980s, female migration has been growing faster than male migration. Female migrants work in foreign firms or joint ventures in southern coastal China, typically as hostesses in restaurants and clubs and performing manual labor that is shunned by urbanites. Most of them have no health-care insurance and do not consult a doctor when ill. According to a 2003 Ministry of Health report, in Beijing 93 percent of female residents gave birth in hospitals, but only 10 percent of migrant women did so. Seventy-one percent of women who died during or as a result of childbirth were migrants. The figures were similar for Guangdong and Shanghai, major migration magnets.[78] The estimated population growth of Guangdong from migration was 24 percent. Recently,

Fujian Province passed a law requiring that migrant women submit to sterilization after the birth of their first child.

Not only do migrants perform the most arduous and low-paying work, they live cheek by jowl in substandard housing. Urban housing for rural migrants often lacks basic amenities, such as access to a kitchen. Most migrants share housing with other migrants, with several occupants per room. Few residences have a private toilet or shower. Because of the risk of infection in cramped housing, Beijing authorities cleared the city of migrants during the 2003 SARS crisis. On the eve of the 2008 Olympics, Beijing authorities cleared the city of migrants.

Not only are migrants exploited for their cheap labor, but they are often cheated out of the meager wages due them. It is not unusual for migrants to be laid off after not being paid for months. The 2008 global economic crisis made the situation worse. Many factories closed in fall 2008 due to an export slowdown. Migrants who returned to their hometowns held out hope that they could return to their jobs after the global economy picked up after the Lunar New Year. Without a national health-care program, migrants may find themselves in health insurance limbo. They are ineligible for urban health insurance because they lack the requisite *hukou*. Migrants seeking care would need to return home to receive care under their village or township medical plan (NRCMCS).

Migrant workers are also ineligible for social relief, the government program of social assistance in the form of minimum living allowance. Urban residents who have no work, no family, and no means of livelihood ("three-no personnel") are covered by the state's social relief scheme. A new state-funded scheme, called *dibao,* is an income supplement for the urban poor, who for a variety of reasons lack sufficient means for basic living. The *dibao* scheme is an urban safety net. In 2006, there were 22.3 million beneficiaries, but migrant workers do not qualify.[79] The only recourse for state aid is emergency relief for vagrant beggars who fall into destitution, called the Relief and Management Measures for Destitute Vagrant Beggars in the Cities. Most migrants do not qualify for this short-term refuge. Exclusion from social relief and poor access to insurance deprive migrants from resources when they fall on hard times. Migrants often return home, if possible, under such circumstances.

The Impact of Migration on Urban and Rural Areas

Migration has both its pluses and minuses. On the plus side, migration benefits business by keeping urban wages low. With a seemingly inexhaustible supply of cheap labor, wages in urban areas are lower than what they would be without migration. Migration also stimulates economic growth in cities. Migrants spend some of their earnings in the cities of their residence, and pay for housing and food, and some other commodities and services. Most migrants also send at least some of their earnings home in the form of remittances, which helps rural economies. In 2009, rural incomes in real terms grew by 8.5 percent, driven mainly by remittances of migrant farmers who moved to cities for better jobs.

On the downside, migration has resulted in infrastructure overload, stressing transportation systems, putting a further crunch on availability of housing, increasing crime, and spreading disease. Beijing has a "floating population" of 3 million and Shanghai has 2 million. The largest concentration of migrants appears to be in the Pearl River Delta in Guangdong Province, where there are an estimated 10 million migrants, including a half million child laborers. Around 7 to 10 million new migrants leave their villages every year, arriving by bus and by train in the cities, stressing transportation networks. These migrants need housing, food, and health care, as well as education for their children.

Migration is also difficult for both the children and elderly parents left behind. The flight to the cities is causing the graying of rural China as a generation of parents migrates to interior cities or to coastal regions to find work. Hubei, Hunan, Anhui, and Sichuan Provinces are China's biggest suppliers of migrant labor, and these working-age migrants are leaving behind a growing number of rural ghost towns in China. Eighty percent of Chinese over the age of sixty now live in rural areas. In one case, an elderly woman living in rural Sichuan Province successfully sued her son and daughter for abandonment. She won a judgment allowing her to live with her daughter and ordering her son to pay monthly support.[80] The case is remarkable for its novelty. More common are suicides among the rural elderly. The suicide rate among elderly Chinese is four to five times higher than the world average. Rural elderly commit suicide to avoid being a burden to their children.

Most rural residents are engaged in agricultural activities. Although migrants often return home for spring planting and fall harvest, they are not available at other times of the year to help with other tasks required on a farm. These activities become more difficult as one ages. With their children gone, the elderly are left to farm the land with little help. Rural incomes will likely stagnate or fall if arduous farmwork is left only to the elderly. With meager incomes, they and their grandchildren will be stuck in a cycle of poverty. Health care, as mentioned earlier in this chapter, is also a problem for the rural poor. Migrants are not available to take care of their elderly parents or to encourage them to see a doctor when necessary. Unless remittances can help cover health care, rural elderly are not likely to see a doctor. They will likely neglect their health until the situation necessitates expensive and invasive catastrophic care. Although there are no official statistics measuring the effect of migration on life expectancy, it is possible that migration of working-age people leads to lower life expectancy of the elderly in rural China.

Migration is also hard on children who follow migrant-worker parents. Children of urban migrants are legally permitted to attend free public schools. However, access to schooling is still not routine, and many migrant children enroll in private schools that charge tuition. Many migrant parents cannot afford the fees, so they leave their children in their home villages, often under the care of elderly parents. Most elderly parents in rural China cannot afford school fees for their grandchildren and must rely on remittances from their children to pay for schooling. If there is not enough money, the children cannot attend school. Many rural grandparents are illiterate, so leaving children in their care places them at a strong disadvantage.

Discontent and Protest in Rural China

It is undeniable that discontent is on the rise in rural China. The primary causes of discontent among China's rural inhabitants include imposition of excessive fines and illegal taxes by village leaders; local authorities' embezzlement of village finances; land seizures; the deterioration of rural health services; the imposition of the one-child policy by overzealous, local family-planning officials; abuse of power on the part of rural party bosses; degradation of the rural environment in the name of industrialization and development; and the rise in industrial pollution of rural waterways. Much of the discontent stems from the inability of rural Chinese to legally challenge local party bosses and administrative officials. The rule of law is still weak in rural China. China's peasants have found it useless to file lawsuits because they are regularly ignored. Instead, many Chinese turn to the petition system, which is a tradition from imperial times and is enshrined in China's constitution. Petitioners can file a grievance with one or more of the "letters and visits offices" (*xinfang ban*) associated with each of China's state and party organs at each level of government. The number of complaints lodged at these offices increased 115 percent between 1995 and 2000. In 2000, there was a total of 10.2 million complaints lodged at the provincial, county, and municipal offices nationwide.[81]

Failing to get a favorable response from the local offices, millions of peasants travel to Beijing every year to submit their grievances to the relevant ministry's office of letters and visits. These offices are hidden in alleyways and difficult to find. The offices rarely make a decision favorable to the peasants, so many peasants stay in Beijing day after day, month after month, year after year. Often, short of a positive outcome, they have nothing to go home to. Many of the petitions rural Chinese bring to Beijing are simply referred right back to the local officials whom the petitions are against. A survey in 2004 found that only three out of two thousand petitioners found a favorable settlement.

For some petitioners there is a worse fate. Increasingly, local officials use illegal detention and intimidation to deter petitioners from even submitting their grievances to national authorities. The central government has demanded a decrease in the number of petitions from the provinces. Some local officials hire people, called "retrievers," to abduct petitioners and detain them in secret houses or hotel rooms (known as "black jails"), and then send the petitioners back to their homes.[82] Another method of deterrence is incarceration of petitioners in mental hospitals. Such extralegal imprisonment is easy due to laws that give officials broad authority to have people committed without recourse.[83]

Without effective legal recourse, China's peasants protest, demonstrate, and riot to express their ire. The number of protestors and the severity of protests in rural areas have increased. China's Ministry of Public Security recorded steady increases in rural unrest in 2004 and 2005, and reported twenty-three thousand protests in 2006.[84]According to Chinese official statistics, there were 57,817 group protests in rural areas in 2008.[85] For instance, in November 2008, up to two thousand people attacked a local party headquarters in northwest Gansu Province in protest over a land dispute and demolition of homes of rural residents.[86]

Although most protests by farmers are over land disputes, thousands of protests are held over other issues as well, such as pollution, improper arrests, lax safety standards, and corruption among party and state officials. For example, in Hunan Province in March 2007, up to twenty thousand people fought with a thousand police in a clash sparked by rising public transport costs.[87] In Weng'an, Guizhou Province, up to thirty thousand people took part in a protest in June 2008, torching government buildings and smashing and burning cars. Residents protested against the authenticity of a police report on a seventeen-year-old girl's death, which officials deemed a suicide but residents believed to be a murder.

Addressing Rural Poverty and Closing Disparity Gaps

Under Deng Xiaoping, China adopted a regional development approach that favored eastern and southern provinces. China's reform-era Five-Year Plans reflect this desire and propose rapid rates of economic growth. In 1982, the Twelfth Party Congress set the goal of quadrupling industrial and agricultural output and raising the living standard to a "comparatively well-off level" (*xiaokang shuiping*) by the end of the century. This goal would be achieved by reforming the economy and opening China to outside investment. The eastern coastal region would take the lead in development, with the interior following some years later. In the early 1980s, Deng Xiaoping began an opening and reform campaign in southern coastal China by allowing Guangdong Province to move "one step ahead" of the rest of China in introducing new economic and political policies.[88] Deng claimed that the coastal region, home to more than 200 million people, should open to the outside world and develop rapidly first. Afterward, they could lead the development of the interior.

By the late 1990s, China had made great strides in achieving the "well-off level." By 1999, per capita GDP had more than doubled since the beginning of reform in 1978. It was clear, however, that the coastal focus had come with a cost to the interior. If Guangdong was "one step ahead," the interior was "left behind." At the end of 1999, the western regions accounted for less than 20 percent of China's GDP. GDP levels per capita were 40 percent of those in the east. For instance, GDP per capita in Guizhou was only one-twelfth that of Shanghai. The western region also included 62 percent of China's officially designated poor counties.

In the mid-1990s, China's leaders became increasingly alarmed by the growing urban-rural disparity. Having largely achieved Deng's goals for economic growth and development, China's leaders turned to the second part of Deng Theory, namely to narrow the gap in society. In the 1990s, they began several programs to alleviate rural poverty. For instance, China's leaders in 1994 launched the 8-7 National Poverty Reduction Program, designed to lift 80 million people out of poverty in seven years. One of the goals of the Ninth Five-Year Plan (1996–2000) was to reduce poverty. Under this plan, Beijing gradually reduced rural taxes, and President Hu eliminated the tax on land and agricultural production. In 2004, the government began giving direct subsidies to grain farmers to encourage them to keep growing grain and to curb grain price rises. The result has been a rise in grain output. In 2000, China began the Develop the West Campaign to facilitate greater regional equality and slow migration to urban and coastal areas. The Eleventh and Twelfth Five-Year Plans continue these efforts to reduce poverty and inequality.

Developing the West

A disproportionate number of China's poor live in western China.[89] Western China is characterized by very high mountains and plateaus, great basins, and arid deserts.[90] The mountains block moisture from the south, making the west extremely dry and difficult, if not impossible, to cultivate. Its vegetation is composed of grasses and hardy shrubs. Xinjiang's Tarim Basin is one of the driest places on earth. Rimmed by tall mountains, most of the basin is uninhabited desert, the Taklamakan, with very little vegetation. For thousands of years, China's west has been sparsely populated. Although the west constitutes 57 percent of China's landmass, it holds only 23 percent of China's population. Government policies and the urban bias have perpetuated the region's grinding poverty. Its isolation and inhospitable environment offered little incentive for the central government and private entrepreneurs to invest there.

Recognizing the growing disparity between the coastal regions and the west, former PRC president Jiang Zemin in 1999 proposed a Develop the West (*Xibu da kaifa*) Campaign.[91] In his 2000 speech introducing the Develop the West program, former premier Zhu Rongji announced that the central government would channel more development investment to the central and western parts of China, especially western China. One explanation for the regional disparity is the uneven distribution of cities in China. More than 80 percent of China's cities are in the east and the center. Accordingly, Beijing funnels its financial resources toward the more populous eastern area of the country, with the less populated and poorer regions getting less and less funding. Residents of the west follow the money to eastern China, resulting in even less funding for their home region. The Chinese government vowed to dedicate the Tenth Five-Year Plan (2001–2005) to improving small and medium-sized cities in central and western China.

The Tenth Five-Year Plan endorsed the Develop the West Campaign. It proposed developing eleven provinces and autonomous regions as well as urban areas in the west. The plan aims to develop infrastructure, improve agriculture, and protect the environment. Programs to develop infrastructure include construction of the Qinghai-Tibet railway and of inland water transport, expansion of telecommunications to rural areas, highway projects, and an increase in the transmission of natural gas and electricity. The plan proposes to develop agriculture and agriculture infrastructure by introducing new varieties of spring wheat and local traditional crops and by strengthening the market system for agricultural products and paving county roads. It proposes to protect the environment by way of the "five combinations" of combining restoration of forests and grassland with strengthening farm management, developing rural energy, encouraging environmentally friendly migration, and closing mountains to animal grazing. To encourage investment in the west, the plan endorses liberalizing rules restricting investment in the public economy to improve infrastructure. To improve science and technology in the west, the plan suggests that the west be given preference with respect to education funding. It also recommends a three-tier (county, township, and village) health network to improve health services in the west.

Since 2000, economic growth in the western region has accelerated. Overall GDP for the western region has grown nearly 12 percent, surpassing the national average of 10 percent. Per capita income grew 342 percent, slightly higher than the 313 percent national growth average.[92] These figures, particularly the per capita income figures, can be misleading, however, since they do not show how the local population fares compared to the immigrants from the east. Although the Chinese government offers impressive growth figures, it is often the Han migrants to the area who dominate the high-paying jobs. Moreover, much of the revenue generated in the region does not remain in the region. For instance, oil revenue from Xinjiang and hydroelectric resources from Guizhou flow to the east and are not invested in the western regions.

The ongoing Develop the West Campaign offers incentives and subsidies to encourage domestic and foreign businesses to invest in industrial production and infrastructure projects in China's interior. The west's economy is overwhelmingly based on SOEs, which have been eclipsed by the private-sector industries in the east. State factories make up 70 to 80 percent of the west's economy, but constitute only 40 percent of that of the east. In the late 1990s, many SOEs in the west closed, laying off thousands of employees and contributing to the existing labor surplus. At the same time, approximately 80 percent of foreign investment is along the east coast. The west accounts for only 4 percent of total FDI. The west is not attractive to foreign investors because of its lack of telecommunications, transportation, and energy. Another obstacle is the entrenched bureaucracy of western provinces. Local bureaucrats, who have close ties with state industry, are reluctant to open their districts to competition from private sources.[93] Finally, years of outward migration of both higher-level skilled technicians and unskilled labor have resulted in a loss of valuable workers. Outbound migration, environmental degradation, and the increase in instances of AIDS are further obstacles to attracting external investment.

The fact that both President Hu Jintao and Premier Wen Jiabao climbed their career ladders in western China implies that they are more aware of the problems in the west. Hu was secretary of the Gansu provincial construction ministry, provincial governor of Guizhou Province, and party chief of Tibet. Wen Jiabao, a former geologist, was deputy director general of the Gansu provincial geological bureau. Under Hu and Wen, the central government has redirected both public and private financial resources toward the interior. The central government has increased state funding of projects in the interior and offers incentives and subsidies to domestic and foreign investors to encourage them to invest in projects in the interior. Most of the program projects occur in selected areas that are attractive for development. These areas have financial, human capital, or infrastructural assets such as a firm economic base, high population density, or location near transportation routes.[94] The region's abundant natural resources, such as oil, natural gas, and minerals, are in great demand for China's economic development and present opportunities for investment.

Developing the West as Domestic Security Strategy

China's leaders claim that developing the west also would promote national unity. Having a peaceful domestic environment is vital to China's overall economic development, and containing separatism is a prerequisite to a stable environment. China shares borders with fourteen countries, and most of the borders are in the central and western regions. Those regions also share ethnic minorities across borders. For example, Uygurs straddle Xinjiang and Afghanistan, Pakistan, and India; Tibetans straddle Tibet and India and Nepal; Mongolians bridge Inner Mongolia and (Outer) Mongolia; and Koreans span Jilin and North Korea. As mentioned earlier in this book, there are separatist movements in some of these areas, particularly in Xinjiang and in Tibet. To contain separatism, China's leaders have accelerated economic development and minority integration into a Han-dominated society. One of the goals of the Develop the West program is to invest in the economic infrastructure and apply incentives to attract the surplus population from the east. Ongoing ethnic tension and conflict in Tibet and Xinjiang discourage migration. The spring 2008 anti-Han riots in Lhasa and other Tibetan-populated areas dampened Han enthusiasm for westward migration. At the same time, it should be noted that the migration itself, and the Han Chinese domination of the best jobs and official positions, exacerbate tensions. Government-incentivized Han migration to minority regions is both a cause of, and a reaction to, ethnic tension.

Rural Development and China's Recent Five-Year Plan

The Eleventh Five-Year Plan continues the work begun under the Tenth Five-Year Plan in calling for increased investment in China's western regions. In particular, the Eleventh Five-Year Plan calls for 80 percent of development monies to be spent on developing the interior and western regions. The underlying principle of the plan is to build a "harmonious society" (*hexie shehui*) by giving priority to employment, social security, poverty reduction, education, medical care, environmental protection, and safety. On social security, the plan seeks to improve the insurance system of pensions, basic medical care, and unemployment. It specifically addresses the need to resolve social security issues for migrant farmworkers in cities and set up a security system of minimum living standards for rural residents.[95] The goal of the Eleventh Five-Year Plan is building an "all-around well-off society" (*quanmian xiaokang*) by 2020. Under the umbrella of building a comprehensively well-off society, Hu Jintao set an ambitious target of quadrupling per capita GDP from 2000 to 2020 and also proposed an extensive list of welfare goals, including equal access to quality education and employment, as well as universal health care and universal social security.

Chapter 2 of the plan specifically addresses the need to develop the rural economy, under the mantra of building a "new socialist countryside." Rather than continue the policy of economic growth at all costs, China's new leadership of President Hu Jintao and Premier Wen Jiabao shifted emphasis to balanced development that takes into account the country's poor. The plan also puts Hu's theory on scientific development on par with Mao Thought and Deng Theory. To achieve a harmonious society, it is necessary for China to maintain a solid pace of economic growth and development. According to Hu, this growth and development is achieved through "scientific development," which calls for China to adopt an economic model that is more balanced, efficient, technologically intensive, environmentally friendly, and equitable. The model grew out of the realization that the past three decades of China's rapid economic growth had been driven largely by expansion in investment at relatively low technical levels and at high costs, particularly in terms of exploitation of natural resources and degradation of the environment. The emphasis of scientific development is on long-term sustainable growth and more equitable distribution of resources. For instance, the plan recommends a per capita income growth rate of 6 percent for both urban and rural residents. To relieve unemployment and to raise rural income, the plan seeks to shift some 45 million rural laborers to nonfarming sectors. To improve the health of rural residents, the number of people covered by the New Rural Cooperative Medical Care System is expected to increase from 23.5 percent to more than 80 percent.[96]

Another approach to developing the interior is the concept of the sister city. In 1995, the State Council decided to link wealthy coastal cities with backward regions. For example, the State Council selected the wealthy coastal cities of Shenzhen, Ningbo, Dalian, and Qingdao to partner with two of Guizhou's eight districts. In the first few months after the relationships were established, the four cities signed agreements with Guizhou on more than 100 projects, mainly in education, health care, and tourism development, totaling $225 million.[97] The financial support offered by the developed cities provides capital to create education and health-care opportunities otherwise not possible. The central government promotes the sister-city concept because it saves the central government capital. By letting the wealthy cities foot the bill for development aid, the central government is able to provide social services such as education and health care without having to pay for them.[98]

The Twelfth Five-Year Plan (2011–2015) puts less emphasis on economic growth than on economic equity.[99] The new targets in the plan, which call for reducing the scale and pace of development, describe a nation that has hit a peak growth rate. The plan targets growth at 7 percent annually, a marked slowdown from the double-digit growth over the past thirty years. The plan recognizes the yawning urban-rural gap and gives priority to spreading economic growth evenly from the wealthier coastal areas to poorer and rural parts of China. Specifically, it calls for striking a balance between urban and rural development, gradually minimizing the gaps between urban-rural and regional living standards, and building a moderately prosperous society by 2020. The plan calls for further modernizing agriculture, expanding rural credit and finance, raising farmers' incomes and living standards, and improving rural infrastructure. While many regional development plans will continue under the Twelfth Five-Year Plan, it retires the ten-year Develop the West Campaign and merely incorporates its programs into the national master Five-Year Plan.

Conclusion

Despite economic advances for millions of Chinese, China's urban-rural gap is widening. Structural impediments, such as the *hukou* residency system and poor agricultural infrastructure, impede the rural poor's efforts at economic and social mobility. Continued urban bias funnels resources to China's cities, to the neglect of rural areas. While China has made advances in rural education, rural health care remains inferior to that in the cities. Less than 10 percent of rural residents have health insurance, imposing crushing hardships on those who do require medical care. The result is a spread of HIV/AIDS in China's rural areas.

The Chinese government has increasingly turned its attention to the problems of rural China. In the past decade, the Chinese government has implemented programs to address the rural health-care crisis. One of these programs, the New Rural Cooperative Medical Care System, seeks to insure rural residents for the treatment of serious diseases. Since 2003, the government has made a greater effort to reduce the transmission of HIV/AIDS in rural areas. The government also introduced a rural old-age insurance scheme to improve living conditions for China's rural elderly.

Migration continues to put tremendous stress on Chinese cities, rural areas, and families. Although migration offers migrant workers higher wages than those found at home, the large numbers of migrants stress transportation systems, housing, and urban infrastructure; create rural ghost towns; and break up families. Another issue stressing rural residents is the actions of corrupt state and party officials. Many local officials tax and abuse residents with impunity, forcing a backlash from the people. Anticorruption and other protests officially number eighty thousand a year.[100]

China's leaders have implemented two key programs to respond to the urban-rural gap. The first of these programs, the 8-7 National Poverty Reduction Program, seeks to lift 80 million people out of poverty. The Develop the West program likewise seeks to lift out of poverty millions of people who live in China's interior by attracting both domestic and foreign investment to this long-neglected area. China's leaders also endorsed Hu Jintao's concept of harmonious society, and integrated into the Eleventh Five-Year Plan a better balance between urban and rural development. The Twelfth Five-Year Plan continues many of the policies of its predecessor. Finally, the central government encourages the creation of sister-city relationships between municipalities on the richer coast and areas in the poorer interior. In this manner, the wealthy coastal cities have been instrumental in providing capital for social services in poorer rural areas.

Notes

1. China's per capita income doubled from 1978 to 1996 and again from 1997 to 2005. In comparison, to double once, it took Britain fifty-eight years (1780–1838), the United States forty-seven years (1839–1886), and Japan thirty-four years (1780–1838). Dollar, "Poverty, Inequality, and Social Disparities During China's Reform," 2.

2. United Nations Development Programme (UNDP), *International Human Development Indicators: China.*

3. United Nations, *Social Indicators: Indicators on Health* (New York: United Nations Statistics Division, 2009), http://unstats.un.org; United Nations Children's Fund,

The State of the World's Children 2009: Newborn and Maternal Health (New York: United Nations Children's Fund), 118, http://www.unicef.org.

4. The comparison between rural and urban incomes in China is distorted because although purchasing power of rural incomes is generally higher (because urban prices are higher), urban incomes exclude all sorts of benefits available mostly (more likely only) to urbanites. These benefits include accumulation of pension rights, gifts or sale among friends, prices of real estate, superior education (at nominal cost or even free) for children, and so on. Despite these caveats, Western economists believe that comparison of income figures from Chinese government yearbooks understates the urban-rural income gap by a large margin.

5. UNDP, *Human Development Report 2010*, 153.

6. National Bureau of Statistics (NBS) of China, "2008 China Statistical Summary," in UNDP (China), *China Human Development Report 2007–2008: Basic Public Services for 1.3 Billion People.*

7. "China's Growth Spreads Inland," *Economist,* November 20, 2004, 13.

8. Fan, "Migration, *Hukou,* and the City," 67.

9. Fan, "Migration, *Hukou,* and the City," 68.

10. Jim Yardley, "Farmers Being Moved Aside by China Real Estate Boom," *New York Times,* December 8, 2004, A1, A10.

11. Sky Canaves, "Gangster Trials Highlight China's Crime Battle," *Wall Street Journal,* December 29, 2009, A12; Philip Pan, *Out of Mao's Shadow,* Chapter 7, "The Party Boss."

12. Accounts of abuse of peasants by government and party officials are too numerous to chronicle here. Excellent sources of information on abuse of rural residents are Philip P. Pan, *Out of Mao's Shadow,* especially Chapter 7, "The Party Boss," and Chen and Wu, *Will the Boat Sink the Water?,* 151.

13. NBS of China, *China Statistical Yearbook 2010,* 6–7.

14. NBS of China, *China Statistical Yearbook 2010,* 363.

15. Long Gen Ying, "China's Changing Regional Disparities During the Reform Period."

16. Park, "Rural-Urban Inequality in China," 43.

17. NBS of China, *China Statistical Yearbook 2010,* 342. Official Chinese statistics use per capita annual disposable income for urban households, and per capita annual net income for rural households. Disposable income refers to the actual income at the disposal of members of the households that can be used for final consumption, other noncompulsory expenditure, and savings. Net income refers to total income of rural households from all sources minus all corresponding expenses such as taxes and fees and household operation expenses (e.g., the purchase of seed, animal feed, insecticide, fertilizer, fuel for farm machinery, plastic sheeting, and so on).

18. NBS of China, in *China by Numbers 2007.*

19. NBS of China, *Statistical Communiqué of the People's Republic of China in 2007: National Economic and Social Development,* Beijing, February 28, 2008, http://www.stats.gov.cn.

20. Chen and Wu, *Will the Boat Sink the Water?,* 151.

21. Chen and Wu, *Will the Boat Sink the Water?,* 153–155; and Philip Pan, *Out of Mao's Shadow,* Chapter 7, "The Party Boss."

22. Chen and Wu, *Will the Boat Sink the Water?,* 155.

23. Chen and Wu, *Will the Boat Sink the Water?,* 158; and Philip Pan, *Out of Mao's Shadow,* Chapter 7, "The Party Boss."

24. UNDP, *Human Development Report 2007–2008.*

25. UNDP, *International Human Development Indicators: China.*

26. UNDP (China), *China Human Development Report 2009–2010,* 12.

27. Eric Eckholm, "Order Yielding to Lawlessness in Rural China," *New York Times,* May 29, 2002, A1, A6.

28. NBS of China, *China Statistical Yearbook 2010,* 780.

29. Development Research Center of China's State Council, 2005, in UNDP (China), *China Human Development Report 2007–2008.*

30. Wright, *Promise of the Revolution;* Tooley, *Beautiful Tree.*

31. National Development and Reform Commission, PRC, in UNDP (China), *China Human Development Report 2007–2008.*

32. Amei Zhang, "Poverty Alleviation in China: Commitment, Policies, and Expenditures," Occasional Paper 27 (New York: United Nations Development Programme, 1993), http://hdr.undp.org.

33. These figures are based on the 2000 census, the only census figures available at the time of publication of this book. World Bank, *Gender Gaps in China: Facts and Figures.*

34. World Bank, *Gender Gaps in China: Facts and Figures.*

35. UNDP (China), *China Human Development Report 2007–2008,* 84.

36. Liu Ji'an, "Compulsory Education and Equality in Human Development," background paper for HDR 2007/08, in National Development and Reform Commission, PRC, in UNDP (China), *China Human Development Report 2007–2008,* 74.

37. Liu Ji'an, "Compulsory Education and Equality in Human Development."

38. "China Education Statistical Yearbook" in UNDP (China), *China Human Development Report 2007–2008,* 75.

39. UNDP (China), *China Human Development Report 2009–2010,* 12.

40. Many middle- and low-income countries ranked above China. WHO, *World Health Report 2006: Working Together for Health.*

41. Blumenthal and Hsiao, "Privatization and Its Discontents," 1166.

42. Liu Yuanli, "China's Public Health-Care System," Table 2: 535.

43. Liu Yuanli, "China's Public Health-Care System," Table 2: 535.

44. Blumenthal and Hsiao, "Privatization and Its Discontents," 1167.

45. *Shanghai Daily,* March 13, 2009, http://www.shanghaidaily.com; United Nations Children's Fund, *State of the World's Children 2009,* 118.

46. Blumenthal and Hsiao, "Privatization and Its Discontents," 1168.

47. "China Says HIV/AIDS Cases Are Soaring," Reuters, November 30, 2011.

48. *China by Numbers* 2007, 152.

49. National Narcotics Control Commission of China, "Drugs Harm the Chinese Youth More Seriously in Recent Twelve Years," http://www.acyf.org.cn.

50. Kulsudjarit, "Drug Problem in Southeast and Southwest Asia."

51. Gill, Yanzhong, and Xiaoqing, *Demography of HIV/AIDS in China.*

52. Gill, Yanzhong, and Xiaoqing, *Demography of HIV/AIDS in China,* 28.

53. UNAIDS, "Key Data," http://www.unaids.org.cn.

54 "AIDS Spreading in China 'Like Africa,'" Reuters, October 17, 2006, http://www.smh.com.au/news.

55. UNAIDS, "Key Data."

56. United Nations Educational, Scientific, and Cultural Organization (UNESCO), *Yunnan Province of China: HIV/AIDS Profile,* n.d., http://www.unescobkk.org.

57. Jim Yardley, "Chinese City Emerges as Model in AIDS Fight," *New York Times,* June 16, 2005, A1, A13.

58. Li Jianghong et al., "Reasons for Initiating Drug Use in Adolescents in Southwest China" (Kunming, Yunnan Province, China: Drug Prevention and Research Institute, n.d.), http://cih.curtin.edu.au.

59. Wang Wedong, "Using AIDS to Get Away with Crimes," *China Daily,* June 5, 2004, 3.

60. UNAIDS, "UNAIDS Recognized Leaders in China's AIDS Response," September 17, 2007, http://www.unaids.org.

61. US Department of State, *Partnership to Fight HIV/AIDS in China.*

62. Kristi Heim, "Gates Foundation, China to Partner in HIV Prevention," *Seattle Times,* November 14, 2007.

63. "Rural Dwellers in Central, West China to Enjoy Health Care Subsidies in 2003," Xinhua News Agency, October 30, 2002, http://www.lexisnexis.com/hottopics /lnacademic/.

64. Liu Yuanli et al., "China's Health System Performance."

65. John G. Taylor, "Poverty and Vulnerability," 96.

66. Blumenthal and Hsiao, "Privatization and Its Discontents," 1169.

67. World Health Organization, "Rural Health Insurance—Rising to the Challenge," Rural Health in China Briefing Notes Series, Briefing Note 6 (Washington, DC: World Health Organization, May 2005), 4.

68. UNDP (China), *China Human Development Report, 2007–2008,* 50.

69. NBS of China, *Statistical Communiqué of the People's Republic of China on the 2009 National Economic and Social Development.*

70. NBS of China, *Statistical Communiqué of the People's Republic of China on the 2007 National Economic and Social Development* (Beijing: National Bureau of Statistics of China, 2008), http://www.stats.gov.cn.

71. UNDR (China), *China Human Development Report, 2007–2008,* 58.

72. John G. Taylor, "Poverty and Vulnerability," 93.

73. NBS of China, *Statistical Communiqué of the People's Republic of China on the 2009 National Economic and Social Development.*

74. "Pretend You're a Westerner," *Economist,* February 21, 2009, 44.

75. Lauren Keane, "Chinese Migrants Return to Rural Roots," *Washington Post,* January 2, 2009, A8. See Wright's *Promise of the Revolution* for a firsthand account of riding the rails with China's migrants.

76. "Winning the Food Race," Population Reports, Series M, no. 13, Johns Hopkins School of Public Health, Baltimore, MD, 1997, http://info.k4health.org.

77. Park, "Rural-Urban Inequality in China," 44.

78. John G. Taylor, "Poverty and Vulnerability," 95.

79. Wong and Zhang, "Getting By Without State-Sponsored Social Insurance," 165.

80. Howard W. French, "Rush for Wealth in China's Cities Shatters the Ancient Assurance of Care in Old Age," *New York Times,* November 3, 2006, A8.

81. O'Brien and Li, *Rightful Resistance in Rural China.*

82. Jim Yardley, "Farmers Being Moved Aside by China Real Estate Boom," *New York Times,* December 8, 2004, A1, A10.

83. Christopher Bodeen, "Chinese Paper: Government Critics Sent to Mental Wards," Associated Press, December 8, 2008.

84. Zhao Huanxin, "Farmers' Protests Drop 20% Last Year," *China Daily,* January 31, 2007.

85. Mu Mu-ying, "Number of Group Protests Exceeds 120,000 in 2008," *Cheng Ming* (Hong Kong), February 1, 2009, 10–11.

86. "Protest in China Flares over Land Dispute: State Media," Agence France-Presse, November 18, 2008.

87. "'Thousands Riot' in China Protest," *BBC News,* March 12, 2007, http://news .bbc.co.uk.

88. Vogel, *One Step Ahead in China.*

89. The western region consists of Xinjiang, Tibet, Ningxia, Guangxi, Inner Mongolia, Qinghai, Gansu, Shaanxi, Sichuan, Yunnan, Guizhou, and Chongqing.

90. Remarkably, the center of the Turfan Basin in Xinjiang is 505 meters below sea level; parts of the Tarim Basin are only 1,000 meters above sea level.

91. Alternatively, "Go West," "Open Up the West," and the "Great Western Development" campaigns.

92. Ma and Summers, "Is China's Growth Moving Inland?" 7.

93. Luo, "The Cities vs. the Countryside."

94. Lai, "China's Western Development Program," 450.

95. Hu Zhengyi, "Wen Explains Proposal on Eleventh Five-Year Plan," Chinese government's official web portal, October 20, 2005, http://www.gov.cn.

96. National Development and Reform Commission of the PRC, *Outline of the Eleventh Five-Year Plan for National and Economic Development of the People's Republic of China,* March 8, 2006, http://en.ndrc.gov.cn.

97. Wright, *Promise of the Revolution,* 57.

98. Wright, *Promise of the Revolution,* 58.

99. The CCP Central Committee approved the plan in late 2010. The National People's Congress had not yet approved the plan at the time of publication.

100. L. Gordon Crovitz, "China's Web Crackdown Continues," *Wall Street Journal,* January 11, 2010, A17.

9 The Military and Defense Policy

This army is powerful because all its members have a conscious discipline; they come together and they fight not for the private interests of a few individuals or a narrow clique, but for the interests of the broad masses and of the whole nation. The sole purpose of this army is to stand firmly with the Chinese people and to serve them whole-heartedly.
                                    —Mao Zedong, "On Coalition Government"

"The troops are coming from the northwest corner of Second Ring Road and are already at Muxidi. They're firing real bullets, and the people are burning their trucks," he said, hardly taking a breath between sentences. "I just came from Muxidi. One of the students I was with died—I'm covered with his blood. I've got to run to the square and warn the others."
                                    —Eyewitness report of June 3, 1989, Beijing
                         (in Shen Tong and Marianne Yen, *Almost a Revolution*)

The soldiers are killing the people, the people are killing the soldiers, right in the middle of the capital.
              —Shen Tong, on the Tiananmen Square Massacre of June 4, 1989
                         (in Shen Tong and Marianne Yen, *Almost a Revolution*)

The coverage of the military crackdown in Beijing on June 3–4, 1989, beamed to millions of televisions around the globe, shocked the world for its images of military brutality. More significant, however, was the fact that the images showed the Chinese military attacking civilians. This was incomprehensible to most Chinese. Throughout the history of the People's Republic of China, China's leaders had stressed that the military loves the people, and that the Chinese people love the military. After all, the military was the *People's* Liberation Army. The Chinese military defeated the Japanese occupiers of China and helped create a new China free of foreign interference. It had helped rebuild China after the devastating years of World War II and civil war. It assisted the Korean communists in pushing Western forces away from the China-Korea border. It had loyally disarmed the Red Guards when Mao told it to do so. It had dutifully protected China's borders from foreign troops and had assisted in innumerable humanitarian missions. The images of the 1989 crackdown, beamed by CNN from its base in Tiananmen, did not square with this history. The crackdown against Chinese civilians raised the question of whom, or what, the military served. From its inception some eighty years ago, the Chinese military has always served one master—the Chinese Communist Party (CCP). Consistent with Mao's adage that "political power comes out of the barrel of a gun," the CCP created and controls the military to serve the party first and the nation second. To this end, the party has always made sure that it controls the gun. Party control of the military explains some of the unique features of the military. For instance, the party, state, and military leadership have interlocking memberships. The military, technically an army, has a navy. Until recently, the military owned a vast empire of companies that produced everything from footwear to pirated CDs.

China's military evolved from a loose band of guerrillas to one of the largest conventional militaries in the world. China's military commands a large land force, thousands of missiles, and a navy that continues to expand its presence beyond a defensive perimeter. It also controls an arsenal of nuclear weapons. China claims that its national military policy is purely defensive in nature, and that its defense priorities are to ensure the country's sovereignty, security, and territorial integrity, and to help safeguard the interests of national development and China's expanding national interest. This chapter examines the history of China's military, China's contemporary views of national security, its defense policy, and transformation of the military to meet those needs.

History of the PLA

The Chinese military is collectively known as the People's Liberation Army (PLA). The ground forces are referred to simply as the PLA, but the navy is called the PLA Navy (PLAN) and the air force is known as the PLA Air Force (PLAAF). The PLA's independent strategic missile forces are often referred to as the PLA Second Artillery Corps. The PLA has grown from a loose collection of armed communist revolutionaries seeking the overthrow of the Nationalist government to a modern force of some 2 million men and women seeking regional and possibly global military power.

The PLA was founded on August 1, 1927, in the Jinggang mountainous region of Jiangxi Province. Chinese communists, who had rebelled against the Kuomintang (KMT) in the Nanchang Uprising, joined Nationalist deserters, impoverished peasants, and bandits under the direction of Mao Zedong and Zhu De to form the Workers' and Peasants' Red Army, or Red Army. Under Mao, the Red Army adopted guerrilla tactics against Kuomintang forces. Under pressure from Soviet advisers, however, Mao abandoned guerrilla warfare, and the Red Army was forced to flee Kuomintang forces during the Long March of 1934–1935. Of the eighty-six thousand party members who fled KMT forces, only one-tenth made it to Yan'an in Shaanxi Province. The Long March remains a legend in PLA history, and it enhanced the political power of its survivors.

During the Japanese invasion and occupation of China, the CCP used the Red Army to expand its influence. Red Army units used guerrilla tactics against the Japanese in North China, ultimately defeating Japanese forces there. Drawing on the ability of a highly motivated, largely peasant communist force to defeat a superior foe, Mao in the 1930s and 1940s developed his concept of "people's war," the defining principle of the Red Army and PLA. *People's war* is a political-military doctrine for waging a revolution against a strong, established, governing authority. In addition to the political and military aspects, the third fundamental aspect of this doctrine is the open-ended timeline in which insurgents plan their revolution. People's war involves the whole populace and mobilization of the countryside's resources to wage low-intensity warfare for as long as it takes to defeat an enemy. After Japan's defeat in World War II, Mao used people's war tactics against Kuomintang forces during the Chinese civil war, ultimately defeating them in 1949. The importance of the open-ended aspect of people's war is illustrated by the fact that it is often referred to as "protracted people's war." This long-term aspect of people's war places the impetus of overall military victory on the enemy. As long as the revolutionary force can avoid defeat, while at the same time maintaining the support of the people, they are succeeding in their struggle. The military aspect of people's war focuses on a strategy of exploiting the enemy's weaknesses. This strategy avoids large-scale, open battles with the enemy's technologically superior, better-equipped army. Instead, protracted warfare and fighting small-scale, strategic battles that can be won characterize people's war. Its strategy is based on three phases.

First, the local peasant militia lures a superior foe deep into the countryside to overextend and isolate them. Second, the Red Army bogs the enemy down in a war of attrition using guerrilla tactics. Finally, the Red Army engages the exhausted enemy in regular warfare, ultimately defeating them. The political aspect of people's war is the most important aspect for the victory of the revolutionary force. Guerrilla warfare involves both the military defeat of the enemy and winning over the population. Mao argued that the revolutionary leaders had to spend more time in organization, instruction, agitation, and propaganda work than they did fighting, because their most important job was to win over the people.[1] Without cultivating the fervent support of the people, the long-term military strategy of people's war cannot be sustained.

In 1949, the party renamed the military the People's Liberation Army. The PLA had grown from 1 million soldiers at the end of World War II to 5.5 million troops. Much of the PLA leadership was party members, illustrating the close relationship between party and military. In 1950, Mao sent forces to Tibet to establish PRC control there. Later that year, Mao deployed PLA forces during the Korean War. In June 1950, North Korea invaded the South. The United Nations invoked collective security and sent forces led by US Army general Douglas MacArthur to the South to push back the invasion. Mao became alarmed as UN forces approached the Yalu River, China's border with North Korea. Concerned over how far the UN forces would go, China's leaders launched the Resist America and Aid Korea Campaign. Mao deployed more than two hundred thousand PLA troops under the banner of Chinese People's Volunteers to fight the UN forces. Using "human wave tactics," in which large numbers of troops face a better-equipped military, Chinese troops ejected UN forces from North Korea and continued the fight until June 1953. However, they also incurred heavy casualties. The war in North Korea showed China's leaders just how deficient the PLA was in technology and equipment. Under the 1950 China-Soviet Treaty of Friendship, Alliance, and Mutual Assistance, the PLA received large amounts of military aid from the Soviet Union in the form of equipment and advisers.

With the help of the Soviets, China's leaders in 1951 began large-scale modernization of the PLA. China's leaders wanted to transform a largely infantry army with limited technology and equipment into a modern military force. Soviet advisers helped develop a defense industry along Soviet organizational lines. The PLA adopted Soviet-style armor and artillery-heavy mobile forces, and throughout the 1950s built a wide variety of Soviet-design military equipment. Between 1953 and 1958, China undertook a program of military professionalism. In 1954, China's leaders established the National Defense Council, Ministry of National Defense, and thirteen military regions. In the 1950s, the PLA adopted uniforms, ranks, and insignia, a conscription system, a reserve system, and new rules of discipline all based on the Soviet system. Under Minister of National Defense Peng Dehuai, the PLA created a professional officer corps. Previously, there was little or no distinction among soldiers and officers. Soviet-style modernization of the military disturbed Mao, however, because he believed it was moving the PLA away from his concept of people's war and creating a military bureaucracy. The party wanted to deemphasize military professionalism in favor of Mao's belief in revolutionary purity, economic development, and supremacy of man over weapons. Party-military tensions increased throughout the 1950s. In particular, many top PLA officers resisted Mao's attempt to increase political education of troops, which intensified during the political campaigns of the 1950s. In addition, the military resented Mao's use of PLA troops to carry out economic programs rather than engage in military training during the Great Leap Forward. Party-military tensions came to a head at the 1959 CCP plenum at Lushan, when Mao replaced Minister of National Defense Peng Dehuai, the chief advocate of military modernization, with Lin Biao, who supported the party's position. Under Lin Biao, political training occupied 30 to 40 percent of a soldier's time.

Lin Biao ordered a restructuring of the PLA during the Cultural Revolution. In early 1967, Lin purged the military high command and ordered regional military forces to maintain order, establish military control, and support the revolutionary left. Lin purged any regional force commanders who continued to support his more conservative opponents. During much of the Cultural Revolution, Mao instructed PLA troops to stay in their barracks, even when urban militias engaged in armed battles. In 1967, leftist radicals attacked regional military organizations, obtaining weapons. As China teetered on the brink of civil war, Mao called on the PLA to pacify the students. In July 1968, Mao abolished the Red Guards and ordered the PLA to disarm radical Guards and oversee their exile to the countryside.

Lin Biao's rise had exacerbated growing tensions with the Soviet Union. In 1960, the Soviet Union withdrew from China, which disrupted China's defense industry and weapons development, forcing China to become more self-reliant. China-Soviet relations deteriorated almost to the point of war in 1969. China's leaders ordered the industries located in the China-Soviet border area to be moved hundreds of miles inland. Lin Biao launched a "war preparations" campaign and resumed military training. He increased military procurement, which had slowed in the early years of the Cultural Revolution. He enhanced military preparedness along the China-Soviet border and reorganized thirteen military regions into eleven. After Lin Biao's death in 1971, the PLA began to disengage from politics, and the party purged Lin's supporters from the PLA. Military representation in the National Party Congress, which had reached an all-time high in the 1969 Ninth Party Congress, fell sharply in the 1973 Tenth National Party Congress.

The 1970s PLA Military Reform and Modernization

In 1974, the PLA deployed to the South China Sea to resolve a long-simmering dispute with the Republic of Vietnam over the Paracel (Xisha) Islands. In January of that year, China's leaders claimed that the Paracels were under the "indisputable sovereignty" of the PRC and soon thereafter sent naval forces to the archipelago occupied by Vietnam. The PLA defeated the South Vietnamese forces in the area and occupied the islands.

In the 1970s, unease about Soviet economic and military activities in Vietnam, Afghanistan, and India motivated China's leaders to resume military modernization. Modernization began with two steps. First, the party needed to fill key vacant positions in the military structure. To maintain control of the PLA, the party appointed civilians, rather than military men, to these positions. For instance, the party appointed Deng Xiaoping chief of general staff. Second, the party needed an overall framework for modernization. In 1975, Premier Zhou Enlai announced the Four Modernizations, a program to further develop Chinese agriculture, industry, science and technology, and national defense. Regarding national defense, Zhou aimed to achieve military parity with the developed nations by the middle of the next century. Zhou ranked military modernization last, indicating that the party viewed technical modernization and professionalization as long-term goals. In 1975, the party codified a military modernization program, which instructed the military to withdraw from politics and to concentrate on military training and other defense matters. Factional struggles between party moderates and leftists in the late 1970s led to the dismissal of Deng from all of his posts and stalled military modernization until after the death of Mao Zedong. Mao's death in 1976 and the subsequent arrest of the Gang of Four allowed the PLA to shift away from the concept of people's war and begin modernization. The PLA sought military contacts with the United States and other Western powers. It also stepped up arms sales to parts of the third world, including Cambodia, Burma (Myanmar), Pakistan, Tanzania, North Korea, and several African countries.

PLA Modernization Under Deng Xiaoping

The 1979 China-Vietnam border war was a watershed event in China's military modernization. The war revealed weaknesses in China's military capabilities and motivated China's leaders to accelerate military modernization. The China-Vietnam war was sparked by a dispute over Cambodia. Vietnam had invaded Cambodia in 1978 to depose the PRC-supported communist Khmer Rouge regime with a Vietnam-backed one. In February 1979, China launched a punitive attack against Vietnam over their shared border. The PLA carried out its largest military operation since the Korean War in a limited, offensive, ground-force campaign. Although the 1979 China-Vietnam conflict lasted only sixteen days, China's troops suffered heavy casualties. PLA troops suffered from deficiencies in command and control and supply, as well as from poor mobility and outdated weaponry. The PLA withdrew in March after suffering some twenty thousand casualties.

Deng's first move in accelerating military modernization was to separate the military from politics. To do this, Deng first needed to carry out key personnel changes. Soon after becoming chairman of the party's Central Military Commission (the highest level in the PLA's chain of command) in June 1981, Deng maneuvered his supporters into key appointments. His supporters assumed key positions in the CMC, Ministry of Defense, and the PLA's high command. He replaced some military region and district commanders with supporters. Deng also created the *state* Central Military Commission in 1982 to strengthen civilian control over the armed forces. Although its membership is identical to that of the party's CMC, the state commission stresses the PLA's role as defender of the state, and establishes another supervisory body parallel to party supervision.[2] Deng put defense industries under civilian control and converted a number of military facilities, such as airports and ports, to civilian use or to dual party-PLA use. For instance, the PLAAF opened runways for commercial flights and the navy opened docks for civilian use. The military also provided the state with the use of more than 300 railroads and more than 250 telephone lines, which had previously served strictly military purposes. These changes limited the PLA's influence in economic and political matters. Deng was also able to decrease military participation in national-level political bodies. For instance, in 1978 more than half of the party's Politburo members were military men, but in 1982 only one-third were from the military. Military membership in the larger Central Committee likewise declined, from 30 percent in 1978 to 22 percent in 1982.

The PLA also underwent significant reorganization and restructuring. The PLA shed nonmilitary duties, such as railroad construction, and changed its doctrine from defensive war to a more mobile style of war. It also included modernization of weapons and equipment. Restructuring involved improving training, streamlining personnel, and setting age limits for officers. Deng's efforts to streamline the PLA stemmed from his view that weapons and technology were more important than manpower in war. Deng's view was a radical departure from Mao's concept of people's war, which relied on the mobilization of the masses to overcome a superior foe. Deng called his doctrine "people's war under modern conditions." To streamline the PLA, Deng Xiaoping began efforts to transform a mass army designed for protracted wars of attrition into a leaner and stronger fighting force. The goal was to create a military capable of fighting and winning a limited war. To reach this goal, Deng's first task was to reduce the number of troops, which numbered 4.5 million in the early 1980s. It demobilized 1 million troops by streamlining the headquarters staffs of the three general departments, the military regions, and the military districts; reducing the size of the air force and navy; and retiring officers. At this time, the PLA transferred the People's Armed Police (PAP) to the state. These former military troops became an internal security force.

Deng's people's war under modern conditions required a different battle strategy. Under Mao's people's war, the masses would initially absorb an attack before the PLA launched a counteroffensive. By the 1980s, however, Deng recognized that the masses were no match for a high-tech foe. Instead, he gave greater decisionmaking powers to military regional commanders, who would coordinate their efforts. This strategy was a departure from Mao's system in which autonomous units would fight in isolation from one another. To be effective, Deng's doctrine required significant reorganization of the PLA. In the 1980s, the PLA consolidated thirteen military regions into seven, and thirty-six group armies into twenty-four. It reorganized its eleven military regions into seven: Beijing, Chengdu, Guangzhou, Jinan, Lanzhou, Nanjing, and Shenyang. In 1985, the party reorganized the PLA's several field armies (main-force armies) into group armies, increasing its capability to fight combined-arms warfare.[3] The PLA also began to acquire more sophisticated military technology.

The 1980s ended on a tragic note for the Chinese people and the PLA. Deng Xiaoping called on PLA forces to restore order in China's cities during the spring 1989 demonstrations. In the weeks before the crackdown, Deng Xiaoping flew to military regions far from Beijing to seek the cooperation of military commanders. The army had split between divisions loyal to the hardliners and those sympathetic to the students. Many PLA commanders were reluctant to carry out Deng's orders, particularly because the use of the military against unarmed civilians would hurt public perceptions of the PLA. Western nations and Japan responded to the violent crackdown with sanctions, including prohibitions against selling military technology and equipment to the PRC, thereby disrupting the PLA modernization progress. The PLA purged military personnel who showed hesitation to obey orders during the crackdown. In a mass reshuffling of military brass in spring 1990, Deng rewarded officers loyal to him by moving them into positions of power.

Following the crackdown, Deng turned his attention to concerns that the PLA would remain loyal to the party after his passing. At eighty-five years of age, Deng's health was waning, and he needed to resolve the succession question. Zhao Ziyang, the man Deng once thought would succeed him, had just been deposed as party chief. Deng maneuvered Jiang Zemin into position as CCP general secretary and ordained Jiang as his handpicked successor. Jiang, however, lacked military experience, which made PLA trust and loyalty to him questionable. Deng was particularly concerned with the loyalty of the powerful "Yang family village." Yang Shangkun was then president of China and CMC secretary-general; his younger half brother, General Yang Baibing, was head of the PLA's General Political Department. After Tiananmen, several moves on the part of the Yang brothers made Deng become suspicious of a potential Yang power grab. At the 1992 Fourteenth Party Congress, Deng forced Yang Shangkun to resign as PRC president and CMC chief. Yang Baibing lost his position as chief of the PLA's General Political Department, the body that ensures that the military remains loyal to the party. Although Yang Baibing received a seat on the CCP's Politburo, he lost his influence with the military. PLA officers associated with the Yangs also lost their positions. With the Yangs out of the way, Deng had the upper hand in elevating Jiang Zemin to party and government posts.

Jiang was elected chairman of the party CMC in 1989 and elected chairman of the state CMC a year later. His first move was to ensure his command of the PLA and to secure its loyalty. To meet his goal, Jiang carried out four reforms. First, he imposed mandatory retirement ages on senior officers. This move had the effect of removing many senior officers from the PLA, Yang Shangkun being one of them. Second, he rotated senior commanders and commissars among the different duty stations. This action limited their influence in local politics. Third, he ordered pay raises for both officers and troops. Fourth, Jiang made regular visits to military posts throughout China to show concern for the troops' welfare. These last two moves had the effect of boosting military morale.

Despite these efforts at modernization, the PLA was still intended to fight limited ground wars. Ironically, the 1990–1991 Gulf War—in which China's military played no role—was another watershed event in revising China's approach to future warfare. By the late 1980s, China's military establishment had begun to see the United States as a wounded hegemon, meaning that the United

States had reached its peak as a military power and was on a slow decline in international influence. The 1990–1991 Gulf War changed that view. Astounded by US technological advances evidenced by that war, China's leaders realized that its emphasis on fighting and winning a limited ground war was misplaced. China's leaders had expected US forces to get bogged down in a war of attrition, but the reality was that airpower softened the enemy and limited the ground war to only 100 hours. Based on lessons learned from the Gulf War, namely that future wars would rely heavily on technology, the PLA high command decided to revise their strategy. After 1991, the PLA would begin planning for a "limited war under high technology conditions."

Recognizing that China's military was woefully deficient in high-tech warfare capabilities, China's leaders redirected investment into research and development of advanced weapons and technologies. They placed high priority on mastering electronic warfare and electronic countermeasures, improving ballistic missile production and precision-guided munitions, building satellites and early warning and command systems, building an advanced communication relay station, investigating laser technology, developing artificial intelligence, improving avionics and mastering in-flight refueling, and developing anti–ballistic missile systems.[4] Because China had neither the knowledge nor the financing to develop all of these new weapons and technologies, it turned to Russia for assistance. Throughout the 1990s, Russia sold to China some $6 billion in fighters, submarines, destroyers, helicopters, antiaircraft missiles, transport aircraft, aircraft engines, and other equipment.[5]

PLA Structure

The PLA is the military arm of the CCP and serves the goals of the party, not of the state. For instance, the PLA swears allegiance to the CCP, not to the state constitution, as is common in the West. It answers to, but is not controlled by, the National People's Congress, and is not accountable to any elected body.

PLA headquarters is organized into the General Staff Department (GSD), General Political Department (GPD), General Logistics Department (GLD), and General Armaments Department. The General Staff Department (also known as the General Staff Headquarters) is the leading organ of all of the PLA's military work. The General Staff Department includes the headquarters of PLA ground forces. It organizes and leads the construction of the PLA, and organizes and commands its military operations. The General Staff has departments in charge of operations, intelligence, training, adjutant and force structure, and mobilization. The General Political Department is meant to ensure that the PLA remains loyal to the CCP, and the CCP created it in 1931 for this reason. The GPD's functions are to train and supervise political cadres (known as commissars) of the PLA, engage in civil-military relations and propaganda work, monitor members of the military, supervise the military justice system of the PLA, oversee promotions and assignments in the PLA, and manage the Communist Youth League in the PLA.

The General Logistics Department is responsible for transportation and supply, communications, supply of fuel and ammunition, and construction of military installations and barracks. Its Production Management subdivision manages PLA enterprises and businesses. The GLD also has a Health Division and a Foreign Affairs Division, responsible for increasing business contacts with the outside world. To enhance understanding of advanced logistic operations, the GLD maintains logistics academies and universities, sends GLD personnel overseas for study, and seeks military-to-military contacts with other countries, including the United States.

The General Armaments Department (also known as the General Equipment Department) manages the procurement, research and development, and production of arms and equipment for the PLA, primarily through contractors. The director of each of the general departments is a member of the CMC.

Military Units

The PLA has 2.3 million active-duty forces. Ground forces comprise the vast majority (74 percent) of the total force structure. An estimated 1.7 million military personnel are in the ground forces, 250,000 in the navy (including 26,000 in naval aviation, 10,000 marines, and 28,000 coastal defense forces), an estimated 400,000 to 420,000 in the air force, and 90,000 to 100,000 in the strategic missile forces. Reservists number an estimated 500,000 to 800,000. Paramilitary forces in the People's Armed Police number an estimated 1.5 million. Recruitment into the armed forces is both voluntary and involuntary. The involuntary component comes from a system of conscription that is somewhat different from that commonly used in the West. Under the Chinese variation, the PLA determines the number of conscripts needed, which produces quotas that are imposed on local governments. Local cadres are charged with providing a set number of soldiers or sailors. If they fail to find enough volunteers to fill the quota, they must order unwilling local residents to enter service. The term of service is two years. Annual quota numbers for PLA and PAP conscripts are estimated to be five hundred thousand. The vast majority of noncommissioned officers are thought to have been conscripts who opted to stay in the military.[6]

PLA ground forces are organized into seven military regions, headquartered in Shenyang in the northeast, Beijing in the north, Lanzhou in the west, Chengdu in the southwest, Guangzhou in the south, Jinan in central China, and Nanjing in the east. There are twenty-eight provincial military districts, four centrally controlled garrison commands (which coincide with the centrally administered municipalities of Beijing, Tianjin, Shanghai, and Chongqing), and twenty-one integrated group armies. The group armies have strengths of between thirty thousand

and sixty-five thousand troops. Each group army typically has two or three infantry divisions, one armored division or brigade, one artillery division or brigade, and one joint surface-to-air missile or antiaircraft artillery brigade.[7]

The navy (PLAN) is organized into North Sea (headquartered at Qingdao, Shandong Province), East Sea (headquartered at Ningbo, Zhejiang Province), and South Sea (headquartered at Zhanjiang, Guangdong Province) Fleets. Each fleet has destroyer, submarine, and coastal patrol flotillas, and naval air stations. China has thirty-one major naval bases: seven associated with the North Sea Fleet, eight with the East Sea Fleet, and sixteen with the South Sea Fleet. The air force (PLAAF) has five air corps and thirty-two air divisions. The major air force headquarters coincide with the seven military regions. The PLAAF has more than 140 air bases and airfields, including ready access to China's major regional and international airports. The Second Artillery Corps, or strategic missile forces, is organized into seven missile divisions based in the military regions, with the central headquarters at Qinghe, north of Beijing. The corps also maintains training and testing bases. The six operational bases have twenty-one launch brigades. Figure 9.1 presents the organization of China's military.

Defense Industries and PLA, Inc.

China's defense industry produces weapons systems for national defense. China's defense industry consists of the following ten corporations:

- China First Aviation Corporation (AVIC), responsible for fighter aircraft, bombers, transports, advanced training jets, and commercial airliners
- China Second Aviation Corporation, responsible for helicopters and unmanned aerial vehicles
- China Aerospace Science Technology Corporation, responsible for satellites and space launch vehicles
- China Aerospace Machinery Electronics Corporation, responsible for missiles, electronics, and ballistics
- North China Industrial Group Corporation (NORINCO), responsible for armored vehicles, artillery, and ordnance
- South China Industrial Group Corporation, responsible for trucks, cars, and motorcycles
- China State Shipbuilding Corporation (North), responsible for destroyers, submarines, and large-container and commercial vessels
- China State Shipbuilding Corporation (South), responsible for frigates and smaller surface combatants, submarines, and merchant ships
- China National Nuclear Corporation (CNNC), responsible for nuclear fuel, energy, and weapons
- China Nuclear Engineering and Construction Corporation, responsible for nuclear power plants[8]

Figure 9.1 Organization of China's Military

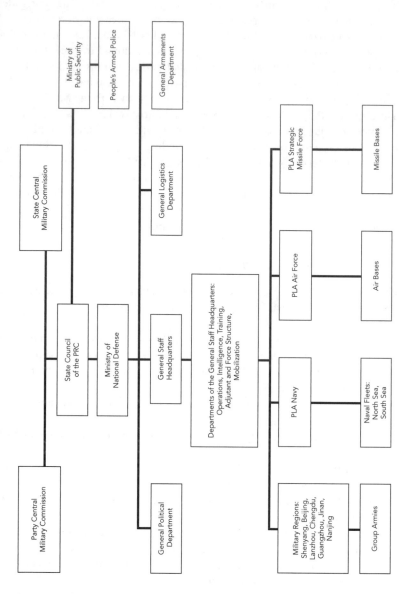

Although it is difficult to obtain exact numbers of defense-related enterprises, scholars have estimated that in the 1990s, China's military-industrial complex consisted of as many as a thousand enterprises employing some 3 million workers and some three hundred thousand engineers and technicians. NORINCO employed approximately eight hundred thousand people, China Nuclear Corporation employed three hundred thousand, and AVIC employed some 1.3 million.[9] These numbers do not include subcontractors and support services, many of which are state-owned enterprises. Many of these SOEs were money-losers in the 1990s and were closed or merged in the early 2000s. The quality of product that these industries produce is questionable. For the most part, they fail to measure up against other major military producers in the world. Chinese conventional weapons and technologies appear to be about twenty years behind the state of the art.

China has made progress in developing a domestic weapons industry, but also pursues joint development with Israel and Russia, receiving their technical assistance in developing a domestically produced modern jet fighter and trying to develop and improve its midair refueling and aerial troop transport capabilities.[10] It also purchases weapons from Russia and has allegedly stolen classified

The North China Industrial Group Corporation (NORINCO)

Probably the Chinese defense company best known to Westerners is the North China Industrial Group Corporation (Beifang Gongye), popularly known as NORINCO. NORINCO is an important supplier for the Chinese military, and produces high-tech defense products such as precision strike systems, amphibious assault weapons and equipment, and antiaircraft and antimissile systems. It produces night antiterrorism and antiriot equipment and small arms. It also develops high-technology civilian-use machinery, chemicals, construction machinery, and other products. Established in 1980 by the State Council, NORINCO is a state-owned corporation managed by the central government. It maintains factories, research institutes, and trading companies. It has established more than 100 joint ventures and has eighty-two overseas companies and offices. NORINCO subsidiaries in the United States include Beta Chemical, Beta First, Beta Lighting, Beta Unitex, China Sports, Forte Lighting, Larin, and NIC International. In 2003, the Bush administration imposed sanctions on NORINCO for allegedly selling missile-related equipment and technology to Iran. NORINCO denied that the items were for missile-related purposes and called the sanctions "groundless and unjustified" and "entirely unreasonable." Some rifles built by NORINCO are still allowed to be imported into the United States. (Information drawn from the North China Industrial Group Corporation website, http://www .norinco.com) information, specifically US nuclear warhead and ballistic missile technology. China is strengthening its air force with the purchase of advanced fighters from Russia and is improving its navy with purchases of Russian ships, particularly better submarines. Its domestic nuclear submarine program remains unimpressive, however.[11] China also has improved its antisatellite program. In January 2007, China conducted its first antisatellite weapon demonstration, successfully hitting its own satellite and raising concerns in the United States about China's ability to destroy US satellites. In early 2011, China rolled out its first stealth fighter, the J-20 prototype, surprising some analysts who thought that such development was still years away. The US government was forced to acknowledge that China's aggressive military investment is paying off in faster-than-expected development of sophisticated weapons systems. China's stealth fighter is designed to challenge the US F-22 Raptor, the world's only fully operational stealth fighter, and its increasingly sophisticated weapons systems increase China's ability to challenge US defense of Taiwan or naval superiority in Asia.

PLA Enterprises and Businesses

Distinct from the defense industry are PLA business units. PLA businesses directly involve and employ PLA personnel, and their business activities directly contribute to the military's total expenditure.

Traditionally, these businesses provided food service, equipment repair, and transport for the military. PLA businesses trace back to the 1930s, when self-sustaining Red Army units maintained farms, factories, and businesses for their own resources. The PLA retained these businesses throughout the decades, but changed their mission in the 1970s. PLA businesses began producing civilian goods in the 1970s, a practice that accelerated under the Four Modernizations. Following adoption of the Four Modernizations, in which national defense was ranked last, the government cut the military budget and slowed procurement of arms. To make up for lost revenue, the Chinese government in the 1980s encouraged PLA businesses to convert to the production of nonmilitary goods or engage in arms sales. In the 1980s, China increased its arms sales to the third world, becoming the world's fifth largest supplier of weapons to developing countries.[12] Low budgets led the PLA to establish commercial industries, beginning with the sale of excess weapons and equipment. By the late 1990s, 80 percent of PLA business output was consumer goods. The PLA had more than ten thousand enterprises employing some seven hundred thousand people. PLA companies had developed more than twenty-five hundred civilian products, constituting 55 percent of PLA industrial output. In the 1990s, direct PLA economic involvement produced profits between $1 billion and $2 billion a year. With more than fifty worldwide conglomerates, PLA businesses comprised approximately 3 percent of China's GDP in the late 1990s. Total revenue of the PLA's businesses equaled the annual national defense budget allocation.

The military's business activities resulted in corruption. The CMC gave the PLA significant freedoms in which to conduct economic activities, but demanded little financial accountability. A 1992 audit by the GLD found more than $100 million in unreported funds in more than three hundred illegal bank accounts. Many businesses underreported profits to avoid paying the GLD. Money not collected by the GLD was supposed to be invested in training or upgrading the standard of living for PLA units. Instead, units used these profits to purchase luxury goods, such as expensive cars, or to provide officers with bonuses. Many PLA businesses also failed to pay taxes. By the 1990s, the CMC was no longer capable of monitoring all of the PLA's financial activities. Rampant smuggling by the military during the economic crisis in Asia in early 1998 cost the government hundreds of billions of yuan of customs revenue. For instance, six PLA and PAP companies had been smuggling oil, bankrupting the country's two geographical oil monopolies. In another case, Premier Zhu Rongji accused the GPD's Tiancheng Group of having avoided paying 50 million yuan ($6.1 million) in import and sales taxes after purchasing a shipment of partially processed iron ore from Australia.[13]

Fed up with military corruption, Jiang in 1998 ordered the PLA to divest itself of its business holdings. Jiang saw the businesses as a source of corruption in the PLA and as a distraction from the PLA's military duties. By the end of the year, the PLA and PAP transferred nearly three thousand businesses to local governments and closed another four thousand. More than 82 percent of GLD enterprises transferred or closed. In the early 2000s, however, up to ten thousand smaller businesses remained in the military. The PLA reorganized, but retained, some of the larger conglomerates.[14]

The PLA currently manages a number of businesses in the service industry, owns factories, and sells products on the global market. PLA businesses provide revenue for its modernization. Most PLA factories manufacture consumer goods such as motorcycles, minivans, trucks, televisions, refrigerators, satellite television dishes, cameras, cell phones, and contact lenses. Other factories are engaged in state-of-the-art weapons. PLA businesses are engaged in pharmaceuticals, transportation, construction, hotel management, agriculture, production of civilian goods, and sales of nuclear arms and technology. These businesses directly involve and employ PLA personnel. The PLA owns up to 50 percent of all hospitals in China. Some of the PLA's largest businesses are trading companies that engage in arms sales and the export of other nonmilitary goods. The PLA uses the foreign exchange generated by these sales to buy raw materials for PLA factories. The four most profitable PLA businesses are China Poly Group (also known as Polytechnologies Corporation), China Xinxing, China Carrie, and China Songhai.

PLA enterprises operate at three levels: national, regional or provincial, and units. The party's CMC has given authority to the GLD to manage PLA businesses. The GLD requires larger PLA businesses to associate with a military command organization or with a military region. Each national-level military command organization has at least one conglomerate under its control. For instance, the GSD controls the China Poly Group. The GPD, which is responsible for the PLA's political education, controls China Tiancheng Corporation, a group with seventeen subsidiaries throughout China. The GLD runs China Xinxing Corporation, which employs one hundred thousand workers in sixty factories throughout China and has more than seventeen joint ventures with Western companies. It exports military supplies, logistical equipment, and other goods produced by GLD factories. It also manages joint-venture hotels for the PLA. Poly Group (Baoli, literally "keep the profit"), a General Staff company, is the PLA's primary arms exporter, but also engages in property development. It was founded in 1984 when the General Staff, which determined that it wanted its own arms trading company, concluded that it would be appropriate to do so openly. Poly Group reports to the armament department of the GSD and is authorized to sell almost any Chinese conventional weapon, including short- and medium-range ballistic missiles.

PLA joint ventures partner with both domestic and foreign firms. Although they are subordinate to military units, they receive no funds from the defense budget. They are self-run and are responsible for their own profits and losses.[15] PLA enterprises provide resources and services to the military. They are spurred by the profit motive and participate in the domestic and global market. For instance, the PLA runs trading companies that import nonmilitary equipment and technology, such as advanced medical equipment for hospitals and raw materials for PLA business ventures.

Regional and provincial military units also manage conglomerates and trading companies. For instance, a trading company affiliated with the Chengdu Military Region exports to more than a hundred countries and regions, making it one of the PLA's top foreign exchange earners. Individual military units also manage their own businesses. In the 1980s, PLA combat units began opening various businesses, some in the service sector, such as hotels and restaurants. Other units hired themselves out to work on projects, or engaged in smuggling and other illicit activities. These activities were not the work of rogue elements, but were approved at the upper echelons of PLA headquarters. Heavy PLA involvement in these ventures led to high levels of graft and corruption. In 1993, CMC chief Jiang Zemin ordered military units to divest themselves of these businesses or relinquish their control to a higher PLA organization. Jiang ran into significant resistance, because even though many of the businesses were money-losers, the officers who ran them enjoyed significant perks as businessmen.

Civil-Military Relations

Civil-military relations refers to the relationship between a nation's military and a nation's civilian society, which includes the government. Civil-military relations in China are unique due to the role of the CCP within China. Unlike many countries, such as the United States, the civilian government of the PRC does not control the military. Instead, the CCP holds the ultimate authority over the PLA, other security services, and national defense policy in general.

Consistent with Mao's dictum that "the party commands the gun, and the gun must never be allowed to command the party," the party has ultimate authority over the PLA.[16] To maintain control of the military, leadership of the PLA is housed in the party's Central Military Commission. The CMC is the command authority of the military. It sets policy for the PLA and enables the party to meet with top military leaders to make major decisions and coordinate policy. Essential to the party's control of the military is a system of interlocking membership of CMC and PLA officials. The commission, which is chaired by China's president, has three vice chairmen, each a general in the PLA ground forces, and seven members representing various components of the PLA. The CMC and Ministry of National Defense dually administer operational control of the military. The chair of the CMC functions essentially as the commander in chief of the PLA, with final say on military matters. The CMC chair is always a senior party member and is usually the chair or general secretary of the CCP. The first CMC chair was the founder of the Red Army, Zhu De. Previous CMC chairs include Mao, Hua Guofeng, Deng Xiaoping, Jiang Zemin, and Hu Jintao. The minister of defense is a member of the CMC. The rest of the CMC are senior party leaders or senior PLA officers.

Despite the legal authority of the CMC chair, the loyalty and obedience of the PLA historically was based on the personal relationship between the party leader and the PLA, as was the case with Mao and Deng. Such a personal basis for a leader's authority can be hazardous to a country's long-term stability, especially during transfers of power. The smooth succession of Jiang, who had almost no connections with the PLA, as the head of the party, the state, and the CMC was helped by several measures he took to win over the military. These measures included compelling older officers (who were more resistant to new leadership) to retire, increasing military pay and benefits, and increasing the military budget in general. Jiang's successor, Hu Jintao, also came to power without a strong relationship with the military. Hu's 2004 succession as CMC chair from Jiang (who was still legally eligible to remain in that post) to the new PRC president and party head illustrates that civilian, or at least party, control of the PLA is shifting from a precarious personal basis to a more stable institutional basis.

Military membership in key state and political offices reached the highest point under Lin Biao, but decreased after 1978. In 1969, 44 percent of the party's Central Committee had military backgrounds; in 2002, only 22 percent of the Central Committee came from the PLA.[17] The Politburo saw a similar decline in the percentage of members from military backgrounds. In 1969, 40 percent of the Politburo had military backgrounds. By 2002, the proportion of members from the military fell to 8 percent.[18] As of 2009, there are no PLA personnel on the Politburo's Standing Committee.

Ensuring that the PLA stays loyal to the CCP is the job of the General Political Department. The GPD is responsible for party propaganda and political indoctrination in the PLA. It also monitors the behavior of military personnel, the military justice system, and military assignments. An important method of maintaining party control throughout the military is the GPD's use of political commissars, sometimes called political directors or instructors. The GPD assigns commissars to military units, at all levels, to serve as the party's representative in that unit.[19] In the past, commissars held the ultimate authority in their units, even able to dictate orders to units' commanding officers. These original commissars were civilian CCP members. However, since the mid-1930s, CCP leaders have decreased the power of the political commissar significantly, because the overpoliticization of the PLA had a negative impact on military effectiveness. Today most commissars come from the PLA officer corps and no longer exercise as much control over their units.[20] A key function of commissars today is approving all promotions within their unit, which is an attempt to ensure that only those loyal to the CCP rise in the ranks of the PLA.[21] The CCP also exercises control over the PLA through party committees, called party branches in smaller units, which are within every unit in the PLA.

In the 1990s, part of the PLA shifted to the People's Armed Police. The PAP was founded in 1982, with the task of providing domestic security for the PRC. The PAP was composed of PLA units, which had similar missions. Over time, the PAP's mission had expanded to include border security; suppressing civil unrest (although the public security police are often used to suppress riots or break up protests among farmers, minorities, and the unemployed); securing important state facilities such as mines, transportation infrastructure, and communications facilities; firefighting; guarding prisons; and protecting high-ranking Chinese and foreign officials. The PAP put down ethnic unrest in Tibet in 2008 and Xinjiang in 2009.

In the 1990s, there were further personnel transfers to the PAP from the PLA.[22] Western analysts estimate that the PAP has 1.5 million members.[23] As in the PLA, PAP units have political commissars assigned to them. Although the PAP is not a part of China's military, it is a part of the armed forces, and as such falls under the command of the CMC. However, the appropriate ministry oversees the daily operations of the PAP's special sections. For example, the railway ministry oversees the PAP units responsible for railroads.

The Military Budget and Expenditures

In the early reform era (1978 to late 1980s), China's leaders subordinated military modernization to economic development. During the 1980s, China's official defense budget decreased nearly 13 percent. Low defense budgets and the lack of domestic technical capabilities hampered the PLA's modernization throughout the 1980s and early 1990s. China's leaders began to reverse this trend in 1989 by launching an ambitious army modernization program. Since then, Chinese defense spending has increased by an average of 12.9 percent annually. The defense budget doubled between 1989 and 1994, and almost doubled again between 1994 and 1999.[24] Throughout the early twenty-first century, China continued double-digit increases in its defense spending. China's defense budget grew a whopping 17.5 percent in 2008 and 18.5 percent in 2009. The defense budget rose 12.7 percent in 2011 to 602 billion yuan ($91.7 billion) (see Figure 9.2).

Foreign scholars estimate the budgets' actual sizes to be between three and four times the official amount. Official budgets are low because, unlike military budgets of other countries, China does not include some portions of personnel cost (which are covered locally), research and development for nuclear weapons, purchases of foreign weapons and equipment, and income from PLA businesses. The much lower pay of PLA troops also significantly reduces the defense budget.

Figure 9.2 China's Defense Budget

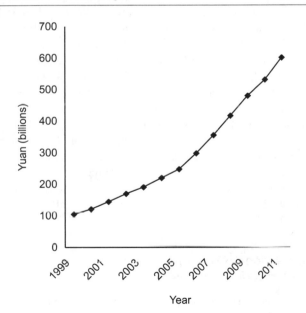

Source: Information Office of the State Council, PRC, *China's National Defense* for the years 2000, 2002, 2004, 2006, 2008, 2010 (Beijing: Information Office of the State Council). http://www .china.org.cn/e-white/index.htm. The 2011 figure is an estimate.

China's National Defense Policy

China claims that its national defense policy is purely defensive in nature. Its defense priorities are protection of national sovereignty, security, and territorial integrity; safeguarding the interests of national development; and safeguarding the interests of the Chinese people.[25] However, its military modernization and defense buildup indicate that China has more than merely defensive capabilities in mind. The PLA is currently in the process of transforming from Deng's "people's war under modern conditions," in which a mass army engages in protracted wars of attrition on its territory, to one capable of winning short-duration, high-intensity conflicts along its periphery against high-tech adversaries (namely the United States).[26] China refers to this approach as preparing for "local wars under conditions of informationization."

China's assertions that its military buildup and modernization are merely defensive can only be fully understood within the context of what the PRC means by *defensive*. According to both nationalist sentiment and Chinese law, the sovereign territory of the PRC includes not only mainland China and nearby islands, but also Taiwan, the Diaoyu Islands (also called the Senkaku Islands), the Penghu Islands (the Pescadores), the Dongsha Islands (the Pratas Islands), the Xisha Islands (the Paracel Islands), and the Nansha Islands (the Spratly Archipelago), among others.[27] Each of these entities is claimed by at least one other country. China also claims the whole South China Sea and part of the East China Sea, a violation of the Law of the Sea Convention, which China has ratified. These maritime claims are reflected in the first island chain of the PLAN's island chain policy, which delineates the area China views as its defensive maritime perimeter. China has demonstrated its willingness to use or threaten military force if it believes that other nations are infringing on its sovereignty. For example, in 1988 the PLAN sank two Vietnamese naval vessels, killing dozens, near the Spratly Islands, and in 2001 a PLA fighter jet collided with a propeller-driven US Navy reconnaissance plane as the Chinese jet was harassing the slower US plane, seventy miles offshore from Hainan. China's use of terms such as *far sea defense* and *defensive counterattack* to describe military action beyond its borders illustrates the offensive potential of the PRC's so-called defensive military buildup.[28]

Safeguarding National Sovereignty, Security, and Territorial Integrity

China's security situation is stable on the whole. China's economic and military modernization has increased China's national strength. In the 1960s and 1970s, China actively supported insurgency movements and the destabilization of governments in Southeast Asia, the Middle East, Africa, and Latin America. Since Mao's death in 1976, however, China has transitioned from a revolutionary state that supported communist revolution abroad to a status quo power that seeks a peaceful and stable international environment. China's post-Mao leaders recognize that a peaceful international environment best facilitates China's economic growth and development.

External threats to China's security have greatly diminished since the collapse of the Soviet Union. In recent years, China has moved large numbers of troops from the 2,700-mile-long border it shares with Russia. Nevertheless, the PLA stresses the need to be prepared for potential conflict along the country's continental periphery. China shares a border with fourteen nations and maritime boundaries with seven. In addition to border disputes with the former Soviet Union, India, and Vietnam, China has had territorial disputes with nearly all of its continental and maritime neighbors. For instance, China is still engaged in a border dispute with India over Kashmir. India does not recognize Pakistan's ceding of historic lands to China in 1964. Although China and India in 2005 signed an agreement on guiding principles, the dispute remains unresolved. China and Bhutan are also engaged in negotiations to demarcate their border. China asserts sovereignty over the Spratly Islands, together with Malaysia, the Philippines, Taiwan, Vietnam, and Brunei. China disputes with North Korea certain islands in the Yalu and Tumen Rivers. China also wants to stem the flow of illegal migration from North Korea by building a fence along portions of their border.

In the past decade, however, China has reached agreements with at least some of its neighbors over territorial disputes. For instance, China and Russia have demarcated islands at the Amur River border, and China and Tajikistan have begun demarcating their boundary. China has been willing to compromise with its neighbors on some territorial issues, but is less willing to compromise on others. For instance, China and Vietnam in 2008 signed a treaty demarcating their land borders, but did not address the sea border, which they continue to dispute. Although China and Japan in 2008 signed an agreement to temporarily set aside an EEZ (exclusive economic zone) dispute and jointly develop the Chunxiao/Shirakaba gas field, the two countries continue to dispute possession of the Senkaku Islands. China also continues to reject Japan's unilaterally declared line in the East China Sea, the site of intensive hydrocarbon exploration and exploitation.

Since the mid-1990s, China has pursued a security policy consistent with its New Security Concept (*xin anquan guan*), which seeks to replace Cold War antagonisms with a policy of security through diplomatic and economic interaction.[29] Since adoption of the New Security Concept, China has increased its presence and participation in international nongovernmental organizations (INGOs). China belongs to seventy major international organizations, including almost all key security regimes. The New Security Concept has had some positive effect on China's security environment in the 1990s and early twenty-first century, including better relations with the Association of Southeast Asian

Nations (ASEAN), the formation of the Shanghai Cooperation Organization, and participation in six-party talks to control nuclear proliferation in North Korea.[30] Since 1990, China has contributed about 7,500 peacekeepers to United Nations peacekeeping operations. For instance, in early 2008, 1,963 Chinese peacekeepers were serving on UN missions in countries including the Democratic Republic of Congo, Liberia, Lebanon, and Sudan.[31]

Nationalism

China's desire to safeguard national sovereignty, security, and territorial integrity is firmly rooted in its past. Few Westerners fathom the depths of Chinese nationalism and the drive to protect territorial integrity. To grasp Chinese nationalism and territorial integrity, one needs to understand the One Hundred Years of Humiliation the Chinese suffered under foreign occupation. Beginning with the Opium Wars of the early nineteenth century, Western powers divided and occupied China's territory, wresting concessions from the weak and corrupt Qing Dynasty. The Western powers also gained significant control over the Chinese economy through their trade practices (Chapter 2). Because of this history, China's leaders are sensitive to real and perceived threats to its sovereignty, security, and territorial integrity. China has not shied away from using military force to settle territorial disputes. For instance, China fought a border war with India in 1962 and fought Vietnam over control of the Paracel Islands in 1974. In more recent years, China has settled territorial disputes peacefully. Since 1998, China has settled eleven land territorial disputes with six of its neighbors. Several disputes remain, however, particularly over China's EEZ claims and ownership of offshore oil and gas deposits. China is also mindful of internal threats to its security. For instance, China's leaders claim that separatist movements in Tibet and Xinjiang threaten to undermine national stability and have cracked down hard on separatists in those regions, whom the Chinese government accuses of threatening China's territorial integrity. China's leaders view the political separation of Taiwan from mainland China in the same light. They claim that pro-independence activists on Taiwan hinder the island's unification with mainland China. China's leaders reserve the right to use force to unite Taiwan with China if they determine that Taiwan seeks permanent separation from the mainland.

The PLA believes that a large and powerful armed force is necessary to safeguard China's territorial integrity, and they extend this belief to the Taiwan question. Under the PRC's One-China principle, Taiwan is an inseparable part of China. China's 2005 Anti-Secession Law states that China may use nonpeaceful means if "secessionist forces" secede from China or if possibilities for peaceful reunification have been exhausted. In recent years, China has increased its ability to take military action against Taiwan, and the balance of military power is shifting in China's favor. For many years, Taiwan enjoyed dominance of the airspace over the Taiwan Strait. This is no longer so, and the reversal has given China more military options with which to coerce Taiwan. These options include a maritime quarantine or blockade; electronic warfare to knock out Taiwan's political, military, and economic infrastructure and damage public confidence in the Taiwan government; a missile campaign; and an amphibious invasion. The last option is unlikely at this time as China does not yet have the capability to invade and conquer Taiwan, particularly if the United States were to intervene. To deter Taiwan from considering permanent separation from the mainland, the PLA has built up its short-range missiles opposite the island. It currently has more than a thousand missiles pointed at Taiwan.

Safeguarding the Interests of National Development: Maritime Security

China's defense strategy includes protecting and advancing China's broader political and economic interests. China's 2008 Defense White Paper states explicitly that a key component of China's defense policy is to safeguard the interests of national development. China's civilian and military leaders agree that China's economic and political power is contingent upon access to and use of the sea, and that China needs a strong navy to safeguard its maritime interests.

To defend national interests, PLA leaders have devised the Far Sea Defense, a new concept that emphasizes offensive operations beyond the first island chain and China's two-hundred-nautical-mile EEZ. The Far Sea Defense requires more large and medium-sized warships and aircraft carrier groups. The PLAN is considering building several aircraft carrier groups by 2020. China's goal is to become a global maritime force by 2050. As a global naval power, China would be able to challenge US naval supremacy in China's maritime periphery and would have access to vast sums of sea-based resources, such as oil and gas, critical to fueling its rapid economic modernization. Reaching this goal depends on China's ability to control the areas delineated by its first and second island chains. The first island chain runs north to south from the Aleutians through the Kuriles, Japan, the Ryukyus, Taiwan, the Philippines, and Indonesia. It includes all of the South China Sea (see Figure 9.3). Although the PLAN has improved its navy with the purchase of Russian ships, particularly their better submarines, and has developed amphibious assault capability, it has already fallen behind on plans for it to be able to control the first island chain. An essential component of the strategy, China's domestic nuclear submarine program remains unimpressive. China's inability to control the first island chain has set back plans to control the second island chain, which reaches as far as the Bonin, Mariana, and Carolina Islands.

Of particular interest to China is the South China Sea. The maritime area of the South China Sea is important because it has extensive natural resources, including fish, oil, natural gas, and minerals. In addition, more than half of the

Figure 9.3 Map of China's First and Second Island Chains of Defense

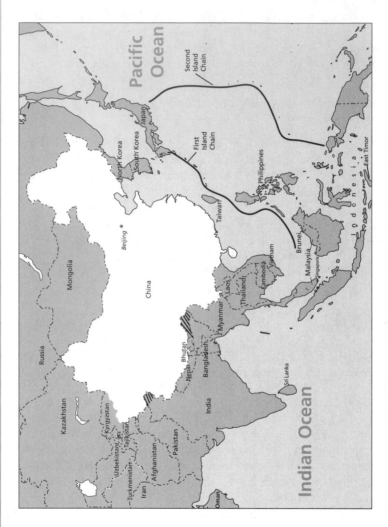

Source: Adapted from map courtesy of the University of Texas Libraries, University of Texas at Austin.

world's merchant fleet (by tonnage) sails through the South China Sea each year. Eighty percent of oil shipped to Japan, South Korea, and Taiwan passes through South China Sea shipping lanes. China asserts sovereignty over the Spratly Islands, together with Malaysia, the Philippines, Taiwan, Vietnam, and Brunei. China bases its claims to the Spratlys and Paracels on historical ties to the islands. China's leaders claim that the Spratly and Paracel Islands have been part of Chinese territory since the Han Dynasty in the second century. China's leaders base their legal claim on the principle of first discovery, citing visits by Chinese fishermen based at Hainan Island.

In 1992, the National People's Congress passed the Law of the Territorial Sea and Contiguous Zone, claiming jurisdiction over the entire South China Sea. Adoption of the law marks a major development in China's maritime policy. By claiming the territory by legal fiat, the law contradicts China's promise to resolve territorial disputes through friendly discussions. The law claims inviolable sovereignty over not only the mainland and its offshore islands, but also Taiwan and its affiliated islands (such as the Pescadores/Penghu), and the Paracel and Spratly Islands. Although the law permits nonmilitary ships passage through its territorial sea, it asserts a right to evict other nations' naval vessels from its territorial waters and authorizes the navy to pursue foreign ships violating its regulations.[32] To defend its interests in the South China Sea, China has established a major presence in the Paracels. China views the Spratlys and Paracels as an essential part of its defense plan to keep hostile naval forces away from the coast. China has built a pier and airstrip on the disputed Spratlys capable of handling PLA ships and aircraft, as well as oil tanks, gun emplacements, and ammunition storage bunkers, all essential for staging offensive operations in the Spratlys. A signal intelligence station on Rocky Island, one of the highest points in the area, covers military signal activity in the area. Silkworm antiship cruise missile installations have also been reported in the Paracels. The Silkworm has a range of some fifty-nine miles and could be used to threaten shipping traffic. The possibility of this sort of militarization by China in the Spratlys is of real concern to regional military security planners and in Washington due to the ability of China to then command the sea-lanes.

In 2002, China signed the Declaration on the Conduct of Parties in the South China Sea, which eased tensions in the Spratlys. Since then, Vietnam and China have expanded construction of facilities in the Spratlys. In March 2005, the national oil companies of China, the Philippines, and Vietnam signed a joint accord on marine seismic activities in the Spratly Islands. Tensions remain, however. For example, China occupies some of the Paracel Islands also claimed by Vietnam and Taiwan and has interrupted Vietnamese hydrocarbon exploration in the South China Sea. Tensions flared in June 2011 when Vietnam accused Chinese ships of cutting cables belonging to Vietnamese oil survey vessels in two separate incidents. Vietnam responded with live-fire drills in the South China Sea.

Force Projection

Force projection refers to the ability of a nation's military to conduct military operations away from its borders. The following sections on China's military modernization address some of China's efforts to develop such capabilities. China's current force projection capabilities are limited, but improving. China has made improvements in relevant technologies such as airlift, sealift, carriers, amphibious capability, missiles, and logistics. To meet its national defense goals, China is making advances in its missile capabilities, naval power, space program, and cyber warfare.

Revolution in Military Affairs (with Chinese Characteristics)

The term *revolution in military affairs* (RMA) refers to the fundamental changes in the nature of warfare that occur over time.[33] For example, World War I was dominated by largely static trench warfare centered on infantry and artillery, but by World War II, warfare became more dynamic with the rise of military aircraft and mechanization.

China's Defense White Paper of 2008 cited "strategic nuclear forces, military astronautics, missile defense systems, and global and battlefield reconnaissance and surveillance" as some of the focuses of the current global RMA. The same white paper noted that, since the 1990s, China has been pursuing "RMA with Chinese characteristics." This effort has centered on transitioning the PLA away from a force built on the concept of quantity over quality, of both personnel and equipment. China has been reducing the size of the PLA since the early 1980s and has been devoting more resources to purchasing or domestically developing weapons and equipment that are more advanced. Some defense technologies that China views as critical are ballistic and cruise missiles, particularly to counter other nations' more advanced warships, as well as antisatellite weapons, which could devastate a high-tech military's communications and reconnaissance capabilities. China is also developing nontraditional strategies to complement its military operations, such as using economic, legal, and political leverage.[34]

The Missile Program

China has the most active ballistic missile program in the world. By late 2007, it had deployed more than a thousand short-range missiles across the strait from Taiwan. It has been increasing the size of this force at a rate of more than 100 missiles per year. China has acquired large numbers of highly accurate cruise missiles from Russia. For instance, China has outfitted the Russian SS-N-22 Sunburn supersonic antiship cruise missile on two Sovremenny- and Sovremenny-II-class guided missile destroyers, and outfitted SS-N-27B Sizzler supersonic antiship cruise missiles on eight of its Russian-built Kilo-class diesel electric submarines. It is also developing an anti-(ship)ballistic missile with a range of about a thousand miles, which will provide the PLA with the ability to attack ships at sea, including aircraft carriers, at a great distance.[35]

The Nuclear Weapons Program

China exploded its first atomic bomb on October 16, 1964. China maintains a policy of no first use of nuclear weapons, but is willing to use nuclear weapons to counterattack against an enemy using nuclear weapons against China. China's official nuclear defense strategy prohibits the use of nuclear weapons against nonnuclear states. China's nuclear missile program is off budget, meaning that it is not reflected in the Ministry of Defense's annual budget. The PLA's Second Artillery Corps controls China's nuclear arsenal and conventional long-range missiles. It maintains both solid-fueled and liquid-fueled missiles; long-, medium-, and short-range missiles; and various types of warheads.

Before 2000, the purpose of China's missile program was to deter attacks from potential foes. The program relied on liquid-fueled intercontinental ballistic missiles (ICBMs) at fixed locations. The fixed locations left China's arsenal vulnerable to attack. Since 2000, however, China has shifted toward a more survivable and flexible strategic nuclear force.[36] It recently introduced two new classes of ICBMs (the DF-31 and DF-31A), which are road-mobile and solid-propellant and capable of targeting any location in the United States. These missiles, coupled with a sea-based deterrent provided by a new class of nuclear-powered submarines and submarine-launched ballistic missiles, give China new flexibility and more options than ever for strategic strikes. Although US forces far exceed those of China, China is now able to inflict serious damage on major US cities with these survivable systems.[37] In 2006, Western sources estimated that China's nuclear stockpile consisted of approximately 200 warheads, with about 145 deployed on delivery systems.[38]

Cyber Warfare

China's goals for future warfare include the ability to fight and win information wars (IW). Information warfare is actions taken to adversely affect an adversary's information and information systems while defending those of one's own. It includes both combatant situations, such as a precision attack to destroy an adversary's command and control capability, and noncombatant situations, such as electronic intrusion into an information and control network. The latter includes infiltrating computer networks, stealing information and data off computers and laptops, and disrupting military and civilian communications capabilities and systems. The purpose of IW is to convince, confuse, or deceive the adversary's military decisionmakers so that the enemy makes wrong decisions, late decisions, or no decisions at all. For IW to succeed, one must achieve superiority over the enemy by collecting, processing, and disseminating information while preventing the adversary from doing the same.[39] Information warfare can be carried out by physical attack and destruction, electronic interference, computer network attack, deception, psychological operations, and counterintelligence.

In its 2008 white paper on national defense, China unveiled the ambition of making major progress in IW by 2020. Vowing to strengthen the military by means of science and technology, the paper said China was working to "develop new and high-tech weaponry and equipment, conduct military training in conditions of IW, and build a modern logistics system in an all-round way."[40] On China's military strategic guideline of active defense, the paper said this guideline "aimed at winning local wars in conditions of informationization." China's leaders recognize that China does not have the ability to threaten major powers, such as the United States, with nuclear weapons. However, it can seriously disrupt the economic, political, and social systems of its potential adversaries using electrons.

The PLA is quickly integrating IW into its national defense strategy. Hacker attacks in government facilities worldwide point back to China, indicating that Chinese IW is moving from theory to implementation. For instance, in August 2000, hackers suspected of working for a Chinese government institute broke into a Los Alamos National Laboratory computer system and stole large amounts of sensitive but unclassified information.[41] Chinese hackers accomplished this feat by hitting open sites, and the hacking at Los Alamos continues on a nearly continuous basis.[42]

Chinese hackers have succeeded in infiltrating computer systems of foreign governments. GhostNet, an Internet spying network traced back to China, has hacked the computer systems of the embassies of India, Pakistan, Portugal, and Germany. The ministries of foreign affairs of Iran, Indonesia, and Brunei also reported compromised computers. Other targets are nongovernmental organizations and the media. The hackers use *malware*—software that infects computer systems—allowing hackers to extract top-secret information. In 2007, Chinese hackers infiltrated the computer systems of several government offices in Great Britain. A year earlier, Chinese hackers succeeded in shutting down part of the House of Commons computer systems. In 2007, Chinese hackers infiltrated the Pentagon's computer network, including the e-mail system used by Defense Secretary Robert Gates. The Indian and Belgian governments also claim that China has targeted their government computer network systems. The size and sophistication of these operations indicate that the Chinese government, and not rogue individuals, is behind the hacking. The Chinese government denies any hacking. Although it is not clear that the Chinese government or the PLA were behind the attacks, developing capabilities for cyber warfare is a stated goal of the PLA. The accesses and skills required for these intrusions are similar to those necessary to conduct computer network attacks.

Hacking is not limited to GhostNet and other Internet spy networks. Cyber spies seek opportunities as they arise. For instance, it appears that Chinese cyber spies snagged an unattended US government laptop during a December 2008 visit to China by the US commerce secretary. After copying the data, the spies tried to use the information to hack into US government computers. In June 2011, it appears that China-based hackers broke into Google's Gmail accounts, targeting US government officials, including people who worked at the White House. The attacks appear to have come from Jinan (Shandong Province), an area that is home to a national security arm of the PLA. Jinan is also home to a military unit dedicated to cyberspace, popularly known as the Blue Army.[43] Chinese authorities deny that the country was the source of the attack.

China engages in nearly continual cyber warfare with Taiwan, probing vulnerabilities in Taiwan's computer systems. Taiwan's defense ministry claims that cyber warfare is of great concern to Taiwan, and that the Chinese are becoming increasingly sophisticated in their methods.[44]

The Space Program

China's space program can be traced back to the 1950s when the PLA established a remote missile and rocket testing site in Jiuquan, Gansu Province, in the remote Mongolian Desert. By 1970, China launched its first satellite into orbit. Today, Jiuquan is an expanding metropolitan city, centered on the modern Jiuquan Space Center. In October 2003, China launched its first manned spaceflight, becoming only the third nation to do so. China's pursuit of advances in space exploration and technologies is driven by strong nationalist sentiment as well as the desire to advance its commercial and security interests. While China has taken advantage of technical help and cooperation from other countries, especially Russia, there is a strong focus on developing technologies domestically.[45] China's manned space mission is indicative of its significant advances in space technology. China has developed and launched a number of communications and remote-sensing satellites for civil, commercial, and military purposes. China has even begun to export space technologies to other countries. Future plans for China's space program include the construction of a space station and an unmanned lunar landing by 2020.[46]

China also has been pursuing military space technologies. Military operations in space may form an important part of China's efforts to increase its ability to wage high-tech, or informationized, warfare. High-tech militaries, such as the US military, are extremely dependent on satellites. China has purchased or developed several technologies for attacking satellites in orbit, such as jammers to block satellite communications or using lasers to disrupt or destroy satellites' optical sensors. In 2007, China surprised the world by shooting down one of its old weather satellites with an antisatellite (ASAT) missile. Beyond being an aggressive show of force, the ASAT test created a large debris field that will linger in orbit for decades, endangering other satellites and space vehicles. A year after the ASAT test, China with Russia introduced a draft treaty at the UN calling for a ban on weapons in space as well as on using or threatening force in space.[47]

Naval Power

China's leaders claim that the PLAN's role is to protect China's sovereignty, national security, and territorial integrity. On the sixtieth anniversary of the founding of the PLA, Chinese president and CMC chief Hu Jintao stated that modernization of the navy was purely defense-oriented, and that China's armed forces, including the navy, would never be a threat to other nations.[48] His comments echoed earlier assertions made by China's leaders that PLAN modernization is solely for defensive and peaceful purposes. To support their claim, China's leaders in the early 2000s promoted a campaign to publicize the peaceful exploration by Ming Dynasty explorer Zheng He. Zheng He was a fifteenth-century Chinese eunuch who commanded a fleet of ships that reached as far as Africa. Unlike the Western powers during their age of exploration, Zheng did not colonize any of the areas where his ships docked. These claims by modern Chinese leaders contradict thirty years of Chinese expansion on the South China Sea, however. This expansion includes the capture of the Paracels from Vietnam in 1974; the 1988 naval seizure of eight Vietnamese-claimed and -held islets; the 1992 enactment of the Territorial Waters Law; and the 1995 takeover of the Mischief Reef off the Philippines, claimed by Manila; and its stepped-up oil and gas exploration in contested territorial waters.

China has made significant progress in modernizing its surface fleet. While China continues to purchase ships and technology, primarily from Russia, it is making progress in domestic production of advanced ships. Significant advances in the PLAN's surface fleet include greatly improved air-defense systems, improved radar, and antiship cruise missiles. The PLAN is not only integrating these improvements into new vessels, but is also upgrading older surface ships with them. The PLAN is also developing and building new high-speed coastal patrol vessels. As of 2008, forty of these vessels were operational, with more in production. These boats are armed with advanced antiship cruise missiles, and their speed and small size make them difficult to target. While they have a limited range of operation, these ships would provide excellent offense or defense in the coastal waters of mainland China or Taiwan. China has also been developing new amphibious vessels. These ships include larger amphibious ships, which can carry men and matériel far from China's shores, as well as smaller landing crafts. These vessels would be a crucial part of any attack on Taiwan or other disputed islands, but they are also important for humanitarian and rescue operations overseas.[49]

The PLAN has made small progress in maritime logistics. China has demonstrated an ability to resupply ships in coastal waters, although logistical difficulties remain an obstacle for the PLAN in conducting long-term, long-distance deployments. Nevertheless, in late 2008, the PLAN deployed two destroyers and a supply vessel off the coast of Somalia for antipiracy operations.[50]

China has been improving its submarine force, building an average of two vessels per year since the mid-1990s, as well as purchasing advanced submarines from Russia. In addition to domestic production, China continues to purchase advanced submarines and submarine technology from Russia and other nations. As of 2009, the PLAN's submarine fleet includes about sixty vessels. The PLAN operates two nuclear-powered, ballistic missile submarines (SSBNs) and is building at least two more. These vessels will be able to strike anywhere in the United States from the central Pacific once armed with the newest ballistic missile China is developing. However, China has yet to send these vessels on regular patrols away from its territorial waters. While some of China's submarines are older, relatively obsolete vessels, China began producing nuclear-powered vessels in the late 1970s and is continually advancing its submarine technology. Some notable submarine capabilities China has developed or purchased are greater stealth, improved sonar, and the ability to launch antiship cruise missiles while submerged.[51]

An important aspect of naval power China lacks is an aircraft carrier. Aircraft carriers are the largest and most complex warships in the world, which enable a country to project military power throughout much of the world. China has shown increasing interest in studying and developing aircraft carriers and aircraft carrier operations. Since 1985, China has purchased four inoperable carriers from other nations for study, eventually converting three of them to floating attractions or scrap. In late 2011, however, China carried out a sea trial of its first aircraft carrier, a refitted former Soviet carrier called the *Varyag*. As of early 2009, China was continuing negotiations with Russia, begun in 2006, for the purchase of about fifty advanced carrier-capable fighter aircraft. The PLAN has built a mock carrier flight deck on land for pilot training and, in 2008, established a carrier pilot-training program at the Dalian Naval Academy.[52] Officials in the Chinese government and PLAN officers have cited national pride, status as a world power, and offshore defense as reasons China is researching, and may build, aircraft carriers. Chinese assertions that any carriers it might build would be purely defensive produce disbelief and concern among other nations because the primary purpose of such vessels is to project military force far beyond a nation's borders. Even in a supposed conflict with Taiwan, several dozen carrier-based aircraft would not significantly improve the offensive and defensive capabilities over the East China Sea already provided by

China's navy and its land-based missiles and aircraft. On the other hand, carriers would be important for protecting the maritime supply lines for China's economy. They would also serve as a potent reminder of China's power and reach. A Chinese aircraft carrier could be sent to trouble spots as a display of resolve, as US carriers sometimes are.[53] Sources outside China have made varying reports on the future of China's aircraft carrier program. These range from China having the capability to produce a medium-sized carrier by 2015 to deploying four battle groups (each consisting of one medium-sized carrier and supporting vessels) by 2020.[54]

Conclusion

The PLA began as a peasant-based army employing guerrilla tactics and, during the Mao years, following the doctrine of people's war. China's leaders began to modernize the military in the 1970s, instructing the armed forces to withdraw from politics and to focus on military training and other defense matters. Mao's death and the subsequent arrest of the Gang of Four allowed the PLA to shift away from the concept of people's war, as the PLA initiated military contacts with the West and sold arms to developing countries. Deng Xiaoping tried to further separate the military from politics and carried out significant reorganization and restructuring of the PLA. Observing US military prowess in the 1990–1991 Gulf War, China's leaders put more emphasis on the development of military technology. China has increased its defense budget by double digits each year since 1989. Deng's successors, Zhao Ziyang and Hu Yaobang, further transformed China's military, enhancing systems that project power beyond China's shores. As external threats to China's national security have diminished since the end of the Cold War, China has turned its focus to safeguarding China's territorial integrity and maritime security. The former includes its claims to Taiwan and the latter enables China to extend its military reach throughout the South China Sea region. Currently, China's leaders are most concerned with the concept of force projection, so that China can conduct military operations away from its borders. China's greatest potential military adversary remains the United States, and China's leaders are developing a number of systems to counter US military superiority, such as cyber warfare, antisatellite capability, and enhanced naval power. If the trend of double-digit military budget increases continues, China will undoubtedly make advances in its military capabilities and seek to challenge US military supremacy in Asia.

Notes

1. Mao, *On Guerrilla Warfare*.
2. The state CMC stresses the military's role as defender of the state, as opposed to defender of the party.

3. Combined arms warfare integrates different arms of a military.

4. Shambaugh, *Modernizing China's Military,* 70.

5. Shambaugh, *Modernizing China's Military,* 71.

6. US Department of Defense, *Military Power of the People's Republic of China, 2008,* 46.

7. US Library of Congress, *Country Profile: China,* 39.

8. Shambaugh, *Modernizing China's Military,* 234.

9. Shambaugh, *Modernizing China's Military,* 242.

10. Graff and Higham, eds., *Military History of China,* 298.

11. Information drawn from Shambaugh, *Modernizing China's Military;* Graff and Higham, *Military History of China;* Mulvenon and Yang, eds., *People's Liberation Army.*

12. For more information on China's arms sales to the third world, see Bitzinger, "Arms to Go."

13. James Mulvenon, testimony before the US-China Economic and Security Review Commission, Washington, DC, December 7, 2001, http://www.uscc.gov/textonly /transcriptstx/txtesmul.htm.

14. James Mulvenon, testimony before the US-China Economic and Security Review Commission.

15. Bickford, "Chinese Military and Its Business Operations," 461.

16. Mao, "Problems of War and Strategy," 224.

17. Cheng and White, "Sixteenth Central Committee of the Chinese Communist Party."

18. Cheng and White, "Sixteenth Central Committee of the Chinese Communist Party."

19. Mulvenon and Yang, eds., *People's Liberation Army.*

20. Li Nan, *Chinese Civil-Military Relations.*

21. Mulvenon and Yang, eds., *People's Liberation Army.*

22. Shambaugh, *Modernizing China's Military;* Haberfeld and Cerrah, *Comparative Policing.*

23. Wayne, *China's War on Terror.*

24. US Department of Defense, *Military Power of the People's Republic of China, 2009,* 31.

25. State Council of the People's Republic of China, *China's National Defense in 2008,* 7.

26. US Department of Defense, *Military Power of the People's Republic of China, 2009.*

27. Dutta, "Securing the Sea Frontier," 275.

28. For more information on the offensive nature of China's so-called national defense policy, see Dutta, "Securing the Sea Frontier," 269–294; US Department of Defense, *Military Power of the People's Republic of China, 2010;* and Graff and Higham, eds., *Military History of China.*

29. Ministry of Foreign Affairs of the PRC, "China's Position Paper on the New Security Concept."

30. The Shanghai Cooperation Organization is an INGO created in 2001 by the governments of Russia, Kazakhstan, Kyrgyzstan, and Tajikistan to strengthen confidence building and disarmament in the border regions.

31. Ian Taylor, "Future of China's Overseas Peacekeeping Operations."

32. "Law on the Territorial Sea and Contiguous Zone of 25 February 1992," http:// www.un.org/Depts/los/legislationandtreaties/pdffiles/chn_1992_Law.pdf.

33. Tilford, *Revolution in Military Affairs: Prospects and Cautions.*

34. US Department of Defense, *Military Power of the People's Republic of China, 2010,* 22.

35. US Department of Defense, *Military Power of the People's Republic of China, 2010,* 2.

36. US Department of Defense, *Military Power of the People's Republic of China, 2010,* 34.

37. US Department of Defense, *Military Power of the People's Republic of China, 2009,* 13.

38 Kristensen, Norris, and McKinzie, *Chinese Nuclear Forces and U.S. Nuclear War Planning.*

39. Shalikashvili, *Joint Vision 2010,* 16; and US Department of Defense, *Military Power of the People's Republic of China, 2010,* 37.

40. State Council of the People's Republic of China. *China's National Defense in 2008.*

41. Los Alamos National Laboratory in New Mexico is one of the US government's major nuclear weapons labs.

42. Thomas, "Like Adding Wings to the Tiger."

43. The name apparently distinguishes the unit from the CCP-dominated military, commonly known as the Red Army.

44. General Chen Chao-min, ROC Minister of National Defense, interview with the author, Taipei, Taiwan, June 22, 2009.

45. Gifford, *China Road;* and Harvey, *China's Space Program.*

46. Harvey, *China's Space Program;* US Department of Defense, *Military Power of the People's Republic of China, 2009.*

47. "Disharmony in the Spheres—The Militarisation of Space," *Economist,* January 19, 2008; State Council of the People's Republic of China, *China's National Defense in 2008,* sec. 14: Arms Control and Disarmament; US Department of Defense, *Military Power of the People's Republic of China, 2009.*

48. "Hu Urges Further Modernization of the PLA Navy," Xinhua, April 25, 2009.

49. O'Rourke, *China Naval Modernization: Implications for U.S. Navy Capabilities;* US Department of Defense, *Military Power of the People's Republic of China,* years 2009 and 2010; and Yoshihara and Holmes, eds., *Asia Looks Seaward.*

50. US Department of Defense, *Military Power of the People's Republic of China, 2009,* 46.

51. Erickson et al., eds., *China's Future Nuclear Submarine Force;* O'Rourke, *China Naval Modernization: Implications for U.S. Navy Capabilities;* US Department of Defense, *Military Power of the People's Republic of China, 2009;* and Yoshihara and Holmes, eds., *Asia Looks Seaward.*

52. Ronald O'Rourke, "China to Buy Su-33 Carrier-Based Fighters from Russia?" *Defense Industry Daily,* March 26, 2009.

53. Choong, "Chinese Navy Needs a PR Frontman"; Robert Karniol, "Long-Brewing Carrier Programme," *Straits Times* (Singapore), January 5, 2009; and O'Rourke, "China to Buy Su-33 Carrier-Based Fighters from Russia?"

54. Minnie Chan, "PLA Said to Eye Four Carriers," *South China Morning Post,* January 2, 2009; Karniol, "Long-Brewing Carrier Programme"; O'Rourke, *China Naval Modernization: Implications for U.S. Navy Capabilities;* and Oster, "Beijing Considers Upgrades to Navy."

10 Foreign Policy

China has historically viewed itself as the world's central civilizing force, or the Middle Kingdom (Zhongguo). For much of its history, China lived in self-imposed isolation, partly because it viewed its cultural superiority as one not to be tarnished by outsiders, or barbarians (*yiti*). Surrounding areas—Korea, Japan, Burma (Myanmar), Annam (Indochina), and Nepal—either were under China's military control or were its satellite states. Delegations of barbarians wishing to approach the Chinese were required to bring tribute and recognize the superiority of Chinese culture.

China began to have contact with Western nations in the early sixteenth century with the arrival of foreign traders. Imperial China limited foreign contact by restricting trade to the area of Canton (present-day Guangzhou). Dissatisfied with the limitation, the British tried to open the Chinese coast and Peking to trade. The war over opium finally created an opening for foreigners. The Opium War of 1839, which ended in 1842 in a complete victory for the British, and subsequent treaties gave foreign governments certain economic and legal rights in China. Throughout the remainder of the Qing Dynasty, imperial China surrendered more and more of its sovereignty to foreign powers. Foreign trade grew, but Chinese industries, particularly the handicraft industry, suffered and failed due to foreign competition. Corruption, rebellion, natural disasters, and foreign domination all had a hand in the collapse of the Qing Dynasty in 1911 (see Chapter 2). Unable to negotiate with the foreign powers from a position of strength, the new Nationalist government honored China's treaties. The heyday for foreign powers in China ended soon after the 1949 communist revolution. The new communist government negated the "unequal treaties" signed between imperial China and foreign powers.

China's foreign policy has changed dramatically since the establishment of the PRC in 1949. For most of the Mao years, China pursued a foreign policy that divided the world into friend and foe, and China's relations with the major powers (the United States, the Soviet Union, and Japan) were largely antagonistic. Deng Xiaoping and his successors adopted a less antagonistic foreign policy and have sought smoother foreign relations so they can better concentrate on China's domestic economic development. Determinants of China's relations with another country usually include historical, economic, and security considerations. Another determinant is the web of foreign relations that each country has. Each bilateral relationship is impacted by each party's other relationships, with certain "triangular" relations particularly important, such as the US-China-Soviet/Russian dynamic, as well as the Japan-China-US triangle and the India-China-Soviet dynamic. These triangular relationships are exceedingly complex and beyond the scope of this chapter. This chapter focuses largely on bilateral relations but refers to the triangular dynamic where necessary.

Foreign Policy Decisionmaking

China's foreign policy decisionmaking process, though highly centralized and personalized, is becoming increasingly diverse with additional bureaucracies, localities, businesses, and interests playing a role. The foreign policy decisionmaking structure consists of China's central leadership, relevant bureaucracies, and bureaucratic cadres. The central leadership consists of an exclusive, or core, leadership circle; members of the Politburo Standing Committee; and some members of the Politburo, usually members who reside in Beijing and the Secretariat. It appears that China's leaders are increasingly influenced by public discourse when formulating policy. These public actors include university-based scholars, analysts associated with think tanks, academic journals, and newspapers.[1]

At the apex of China's foreign policy decisionmaking structure is the core leadership circle, consisting of the paramount political leader (e.g., Mao Zedong, Deng Xiaoping, Jiang Zemin, and Hu Jintao) and one or two of his closest associates. The CCP Politburo is the most important formal institution in the foreign policy apparatus under the informal, personalized, core leadership circle. However, the Politburo includes members from provinces and cities other than Beijing, and its size is comparatively large. These two factors hinder its ability to act with dispatch on foreign policy issues that require immediate attention. Hence, de facto decisionmaking power actually rests with the smaller Standing Committee. However, the Politburo does deliberate on important foreign policy decisions on broad issues such as peace, national security goals, and diplomatic strategy. Foreign policy initiatives usually originate in the Politburo's Standing Committee, which makes decisions by consensus. Lacking a consensus, China's top political leader makes the call.[2]

The body most directly responsible for the conduct of foreign affairs is the CCP Central Committee Foreign Affairs Leading Small Group. The Central Foreign Affairs LSG supervises policy implementation and coordination of the foreign affairs sector. It consists of a head, who is always a member of the Politburo's Standing Committee, key members of the Standing Committee, and top bureaucrats of relevant government and party agencies. It may also include a high-ranking member of the military. The Central Foreign Affairs LSG gives China's leaders the opportunity to meet with bureaucrats responsible for the practice of foreign affairs. Although the LSG is not a decisionmaking body, China's leaders take its recommendations into consideration when China formulates policy. The key state organs with foreign policy responsibility are the Ministry of Foreign Affairs and the Ministry of Commerce.[3] In the military, there is the PLA General Staff Department. The Ministry of Foreign Affairs (MOFA, or Waijiao bu) technically falls under the State Council (cabinet). In reality, it reports directly to the Politburo's Standing Committee through the Central Foreign Affairs LSG. It carries out China's foreign policy. It interprets foreign policy decisions made by the core leadership circle and devises policy to implement those decisions. The minister of foreign affairs is responsible for running the bureaucracy. He is assisted by vice ministers and assistant ministers, each of whom is responsible for regional or functional departments. For instance, the Department of Asian Affairs is responsible for implementing policy toward China's Asian neighbors. The Department of Hong Kong, Macao, and Taiwan Affairs is responsible for carrying out policy toward those entities. Foreign policy concerning the United States is the responsibility of the Department of North American and Oceanian Affairs. The Ministry of Commerce is responsible for administering China's foreign trade, economic cooperation, and foreign investment. In addition, the Xinhua News Agency reports on China's foreign affairs. Its officials sometimes lobby on behalf of the Chinese government and its interests.[4] For instance, the Hong Kong office of Xinhua was the eyes and ears of the CCP in the territory before the 1997 transition to Chinese rule. Many Xinhua employees double as reporters and spies.

In the early years of the PRC, Chinese foreign policy decisionmaking occurred under the joint control of the CCP's Central Committee and the State Council. From 1949 until his death in 1976, Mao Zedong dominated foreign policy decisionmaking. He determined if China waged war, sought peace, exported revolution, or closed its doors to foreigners. Premier Zhou Enlai, who served as foreign minister from 1949 to 1958, was in charge of the actual conduct of foreign affairs. During the Cultural Revolution, when all political institutions ceased normal functioning, Mao and special bodies such as the Cultural Revolution Small Group assumed control over many functions formerly exercised by the party. China became xenophobic and closed itself off to most of the world (the exception being Albania, which according to Mao had created a pure communist system). During the Deng years, foreign policy decisionmaking became more consensual, but the decisions continued to originate at the top. In the post-Deng era, it appears that voices outside of the traditional policymaking channels are increasingly influencing China's leaders. It used to be that think tank analysts and university-based scholars were irrelevant to China's foreign policymaking. Analysts and scholars now regularly interact with government officials and have become both advisers to the government and conveyors of public opinion.[5]

Major foreign policy initiatives originate from written instructions or comments by members of the core leadership circle. Other initiatives, such as those concerning the implementation of policy, originate in the relevant bureaucracy, which drafts a memorandum proposing a specific plan of action. Bureaucratic cadres submit the memo to the staff office of the Foreign Affairs LSG for the core leadership's approval. Personal connections (*guanxi*) with members of the core leadership can help smooth a policy initiative's path to the top.[6] Once the core leadership approves a policy, documents are drawn up to create rules under which the policy will be implemented. Some rules can be narrow, permitting little leeway in implementing a policy; other rules are purposely vague to allow flexibility in implementation. The actual implementation of a policy is carried out by the relevant bureaucracy, such as the MOFA or the Ministry of Commerce (MOFCOM, or Shangwu bu).

China's Foreign Relations, 1949–1972

Following establishment of the PRC in 1949, China's leaders voided diplomatic relations established by the Nationalist government, ended recognition of diplomats accredited by the Nationalist government, and abrogated many of the international treaties and agreements signed by the previous government. Diplomatic relations could be reestablished only on the basis of mutual respect for sovereignty, territorial integrity, and mutual benefit. In the early days of the PRC, all of the communist governments rushed to recognize China. Great Britain and the Scandinavian countries did so as well. One condition of normalization of relations was that countries drop formal recognition of the Republic of China (Taiwan). The United States chose to maintain diplomatic relations with the Republic of China (ROC), as did Japan and many Latin American countries. Although some members of the US government advocated recognition of the PRC, Chinese intervention in the Korean War ended any discussion in the United States of shifting diplomatic relations from the ROC to the PRC.

China's foreign policy in the early years of the PRC (1949–1953) followed the principles of Mao's "two camp" theory. Mao divided the world into two camps: a communist one and the capitalist one. Countries fell into either of the camps; there could be no fence-sitting. According to Mao, China leaned toward the side of international communism to combat the forces of colonialism and imperialism. Although China normalized relations with some noncommunist countries, it largely conducted trade and other relations with communist countries. For instance, in 1950, China signed a Treaty of Peace, Friendship, and Mutual Assistance with the Soviet Union. Although the treaty called for mutual aid, in reality Soviet financial and technical assistance came with a cost. It indebted

China to the Soviet Union and subordinated the Chinese government to the Soviets. Under Soviet influence, China's foreign policy was unequivocally revolutionary and nationalistically militant, meaning that China encouraged open armed struggle and subversion beyond its borders. Meanwhile, Mao's policy of "leaning to one side" compelled him to support communist insurrections in developing countries such as Burma (later Myanmar), India, Malaya, the Philippines, and Indonesia.

Stalin's death in 1953 offered China the opportunity to moderate its foreign policy. Stalin's death allowed Mao to break out of the Soviet camp and to formulate an independent foreign policy. After 1953, China adopted a more moderate policy of mutual assistance and nonaggression, summed up in Zhou Enlai's Five Principles of Peaceful Coexistence. The Five Principles states that relations among nations should be established on the basis of mutual respect for territorial integrity and sovereignty, nonaggression, noninterference in each other's internal affairs, equality and mutual benefit, and peaceful coexistence. The Five Principles of Peaceful Coexistence continues to be the cornerstone of China's foreign policy. Zhou articulated the Five Principles to leaders of the undeveloped world at the Bandung Conference, a meeting of twenty-nine Asian and African nations in April 1955 in Bandung, Indonesia. At the meeting, the Asian and African leaders expressed neutrality in Cold War squabbles between the United States and the Soviet Union. Not only was the Bandung Conference the genesis of the Non-Aligned Movement, but it was China's debut on the world stage as a moderate state. Other countries had grown suspicious of China because of its support for insurrection. At Bandung, skillful Chinese diplomat Zhou Enlai explained that China was becoming a more responsible member of the international community, despite its urges to eradicate the lingering evils of imperialism. In the "Bandung Spirit," China and India put aside their border dispute and sought better relations. US and Chinese ambassadors began in 1955 to hold periodic talks. By 1966, they had held more than 130 talks in both Geneva and Warsaw. China walked away from the Bandung Conference as a rising star among emerging nations.

In the late 1950s, China moved away from the Bandung Spirit and became more militant. The foreign policy pendulum swung away from neutrality and back to class warfare. Mao argued that peaceful coexistence between the communist East and the capitalist West was impossible, and he once again argued that active struggle was necessary for undeveloped countries. Most of these countries rejected Beijing's interference, and by 1960, China found itself isolated from all important noncommunist third world countries. Zhou's statements on peaceful coexistence rang hollow in the ears of third world leaders.

China's foreign policy became more confrontational in the early 1960s. In 1962, Mao devised his "three worlds" theory, which divided the world into three spheres: the first world of the superpowers, the United States and the Soviet Union; the second world of the developed countries of Japan, Europe, and

Canada; and the third world of the developing countries in Asia, Latin America, and Africa. Mao described the third world as the "main force in the worldwide struggle against imperialism and hegemonism" and maintained that the second world, controlled by the first, oppresses the third world. Mao claimed that this oppression could be overcome if the third world won over the second and united with it in a struggle for self-determination. In this context, and following the Sino-Soviet split of the early 1960s, China began to compete with Russia in Africa. China declared itself the friend of "anti-imperialism" in Africa and the Middle East and offered economic aid and technical assistance, particularly for conspicuous development projects. China's leaders expanded their propaganda efforts, holding up Mao as a guide to revolution. Mao advocated violent revolution in African colonies and saw China as a leader of the third world in its struggle for independence. Although many African countries accepted Chinese economic aid, most African independence activists rejected China's self-appointed leadership. Beijing's support of national revolutionary groups cost China diplomatic partners. In the Middle East, China supported the Arab countries against the State of Israel in the 1967 war and shipped small amounts of weapons to the Palestine Liberation Organization. Promotion of the doctrine of Lin Biao's "people's war" during the Cultural Revolution seriously damaged China's third world standing. Not satisfied with revolutionary gains, after 1965 China began an ideological war. Inflated by self-worth, Mao saw himself as a model revolutionary and revolutionary innovator. Always the supporter of violent and continuous revolution, Mao waged war on the Soviet position that peaceful transition to socialism was possible. China's militancy in the third world cost the country diplomatic recognition. In the 1960s, six countries, all in the third world, ended or suspended diplomatic relations with China.

The winding down of the Cultural Revolution after 1969 allowed a shift in China's foreign policy. China had recalled most of its ambassadors during the Cultural Revolution. After the height of the Cultural Revolution, China in 1969 began to return its ambassadors to their posts. Zhou Enlai began to take steps to moderate China's policy and tried to return to the more neutral position of the Bandung Spirit.

The August 1968 Soviet invasion of Czechoslovakia was a watershed event in moving China away from belligerence and toward better relations with the West. Throughout the 1960s, China had grown increasingly concerned about the Soviet threat to China's security. Despite this growing threat, China's leaders continued to refer to the United States as its "number one enemy." The Soviet invasion of another communist country rattled China's leaders, who labeled the invasion as "social-imperialism." At the same time, US president Lyndon Johnson's attempts to limit the war in Vietnam reduced the US threat to China's security. China's leaders began to see Moscow as a greater danger to China's security than the United States. As China-Soviet relations soured, Mao began to make overtures to the United States. With most of his adversaries muted or silenced by the Cultural Revolution, Mao was able in the late 1960s and early 1970s to make his own foreign policy decisions. In 1968, he resumed the sporadic Warsaw talks with the United States, and in 1971, announced his desire to establish ties with the United States by inviting the US table tennis team to visit China.

In the 1970s, China sought a greater role as a peaceful leader of the third world. In 1974, Deng Xiaoping in a speech to the UN expounded Mao Zedong's theory of the differentiation of the three worlds and proclaimed China's foreign policy. In his UN speech, Deng stated that China would always be a member of the third world, and that China firmly supported the third world countries in their struggles, indicating that China would pursue a foreign policy of third world leadership. After Mao's passing, however, Deng quietly dropped references to class struggle and international conflict in favor of international cooperation.

Relations with the United States

Undoubtedly, the most important foreign relations China has are with the United States.

China-US relations date back to the US Open Door policy (1899 and 1900), which claimed equal access to China's treaty ports and stressed the importance of preserving China's territorial and administrative integrity at a time of colonial expansions into China. The United States supported the Nationalist ROC government with military aid during Japan's occupation of China. For instance, US general Claire L. Chennault's famous Flying Tigers, based in southern Yunnan Province, conducted air operations against the Japanese air force in China.[7] During World War II, US general Joseph Stilwell ("Vinegar Joe") served as chief of staff to Generalissimo Chiang Kai-shek and as commander of the China-Burma-India Theater. The United States supported the Nationalist ROC government throughout World War II, sending untold millions of dollars of US military and economic aid to the Chiang regime. By the end of World War II, China had 6 million ounces of gold and US dollar reserves of more than $900 million, all from US taxpayers. At the end of World War II, US air and naval forces airlifted and shipped KMT forces to China's major cities to try to prevent a communist takeover of China. During the Chinese civil war, the United States increased military and economic aid to the KMT. The United States continued to funnel both military and economic support to the ROC following the Nationalists' retreat to the island of Taiwan.

Despite Mao's 1949 proclamation of the PRC on mainland China, the United States refused to recognize the new state and instead maintained diplomatic relations with the ROC. Relations between China and the United States further soured during the Korean War. In the first days of the war, US president Harry Truman inserted the Seventh Fleet into the Taiwan Strait and blockaded the Chinese coast. President Truman took this action to prevent PRC military action against Taiwan, but also to prevent Chiang Kai-shek from organizing an offensive to recover the mainland. US forces fought PLA soldiers in Korea, suffering significant casualties. By the end of 1951, the United States had suffered 135,000 casualties (dead, wounded, or missing); up to 800,000 Chinese soldiers had died on Korean soil.

The Korean War had a significant impact on US-ROC relations. The United States saw Taiwan, like Japan, as a bulwark against the spread of communism in Asia. Throughout the 1950s, the United States strengthened and increased its military bases on Taiwan, dubbed America's "unsinkable aircraft carrier" in the Pacific. In 1954, the United States and the government of the ROC signed a mutual defense treaty, under which the ROC granted the United States the right to maintain troops on the island, and the United States offered Taiwan both military aid for its defense and economic aid for its economic and social development. In 1955, the US Navy patrolled the Taiwan Strait after China shelled the ROC-controlled offshore islands of Quemoy and Matsu.

The China-Soviet split in the 1960s offered the United States an opportunity to use China to threaten the Soviet Union. Playing the "China card," the United States began to send out feelers to Beijing indicating a rapprochement between the two countries. The Vietnam War, in which both US and Chinese troops fought, put off any attempt by the United States to have closer relations with China. US-China relations began to improve in the early 1970s, however. President Richard Nixon, who had written in a 1967 *Foreign Affairs* article that a long-term policy of isolating China was irrational, began a series of unilateral moves, called "small steps," to improve US-China relations. For instance, the US government began to use the term *People's Republic of China* instead of *mainland China* and relaxed restrictions on trade with and travel to China. It ended Seventh Fleet patrols of the Taiwan Strait and halted reconnaissance flights over Chinese territory. Although China's leaders publicly ignored these and other moves, they signaled their interest in normalizing relations with the United States by engaging in indirect talks through intermediaries such as Pakistan's president, General Yahya Khan. After the Second Plenum of the CCP Central Committee, held from late August to early September 1970, Chinese premier Zhou Enlai announced China's willingness to receive a US special envoy to discuss the status of Taiwan. The United States disregarded the wording of the message and began preparations for Nixon's visit to China.

The first step in normalizing China-US relations was Beijing's invitation to the US table-tennis team, which had been competing in the world championships in Japan. The March 1971 visit by the US team to China, in which they were feted and hosted by Zhou Enlai, ushered in a new era of people-to-people diplomacy, dubbed *ping-pong diplomacy*. The US government relaxed visa restrictions for individuals and groups from China, and relaxed trade restrictions on US exports to China. In July 1971, President Nixon's national security adviser, Henry Kissinger, paid a secret visit to China. Officially, Kissinger flew to Pakistan to meet with Pakistan's president Khan and then accepted Khan's invitation to rest for a few days in the mountains. In fact, Kissinger flew on to Beijing where he met with Zhou Enlai and other Chinese officials. Upon Kissinger's return to the United States, China and the United States simultaneously issued a communiqué indicating that President Nixon would visit China to establish normal relations between the two countries.

The US rapprochement toward China also meant that it would no longer obstruct the PRC's admission to the United Nations. An original signatory of the UN Charter, the Nationalist ROC was a member of the UN General Assembly as well as a permanent member of the exclusive Security Council. Under the UN Charter, the General Assembly determines whether new members are accepted into the United Nations. For twenty years, the Soviet Union had tabled a resolution seeking the admission of the communist PRC and the expulsion of the ROC. Although the resolution failed, it was defeated by smaller margins as the UN membership expanded. In 1971, the United States changed its position and proposed that the PRC be seated in both the General Assembly and the Security Council, but stipulated that the ROC retain its seat in the General Assembly. The US proposal had little traction, and in October 1971, the United Nations voted to accept the PRC and expel Taiwan. Shocked to hear the news on the eve of its imminent expulsion, the Taiwan representative to the UN walked out of the organization rather than face defeat.

Nixon's 1972 trip to China came as a complete shock to the world. President Nixon had been a staunch anticommunist. One of the most shocked parties was the government of Japan, which, under enormous US pressure, had been unable to establish normal relations with China. Immediately following the announcement of Nixon's pending trip, Japan moved to establish formal relations with China. In February 1972, Nixon, accompanied by Kissinger, traveled to Beijing where he met with Mao Zedong and worked out with Zhou Enlai the first Shanghai Communiqué, which set China-US relations on a new course. The 1972 Shanghai Communiqué expressed the desire of both countries to begin the process of normalizing relations. To do this, China and the United States had to put aside questions on which the two sides disagreed. The foremost question was the status of Taiwan. Because China and the United States could not agree on this issue, it needed to be laid aside. In the 1972 Shanghai Communiqué, the Chinese reaffirm their position that "the Government of the People's Republic of China is the sole legal government of China," that "Taiwan is a province of China," and that "the liberation of Taiwan is China's internal affair in which no other country has the right to interfere." President Nixon did not want to commit to Beijing's view, so the US version of the communiqué merely acknowledges that it is Beijing's view that Taiwan is a part of China, but does not state that the United States shares that view. The US side of the communiqué states that the United States "acknowledges" that "all Chinese" on either side of the Taiwan Strait maintain there is but one China and the US government does not challenge them for saying so. The wording of the communiqué is crucial. Essentially, the United States acknowledged that Beijing had its own view regarding Taiwan's status, without actually agreeing with it. What the United States does not do in the Shanghai Communiqué is define the term *China*. By stating that "there is but one China and that Taiwan is a part of China," the United States left open to interpretation whether the term *China* referred to the PRC or to the ROC. By using vague terminology, the United States was able to lay aside the Taiwan question and move toward diplomatic recognition of the PRC.

Contemporary Foreign Relations

China's contemporary foreign policy has less to do with sorting the world into antagonistic and friendly camps and more to do with placating countries wary of China's economic and military rise and with gaining access to precious resources necessary for its continued economic development. To these ends, China has been working to improve relations with its diplomatic partners and neighbors, has expanded its presence into resource-rich poor countries, and has increased participation in international organizations. China has put forth a policy of peaceful rise or peaceful development designed to mollify neighbors who are threatened by a stronger China. It increasingly uses soft power in the form of foreign aid and investment to project a positive image. Despite these positive efforts, however, areas of tension remain. Western powers and international organizations, for example, are leery of China's investments in poor countries that gain China access to natural resources, while propping up unsavory regimes. Other countries complain of unfair trade practices and an artificially low currency that benefits China to the detriment of others.

Asian Pacific countries in particular fret over China's military rise and its increasingly assertive claims to disputed territories—claims that have recently turned antagonistic. Traditionally a continental power, China borders on fourteen countries and, with the exception of Russia, all of its neighbors are Asian. China also faces the Pacific. In addition to its Pacific Ocean neighbors, it has a host of neighbors in the East China and South China Seas. In antiquity, China exercised suzerainty over many of its neighbors. Kingdoms sent tribute to the Chinese emperor, the Son of Heaven. China's relations with its neighbors changed as the Qing Dynasty decayed and eventually collapsed. It watched as one of its closest neighbors, Japan, industrialized and militarized. In the early twentieth century, China was eclipsed by an industrialized and militarized Japan. Japan in the 1930s annexed Manchuria as a puppet state and used it as a springboard to invade China in 1937 and occupy it until the end of World War II. Throughout the Mao years, China supported communist movements and insurgencies in the Asia Pacific, earning the distrust and disdain of many of its neighbors. Under Deng, China pursued a more cooperative stance with its Asian neighbors and joined many regional intergovernmental organizations. Today, China's most important Asian relationships are those with Japan, India, and Southeast Asia.

Relations with the United States

China-US relations from 1972 until the end of the Cold War can best be described as strategic cooperation designed to deter Soviet expansion. The Nixon administration began to investigate a military relationship with China and began to relax restrictions on the export of advanced technology to China. Successive administrations continued to relax the restrictions, but to Beijing's disappointment failed to sell US arms to China. China's relations with the United States improved after Nixon's 1972 trip to China, and Americans who travelled there came away with an infatuation for China bordering on euphoria.[8] The US government and businesses took a more jaundiced view, and China-US trade dropped in 1976 and 1977. Nixon's resignation in 1973 retarded any progress toward diplomatic relations. China's relationship with the United States advanced when the Carter administration switched diplomatic relations from the ROC on Taiwan to China in 1979. The United States agreed to move its embassy from Taipei to Beijing. Washington downgraded the former embassy in Taiwan to the American Institute in Taiwan, agreed to remove military forces by the end of April 1979, and set certain limits on the sale of defensive arms to Taiwan. In 1980, President Carter extended most-favored-nation (MFN) trading status to China. MFN status reduced US tariffs on imports from China, which was necessary for expanding trade relations between the two countries.

Despite advances in bilateral relations in the 1970s, China-US relations deteriorated some during the early 1980s. The main bone of contention between China and the US was President Reagan's commitment to sell defensive arms to Taiwan. The United States sold arms to Taiwan under the former 1954 Security Treaty, and China opposed the continued sale of US arms to Taiwan after the normalization of China-US relations. In 1981, China raised new demands against US arms sales, and after a year of negotiations, the United States and China signed the Arms Reduction Act. The 1982 act states that the United States will not exceed, either in quality or quantity, the level of arms supplied since the resumption of formal relations, and that the United States will gradually reduce its arms sales to Taiwan.[9] The act did not commit the United States to a timetable for termination of arms sales, and as indicated above, the United States continues to sell defensive arms to Taiwan. China and the United States enjoyed better relations in the second half of the 1980s, and the two countries expanded economic and cultural ties. The United States relaxed restrictions on technology transfers to China, US businesses invested in China's SEZs (Chapter 7), Chinese and American students travelled abroad to study in each other's countries,

American and Chinese scholars participated in bilateral conferences, and US tourists flocked to China as more Chinese visited the United States. US public opinion of China was very positive, perhaps even a bit romanticized, during this time.[10] The Chinese people's adoption of Michael Jackson, Madonna, and McDonald's led many Americans to identify their Chinese counterparts as "just like us." Increasing friction in trade relations, and then the Tiananmen Square Massacre (Chapter 5) in the late 1980s, shattered this overly optimistic view.

China-US relations deteriorated after the crushing of the 1989 Tiananmen protests and continued to deteriorate throughout much of the 1990s. In response to the massacre at Tiananmen, the George H. W. Bush administration imposed a package of sanctions on China, to include the suspension of all government-to-government sales and commercial exports of weapons, and the suspension of visits between US and Chinese military leaders. Disappointed by President Bush's tepid response, the US Congress passed legislation making the lifting of sanctions contingent on political reform in China. In 1992, President Clinton tried to tie China's human rights record to renewal of China's MFN status with the United States. In the early 1990s, the United States Congress influenced the International Olympic Committee to reject China's bid to host the 2004 Olympics. In 1995, the United States permitted Taiwan's president Lee Teng-hui to visit the United States, the first sitting Taiwan president to do so. Initially, the Clinton administration had told China's leaders that it would not issue a visa to Lee. However, the US Congress passed a resolution forcing Clinton's hand. The US State Department issued the visa after Chinese ambassador Qian Qichen had told Beijing that the United States would not do so. The US act humiliated Qian and left Beijing unable to trust the United States. In response to Lee's visit to the US, China responded by holding live-fire missile exercises toward Taiwan. In 1996, China again conducted live-fire military exercises in the Taiwan Strait, this time to try to influence the Taiwan presidential elections. The Chinese leadership believed that Lee Teng-hui—despite his position as leader of the pro-unification Nationalist Party—was a closet supporter of Taiwan independence, and wanted to intimidate voters in Taiwan from reelecting Lee. A red-faced Premier Zhu Rongji warned of dire consequences if the people of Taiwan voted for "the wrong man." In response, President Clinton moved an aircraft carrier group near Taiwan. Beijing accused the United States of acting like a hegemon in the region.[11] (Beijing's threats backfired, and voters reelected Lee by a wide margin.)

In 1999, relations soured further when NATO missiles dropped by an American B-2 bomber accidentally struck the Chinese embassy in Belgrade, killing three Chinese and injuring twenty. Many people in China thought that Beijing should retaliate against the United States.[12] The rationale for retaliation rested on the premise that the embassy is Chinese territory. By extension, many Chinese viewed the bombing as an attack against China itself, requiring some military response. Spontaneous and government-orchestrated protests against the United States turned violent in China, and mobs attacked the US embassy in Beijing, burning some of it. Despite expressions of sincere regret and remorse from Washington, most Chinese could not believe that the United States, a superpower, could make such a stupid mistake. Susan Shirk, the deputy assistant of state responsible for China at the time, claimed that the Belgrade bombing "profoundly damaged" trust in US intentions toward China.[13]

China-US relations sunk to a new low in spring 2001. On April 1, a US EP-3 surveillance plane was flying a reconnaissance mission over international waters in the South China Sea when a PLA Navy fighter jet collided with it. The Chinese jet crashed into the sea; the pilot ejected from his aircraft but was killed by the EP-3's propellers. The US plane made an emergency landing at a naval airfield on Hainan, where the Chinese military held the US crew prisoner for eleven days. China's leaders insisted that the United States take full responsibility for the crash. US military and aviation experts argued that it was unlikely that the slower-flying EP-3, a lumbering turbo-prop known as a "flying cow," maneuvered into the faster fighter jet. They claimed that the intercepts by Chinese fighters over the past couple of months had become more aggressive to the point the United States felt the fighters were endangering the safety of Chinese and US aircraft. US crews claimed that the Chinese pilot, Wang Wei, had flown so close to US planes in previous missions that they could read the e-mail address he held up to his fighter's window. Despite these arguments and an oral statement of regret for the loss of life from US secretary of state Colin Powell, Chinese authorities released the US crew only after receiving a written letter of apology. The Chinese also refused to allow the United States to fly the plane off the island, and to further humiliate the United States, insisted on disassembling the plane and shipping it out as freight.

China's relations with the United States are much better in the twenty-first century than they were in the 1990s. China has enjoyed mostly positive relations with the United States and is its second largest trading partner. The United States and China also cooperate on North Korea, piracy, and climate change. However, several areas of significant tension continue to flare up periodically. These issues involve mostly Taiwan, Tibet, trade, human rights, and security concerns. The following section of the chapter analyzes these burning issues in China-US relations, and references other areas of the book that also cover these issues.

The Taiwan question. Taiwan continues to be a major issue in China-US relations. The 1972 Shanghai Communiqué is the first of the so-called four pillars of China-US relations. The three other pillars are the 1979 Normalization Act, the Taiwan Relations Act (TRA) of 1979, and the 1982 Arms Reduction Act. Each of these addresses the question of Taiwan. The status of Taiwan is arguably the most contentious issue in China's relations with the United States.

China maintains a One-China *principle,* which claims that there is but one China and Taiwan is a part of China. The term *China* in this case refers to the PRC. For its part, the United States maintains a One-China *policy,* under which it maintains diplomatic relations with the PRC and informal relations with the ROC on Taiwan. Because China's leaders consider Taiwan to be a part of the PRC, China regards US support of Taiwan as meddling in China's domestic affairs. In particular, China's leaders claim that Taiwan would have united with the mainland many years ago if it were not for US arms sales to the ROC.

In the 1972 communiqué, the United States reaffirmed its interest in a peaceful settlement of the Taiwan issue by the Chinese themselves and affirmed the United States' long-term objective of withdrawing all US forces and military installations from Taiwan. The issue of Taiwan came up again in the second pillar of China-US relations: the 1979 normalization agreement. In a December 1978 joint communiqué, China and the United States announced that they would establish diplomatic relations on January 1, 1979. In the English translation of the communiqué, the United States "acknowledges" the Chinese position that Taiwan is a part of China, but would maintain "cultural, commercial, and other unofficial relations with the people of Taiwan." In unilateral statements made after the announcement of the communiqué, the United States in press briefings pledged to remove troops from Taiwan; it reiterated its position that it sought a peaceful resolution of the Taiwan issue and offered to sell limited quantities of defensive arms to Taiwan. Unilateral statements by the Chinese revealed China's opposition to US arms sales to Taiwan and reiterated its position that unifying Taiwan with the mainland is China's internal affair. Following normalization of relations with China, the United States broke off formal relations with Taiwan. To maintain unofficial relations, however, the United States replaced its embassy with an unofficial agency, called the American Institute in Taiwan (AIT), staffed by former government officials. Taiwan's counterpart in the United States is called the Taipei Economic and Cultural Representative Office (TECRO). Taiwan maintains TECRO offices in major US cities.

A tougher question concerned the US commitment to defend Taiwan. Deng Xiaoping insisted that the United States immediately abrogate its 1954 mutual defense treaty with Taiwan. Instead, the United States issued a statement reiterating its interest in the peaceful resolution of the Taiwan question. It assured China that it would sell only a reasonable amount of defensive arms to Taiwan and implied that it could reduce arms sales if tensions between China and Taiwan declined. Congress, however, was incensed that the Carter administration negotiated without its consultation on the normalization agreement. Unable to reverse the normalization agreement, Congress in spring 1979 passed the Taiwan Relations Act (TRA), a law that commits the United States to help Taiwan defend itself. To protect Taiwan from the threat of force from China, the TRA allows the United States to sell defensive weapons to Taiwan. The TRA also states that the United States considers any effort to determine the future of Taiwan by other than peaceful means, including boycotts or embargoes, a threat and of "grave concern" to the United States.[14] The president is to inform Congress of any threat to Taiwan's security, and the executive branch, with the US Congress, is to determine the appropriate response. Beijing has never recognized the validity of the TRA and insists that it conflicts with the 1979 normalization communiqué. To Beijing, the 1972 and 1979 communiqués are literal statements of truth.

The fourth pillar of US-China relations, and one that directly concerns US support of Taiwan, is the 1982 Joint Communiqué on Arms Sales to Taiwan. China had opposed US arms sales to Taiwan after normalization of China-US relations, particularly because it viewed continued arms sales as an unacceptable infringement of Chinese sovereignty. In the early years of the Reagan administration, China's leaders sought promises from the United States that its arms sales to Taiwan would not exceed, in quality or quantity, the level reached during the Carter administration; that it would gradually reduce its supply of weapons to Taiwan; and that it would set a timetable for ending arms sales to Taiwan. In August 1982, the United States committed itself to gradually reduce and eventually terminate arms sales to Taiwan. Much to Beijing's chagrin, the United States continues to sell large quantities of high-quality defensive arms to Taiwan. In 2010, the US government approved a $6 billion arms sales package to Taiwan, including sophisticated weaponry such as Harpoon antiship missiles, Black Hawk helicopters, and Patriot interceptor missiles. China loudly protested the sale of defensive weapons to Taiwan. China's governments have long argued that Taiwan would have united with the PRC a long time ago if not for US interference in the matter, which China considers its internal affairs. Unable to stop the sales, China commonly responds with words of indignation and suspension of military dialogue. For instance, in response to the 2010 sale, China summoned the US ambassador and chastised him for meddling in China's "internal affairs," cut off military-to-military ties, and threatened to impose sanctions on those US companies supplying the arms to Taiwan.[15] While US arms sales to Taiwan greatly perturb China's leaders and China's response to the sales may chill relations between the two countries, the arms sales so far have not caused any permanent fallout in China's relations with the United States.

Since the election of Ma Ying-jeou as president of the ROC in 2008, China and Taiwan have enjoyed unprecedented good relations. These relations follow nearly twenty years of rocky relations during the ROC presidencies of Lee Teng-hui (1988–2000) and Chen Shui-bian (2000–2008). China accused Lee of being a separatist, although Lee—who also was chair of the Nationalist Party on Taiwan—publicly espoused reunification. Chen Shui-bian of the Democratic Progressive Party had built his political career around advocating permanent Taiwan independence from mainland China. Even during these rocky times, however, China became Taiwan's largest trade partner. Since the election of Ma, the government of Taiwan has signed several cooperative agreements with China, and Taiwan cumulative investment in China has grown to more than $100 billion.[16] China and Taiwan have also strengthened trade and tourist links. In 2009, China and Taiwan established direct air links for the first time in sixty years. In the absence of direct flights, people living on Taiwan had to travel to China via a third territory, usually Hong Kong. Cutting out this extra leg saves tourists and business travelers time and money. In 2009, Taiwan businesses invested $7.14 billion in China, and bilateral trade reached $109 billion.[17] In 2009, the number of visits by Taiwan citizens to mainland China reached 4.5 million. From July 2008, when tourists from mainland China were first allowed to travel directly to Taiwan, to the spring of 2010, mainland tourists made 1.3 million visits.[18] Despite the economic integration and recent good feelings across the Taiwan Strait, China is no closer to its goal of "peaceful reunification." Most people on Taiwan continue to prefer the status quo to unification or Taiwan independence.[19] China still has more than one thousand missiles pointed directly at the island. Improved China-Taiwan relations benefit the China-US relationship by diffusing one of the most irksome aspects of China-US relations.

Tibet. Chapter 6 has already introduced China's policy toward Tibet and the central government's violation of Tibetans' human rights. The United States does not dispute China's claim to Tibet, but objects to Chinese authoritarian control of Tibet. In particular, the United States objects to religious restrictions in Tibet and to a number of human rights violations in Tibet. It also does not support Beijing's claim that the Dalai Lama is a separatist. Tibet and the Dalai Lama have supporters both in the White House and in Congress. In 1991, President George H. W. Bush met with the Dalai Lama, the first US president to do so. Presidents Clinton, George W. Bush, and Obama all have received the Dalai Lama and have called for dialogue between the Chinese government and the Dalai Lama. China lodges a diplomatic protest every time a sitting US president meets the Dalai Lama at the White House. The United States replies that these visits are "private," and that they never occur in the Oval Office.

Congress regularly calls for China to change its policies in Tibet. In 1987, the Dalai Lama gave his first political speech in the United States, at the invitation of the Congressional Human Rights Caucus. After his visit, Congress passed nonbinding resolutions declaring that the United States should make Tibet's situation a higher policy priority and should urge China to establish a constructive dialogue with the Dalai Lama. The US Congress authorized funding for broadcasting Voice of America and Radio Free Asia programs in Tibet and in the Tibetan language. In the 1990s, several foreign affairs authorization acts referred to Tibet as an occupied sovereign nation. In 2007, the US Congress awarded the Dalai Lama the Congressional Medal of Honor, a move that Beijing denounced as interfering in China's internal affairs and damaging to China-US relations.[20] Congress also regularly denounces China's military campaigns against Tibetans, such as the ones that occurred in 2009 and 2010, as Tibetans tried to mark the anniversary of the 1959 failed Tibetan uprising against China. Although it does not appear that US calls for Chinese-Tibetan dialogue and congressional resolutions concerning Tibet have resulted in a change of policy in Beijing, these efforts let China's leaders know that the world is watching. Ultimately, it appeared that Beijing's strategy was to simply wait out the aging Dalai Lama. That strategy seems to be paying off. In March 2011, the Dalai Lama stepped down as political leader of Tibet, saying that rule by "spiritual leaders or by kings" is now "out of date." The Dalai Lama claimed that he wanted to set an example of a nonelected leader who is happy to relinquish power in the name of democracy.[21] He called for an elected political leader with greater power and responsibilities.

Trade. Trade issues are often contentious between China and the United States. While running for election to the US presidency in the early 1990s, Bill Clinton linked China's human rights record to renewal of granting most-favored-nation status to China. Although the US Congress annually threatened to revoke MFN status if China did not improve its human rights record, it never followed through, and China labeled the United States a "paper tiger" (meaning something that seems as threatening as a tiger, but that is actually harmless). The whole point became moot after China joined the World Trade Organization, but the US attempts left a sour taste in Chinese mouths. The US trade deficit with China continues to be a thorn in the side of China-US relations. The trade deficit was discussed in more detail in Chapter 7. US trade deficits continue to climb to record highs, much to the chagrin of US manufacturers and politicians. By late 2010, the US trade deficit with China had reached $273 billion, the largest in the world between two states. As it stands, however, the United States and China need each other. History professor Nial Ferguson coined the term *Chimerica* to describe the China-US economic relationship. According to Ferguson, a symbiotic relationship exists between a productive China and a consumptive United States that has aligned the world's status quo power with its most significant challenger for much of the past decade. Despite a marked retrenchment in US consumption during the economic downturn of recent years, it appears that China and the United States continue to be locked in some sort of embrace, even if it is with knives at each other's throats.

China is not just looking to trade with the United States, but to invest in it. China in the twenty-first century has made significant forays into the US economy. China invested in deals valued at $11.7 billion between 2003 and 2010. In 2009 alone, China invested nearly $1 billion in the United States despite a slowdown in the global economy.[22] Visible signs of Chinese investment are Chinese laptop-computer maker Lenovo, appliance maker Haier, construction-machinery maker SANY, and automotive-parts maker Wanxiang, just to name a few. Lenovo is now one of the most recognized brands of laptop computers in the

United States. Haier employs hundreds of US workers in its South Carolina factory. SANY is opening a plant in Georgia. Chinese firms are also making major investments in the US energy sector, for example in clean energy and shale gas.

The United States reviews certain foreign acquisitions of existing businesses. Under the 2007 Foreign Investment National Security Act (FINSA), the US government must evaluate the national security implications of acquisitions of US businesses by foreign entities that may be connected to foreign governments.[23] In the early twenty-first century, the Committee on Foreign Investment in the United States—the body responsible for review of transactions under FINSA—turned down a few high-profile cases, such as the China National Offshore Oil Company's 2005 attempted acquisition of UNOCAL, and Huawei Technology's 2007 proposed acquisition of a significant ownership stake in 3Com (a digital electronics manufacturer, since acquired by Hewlett-Packard), giving the impression that the United States was hostile to Chinese acquisitions in the United States. Despite these cases, Chinese investment and business acquisitions in the United States are robust. Chinese foreign direct investment (FDI) in the United States doubled in 2010 alone.[24] Chinese companies are invested in projects in thirty-five US states. Recent Chinese investments in the United States include Tianjin Pipe's new steel pipe mill in Texas, Suntech Power's solar-panel manufacturing plant in Arizona, and American Yuncheng Gravure Cylinder's print plant in South Carolina. These and other Chinese investments faced no significant opposition, and in some cases benefitted from state and local government investment incentives.

Human rights. Human rights was not an issue in the first decade after China's normalization of relations with the United States. China's crushing of the protests at Tiananmen in June 1989, however, put human rights at the front and center of the China-US relationship. The United States viewed the Tiananmen Square Massacre as a gross violation of human rights and responded with sanctions and other punitive measures. Congress and the Clinton administration in the early 1990s used MFN status as the main tool within US human rights policy toward China. After the separation of this link in 1994, the Clinton administration promoted its human rights agenda by calling for US businesses engaged in work with the Chinese government to protect human rights, by increasing Voice of America broadcasts in China, focusing more of its reporting on politics, and drawing international attention to China's human rights record. From 1990 to 2002, the United States introduced annual resolutions to the UN Human Rights Commission criticizing China's human rights practices and requiring Beijing to follow international human rights standards. Failing to see any positive improvement over the years, President George H. W. Bush in 2003 opted not to offer the annual resolution, but argued that the United States could discuss human rights issues directly with China's leadership. The US State

Department, however, continues to issue annual reports on China's human rights and religious freedom.

Despite its vocal criticism of China's human rights record, the United States has little power to compel China's leaders to improve the situation. China's leaders think that the United States uses human rights as an excuse to interfere in the affairs of other countries and to advance its own strategic goals. In particular, Beijing believes that the United States uses human rights as a tool to undermine China's socialist system.[25] China's leaders use a socioeconomic definition of human rights that includes food, shelter, health, and education, rather than the Western definition, which protects individual freedoms and civil liberties (see Chapter 5). China's leaders see socioeconomic rights as positive rights because they require the state to take a proactive role. In contrast, they regard civil and political rights as negative rights because they limit the powers of the state. China's leaders argue that human rights are within China's own jurisdiction of sovereignty, and that other countries have no right to interfere. China condemns US criticism of China's human rights record as intervening in its internal affairs and for ignoring China's sovereignty over what it sees as a domestic issue.[26]

Security concerns. Despite recent improvements in bilateral relations, both China and the United States remain wary of each other's security interests in the Asia Pacific. The United States remains suspicious of China's annual double-digit rise in military expenditures (Chapter 9) and views China as a rising military power that seeks to challenge US influence in the Asia Pacific. From China's perspective, the United States unduly dominates the region and regularly interferes in regional issues, often meddling in the internal affairs of Asian countries.

Japan

China's most important relationship in Asia is that with Japan. China's post–World War II relations with Japan have never been characterized by the hostility that China exhibited toward the United States and the Soviet Union, though relations have been quite tense since the beginning of the twenty-first century. Geographic proximity, history, and cultural and economic ties explain this relationship. As early as the Tang Dynasty, Japanese missions sent to China imported Buddhism, Confucian values, Chinese political principles, forms of governmental organization, codes of law, art, and music to Japan. Although these elements developed differently in China and Japan—largely due to being separated by water and periods of isolation—there remains a sense in Japan that China is an important source of Japanese culture. Guilt over Japanese behavior in China during World War II may have made Japan less antagonistic than the United States, and eventually the Soviet Union, in its relations with China.

Following its defeat at the end of World War II, Japan no longer posed a direct military threat to China. However, it posed a potential threat because it served as the main US military base in Asia. According to Mao's bipolar world, the United States was the enemy, and Japan under US occupation belonged to the enemy camp.[27] To strengthen defenses against the United States, China in 1950 entered into a treaty with the Soviets. In 1951, Japan signed a security treaty with the United States, ostensibly against China and the Soviet Union. Japan's government was also put off by Chinese attempts to manipulate public opinion in Japan. Chinese Communist Party activists worked with Japanese trade, fishing, and labor groups to strengthen their pro-China voices. Despite China's efforts, Japan—occupied by the United States until 1952—signed a peace treaty with the Nationalists on Taiwan and normalized relations with Taipei rather than Beijing.

Despite these tensions, Japanese businesses saw trade opportunities with China, and in 1952, China and Japan signed an unofficial trade agreement. In 1962, China and Japan signed the semiofficial Memorandum on Trade Agreement, which opened the door to better relations. In 1964, Mao developed his three worlds theory, in which he saw Japan and other small and medium-sized capitalist countries as belonging to an intermediate zone between the superpowers. This view implied that China could work with Japan. Despite this attitude and the growth of trade and informal exchanges between the two countries, Mao suspended any idea of normalization with Japan during the first half of the Cultural Revolution. China-Japan relations deteriorated during the Cultural Revolution and further declined after Japan renegotiated the 1960 Security Pact with the United States, which reaffirmed the Japan-US security alliance. China-Japan relations improved after the thaw in China-US relations in 1971. For many years, the United States had put pressure on Japan to maintain diplomatic relations with Taiwan rather than with China. Japan resumed formal relations with China in 1972, soon after Nixon's visit to China. Throughout the 1970s and 1980s, China-Japan relations focused on economic relations as Japan followed a policy of *seikei bunri,* namely, the separation of economics and politics. Japan has been China's top trading partner since the 1960s. In 2004, China became Japan's largest export market, eclipsing trade with the United States for the first time since 1945. Exports and imports between Japan and China, including Hong Kong, reached $213 billion, accounting for more than 20 percent of Japan's total trade. In fact, China now consumes more Japanese goods than all European countries combined. China is also Japan's largest source of imports. In 2010, the two countries' bilateral trade value totaled a record $302 billion. Japan is China's second largest source of foreign investment. In 2010, China's FDI in Japan totaled $314 million; Japan's FDI in China totaled $7.3 billion.[28]

Despite these good economic relations, there is still considerable tension between China and Japan. Much of this tension stems from Japan's occupation of China during World War II. Bitterness remained in China long after Japanese troops left the Chinese mainland. One of the areas of tension is China's claim that Japan fails to acknowledge the atrocities it committed during the occupation. Two issues related to this failure particularly perturb the Chinese. The first issue concerns the visits by government officials to the Yasukuni Shrine in Japan. Built in 1869 by the Meiji emperor to honor the war dead, the shrine memorializes nearly two and a half million soldiers who fought and died for Japan. Since World War II, Japanese prime ministers have visited the shrine. The visits became controversial, however, after 1978 when shrine administrators decided to enshrine and commemorate fourteen Class A war criminals, including General Hideki Tojo, at the shrine.[29] The Chinese government later strongly criticized the decision. The Chinese were further angered by the visits of government officials to the shrine. From 1985 to 2001, there was a virtual moratorium on prime ministerial visits in response to protests from China.[30] Some senior government officials, who subscribed to a nationalist narrative of World War II, continued their public visits. Each year on the anniversary of the end of World War II (August 15), ultranationalist politicians visit the shrine. Prime Minister Koizumi Junichiro of the ruling Liberal Democratic Party visited the shrine every year from 2001 to 2006. Koizumi's visits to the shrine, which constituted his keeping a promise to domestic pressure groups, inflamed Chinese sensitivities, and between 2001 and 2007, Beijing refused to arrange summit meetings between the two countries. Because of the anti-Japanese feelings that the shrine invokes, the Democratic Party of Japan, which came into office after their victory in the summer 2009 parliamentary elections, pledged not to visit the shrine.

Another area of tension is the revision of Japanese textbooks. The Chinese government and people claim that Japanese textbooks gloss over Japan's wartime atrocities. In the most recent case, the Japanese government in 2001 sanctioned a textbook produced by the nationalist Japanese Society for History Textbook Reform for use in Japan's middle schools. Contributors to this book argued that Japan fought in self-defense and that accounts of atrocities were exaggerated to vilify Japan. In fact, the offending title, just one of a selection of textbooks available to middle schools, is unpopular in Japan as well. Government approval of the book attracted significant attention and protest in China, while the second stage of the adoption process—review by local school boards, where the book has been widely rejected due to intense pressure from parents and teachers—was not widely reported in China. The 2001 and 2005 editions of the book were each used by less than a half percent of middle schools in Japan.[31] While the 2009 edition of the book broke the 1 percent barrier, the textbook has a long way to go before its narrative becomes the norm in Japanese history education.

Japan is also increasingly wary of China's growing military might. Before and during World War II, Japan had been militarist and expansionist. After suffering defeat in World War II, Japan adopted a pacifist constitution, which states that Japan will never maintain any offensive military capability. However, Japan maintains a self-defense force of 250,000 troops.[32] Although Japan's post–World War II military was established on the assumption that it is strictly and exclusively defensive, lingering memories of Japanese aggression during World War II have made China's leaders suspicious of any real or perceived Japanese military modernization. Almost without exception, Japan since 1976 has capped military spending at 1 percent of GDP. Due to the sheer size of its economy, however, Japan maintains the fourth largest military budget in the world in absolute terms. During the Cold War, Japan built a world-class army, complete with tanks, aircraft, and submarines. While there continue to be important restrictions on military operations, Japan has upgraded its weapons systems and acquired new technology and systems when necessary. Japan continues to partner with the United States in its defensive alliances, and China's leaders are concerned that Japan will tighten its alliance coordination with the United States and present a united front against China on either political or security issues in the Asia-Pacific region.

India and Pakistan

China and India established diplomatic relations in 1950. India was one of the first Asian countries, and the second noncommunist country, to formalize relations with China. In 1954, Premier Zhou Enlai and Indian prime minister Jawaharlal Nehru jointly announced the Five Principles of Peaceful Coexistence. The Bandung Spirit did not last, however, and by the late 1950s, China and India were involved in a serious border dispute. Small-scale fighting over the border escalated into a more intensive war in 1962. The border war was followed by more than twenty years of chilly relations between the two countries. The turning point in China-India relations occurred in December 1988, when India's prime minister Rajiv Gandhi visited China. Gandhi's visit began a warming trend in bilateral relations. During his visit, Gandhi signed bilateral agreements on science and technology cooperation, on the development of direct air links, and on cultural exchanges. China and India agreed to hold annual meetings between foreign ministers, to create a joint ministerial committee on economic and scientific cooperation, and to work to resolve the boundary issue. In 1991, Chinese premier Li Peng visited India. In July 1992, border trade resumed after more than thirty years.

Today, India is one of China's largest trade partners. It is China's seventh largest export market and China's tenth largest trade partner. While India-China trade increased by more than 50 percent annually from 2004 to 2008, Indian officials are increasingly concerned about its trade deficit with China, which grew 70 percent during the same time. China's trade surplus, which stood at more than $20 billion in 2011, represents a 26 percent increase over the 2009 figure. They complain that Chinese barriers to trade mean that India exports mostly lower-value raw materials and primary goods, but imports higher-value finished products in return. For instance, while India exports to China mostly minerals, metals, cotton, organic chemicals, precious stones, and some iron and steel, India imports electrical machinery, electronic products, and machineries from China.

Despite vigorous trade relations, China-India relations in the early twenty-first century remain testy. Long-simmering territorial disputes and China's support for Pakistan continue to hamper good diplomatic relations (see Figure 10.1). In the fallout of the 1962 border war, both China and India claim territory held by the other. India claims an area of Chinese-held territory in Kashmir (called Aksai Chin by China), while China claims a larger territory in India's northeastern state of Arunachal Pradesh. (China calls the Indian-held territory South Tibet.) As China-India relations warmed up in the early 1990s, the two countries agreed in 1993 to respect the 2,520-mile border (officially called the Line of Actual Control) and to reduce military forces along the border pending a peaceful, final boundary settlement. While it appears that both China and India preferred the status quo to fighting a new border war, Chinese words and actions are making India nervous.

In recent years, China has upped the rhetoric asserting its claim to South Tibet, arousing India's suspicion over China's intent. China has invested heavily in infrastructure projects in the disputed region. In response, India in 2009 deployed up to sixty thousand troops along the Arunachal Pradesh border and opened a refurbished air base while beginning a number of its own infrastructure projects there. By deploying troops and engaging in development, India is making a statement that Arunachal Pradesh is not a part of China, as Beijing claims.

China's growing investments in Pakistan-controlled Kashmir also concern India.[33] China helped Pakistan develop a deep-sea port at Gwadar on the Arabian Sea. Beijing provided some $200 million in grants and loans for the project. In what China expert Jonathan Holslag has termed "tarmac diplomacy," China is assisting Pakistan in railway and highway development.[34] China also is funding the construction of hydroelectric power plants, among other infrastructural development within Pakistan-controlled Kashmir. In 2010, China sent thousands of troops to Pakistan-controlled Kashmir to assist in a roads project there. In 2010, China hinted that it considered the northern parts of Indian-controlled Kashmir as parts of Pakistan.

In early 2011, the Indian government announced that it plans to build 558 roads by 2030 in an effort to shore up its infrastructure along its China and Pakistan borders. India's roads project appears to be a response to China's recent infrastructure development in Tibet and China-assisted roads projects in Pakistan-occupied Kashmir. During the last decade, China constructed three major highways and fifty-five other roads along the Indian border. One of the highways, which runs between Lhasa in Tibet and Aksai Chin in Chinese-held Kashmir,

Figure 10.1 Map of Territories Disputed with India

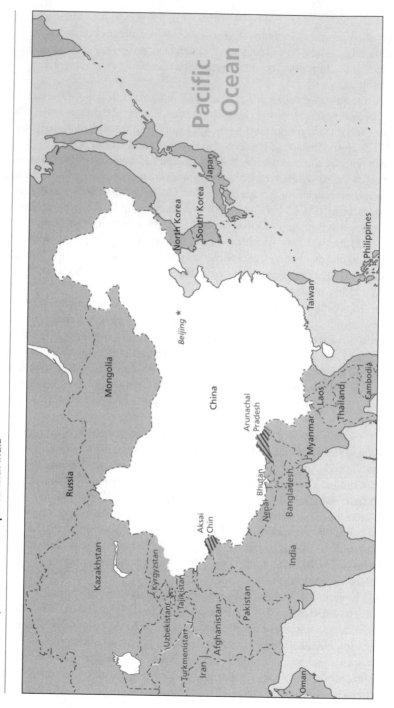

appears to be an attempt to solidify China's claims to the disputed territory. There also appears to be a military component to the roads projects. For both China and India, the roads not only help bolster claims to disputed territory, but facilitate troop and equipment mobilization.

India is increasingly nervous over China's assertiveness in the Asia Pacific. China is rapidly developing a blue-water navy (Chapter 9) and has rankled Southeast Asian countries with its claim to nearly the entire South China Sea. Increasingly wary of China's diplomatic and military influence in Asia, India in 2010 suspended regular bilateral defense meetings. On land, China not only supports India's longtime rival Pakistan, but is nurturing closer relations with India's neighbors—Pakistan, Sri Lanka, and Myanmar—leaving India feeling encircled by allies of China. In response, India is reaching out to other Asian democracies that share India's concern about an increasingly nationalistic China. For instance, in late 2010, India signed a trade deal with Japan and pushed for rapid implementation of an existing one with Southeast Asian allies.

The United States is also a part of the China-India dynamic. China's hardened position on Tibet and Kashmir has pushed India strategically closer to the United States. Increasingly strong ties with the United States are emboldening India in dealing with China. On a visit to India in late 2010, US president Obama indicated support for India's bid for permanent membership on the UN Security Council, which rankled Beijing and made China wary of warmer US-India relations. A 2008 agreement facilitating nuclear cooperation between the United States and India rankled Beijing as well. It provides US assistance to India's civilian nuclear energy program and expands US-India cooperation in energy and satellite technology. Beijing has supported a similar deal for Pakistan.

Southeast Asia

During the Mao years, China supported communist insurgencies and revolution in Southeast Asia. Tensions between Southeast Asian nations and China continued in the 1980s and 1990s, mostly due to perceived Chinese expansion in the South China Sea. For example, China in 1974 sank a Vietnamese naval ship, resulting in the drowning death of some 100 Vietnamese sailors, in its successful attempt to occupy the Paracel Islands. In the 1990s, China challenged the Philippines' claims to parts of the Spratly Islands. The Philippines accused China of placing a satellite dish on the contested Mischief Reef and of building military structures near the Philippine-held islands in the Spratlys. Consistent with its attempts at a peaceful rise, China in the early twenty-first century replaced belligerence and aggression with a more cooperative position in projecting power and influence in Southeast Asia. It appears, however, that China's line toward the South China Sea has hardened again. In 2010, China's leaders stated that they regarded the South China Sea as a "core interest" on a par with Taiwan and Tibet, and they reacted with anger after the United States raised the territorial claims at a July regional meeting. Washington called for a multilateral approach to resolving the claims, which gained the support of most of the Asian countries at the meeting. China responded by carrying out naval drills in the disputed southern waters. In a bizarre effort to solidify its claim, China in August sent a tiny submarine down more than two miles to plant a Chinese flag on the seabed. In fall 2010, China suspended high-level exchanges with Japan and limited export of rare earths to Japan after that country detained the captain of a Chinese boat that had collided with two Japanese coast guard ships near disputed islands in the South China Sea.

The dispute over the South China Sea seems to contradict China's efforts to use soft power to increase its influence in Southeast Asia. In his 2004 book *Soft Power,* Joseph Nye calls soft power "the second face of power." Rather than use inducement or threats to get the outcomes it wants, a country may obtain the outcomes it wants because other countries want to follow it. This soft power, namely getting others to want the outcomes that you want, co-opts rather than coerces.[35] Elements of soft power are attractions, agenda-setting, values, culture, policies, institutions, public diplomacy, and bilateral and multilateral diplomacy.[36] China's soft power includes economic assistance, security and trade relations, multilateral and bilateral diplomacy, confidence-building (measures that gradually increase trust between or among nations), tourism, and education.

In Southeast Asia, for example, China is playing down territorial disputes and touting its "peaceful rise." China ended its border disputes and signed Southeast Asia's Treaty of Amity and Cooperation, which commits signatories to mutual respect for a country's sovereignty and equality. It signed bilateral cooperative agreements with several Asian states, and China has signed oil and gas exploration agreements with India and Vietnam, former foes. China also stepped up activities with developing nations whose relations with the US or Japan are waning. China has aggressively wooed the Philippines with offers of greater cooperation and aid. China also is boosting its image through public diplomacy. Efforts include museum exhibits in Malaysia and Singapore to celebrate the six-hundredth anniversary of the voyage of Chinese admiral Zheng He, who sailed to foreign countries but did not conquer them; increasing cultural exchanges with Southeast Asia by hosting overseas scholars; and creating a Chinese peace corps to send Chinese youth to assist in development programs in developing nations like Laos and Myanmar.[37]

China also practices multilateral diplomacy and in recent years has increased its participation in regional multilateral groups. China's main avenue for multilateral diplomacy with Southeast Asia is its involvement with the Association of Southeast Asian Nations (ASEAN) and the ASEAN Regional Forum (ARF).[38] ASEAN seeks to accelerate economic growth through market liberalization and integration of member economies and to promote regional peace and stability in the region. The ARF seeks regional security through confidence-building measures (namely meetings and exchanges) and the use of diplomacy to prevent disagreements among states from escalating into conflict. ASEAN is currently in the process of creating a free-trade area, in which member states would eventually reduce intraregional tariffs and eliminate nontariff barriers to trade. Association leaders are currently working to transform the organization into an economic community, called the ASEAN Economic Community (AEC), by 2020. The AEC would create an economic region in which there is a free flow of goods, services, investment, capital, and skilled labor. In a formula called the ASEAN Plus Three framework, China, along with Japan and South Korea, would join the regional free-trade area. ASEAN currently has free-trade agreements with China only in the areas of investment and goods and services.

Since the 1990s, China has downplayed territorial disputes while focusing on development aid, investment, and trade. In recent years, China has provided ASEAN countries with a total of $750 million in loans and other investments. Chinese companies are building power plants in Indonesia, helping the Philippines feed itself by assisting that country in developing hybrid rice and corn, and offering economic assistance and investment to Cambodia, Laos, Myanmar, Thailand, and Vietnam through the Greater Mekong Subregion program.[39] There has also been a rapid rise in China-ASEAN two-way trade. According to Chinese data, China's exports to ASEAN countries rose by 220 percent from 2000 to 2005. China is the largest importer of goods made in the six ASEAN countries. China's combined imports from ASEAN countries rose by nearly 240 percent from 2000 to 2005.[40]

Economic assistance, investment, and trade in Asia are part of China's efforts to build an image as a constructive, cooperative, and peaceful partner in the region. Most important, China wants to demonstrate that its growing economic, political, and military power does not threaten the peace and stability of the region. For decades, the United States and Japan have been the dominant powers in Asia. China's rise challenges that dominance. In the mid-1990s, China's leaders were aware that the United States found China's economic and military rise threatening. Hegemonic stability theory posits that a rising power will challenge an existing power, resulting in war between the two. In response, China's leaders in 1996 devised a new security policy, called the New Security Concept (*xin anquan guan*). This policy argues that the Cold War mentality of competing and antagonistic blocks is outdated. It argues that the international system is moving toward relaxation of tensions and that peace and development are the main themes of the times. The New Security Concept is based on principles of mutual trust, mutual benefit, equality, and coordination among nations. This means that all nations should transcend differences in ideology, discard power politics, respect each other's security interests, recognize all countries as equal members of the international community, and seek peaceful settlement of their disputes. Its primary focus is enhancing trust through dialogue and promoting security through cooperation. For instance, the New Security Concept calls on nations to resolve territorial and border disputes peacefully through negotiations consistent with the UN Charter and international law; to reform and improve existing international economic and financial organizations and promote common prosperity; to address nontraditional security areas such as combating terrorism and transnational crimes, in addition to the traditional security areas of preventing foreign invasion and safeguarding territorial integrity; and to conduct effective disarmament and arms control.

The New Security Concept embraces concepts of common, comprehensive, and cooperative security, and is directed primarily at China's relations with its Asian neighbors. The New Security Concept is reminiscent of Zhou Enlai's Five Principles of Peaceful Coexistence. The thrust of the NSC is enhancing trust through dialogue and promoting security through cooperation. The core of the NSC is mutual trust, mutual benefit, equality, and coordination:

- *Mutual trust* means that all countries should discard power politics and maintain frequent dialogue on each other's security and defense policies and major operations.
- *Mutual benefit* means that all countries should meet the objective needs of social development in the era of globalization and respect each other's security interests.
- *Equality* means that all countries, big or small, are equal members of the international community and should refrain from interfering in another country's internal affairs.
- *Coordination* means that all countries should seek peaceful settlement of their disputes through negotiations and engage in ongoing cooperation on security issues to diffuse tension, avoid misunderstanding, and prevent the outbreak of wars and conflicts.

The New Security Concept supports the foreign policy approach known as China's Peaceful Rise (*Zhongguo heping jueqi*). China uses the term *peaceful rise* primarily to reassure its neighbors that China's economic and military prominence will not threaten peace and stability in the region, and that other nations will benefit from China's rise. China's leaders continually stress that China seeks neither hegemony nor military expansion, no matter how much the country develops. The doctrine emphasizes the importance of soft power and is based on the premise that good relations with its neighbors will enhance rather than diminish Chinese comprehensive national power. As an economic policy, the Peaceful Rise doctrine argues that other countries can materially benefit from China's economic rise through trade and investment. As a foreign policy, the doctrine emphasizes diplomacy and multilateral cooperation. For instance, China played a key role in the six-power talks concerning North Korea's nuclear program. It also created the Shanghai Cooperation Organization (SCO) to strengthen ties with its neighbors Russia, Kazakhstan, Kyrgyzstan, Tajikistan, and Uzbekistan. China's Peaceful Rise doctrine also calls for a less assertive policy toward territorial disputes in the East China and South China Seas (namely, the disputes over claims to the Spratly Islands and Diaoyu/Senkaku Islands).

Chinese supporters of the New Security Concept and Peaceful Rise doctrine claim that China is in the process of reidentifying itself by constructing a peaceful image. They claim that China had a revolutionary national identity in the Mao era and a detached national identity in the Deng and Jiang era. More than twenty years of opening and reform have moved China toward a status quo national identity.[41] The more China has integrated into international institutions, the more it identifies itself as a status quo state. For instance, between 1949 and 1979, China had signed only thirty-four international conventions. By 2002, however, it had signed 220 international conventions, the same number as those signed by the United States and Great Britain. The most significant multilateral agreement is China's accession to the World Trade Organization. China's willingness to sign these conventions indicates that China's leaders are open to dialogue on a host of important issues. In July 2006, China reinforced its image of a nonthreatening state by hosting the first China-ASEAN workshop on regional security. More than thirty senior defense officials from China and ASEAN member states gathered in Beijing to discuss military and security cooperation. Also that year, China hosted the sixth annual SCO summit, at the end of which participants signed an agreement to enhance economic cooperation by collaborating in the fields of energy, information technology, and transportation.[42] China also seeks to promote regional security through its association with the ASEAN Regional Forum (ARF). The ARF seeks to foster dialogue and consultation on political and security issues in the Asia Pacific. China has hosted numerous ARF workshops on nontraditional security concerns, such as terrorism, piracy, and the proliferation of weapons of mass destruction.

The integration of the New Security Concept and China's Peaceful Rise into China's foreign policy gives us an indication of China's future aspirations. China's ascendancy can be threatening to other countries in the region. As China's economy strengthens, it is likely to challenge, and attempt to replace, the United States and Japan as the dominant regional power. In touting the New Security Concept and Peaceful Rise, China's leaders argue that China does not seek to replace the United States as regional hegemon, but that the shift of power from a decreasingly powerful United States or Japan to a rising China will be peaceful. In fact, China is gradually replacing reference to its "peaceful rise" (*heping jueqi*) with "peaceful development" (*heping fazhan*), believing that the latter sounds less threatening.

Central Asia

Since the collapse of the Soviet Union and the end of the Cold War, Central Asia has become a region of immense importance for China.[43] China's primary interests in Central Asia are to strengthen domestic and national security, which includes energy security, and to build strong economic ties.

Good relations with Central Asia are vital for China's domestic stability, particularly in the Muslim northwest. China is home to more than 8 million Uygurs; about 300,000 more live in the former Soviet republics of Uzbekistan, Kazakhstan, and Kyrgyzstan. Beijing considers Xinjiang a destabilizing region beset by the so-called three evils of separatism, fundamentalism, and terrorism. The independence of the Central Asian republics following the collapse of the Soviet Union inspired some Uygurs in Xinjiang to call for an independent state of Uyguristan or Eastern Turkmenistan. Uygurs in the Central Asian republics supported their brethren in Xinjiang. As described in Chapter 6, Beijing responded to Uygur agitation with a Strike Hard campaign in 1996, further compounding Uygur efforts at separation. However, China recognized that it needed better relations with the Central Asian republics to prevent Uygur separatists from using the republics as a base for their activities. In 1996, China held a landmark summit with Russia, Kazakhstan, Kyrgyzstan, and Tajikistan. The so-called Shanghai Five pledged to resolve border disputes, demilitarize their borders, and engage in confidence-building measures. In June 2001, the Shanghai Five plus Uzbekistan launched the Shanghai Cooperation Organization (SCO), which calls for closer political and economic cooperation and coordinated action among the member states to fight separatism, fundamentalism, and terrorism. Specifically, China's initiative in creating the SCO was part of a security strategy to prevent Uygur separatists from using Central Asian states as a base for their activities. The SCO has proven instrumental in China's efforts to subdue Xinjiang. For instance, SCO members have responded positively to China's appeals that they crack down on the Uygur insurgency in their own countries and cut off funding to Uygur and Islamist groups suspected of supporting separatists in Xinjiang. Under pressure from China, the governments of Kazakhstan and Kyrgyzstan have shut down Uygur political parties and newspapers operating in those countries.[44]

After the September 11, 2001, terrorist attacks on the United States, China began to view violence in Xinjiang as part of a larger problem of Islamic terrorism. Uygur unrest became not just a domestic stability problem for China but a national security issue. Although the governments of the Central Asian republics are currently secular, Beijing is concerned that fundamentalist terrorist groups will provide aid and matériel to Xinjiang separatists. The SCO provides China a multilateral forum from which to crack down on terrorist activities. For instance, in 2002, units from China's Xinjiang Military District and Kyrgyzstan conducted a joint military exercise at the Kyrgyz-Chinese border aimed at combating cross-border terrorist activities. In 2005, China and Russia held their first joint military exercise. The exercise was aimed at strengthening the capabilities of the two countries in fighting international terrorism, extremism, and separatism. In 2007, all SCO members held their first joint military exercise. Conducted in a military district in Russia, the Peace Mission 2007 exercise was aimed at countering terrorism. Following a 2009 surge in violence in Xinjiang, in which 197 people were killed, China and Russia held joint exercises in northeast China designed to strengthen antiterrorism cooperation between the two countries.

The collapse of the Soviet Union raised security issues on China's borders. In particular, China is concerned about the United States' presence in the region. During the Cold War, Russia had been the dominant power in Central Asia. After the end of the Cold War and the emergence of the Central Asian republics, the United States began to pursue its own interests in the region. The creation of the Central Asian republics, coupled with the War on Terror, allowed the United States to increase its diplomatic and military presence and influence in the region. The United States, having established military bases in Central Asia after September 2001, has now become a force in what was previously a predominantly Russian sphere of influence. China now has two major powers on its border—the United States and Russia. Beijing views US military bases in Kazakhstan and Kyrgyzstan as an attempt to outmaneuver China, Russia, and Iran in Central Asia.[45] China viewed the demise of the Soviet Union as an opportunity to build political, economic, and strategic clout in Central Asia. Much to Beijing's chagrin, however, the United States saw the same opportunity and moved into Central Asia after the September 11 terror attacks. Strong diplomatic relations with the Central Asian republics, coupled with its military bases there, puts the United States in a good position to challenge China's power and influence in Central Asia. Of course, the United States also has liabilities in Central Asia, particularly the tension generated between its professed democratic ideals and the authoritarian reality of the region's polities. These liabilities limit US ability to challenge China's rising influence in Central Asia.

While Uygur unrest in Xinjiang Province and the increasing US presence in Central Asia are two factors driving China's interest in the region, it is China's quest for energy security that really drives China to strengthen ties with Central Asia. Beijing relies heavily on Middle East oil for its energy needs because China's own oil and gas resources cannot meet rising oil consumption. Over the next twenty-five years, China's energy consumption is expected to double (Chapter 7 discusses China's increasing energy needs). Central Asian gas and oil lessen China's reliance on Middle Eastern oil and the US goodwill that protects the transport of oil through the Persian Gulf. The discovery and extraction of vast amounts of oil and gas in Central Asia in the 1990s stimulated Beijing's interest in the region as a source of energy for China's continued economic development. However, China must compete with the United States and Russia for those resources. In recent years, China has worked with the Central Asian republics to build a network of pipelines to deliver Central Asian oil and gas to China. The major natural gas pipeline remains the Central Asia–China pipeline, a natural gas pipeline from Turkmenistan to Xinjiang. The 1,139-mile-long pipeline traverses parts of Turkmenistan, Uzbekistan, and Kazakhstan. It is notable for being the first major pipeline for natural gas that does not pass through Russia. Soviet-era pipes supplied Central Asian oil and gas to Eastern Europe via Russia. Russia enjoyed a monopoly on energy resources and transfers, giving it tremendous economic, political, and strategic power. The new Central Asia–China gas pipeline breaks the Russian monopoly on gas flows. The pipeline also serves to contain US military presence in Asia. The 2007 signing agreement between China and Turkmenistan contains a provision that discourages the latter from accepting a US military presence in the country.[46] China's interest in these pipelines means that Beijing has a vested interest in maintaining good relations with these states and ensuring their internal stability. In this sense, China is somewhat a status quo power in the region. As such, China's presence in the region drags it into internal disputes—such as border issues, water disputes, diasporas, and migration—between and among these states.

The major Central Asian oil pipeline serving China is the Kazakhstan-China pipeline. The 1,384-mile pipeline originates on Kazakhstan's Caspian shore and ends in Xinjiang. The pipeline was a joint development between the China National Petroleum Corporation (CNPC), China's largest integrated oil and gas company, and the Kazakh state-owned oil company, KazMunayGas. It has a capacity of 120,000 barrels a day. Because of these pipelines, Kazakhstan sells one-quarter of its oil to China, and Turkmenistan, which holds the fourth largest gas reserves in the world, sells more gas to China than to Russia.[47] Even Russia is selling more oil and gas to China than it did in the past. As European energy growth slows, Russia has found a new market in China. A pipeline from Siberia to China commits 15 million tons of Russian oil a year.

Beyond merely buying oil and gas from Central Asia, China is investing in energy projects there, gaining majority shareholding status in some of Central Asia's largest energy companies. For instance, CNPC acquired PetroKazakhstan in 2005. PetroKazakhstan has the second largest amount of Kazakh oil reserves after ChevronTexaco's TengizChevroil. In 2007, China's CITIC Bank Corporation acquired a 50 percent share in KazMunayGas. In 2009, CNPC gained a majority of shares in MangistauMunaiGaz, Kazakhstan's fourth largest oil company, with reserves of 500 million barrels, in exchange for a $10 billion credit line to Kazakhstan, whose economy was severely weakened by the 2008 global financial crisis. China currently seeks to acquire KarazhanbasMunai, a joint-stock company whose oil field has reserves of 46.6 million tons of oil. As a result of these and other acquisitions, Chinese companies control about 1 billion tons of oil reserves in Kazakhstan.[48]

Beyond oil, China has other economic interests in Central Asia. China wants to expand trade and investment opportunities in Central Asia. China offers the Central Asian republics huge amounts of credit in exchange for oil deals. Unlike the West, China offers financial assistance without demanding improvements in democracy and human rights. For instance, in 2008, China agreed to supply fifteen locomotives to Uzbekistan's railway, financed by long-term soft credit from Chinese state banks.[49] In 2009, the president of Kazakhstan travelled to Beijing and signed several deals with Hu Jintao, one of them involving the aforementioned MangistauMunaiGaz.

The SCO is also instrumental in fostering economic development in Central Asia. Annual SCO meetings are commonly accompanied by the signing of trade and investment agreements. For instance, on the eve of the 2006 meeting, China signed a deal to build a highway in Tajikistan and announced a financial plan to build a hydroelectric station in Kazakhstan. China's National Oil and Gas Exploration and Development Corporation (CNODC) announced at the meeting that it would spend $210 million to explore for oil and gas in Uzbekistan.[50]

Trade is thriving between China and Central Asia, and Chinese state firms are busy building railways and highways to facilitate trade. Trade between China and the Central Asian republics reached $25.2 billion in 2008.[51] Kazakhstan is China's most important economic partner in Central Asia, with China-Kazakhstan trade amounting to $17.5 billion in 2008. While China floods Kazakhstan and the other Central Asian republics with clothing, electronics, and household appliances, the republics supply China with a range of raw materials, most commonly extractive resources such as gas, uranium concentrate, and precious and rare earth metals, as well as agricultural products such as cotton fibers and fertilizers. For instance, in spring 2011, Uzbekistan and China signed investment deals worth more than $5 billion. Chinese banks agreed to open credit lines worth $1.5 billion to Uzbek banks to help fund investment projects in the Central Asian state. The two countries also agreed to build an Uzbek branch of the Central Asia–China natural gas pipeline, which will allow Uzbekistan to expand natural gas supplies to China. Trade between the two countries has quadrupled in the last five years.[52]

China has also played a key role in financing the so-called Silk Road transit corridor. The corridor is part of a larger infrastructural effort to bind Central Asia to China and make the region a transit corridor for Chinese goods to world markets. Formally known as the Transport Corridor Europe-Caucasus-Asia (TRACECA), the corridor seeks to revive the ancient Silk Road, which facilitated trade between Asia and Europe.[53] The corridor features a Eurasian continental railroad bridge, a major highway, and a pipeline network, to be complemented eventually with a fiber-optic network. Backed by thirty-two countries, the new transit corridor features routes from Tokyo to Bulgaria through a unified highway system. Since December 2004, TRACECA has linked China's east coast to Rotterdam through Mongolia, Kazakhstan, Russia, and Western Europe. While these projects enjoy the backing of major international financial institutions, China has also been a major source of funding. For instance, China is financing a $660 million, 132-mile expressway between Kashgar in Xinjiang Province and Irkeshtam, a border point in Kyrgyzstan, which is expected to open in 2013. The link, which crosses the Pamir Plateau, is a key link in facilitating improved China-Eurasian transport and trade.[54]

Africa

China's interests in Africa have shifted from supporting revolution to gaining access to its vast supplies of natural and energy resources, access to export markets, and to exploiting commercial opportunities. China's continued economic development is premised on the availability of energy resources and raw materials, of which Africa has plenty. Since the 1990s, China, under the "going out" strategy (see Chapter 7), has aggressively tapped African countries for their resources. Chinese state and private firms are active in Africa, pumping oil, mining minerals, exploiting hardwoods, rebuilding infrastructure, and investing in new hospitals and schools. In 2008, China's two-way trade with Africa was $115 billion, making China the continent's third largest trading partner after the United States and France. China-Africa trade tends to be concentrated in extractive industries and mining, such as oil, mineral products, diamonds, ferromanganese, and copper; industrial products such as iron and steel products; and raw materials such as wood, cotton, and tobacco. China's exports to Africa consist of mostly light industrial products, textiles, clothes, electronics, and consumer goods. Although most trade with China is concentrated in oil and mining, China is beginning to import more value-added commodities. These commodities, such as food products, have undergone some labor-intensive processing in Africa and will be further processed in Asia for industrial or consumer use.[55]

China's trade and investment in Africa are concentrated in a few countries, most of it in the oil-exporting nations of Angola, Equatorial Guinea, Nigeria, Republic of Congo, and Sudan. One-quarter of China's trade with Africa is with one country—Angola. In 2008, two-way trade reached $25.4 billion, making Angola China's largest trading partner in Africa.

Chinese trade and investment in Africa are driven largely by its multinational corporations that retain strong ties to the central government. Highly competitive and subsidized by the state, Chinese corporations are capturing key resources and market share across Africa. More than eight hundred Chinese state-owned firms are active in the African economy. One of these multinational corporations, the China National Offshore Oil Company, in 2005 bought a 45 percent stake in an offshore Nigerian oil field. China's Sinopec outbid an Indian oil company in Angola, offering the Angolan government $2 billion at the eleventh hour, freeing it from its reliance on International Monetary Fund sources. Chinese communications giant Huawei Technologies has expanded its business into thirty-nine sub-Saharan African countries, including a contract to build the infrastructure for Nigeria's lucrative mobile phone market. The Algerian government has awarded $20 billion in government construction contracts in Algeria, or 10 percent of its massive investment plan, to some fifty Chinese firms. The Chinese firms, most of them state-controlled, are building an airport, the country's first shopping mall, its largest prison, sixty thousand new homes, two luxury hotels, and the longest continuous highway in Africa.

Many Africans are increasingly unsettled by China's presence on the continent. Although this investment is designed to benefit Algerians in the long run, critics of China's investment in Africa claim that there is no trickle-down for the average citizen. Chinese small and medium enterprises are likewise expanding their presence in Africa, and Chinese small-scale retailers threaten to undermine traditional retailers. These businesses are able to offer up low-cost consumer products, but they also drive out traditional suppliers. In recent years, Chinese textile firms exploited workers with low wages and low labor standards, forcing domestic firms out of business. In Algeria, as in other countries in which they have won large contracts, Chinese firms import everything from the heaviest equipment to water for their water coolers. At the same time, Chinese firms imported thousands of Chinese workers, ignoring the African unemployed. The establishment of Chinese businesses in Africa has fueled Chinese immigration to the continent. Some cities, such as Algiers, have Chinatowns. Chinese firms import workers for cheap labor, and Chinese provincial authorities encourage emigration to Africa as a means of acquiring foreign remittances. (At the same time, a growing number of Africans are living in China. Forty percent of foreigners in Guangzhou are African workers, who have created their own "Little Africa," complete with shops, restaurants, and travel agencies.) In some cases, the influx of Chinese laborers to Africa has exacerbated existing unemployment. African laborers employed in Chinese firms complain of low wages, low labor standards, and discrimination.[56] On construction sites in Africa even the unskilled workers are usually Chinese, not local workers. Chief engineers of construction projects in Africa, who are Chinese, argue that the Chinese work longer and harder than Africans, and without complaint. These tensions can lead to violence. In summer 2009, an Algerian got into a fight with a Chinese trader over a parking space in Algeria, sparking an anti Chinese riot that took on Islamic overtones. After the fight, an Algerian mob looted Chinese shops and vandalized cars. Anti-Chinese sentiment also rose that summer after Chinese authorities repressed the Uygur Muslims in Xinjiang. Al-Qaida in the Islamic Maghreb threatened retaliation.[57]

China's expanding role in Africa is an important issue in international relations. China's support for dictators and weak democracies is changing Africa's relations with the West. China follows a policy of noninterference in the countries with which it does business. As an alternative to the Washington Consensus imposition of political and economic preconditions, China offers African leaders a "Beijing Consensus," wherein China offers loans and forgives debt without any political preconditions. Africa commands the largest percentage of China's development assistance (44 percent). Much of this aid is gift in kind, in the form of soccer stadiums and government buildings, which are built by Chinese engineering firms with Chinese-sourced materials. The China Export-Import (Exim) Bank and the China Development Bank are key sources of funding for African projects. The Chinese Exim Bank has a portfolio thirty times greater than its nearest Western rival in Africa. Chinese aid also props up undemocratic African regimes. For example, Angola is one of Africa's largest beneficiaries of Chinese largess, having received $2 billion in loans from China's Exim Bank to build an oil refinery, a new international airport, diamond mines, and the fisheries industry. Seventy percent of the funds will go to Chinese companies, which will subcontract the remaining 30 percent to local companies. Angola is paying back the loans in oil exports to China and has given China access to highly coveted offshore oil fields. Angola is China's largest foreign supplier of oil, supplying 18 percent of its total imports of petroleum, outpacing China's previous largest supplier, Saudi Arabia. Several Western lending institutions and human rights organizations have called the government of Angola corrupt, fraught with cronyism, abusive of human rights, and a violator of citizens' political rights and civil liberties.

Beyond trade, aid, and investment, China is also engaged in arms sales and PLA deployments in Africa. China has sent PLA troops to Africa under United Nations auspices, as observers to several African missions, and as peacekeepers to UN missions in the Democratic Republic of Congo and Liberia. It has also pledged engineering and medical troops to support the UN mission in Sudan. China also sees Africa as vital for the development of its space program. China operates a space tracking station in Namibia. In Nigeria, Beijing's willingness to sell arms in support of military action in the Niger Delta secured a lucrative oil deal for China. In Sudan, Chinese firms and laborers are upgrading one of the country's largest construction projects, an oil refinery being upgraded outside of Khartoum. China has long sold arms to third world countries, many of them in Africa. China has sold light arms to many African nations and sells higher-priced items such as aircraft, aircraft parts, and armored personnel carriers to Zimbabwe, Namibia, and Sudan. China's arms sales to Africa may turn back any progress the continent has made toward democracy. China supplies arms to regimes barred from obtaining weapons from Western sources. China's arms sales to Africa stood at $1.3 billion in 2003, making it the second largest arms dealer in Africa, after Russia. Chinese arms have fueled civil war in Sudan and Ethiopia and have kept Zimbabwean dictator Robert Mugabe in power.

China also sees African countries as important diplomatic partners and friends as it seeks greater influence on the world stage. To facilitate relations with African nations, China has engaged Africa through the Forum on China-Africa Cooperation (FOCAC). Beijing hosted the first FOCAC meeting in 2000. The meeting conference proposed the development of a new, stable, and long-term partnership with African countries, based on China's Five Principles of Peaceful Coexistence and noninterference in a country's sovereign affairs. Chinese and African leaders met in Ethiopia in 2003. Through the FOCAC process, China has cancelled African debt, developed market access, and expanded its cooperation with African firms in oil and natural resource exploration and extraction. As an indication of China's growing interest in Africa,

China's leaders dubbed 2006 as the "Year of Africa." In November 2006, Chinese leaders hosted the Beijing summit of the Forum on China-Africa Cooperation. Forty-one heads of state and senior officials from forty-eight African countries participated in the event, the highest-level and largest meeting that had taken place between Chinese and African leaders since the establishment of diplomatic relations in the 1950s. These leaders look positively upon China's engagement in Africa, particularly China's active involvement in construction and infrastructure development. They hope that engagement with China will raise the continent's status; develop competitive markets; assist them in fighting AIDS, tuberculosis, and malaria; and better integrate the continent with the global economy. At the conclusion of the summit, Chinese and African leaders issued a declaration and an action plan. The declaration confirms establishment of a strategic partnership between China and Africa. The action plan includes a detailed program for investment, trade, and development assistance. For instance, China pledged to engage in joint energy exploration and exploitation and signed fourteen commercial contracts and agreements covering natural resources, infrastructure, finance, technology, and communications. Since the initiation of FOCAC, China-Africa trade has increased ten times, from $10.6 billion in 2000 to $100 billion in 2008. (At the Beijing summit in 2006, China had pledged to double trade to $100 billion by 2010.) It also pledged to double its aid to Africa by 2009.

China's engagement in Africa and the FOCAC process confirms China's role as a global power in Africa. China has become a key aid donor and investor in Africa, and Chinese aid, trade, and investment have reduced Africa's traditional dependence on Western donors. African leaders, particularly authoritarian leaders, are attracted to China's development model, based on strong state management of economic liberalization, but with limited political liberalization. Chinese aid and investment do not come with the preconditions demanded by Western donor nations. In addition to its interests in developing economic relations with African countries, China views its engagement in Africa as an opportunity to advance the South-South agenda. Reminiscent of the Bandung Spirit, China and Africa are seeking a larger role for developing countries in international affairs. For instance, China has pledged to support programs that enhance Africa's agenda, such as encouraging Western donor nations to carry through on development pledges consistent with the United Nations Millennium Development Goals, a conclusion of the Doha round of world trade negotiations that benefits Africa, and better representation for Africa on the world stage. Chinese diplomacy and friendships with African countries can bring good things to Beijing. In recent years, Chinese largess persuaded some African countries to switch diplomatic relations from Taiwan to China. Flush with more than $3 billion in foreign reserves, China has used economic diplomacy to buy diplomatic partners. Between 2003 and 2008, four African countries switched recognition from Taiwan to China. Liberia switched in 2003 after China put pressure on Liberia by threatening to block a $250 million budget for the UN's peace-keeping troops in that country. Senegal switched to China in 2006 after the latter offered it up to $200 million in aid on the condition that it switch ties. China offered to stop arming rebel forces in Chad's bitter civil war if it switched to China. After forty-two years of diplomatic relations with Taiwan, Malawi in 2008 switched to China after China offered it $6 billion in aid. China's attempts to restrict Taiwan's diplomatic space in Africa have paid off. Today, only five African countries recognize Taiwan. With more than fifty of the world's countries located in Africa, Africa provides a significant voting bloc in international organizations. Supported by this bloc, China will have more clout in international organizations.

Russia

China had close, albeit sometimes very strained, relations with Russia in the early years of the PRC. On a trip to Russia, Mao signed the Sino-Soviet Treaty of Friendship, Alliance, and Mutual Assistance in February 1950. Russia, as the core of the Soviet Union, offered Mao's government $300 million in loans to rebuild China's economy after World War II. Strains in the relationship were evident as early as the Korean War (1950–1953), when Mao became angry with Soviet leader Joseph Stalin for neither committing Soviet troops to the conflict nor threatening to use nuclear weapons to end the conflict. Mao also was bitter that the Soviets would not forgive loans to China. Despite these disagreements, the Soviet Union extended some $2 billion in loans, credits, technical assistance, and training to China throughout the 1950s. Tensions worsened, however, after Stalin's successor, Nikita Khrushchev, criticized Stalin's excesses in a 1956 Soviet Communist Party gathering and made overtures toward peaceful coexistence with the West. China's leaders were also dissatisfied with Soviet neutrality during the 1962 China-India border war, and with its failure to honor an agreement to provide nuclear weapons technology to China. Mao also unsuccessfully challenged Khrushchev for the leadership of the Comintern. The tipping point in China-Russia relations came in 1958 when Mao unleashed the Great Leap Forward and broke with Soviet-style central planning. The break became final in 1960 when the Soviet Union recalled all of its advisers in China. The nearly ten thousand advisers took their blueprints and plans with them, leaving the Chinese with Soviet-designed factories with no blueprints, and military equipment with no design information.[58] Chinese-Russian relations were extremely tense throughout the 1960s and 1970s. During the Cultural Revolution, Red Guards attacked the Soviet embassy and harassed Soviet diplomats. Relations hit a low point in 1969, when bloody armed clashes broke out on China's northeast border with Russia.

China-Russia relations began to improve in the 1980s as both Chinese and Soviet leaders called for a relaxation of tensions between the two countries. In 1982, China and the Soviet Union indicated the desire to resume diplomatic relations. In late May 1989, Soviet leader Mikhail Gorbachev visited China, the first Soviet leader to do so in thirty years. Because of the student occupation of Tiananmen Square, China's leaders were unable to offer Gorbachev a state welcoming ceremony there. Nevertheless, Gorbachev's visit underscored Chinese and Soviet desire to improve bilateral relations. Following the December 1991 collapse of the Soviet Union, China and Russia in March 1992 ratified a border agreement, ending the Chinese-Russian split.

China's relations with Moscow warmed considerably in the late twentieth and early twenty-first centuries. In 2001, Russian president Vladimir Putin and PRC president Jiang Zemin signed a friendship pact to defend mutual interests and boost trade. In 2005, China and Russia held their first joint military exercises. Russia declared 2007 the "Year of China" and held hundreds of China-related business, educational, and sports events throughout the year. Moscow opened a massive new Chinese culture exhibit, and China pledged to build a series of cooperative energy projects.[59]

China enjoys good economic relations with Russia. Unlike their earlier relationship, which was characterized by Russia's superiority, China-Russia relations are on a more equal footing. In 2004, Chinese premier Wen Jiabao and Russian president Vladimir Putin signed an agreement on expanding trade. China-Russia trade volume has risen nearly ten times between 1998 and 2007. By 2007, bilateral trade had grown to $48 billion, registering an $8.8 billion trade surplus in China's favor.[60] Compared with these trade flows, investment flows between China and Russia seem small. In 2006, China had more than seven hundred projects in Russia, but which totaled only $1 billion. Russian investment in China was even lower, totaling only $7 million in FDI in China.[61] During a 2007 visit to Russia, however, President Hu moved to boost investment flows by signing commercial deals worth $4 billion and pledging to invest $12 billion in Russia by 2020. China and Russia have also signed numerous agreements on strengthening cooperation on energy. For instance, Russian gas giant Gazprom signed a strategic partnership deal with China National Petroleum Corporation in 2004 to build a gas pipeline for the delivery of Russian natural gas to China. And in 2006, Chinese president Hu Jintao and Russian president Putin further agreed to extend energy cooperation. The pipeline project became less feasible, however, and ultimately stalled after China agreed to import more than 2 million tons of liquefied natural gas from Australia. The delay in the project is an indicator of China's rising influence with Russia. Despite their agreements on trade and energy cooperation, China's leaders do not hesitate to toss aside agreements with Russia if a more favorable one comes along.

Europe

For much of the postwar era, China considered relations with Europe to be secondary to those with the United States, Japan, and neighboring powers. Only a few European countries, namely Denmark, Finland, France, Norway, Sweden, and the United Kingdom, established relations with China in the 1950s and 1960s. Today, China engages in both bilateral and multilateral relations with most of Europe. China has diplomatic relations with all European nations, except for the Holy See (Vatican). China also engages Europe in multilateral relations through many international organizations, such as the United Nations, World Trade Organization, World Bank, International Monetary Fund, International Atomic Energy Agency, World Intellectual Property Organization, and International Olympic Committee. China established relations with the European Union (EU) in 1975, but did not engage in regular summits until 1998. A watershed event in China's relations with Europe was the agreement between the two sides in 2001 to create a "comprehensive strategic partnership." Since then, China and Europe have strengthened their relations through a number of initiatives. Chinese and European leaders have engaged in top-level exchanges. In the past decade, heads of state or government of fourteen European countries have visited China, as have two-thirds of the EU commissioners and more than seventy members of the EU parliament. The president of the European Parliament, Josep Borrell, visited China in 2006, the first visit to China by a European Parliament president in thirteen years.[62] The highest-profile visitors were German chancellor Angela Merkel, former French president Jacques Chirac, and former Italian prime minister Romano Prodi. In 2005, China's president Hu Jintao visited several European nations, and in September 2006, China's premier Wen Jiabao visited Finland, Germany, and the United Kingdom, and attended the Ninth EU-China Summit meeting in Helsinki. In August 2007, German chancellor Angela Merkel made her second visit to China in two years. During her visit, Merkel pleased her hosts by welcoming China's economic development and increasing participation in international affairs, and reiterated Germany's adherence to the One-China policy.

Despite these visits, however, Europe became increasingly critical of China. Europeans became increasingly wary of Chinese competition with European manufacturing and vocally critical of China's human rights abuses and its treatment of the Dalai Lama. In a speech to the Chinese Academy of Social Sciences (CASS) during her 2007 visit to China, Chancellor Merkel stated that China should view the 2008 Beijing Olympics as an opportunity to promote human rights. Shortly after her visit, Chancellor Merkel received the Dalai Lama in Berlin, the first German chancellor to do so. In response to the meeting, China cancelled a human rights dialogue with Germany and temporarily suspended senior-level contacts with Berlin. Merkel further enraged China's leaders in 2008 when she announced that she would not attend the opening ceremony of the Beijing Olympics in protest at China's human rights record. Poland's prime minister Donald Tusk and Czech president Vaclav Havel echoed her decision. China-EU relations have improved somewhat in recent years. Today, China and the EU regularly engage in political trade and economic dialogue meetings. The substance of the meetings ranges from environmental protection to industrial policy to education and culture. China and Germany have made efforts to repair relations. During the Tenth China-EU Summit in 2007, China and Germany agreed to initiate high-level dialogue to address economic and trade issues. In October 2008, Merkel visited China a third time, this time to attend the Seventh Asia-Europe Meeting. Merkel could rightly claim that she had visited China every year since becoming chancellor, an indication of the great importance Berlin attaches to ties with China.

China and the EU also engage in high-level military exchanges. The North Atlantic Treaty Organization (NATO) has gradually stepped up its ties with China in recent years and seeks closer cooperation with Beijing. Recognizing that China is one of the permanent members of the UN Security Council, NATO has called for regular contacts with China. These ties are a major advance in China-NATO relations. Historically, China has been critical of NATO deployments and expansion. It criticized the expansion of NATO in the 1990s and viewed the deployment of forces in Bosnia in the 1990s as US hegemonism. The terrorist attacks against the United States on September 11, 2001, made clear the need to face security threats and reinforced the concept of international cooperation in combating them. In 2005, China and NATO started direct contact at the working level at NATO headquarters in Brussels. Despite China's interest in NATO, major areas of disagreement remain. For instance, China backs Russia and its allies against a US-NATO global missile shield and disagreed with NATO involvement in Bosnia in the 1990s and in Libya in 2011.

Despite the desire for agreement between China and the European Union, the two parties disagree in key areas of combating climate change and protecting the environment, sustainable development, and protection of human rights. China and the European Union also disagree over a number of key economic issues, such as trade deficits, exchange rates, and intellectual property rights. The European Union is also critical of China's investments in Africa and seeks coordination with China in building sustainable economic growth. Europe is also critical of China's lack of preconditions in offering development aid to Africa and wants China to support regional efforts to improve governance in African countries.[63]

While these diplomatic channels and discussions are important, trade forms the foundation of China-Europe ties. The European Union is China's largest trading partner and China is the second largest trade partner of the European Union after the United States. Europe's imports from China grew 16.5 percent a year between 2004 and 2008, but declined in 2009 due to fallout from the global financial crisis. European imports from China came roaring back in 2010, increasing 31 percent from a year earlier. China remains Europe's largest source of manufactured imports, importing mostly industrial goods such as machinery, transport equipment, and miscellaneous manufactured articles. China is also Europe's fastest-growing export market. Europe's exports to China increased 4 percent in 2009 from a year earlier, and 38 percent in 2010.[64] Europe exports to China technology and infrastructure vital to China's economic development. Despite the increase in exports to China, the European Union runs a trade deficit with China. Europe's trade deficit in 2010 was $242 billion.[65] Europe's trade deficit is mostly in the areas of office and telecom equipment, textiles, and iron and steel.

Europeans are increasingly investing in China. European FDI in 2009 grew 26 percent over 2007.[66] Europeans are finding that their investments in China come with their share of problems. Intellectual property rights (IPR) infringement remains a problem for European businesses in China. In 2007, 70 percent of European businesses operating in China claimed to have been a victim of IPR violations, and European manufacturers estimated that IPR theft cost them 20 percent of their potential revenues in China.[67] European service companies have found it difficult to break into the Chinese market. China maintains investment and ownership caps in many sectors such as banking, construction, and telecommunications despite signing agreements that it would open its market.[68] Foreign law firms in China are still not allowed to employ Chinese lawyers and are not permitted to participate in bar exams to gain Chinese qualifications. Once in China, European service companies find it difficult to navigate China's bureaucracy.

China's investment in Europe is disproportionately small considering the high proportion of China's trade with the European Union. Europe accounts for only 4 percent of China's outward FDI, as compared with 67 percent for Asia and 21 percent for Latin America.[69] The relatively insignificant amount of Chinese FDI in Europe may indicate that Chinese firms are merely seeking a toehold in European markets, but are not yet interested in, or ready for, a strong business presence there. When Chinese companies do invest in the European Union, their preferred locations are Great Britain (particularly London), Germany, France, and Spain.

Latin America

During the Cold War, China's relations with Latin American countries were heavily influenced by its revolutionary ideology and by those countries' relations with the superpowers. China's formal relations with Latin American countries are relatively recent. No Latin American country recognized the PRC until Cuba did so after its own communist revolution in 1959, and no South American country recognized the PRC until Chile did in 1970 after the election of Salvador Allende. After the Sino-Soviet split, China tried to form cooperative relations with, and to take a leadership role among, third world nations. Latin American nations formed a part of the third world with which China most identified. Like its foreign policy toward Asia and Africa, China's main foreign policy principles toward Latin America shifted at the end of the Cold War from encouraging or supporting revolution toward peace and economic development.

China's most important partners in Latin America are Venezuela, Mexico, Brazil, and Argentina. China's selection of these particular countries is strategic. Each of the countries is important to Beijing not only for the resources they may contribute to China's economic development, but also for their leverage over other countries on the continent. As the political and economic powers in South America, Brazil and Argentina have influence over other South American countries. Mexico influences the Central American states, and Venezuela influences Caribbean countries. Beijing refers to these four countries as strategic partners, meaning that it enjoys the highest degree of mutual trust and interdependence with those countries and with their goodwill can increase its influence in the region. China's support of populist regimes, such as Venezuela, Ecuador, and Bolivia, is also strategic. Those regimes' opposition to the US presence in Latin America serves China's interests because they prevent the United States from dominating the continent's financial, economic, and political institutions.[70] China's support of populist regimes and its desire to check US power in Latin America have their limits, however. Although China is no fan of US dominance in Latin America, or anywhere else, it values its stable, somewhat pleasant relations with the United States. For instance, China's interest in Venezuela focuses primarily on trade, even though Chavez wants China to be another vocal anti-US ally in the diplomacy and security arenas, similar to Venezuela's relationship with Iran and Russia. Beijing has no interest in being closely associated with Chavez's anti-US rhetoric or his support of Colombian rebels and North Korea's nuclear activities. China's leaders appear willing to hold Chavez at arm's length. As of 2008, Hugo Chavez had visited China five times since becoming president in 1999. Former Chinese president Jiang Zemin visited Venezuela only once, and Chinese president Hu Jintao avoided the country while visiting other Latin American nations in 2004, and again when he returned to the region in 2005, on a visit to Mexico. China is reluctant to be seen as directly challenging the United States in Latin America because of the diplomatic and possible economic problems that could result.

Latin America's growing importance to China is reflected in Latin America's gradually growing share of China's foreign trade. In 2000, Latin America accounted for only 2.7 percent of China's trade. By 2009, however, Latin America's share was 5 percent.[71] China–Latin America trade rose from $12.2 billion in 2000 to $102 billion in 2007. Since 2000, there has been a surge in Chinese consumption of metals, petroleum, food, and other commodities from Latin America. China's surging demand has been pushing up prices for Latin American commodities such as soy, iron ore, copper, and other metals, creating a boom for the economies of Argentina, Brazil, Chile, and Peru. China's largest trade partner in Latin America is Brazil. China-Brazil bilateral trade reached $56 billion in 2010. China is Brazil's largest trading partner, displacing the United States. The main products that Brazil exports to China are soy (accounting for 33 percent of the total), iron ore (25 percent), and petroleum (10 percent). Since establishing a strategic partnership with Brazil in 1993, fifteen senior Chinese leaders and seven top Chinese military personnel have visited Brazil, with nearly as many Brazilian leaders visiting China.

Mexico is quickly becoming a major market for Chinese goods. China is Mexico's second largest import partner. Imports from China reached $12.3 billion in 2009, nearly five times more than in 2000. Mexico's trade deficit with China grew from under $1 billion in 2000 to $6 billion in 2006, but settled back to around $1 billion after the 2008 global financial crises.[72] Mexico also suffers from competition with China in the global market. Mexico competes with China in the manufacture of shoes and clothing for the US market. China has replaced Mexico as the second largest exporter of goods to the United States. Foreign investment in Mexico's assembly industries has also shifted to China because wages there are generally much lower.

China has also stepped up relations with Venezuela. China-Venezuela two-way trade grew from $350 million in 2000 to $10 billion in 2011. China is increasingly investing in energy projects in Venezuela, the country with the largest proven oil reserves in the Western Hemisphere. These projects range from a $350 million infrastructure project in fifteen oil fields to a $60 million gas field project to further upgrade the country's railways and refineries. China's largest energy company, China National Petroleum Corporation, has acquired access to develop oil and gas fields in the country. In return, Venezuela provides China with oil, and daily exports have reached 500,000 barrels a day.[73] Venezuela exports as much as 15 percent of its petroleum and related products to China and hopes to increase the percentage to 45 percent by 2012.[74]

Chinese investment in Latin America has increased as well. Trade with Latin America has grown at an average annual pace of 30 percent since 2001, rising from $15 billion to $179 billion in 2010. One of China's more notable investments in Latin America is the concession for container ports at each end of the Panama Canal. In 1997, Hong Kong–based shipping giant Hutchison Whampoa won a twenty-five- to fifty-year contract to run the two major ports at the Atlantic and Pacific entrances of the Panama Canal. The ports are managed by a Hutchison subsidiary, Panama Ports, which is partly owned by China Resources Enterprise, the commercial arm of the Chinese Ministry of Trade. Although some US critics of the Chinese concession argued that China's control of the ports threatened US trade and maritime interests, treaties with the Panamanian government give the United States the right to defend the canal's neutrality, and the United States may deploy security forces to the Canal Zone without consulting with the Panamanian government. Incidentally, the other two ports for the canal are operated by a US or Taiwanese firm.

Consistent with its New Security Concept and Peaceful Rise doctrine, China has increased membership or participation in several international organizations in Latin America. China is a member of the Asia-Pacific Economic Cooperation forum and the Inter-American Development Bank, and is an observer to the

Organization of American States. China is also involved in regional organizations such as the China–Latin America Forum, China–South American Common Market Dialogue, and China–Andean Community consultations. During Hu Jintao's 2004 sixteen-day trip to Latin America, he signed thirty-nine agreements ranging from energy to investment, to education, and to tourism. The goal of Hu's visit was partly to secure future sources of resources for China's development, such as oil, iron ore, aluminum, timber, and other commodities. In recent years, several Chinese state companies have signed deals to develop oil fields and mines and to purchase commodities in Argentina, Bolivia, Brazil, Chile, Cuba, and Venezuela.

China's foreign policy in Latin America involves more than trade and investment. China also cooperates on science and technology, security and military affairs, and education and cultural projects. For instance, China is helping Venezuela build and launch new communications satellites, and China and Brazil have been conducting joint research and development of satellite remote-sensing technology since the late 1980s. The two countries have even launched two joint satellites. China also cooperates with Latin American countries in arms sales and military exchanges. In recent years, China has sold air-defense radar and aircraft to Venezuela, and PLA air force trainers have served as instructors for a new fleet of Chinese aircraft that Beijing sold to Venezuela.[75] China and most Latin American nations exchange visits of defense officials, including defense ministers and senior military officers.

China's interest in Latin America is political as well. More than half of the twenty-four countries that maintain diplomatic relations with Taiwan are in Latin America. For many years, China competed with Taiwan in checkbook diplomacy, the offering of generous aid packages in return for diplomatic recognition. Although a few countries switched diplomatic relations from Taiwan to China, such as Costa Rica, most have opted to maintain formal relations with Taiwan. Since the election of Ma Ying-jeou as president of Taiwan in 2008, Beijing has called a truce in this diplomatic competition. Since Ma's election, China's leaders have tried to improve relations with Taiwan, and recognize that wooing Latin American states from Taiwan hurts Taiwan more than it helps Beijing.

Conclusion

China's foreign policy has experienced a dramatic sea change, from exporting revolution during the Mao years to forging strong relations with other countries through economic and diplomatic ties in the post-Mao years. The world has welcomed this change. Professing its Peaceful Rise doctrine, China presents itself as a positive force in world affairs and argues that China's economic and military prominence benefits all people. Since 1978, China has enjoyed more peaceful relations with its neighbors and has entered into significant agreements reducing tensions with former adversaries Russia, India, Vietnam, and Japan. China-US relations have improved immensely since 1978, although the two countries continue to disagree on such important issues as Taiwan, Tibet, trade, and China's economic support and arms sales to despotic regimes.

In addition to improving bilateral relations, China has sought to enhance its presence in international organizations. China belongs to more than seventy-one international organizations, up from fewer than thirty in the 1980s. The major organizations to which China belongs are the African Development Bank, International Monetary Fund, Interpol (the international investigative service), World Bank, World Trade Organization, and the United Nations and its Security Council. China is also active in several regional international organizations either as a member or as a nonvoting observer.

Under Deng and his successors, China has achieved Deng's twin goals of making China a player in the world economy and in making China a world economic power. Such goals would have been inconceivable before 1978. Today, governments worldwide are eager to trade with China, and most actively seek China's investment in their countries. In return, trade with China has bolstered the economies of developed and developing countries alike, albeit China's large trade surpluses continue to irk some of China's trade partners.

The picture is not all rosy, however. Environmentalists are alarmed by the exploitation of Africa's forests and minerals.[76] Chinese-financed dams have displaced indigenous populations in Africa, and Chinese criminal organizations engage in poaching of endangered wildlife products. Chinese firms present a challenge to Western companies for resources and market share. Western governments and lending institutions are increasingly critical of China's financial largess. With more than $3 billion in foreign reserves, China has become a major source of capital in Asia, Latin America, and Africa. What is attractive about Chinese capital is that it comes with no preconditions, unlike the economic reforms required by the IMF or World Bank structural adjustment programs. Unlike the US Millennium Challenge Corporation, which requires investment in education, health care, and good governance, Chinese money requires no behavior modification or stringent spending guidelines. With the availability of China's aid, third world dictators can shun multilateral lending institutions and the United States and carry on as usual. Western capitals, and Washington in particular, view China's policy as undermining recent advances in human rights and democratization in developing countries. Despite the West's disdain for the use of China's largess, it appears that China will increasingly invest in dictatorships and solidify ties with less savory governments, just as it seeks strong relations with developed and democratic countries. As China rises as a regional and global power, the world's dominant countries will need to devise new policies to deal with a stronger China that at times is willing to accommodate, but at other times seeks its own way.

Notes

1. Glaser and Medeiros, "The Changing Ecology of Foreign Policy-Making," 307.
2. Lu Ning, *Dynamics of Foreign-Policy Decisionmaking in China,* 19.
3. Formerly the Ministry of Foreign Trade and Economic Cooperation.
4. Lampton, *Making of Chinese Foreign and Security Policy.*
5. Glaser and Medieros, "The Changing Ecology of Foreign Policy-Making," 307.
6. Lu Ning, *Dynamics of Foreign-Policy Decisionmaking in China,* 39.
7. Formally, the China Air Task Force, successor of the American Volunteer Group.
8. Harding, *Fragile Relationship,* 60.
9. Ronald Reagan Presidential Library, "United States–China Communiqué on United States Arms Sales to Taiwan."
10. For Gallup Poll data on US public opinion of China from 1972 until 1991, see Harding, *Fragile Relationship,* 363.
11. The 1979 TRA requires by law that the US president inform Congress of any threat to the security or the social or economic system of the people of Taiwan and that the president and Congress determine appropriate action.
12. See Gries, *China's New Nationalism,* for a thorough treatment of nationalism in contemporary China and a discussion of the Belgrade bombing.
13. Shirk, *China: Fragile Superpower,* 218.
14. Public Law 96-8, Taiwan Relations Act, sec. 2, b4.
15. One of these companies is Boeing, which makes the Harpoon antiship missiles. Boeing produces more than half of China's commercial jets, and services them with spare parts. China's leaders recognize that Boeing has major operations in many US states, and that congressional action would be swift if China carried through on its threats.
16. Government Information Office, Republic of China, *Republic of China Yearbook, 2009.*
17. Government Information Office, Republic of China, *Republic of China Yearbook, 2010,* 110, 111.
18. Government Information Office, Republic of China, *Republic of China Yearbook, 2010,* 87.
19. Election Study Center, National Chengchi University, "Important Political Attitude Trend Distribution" (Taipei: Election Study Center, National Chengchi University), http://esc.nccu.edu.tw.
20. Dumbaugh, *Tibet: Problems, Prospects, and US Policy,* 20.
21. "Dalai Lama Rejects Appeals," Radio Free Asia broadcast, March 17, 2011, http://www.rfa.org.
22. NBS of China, *China Statistical Yearbook 2010,* 257.
23. US Congress, Foreign Investment National Security Act of 2007, Public Law 110-49 (Washington, DC: Government Printing Office, July 26, 2007), http://www.gpo.gov.
24. Rosen and Hanemann, *An American Open Door?,* 28.
25. Zhou, "Conflicts over Human Rights Between China and the United States," 111.
26. For more on China's views of the disagreement between China and the United States on the issue of human rights, see Zhou, "Conflicts over Human Rights Between China and the United States."
27. Barnett, *China and the Major Powers in East Asia,* 93.
28. See the following articles from the Japan External Trade Organization (JETRO): "Value of Exports and Import by Area and Country" (December 2008), "Japan's Inward FDI by Region/Country," "Japan's Outward FDI by Region/Country." All may be found at http://www.jetro.go.jp.

29. Tojo was not only prime minister but ran several different ministries at the same time during the war.

30. For a discussion of China's reaction to the Yasukuni Shrine visits, see Deans, "Diminishing Returns?"

31. Penney and Wakefield, "Right Angles: Examining Accounts of Japanese Neo-Nationalism," 548.

32. Article 9 of Japan's constitution states that Japan will not maintain offensive military capability.

33. Kashmir has been divided between India and Pakistan since 1947. Both India and Pakistan claim jurisdiction over Kashmir in its entirety.

34. Holslag uses the terms *tarmac diplomacy* and *road diplomacy* to refer to China's many roads and highway projects in Central Asia, South Asia, and the Middle East, extending as far as Afghanistan, Iran, and Myanmar (Burma). Holslag, *China and India.*

35. Nye, *Soft Power,* 5.

36. Nye, *Soft Power,* 31.

37. Kurlantzick, "China's Charm Offensive in Southeast Asia."

38. ASEAN includes Brunei, Burma (Myanmar), Cambodia, Indonesia, Laos, Malaysia, Philippines, Singapore, Thailand, and Vietnam.

39. Cruz De Castro, "Limits of Twenty-First-Century Chinese Soft-Power Statecraft in Southeast Asia," 95.

40. Vaughn and Morrison, *China–Southeast Asia Relations,* 9.

41. Status quo nations seek to preserve the existing territorial, ideological, and power distribution. Defenders of the status quo regard stability and order as key values. International law, treaties, and orthodox diplomatic procedures are portrayed as legitimizing or codifying the system.

42. "Joint Communiqué of the 2006 SCO Summit," Xinhua, June 15, 2006, http://english.scosummit2006.org.

43. The term *Central Asia* in this book refers to the former Soviet Central Asian republics of Kazakhstan, Kyrgyzstan, Uzbekistan, Tajikistan, and Turkmenistan.

44. Chung, "Defense of Xinjiang."

45. Manas air base in Kyrgyzstan is only two hundred miles from the Chinese border and is a major base of support for air operations and the hub of a regional electronic intelligence network that covers western China. Chung, "Defense of Xinjiang."

46. Robert M. Cutler, "Gas Pipeline Gigantism," *Asia Times,* July 17, 2008.

47. James Brooke, "China Displaces Russia in Central Asia," Voice of America broadcast, November 16, 2010, http://www.voanews.com.

48. Hal Foster, "China Will Be Involved in 50 Percent of Kazakhstan's 2010 Output," Central Asia Newswire, August 20, 2010, http://centralasianewswire.com.

49. "Uzbekistan Receives New Passenger Locomotives from China," Uzbekistan National News Agency, June 4, 2010, http://uza.uz.

50. "Shanghai Cooperation Organization Summit Opens," Radio Free Europe, Radio Liberty, June 15, 2006, http://www.rferl.org.

51. "China Plans a New Silk Road," Indo Asian News Service, April 15, 2011, http://in.finance.yahoo.com.

52. "Uzbekistan Says Signs China Deals Worth $5 Billion," Reuters, April 21, 2011, http://uk.reuters.com.

53. While the project will not follow the exact China-to-Europe routes taken by the ancient Silk Road, it will develop six corridors connecting the Central Asian republics, Russia, and China with South Asia and the Persian Gulf countries. The project's financing will be shared among the eight countries involved and the Asian Development Bank.

54. Xin Dingding, "Wheels Turning to Create New Silk Road," *China Daily,* April 15, 2011.

55. Broadman, "China and India Go to Africa."

56. Serge, *China Safari,* 233–240.

57. Alfred de Montesquiou, "China's Africa Footprint: A Makeover for Algeria," *Washington Post,* January 19, 2010.

58. Kornberg and Faust, *China in World Politics,* 102.

59. Josh Kurlantzick, "Beijing's Big Push," *Newsweek International,* April 7, 2007.

60. NBS of China, *China Statistical Yearbook 2008,* 719.

61. "China-Russia Border Trade Reaches US$7b in 2006," Xinhua, March 2, 2007, http://www.china.org.cn; NBS of China, *China Statistical Yearbook 2008,* 731.

62. Murphy and Murphy, *China-Europe Relations,* 5.

63. Commission of the European Communities, *EU-China,* 6.

64. European Trade Commission, *Trade: China,* June 2010, http://ec.europa.eu /trade/creating-opportunities/bilateral-relations/countries/china.

65. European Trade Commission, *Trade: China,* June 2010.

66. Calculated from NBS of China, *China Statistical Yearbook 2008,* 730 and 252.

67. European Trade Commission, *Trade: China,* June 2010.

68. European Trade Commission, *Trade: China,* June 2010.

69. In 2007, China invested $1.5 billion in Europe, but this dropped 43 percent in 2008 due to the global financial crisis. Chinese FDI in Europe rebounded to $3.3 billion in 2009.

70. Ellis, *China in Latin America,* 17.

71. NBS of China, *China Statistical Yearbooks* for 2001 and 2010.

72. NBS of China, *China Statistical Yearbooks* for 2002, 2008, and 2010.

73. Chietigj Bajpaee, "Chinese Energy Strategy in Latin America."

74. BBC news in Chinese, "Weineiruila xiang Zhongguo goumai 18 sou youlun," broadcast May 12, 2006, http://news.bbc.co.uk/chinese/simp/hi/newsid_4760000/newsid _4764200/4764241.stm.

75. Cheng and Huangao Shi, "Sino-Venezuelan Relations," 116.

76. Alden, *China in Africa,* 87.

11 China's Future

On October 1, 2009, China celebrated the sixtieth anniversary of the founding of the People's Republic of China (PRC). National Day celebrations were extravagant. In Tiananmen Square, China's top leaders hosted a parade of more than ten thousand soldiers and a display of high-tech weapons—including nuclear missiles capable of reaching the United States—followed by a civilian parade of more than one hundred thousand people. Cheering throngs lined Beijing streets, where some 40 million potted flowers had been planted. Chinese state television broadcast the National Day Gala and massive fireworks display on TV and the Internet. For months, Chinese citizens and government employees worked on preparations for the big day. For instance, special parade villages were created on military grounds outside of Beijing to drill soldiers participating in the parade. Parts of Beijing were shut down on several occasions for rehearsals of the anniversary parade. Well in advance of National Day, professional exterminators targeted mosquitoes, rats, flies, and cockroaches.

The 2009 National Day celebration was designed to celebrate Chinese nationalism and to demonstrate to the world that China was a modern nation capable of holding its own on the world stage. Sixty years on from its founding as the PRC, China observers can look back and assess the country's achievements. In 2009, China became the world's second largest economy after the United States and is now a major player in the world economy. It has an extremely active stock market, with 1,550 stocks. Millions have been lifted out of poverty, and the standard of living for most urban Chinese is better than ever. Rural Chinese no longer suffer regular famine. A thriving middle class drives imported sport utility vehicles, sends its children to private schools, and freely travels the world.

Despite these advances, there are still many problems, some of them government-created or at least government-contributed. For instance, urban-rural disparity is reaching destabilizing proportions. In the cities, the gap between rich and poor is increasing. The rise of a new rich urban class, with accompanying disdain for the rule of law, rankles many Chinese, some of whom long for the days of Mao-imposed egalitarianism. Although Chinese enjoy more economic and political freedoms than at any time since the Mao years, the media is still state-controlled. Churches must register with the proper authorities and submit to oversight by those authorities. Under pressure from their husbands, families, clans, or the state, mothers abort or abandon their little girls in the hopes of having a male child.[1] Individual and official corruption has skyrocketed. The inability of China's leaders to resolve these problems raises the question of whether they will negatively impact China's future development. This chapter addresses China's remaining problems and assesses their impact on China's future. It also offers possible scenarios for China's political future.

Consumerism

China has been the world's fastest-growing economy for more than thirty years. This growth has resulted in an extraordinary increase in the standard of living for most Chinese. Since the beginning of the reform era in 1978, nearly 500 million people have been lifted out of poverty. China's middle class includes not just intellectuals and professionals, but office workers and support staff. The Chinese people appear eager to spend their newfound wealth. Since the early 1980s, consumerism has escalated in China. The once-drab department stores on Nanjing East Road in Shanghai that used to display bottles of Head and Shoulders–brand shampoo in their glass cases have been replaced by glittering palaces to consumerism bearing the latest designer imports from Paris and Milan and an unparalleled array of brightening creams from Tokyo.

In 1984, Deng Xiaoping introduced to the Chinese people "socialism with Chinese characteristics," and exhorted the Chinese people to embrace market-oriented principles and activities. To spur them to action, Deng proclaimed, "To Get Rich is Glorious!" The Chinese people appear to have taken this advice to heart. China is now one of the world's largest consumer nations. In 2005, China became the world's biggest consumer of four of the main five food, energy, and industrial commodities. China uses more grain (namely, rice and wheat), meat, coal, and steel than the United States.[2] Higher standards of living, especially in urban China, have increased Chinese appetites. Chinese households tend to consume more meats, poultry, fish, dairy products, and fruit as their incomes rise, while consumption of staple grains tends to decrease. For instance, Chinese ate 20 percent more chicken in 2010 than in 2006, while consuming almost 11 percent more pork. Despite being a nation of tea drinkers, the Chinese are increasingly consuming coffee and beer. The Chinese coffee market is growing 30 percent a year. In the past decade, Starbucks has built forty-four stores in Beijing alone. China is the world's largest market for beer. The average Chinese adult drank about a half bottle of beer in 1961. In the early twenty-first century, beer consumption increased 34 percent. Today, the average Chinese adult drinks 103 bottles of beer a year.

China's booming economy and industrial development also created increased demand for building materials, real estate, and consumer goods. China uses more than double the amount of steel the United States uses and has a nearly insatiable appetite for cement, pushing up prices for those materials. China is importing vast quantities of raw materials from Africa, Latin America, and Asia, forcing up commodity prices and shipping rates. The real estate market is on fire, swelling demand for appliances and furniture. Traditionally great savers, Chinese individuals are spending more than ever on consumer goods and consumer durables. China has more household appliances, such as refrigerators and televisions, than does the United States. Cable TV reaches 163 million households. Chinese people also want to stay connected. China has more than 900 million cell phone users and 477 million Internet users, making China the world's largest online market. Chinese increasingly use the Internet for personal shopping. The market value of online shopping in 2005 was 19 billion yuan ($2.3 billion), up from less than 1 billion in 2001 ($122 million).[3] The vast majority (83 percent) of China's online shoppers are aged eighteen to thirty-five, and two-thirds of online shoppers are male.[4]

China is the world's second largest user of oil, behind the United States. While the 9 million barrels of oil per day that China consumes is less than half of the 19 million barrels that the United States uses, China's demand is increasing at a faster rate than that of the United States. Until the global financial crisis in 2008, US oil demand increased 5 percent in the early twenty-first century. At the same time, China's consumption more than doubled. Although industry accounts for more than half of China's oil consumption, 25 percent of its oil is used for transportation. The growing demand in the transportation sector partly reflects growing affluence in China. Sales of passenger cars and other light vehicles grow nearly 50 percent in China in 2009, propelling it past the United States as the world's leading automobile market. There are more than one thousand more cars on Beijing's streets every day. China's major producers, in order of market share, are Shanghai GM, Shanghai VW, FAW-VW, Chery, Beijing Hyundai, FAW-Toyota, FAW-Xiali, Jili, Guangzhou Honda, and Shenlong.[5] Foreign automotive companies such as General Motors, Volkswagen, Mercedes-Benz, Ford, Suzuki, Daihatsu, Honda, Subaru, Citroën Toyota, BMW, Daimler, and Nissan all have plants in China. In 2009, an obscure Chinese construction-equipment maker, Sichuan Tengzhong Heavy Industrial Machinery, bought GM's Hummer brand, a collection of rugged sport utility vehicles based on the concept of the US military Humvee vehicle. Despite the booming sales, China still has a low rate of personal car ownership. There are about 35 cars per thousand people in China, compared with 439 in the United States and 100 in Brazil. Auto sales in China have the potential to double by 2015.

China is the world's second largest consumer of luxury goods following Japan. More Bentleys are sold in Beijing than in any other city in the world. The Rolls-Royce outlet in Beijing is one of the brand's top-selling dealerships. Gucci's fastest-growing market is China. In 2011, China had 115 billionaires, the second largest number in the world behind the United States. China's luxury market is expected to become the world's largest by 2020. Much of the desire for luxury goods is driven by women, and women are increasingly able to afford luxuries. Eleven of the world's twenty richest self-made women live in China. China is home to 153 female yuan billionaires (around $150 million). Buyers from China account for 20 percent of purchases at Christie's International Auctions in Hong Kong. Chinese art collectors also bid on Renoirs, Monets, and van Goghs at Christie's houses in New York and London.

Despite these impressive figures, China's consumption figures are not as high as leaders think they should be. Billionaires and millionaires aside, China has a long way to go to catch up with Americans in their consumption patterns. Per capita income in China was $4,382 in 2010, less than one-tenth of the $47,284 in the United States. Food consumption is far lower per individual in China than in the US. For example, the average Chinese person eats 119 pounds a year compared with 271 pounds in the United States.[6] The contribution of the Chinese consumer to China's economic growth had actually diminished in the first decade of the twenty-first century. Personal consumption accounted for nearly 80 percent of China's economic growth in the first half of the 1980s. Consumption's share of GDP declined in the 1990s. In the 2000s, China's booming economy was largely due to exports and government investment in the commercial sector, and not due to domestic consumption. From 2000 to 2006, growth in household consumption lagged behind the underlying growth of the overall economy, despite a doubling of household consumption outlays.[7] China's leaders want people to increase domestic consumption rates to reduce the reliance on exports and government spending. Since 2004, China's leaders have endorsed plans to expand domestic consumption as a major source of economic growth. A major goal of the Twelfth Five-Year Plan (2011–2015) is to increase domestic consumption. The plan seeks a shift from the export-led sectors to domestic consumer demand by raising Chinese workers' incomes to stimulate demand. Most developed countries with sound economies possess a relatively high level of domestic consumption, meaning consumers purchase goods produced by domestic firms. The US level of consumption is 70 percent of GDP. China's level of consumption in 2005 dropped to 38 percent of GDP, the lowest share of any major economy in the world.[8]

Many Chinese save to deal with the "New Three Mountains" of the high costs of housing, schooling, and medical care. Chinese household savings are about 29 percent of disposable income, one of the highest savings rates in the world.[9] High levels of household savings in China are due to the lack of a government-provided social safety net. China's total expenditure on health care is less than 4.6 percent of GDP, low compared with the rest of the world. Only half of China's urban population has basic health insurance. The basic government pension scheme is limited and provides a pension equal to only 20 percent of local average wages. Less than 20 percent of those employed have pensions, and many former state-owned enterprise (SOE) employees lost their pensions or saw them reduced. Government funding of education is modest, too. China spends only about 3 percent of GDP on education. Primary school fees are high and are often prohibitive for poorer rural households. The lack of national health care, social security, and welfare systems, as well as the lack of secure pensions, means that Chinese citizens must save a substantial portion of their income to fund their own health-care costs, education for their children, and their retirements and that of their parents. If China's leaders are sincere in their desire to increase household consumption, they would need to divert funds from government support of industry to domestic social programs, such as health care, pensions, education, and housing.

Younger consumers, however, are saving less than did older generations. Young urbanites in particular are grabbing up credit cards and are more willing than their parents to use them. Consumers aged eighteen to twenty-four were the most eager credit-card users by 2007. In the southern coastal city of Xiamen, four out of ten consumers owned at least one credit card. Shanghai had the biggest population of credit-card holders, with residents owning more than one card on average. Half of credit-card holders reported using them at least once a week.[10]

While the Chinese middle class and its new rich are happily spending and consuming, China still faces some major challenges. The next section addresses unresolved issues that may hold China back from becoming the world power to which it aspires.

Major Outstanding Challenges

China's economy is projected to overtake that of the United States by 2035 and be twice its size in the mid-twenty-first century.[11] China's rapid growth is due more to domestic demand than to exports, which allowed it to weather the economic crisis of 2008–2009. China's GDP in 2010 was $5.9 trillion, compared to $14.6 trillion for the United States. What is key is China's economic expansion. China has averaged 10 percent annual economic growth since 2000 and was still going strong in early 2010, despite the global economic slowdown. Goldman Sachs anticipates that China will surpass the United States in economic output in 2027. Economist Albert Keidel predicts that China's GDP will reach about $82 trillion in 2050, compared with $44 trillion for the United States.[12] China economist Thomas Rawski concurs that China's economy will continue to grow rapidly between 2010 and 2030, and he predicts annual growth averaging 6 to 8 percent. Although this rate is lower than the average 10 percent growth that China has experienced in the reform era, the projected rate would certainly increase the scale of China's economy and the standard of living for the Chinese people.[13]

China's rise may be checked by internal problems such as rising income disparity, urban-rural disparity, a massive floating population, expanding pockets of unrest and social discontent, an aging labor force, and corruption. This book has already examined the first four problems. It now turns to the fifth and sixth problems: changing demographics and corruption.

Demographics

In 1953, more than 36 percent of the population was under fourteen years of age, and only 4 percent of the Chinese population was over sixty-five years of age. According to the 2000 census, the percentage of population under fourteen dropped to less than 23 percent, and the figure for those over sixty-five rose to 8.5 percent.[14] Life expectancy has also increased, from an average of 68.5 years in 1990 to 73 years in 2009. Most China watchers anticipate that the country will experience a labor shortage as the Chinese population ages. At the same time, wages are likely to rise as education levels increase due to China's education reforms and as fewer people compete for jobs due to changing demographics. The labor shortage may mean that Chinese companies will move their operations abroad to countries such as Burma (Myanmar) and Vietnam, where wages are even cheaper. US companies may opt to stay in the Western Hemisphere and operate in Mexico and Central American countries rather than pay higher wages in China and shipping across the oceans.

A contraction in the workforce would likely slow China's economy unless it moves away from reliance on labor-intensive industries to more capital-intensive and high-tech industries. It could mitigate the potential economic damage of the loss of assembly jobs overseas by moving away from assembly work to electronics and other higher-end goods.

Another result of an aging population is the increasing burden on young Chinese adults to care for their elderly parents. After thirty years of implementing the one-child policy, many families have only one child to look after two parents. The need to set aside money to support one's elderly parents helps explain China's high household savings rate. While saving for the future is prudent, the Chinese government increasingly wants more of China's economic growth to come from domestic consumption and less from exports and government expenditure. The need to save for one's parents' retirement, as well as for one's own retirement, means that consumption levels will fall below Chinese government expectations.

Corruption

The consumerism described above has a more insidious side. Increasingly, China's rich urban youth are committing crimes, and often getting away with them. For instance, in May 2009, a street-car racer hit and killed a pedestrian, creating an outcry. The driver was the son of a merchant family rich enough to own several sports cars. His victim was the son of unemployed workers who lived in a rural town, and who struggled to pay their son's college tuition so he could have a better life. The driver was sentenced to only three years in prison, an especially lenient sentence. It was even rumored that the family paid a stand-in for him at the trial.[15]

Lack of respect for the law at the street level is replicated and magnified at the upper echelons of business and government in China. As this book has described, politically connected businesspeople artificially inflated dividend payments to investors, engaged in insider trading, stole shares of stock meant for staff, diverted funds raised in initial offerings, and otherwise engaged in assorted economic irregularities. Former Beijing mayor Chen Xitong was convicted of corruption and dereliction of duty. Several top managers of the Sanlu Group, a company manufacturing infant formula, were sentenced to long prison terms after being convicted of adulterating the milk powder with melamine. An estimated three hundred thousand babies became ill, and six cases resulted in death. Rural farmers regularly demonstrate against corrupt local officials. Former Shanghai Communist Party chief Chen Liangyu was sacked from his party and government posts for stealing from the city's pension fund. Several top media officials in Guangzhou were arrested for allegedly selling advertising slots privately. China's stock market also suffered from corruption, with eleven firms blacklisted and nearly three hundred people penalized for generating fake company reports and false auditing. In an attempt to clamp down on corruption and save its reputation, the CCP has told officials to dump their mistresses, stop frequenting girlie bars, and avoid extravagances.

Corruption is not new in China and is not unique to China. What makes Chinese graft distinctive is the senior levels at which graft takes place. Corruption, the abuse of power for political gain, is now found at every level of government in China. Corruption in China is particularly hideous because it often involves groups more than individuals. This web of deception makes Chinese graft particularly egregious and difficult to track. Despite the party's pronouncements to crack down on graft, loyalty to friends and family, and to those with whom one has special connections, commonly overrides efforts to prosecute corruption. Foreign businesses find it particularly frustrating to deal in China, because so many individuals involved in the business relationship require greasing of the palms. And at a time when capital is king in China, greasing the skids seems like an acceptable way to move negotiations along, or to accrue a little something extra for retirement or future needs.

From the time of its founding in 1921 and throughout its eighty-odd year history, the CCP has prided itself on being better than the corrupt Nationalists and capitalists. It appears, however, that corruption grew significantly in the 1990s, to coincide with the full implementation of market-oriented reforms. As members of the CCP, party cadres have access to inside information and to public funds, and they have the clout and the connections to take advantage of opportunities unavailable to other citizens. Some of the most common forms of corruption involving party and government officials are kickbacks for contracts for infrastructure projects, bribes paid by developers for land deals, fraud in the financial services sector, illegal purchase and sale of pharmaceuticals, and dishonest valuation of assets of state firms slated to be privatized.[16] Since 2000, more than one hundred thousand party members have been disciplined or punished each year for various offenses. Transparency International, which each year measures perception of corruption in countries throughout the world, ranked China as seventy-ninth out of 180 countries surveyed, with the rank of 1 being least corrupt and 180 being the most.[17]

Chinese society sees corruption as a negative development, and official corruption threatens the legitimacy of the CCP. In the 1990s and early 2000s, the Chinese countryside witnessed millions of cases of protest against graft and corruption, many of which resulted in injury to persons or property. City dwellers also protest corruption, as was evidenced during the spring 1989 demonstrations. Although China has more than 1,200 laws, rules, and regulations to curtail corruption, they are inadequately enforced. In recent years, China has taken various measures to help curb corruption. These measures include rotating anticorruption chiefs among the provinces, establishing oversight bureaus to enforce land acquisition laws, opening environmental inspection centers to monitor local compliance with environmental regulations, and creating a special hotline to allow whistle-blowers to report cases of corruption. In addition, the government plans to publish the names of people who pay bribes and to set up an electronic database on individuals who have engaged in bribery.[18]

Rising Social Discontent

China is facing rising discontent. A series of riots in several cities throughout three weeks in May and June 2011 tested the CCP's ability to maintain order and contain public anger over economic and political grievances. In mid-June, hundreds of migrant workers overturned police cars, smashed windows, and torched government buildings in Guangdong Province before being subdued by armed police. The migrants were protesting the rough treatment of a pregnant migrant street vendor by security guards. The riot followed the bombing of local government offices in Tianjin and in two other cities in the previous two weeks and ethnic unrest in Inner Mongolia in May.

Antigovernment protests are becoming increasingly common in China. In the past, serious rioting mostly occurred in rural areas as farmers protested land grabs by property developers and local officials. In recent years, however, violent protests have spread to China's cities. The 2011 unrest occurred nearly simultaneously in several cities as people became increasingly frustrated by rising inflation and poor working conditions. Social unrest has been rising steadily as well. In 2007, China had more than 80,000 "mass incidents," up from some 60,000 in 2006. China watchers estimated 127,000 such incidents in 2008.[19]

Recent antigovernment protests occurred in the midst of a sustained crackdown on dissent. China's leaders in early 2011 got a bad jolt after anonymous posts online called for popular rallies like those that toppled Middle East regimes. Anxious over a possible "Jasmine Revolution," Chinese authorities began cracking down on Internet security over fear that antiregime sentiment in the Middle East would spread to China. In addition to added Internet scrutiny, Chinese authorities detained dozens of Internet bloggers, journalists, writers, and human rights lawyers in an attempt to silence them. Included in the sweep was Ai Weiwei, a prominent Chinese artist and outspoken critic of the government.[20] Chinese authorities released Ai on bail after eleven weeks, on the condition that he not talk with the media.

China's leaders have responded to social discontent with beefed-up security and measures designed to pacify and placate the population. They deployed thousands of riot police armed with tear gas and shotguns to restore order after the Guangdong riot and plan to increase spending on police, courts, prosecutors, and other domestic security. China's leaders called for controls on inflation, measures to close the rich-poor gap, and higher social spending with bigger outlays for education, job creation, low-income housing, health care and pensions, and other social insurance. These policies are designed to thwart unrest among a population suffering from ratcheting discontent, a phenomenon in which society has grown accustomed to greater prosperity and expects more.

Scenarios for the Future

It is always dangerous to make predictions, and this book has no intention of doing so. It is possible, however, to look at China's past and present to come up with possible scenarios for China's future. The remainder of this chapter offers some comments on the potential future of China's domestic politics, prospects for democracy, and China in world affairs.

Domestic Politics

One pressing question that China watchers have is, what are the prospects for democracy in China? There are several factors to consider in answering this question. First, what is the future of the CCP, and will the CCP allow further political liberalization? Second, what model of political order would China follow, if any, or will China's leaders design a new political order with Chinese characteristics?

The most likely scenario is that China models itself on Singapore. Former premier Zhu Rongji and several other Chinese leaders have publicly expressed admiration for the city-state. Singapore's political system has both authoritarian and democratic elements.[21] Singapore is a democratic republic, with political power divided among the executive, legislative, and judiciary branches. The president is head of state and appoints the prime minister. The prime minister chairs the cabinet and is responsible for the general direction of the government and accountable to parliament. However, Singaporean democracy is procedural rather than substantive. While Singaporeans enjoy the right to elect their own representatives, the government largely fails to protect their civil rights and liberties. Moreover, Singaporean politics is characterized by a dominant-party system. A dominant-party system is open to all, but for a variety of reasons, over long periods, only one party has any real chance to attain power. The People's Action Party (PAP) dominates Singaporean politics and has won control of parliament in every election since 1959. Part of PAP's success is the legitimacy it attained by being the party of independence, its strong leadership under veteran leader Lee Kwan-yew, and its ability to bankrupt opposition parties by suing them for libel and by incarcerating opposition politicians for a variety of charges.[22] The government regularly prohibits the publication of particular Western media in the city-state, such as the *Asian Wall Street Journal* and *Cosmopolitan* magazine. The Singaporean government banned the former because a reporter wrote an article taking exception to Lee Kwan-yew's persecution of opposition politicians, and the latter because it constituted pornography. Many Singaporean intellectuals, such as university professors, work abroad to avoid government oversight of their research. Freedom House, which ranks states according to a slate of indicators of freedom, does not consider Singapore an electoral democracy and ranks the country as only partly free. It gave Singapore a rating of five for political rights and four for civil liberties, where one represents the most free and seven represents the least free.[23] Reporters Without Borders ranked Singapore 136 out of 175 countries in its 2010 worldwide press freedom index.[24]

Another economy that has aspects of both democracy and authoritarianism is Hong Kong. The people of Hong Kong elect representatives to the legislature and to their urban councils. However, Beijing, through a China-sympathetic electoral committee, elects the chief executive. Candidates for chief executive must first pass muster with Beijing. In contrast to its poor ranking for Singapore, Reporters Without Borders ranked Hong Kong 34 out of 175. Despite this ranking, journalists in Hong Kong engage in self-censorship. Most of Hong Kong's journalists who were critical of China left journalism or Hong Kong under pressure either before or immediately after the 1997 handover. University professors are freer than their Singaporean counterparts but can feel the heat from university administrators if they delve too deeply into the issues of human rights and civil liberties in China and Hong Kong. Freedom House ranks Hong Kong as partly free, with a rank of five for political rights but a relatively high ranking of two for civil liberties.

Despite Singapore's low rankings on the freedom scales and Hong Kong's low ranking for political rights, Singapore and Hong Kong are the two freest economies in the world, outranking all of the more democratic countries. It is possible that China's leaders will adopt the Singaporean model of broad economic liberalization accompanied by only limited political liberalization. Already there is evidence that China is following this road. China's leaders have publicly praised the Singapore model, while dismissing the democratic yet free countries of India and the Philippines as unworthy models. As this book has demonstrated, China in the past thirty years has liberalized the economy, but has not accompanied that liberalization with political freedom. Freedom House ranks China as "not free," and gave China a seven for political rights and a six for civil liberties. Reporters Without Borders ranked China 171 out of 175 countries in its 2010 press freedom index. It appears that China's leaders are creating a sort of corporate authoritarian system in which the CCP controls civil society by overseeing all civic organizations and maintains power by being the only legitimate ruling party of China.

However, there are huge differences between Singapore and China that will make it difficult for China to emulate Singapore. Corruption is much lower in Singapore. Transparency International ranked Singapore as 1 out of 180 countries surveyed. It ranked Hong Kong 13 (ahead of the US rank of 22). As we saw above, Transparency International ranked China 78.[25] If China's leaders want to emulate Singapore, they need to crack down harder on official corruption. Second, Singapore's population is highly educated, far above China's standards. China's leaders will need to work harder to educate the Chinese people. As we saw in Chapter 6, China's leaders are aware of this need and are in the midst of building top-notch research universities. Singapore also has world-class infrastructure. This infrastructure did not happen by chance, but is the result of heavy state investment. Singapore developed a thriving urban city-state by building high-density satellite towns connected to the central business district by expressways and rail systems. This development followed the clearing of slums and building extensive public housing. China has adopted this model in some of its cities, the downside, however, being the demolition of traditional neighborhoods to make way for modern high-rises. Singapore also has the world's largest container port and the world's largest port for transshipment of goods. In the 1990s, China's leaders invested heavily in the port of Shanghai. Since 2005, Shanghai has been the world's busiest port by freight tons handled. The port is China's most important gateway for foreign trade. Not only is it a critical hub for goods moving up and down the Yangtze River valley, but it allows China to ship goods more efficiently, as China can ship goods directly out of Shanghai, rather than having to transship through Hong Kong, as had been the practice in the past.

Emulating the Singapore model is the most likely scenario. In another scenario, however, the CCP remodels itself along the lines of the former communist parties of Eastern Europe. After the fall of the Soviet Union, most communist parties found their political fortunes waning. Some of them, such as the Communist Party of the Soviet Union, ceased to exist. Some of the parties reemerged as socialist parties, such as the Socialist Party of Serbia and the United Russia Party. While Slobodan Milosevic's Socialist Party allied with Serbian ultra-nationalists, United Russia and most of the other reconstituted parties espoused a mixture of state regulation and market freedoms. Because they were born in an era of democratization after the fall of the Soviet Union and the end of the political monopoly of the Soviet Communist Party, the reformulated parties recognized multiparty systems. While recognizing other political parties, the reconstituted socialist parties continued to dominate politics in their respective countries. It is possible that the CCP, having allowed entrepreneurs to join the party, will take another step and tolerate political pluralism. This metamorphosis is possible if the CCP does two things. First, the CCP would have to determine that political competition further legitimates the party. As we have seen in Chapter 4, allowing private entrepreneurs into the CCP was a pragmatic decision. As the country adopted capitalism and the number of capitalists grew substantially, it was important not to isolate politically the drivers of China's economy. When those drivers increasingly expressed interest in joining the party—and did so quietly in the 1990s—it made political sense to welcome them, and the knowledge and views that they had, into the party. Allowing private entrepreneurs into the party made the CCP more inclusive of China's population.

Second, the CCP will only embrace political pluralism if it believes it will maintain control of the levers of power. Several authoritarian leaders, such as Augusto Pinochet in Chile, the military government in Brazil, and Indira Gandhi in India, allowed elections after autocratic rule, believing that they would retain power. Each of these was surprised by the outcome. China's rulers are also all too aware of the untimely demise of the Soviet Union. China's leaders fault former Soviet president Mikhail Gorbachev for introducing both economic and political reforms at the same time. China's leaders saw no sense in giving the people the right to criticize the government and its leaders publicly before satisfying them in their pocketbooks. Unlike Gorbachev, China's leaders allowed economic liberalization first, raising the people's standard of living, and thereby further legitimizing the CCP. After thirty years of booming economic growth and dramatic increases in standards of living, the CCP is in a better position to expand political liberties. Most Chinese support the CCP, and while they may seek greater political freedom, do not seek the overthrow of the party responsible for China's rise. The expansion need not be radical. The CCP is one of the best-organized political parties in the world. Tight discipline, control of the military, and control of the media give the CCP an advantage against any burgeoning parties. In fact, the CCP is likely to be even stronger in the future. Allowing private entrepreneurs into the party and attempts at intraparty democracy have also strengthened the CCP by allowing different voices to be heard. China's economic rise has legitimated the CCP. As we have seen in this book, the CCP has already carried out limited political liberalization. For instance, we have seen that the party encourages use of the Internet (albeit with some degree of censorship), tolerates and benefits from environmental activism, and has encouraged the growth of the legal profession in China.

One significant caveat makes this scenario less likely than the Singaporean scenario: party leaders have ruled out adopting Western-style political institutions. They claim not only that Western-style democracy is unsuited to China, but that China's one-party system is superior to the democratic model. The fear is that without a single communist party in control, China would descend into chaos and its government would be incapable of accomplishing anything. Until China's leaders change this mentality, we will not likely see pluralism in China's political institutions. That said, crazier things have happened. For instance, few people anticipated the fall of the Berlin Wall in 1989 or Fidel Castro's resignation. Few Westerners predicted that the CCP would welcome private entrepreneurs into its fold. The phenomenon of private entrepreneurs in the CCP raises the question of what one calls these new party members. Communist capitalists? Capitalist communists? If the CCP can embrace capitalists, it may be willing to reconsider reforming its political institutions.

Prospects for Democracy

Despite their reluctance to embrace political pluralism, China's leaders have experimented with elections at lower levels of government. Those who hold out hope for democracy in China point to the 1987 Organic Law of Village Elections, which allows villagers to elect members of their village committee and their village chief. They claim that it is a start. The right of villagers to elect their village government does not necessarily indicate that China is democratizing. For instance, the law merely stipulates and does not mandate village elections, and as we saw in Chapter 4, the law actually reinforces the power of the party in rural villages—most elected village chiefs are party members and the law stipulates that the local party chief has final say in matters of local governance. Even at this lowest level of political participation, the CCP is still in control. The control that the CCP maintains over elections even at the lowest level of government indicates that it is unwilling to relinquish control at higher levels. Although elections to the National People's Congress are competitive and open, and despite the existence of smaller political parties, most delegates elected to the congress belong to the CCP. There is no true party competition, and the other parties must recognize the CCP as supreme.

China's economic growth raises questions concerning the prospects for democracy in China. Although many observers of economic liberalization posit that economic liberalization drives democratization, it is a spurious link. As we have seen, neither of the two freest economies in the world (Singapore and Hong Kong) is a liberal democracy. China's nascent democracy movement was crushed under the heavy imprint of PLA tracks in June 1989. Since then, most Chinese have shied away from outright advocacy of democratization. However, there are still many individuals in China who support democracy for China. One of them is Yu Keping, member of a think tank that reports to the party's Central Committee. In 2006, the *Beijing Daily News* published his essay "Democracy Is a Good Thing." The essay has since then been discussed widely inside and outside of China.

Yu bolsters his argument in favor of democracy for China with reference to Marx and China's leaders. For instance, Yu adds: "The classical authors of Marxism said: 'There is no socialism without democracy,'" and "Hu Jintao pointed out further: 'There is no modernization without democracy.'" Like China's leaders, however, Yu argues that China should not adopt a foreign model of democracy, but should develop its own, just as it developed socialism with unique Chinese characteristics: "We will not import an overseas political model. Our construction of political democracy must be closely integrated with the history, culture, tradition, and existing social conditions in our nation."[26]

In recent years, China's leaders have spoken of democracy in positive terms. Both President Hu Jintao and Premier Wen Jiabao have integrated references to democracy in many of their speeches. For instance, in his address to the Seventeenth Party Congress in 2007, Hu referenced democracy more than sixty times. In particular, he stated that the CCP will expand intraparty democracy by increasing transparency in party affairs and will oppose and prevent arbitrary

---

Democracy Is a Good Thing

"Democracy is a good thing, and this is not just for specific persons or certain officials; this is for the entire nation and its broad masses of people. Simply put, for those officials who care more about their own interests, democracy is not only not a good thing, in fact, it is a troublesome thing, even a bad thing. Just think, under conditions of democratic rule, officials must be elected by the citizens and they must gain the endorsement and support of the majority of the people; their powers will be curtailed by the citizens, they cannot do whatever they want, they have to sit down across from the people and negotiate. Just these two points alone already make many people dislike it. Therefore, democratic politics will not operate on its own; it requires the people themselves and the government officials who represent the interests of the people to promote and implement it.

"Democracy is a good thing, but that does not mean that everything about democracy is good. Democracy is definitely not 100 percent perfect; it has many internal inadequacies. . . . But among all the political systems that have been invented and implemented, democracy is the one with the least number of flaws. That is to say, relatively speaking, democracy is the best political system for humankind." (Yu Keping, "Democracy Is a Good Thing," *Beijing Daily News,* October 23, 2006)

decisionmaking by an individual or a minority of people. In a 2006 visit to Peking University, Premier Wen said that China must pursue both democracy and science if China wants to transform itself into a modernized country. During a chat with Internet surfers in which "netizens" complained of official corruption in China, Wen commented that only democracy could help curb corruption.[27]

Their comments beg the question, what would democracy look like in China? Even the student leaders of the spring 1989 demonstrations believed in an elite form of democracy in which they, the elite of society, would have greater decisionmaking power than their fellow citizens. Part of this mentality was evidenced by the ropes they used to mark off their marchers from fellow marchers during the demonstrations, indicating that their pursuit of democracy did not necessarily include all of Chinese society. What this book has made clear is that China's leaders are referring not to Western-style, classical, liberal democracy characterized by pluralism and protection of civil rights and liberties, but to a sort of democracy led by the CCP. This may seem oxymoronic (although so do the concepts of communist capitalists or capitalist communists), but may actually follow a more classical style of democracy in which elites gather information and opinion from the masses, but deliberate and make policy independently of the masses. What this book has made clear is that the CCP's leadership is paramount and it still believes in the tenet of democratic centralism, where opinions are expressed but the party makes the ultimate decisions. Under this "democracy with Chinese characteristics," the party would expand elections at the lower levels of government, curb official corruption, and more adamantly pursue the rule of law. China's leaders believe that this form of democracy would strengthen the country's political institutions without the party having to relinquish power to competitors.

China in World Affairs

China's economic power is already unsettling to many foreign governments. As we saw in Chapter 7, China's chronic trade surpluses with the United States have prompted US manufacturers and politicians to charge China with playing unfairly. Western economists agree with them that China's leaders intentionally undervalue their currency. China's new influence due to its economic rise has given Chinese leaders the ability to shun these criticisms and to turn around and lecture the United States on its chronic budget deficits. Other countries will have to learn not to lecture China, as they once were prone to do.

The effects of China's dramatic economic rise will carry over into other areas such as military and diplomatic affairs. Growing economic dominance will enhance China's diplomatic prowess, which is already putting other countries on edge. For instance, China's penchant for signing contracts with dodgy states and selling arms to troublesome regimes does not play well in the West. However, China is not going to give up anytime soon these lucrative contracts that give China access to materials necessary for its development. At the same time, China cannot afford to snub international opinion of these deals, and will seek to position itself so that it can benefit from trade relations with unsavory states while maintaining good relations with Western powers.

China's double-digit increases in military expenditures are another area of concern for Western countries, particularly the United States. As threats against the Chinese mainland have diminished in the post–Cold War era, China's military buildup can hardly be considered defensive. Military modernization is designed to project China's power and influence throughout Asia and to deter the United States from military action near China, especially in defense of Taiwan. Despite robust China-US relations and cooperation on North Korea, antiterrorism, and antipiracy, China and the United States are not strategic partners in Asia. The United States has by far the strongest military in Asia and has the strongest navy in the region. As China continues to modernize its military, it directly challenges that position. The outstanding question is, why does China feel the need to challenge US military supremacy in Asia?

China's militarization is somewhat moderated by its increasing participation in international organizations. China already belongs to some seventy international organizations and will likely seek a louder voice in the major ones, such as the World Bank, the International Monetary Fund, and the United Nations and its associated bodies. These groups offer China a platform from which to put forth its agenda as well as to cooperate with other countries.

Summary

China has undergone dramatic changes since the founding of the PRC in 1949. The Chinese communists took the Chinese people on a roller-coaster ride from land-to-the-tiller distribution of farmland to collectivization of agriculture and back again to household farming; from nationalization of industry to corporatization; from a planned economy to a market economy; from persecution of capitalists to inclusion in the party; from subsistence farming to famine to agricultural abundance; from condemnation of the West to extreme xenophobia to a seat on the UN Security Council; from a peasant revolutionary army to a modern military; from extreme egalitarianism to consumerism and accumulation of wealth; from ideological orthodoxy to political pragmatism; and from national humiliation to national pride. It is doubtful that any people have endured such radical changes in the past sixty years. The transitions have been in many ways unsettling, and often painful, and each change has had its winners and losers. While the future for China as a country looks positive, there are still many people in China who have been left behind. China's challenge in the coming decades will be to continue its positive trajectory while helping those left behind.

Notes

1. For a heartbreaking account of the anguish these mothers feel, read Xinran, *Message from an Unknown Chinese Mother.*
2. Individuals in the United States remain the world's greatest consumers.
3. iResearch, in *China by Numbers 2007*, 101.
4. "Young Male [sic] Take Up 2/3 of China's Online Shoppers: Report," *China View*, July 18, 2006, http://news.xinhuanet.com.
5. FAW is the acronym for First Auto Works, founded in 1953.
6. Food and Agriculture Organization of the United Nations, Statistics Division (FAOSTAT), November 25, 2008, http://faostat.fao.org.
7. Joseph Quinlan, "Some Inconvenient Truths About the Chinese Consumer," *China Post*, September 28, 2007.
8. Lardy, "China: Toward a Consumption-Driven Growth Path."
9. In contrast, the US household savings rate was 3.6 in 2011.
10. "Young Consumers Show Little Interest in Saving," *China Daily*, November 1, 2007.
11. Keidel, *China's Economic Rise.*
12. Keidel, *China's Economic Rise*, 6.
13. Perkins and Rawski, "Forecasting China's Economic Growth to 2025."
14. NBS of China, *China Statistical Yearbook 2010*, 96.
15. The driver appeared much heavier at his sentencing than in photos from the accident scene, prompting the rumors. Shai Oster, "China's Rich Youth Spark Bitter Divide," *Wall Street Journal*, September 22, 2009, A1, A22.
16. For more information on official corruption, see Pei, "Fighting Corruption," 228.
17. Transparency International, *Corruption Perception Index 2009*, http://www .transparency.org.
18. Pei, "Fighting Corruption," 246.
19. Figures are according to the Chinese Academy of Social Sciences, cited in Jeremy Page, "Wave of Protests Rocks China," *Wall Street Journal*, June 14, 2011, A1, A11.
20. Readers might recognize Ai Weiwei as the artistic director of the "Bird's Nest" Olympic Stadium.
21. The term *hybrid* describes political systems that are both democratic and authoritarian.
22. A former colony of Great Britain, Singapore ceased to be a part of the British Empire when it joined Malaysia in 1963 and gained full independence after it separated from that country in 1965.
23. Freedom House, *Freedom in the World 2010* (Washington, DC: Freedom House, 2010), http://www.freedomhouse.org.
24. Reporters Without Borders, *Worldwide Press Freedom Index 2010.*
25. Transparency International, *Corruption Perception Index 2010*, http://www .transparency.org.
26. Yu Keping, "Democracy Is a Good Thing," *Beijing Daily News*, October 23, 2006, http://www.zonaeuropa.com.
27. "Wen: Only Democracy Sustains Governance," *China Daily*, February 28, 2009.

Acronyms

APC	agricultural producers' cooperative
CCP	Chinese Communist Party
CCRSG	Central Cultural Revolution Small Group
CMC	Central Military Commission
CPPCC	Chinese People's Political Consultative Conference
CSRC	China Securities Regulation Commission
CYL	Communist Youth League
DPP	Democratic Progressive Party
EDZ	economic development zone
FDI	foreign direct investment
GDP	gross domestic product
HRS	household responsibility system
IMF	International Monetary Fund
IO	international organization
IW	information warfare
KMT	Kuomintang (Nationalist Party)
MES	Modern Enterprise System
NCEE	National College Entrance Examination
NPC	National People's Congress
OFDI	outward foreign direct investment
PBC	People's Bank of China
PLA	People's Liberation Army
PRC	People's Republic of China
ROC	Republic of China
SAR	special administrative region
SARS	severe acute respiratory syndrome
SEZ	special economic zone
ShSE	Shanghai Stock Exchange
SOE	state-owned enterprise
SzSE	Shenzhen Stock Exchange
WHO	World Health Organization
WTO	World Trade Organization

Chinese Pronunciation Guide

China uses the pinyin romanization system. It has what are called initials and vowels. Most of the letters are pronounced the same as in English, but a few of them are pronounced differently. Below is a guide to letters that differ in pronunciation from their English equivalents.

Letter   Chinese Pronunciation

Initials:

c	ts, as in *ts*ar or *tsetse* fly
q	ch, as in *ch*eap
r	a cross between the English *j* and *r*
x	sh, as in *sh*eet
zh	j, as in *j*am

Vowels:

a	a, as in f*a*ther
ai	i, as in h*i*gh
ao	ow, as in h*ow* and n*ow*
e	a, as in *a*bout and *a*go
ei	ay, as in n*ei*ghbor and w*ei*gh
ia	ye, as in *ye*t and *ye*s
iong	y+oong
iu	y+long u
o	aw, as in s*aw*
ong	as in s*ong*
ou	as in s*ou*l
u	as in r*u*le
ua	wa, as in *wa*ter
uai	why, like the word *why*
uo	wa, as in *wa*r
ü	long *u* (spoken with rounded lips)

Bibliography

Abraham, Thomas. *Twenty-First Century Plague: The Story of SARS*. Baltimore, MD: Johns Hopkins University Press, 2005.

Adams, Ian, Riley Adams, and Rocco Galanti. *Power of the Wheel: The Falun Gong Revolution*. Toronto: Stoddart Publishing, 2000.

Ahn Byung-joon. *Chinese Politics and the Cultural Revolution: Dynamics of Policy Processes*. Seattle: University of Washington Press, 1976.

Alden, Chris. *China in Africa*. London: Zed Books, 2007.

Amnesty International. *Amnesty International Report 2008: The State of the World's Human Rights*. London: Amnesty International, 2008. http://thereport.amnesty.org.

———. *Amnesty International Report 2009: The State of the World's Human Rights*. London: Amnesty International, 2009. http://report2009.amnesty.org.

———. *Undermining Freedom of Expression in China: The Role of Yahoo!, Microsoft, and Google*. London: Amnesty International, 2006. http://irrepressible.info.

Ash, Robert. "Squeezing the Peasants: Grain Extraction, Food Consumption, and Rural Living Standards in Mao's China." *China Quarterly* 188 (2006): 959–998.

Auffhammer, Maximilian, and Richard T. Carson. "Forecasting the Path of China's CO_2 Emissions Using Province-Level Information." *Journal of Environmental Economics and Management* 55, no. 3 (May 2008): 229–247.

Bachman, David. *Bureaucracy, Economy, and Leadership in China: The Institutional Origins of the Great Leap Forward*. Cambridge, UK: Cambridge University Press, 1991.

Bajpaee, Chietigj. "Chinese Energy Strategy in Latin America." *China Brief* 5, no. 14 (June 21, 2005).

Bao, Shuming, Shuanglin Lin, and Changwen Zhao, eds. *The Chinese Economy After WTO Accession*. Burlington, VT: Ashgate Publishing, 2006.

Baradat, Leon P. *Political Ideologies: Their Origins and Impact*. 9th ed. Upper Saddle River, NJ: Pearson Prentice Hall, 2006.

445

Barnett, A. Doak. *China and the Major Powers in East Asia.* Washington, DC: Brookings Institution Press, 1977.

———. *The Making of Foreign Policy in China: Structure and Process.* Boulder, CO: Westview Press, 1985.

Barnett, A. Doak, and Ezra Vogel. *Cadres, Bureaucracy, and Political Power in Communist China.* New York: Columbia University Press, 1967.

Becker, Geoffrey S. *Food and Agricultural Imports from China.* Washington, DC: Congressional Research Service, September 26, 2008. http://www.fas.org.

Becker, Jasper. *Hungry Ghosts: Mao's Secret Famine.* New York: Free Press, 1996.

Benton, Gregor, and Alan Hunter, eds. *Wild Lily, Prairie Fire: China's Road to Democracy, Yan' an to Tian' anmen, 1942–1989.* Princeton, NJ: Princeton University Press, 1995.

Bergsten, Fred C., Gill Bates, Nicholas R. Lardy, and Derek Mitchell. *China: The Balance Sheet.* New York: Public Affairs, 2006.

Bernstein, Thomas P. "Farmer Discontent and Regime Responses." In *The Paradox of China's Post-Mao Reforms,* edited by Merle Goldman and Roderick MacFarquhar, 197–219. Cambridge, MA: Harvard University Press, 1999.

———. *Up to the Mountains and Down to the Villages: The Transfer of Youth from Urban to Rural China.* New Haven, CT: Yale University Press, 1977.

Bianco, Lucien. *Origins of the Chinese Revolution, 1915–1949.* Stanford, CA: Stanford University Press, 1971.

Bickford, Thomas J. "The Chinese Military and Its Business Operations: The PLA as Entrepreneur." *Asian Survey* 34, no. 5 (May 1994): 460–474.

Bitzinger, Richard A. "Arms to Go." *International Security* 17, no. 2 (Autumn 1992): 84–111.

Bo Zhiyue. "The Seventeenth Central Committee of the Chinese Communist Party: Institutional Representation." *Issues and Studies* 44, no. 3 (September 2008): 1–41.

Bogg, Lennart, Hengjin Dong, Keli Wang, Wenwei Cai, and Vinod Diwan. "The Cost of Coverage: Rural Health Insurance in China." *Health Policy and Planning* 11, no. 3 (1996): 238–252.

Blumenthal, David, and William Hsiao. "Privatization and Its Discontents: The Evolving Chinese Health Care System." *New England Journal of Medicine* 353, no. 11 (2005): 1165–1170.

Brandt, Loren, Thomas G. Rawski, and John Sutton. "China's Industrial Development." In *China's Great Economic Transformation,* edited by Loren Brandt and Thomas G. Rawski, 569–632. Cambridge: Cambridge University Press, 2008.

Brautigam, Deborah. *The Dragon's Gift: The Real Story of China in Africa.* Oxford: Oxford University Press, 2009.

Broadman, Harry G. "China and India Go to Africa: New Deals in the Developing World." *Foreign Affairs* 87, no. 2 (March–April 2008): 95–109.

Brown, Lester. "China Replacing the United States as World's Leading Consumer." *Plan B Updates.* Earth Policy Institute, February 16, 2005. http://www.earthpolicy.org.

Browning, Graeme. *If Everybody Bought One Shoe: American Capitalism in Communist China*. New York: Hill and Wang, 1989.

Bryce, James. *The American Commonwealth*. Vol. 1. New York: Macmillan, 1893.

Bureau of Economic Analysis (BEA). *U.S. International Transactions Accounts Data*. Washington, DC: US Department of Commerce, Bureau of Economic Analysis, August 2, 2009. http://www.bea.gov/international.

Bureau of the Public Debt. "The Debt to the Penny and Who Holds It." Washington, DC: US Department of the Treasury, Bureau of the Public Debt, 2009. http://www.treasurydirect.gov.

Burki, Shahid Javed. *A Study of Chinese Communes, 1965*. Cambridge, MA: Harvard University Press, 1969.

Byrd, William A., ed. *Chinese Industrial Firms Under Reform*. New York: Oxford University Press, 1992.

Cai, Yongshun. "Local Governments and the Suppression of Popular Resistance in China." *China Quarterly* 193 (2008): 24–42.

Central Intelligence Agency. *The World Factbook*. Washington, DC: US Central Intelligence Agency, 2009. https://www.cia.gov/.

———. *World Factbook: China*. Washington, DC: US Central Intelligence Agency, 2009.

———. *World Factbook: China*. Washington, DC: US Central Intelligence Agency, 2011.

Chai, Winberg, ed. *The Foreign Relations of the People's Republic of China*. New York: G. P. Putnam's Sons, 1972.

Chan, Anita. "The Social Origins and Consequences of the Tiananmen Crisis." In *China in the Nineties: Crisis Management and Beyond,* edited by David Goodman and Gerald Segal, 105–130. Oxford: Oxford University Press, 1991.

Chang, Iris. *The Rape of Nanking: The Forgotten Holocaust of World War II*. New York: Penguin Putnam, 1997.

Chang King-yuh, ed. *The Impact of the Three Principles of the People on China*. Taipei, Taiwan: Institute of International Relations, National Chengchi University, 1988.

Chao, Jane, Frank Ge, Martin Joerss, Shirley Li, Larry Wang, Johnathan Woetzel, and K. K. Wong. *From Bread Basket to Dust Bowl?* San Francisco: McKinsey and Company, November 2009.

Chen Fang. *The Wrath of Heaven: Scandal at the Top in China*. Hong Kong: Edko Publishing, 2000.

Chen Guidi and Wu Chuntao. *Will the Boat Sink the Water? The Life of China's Peasants*. New York: Public Affairs, 2006.

Chen Jianfu. "The Revision of the Constitution in the PRC: A Great Leap Forward or Symbolic Gesture?" *China Perspectives* no. 53 (May–June 2004): 15–32.

Chen Jie. "Attitudes Toward Democracy and the Political Behavior of the Chinese Middle Class." In *China's Emerging Middle Class,* edited by Cheng Li, 334–358. Washington, DC: Brookings Institution Press, 2010.

Chen Yiu Por and Zai Liang. "Educational Attainment of Migrant Children: The Forgotten Story of China's Urbanization." In *Education and Reform in China,* edited by Emily Hannum and Albert Park, 117–132. Oxford, UK: Routledge, 2007.

Chen Zhu, Hong-Guang Wang, Zhao-Jun Wen, and Yihuang Wang. "Life Sciences and Biotechnology in China." *Philosophical Transactions of the Royal Society: Biological Sciences* 362, no. 1482 (2007): 947–957.

Ch'en Chieh-ju, and Lloyd E. Eastman. *Chiang Kai-shek's Secret Past: The Memoir of His Second Wife, Ch'en Chieh-ju.* Boulder, CO: Westview Press, 1993.

Cheng, Joseph Y. S., and Huangao Shi. "Sino-Venezuelan Relations: Beyond Oil." *Issues and Studies* 44, no. 3 (September 2008).

China by Numbers 2007. Hong Kong: China Economic Review Publishing, 2006.

Chiou, C. L. *Maoism in Action: The Cultural Revolution.* St. Lucia, Queensland: University of Queensland Press, 1974.

Chiu, Becky, and Mervyn K. Lewis. *Reforming China's State-Owned Enterprises and Banks.* Northhampton, MA: Edward Elgar, 2006.

Chung Chien-peng. "The Defense of Xinjiang: Politics, Economics, and Security in Central Asia." *Harvard International Review* 25 (Summer 2003): 58–62.

———. "'Regional Autonomy' for Minority Nationalities in the People's Republic of China: Rhetoric or Reality?" *Selected Papers in Asian Studies* 23. Western Conference of the Association for Asian Studies, 1996.

Clark, Paul. *The Chinese Cultural Revolution: A History.* Cambridge, UK: Cambridge University Press, 2008.

Clarke, Donald. "China Reins in Rural Protest, but Not Resentment." *Washington Post,* November 19, 2006, A24.

———. *China's Legal System: New Developments, New Challenges.* Cambridge: Cambridge University Press, 2008.

———. "The Chinese Legal System Since 1995: Steady Development, Striking Continuities." *China Quarterly* 191 (September 2007): 555–566.

Commission of the European Communities. *EU-China: Closer Partners, Growing Responsibilities.* Brussels: European Union, October 24, 2006.

Congressional-Executive Commission on China. *Annual Report 2005.* Washington, DC: US Government Printing Office, October 11, 2005. http://www.cecc .gov.

———. *Annual Report 2008.* Washington, DC: US Government Printing Office, October 31, 2008. http://www.cecc.gov.

———. *Freedom of the Press in China After SARS: Reform and Retrenchment.* Washington, DC: US Government Printing Office, September 22, 2003. http://www.cecc.gov.

———. *Village Elections in China.* Washington, DC: US Government Printing Office, July 8, 2002.

Connelly, Rachel, and Zhenzhen Zheng. "Educational Access for China's Post–Cultural Revolution Generation, Enrollment Patterns in 1990." In *Education and Reform in China,* edited by Emily Hannum and Albert Park. Oxford, UK: Routledge, 2007.

"Constitution of the People's Republic of China." *People's Daily Online,* December 4, 1982. http://english.peoplesdaily.com.cn.

Crane, Keith, Roger Cliff, Evan Medeiros, James Mulvenon, and William Overholt. *Modernizing China's Military: Opportunities and Constraints.* Santa Monica, CA: RAND Corporation, 2005.

Creel, Herlee G. *Chinese Thought from Confucius to Mao Tse-tung.* Chicago: University of Chicago Press, 1953.

———. *Confucius and the Chinese Way.* New York: Harper and Row, 1949.

Croll, Elisabeth J. *From Heaven to Earth: Images and Experiences of Development in China.* London: Routledge, 1994.

Cruz De Castro, Renato. "The Limits of Twenty-First-Century Chinese Soft-Power Statecraft in Southeast Asia: The Case of the Philippines." *Issues and Studies* 43, no. 4 (December 2007): 77–116.

Davis, Deborah, ed. *The Consumer Revolution in China.* Berkeley: University of California Press, 2000.

Davis, Deborah, and Helen Siu. *SARS: Reception and Interpretations in Three Chinese Cities.* London: Routledge, 2006.

Deans, Phil. "Diminishing Returns? Prime Minister Koizumi's Visits to the Yasukuni Shrine in the Context of East Asian Nationalisms." *East Asia* 24 (2007): 269–294.

De Barry, William Theodore, Wing-Tsit Chan, and Burton Watson. *Sources of Chinese Tradition.* Vol. 1. New York: Columbia University Press, 1960.

Dickson, Bruce J. "China's Cooperative Capitalists: The Business End of the Middle Class." In *China's Emerging Middle Class,* edited by Cheng Li, 291–309. Washington, DC: Brookings Institution Press, 2010.

———. "Integrating Wealth and Power in China: The Communist Party's Embrace of the Private Sector." *China Quarterly* 192 (December 2007): 827–854.

———. *Red Capitalists in China: The Party, Private Entrepreneurs, and Prospects for Political Change.* Cambridge, UK: Cambridge University Press, 2003.

———. *Wealth into Power: The Communist Party's Embrace of China's Private Sector.* Cambridge: Cambridge University Press, 2008.

Dollar, David. "Poverty, Inequality, and Social Disparities During China's Reform." World Bank Policy Research Working Paper 4253. Washington DC, 2007. http://www-wds.worldbank.org.

Dreyer, June Teufel. *China's Political System: Modernization and Tradition.* 7th ed. New York: Longman, 2006.

Dumbaugh, Kerry. *Tibet: Problems, Prospects, and U.S. Policy.* Washington, DC: Congressional Research Service, Library of Congress, 2008.

Dutta, Sujit. "Securing the Sea Frontier: China's Pursuit of Sovereignty Claims in the South China Sea." *Strategic Analysis* 29, no. 2 (April–June 2005): 269–294.

Dwyer, D. J. "The Coal Industry in Mainland China Since 1949." *Geographical Journal* 129, no. 3 (September 1963): 329–338.

Economy, Elizabeth. "Environmental Enforcement in China." In *China's Environment and the Challenge of Sustainable Development,* edited by Kristen A. Day, 103–120. Armonk, NY: M. E. Sharpe, 2005.

———. *The River Runs Black.* Cornell, NY: Cornell University Press, 2004.

Economy, Elizabeth, and Adam Segal. "The G-2 Mirage: Why the United States and China Are Not Ready to Upgrade Ties." *Foreign Affairs* 88, no. 3 (May/June 2009): 14–23.

Ellis, R. Evan. *China in Latin America: The Whats and Wherefores.* Boulder, CO: Lynne Rienner Publishers, 2009.

Erickson, Andrew S., Lyle J. Goldstein, William S. Murray, and Andrew R. Wilson, eds. *China's Future Nuclear Submarine Force.* Annapolis: Naval Institute Press, 2007.

Esarey, Ashley. "Cornering the Market: State Strategies for Controlling China's Commercial Media." *Asian Perspective* 29, no. 4 (2005): 37–83.

———. *Speak No Evil: Mass Media Control in Contemporary China.* Washington, DC: Freedom House Special Report, February 2006.

Esherick, Joseph W., Paul G. Pickowicz, and Andrew Walder, eds. *The Chinese Cultural Revolution as History.* Stanford, CA: Stanford University Press, 2006.

European Commission. *Intellectual Property: IPR Enforcement—The Countries.* Brussels, Luxembourg: EU European Commission, October 4, 2006. Accessed August 15, 2009. http://ec.europa.eu.

Evans, Richard. *Deng Xiaoping and the Making of Modern China.* New York: Penguin, 1995.

Fan, C. Cindy. "China's Eleventh Five-Year Plan (2006–2010): From 'Getting Rich First' to Common Prosperity." *Eurasian Geography and Economics* 47, no. 6 (2006): 708–723.

———. "Migration, *Hukou,* and the City." In *China Urbanizes: Consequences, Strategies, and Policies,* edited by Shahid Yusuf and Tony Saich, 65–89. Washington, DC: World Bank, 2008.

Fairbank, John King. *The Great Chinese Revolution: 1800–1985.* New York: Harper and Row, 1987.

———. *The United States and China.* 4th ed. Cambridge, MA: Harvard University Press, 1983.

Fairbank, John King, and Merle Goldman. *China: A New History.* Cambridge, MA: Belknap Press of Harvard University Press, 1998.

Fairbank, John King, Edwin O. Reischauer, and Albert M. Craig. *East Asia: Tradition and Transformation.* Boston: Houghton Mifflin Company, 1989.

Feaver, Peter D., Takako Hikotani, and Shaun Narine. "Civilian Control and Civil-Military Gaps in the United States, Japan, and China." *Asian Perspective* 29, no. 1 (2005): 233–271.

Federal Bureau of Investigation. "Counterintelligence Cases Past and Present." Washington, DC: Department of Justice, Federal Bureau of Investigation, January 1, 2009. http://www.fbi.gov.

Federal Reserve Board. "Major Foreign Holders of Treasury Securities." Washington, DC: US Department of the Treasury, Federal Reserve Board, July 16, 2009. http://www.treas.gov.

Fenby, Jonathan. *Modern China: The Fall and Rise of a Great Power, 1850 to the Present.* New York: HarperCollins Penguin, 2008.

Feng Jicai. *Voices from the Whirlwind: An Oral History of the Chinese Cultural Revolution.* New York: Random House, 1991.

Fewsmith, Joseph. "China and the Politics of SARS." *Current History* 102, no. 665 (September 2003): 250–255.

Freedom House. *Freedom of the Press 2010.* Washington, DC: Freedom House, 2010.

French, Patrick. *Tibet, Tibet: A Personal History of a Lost Land.* New York: Alfred A. Knopf, 2003.

Freund, Elizabeth M. "Bill Clinton's 'Three Noes' and the Taiwan Question." In *Across the Taiwan Strait: Exchanges, Conflicts, and Negotiations,* edited by Winston L. Wang and Deborah A. Brown, 221–251. New York: St. John's University, 1999.

———. "Falling Flat: The Challenges of Corporatizing China's State Industry." In *Remaking China's Public Management,* edited by Peter Nan-shong Lee and Carlos Wing-Hung Lo, 167–182. Westport, CT: Quorum Books, 2001.

———. "Fizz, Froth, Flat: The Challenge of Converting China's SOEs into Shareholding Corporations." *Policy Studies Review* 18, no. 1 (Spring 2001): 96–111.

Fung, Hung-gay, and Kevin H. Zhang, eds. *Financial Markets and Foreign Direct Investment in Greater China.* New York: M. E. Sharpe, 2002.

Gamer, Robert E., ed. *Understanding Contemporary China.* 3rd ed. Boulder, CO: Lynne Rienner, 2008.

Garnaut, Ross, and Ligang Song, eds. *China: Linking Markets for Growth.* Canberra: ANUE Press and Asia Pacific Press, 2007.

———. *The Turning Point in China's Economic Development.* Canberra: ANUE Press and Asia Pacific Press, 2006.

Ge Wei. *Economic Ideas Leading to the 21st Century.* Singapore: World Scientific, 1999.

Gifford, Rob. *China Road: A Journey into the Future of a Rising Super Power.* New York: Random House, 2007.

Gill, Bates, Jennifer Chang, and Sarah Palmer. "China's HIV Crisis." *Foreign Affairs* 81, no. 2 (March/April 2002): 96–110.

Gill, Bates, Huang Chin-hao, and J. Stephen Morrison. *China's Expanding Role in Africa: Implications for the United States.* Washington, DC: Center for Strategic and International Studies, 2006.

Gill, Bates, Yanzhong Huang, and Xiaoqing Lu. *Demography of HIV/AIDS in China.* Washington, DC: Center for Strategic and International Studies, July 2007. http://www.csis.org.

Gilley, Bruce. "Not So Dire Straits: How the Finlandization of Taiwan Benefits U.S. Security." *Foreign Affairs* 89, no. 1 (January/February 2010): 44–60.

————. *Tiger on the Brink: Jiang Zemin and China's New Elite*. Berkeley: University of California Press, 1998.

Glaser, Bonnie S., and Evan S. Medeiros. "The Changing Ecology of Foreign Policy-Making in China: The Ascension and Demise of the Theory of 'Peaceful Rise.'" *China Quarterly* 190 (June 2007): 291–310.

Goldman, Merle. "The Reassertion of Political Citizenship in the Post-Mao Era: The Democracy Wall Movement." In *Changing Meanings of Citizenship in Modern China,* edited by Merle Goldman and Elizabeth J. Perry. Cambridge, MA: Harvard University Press, 2002.

————. *Sowing the Seeds of Democracy in China: Political Reform in the Deng Xiaoping Era*. Cambridge, MA: Harvard University Press, 1994.

Goldman, Merle, and Roderick MacFarquhar, eds. *The Paradox of China's Post-Mao Reforms*. Cambridge, MA: Harvard University Press, 1999.

Goncharov, Sergei N., John W. Lewis, and Xue Litai. *Uncertain Partners: Stalin, Mao, and the Korean War*. Stanford, CA: Stanford University Press, 1993.

Goodman, David S. G. "The Campaign to 'Open up the West': National, Provincial-Level, and Local Perspectives." *China Quarterly* 178 (June 2004): 319–334.

————, ed. *China's Provinces in Reform: Class, Community and Political Culture*. London: Routledge, 1997.

Government Information Office, Republic of China. *The Republic of China Yearbook, 2008*. Taipei, Taiwan: Government Information Office, 2008. http://www.gio.gov.tw.

————. *The Republic of China Yearbook, 2009*. Taipei, Taiwan: Government Information Office, 2009. http://www.gio.gov.tw.

Graff, David A., and Robin Higham, eds. *A Military History of China*. Boulder, CO: Westview Press, 2002.

Grasso, June M., Jay Corrin, and Michael Kort. *Modernization and Revolution in China: From the Opium Wars to World Power*. 3rd ed. New York: M. E. Sharpe, 2004.

Green, Stephen Paul. *The Development of China's Stock Market, 1984–2002: Equity Politics and Market Institutions*. New York: RoutledgeCurzon, 2004.

Greenhalgh, Susan. *Just One Child: Science and Policy in Deng's China*. Berkeley: University of California Press, 2008.

Greenhalgh, Susan, and Edwin A. Winckler. *Chinese State Birth Planning in the 1990s and Beyond*. Washington, DC: US Department of Justice, Immigration and Naturalization Service, September 2001.

————. *Governing China's Population: From Leninist to Neoliberal Biopolitics*. Stanford, CA: Stanford University Press, 2005.

Gries, Peter Hays. *China's New Nationalism: Pride, Politics and Diplomacy*. Berkeley: University of California, 2004.

Guo Gang. "Party Recruitment of College Students in China." *Journal of Contemporary China* 14, no. 43 (2005): 371–393.

————. "Persistent Inequalities in Funding for Rural Schooling in Contemporary China." *Asian Survey* 47, no. 2 (March–April 2007): 213–230.

Guo Jian, Yongyi Song, and Yuan Zhou. *Historical Dictionary of the Chinese Cultural Revolution*. Lanham, MD: Scarecrow Press, 2006.

Haberfeld, M. R., and Ibrahim Cerrah. *Comparative Policing: The Struggle for Democratization*. London: Sage Publications, 2008.

Han, Dongping. *The Unknown Cultural Revolution: Life and Change in a Chinese Village*. New York: Monthly Review Press, 2008.

Hannum, Emily, Jere Behrman, Meiyan Wang, and Jihong Liu. "Education in the Reform Era." In *China's Great Economic Transformation,* edited by Loren Brandt and Thomas G. Rawski, 215–249. Cambridge, UK: Cambridge University Press, 2008.

Hannum, Emily, and Albert Park, eds. *Education and Reform in China*. Oxford, UK: Routledge, 2007.

Hannum, Emily, Albert Park, and Kai-Ming Cheng. "Introduction: Market Reforms and Educational Opportunity in China." In *Education and Reform in China,* edited by Emily Hannam and Albert Park. Oxford, UK: Routledge, 2007.

Harding, Harry. *China's Second Revolution: Reform After Mao*. Washington, DC: Brookings Institution Press, 1987.

————. *A Fragile Relationship: The United States and China Since 1972*. Washington, DC: Brookings Institution Press, 1992.

Harvey, Brian. *China's Space Program*. New York: Springer, 2004.

Hassid, Jonathan. "China's Contentious Journalists: Reconceptualizing the Media." *Problems of Post-Communism* 55, no. 4 (July–August 2008): 52–61.

Henderson, Gail, et al. "Distribution of Medical Insurance in China." *Social Science and Medicine* 41, no. 8 (1995): 1119–1130.

Hesketh, Therese, Li Lu, and Zhu Wei Xing. "The Effect of China's One-Child Policy After 25 Years." *New England Journal of Medicine* 353 (September 15, 2005): 1171–1176.

Hinton, William. *Fanshen: A Documentary of Revolution in a Chinese Village*. New York: Random House, 1966.

Ho, Lok Sang. "Market Reforms and China's Health Care System." *Social Science and Medicine* 41, no. 8 (1995): 1065–1072.

Holslag, Jonathan. *China and India: Prospects for Peace*. New York: Columbia University Press, 2010.

Horowitz, Michael. C. *The Diffusion of Military Power: Causes and Consequences for International Politics*. Princeton, NJ: Princeton University Press, 2010.

"How It Works and How It Might Grow." Asia Programme Working Paper 8. The Royal Institute of International Affairs, October 2003. http://www.chathamhouse.org.uk.

"How to Run a People's Commune." *Renmin Ribao* [*People's Daily*] editorial, September 4, 1958. In *People's Communes in China,* 84. Peking: Foreign Languages Press, 1958.

Howell, Jude. *China Opens Its Doors: The Politics of Economic Transition.* Boulder, CO: Lynne Rienner Publishers, 1993.

Hu Jintao. "Hold High the Great Banner of Socialism with Chinese Characteristics and Strive for New Victories in Building a Moderately Prosperous Society in All Respects." Paper presented at the Seventeenth National Congress of the Communist Party of China, Beijing, China, October 15, 2007.

Huang Jikun, Keijiro Otsuka, and Scott Rozelle. "Agriculture in China's Development: Past Disappointments, Recent Successes, and Future Challenges." In *China's Great Economic Transformation,* edited by Loren Brandt and Thomas G. Rawski, 467–505. Cambridge: Cambridge University Press, 2008.

Huang Jikun and Scott Rozelle. "The Impact of Trade Liberalization on China's Agriculture and Rural Economy." *SAIS Review* 22, no. 1 (Winter–Spring): 115–131.

Huang Yasheng. *Selling China: Foreign Direct Investment During the Reform Era.* New York: Cambridge University Press, 2003.

Hudson, Christopher, ed. *The China Handbook.* Chicago: Fitzroy Dearborn Publishers, 1997.

Hughes, Richard. *The Chinese Communes: A Background Book.* London: Bodley Head, 1960.

Inoguchi, Takashi, and Paul Bacon. "Rethinking Japan as an Ordinary Country." In *The United States and Northeast Asia: Debates, Issues, and New Order,* edited by G. John Ikenberry and Chung-in Moon, 79–98. Lanham, MD: Rowman and Littlefield, 2008.

Institute of Current China Studies. *Zhong gongchang yong ziyu zidian* [A Lexicon of Chinese Communist terminology]. Vols. 1 and 2. Taipei, Taiwan: Institute of Current China Studies, 1991.

International Energy Agency. *World Energy Outlook 2010 Factsheet.* Paris, France: International Energy Agency, 2010. http://www.worldenergyoutlook.org.

International Food Policy Research Institute. *China: Impact of Public Investments at the Village Level.* http://www.ifpri.org/country/china.asp.

International Intellectual Property Alliance (IIPA). "2009 Special 301 Report on Copyright Protection and Enforcement: People's Republic of China." Washington, DC: International Intellectual Property Alliance, February 17, 2009.

International Republican Institute. *People's Republic of China: Election Observation Report.* Washington, DC: International Republican Institute, 1995.

Ip, Cliff, Si-Si Liu, and Bonny Ling. *China's Death Penalty Reforms.* Human Rights in China, 2007. http://hrichina.org.

Japan External Trade Organization. *Japan's Inward FDI by Region/Country.* Japan External Trade Organization, 2008. http://www.jetro.go.jp.

———. *Japan's Outward FDI by Region/Country.* Japan External Trade Organization, 2009. http://www.jetro.go.jp.

———. *Value of Exports and Import by Area and Country (2008/12).* Japan External Trade Organization, 2008. http://www.jetro.go.jp.

Jian Xie et al. *Addressing China's Water Scarcity: Recommendations for Selected Water Resource Management Issues.* Washington, DC: World Bank, 2009.

Jiang Xiaojuan. *FDI in China: Contributions to Growth, Restructures, and Competitiveness in China in the 21st Century.* Hauppauge, NY: Nova Science Publishers, 2004.

Jiang Xiaowei. "An Assessment of Major Theoretical Perspectives of Elite Recruitment in China." Paper presented at the 47th meeting of the American Association for Chinese Studies, Richmond, VA, October 5–7, 2007.

Jiang Zemin. "Hold High the Great Banner of Deng Xiaoping Theory for an All-Round Advancement of the Cause of Building Socialism with Chinese Characteristics to the 21st Century." Address to the Fifteenth National Congress of the Communist Party of China, Beijing, China, September 12, 1997. http://www.fas.org.

Joffe, Ellis. "The People's Liberation Army and Politics: After the Fifteenth Party Congress." In *China Under Jiang Zemin,* edited by Hung-mao Tien and Yun-han Chu, 99–114. Boulder, CO: Lynne Rienner, 2000.

Johnston, Reginald F. *Twilight in the Forbidden City.* Reprint. Wilmington, DE: Scholarly Resources, Inc., 1934.

Kan, Shirley. *China's Anti-Satellite Weapons Test.* Washington, DC: Congressional Research Service, April 23, 2007.

———. *Taiwan: Major Arms Sales Since 1990.* Washington, DC: Congressional Research Service, February 24, 2011. http://www.fas.org.

Kaup, Katherine Palmer. *Ethnic Politics in China.* Boulder, CO: Lynne Rienner Publishers, 2000.

Keidel, Albert. *China's Economic Rise—Fact and Fiction.* Policy Brief 61. Washington, DC: Carnegie Endowment for International Peace, July 2008.

Kim, Jae Cheol. "From the Fringe to the Center: The Political Emergence of Private Entrepreneurs in China." *Issues and Studies* 41, no. 3 (September 2005): 113–143.

Kleinman, Arthur, and James L. Watson, eds. *SARS in China: Prelude to Pandemic?* Stanford, CA: Stanford University Press, 2006.

Kornberg, Judith F., and John R. Faust. *China in World Politics.* 2nd ed. Boulder, CO: Lynne Rienner Publishers, 2005.

Kristensen, Hans M., Robert S. Norris, and Matthew G. McKinzie. *Chinese Nuclear Forces and U.S. Nuclear War Planning.* Washington, DC: Federation of American Scientists/Natural Resources Defense Council, 2006.

Krkoska, Libor, and Yevgenia Korniyenko. "China's Investments in Russia: Where Do They Go and How Important Are They?" *China and Eurasia Quarterly* 6, no. 1 (2008): 39–49.

Kulsudjarit, Kongpetch. "Drug Problem in Southeast and Southwest Asia." *Annals of the New York Academy of Sciences* 1025 (2004): 446–457.

Kurlantzick, Josh. "China's Charm Offensive in Southeast Asia." *Current History,* September 2006.

Kwan, Clarence, and Karl P. Sauvant. *Chinese Direct Investment in the United States—The Challenges Ahead.* Westbury, NY: Halcyon Business Publications, 2008. http://www.vcc.columbia.edu.

Kwong, Julia. *Cultural Revolution in China's Schools, May 1966–April 1969*. Stanford, CA: Hoover Press, 1988.

Kynge, James. *China Shakes the World: A Titan's Rise and Troubled Future*. New York: Houghton Mifflin, 2007.

Lai, Hongyi Harry. "China's Western Development Program: Its Rationale, Implementation, and Prospects." *Modern China* 28, no. 4 (October 2002): 432–466.

Lam, Willy Wo-lap. "China's 11th Five-Year Plan." *China Brief* (November 23, 2005). http://www.asianresearch.org.

Lampton, David M. *The Making of Chinese Foreign and Security Policy in the Era of Reform, 1979–2000*. Stanford, CA: Stanford University Press, 2001.

Lardy, Nicholas R. "China: Toward a Consumption-Driven Growth Path." Policy Briefs in International Economics, No. PB06-6. Washington, DC: Institute for International Economics, September 2006.

Larus, Elizabeth Freund. "China's New Security Concept and Peaceful Rise: Trustful Cooperation or Deceptive Diplomacy?" *American Journal of Chinese Studies* 12, no. 2 (October 2005): 219–241.

———. *Economic Reform in China, 1979–2003: The Marketization of Labor and State Enterprises*. Lewiston, NY: Edwin Mellen Press, 2005.

———. "Soft Power Versus Hard Cash: Maintaining Democratic Allies." In *Taiwan and the International Community,* edited by Steven Tsang, 153–188. Oxford: Peter Lang, 2008.

Lee, Lai To. "Political Reforms in Post-Deng China." Paper presented at the Conference on Asian Perspectives on the Challenge of China, Cambridge, MA, Commonwealth Institute, March 7–8, 2000. http://www.comw.org.

Leng Shao-chuan. "The Role of Law in the People's Republic of China as Reflecting Mao Tse-tung's Influence." *Journal of Criminal Law and Criminology* 68, no. 3 (September 1977): 356–373.

Leng Shao-chuan and Hungdah Chiu. *Criminal Justice in Post-Mao China: Analysis and Documents*. Albany: State University of New York Press, 1985.

Lenin, V. I. "The State and Revolution." In *The Lenin Anthology,* edited by Robert C. Tucker, 311–398. New York: W. W. Norton, 1975.

———. "What Is to Be Done? Burning Questions of Our Movement." In *The Lenin Anthology,* edited by Robert C. Tucker, 12–114. New York: W. W. Norton, 1975.

Levin, Richard. "Top of the Class: The Rise of Asia's Universities." *Foreign Affairs* 89, no. 3 (May–June 2010): 63–75.

Li Cheng, ed. *China's Emerging Middle Class*. Washington, DC: Brookings Institution Press, 2010.

Li Cheng. "Ethnic Minority Elites in China's Party-State Leadership: An Empirical Assessment." *China Leadership Monitor* 25 (June 17, 2008).

Li Cheng and Lynn White. "The Sixteenth Central Committee of the Chinese Communist Party: Hu Gets What?" *Asian Survey* 43, no. 4 (July–August 2003): 553–597.

———. "The Thirteenth Central Committee of the Chinese Communist Party: From Mobilizers to Managers." *Asian Survey* 28, no. 4 (April 1988): 371–399.

Li Lianjiang and Kevin J. O'Brien. "Protest Leadership in Rural China." *China Quarterly* 193 (March 2008): 1–23.

Li Nan. *Chinese Civil-Military Relations: The Transformation of the People's Liberation Army.* London: Routledge, 2006.

Li Zhisui and Anne F. Thurston. *The Private Life of Chairman Mao: The Memoirs of Mao's Personal Physician.* New York: Random House, 1994.

Liang, Heng, and Judith Shapiro. *Son of the Revolution.* New York: Alfred A. Knopf, 1983.

Lieberthal, Kenneth. *Governing China: From Revolution Through Reform.* 2nd ed. New York: W. W. Norton, 2004.

Lilley, James R., and David L. Shambaugh. *China's Military Faces the Future.* Armonk, NY: M. E. Sharpe, 1999.

Lin Jing. "Emergence of Private Schools in China." In *Education and Reform in China,* edited by Emily Hannum and Albert Park, 44–63. Oxford, UK: Routledge, 2007.

Lin Shuanglin and Xiaodong Zhu. *Private Enterprises and China's Economic Development.* London: Routledge, 2007.

Lin Teh-chang. "Environmental NGOs and the Anti-Dam Movements in China: A Social Movement with Chinese Characteristics." *Issues and Studies* 43, no. 4 (December 2007): 149–184.

Lippit, Victor D. "The Maoist Period, 1979–78: Mobilizational Collectivism, Primitive Accumulation, and Industrialization." In *The China Handbook,* edited by Christopher Hudson, 3–18. Chicago: Fitzroy Dearborn, 1997.

Liu Binyan. *A Higher Kind of Loyalty: A Memoir by China's Foremost Journalist.* New York: Random House, 1990.

Liu Jihong, Ulla Larsen, and Grace Wushak. "Factors Affecting Adoption in China, 1950–1987." *Population Studies* 58, no. 1 (2004): 21–36.

Liu Ti and Stephen Paul Green. "China's Informal Stock Market: How It Developed, How It Works, and How It Might Grow." Royal Institute of International Affairs, Asia Programme Working Paper 8, October 2003. http://www.chathamhouse.org.uk.

Liu Yuanli. "China's Public Health-Care System: Facing the Challenges." *Bulletin of the World Health Organization* 82, no. 7 (July 2004): 532–538.

Liu Yuanli, William C. Hsiao, and Karen Eggleston. "Equity in Health and Health Care: The Chinese Experience." *Social Science and Medicine* 49, no. 10 (1999): 1349–1356.

Liu Yuanli, Keqin Rao, Jing Wu, and Emmanuela Gakidou. "China's Health System Performance." *Lancet* 372 (November 29, 2008): 1914–1923.

Lo, Carlos Wing-Hung, and Ed Snape. "Lawyers in the People's Republic of China: A Study of Commitment and Professionalization." *American Journal of Comparative Law* 53, no. 2 (Spring 2005): 433–455.

Loschky, Alexander. "High-Technology Trade Indicators, 2008." Joint Research Centre Scientific and Technical Reports, European Union European Commission, 2008. http://statind.jrc.ec.europa.eu.

Lu Hanlong. "To Be Comfortable in an Egalitarian Society." In *The Consumer Revolution in China,* edited by Deborah Davis, 124–151. Berkeley: University of California Press, 2000.

Lu Ning. *The Dynamics of Foreign-Policy Decisionmaking in China.* 2nd ed. Boulder, CO: Westview Press, 2000.

Lu Xiaoqing and Bates Gill. *China's Response to HIV/AIDS and U.S.-China Collaboration.* Washington, DC: Center for Strategic and International Studies, October 2007.

Luo, Jing. "The Cities vs. the Countryside." *World and I* 16, no. 10 (October 2001): 20–32.

Lynch, Michael. *Mao.* London: Routledge, 2004.

Ma, Doris, and Tim Summers. "Is China's Growth Moving Inland? A Decade of 'Develop the West.'" Asia Program Paper ASP PP 2009/02. London: Chatham House, October 2009. http://www.chathamhouse.org.

MacFarquhar, Roderick. *The Origins of the Cultural Revolution.* Vol. 1. New York: Columbia University Press, 1974.

——. *The Origins of the Cultural Revolution.* Vol. 2. New York: Columbia University Press, 1983.

——, ed. *The Politics of China, 1949–1989.* Cambridge, UK: Cambridge University Press, 1993.

MacFarquhar, Roderick, and Michael Schoenhals. *Mao's Last Revolution.* Cambridge, MA: Belknap Press of Harvard University Press, 2006.

MacKinnon, Rebecca. "Bloggers and Censors: Chinese Media in the Internet Age." Address to the City Club of Washington, Washington, DC, May 18, 2007. http://www.cna.org.

Macridis, Roy C., and Mark L. Hulliung. *Contemporary Political Ideologies: Movements and Regimes.* 6th ed. New York: HarperCollins, 1996.

Mann, James. *The China Fantasy: Why Capitalism Will Not Bring Democracy to China.* New York: Penguin Books, 2007.

Manning, Robert A., Ronald Montaperto, and Brad Roberts. *China, Nuclear Weapons, and Arms Control: A Preliminary Assessment.* New York: Council on Foreign Relations, 2000.

Mao Zedong. "Be Concerned with the Well-Being of the Masses, Pay Attention to Methods of Work." In *Selected Works of Mao Tse-tung.* Vol. 1. Peking: Foreign Languages Press, 1965. First published as part of the concluding speech made at the Second National Congress of Workers' and Peasants' Representatives, Zhujin, Jiangxi Province, January 1934.

——. "On Coalition Government." In *Selected Works of Mao Tse-tung.* Vol. 4. Peking: Foreign Languages Press, 1965. First published April 24, 1945.

——. "On the Correct Handling of Contradictions Among the People." In *Selected Readings from the Works of Mao Tse-tung.* Peking: Foreign Languages Press, 1967.

——. *On Guerrilla Warfare.* Urbana: University of Illinois Press, 2000.

——. "On Practice." In *Selected Works of Mao Tse-tung.* Vols. 1–4. Peking: Foreign Languages Press, 1965. First published July 1937.

————. "Problems of War and Strategy." In *Selected Works of Mao Tse-tung*. Vol. 2. Peking: Foreign Languages Press, 1965. First published November 1938.

————. *Quotations from Chairman Mao*. New York: Award Books, 1971. First published as *Mao Zhuxi Yulu* [Quotations from Chairman Mao]. Beijing: *Zhongguo renmin jiefangjun zhong zhengzhibu bianyin* [China People's Liberation Army Central Politburo Publishing], 1965.

————. "Report on an Investigation of the Peasant Movement in Hunan." In *Selected Works of Mao Tse-tung*. Vol. 1. Peking: Foreign Languages Press, 1965. First published March 1927.

————. "Report to the Second Plenary Session of the Seventh Central Committee of the Communist Party of China [March 5, 1949]." In *Selected Works of Mao Tse-tung*. Vol. 3. Peking: Foreign Languages Press, 1965.

————. *Selected Readings from the Works of Mao Tse-tung*. Peking: Foreign Languages Press, 1971.

————. *Selected Works of Mao Tse-tung*. Vols. 1–4. Peking: Foreign Languages Press, 1965.

————. *Selected Works of Mao Tse-tung*. Vol. 5. Peking: Foreign Languages Press, 1977.

————. *Socialist Upsurge in China's Countryside*. Peking: Foreign Languages Press, 1957.

————. "Some Questions Concerning Methods of Leadership." In *Selected Works of Mao Tse-tung*. Vol. 3. Peking: Foreign Languages Press, 1965. First published June 1, 1943.

Marx, Karl. "Critique of the Gotha Program." In *The Marx-Engels Reader*. 2nd ed. Edited by Robert C. Tucker. New York: W. W. Norton, 1978. First published 1875.

McBeath, Gerald, and Leng Tse-kang. *Governance of Biodiversity Conservation in China and Taiwan*. Northhampton, MA: Edward Elgar, 2006.

McGregor, James. *One Billion Customers: Lessons from the Front Lines of Doing Business in China*. New York: Free Press, 2005.

Medvedev, Roy. *China and the Superpowers*. Oxford, UK: Basil Blackwell, 1986.

Meisner, Maurice. *Li Ta-Chao and the Origins of Chinese Marxism*. Cambridge, MA: Harvard University Press, 1967.

————. *Mao's China and After: A History of the People's Republic*. 3rd ed. New York: Free Press, 1999.

Meng-Kin Lim, Hui Yang, Tuohong Zhang, Wen Feng, and Zijun Zhou. "Public Perceptions of Private Health Care in Socialist China." *Health Affairs* 23, no. 6 (2004): 222–234.

Mertha, Andrew, and Robert Pahre. "Patently Misleading: Partial Implementation and Bargaining Leverage in Sino-American Negotiations on Intellectual Property Rights." *International Organization* 59, no. 3 (Summer 2005): 695–729.

Millward, James. *Violent Separatism in Xinjiang: An Assessment*. Washington, DC: East West Center Washington, 2004. http://www.eastwestcenter.org.

Ministry of Foreign Affairs, People's Republic of China. "China's Position Paper on the New Security Concept." Beijing: People's Republic of China, July 31, 2002. http://www.mfa.gov.cn/eng/wjb/zzjg/gjs/gjzzyhy/2612/2614/t15319.htm.

Ministry of Health of the PRC. *Research on National Health Services: An Analysis Report of the National Health Services Survey in 1993.* Beijing: Ministry of Health, 1994.

Moneyhon, Matthew D. "China's Great Western Development Project in Xinjiang: Economic Palliative, or Political Trojan Horse?" *Denver Journal of International Law and Policy* 31, no. 3 (Summer 2003): 491–519.

Mote, Frederick W. *Intellectual Foundations of China.* 2nd ed. New York: Alfred A. Knopf, 1989.

Mulvenon, James C., and Andrew N. D. Yang, eds. *The People's Liberation Army as Organization.* Santa Monica, CA: RAND, 2002.

Murphy, Gill, and Melissa Murphy. *China-Europe Relations: Implications and Policy Responses for the United States.* Washington, DC: Center for Strategic and International Studies, May 2008.

Myers, James T. *Enemies Without Guns: The Catholic Church in China.* New York: Paragon House, 1991.

Nathan, Andrew J. "China's Constitutionalist Option." In *China's Deep Reform: Domestic Politics in Transition,* edited by Lowell Dittmer and Guoli Liu. Lanham, MD: Rowman and Littlefield, 2006.

National Bureau of Statistics (NBS) of China. *Actual Foreign Direct Investment (FDI) by Country of Origin, 1990–2004.* http://www.china-profile.com.

———. *China Statistical Yearbook 2008.* Beijing: China Statistics Press, 2008.

———. *China Statistical Yearbook 2009.* Beijing: China Statistics Press, 2009.

———. *China Statistical Yearbook 2010.* Beijing: China Statistics Press, 2010.

———. "Yearly Data 1998, 17–13: Utilization of Foreign Capital." Beijing: National Bureau of Statistics of China, 1998. Last accessed July 15, 2009. http://www.stats.gov.cn.

National Commission for UNESCO of the People's Republic of China. *A Study of the Current Situation and Development of Literacy Education in China's Minority Area.* Beijing: National Commission for UNESCO of the People's Republic of China, November 2003.

Naughton, Barry. *Growing Out of the Plan: Chinese Economic Reform, 1978–1993.* Cambridge: Cambridge University Press, 1996.

Nee, Victor, and Don Layman. *The Cultural Revolution at Peking University.* New York: Monthly Review Press, 1969.

Neftci, Salih N., and Michelle Yuan Ménager-Xu. *China's Financial Markets: An Insider's Guide to How the Markets Work.* Burlington, MA: Elsevier Academic Press, 2007.

Newitt, Malyn. *A History of Portuguese Overseas Expansion, 1400–1668.* London: Routledge. 2005.

Nielsen, Ingrid, and Russell Smyth, eds. *Migration and Social Protection in China.* Singapore: World Scientific, 2008.

Nien Cheng. *Life and Death in Shanghai.* New York: Penguin Books, 1986.

North China Industrial Group Corporation (NORINCO) (Beifang Gongye). "About Norinco: Introduction." Beijing, China: Norinco, 2005. http://www.norinco.com.

Nowak, Manfred. "Civil and Political Rights, Including the Question of Torture and Detention: Report of the Special Rapporteur on Torture and Other Cruel, Inhumane or Degrading Treatment or Punishment." New York: United Nations Economic and Social Council, March 10, 2006.

Nye, Joseph S. *Soft Power: The Means to Success in World Politics.* New York: Public Affairs, 2004.

O'Brien, Kevin. "Villagers, Elections, and Citizenship in Contemporary China." *Modern China* 27, no. 4 (October 2001): 407–435.

O'Brien, Kevin, and Li Lianjiang. *Rightful Resistance in Rural China.* Cambridge, UK: Cambridge University Press, 2006.

Oi, Jean C. *State and Peasant in Contemporary China: The Political Economy of Village Government.* Berkeley: University of California Press, 1989.

Organization for Economic Cooperation and Development (OECD). *OECD Science, Technology, and Industry Outlook, 2008.* Paris: OECD Publications, 2008. http:// www.sourceoecd.org.

O'Rourke, Ronald. *China Naval Modernization: Implications for U.S. Navy Capabilities—Background and Issues for Congress.* Washington, DC: Congressional Research Service, October 20, 2011. http://fas.org/sgp/crs/row/RL33153.pdf.

Palmer, Katherine. "China's Nationalities and Nationality Areas." In *The China Handbook,* edited by Christopher Hudson, 276–285. Chicago: Fitzroy Dearborn, 1997.

Palmer, Michael. "Transforming Family Law in Post-Deng China: Marriage, Divorce, and Reproduction." *China Quarterly* 191 (2007): 675–695.

Pan, Philip P. *Out of Mao's Shadow: The Struggle for the Soul of a New China.* New York: Simon and Schuster, 2008.

Pan, Stephen, and Raymond J. de Jaegher. *Peking's Red Guards: The Great Proletarian Cultural Revolution.* New York: Twin Circle Publishing Company, 1968.

Park, Albert. "Rural-Urban Inequality in China." In *China Urbanizes: Consequences, Strategies and Policies,* edited by Shahid Yusuf and Anthony Saich, 41–63. Washington, DC: World Bank, 2008.

Pearson, Margaret M. *China's New Business Elite: The Political Consequences of Economic Reform.* Berkeley: University of California Press, 1997.

Pei Minxin. "Fighting Corruption: A Difficult Challenge for Chinese Leaders." In *China's Changing Political Landscape: Prospects for Democracy,* edited by Cheng Li, 229–250. Washington, DC: Brookings Institution Press, 2008.

———. "Think Again: Asia's Rise." *Foreign Policy* 173 (July–August 2009).

Peng Xizhe. "Demographic Consequences of the Great Leap Forward in China's Provinces." *Population and Development Review* 13, no. 4 (December 1987): 639–670.

Penney, Matthew, and Bryce Wakefield. "Right Angles: Examining Accounts of Japanese Neo-Nationalism." *Pacific Affairs* 81, no. 4 (Winter 2008–2009): 537–555.

Perkins, Dwight H., and Thomas G. Rawski. "Forecasting China's Economic Growth to 2025." In *China's Great Economic Transformation,* edited by Loren Brandt and Thomas G. Rawski, 829–881. Cambridge, UK: Cambridge University Press, 2008.

Perry, Elizabeth J. "From Native Place to Workplace: Labor Origins and Outcomes of China's *Danwei* System." In *Danwei: The Changing Workplace in Historical and Comparative Perspectives,* edited by Xiaobao Lu and Elizabeth J. Perry, 42–59. New York: M. E. Sharpe, 1997.

Pillsbury, Michael. *Chinese Views of Future Warfare.* Washington, DC: National Defense University Press, 1997.

PLA History. GlobalSecurity.org, n.d. http://www.globalsecurity.org.

Postiglione, Gerard A. "School Access in Rural Tibet." In *Education and Reform in China,* edited by Emily Hannum and Albert Park, 93–116. Oxford, UK: Routledge, 2007.

Putterman, Louis. "Ration Subsidies and Incentives in the Pre-Reform Chinese Commune." *Economica* 55, no. 218 (May 1988): 243.

Pye, Lucian W. *China: An Introduction.* New York: HarperCollins Publishers, 1991.

Reporters Without Borders. *Worldwide Press Freedom Index 2007.* Reporters Without Borders, 2007. http://www.rsf.org.

———. *Worldwide Press Freedom Index 2010.* Reporters Without Borders, 2010. http://www.en.rsf.org.

Republic of China Government Office. *Republic of China Yearbook 2010.* Taipei: Government Information Office, 2010.

Richman, Barry M. *Industrial Society in Communist China.* New York: Random House, 1969.

Ronald Reagan Presidential Library. "United States–China Communiqué on United States Arms Sales to Taiwan." Washington, DC: National Archives, August 1982. http://www.reagan.utexas.edu.

Rosen, Daniel H., and Thilo Hanemann. *An American Open Door? Maximizing the Benefits of Chinese Foreign Direct Investment.* New York: Asia Society, May 2011. http://www.rhgroup.net.

Rosen, Stanley. "Contemporary Chinese Youth and the State." *Journal of Asian Studies* 68, no. 2 (May 2009): 359–369.

———. "Education and Economic Reform." In *The China Handbook,* edited by Christopher Hudson, 250–261. Chicago: Fitzroy Dearborn, 1997.

Saich, Tony. *Governance and Politics of China.* New York: Palgrave Macmillan, 2004.

Schell, Orville. *Mandate of Heaven: The Legacy of Tiananmen Square and the Next Generation of China's Leaders.* New York: Touchstone, 1995.

Schoppa, R. Keith. *Revolution and Its Past: Identities and Change in Modern Chinese History.* Upper Saddle River, NJ: Prentice Hall, 2002.

Schram, Stuart. *The Thought of Mao Tse-tung.* Cambridge, UK: Cambridge University Press, 1989.

Schurmann, Franz. *Ideology and Organization in Communist China.* Berkeley: University of California Press, 1968.

Schwartz, Benjamin I. *Communism and China: Ideology in Flux.* Cambridge, MA: Harvard University Press, 1968.

Schwartz, Louis B. *China Renewable Energy and Sustainable Development Report, October 2008.* Vol. 10. Pittsburgh, PA: China Strategies, LLC, October 2008. http://www.geni.org.

Scobell, Andrew. "China's Evolving Civil-Military Relations: Creeping Guojiahua." *Armed Forces and Society* 31, no. 2 (Winter 2005): 227–244.

Seagrave, Sterling. *The Soong Dynasty.* Harper and Row, 1985.

Serge, Michel. *China Safari: On the Trail of Beijing's Expansion in Africa.* New York: Nation Books, 2009.

Shalikashvili, John S. *Joint Vision 2010.* Washington, DC: US Department of Defense, July 1997.

Shambaugh, David. "China Engages Asia: Reshaping the Regional Order." *International Security* 29, no. 3 (Winter 2004–2005): 64–99.

———. *Modernizing China's Military: Progress, Problems, and Prospects.* Berkeley: University of California Press, 2002.

Shanghai Stock Exchange. "Brief Introduction to SSE." Shanghai, China: Shanghai Stock Exchange, 2002. http://www.sse.com.cn.

Shapiro, Judith. *Mao's War Against Nature.* Cambridge: Cambridge University Press, 2001.

Shelton, Garth, and Farhana Paruk. "The Forum of China-Africa Cooperation: A Strategic Opportunity." Monograph no. 156. Pretoria, South Africa: Institute for Security Studies, 2008. http://www.iss.co.za.

Shen Tong and Marianne Yen. *Almost a Revolution.* Boston: Houghton Mifflin, 1990.

Shenzhen Stock Exchange. "SSE Overview." Shenzhen, China: Shenzhen Stock Exchange, 2009. http://www.szse.cn.

Shih Ch'eng-chih. *Urban Commune Experiences in Communist China.* Hong Kong: Union Research Institute, 1962.

Shirk, Susan L., ed. *Changing Media, Changing China.* Oxford: Oxford University Press, 2011.

Shirk, Susan L. *China: Fragile Superpower.* Oxford: Oxford University Press, 2008.

———. *The Political Logic of Economic Reform in China.* Berkeley: University of California Press, 1993.

Short, Philip. *Mao: A Life.* New York: Henry Holt, 2000.

Singer, Martin. "Educated Youth and the Cultural Revolution in China." *Michigan Papers in Chinese Studies*, no. 10. Ann Arbor, MI: Center for Chinese Studies, 1971.

Smil, Vaclav. "China's Great Famine: 40 Years Later." *BMJ Education and Debate* 319 (December 1999): 1619–1621.

Snow, Edgar. *Red Star over China: The Classic Account of the Birth of Chinese Communism.* New York: Random House, 1938.

Spence, Jonathan D. *Mao Zedong.* New York: Penguin, 1999.

———. *The Search for Modern China.* New York: W. W. Norton, 1990.

State Council of the People's Republic of China. *China's National Defense in 2008.* Beijing: Information Office of the State Council of the People's Republic of China, January 2009. http://www.fas.org/programs/ssp/nukes/2008Defense WhitePaper_Jan2009.

———. *China's National Defense in 2010.* Beijing: Information Office of the State Council of the People's Republic of China, March 31, 2010. http://www.merln .ndu.edu/whitepapers/China_English2010.

State Statistical Bureau, PRC. *China Statistical Yearbook 1998.* Beijing: China Statistical Publishing House, 1998.

Sullivan, Michael J. "The 1988–89 Nanjing Anti-African Protests: Racial Nationalism or National Racism?" *China Quarterly* 138 (June 1994): 438–457.

Sutter, Robert G. *Chinese Foreign Relations: Power and Policy Since the Cold War.* Lanham, MD: Rowman and Littlefield, 2008.

Sutton, Donald S. "Consuming Counterrevolution: The Ritual and Culture of Cannibalism in Wuxuan, Guangxi, China, May to July 1968." *Comparative Studies in Society and History* 7, no. 1 (1995): 136–172.

Swaine, Michael D. "The Modernization of the People's Liberation Army: Implications for Asia-Pacific Security and Chinese Politics." In *China Under Jiang Zemin,* edited by Hung-mao Tien and Yun-han Chu, 115–134. Boulder, CO: Lynne Rienner, 2000.

Taiwan Foundation for Democracy. *China Human Rights Report 2006.* Taipei: Taiwan Foundation for Democracy, 2006.

Tanaka, Osamu. "A Study of China's 11th Five-Year Plan—In Contrast with the 10th Five-Year Plan." ESRI Discussion Paper Series no. 170. Tokyo: Economic and Social Research Institute, October 2006. http://www.esri.go.jp.

Tang Tsou. "The Tiananmen Tragedy: The State-Society Relationship, Choices, and Mechanisms in Historical Perspective." In *Contemporary China in Historical Perspective,* edited by Brantly Womack. Cambridge, UK: Cambridge University Press, 1991.

Tang Wenfang. *Public Opinion and Political Change.* Stanford, CA: Stanford University Press, 2005.

Tanner, Murray Scot, and Eric Green. "Principals and Secret Agents: Central Versus Local Control over Policing and Obstacles to 'Rule of Law' in China." *China Quarterly* 191 (September 2007): 644–670.

Tao Chu. *The People's Communes Forge Ahead.* Peking: Foreign Languages Press, 1964.

Taylor, Ian. "The Future of China's Overseas Peacekeeping Operations." *China Brief* 8, no. 6 (March 14, 2008).

Taylor, John G. "Poverty and Vulnerability." In *China Urbanizes: Consequences, Strategies, and Policies,* edited by Shahid Yusuf and Anthony Saich, 91–104. Washington, DC: World Bank, 2008.

Teiwes, Frederick. *China's Road to Disaster: Mao, Central Politicians, and Provincial Leaders in the Great Leap Forward, 1955–1959.* New York: M. E. Sharpe, 1999.

Teiwes, Frederick C., and Warren Sun. *The Tragedy of Lin Biao.* Honolulu: University of Hawaii Press, 1996.

"Tentative Regulations (Draft) of the Weihsing (Sputnik) People's Commune, August 7, 1958." In *People's Communes in China,* 61–77. Peking: Foreign Languages Press, 1958.

Thomas, Timothy L. "Like Adding Wings to the Tiger: Chinese Information War Theory and Practice." Fort Leavenworth, KS: Foreign Military Studies Office, n.d. http://fmso.leavenworth.army.mil/documents/chinaiw.htm. Accessed November 17, 2011.

Thompson, Drew. "China's Emerging Interests in Africa: Opportunities and Challenges for Africa and the United States." *African Renaissance Journal* (July–August 2005): 20–29.

Thornton, John L. "Long Time Coming: The Prospects for Democracy in China." *Foreign Affairs* 87, no. 1 (January/February 2008): 2–22.

Tien, Hung-mao, and Yun-han Chu. *China Under Jiang Zemin.* Boulder, CO: Lynne Rienner Publishers, 2000.

Tilford, Earl H., Jr. *The Revolution in Military Affairs: Prospects and Cautions.* Carlisle Barracks, PA: United States Army War College, Strategic Studies Institute, June 1995.

Tooley, James. *The Beautiful Tree: A Personal Journal into How the World's Poorest People Are Educating Themselves.* Washington, DC: Cato Institute, 2009.

Treiman, Donald. "The Growth and Determinants of Literacy in China." In *Education and Reform in China,* edited by Emily Hannum and Albert Park, 135–153. Oxford, UK: Routledge, 2007.

Tseng, Wanda, and Markus Rodlauer, eds. *China: Competing in the Global Economy.* Washington, DC: International Monetary Fund, 2003.

Tuchman, Barbara W. *Stilwell and the American Experience in China, 1911–1945.* New York: Macmillan, 1971.

Unger, Jonathan, ed. *The Nature of Chinese Politics: From Mao to Jiang.* New York: M. E. Sharpe, 2002.

———, ed. *The Pro-Democracy Protests in China: Reports from the Provinces.* Armonk, NY: M. E. Sharpe, 1991.

United Nations Conference on Trade and Development (UNCTAD). *World Investment Report 2009.* http://www.unctad.org.

United Nations Development Programme. *China's Accession to WTO: Challenges for Women in the Agricultural and Industrial Sectors.* Beijing: UNDP, July 2003.

———. *Human Development Report 2007–2008, Country Fact Sheets: China.* New York: United Nations, 2007. http://hdrstats.undp.org.

————. *Human Development Report 2007–2008, World Development Indicators.* Washington, DC: United Nations, 2007. http://hdrstats.undp.org.

————. *Human Development Report 2010.* New York: United Nations, 2010. http:// hdr.undp.org.

————. *International Human Development Indicators: China.* New York: United Nations, 2010. http://hdrstats.undp.org.

United Nations Development Programme (China). *China Human Development Report 2007–2008: Basic Public Services for 1.3 Billion People.* Beijing: China Publishing Group Corporation, 2008. http://www.undp.org.cn.

————. *China Human Development Report 2009–2010: China and a Sustainable Future: Towards a Low Carbon Economy and Society.* Beijing: China Publishing Group Corporation, April 2010. http://www.undp.org.cn.

United Nations Educational, Scientific, and Cultural Organization, Institute for Statistics. *UIS Statistics in Brief.* Montreal: UNESCO, n.d. http://stats.uis.unesco .org.

United States Department of Defense. *Military Power of the People's Republic of China, 2008.* Washington, DC: Department of Defense, 2008.

————. *Military Power of the People's Republic of China, 2009.* Washington, DC: Department of Defense, 2009.

————. *Military Power of the People's Republic of China, 2010.* Washington, DC: Department of Defense, 2010.

United States Department of State. *Country Reports on Human Rights Practices— 2007.* Washington, DC: Bureau of Democracy, Human Rights, and Labor, March 11, 2008. http://www.state.gov.

————. *Country Reports on Human Rights Practices—2010.* Washington, DC: Bureau of Democracy, Human Rights, and Labor, April 8, 2011. http://www.state .gov.

————. *Partnership to Fight HIV/AIDS in China.* Washington, DC: US State Department Office of the Global AIDS Coordinator and the Bureau for Public Health. http://www.pepfar.gov/countries/china/index.htm. Accessed December 8, 2011.

United States Library of Congress. "Country Profile: China." Washington, DC: Federal Research Divison, August 2006.

US-China Business Council. *US-China Trade Statistics and China's World Trade Statistics.* Washington, DC. http://www.uschina.org/statistics/tradetable.html. Accessed December 8, 2010.

Vaughn, Bruce, and Wayne M. Morrison. *China–Southeast Asia Relations: Trends, Issues, and Implications for the United States.* Washington, DC: Congressional Research Service, Library of Congress, April 4, 2006.

Veeck, Gregory, Clifton Pannell, Christopher J. Smith, and Youqin Huang. *China's Geography: Globalization and the Dynamics of Political, Economic, and Social Change.* Lanham, MD: Rowman and Littlefield, 2007.

Vogel, Ezra F. *One Step Ahead in China: Guangdong Under Reform.* Cambridge: Harvard University Press, 1989.

Walker, Richard L. Introduction to *Enemies Without Guns: The Catholic Church in China,* by James T. Myers. New York: Paragon House, 1991.

Wang, James C. F. *Contemporary Chinese Politics: An Introduction.* Upper Saddle River, NJ: Prentice Hall, 1999.

Wang, Lindsay L. *Dog's Daughter: My Life in Communist China and Liberal America.* Singapore: Times Editions, 2003.

Wang Pufeng. "The Challenge of Information Warfare." In *Chinese Views of Future Warfare,* edited by Michael Pillsbury. Washington, DC: National Defense University Press, 1997.

Wang Shaoguang. "China's 1994 Fiscal Reform: An Initial Assessment." *Asian Survey* 37, no. 9 (September 1997): 801–817.

———. *Failure of Charisma: The Cultural Revolution in Wuhan.* Hong Kong: Oxford University Press, 1995.

Wang Shiwei. "Wild Lily." In *Wild Lily, Prairie Fire: China's Road to Democracy, Yan'an to Tian'anmen, 1942–1989,* edited by Gregor Benton and Alan Hunter. Princeton, NJ: Princeton University Press, 1995.

Wang Zhengxu and Zheng Yongnian. "Key Policy Outcomes of the Seventeenth National Congress of the Chinese Communist Party." Briefing Series Issue 31. Nottingham, UK: University of Nottingham China Policy Institute, November 2007.

Wayne, Martin I. *China's War on Terror: Counter-Insurgency, Politics, and Internal Security.* New York: Routledge, 2008.

Wei Jingsheng. *The Courage to Stand Alone: Letters from Prison and Other Writings.* New York: Penguin, 1998.

———. "Democracy or a New Dictatorship?" In *Wild Lily, Prairie Fire: China's Road to Democracy, Yan'an to Tian'anmen, 1942–1989,* edited by Gregor Benton and Alan Hunter, 181–184. Princeton, NJ: Princeton University Press, 1995. Originally published in *Explorations* [*Tansuo*] (Beijing, 1979).

White, Theodore H., and Annalee Jacoby. *Thunder out of China.* New York: Da Capo Press, 1980.

Whiting, Allen S. *China Crosses the Yalu: The Decision to Enter the Korean War.* Stanford, CA: Stanford University Press, RAND Corporation, 1960.

Williams, Erin. "Ethnic Minorities and the State in China: Conflict, Assimilation, or a 'Third Way'?" Ontario: Canadian Political Science Association, 2008. http://www.cpsa-acsp.ca.

Winckler, Edwin A. "People's Republic of China Law on Population and Birth Planning." *Population and Development Review* 28, no. 3 (September 2002): 579–585.

Womack, Brantly, ed. *China's Rise in Historical Perspective.* Lanham, MD: Rowman and Littlefield, 2010.

———. "From Urban Radical to Rural Revolutionary from the 1920s to 1937." In *Cambridge Critical Introduction to Mao,* edited by Timothy Cheek, 61–86. Cambridge, UK: Cambridge University Press, 2010.

———. "Mao Before Maoism." *China Journal* 46 (July 2001): 95–117.

Wong, John, and Hongyi Lai. *China into the Hu-Wen Era: Policy Initiatives and Challenges.* Singapore: World Scientific Publishing, 2006.

Wong, Linda, and Zhang Gongcheng. "Getting By Without State-Sponsored Social Insurance." In *Migration and Social Protection in China,* edited by Ingrid Nielsen and Russell Smyth, 165–183. Singapore: World Scientific, 2008.

World Bank. *From Poor Areas to Poor People: China's Evolving Poverty Reduction Agenda: An Assessment of Poverty and Inequality in China.* Washington, DC: World Bank, March 2009.

———. *Gender Gaps in China: Facts and Figures.* Washington, DC: World Bank, October 2006. http://siteresources.worldbank.org.

———. *World Development Report 2009: Reshaping Economic Geography.* Washington, DC: World Bank, 2009. http://www.worldbank.org.

World Health Organization. "Rural Health Insurance—Rising to the Challenge." China Briefing Notes Series, Briefing Note 6. Washington, DC: World Health Organization, May 2005.

———. *The World Health Report 2000, Health Systems: Improving Performance.* Washington, DC: World Health Organization, 2000.

———. *The World Health Report 2006, Working Together for Health.* Washington, DC: World Health Organization, 2006.

———. *The World Health Report 2008, Primary Health Care: Now More Than Ever.* Washington, DC: World Health Organization, 2008.

World Trade Organization (WTO). "Trade Profiles." Geneva, Switzerland: World Trade Organization, n.d. http://stat.wto.org/CountryProfile/WSDBCountryPFReporter.aspx?Language=E.

Wright, Daniel B. *The Promise of the Revolution.* Lanham, MD: Rowman and Littlefield, 2003.

Xie Zhuoyan. "Petition and Judicial Integrity." *Journal of Politics and Law* 2, no. 1 (March 2009): 24–30.

Xin Wang. "Divergent Identities, Convergent Interests: The Rising Middle-Income Stratum in China and Its Civic Awareness." *Journal of Contemporary China* 17, no. 54 (February 2008): 53–69.

Xinran. *The Good Women of China: Hidden Voices.* New York: Pantheon Books, 2002.

———. *Message from an Unknown Chinese Mother: Stories of Loss and Love.* London: Chatto and Windus, 2010.

Yang Guobin. *The Power of the Internet in China: Citizen Activism Online.* New York: Columbia University Press, 2009.

Yang Jiang. *Six Chapters from My Life "Downunder."* Seattle: University of Washington Press, 1984.

Ying, Long Gen. "China's Changing Regional Disparities During the Reform Period." *Economic Geography* 75, no. 1 (January 1999): 59–70.

Yoshihara, Toshi, and James R. Holmes, eds. *Asia Looks Seaward: Power and Maritime Strategy.* Westport, CT: Praeger Security International, 2008.

Yusuf, Shahid, and Anthony Saich, eds. *China Urbanizes: Consequences, Strategies, and Policies.* Washington, DC: World Bank, 2008.

Zhang Hong. "From Resisting to 'Embracing'? The One-Child Rule: Understanding New Fertility Trends in a Central China Village." *China Quarterly* 192 (2007): 855–875.

Zhang Le-Yin. "Chinese Central-Provincial Fiscal Relationships, Budgetary Decline, and the Impact of the 1994 Fiscal Reform: An Evaluation." *China Quarterly* 57 (March 1999): 115–141.

Zhang Liang, Andrew J. Nathan, and E. Perry Link. *The Tiananmen Papers*. New York: Public Affairs, 2001.

Zhao Dingxin. *The Power of Tiananmen: State-Society Relations and the 1989 Beijing Student Movement*. Chicago: University of Chicago Press, 2001.

Zhao Ziyang. *Guojia de qiutu: Zhao Ziyang de mimi luyin* [Prisoner of the state: Zhao Ziyang's secret memoir]. New York: Simon and Schuster, 2009.

Zheng Yi. *Hongse jinian bei* [Scarlet memorial]. Taipei: Huashi Wenhua Gongsi, 1993.

Zhou Qi. "Conflicts over Human Rights Between China and the United States." *Human Rights Quarterly* 27, no. 1 (February 2005): 105–124.

Zhu, Wei Xing, Li Lu, and Therese Hesketh. "China's Excess Males, Sex Selective Abortion, and One-Child Policy: Analysis of Data from 2005 National Intercensus Survey." *British Medical Journal* (April 9, 2009). http://bmj.com.

Zusman, Eric, and Jennifer L. Turner. "Beyond the Bureaucracy: Changing China's Policymaking Environment." In *China's Environment and the Challenge of Sustainable Development*, edited by Kristen A. Day. Armonk, NY: M. E. Sharpe, 2005.

Index

abortion, 197–201, 309, 424
acid rain, 276
adoption, 199, 204–205
Afghanistan, 331, 343
Africa, 406–410, 413, 418; Chinese investment in, 294; PLA deployments in, 408; Sino-Soviet competition in, 378. *See also individual nations*
African Development Bank, 418
agricultural producers' cooperatives (APCs), 65, 71, 73, 75
agricultural reform, 9, 62, 65, 146–148, 250–252, 254–256, 298, 306–307, 438. *See also* collectivization
agriculture: cash crops, 150; collectivization of, 65, 70, 72–73, 79, 230; communes and, 75, 77, 147; decollectivization of, 137; Develop the West Campaign and, 329–331; environmental factors, 270, 272, 323; feminization of, 284; during Great Leap Forward, 72, 82; in imperial China, 22; industry and, 78–79; infrastructure of, 306–307; Mao and, 70–71, 76; modernization of, 145, 147, 249, 333, 343; price reform and, 257; rural industrialization and, 254–256; urban bias and, 305–306. *See also* agricultural reform

AIDS. *See* human immunodeficiency virus (HIV)
aircraft carriers, 369
air pollution, 275–277; coal and, 275–276
Algeria, 294, 406–407
All-China Environment Federation, 280
American Institute in Taiwan (AIT), 386
Angola, 267, 406, 408
anti-corruption campaigns, 155–156, 162, 167–168, 172, 353. *See also* corruption
antigovernment protests, 430–431. *See also* separatism; Tiananmen Square protests (1989)
Anti-Rightist Campaign, 68–69, 83, 180, 230
Arms Reduction Act (1982), 385
ASEAN Economic Community (AEC), 399
ASEAN Regional Forum (ARF), 398, 401
Asia-Pacific Economic Cooperation forum, 416
assimilation, 229–230
Association of Southeast Asian Nations (ASEAN), 359–360, 398–399, 401, 420
automotive industry, 425
autonomous counties, 141n28

471

About the Book

This authoritative text captures the dynamism of Chinese politics and society. Elizabeth Freund Larus begins with a broad sweep of China's modern history—from the imperial era to the present—providing essential context for understanding the current political environment. She then makes sense of the dramatic political, social, and economic changes that have occurred across some six decades. The result is a rich and detailed analysis that is both thought-provoking and accessible, appropriate for students at all levels.

Elizabeth Freund Larus is professor of political science and international affairs at the University of Mary Washington. She is author of *Economic Reform in China, 1979–2003: The Marketization of Labor and State Enterprises.*